WET MIND

WET MIND

The New Cognitive Neuroscience

Stephen M. Kosslyn

and Olivier Koenig

THE FREE PRESS
A Division of Macmillan, Inc.
NEW YORK

Maxwell Macmillan Canada
TORONTO

Maxwell Macmillan International
NEW YORK   OXFORD   SINGAPORE   SYDNEY

The Free Press
A Division of Macmillan, Inc.
866 Third Avenue, New York, N.Y. 10022

Maxwell Macmillan Canada, Inc.
1200 Eglinton Avenue East
Suite 200
Don Mills, Ontario M3C 3N1

Macmillan, Inc. is part of the Maxwell Communication
Group of Companies.

Printed in the United States of America

printing number
1 2 3 4 5 6 7 8 9 10

Library of Congress Cataloging-in-Publication Data

Kosslyn, Stephen Michael
    Wet mind : the new cognitive neuroscience / Stephen M. Kosslyn and Olivier Koenig.
        p.   cm.
    Includes bibliographical references and index.
    ISBN 0-02-917595-X
    1. Cognitive neuroscience.   I. Koenig, Olivier.   II. Title.
    [DNLM: 1. Brain—physiology.   2. Cognition—physiology.
3. Neuropsychology.   WL 103 K86w]
QP360.5.K67   1992
612.8'2—dc20
DNLM/DLC
for Library of Congress   91-38404
                                                                CIP

To our families

Contents

Preface

The 1990s were declared by the Congress of the United States of America to be the "Decade of the Brain." In this book we attempt to convey a sense of why this declaration is appropriate. We are finally "cracking the code," and beginning to understand how the brain works and—a more enigmatic question—how it gives rise to the mind. This endeavor has transcended the usual disciplinary boundaries, and has begun to succeed in part because of the contributions of cognitive psychologists and specialists in artificial intelligence in addition to those of neuroscientists.

Our goal is to paint a particular type of picture of how the mind is produced by the brain: We hope to show how the brain gives rise to the structure of the mind and to delineate the major components of that structure; we do not aim to specify the details of what each part does. Moreover, we do not simply review the literature, but rather tell the emerging story as we see it. We do not try to give equal time to all the many worthy researchers in this new field; rather, we pick and choose in order to illustrate salient points.

Furthermore, we aim to speak to the general reader, not the expert in any one field. Indeed, as experts will know, each of these chapters could easily be expanded into several volumes. Even at this relatively early stage, there is already too much known to say anything simple about how the brain works. Nevertheless, it is possible to stake out a middle ground. Our hope is to avoid being so precise as to overwhelm readers with details, but also to avoid being so general as to be vague. We were guided by this hope when we focused on sets of specific questions, and then sought just the information that would speak to the questions. In this book we seek to provide a map of the forest; although the outlines of some of the individual trees may have been left blurry, we believe that they can be filled in at a later date without substantially altering the overall contours we have drawn.

This book had several roots. Perhaps most important, in 1987 Olivier Koenig took a leave from the University of Geneva and went to Cambridge, Massachusetts to work in Stephen Kosslyn's laboratory for a year (which became two years). We began a highly successful collaboration in which we investigated how the cerebral hemispheres store information about spatial relations. This collaboration gradually branched out, and we began to consider many topics and approaches. At the time, Kosslyn had for four years been teaching a somewhat idiosyncratic course called "Minds, Brains, and Computers" in an attempt to integrate the entire range of modern research on the neural basis of cognition. The lecture notes for this course were slowly evolving into prose, and it dawned on Kosslyn that there might be the makings of a book there. But this would have been a false dawn if Koenig had not been enthusiastic about collaborating on such a book or if Susan Milmoe, and then Susan Arellano, at The Free Press had not believed that the time was ripe for such a project.

The book has profited greatly from many additional sources of support and encouragement. Susan Chipman of the Office of Naval Research, Alfred Fregly of the Air Force Office for Sponsored Research, and Joseph Young of the National Science

Foundation, all managers of programs that supported Kosslyn's research, have steadfastly been personally supportive as well, and never failed to provide valuable feedback. The Swiss Science Foundation supported Koenig during his stay at Harvard and also supported his research described in this book. In addition, four generations of students and teaching fellows in Psychology 1185 at Harvard University helped to hone the approach and content; in particular, Elizabeth (Liddy) Olds and Chad Marsolek took much time to comment in detail on the project. Halle Brown, Chris Chabris, James Intriligator, and Lisa Shin not only provided carefully considered and very useful comments and suggestions, but they—along with David Gow and Billy Thompson—also helped to pull this book together when the deadline seemed impossibly near. We are very grateful for their help. We also thank Anthony Korotko Hatch and Adam Anderson for producing the bulk of the original artwork (everything that couldn't be done easily on a computer), and Greg Horwitz and Chris Chabris for producing the remainder.

We also are extremely grateful to David Caplan, Michael Jordan, Steven Pinker, and Larry Squire for reading the manuscript; they helped to prevent us from misrepresenting the state of the field, and made this a better book by prodding us to think more deeply. Shelia Kennison spent many hours working over early drafts of the manuscript, trying to teach us how to make the material flow; this book is far easier to read because of her efforts to help us find a useful organizational structure. Susan Milmoe read numerous drafts of the book, and knew how to mix critical feedback with just the right amount of praise; she helped us to tell a story that others could understand. We are particularly grateful to Susan for believing in the project enough to encourage us even when it was not clear whether much would come of all this effort. Finally, we wish to thank our families and friends, who put up with more than the usual amount of distracted mutterings and late nights while this book was being written.

1

Wet Mind/Dry Mind

Have you ever wondered why dancing is harder than it looks? Or how "mental pictures" spring to mind when you think of an ideal mate? Or why you remember emotional events so vividly? A confluence of developments in several fields has brought us dramatically closer to answering questions like these than one could have imagined even ten years ago. Researchers are now seeking to understand mental abilities by specifying the brain functions that subserve them. Their efforts are not only illuminating how the normal mind works, but also helping to explain the effects of brain damage on cognition and behavior.

Consider the puzzles raised by the maladies of even a single brain-damaged person, described by David Benson and John Greenberg in 1969.[1] A 25-year-old soldier entered the Boston Veterans Administration Hospital seven months after accidental carbon monoxide poisoning. While on leave in November 1966, he had been found stuporous on the bathroom floor after having been exposed to leaking gas fumes while showering. Following initial resuscitation he was sufficiently alert to converse with relatives, but he lapsed into a coma the next day. One month later he was described as alert and talkative, but was thought to be blind.

Seven months later he was readmitted to the hospital. At this point he was demonstrably not blind. He appeared attentive to his surroundings and could navigate corridors successfully in his wheelchair. He was able to name colors and appeared to follow moving visual stimuli. When asked to name objects he was viewing, it was clear that he could see their colors and size (a safety pin was "silver and shiny like a watch or nail clipper" and a rubber eraser was "a small ball"). He identified a photograph of a white, typewritten letter on a blue background as "a beach scene," pointing to the blue background as "the ocean," the stationery as "the beach," and the small typewriter print as "people seen on the beach from an airplane." He could select similar objects from a group, but only if there were strong color and size clues; after training he could name several familiar objects but failed to do so if their colors or sizes were altered. Thus he failed to identify a green toothbrush which was substituted for a previously named red toothbrush. He also called a red pencil, "my toothbrush."

Although he could readily identify and name objects from tactile, olfactory, or auditory clues, he could not identify them by vision alone, nor could he name objects, pictures of objects, body parts, letters, numbers, or geometrical figures when looking at them. His eyes wandered persistently, especially when he was inspecting an object. Moreover, he was unable to select his doctor or family members from a group until they spoke, and he was unable to identify family members from photographs. At one time he identified his own image in a mirror as his doctor's face. He did identify his own photograph, but only by the color of the military uniform. After closely inspecting a scantily attired "cover girl" in a magazine, he surmised that she was a woman because "there was no hair on her arms." That this inference was based on flesh color identification was evident when he failed to identify any body parts. For example, when asked to locate her eyes he pointed to her breasts.

Clearly, common sense will not help us to understand the

details of this patient's problems. Why can he perceive size and color, but not shape? If he cannot recognize objects, how can he see that the arm has no hair? Both an arm and hair are objects. Moreover, the confusion between eyes and nipples is not entirely random; consider the similarity of their shapes. If this sort of similarity affected his judgments, why could he not encode more detailed aspects of shape? And why did he identify objects if he was familiar with the alternatives, but fail dramatically when they were changed? Chapter 3 illuminates the answers to these questions.

Until recently, explanations for puzzles such as these would have been almost entirely speculative, in large part because there were no clear ideas about how the brain functions normally. But there has been a dramatic change in the last decade, primarily because of technological developments. The two most important of these developments both depend on the ready availability of relatively inexpensive, very fast computers.

First, by providing new ways to mimic the activity of complex networks of brain cells (*neurons*), computers allow researchers to formulate more precise theories about brain function. And second, computer-aided brain scanning techniques allow theories to be tested in new ways. We can now monitor the activity of normal, working human or animal brains, and observe which regions are involved in specific cognitive activities.

In short, we have new ways to ask questions about the mind and brain and new ways to answer them. Computer modeling and brain scanning played a critical role in the birth of a new field called *cognitive neuroscience,* which focuses on how mental activities are carried out by the brain.

Wet Mind

Mental capacities such as memory, perception, mental imagery, language, and thought all have proven to have complex underlying structures. Cognitive neuroscientists improve our understanding of them by delineating component processes and specifying the way they work together. (This project has sometimes been described as "carving the mind at its joints.")

Researchers in cognitive psychology and some parts of artificial intelligence share this aim, but they do not consider the brain. Their central metaphor is the computer. Just as information processing operations in a computer can be analyzed without regard for the physical machine itself, mental events can be examined without regard for the brain.[2] This approach is like understanding the properties and uses of a building independently of the materials used to construct it; the shapes and functions of rooms, windows, arches, and so forth can be discussed without reference to whether the building is made of wood, brick, or stone. We call this approach *Dry Mind*.

In contrast, we call the approach of cognitive neuroscience *Wet Mind*. This approach capitalizes on the idea that *the mind is what the brain does:* a description of mental events is a description of brain function, and facts about the brain are needed to characterize these events.

The aim is not to replace a description of mental events by a description of brain activity. This would be like replacing a description of architecture with a description of building materials. Although the nature of the materials restricts the kinds of buildings that can be built, it does not characterize their function or design. Nevertheless, the kinds of designs that are feasible depend on the nature of the materials. Skyscrapers cannot be built with only boards and nails, and minds do not arise from just any material substrate.

The Quest for Components

The claim that different mental functions are carried out by different parts of the brain has been made by *localizationists* for many years, and possibly dates back as far as 5,000 years ago to the ancient Egyptians.[3] Until very recently the idea of localization of function was hotly debated, with *globalists* arguing that the brain works as a single, integrated whole. Three sets of events fueled this debate.

Faculty psychology. In 1796 the Austrian anatomist Franz Joseph Gall began to measure bumps on the head of residents of Vienna. His goal was to use the size and location of the bumps to assess cognitive profiles. J. G. Spurzheim soon joined him, named the theory *phrenology,* and vigorously promoted the ideas.[4] The phrenologists believed that the brain is a collection of separate organs, each governing a distinct mental faculty, with the parts of the brain at the surface (the *cortex*) playing a critical role.

These theorists are often treated as quacks today, but they laid important foundations for the contemporary understanding of how mental functions are embodied in the brain. To see why, we must distinguish those of their claims that can be taken seriously from those that must be discarded.

The notion of distinct brain regions for distinct faculties was not all there was to phrenology. The phrenologists also assumed that (a) the larger the size of the region, the better the faculty, and (b) larger brain regions resulted in larger lumps on the surface of the skull. So, to assess someone's personality, one felt his or her head and noted the size of the lumps over specific regions. Both of these assumptions are probably wrong. In addition, the phrenologists characterized mental functions at the wrong level of specificity. Gall included among the faculties acquisitiveness, sublimity, secretiveness, veneration, firmness, hope, and parental love (said to be located just above parts of the brain now known to be used in vision).

On the other hand, the general idea of specifying and analyzing mental abilities was good, and so was Gall's emphasis on the importance of the cortex. Prior to Gall, the interior regions of the brain were treated as paramount. The cortex is in fact so important that it is literally folded and packed into the skull in a way that maximizes its surface area. And finally, Gall's idea that the brain is not an amorphous, undifferentiated single system also turns out to have been right on target.

The most influential globalist critic of phrenology was the French physiologist Pierre Flourens. Unlike the phrenologists, who were not really scientists, he carried out experiments, mostly on birds, although he hoped to generalize the results to all higher animals. Flourens showed that birds could recover after parts of the nervous system were removed, regardless of the location of the damage. Abilities were not localized, he believed, but rather resulted from the operation of numerous sites working in concert.[5] But birds are not people (the expression "bird brain" is pejorative for good reason), and Flourens did not measure possible deficits very carefully. If his measures were not sensitive enough, he might easily have missed a subtle effect—which is one reason why scientists are reluctant to accept the failure to discover something as evidence that it does not exist.

Later animal experiments challenged the globalist view of the brain. In 1870 the German physicians Eduard Hitzig and Gustav Theodor Fritsch administered mild electrical stimulation to the cerebral cortex of dogs, and found that different muscles contracted when different brain regions were stimulated.[6] In 1881 another German, E. Munk, removed the posterior region of the brain of a dog, and found that it still saw but could no longer recognize objects; it suffered from "psychic blindness."[7] These and similar findings demonstrated that some aspects of vision could be selectively impaired, and suggested that different parts of the brain do have different functions.

Clinical neuropsychology. Another line of research that fed the growing debate about localization was the study of behavioral deficits in patients with brain damage, often undertaken by physicians as part of an effort to characterize the deficit and determine the best program of rehabilitation.

As early as 1825 researchers observed an association between lesions of the anterior part of the brain and language problems.[8] Marc Dax, a French physician, noted in 1836 that language deficits occurred following damage to the left portions of the brain—which was probably the first clear attempted linkage of language deficits to damage in a particular location. (Unfortunately, his paper was so obscure that it was not even published for 25 years.)[9] Dax was not able to find a single case of a right-handed person with language difficulties following right-sided damage.

Clinical data first had a serious impact on the debate about localization of function in 1861, when the French anthropologist/ neuroanatomist Paul Broca displayed the brain of a patient he called "Tan," who had died only one day before the presentation. After suffering a stroke, he had lost the ability to say everything but "tan" (which appears at the end of many French verbs and adjectives). A stroke interrupts the blood supply to a region of the brain, which causes brain cells in that region to die. Tan's stroke had damaged the posterior part of his left frontal lobe. Later that year Broca discovered a second case with similar damage that apparently impaired language production. To Broca, these observations suggested that cognitive functions are carried out by tissue in specific folds in the cortex—which do not correspond well to bumps on the head. Indeed, in later work he emphasized the importance for language production of the left posterior portion of one particular fold, known as the third frontal convolution (see Figure 1.1).[10] Broca noted, however, that left-handed people can sometimes have the reverse relationship, with language seemingly governed by the right side.

Further clinical evidence supported the localizationist view. A little more than a decade after Broca's discovery, the German neurologist Carl Wernicke described a patient who had trouble understanding speech following damage to the left superior temporal gyrus.[11] Whereas Broca had shown that damage to the left frontal lobe could impair language production, Wernicke found that damage to posterior regions could impair language comprehension. The two findings showed that language is not a single function, but has at least two components, which are affected by lesions to different regions of the brain. Another important contribution of Wernicke was to recognize that the phrenologists had not analyzed mental function properly; not complex attributes such as "filial love," but rather much simpler perceptual and motor functions are localized in distinct brain regions.[12]

Following the discoveries of Broca and Wernicke, numerous other brain "centers" for specific functions were reported. Every patient with brain damage and a behavioral deficit was an invitation for researchers to posit a center for the disrupted behavior in the damaged part of the brain (which, as we shall see later in the book, is based on flawed logic). Elaborate speculative diagrams of the brain based on little evidence were published; they included far more detail than was warranted by the specificity of the damage or behavioral deficits.

Meanwhile, in the 1860s the British neurologist John Hughlings Jackson challenged a strict localizationist view. No simple-minded globalist, Jackson was the first, in 1864, to suggest

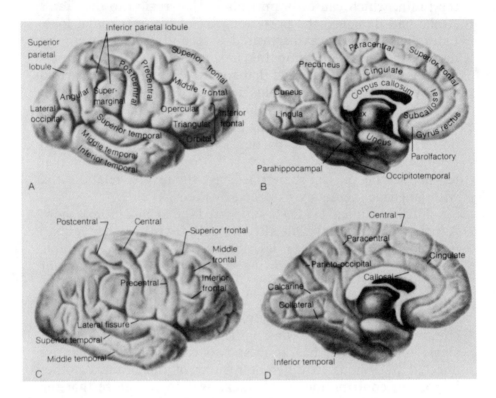

FIGURE 1.1 Major landmarks in the brain; the panel above illustrates lateral (side, A) and medial (interior, B) views of the gyri (bulges), and lateral (C) and medial (D) views of the sulci (creases). The right panel illustrates the location of the major lobes of the brain. Dorsal views are seen from above, ventral views from below. The third frontal convolution is the inferior frontal gyrus. "Superior" means above, "inferior," below, "anterior," front, and "posterior," rear. (*From Fundamentals of Human Neuropsychology, 3rd edition, by Brian Kolb and Ian Q. Whishaw, eds. Copyright © 1990 by W. H. Freeman and Company. Reprinted with permission.*)

that some perceptual processes are more effective in the right side of the brain.[13] And he noticed that epileptic seizures seemed to affect specific regions of the body—which suggested that they may have localized origins in the brain. Nevertheless, he rejected the idea that a particular cognitive function is carried out in a particular brain site. Jackson found that a function was never

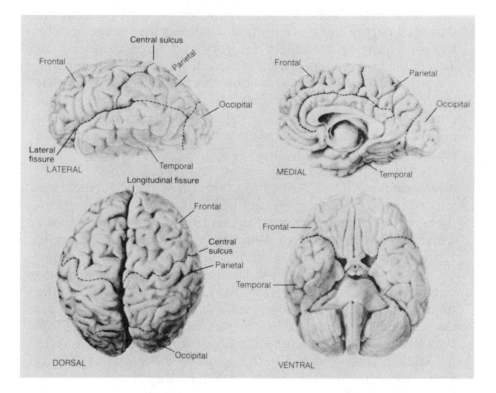

Central sulcus

Frontal

Parietal

Occipital

Lateral fissure

LATERAL

Temporal

Longitudinal fissure

Frontal

Parietal

Occipital

MEDIAL

Temporal

Frontal

Central sulcus

Parietal

Temporal

DORSAL

Occipital

Frontal

Frontal

Temporal

VENTRAL

completely lost following brain damage. He made much of cases in which a patient could perform a behavior involuntarily but not voluntarily. For example, one patient consistently failed, despite repeated requests, to say the word "no." After being goaded to exasperation, however, he finally said, "No, doctor, I never can say 'no!'"

Jackson believed that a specific mental ability is not produced by one distinct group of localized brain cells, but rather arises at several levels of organization, beginning with a low (spinal or brain stem) level, a motor or sensory level, and then at a "high" frontal level. The more complex the activity, Jackson believed, the more brain processes are recruited—more in reading a word than a letter; more in reading a sentence than a word; and more in reading a story than a sentence. And the more complex the activity, the more combinations of different processes can be recruited to carry it out.

Jackson pointed out that even if damaging part of the brain

impairs a certain behavior, we cannot necessarily infer that the damaged part of the brain normally governs that behavior. The British psychologist Richard Gregory compared damaging an area of the brain to removing a resistor from a radio.[14] Removing a resistor may make the radio howl, but this does not mean that the resistor is a "howl suppressor." Rather, the functioning of an entire system of components is altered when one part is damaged. To understand deficits, we need to understand the dynamic relation between different functions.

Neuroanatomy. The localization enterprise was further advanced in the nineteenth century by another important development, namely the discovery of dyes and stains that revealed the distribution and density of different types of cells in the brain. Using such a technique, the Spanish histologist Santiago Ramon y Cajal in 1888 showed that the cortex could be delineated into separate areas and described networks of brain cells under the microscope that seemed compatible with the kinds of diagrams the clinicians constructed.[15] Consistent with these ideas, in 1909 the German anatomist Korbinian Brodmann dissected brains (in his kitchen sink) and numbered some 50 differently appearing areas according to the order in which he cut them.[16] His taxonomy is still used today in many laboratories, although before long, on the basis of minimal clues, other researchers had reported some 200 areas.

The American psychologist Karl Lashley responded to these developments with a new round of attacks on localization. He and his colleagues reported that they could recognize only a few regions of the cortex if they were not expecting a specific region.[17] They also found that the differences between some purportedly distinct regions "were so small as to be imperceptible to all but the anatomists who first described them."[18]

Lashley also removed portions of the brains of rats and found no evidence for selective breakdown in behavior depending on the site of damage. He concluded that only the extent of the damage was important, not its location. He proposed two principles to explain brain function: According to the principle of *mass action,* the brain works as a single system, and so the more that is damaged, the worse performance will be; and according to the principle of *equipotentiality*, all parts have equal ability to perform different tasks, so it does not matter which parts are damaged.[19]

Lashley's views gained a substantial following, but his behavioral tests were relatively crude and he failed to detect effects of the location of a lesion that have since been repeatedly documented. Furthermore, his principles could not account for the selective effects of electrical stimulation on behavior discovered by Hitzig and Fritsch. Indeed, the Canadian neurosurgeon Wilder Penfield and his colleagues found that stimulating different parts of the human brain (prior to surgery) sometimes evoked different memories or experiences.[20] By the end of the 1960s, these findings and the selective effects of brain lesions on behavior (in both humans and animals) provided strong evidence against an extreme globalist view.

Of functions and Functions: A Reconciliation

The recently deceased Soviet neurologist Aleksandr Romanovich Luria offered a way to reconcile the conflicting views and findings concerning localization by drawing an important distinction between two uses of the word "function."[21] We can speak of the functions (with a lowercase *f*) of specific organs; for example, one function of the stomach is to produce digestive fluid. In another sense, we can speak of a Function (with an uppercase *F*) as a complex activity involving a number of different organs; the Function of the digestive system as a whole is to take in food and supply the blood with nutrients. In cognition, a Function such as reading is carried out by functions that detect lines, organize them into patterns, match them to patterns stored in memory, and so forth.

A simple, elementary function often depends on tissue in a particular region, for at least two reasons. First, the brain's structure (i.e., its anatomy) restricts the information available in, and the possible outputs from, any given locus.[22] Some parts of the brain receive input from the eyes, and so process visual input; other parts receive input from the ears, and so process auditory input, and so on. Neurons that are near each other tend to receive similar input and send outputs to similar locations; thus, they will tend to perform the same function. Second, nearby neurons have the opportunity for fast interaction; neurons that are near each other have relatively short connections, and hence can affect each others' operation quickly. (By analogy, think about why cities exist; why don't people distribute themselves more evenly across the countryside? It is clear that lots of interactions are facilitated by physical proximity.) When groups of neurons must interact to carry out a specific function, it makes sense that those neurons will be localized in a particular region of the brain.

A Function, in contrast, often can be performed in a number of ways, depending on the state of the individual tissues, organs, and the organism as a whole. In the brain, different cognitive strategies can be used to accomplish the same end. For example, we can add (a Function) by counting on our fingers, by memorizing the result of adding pairs of numbers and later recalling the sum, by pressing a sequence of keys on a calculator, and so on. Different "strategies" can be composed by combining different simple functions, which will allow one to perform a task in different ways; an integrative Function can be carried out by simpler functions that are localized in many different places in the brain. Thus, we can have it both ways: some functions are localized, but the brain works as a whole to produce Functions that are not localized.

Today the debate between localizationists and globalists has subsided.[23] The issue is not whether different parts of the brain have different functions (at least some do), or whether entire abilities are localized in a single area (probably rarely, if ever). Rather, researchers see their goal as characterizing what the functions are, which parts of the brain are used to carry out each one, and how functions work together.

Regions and Functions of the Brain

To characterize the functions of various brain regions we must not only divide the brain into units, delineated in terms of physical (anatomical) properties and physiological activity, but also must divide Functions into units (functions).

Characterizing Regions of the Brain

It was not until the early nineteenth century that the brain began to be divided into a standard set of lobes or regions.[24] The original conception specified five lobes: the anterior, upper, and lower lobes, the operculum, and the island of Reil. By 1830, many physicians spoke of three lobes, the anterior, posterior, and middle lobes, which were specified relative to the base of the skull; this taxonomy appeared in textbooks until about 1850. Then other parts of the skull began to be used as landmarks for the brain; physicians began to associate regions of the brain with the bones that covered them—a system that is still used today. Researchers generally specify four lobes: the occipital, temporal, parietal, and frontal (Figure 1.1), corresponding to four major bones of the skull. However, the insula (tissue that is folded into the sylvian fissure) and the limbic system (structures that lie deep in the brain) are sometimes considered as additional lobes.

Broca's convention of relating functional regions of the brain to features of the cortex has also been widely adopted. These landmarks consist of *sulci* (which is the plural of sulcus) and *gyri* (which is the plural of gyrus); a sulcus is a crease in the surface layers of the brain (i.e., the cortex), and a gyrus is the bulging area between sulci. Especially important are the *lateral sulcus* (also called the *sylvian fissure*) and the *central sulcus* (also called the *Rolandic fissure*). As illustrated in Figure 1.1, the lateral sulcus (also called the *lateral fissure*) divides the temporal lobe from the frontal and parietal lobes, and the central sulcus divides the frontal lobe from the parietal lobe. The boundaries of the occipital lobe are not so clearly demarcated.

Despite considerable variability from brain to brain, all human brains share the major sulci and gyri. These landmarks are not formed arbitrarily, the way creases and folds arise when one crumbles up a piece of paper. One reason for the consistency is that connections between areas tug at particular locations during gestation, drawing them together. As we noted earlier, connections play a major role in specifying the functions because they determine what input is available in a region of the brain and what output is required from that region. Hence, at least some of the time anatomical regions that are defined by sulci and gyri should have different functions.

And in fact, special dyes and stains reveal that regions of the brain with different input/output connections often also have different physical organizations. The areas discovered in this way sometimes are only a few millimeters wide, and neurons in these areas typically respond in very specific circumstances, as we shall see. These areas may correspond to individual neural processors, and their properties provide important clues as to the function they perform. Their locations are typically specified relative to sulci and gyri.

Characterizing Functions of Brain Areas

In order to characterize brain functions, we need to consider what kinds of things we are looking for in the brain. What sort of "function" is likely to be localized in a piece of tissue? It is not something like "acquisitiveness," but what is it? As was evident in our discussion of the patient with selective visual deficits, common sense alone will not help us to characterize what parts of the brain do. This should not be a surprise because common sense develops as we interact with objects and people, and the principles that govern these sorts of interactions may have little to do with those that determine how the brain works.

The resolution of the localizationist/globalist debate suggests that relatively simple, mechanical functions are localized. One way to formulate hypotheses about this type of function is to discover how to build a machine that exhibits specific abilities, as we shall see in the following chapter. Taking the Wet Mind approach, we apply to the study of brain function a theoretical vocabulary borrowed from computer science, which has been used to guide the construction of intelligent machines. We must consider this vocabulary before we can proceed further.

Plan of the Book

This book consists of nine chapters. In Chapter 2, we develop the idea of computation, and describe one particular kind of computation in detail—namely computation by "neural networks." We discuss how one can generate hypotheses about the existence of neural networks that perform specific computations, and discuss five general principles of brain function that are suggested by this type of theorizing.

In Chapter 3 we consider visual perception. This chapter, like the following five chapters, is divided into two major parts. In the first, we consider a set of individual abilities of the system being discussed (such as the ability to identify objects when they are contorted into unusual shapes), and infer computations that can confer each ability. In the second, we review the primary ways that brain damage can impair the ability. We use the analyses in the first part of the chapter to provide alternative accounts for each deficit. Our aim is to show that the deficits are not simple, and will probably often have several distinct subtypes.

In Chapter 4 we move on to visual mental imagery. We take advantage of the discovery that visual imagery shares mechanisms with visual perception, and build on the analyses of Chapter 3 to understand imagery abilities and deficits following brain damage.

In Chapter 5 we turn to reading. Reading is of interest in part because it is a bridge from basic visual processes to more abstract language processes and in part because it is a learned ability—and hence involves processes that do not contribute to visual perception and mental imagery, which are not acquired via instruction.

In Chapter 6 we consider language more generally. We focus specifically on the perception, comprehension, and production of simple utterances, and illustrate how these evolutionarily late developments apparently took advantage of structures and functions that were present to help carry out other Functions.

In Chapter 7 we discuss movement and action. Even here, we are able to build on what came before. Indeed, many of the principles that govern language production turn out to apply to actions in general. We consider not only complex movements of the limbs, but also the actions that underlie our ability to write. In so doing, we further articulate the relation between these processes and those that underlie perception, imagery, reading, and language.

In Chapter 8 we address memory, a Function that lies at the interstices of virtually all those discussed previously. We show

how memory serves to integrate many facets of mental activity, and how it grows out of specific perceptual and motor functions.

Finally, in Chapter 9 we turn to "gray matters," issues still too poorly understood for us to tell a detailed story. "Gray matters" range from reasoning to cerebral lateralization, from consciousness to emotion and rehabilitation. We show that they can, in principle, be understood from the perspective we take in the rest of the book. We close with some general thoughts about Wet Mind and our particular attempt to chart the present state of the art.

2

Computation in the Brain

In order to appreciate the relevance of computing to understanding the brain, it may be most useful to begin by considering the hand. Would you be satisfied that you had truly understood the nature of the hand if all you had was a detailed description of its physical composition? Say you knew its precise shape, which muscle fibers were connected to which tendons, and so on; would that be enough? Probably not. You probably would want to know what the muscles and tendons are *for,* what purpose they served. Understanding the construction of the hand requires an understanding of its role in manipulation, the kinds of things it does—grasping, jabbing, poking, stroking, and so on.

Similarly, a complete understanding of the brain will require more than a description of its physical composition, its cells and their connections, various chemical and electrical interactions, and so forth. The brain does something different from any other organ: It processes information. The brain registers input from

17

the senses, interprets the input, and makes decisions about how to behave accordingly. Thus, we can characterize brain function in terms of how information is processed.

For example, our two eyes allow us to see how far away an object is from us. In order to do so, the brain takes account of slight disparities in the images registered by each eye. This information serves as input to a "stereo vision" process, which compares the differences between the two eyes and infers how far objects must be to project such differences. In addition, we can recognize the same word when it is spoken by many different people, who have voices that are relatively high or low, talk quickly or slowly, and so on. The auditory system takes the sound pattern as input, and processes information about changes in the sound that are preserved across all of these variations. This information is then used to identify the word.

The language of information processing is derived from computers, so in order to specify how the brain works we must use key concepts from this language.

Computing by Connections

Today's most common computers, from million-dollar mainframes to inexpensive PCs, are based on a design worked out by John von Neumann in the 1940s. Von Neumann explicitly tried to design the computer to mimic what was then known about the brain. It is ironic that less than 50 years later most features of his design are held up as decidedly unlike those of the brain. For example, although standard computers have proven invaluable in many respects, they do only one thing at a time, whereas brains do many things at the same time, such as see, hear, and guide movement. Similarly, computers operate only as explicitly instructed, whereas brains discover new strategies without being explicitly told how to do so. Furthermore, standard computers have a clear distinction between stored information (i.e., data) and operations that manipulate that information. Brains, on the other hand, do not.[1]

These sorts of facts have been widely appreciated for decades, but only recently has a new form of computation been developed that has brain-like features. "Neural network" (also known as "parallel distributed processing" or "connectionist") computation is performed by sets of interconnected units that work together to perform a specific type of information processing. It may be easiest to explain the key ideas of such computation if we begin with some fictional marine zoology.

Professor Jack Costlow was forced to work on a low budget. Having no money to fund deep sea explorations, he explored the mysteries of tidal pools. His rise to fame began with an accidental discovery of a form of recreation practiced by octopi. This game is illustrated in Figure 2.1. The octopi lined up in three rows. The octopi in the first row intertwined tentacles with the octopi in the second row, who in turn intertwined tentacles with the octopi in the third row. Professor Costlow noticed that whenever anything brushed one of the free tentacles of an octopus in the first row, that octopus would squeeze tentacles with all the octopi in the middle row. Those octopi in turn would squeeze tentacles with the octopi in the third row. What caught the Professor's attention, however, was what happened when something brushed against several of the octopi in the first row, leading all of them to squeeze the octopi in the middle row. Now some of the octopi in the middle row squeezed the octopi in the third row harder! Depending on how they squeezed, a different octopus in the third row waved its free tentacles out of the water.

The Professor's first thought was that he had stumbled on a coven of sadistic octopi; he thought that squeezing those in the middle row brought them pain, and the more they hurt, the more they took it out on their brothers and sisters in the third row. But then he noticed something interesting. The octopi in the last row did not always respond in the same way. Depending on how many octopi were brushed in the first row, different octopi in the third row waved their tentacles out of the water.

These intertwined octopi unknowingly were reporting to seagulls the density of small fish in the area: high, medium, or low. The octopi were operating as a kind of computational device, which is illustrated more formally in Figure 2.2.

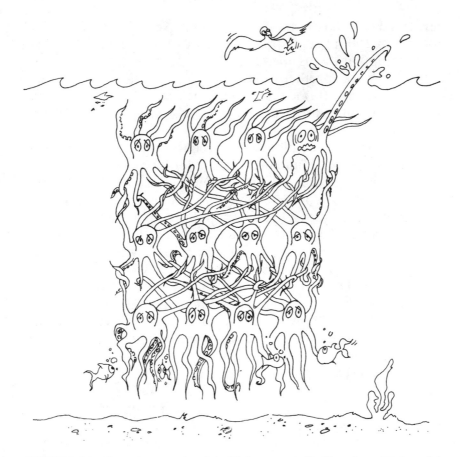

FIGURE 2.1 An octopus network, which purportedly lives in a tidal pool in Southern California

Feedforward Networks

A device that operates in this way is known as a "feedforward" neural network; the input marches through the system to produce an output. Such networks have layers of units, and each octopus corresponds to a unit. The octopi in the first row serve as units in the *input layer;* those in the third row serve as units in the *output layer;* and those in the middle are in a *hidden layer*. The members of the hidden layer have no direct contact with the "world"; they are not directly affected by the stimuli in the world, nor do they directly affect things in the world. Rather, the hidden layer

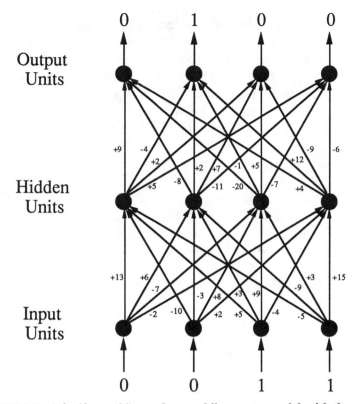

FIGURE 2.2 A feedforward "neural network" computer model, with three layers of units

receives input only from the input layer and sends output only to the output layer.

The input to and output from the network consists of *binary vectors,* ordered series of 1's and 0's. By analogy to the octopi, if an octopus in the first row is brushed, it is "on" (active) and corresponds to a "1." And if an octopus in the third row is squeezed hard enough so that it waves its free tentacles out of the water, it is "on" and corresponds to a "1." A binary vector is simply a series of on and off values in a row.

As has been done for decades in standard digital computers, a series of 0's and 1's can be used as a symbol (it can stand for something else). For example, we can adopt a convention where "0001" means the letter *A,* "0010" means the letter *B,* "0100" means the letter *C,* and so forth. Professor Costlow realized this, and noted the correspondences between the input and output. He discovered that when any three of the octopi in the first row were brushed by fish, the second octopus in the third row waved (corresponding to the code 0100); when only two of the octopi in the first row were brushed, the third octopus waved (0010); and when only one octopus in the first row was brushed, the last octopus in the third row waved (0001).

Turning again to Figure 2.2, each octopus corresponds to a unit. Notice that there are two kinds of connections between units, excitatory and inhibitory. If a unit is connected to another by an excitatory connection, then turning on the first unit will result in its trying to turn on the second. Excitatory connections between octopi were ones where the first octopus used a tentacle to squeeze hard, and led the Professor originally to suspect perverse relationships among the creatures. However, he soon noticed that his initial impression was mistaken; they did not always squeeze: some tentacles tickled other octopi. These were inhibitory connections. If one unit is connected to another by an inhibitory connection, then turning on the first unit causes it to try to keep the second one off. Tickling is very distracting to octopi, and so tickling one tentacle could counteract the effects of squeezing another. In addition, if an octopus is tickled enough, it gets rather giddy and will try to tickle the octopi in the next layer, distracting them from being activated by squeezes.

Brain cells (neurons) have the same two kinds of connections, although they are much more complex than the units in these networks; indeed, in the brain some neurons always try to activate others, whereas other neurons always try to inhibit others. These effects, however, can sometimes be altered by the cell on the receiving end if specific chemicals are present.

In addition, each connection illustrated in Figure 2.2 has a *weight* (strength); the larger the weight (excitatory or inhibitory) on a connection, the more vigorously a unit will try to turn on or off, as appropriate, the unit to which it is connected. The octopi's tentacles varied in strength; the stronger the tentacle, the more squeezing or tickling affects the recipient. When given the input vector "0111," the network always produced the output vector "0100." It did this because certain tentacles were squeezing or tickling vigorously, while others were squeezing or tickling gently, causing the octopi in the hidden layer to squeeze only the appropriate output octopus hard enough so that it waved.

Consider the simplest case, illustrated in Figure 2.3, where two input units are connected via excitatory connections to one hidden unit. When the input vector is "00," nothing happens because neither input unit is turned on. When the input is "01," the critical connection is between the second input unit and the hidden unit. In this example the weight is 9 on that connection, which thus will provide an input to the hidden unit of 9, which turns it on quite a bit. In contrast, an input of "10" will make use of the connection between the first input unit and the hidden unit, which has a weight of 3. When the input is "11," the total input to the hidden unit will be 12, which really gets the hidden unit going. This unit in turn is connected to an output unit, which would fire "1" when the input it receives is over a "threshold" value (e.g., 10), and "0" otherwise. The excitatory connection between the hidden and output unit has a weight of 1, and hence simply passes the accumulated activation at the hidden unit to the output unit. Thus, depending on the pattern of input, the output will be 1 or 0; in this case, the output would indicate

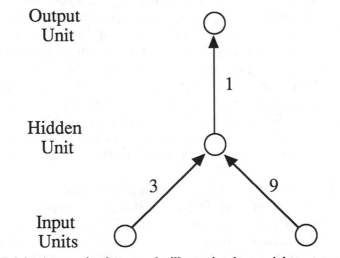

Output
Unit

Hidden
Unit

Input
Units

FIGURE 2.3   A very simple network, illustrating how weights on connections affect processing

whether both input units were on at the same time (which might be helpful in counting fish).

In an actual network model, like our octopus network, each input unit is connected to many hidden units, and each hidden unit is connected to many output units. Thus, depending on the weights on the connections, when a "1" is on one of the input units, it will try to turn on or turn off (depending on whether the connections are excitatory or inhibitory) the various hidden units, having an effect in proportion to the weights on its connections. The degree to which each hidden unit is on depends on the sum of the input it receives from all of the input units to which it is connected.[2] The hidden units in turn try to turn on or off the output units, obeying the same principles.

Training Associations

But how do the weights get adjusted so that the connections have just the right effect? How did the muscles in each of the tentacles of each octopus develop to squeeze or tickle the right amount? Each individual octopus has no idea of what the network is doing; it simply squeezes or tickles in proportion to how much it is squeezed or tickled. As you can imagine, Professor Costlow became fascinated by the octopi, and spent many hours on the beach watching them. It finally dawned on him that their relationship with the seagulls cut two ways: The seagulls not only observed the flailing octopi for a fish report, but also rewarded some of the octopi (with little bits of shredded fish) whenever they gave the gulls the right signal. In order for the seagulls to see the number of fish, they had to dive rather low, which required effort; they wanted to avoid having to swoop low to the water on reconnaisance missions by training the octopi to be good spotters.

The seagulls, then, were "training" a neural network. Such training consists of teaching the network to produce a given output when it receives a given input. The seagulls trained the octopi in the network by getting them to adjust the strengths of the connections. Before training, the weights on the connections were random, so that when the input was first presented, random output was produced. For example, an input of "0111" might have caused all four octopi in the third row to wave happily, producing an output vector of "1111," or none to respond, producing "0000," or any other combination of values, depending on the particular random weights.

The most common training technique is called *backward error propagation,* or "backprop" for short.[3] Here is the basic idea: The network starts off with very small, random weights, and an input is presented. The output that is produced is essentially random. A "teacher" compares the actual output to the desired output at each output unit. For example, if "1111" was produced, for three of the output units a "1" was produced when a "0" was desired. The teacher therefore lowers (by a little bit) all of the weights on the excitatory connections and raises the weights on the inhibitory connections to those three inaccurate output units. Thus, the next time that input is presented, there will be less net excitatory input to those output units. Similarly, if a "0" is obtained at an output unit initially and a "1" is appropriate, the weights on the excitatory connections leading to that unit will be raised, and the weights on the inhibitory connections leading to that unit will be reduced.

On each presentation, the teacher adjusts the weights in this manner to reduce the difference between what was obtained and what was desired. One adjustment usually is not enough, and so many presentations of the input are necessary before the weights are fully adjusted.[4] Small steps are necessary because each connection typically is used as part of many different input/output associations, and the right balance must be struck among the connections to preserve all of the stored associations at the same time. In the octopus network, only three input/output associations were stored (between large, medium, and small amounts of fish and three output symbols), but networks of this type can store many such associations. Thus, training usually involves a large set of associations, all of which are learned at the same time.

In the octopus network, if an output octopus should have been waving but was not, the seagulls strengthened the excitatory connections to this unit in the following way: They gave fish to the octopi in the hidden layer if they tensed the tentacles that squeezed this output octopus; they had them do "sets" of exercises (the octopus equivalent of pumping iron), building up the muscles so that the tentacles that connect to the output unit could squeeze harder in the future. In contrast, octopi in the hidden layer who were tickling the output octopus were rewarded for keeping the offending tentacle still, thereby decreasing their tendency to tickle vigorously. Similarly, if an octopus in the output row was waving but should not have been, the seagulls reinforced octopi in the hidden layer who were tickling this output octopus, building up these muscles so that they could tickle more vigorously and hence be more distracting. And octopi in the hidden layer that were squeezing were rewarded for keeping these tentacles still, thereby decreasing the strength of subsequent squeezes. The same process was done with the octopi in the input layer, now adjusting their squeezing and tickling of those in the hidden layer.

There are many different ways of training networks, but all hinge on adjusting the weights properly so that the input produces the correct output. Some of the methods do not depend on a teacher, but rather make use of internal relations within the network itself to adjust the weights.[5] We focus on the backprop method in large part because the majority of the models we will discuss later in the book rely on it.

Computing Qualitative Relations

The network we have described counts fish, but not all—or even most—computation involves quantitative associations. Professor Costlow was most impressed by a discovery that occurred after he began to study the octopi in depth. He had become so enamored of these octopi that he took to bathing with them, allowing those in the input layer to run their tentacles over his body. He actually convinced some friends to accompany him in this uniquely Californian experience. He soon noticed that the octopi in the last row came to produce different patterns of flailing tentacles, depending on who was being massaged by the input octopi. The network was identifying the people!

The seagulls liked to know who was splashing around in the water because some of the people brought them snacks, and so they trained the network to identify the people. To do so, the seagulls needed to know how to interpret the input and output vectors in a new way; they already knew how to make the right weights on connections. They let each input unit register a feature, either a moustache, a pot belly, a ring on the right hand, or hairy arm pits. For example, "1111" was the input when Sam was massaged; he has all four features. And "0110" was the input when Sally was the object of the affections of the octopi in the input layer; she has a pot belly and a ring on the right hand, but no moustache or hairy arm pits. Only the first octopus in the output layer raised his tentacle when Sam was present (producing the vector 1000), whereas the last one raised his tentacle when Sally was present (producing the vector 0001), thereby signaling the seagulls who was in the tidal pool.

These types of networks function as a kind of associative memory, pairing an input with an output. This sort of memory is very powerful in part because the input and output can stand for practically anything. The interpretation of the inputs and outputs is by convention, and so anything can be paired with anything else. The input might be visual properties of a person, and the output a name; the input might correspond to the smell of a juicy cheeseburger and the output a signal for the salivary glands to start up, and so on.

The pattern of weights established on the internal connections of a network often serves as a *representation*. A representation is something that stands for something else. Consider again the octopus network that could identify people. The pattern of excitatory and inhibitory weights on the connections represents the combinations of features that identify the individual people. These weights store the information about the people that allows the network to identify them, and in that sense represent the people in their absence. If we think about a network that recognizes objects more generally, the patterns of weights in the network will be representations of different objects; without the right weights, the network cannot map the input to the proper output.

Interpreting Input and Output

But how does the network "know" whether to estimate fish density or recognize people? The network does not know how the input and output are interpreted; that is up to the seagulls. And there may be two groups of seagulls, which interpret the same output pattern in different ways. A single output vector could mean lots of fish or Sheila, but when the tide is very low one group of seagulls knows that there will not be any fish, and so that group leaves. The other group knows that the people prefer to loll in low tidal pools, and so it moves in and reads the output vector as indicating people. In fact, in conventional computers the same strings of 0's and 1's can indicate letters, symbols, digits, and even instructions, depending on the effects they have elsewhere in the system.[6]

As noted in Chapter 1, in the brain the actual physical connections between different areas often determine the consequences of an output; the output from one network serves as input to another—and depending on what this second network does, the input has one "interpretation" or another. Depending on which group of seagulls is watching, the same output pattern has a different interpretation. The interpretation corresponds to the impact of the pattern elsewhere in the system, of which an individual octopus network is only one component.

Recurrent Networks: Using Feedback

Not all networks process input in a lock-step fashion to produce output. As illustrated in Figure 2.4, some networks include connections from the output units back to earlier units (typically the input units, as illustrated in the figure). These connections can be precise, as illustrated in the figure, or more diffuse; each output unit could send feedback to every input unit or to any subset of the input units. These *recurrent networks* use excitatory or inhibitory feedback to modulate the input, and in so doing display another important property: If only a fragment of the

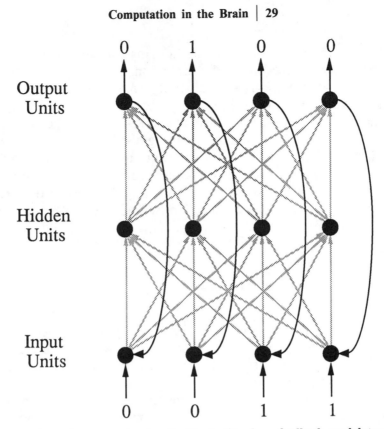

FIGURE 2.4 A recurrent network, illustrating how feedback modulates the performance of the network

input is present, these networks can actually fill in the missing values. This process is called *vector completion.* For example, if a value of .5 were on the input lines instead of 1, the values at the output units probably would fall below their thresholds. But feedback from the recurrent connections could boost the inputs close to a value of 1—allowing the network to function properly. Similarly, individual missing values can be completed.[7]

In terms of our octopus network, imagine that some of the octopi in the output layer stretch back their tentacles and squeeze or tickle input tentacles of the octopi in the first layer. If the output octopi squeeze and tickle appropriately, the octopus network can perform correctly even if the fish don't always brush very hard against the input tentacles. The strengths of the recurrent connections are adjusted during training the same way that strengths of feedforward connections are adjusted.

Vector completion is important for at least two reasons. First, in real neural networks, the input is often noisy. Neurons are not precise devices; they fire probabilistically and cannot fire during a "rebound" period after having just fired. Second, as will be discussed in the following chapter, many—if not most— brain areas that are connected by fibers running one way are also connected by fibers running the other way. Models of recurrent networks help us to understand how feedback interacts with input in such systems.

Recap: The Nature of Computation

These examples illustrate several general points about computation. First, the 0's and 1's in the octopus network correspond to whether the animals are active or quiescent. In a computer, 0's and 1's correspond to whether tiny capacitors are charged or not charged (in older computers, tiny magnets are on or off). In both cases, physical states function to carry information. So too with neurons, the cells that process information in the brain. They "fire" at different rates, and this physical state conveys information.

The second general point is that in both of the examples, reporting fish density and recognizing people, the network is performing computations. By computation we mean an *informationally interpretable systematic mapping from input to output.* Let us take this one piece at a time. The inputs and outputs are patterns of activity. These patterns are "informationally interpretable" because they have a specific impact on the way the seagulls behave; depending on which octopus is waving, the seagulls dive for fish or do not bother. In addition, the connections within the network specify a "systematic mapping," which pairs each input with a particular output. This mapping is "systematic" because it preserves a specific relationship between properties of the input and output; as these properties vary, the input/output pairings vary accordingly. The systematic relationship between inputs and outputs typically can be described by a rule. For example, the inputs and outputs may vary systematically with the number of fish, identity of the person, and so forth.

Computation, then, is nothing more than a rule-based association game; given an input, a particular output is required by the rules. The inputs and outputs have interpretations in the context of the larger system, which includes other components that produce the inputs and act on the outputs. Note that a computational system need not actually include rules that are explicitly specified ("mentioned") and followed; the system need not include a cookbook that specifies recipes, which in turn are read and followed a step at a time. Rather, like our octopus network, the system may not specify rules at all, but rather is "wired" in such a way that the relations between its inputs and outputs can be *described* using rules. By analogy, the motions of the planets are described by Kepler's laws, but the planets do not *follow* these rules. In the brain, physical states (patterns of neural activity) have the effect of producing other physical states that in turn affect other physical states, and laws can describe the interrelations between these physical states and their impact on behavior.

Big Networks and Little Networks

Imagine that our seagulls got lazy, and did not want to have to remember which people were the feeders. Thus, they had the output octopi of the network that names people intertwine their tentacles with those of octopi in the input layer of a second network. This second network categorizes the input as a feeder or nonfeeder, saving the seagulls the effort of remembering who was who. The two networks can be viewed as a single system, with the first encoding the distinctive features of the input and producing an identification, and the second categorizing the identity in a useful way for the seagulls.

If you saw such a thing in a tidal pool, it would look like a bunch of octopi with intertwined tentacles (imagine yourself in

Professor Costlow's position when first stepping into their pool). There is no dotted line telling you where one network ends and the other begins; all you see are interconnected octopi. What distinguishes the two parts of the network is that they do different things; they have different roles in information processing. For some purposes, it would be sufficient to describe the entire intertwined network as a single system, which signals when a person who feeds seagulls is rolling around in the tidal pool. Alternatively, we could discuss the two subnetworks separately— the one that identifies and the one that categorizes, respectively. This would be useful if we wanted to know what would happen if the network were damaged (say one octopus got sick). If we know that there are two subnetworks, we can more easily understand the kinds of errors that would be produced when part of the system were damaged.

As the octopus example illustrates, it sometimes is useful to regard a set of networks as comprising a larger network. Such a larger network functions as a *processing subsystem*. A processing subsystem performs one or more computations that map an input to an output. A processing subsystem is a "black box" that takes inputs and produces specific outputs, which in turn are passed on to some other black box. The operation performed within the box often depends on previously stored information —representations—which are used to transform the input in appropriate ways.

We can characterize networks as carrying out steps, and a single step may itself be composed of smaller steps. The smaller steps can be thought of as an *algorithm* that accomplishes the computation described by the coarser step. An algorithm is a set of steps that, if followed faithfully, will always produce a given output when given a particular input. By characterizing processing at a coarser level we do not need to commit to the details of the algorithms that carry out each step. For example, we can specify that a network classifies objects a good or bad, without concern for the internal steps it takes to do so.

We can regard each step as being accomplished by a processing subsystem. Often processing within a subsystem can be broken down into sets of computations, but this does not matter:

As long as we can specify informationally interpretable systematic mappings from input to output, we are describing a bona fide computational entity.

In this book we conceive of processing subsystems as corresponding to individual neural networks or sets of networks that work together. We will characterize these networks at different levels of coarseness, starting off with big boxes and breaking them down into sets of more detailed boxes as we progress.

Discovering Networks

As would be true in a two-network octopus system, we cannot simply look at the brain and discover processing subsystems; they are distinguished by what they do, not how they look. What a given neural network does is determined in part by the input it receives. Different parts of the brain receive different kinds of input. For example, the occipital lobe receives input from the eyes, and hence it processes visual information; in contrast, part of the temporal lobe receives direct input from the ears, and hence it processes auditory information. But the same information is treated in different ways in different parts of the brain; for example, visual input is used to recognize shapes, locate objects, track moving objects, and so forth. Thus, although the kind of information sent to a network restricts what it can do, the input alone does not determine what a network computes. If we stumbled on the tangled two-network octopus system, with no physical indication that it was composed of two subsystems, we would only discover its subsystems by analyzing more carefully how networks could allow a system to behave in specific ways.

How do we discover which computations are carried out by networks? We begin by performing a *computational analysis,* the method of which was developed in detail by the late artificial intelligence researcher David Marr in the 1970s.[8] A computational analysis is a logical analysis of the information processing that is needed to produce a specific behavior. One analyzes the nature of the input and the goal of the processing, noticing which aspects of the input are critical for establishing the input/output mapping; one then specifies what computations are needed to use that information appropriately. These analyses can be performed in conjunction with an examination of properties of the brain to produce a *theory of a subsystem*. A theory of a subsystem is an argument for inferring that a particular processing subsystem exists in the brain. Once the theory is formulated, it can be tested. Computational analyses help one to come up with the theory in the first place.

To illustrate the idea of a computational analysis, let us consider one of Marr's examples in some detail. A fundamental ability of our visual systems is that they pick out a single region of space as corresponding to an object. This is a prerequisite for later trying to recognize the shape. The input can be regarded as a matrix that specifies the intensity of light at each point on a surface (which is registered by the eye or a TV camera), and the desired output is a shape. Although this ability may seem trivially simple, one lesson we have learned from efforts to program computers to behave intelligently is that some of the things we do effortlessly are in fact very difficult. The depth of the problem should become apparent if you study the digitized output from a TV camera presented in Figure 2.5. The value of each number indicates how intense the light was at that point. At first glance, it is impossible to make out anything meaningful in such a display. The outline of an object is not obvious given the input—it must be discovered.

The theory of what is computed by this subsystem rests in part on an analysis of what information is available for a network to use as input, and what properties of the input would allow it to register an object's edges. The input specifies the absolute intensity at each point in space, which makes it easy to compute the relative intensities at different places. The first part of the analysis is to infer which aspects of the input are critical for producing the requisite output. Marr assumed that shapes could be organized by locating their edges, so he sought properties of the input that would signal edges. Marr noted that edges of objects often correspond to places where intensity changes sharply along a set of contiguous points. These points can be characterized precisely as places where there are "zero crossings" in the second derivative of the function relating intensity to position. (As is evident in Figure 2.6, the second derivative

```
89 89 90 91 90 92 91 90 92 91 90 90 89 86 86 86 82 76 67 64 56 54 49 49 45 40 39 35 33 35 36 34 35 32 35 37 40 42 50 59 65 73 77 75 77 81 80
93 92 92 92 93 91 92 90 94 92 92 92 91 87 85 81 73 65 58 53 53 50 44 45 40 39 38 38 38 38 38 34 42 40 38 35 40 47 55 66 73 76 74 79 79
93 92 92 92 91 92 92 92 92 92 91 90 87 84 79 71 63 53 51 47 47 49 47 40 37 36 39 40 43 47 50 51 44 44 50 45 42 36 35 36 42 50 59 68 70 77 79
94 96 94 92 94 91 91 92 90 88 87 83 77 74 69 59 53 47 46 47 43 42 38 38 36 39 46 48 51 58 60 58 55 58 55 50 45 42 39 42 39 43 52 62 70 73 76
95 91 94 92 92 92 92 91 90 84 77 72 65 60 53 50 45 47 44 40 43 38 38 31 43 50 54 57 62 66 63 61 60 61 60 51 53 50 50 50 44 45 44 53 58 69 73
96 96 94 94 92 91 92 89 84 79 69 56 52 49 45 43 45 45 44 46 42 43 45 54 63 66 67 73 71 71 71 69 69 71 67 64 63 57 55 51 44 44 43 50 60 71
97 98 98 97 94 92 88 82 77 70 56 51 45 42 40 39 38 41 45 51 53 49 52 60 68 71 77 80 83 81 81 82 78 79 79 76 72 70 64 58 53 50 48 43 41 51 64
95 94 94 95 91 87 77 71 62 55 47 44 47 41 39 38 44 52 57 57 57 60 69 76 79 84 85 87 90 87 88 90 87 85 82 81 76 75 73 69 66 63 58 50 44 49 55
93 92 91 87 81 73 65 58 53 49 43 46 46 45 43 48 53 61 61 59 66 77 86 87 88 91 92 91 91 92 94 91 90 87 87 84 82 81 78 77 76 70 65 60 54 49 49
90 87 83 76 70 65 53 49 47 45 49 49 51 47 54 63 66 70 66 70 80 87 91 94 92 94 91 94 95 96 96 93 92 92 87 86 85 82 81 80 76 74 70 65 61 55
83 79 70 64 61 56 50 49 49 51 53 54 59 63 66 75 79 79 79 85 89 92 91 95 94 95 95 94 95 94 97 96 96 96 95 94 91 88 84 83 80 79 77 73 71 65 59
76 73 66 65 58 53 50 51 53 56 59 64 74 75 80 82 85 85 85 87 91 92 92 92 91 92 93 91 93 96 96 96 95 95 94 91 89 86 84 82 80 76 74 74 67
70 67 66 60 59 51 55 56 60 64 72 76 82 84 85 84 87 86 87 88 89 88 89 90 90 90 92 92 92 94 94 96 95 94 92 89 85 83 83 81 78 71 74
71 66 63 60 56 56 61 65 73 77 81 83 86 85 85 84 83 84 82 84 83 84 84 84 85 86 85 86 87 87 87 89 90 90 93 94 94 94 92 91 86 84 84 81 77 80 77
68 68 62 59 60 61 70 74 78 82 81 81 84 85 83 81 81 80 79 79 80 80 81 81 80 81 82 82 84 83 84 85 85 87 87 90 92 90 89 90 87 85 84 82 80 80 80
69 70 69 63 65 73 74 80 81 83 82 80 82 82 80 80 78 77 77 77 80 77 77 78 74 78 79 79 79 78 79 79 79 80 80 80 81 83 85 84 81 88 87 84 84 83 80 81 81
69 74 73 72 75 81 82 85 82 82 81 79 79 81 80 79 77 71 78 77 80 77 75 74 76 75 75 76 75 75 75 75 76 80 83 84 83 84 87 85 85 84 84 82 83 80
75 78 76 81 82 85 86 84 81 80 80 79 79 80 80 80 80 81 81 80 79 79 74 71 70 70 71 71 72 72 71 73 72 73 74 79 80 81 81 82 84 84 82 84 83 82 6
75 77 81 85 86 86 83 82 81 81 81 82 76 79 80 81 80 82 79 75 74 71 69 62 59 63 64 66 65 69 66 73 75 79 81 80 82 82 81 81 7
78 83 84 86 87 84 84 82 80 81 81 81 80 82 82 81 77 75 69 65 61 59 59 55 49 50 55 60 61 64 60 63 62 59 63 69 71 74 80 77 79 81 81 80 80 81 8
84 87 86 86 86 84 84 81 78 79 80 82 83 81 78 74 68 65 61 57 56 53 54 44 43 43 50 56 59 60 60 60 60 59 57 60 63 69 72 73 76 75 79 77 80 80 81
85 89 84 87 85 85 84 80 79 81 80 80 80 73 67 65 61 60 57 54 51 49 45 45 48 53 54 52 53 59 58 56 55 56 56 60 76 70 71 73 75 75 75 80 81
90 91 91 88 86 84 83 82 80 81 76 71 68 65 63 64 61 55 54 44 42 35 32 29 33 34 37 42 42 43 40 46 51 53 58 60 58 57 55 58 54 69 67 66 77 79 80
91 92 90 87 85 82 82 74 70 64 60 49 39 27 19 21 19 11 12 17 17 13 08 05 08 09 11 09 08 11 33 58 55 43 27 12 08 03 05 04 08 16 30 46 51 61 64 63
91 89 88 85 83 81 71 66 61 54 42 30 29 34 35 22 13 15 19 16 07 07 11 12 12 13 13 13 12 42 76 81 71 50 30 19 13 09 06 08 08 12 19 29 34 36 42
91 90 88 86 84 75 70 65 56 45 34 34 35 45 55 53 34 40 32 19 13 11 06 07 06 04 04 04 03 03 02 02 00 01 02 04 07 10 17 24 28 30 36 42 45 43 44 63 77 83 84 84
94 92 88 82 83 86 79 73 66 65 59 55 45 43 22 16 09 11 14 11 10 06 07 04 03 03 04 04 04 06 07 04 04 04 08 11 18 24 27 31 40 53 71 79 82 83 86
92 90 86 84 82 82 77 70 64 59 45 35 23 13 11 10 11 14 16 14 11 10 08 08 12 08 06 10 20 27 21 14 10 06 09 10 12 13 19 32 56 67 75 78 80 81
91 90 87 86 83 82 74 70 64 60 49 37 27 19 21 19 11 12 17 17 13 08 05 06 09 11 09 08 11 33 58 55 43 27 12 08 03 05 04 08 16 30 46 55 61 64 63
91 89 88 85 83 81 71 66 61 54 42 30 29 34 35 22 13 15 19 16 07 07 11 12 12 13 13 13 12 42 76 81 71 50 30 19 13 09 06 08 08 12 19 29 34 36 42
91 90 88 86 84 75 70 65 56 45 34 34 35 45 55 53 34 40 32 19 13 11 09 07 06 08 02 01 13 29 36 42 45 49 47 49 48 56 54 56 66 72 71 74
92 94 94 89 82 75 70 64 52 43 41 50 63 71 68 44 23 20 19 21 23 53 77 65 39 23 19 19 30 73 95 96 86 73 52 37 24 24 22 22 29 30 55 60 66 71
92 94 92 89 80 70 68 59 51 51 54 63 74 79 75 58 35 23 20 21 22 31 43 39 25 17 18 17 47 85 93 86 71 56 38 28 28 29 32 36 42 51 64 69 70 71 74
94 95 92 85 76 70 64 57 49 56 62 71 79 82 81 75 82 81 75 83 85 89 92 91 94 93 94 94 93 93 30 53 33 30 39 42 47 45 45 54 65 68 72 71 74
94 92 86 71 74 66 56 51 55 55 63 73 77 80 82 74 69 52 35 25 20 16 11 17 18 17 21 40 59 59 50 41 34 38 44 44 48 50 49 51 52 58 63 67 71 73 73
86 78 75 70 64 56 54 49 47 49 44 46 54 56 58 61 65 71 78 83 89 92 93 91 93 91 89 89 89 91 94 93 94 94 93 94 92 90 87 88 88 86 84 83 82 84 85 84 82 81
81 77 75 70 59 53 48 44 41 42 47 47 41 51 47 50 44 42 40 43 42 39 44 45 50 58 60 59 60 70 77 80 77 80 79 80 79 74 76 69 68 70 73 75 75 76 76 76 76 79 80
79 80 74 68 56 54 47 47 49 44 44 44 49 56 56 58 58 61 61 70 70 81 71 78 83 87 89 90 89 88 87 80 80 79 80 79 80
82 83 80 70 60 55 61 57 59 56 55 58 60 58 56 55 60 59 64 69 73 75 77 80 86 92 94 91 90 91 94 94 91 90 89 88 84 82 81 80 80 81 80 81 80 81 80
85 85 83 77 71 70 73 75 73 68 64 66 68 68 68 69 73 76 80 85 89 90 90 92 93 96 94 93 94 94 92 90 91 90 89 87 86 83 82 80 81 79 82 81 80 82
85 85 84 83 82 79 81 79 73 71 74 75 77 77 78 83 85 89 92 93 92 91 88 89 91 91 92 90 90 90 91 89 87 82 83 81 82 82 83 83
82 81 82 82 84 82 80 76 76 75 77 77 78 82 82 83 87 87 90 91 93 91 91 89 89 89 91 91 89 89 88 87 88 88 86 86 84 83 82 84 83 82 81 81
83 84 81 79 79 74 74 72 74 75 80 80 80 82 84 86 91 89 90 91 90 91 90 91 89 91 91 92 91 88 89 84 87 88 88 86 86 84 83 82 84 84 82 81
83 82 82 78 79 74 76 77 76 77 80 82 84 82 85 86 89 91 94 93 94 93 95 92 92 91 90 92 89 89 87 89 88 86 88 81 81 81 78 74 78 78
81 82 79 80 79 81 75 77 79 81 82 83 84 85 84 85 88 90 93 92 92 92 94 96 95 92 95 92 91 90 87 85 87 84 82 82 82 82 81 80 79 80 81 81 80 81 83 84
85 85 84 81 81 80 80 80 80 82 81 83 84 84 87 91 92 91 93 92 94 94 95 94 92 92 90 89 86 85 84 82 82 82 81 81 80 79 76 77 79 80 76 80 81 83
89 88 87 85 85 82 81 80 81 79 81 83 86 84 87 88 92 92 92 94 94 91 91 90 90 90 92 91 92 91 87 86 83 80 80 76 79 78 76 77 78 74 74 77 79 81 80 80
89 90 89 87 85 84 84 81 81 82 81 84 85 85 87 90 91 91 90 91 90 90 92 91 92 91 87 86 83 80 80 76 79 78 76 74 76 79 77 77 79 81 80 81
86 89 85 84 85 84 85 87 83 82 81 81 82 82 84 84 87 84 84 87 86 84 85 90 89 84 87 87 85 81 80 80 76 77 77 77 75 77 76 77 77 78 79 80 82 82 80
```

FIGURE 2.5 A digitized output from a TV camera. Can you guess what object is displayed? (Marilyn Monroe's eye. *Figure courtesy of David Mumford, prepared by Mark Nitzberg.*)

indicates the rate of change of a change, and so it indicates how quickly intensity changes over an image.) Marr noticed that sets of such points often can be grouped by connecting them with small line segments, blobs, and so on. This was the first step towards specifying the edges of an object.

However, connecting up places where intensity changes sharply not only captures edges of objects, but also indicates texture changes and small surface deformations. Marr obtained a

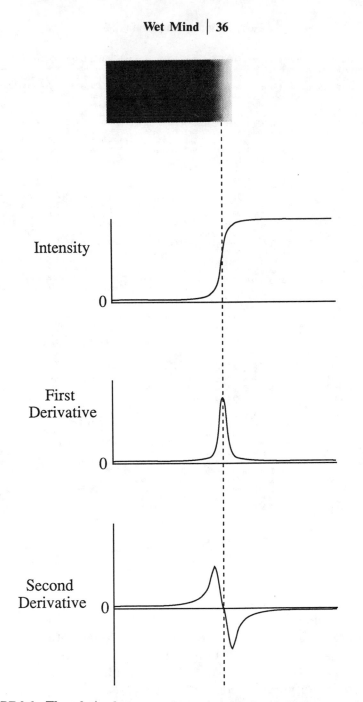

FIGURE 2.6 The relation between a change in intensity, the first derivative (the slope of the intensity), and second derivative (the slope of the first derivative)

hint as to how the brain deals with this problem by observing properties of neurons in the first cortical area to process vision (which will be discussed further in the following chapter). Properties of the cells' *receptive fields* were particularly illuminating. A neuron's receptive field is the region of space in which a stimulus will activate it (and the animal does not move its eyes; more precisely, a receptive field is defined relative to a specific region on the retina, the light-sensitive surface at the back of the eye). For example, if the neuron responds to a spot of light, it will do so only if a spot falls within a set of contiguous locations in front of the animal. That set of locations is the cell's receptive field.

Two properties of these cells' receptive fields hinted at how the brain sorts out whether one is looking at edges rather than textures or surface markings. First, the neurons are "tuned" so that they fire vigorously when the center of the receptive field is stimulated, and are actually inhibited from firing if the area near the edge of the receptive field is stimulated. These neurons are called *on-center/off-surround;* neurons with the opposite properties—*off-center/on-surround*—also exist. When an edge is present, a characteristic pattern of activity arises in sets of these neurons.[9] And second, these receptive fields come in different sizes, and the larger the size the poorer the resolution of the neuron. The neuron responds to the sum total of the stimulation within its receptive field, essentially averaging over the input. Hence neurons with larger receptive fields average over a relatively large area, and fine distinctions are lost. By analogy, comic strips are printed using small dots, which can indicate small variations in shape. If large dots were used, only coarse variations could be made—producing low-resolution pictures. The output from large receptive fields is like seeing large dots. In short, the neural machinery is present to detect contiguous sharp changes in intensity at different levels of resolution.

Marr's insight was that edges, unlike texture and surface marks, show up at many levels of resolution. An edge is signaled by sharp changes along sets of contiguous points that are registered simultaneously by neurons with different-sized receptive fields.

Marr thus was led to develop a theory of a subsystem (which he called a "theory of the computation," i.e., a theory of what is computed), which posited a subsystem that picks out regions of the input likely to correspond to figures. This subsystem can be characterized in terms of its input, operation, and output: The input is a map of intensity at each point in space; the operation consists of finding locations where there are sharp changes in intensity, connecting these locations, comparing these connected locations at different levels of blur, and selecting the connected sets of locations of sharp intensity changes that are present at multiple levels of blur; and the output is a set of edges added to the input map.

Marr's analyses revealed that neurons with the right response patterns do the equivalent of taking the second derivative of the input. Furthermore, because each location in space provides input to sets of neurons with different-sized receptive fields, the zero crossings can be connected up and compared at different levels of blur. Marr not only performed a logical analysis of what computations could produce the desired output given the input, but he also looked at the way the brain happens to be constructed, and used those facts to guide his theorizing.

This example sketches out how logical analyses of the nature of the necessary information processing and observations about properties of the brain can lead to well-motivated hypotheses about what a processing subsystem does. Such hypotheses about the existence of processing subsystems that carry out specific tasks must then be tested by examining the brain in action (as will be illustrated in later chapters). And in fact such tests, as well as attempts to program computers to mimic human performance using Marr's theory, have shown that Marr's ideas do not tell the whole story about how objects are separated from background; in fact, color, texture, relative depth, and other factors that do not involve edges are also at work. Nevertheless, he discovered part of the story, and the reasoning behind his theory serves as a model for how the science is done.

Computer Models

Even relatively simple activities, such as finding edges, are likely to involve complex interactions among multiple networks. For example, individual processing subsystems might find contiguous locations where intensity changes rapidly, organize regions of homogeneous color or texture, and so on. But an edge may be indicated only weakly by any one cue taken alone; in contrast, it may be strongly implicated by the presence of correlated changes in several cues.

The interactions among individual computations can be very complex, which is one reason why the computer has been so important in the development of cognitive neuroscience. Efforts to create artificial intelligence (AI) rest on the idea that complex behavior arises by combining relatively simple operations, and researchers in AI have developed methods of programming computers to perform such operations. The techniques of AI can be used not only to build intelligent machines, but also to build computer models of biological information processing. That is, just as one can test principles of aircraft design by building a model airplane and seeing what it does in a wind tunnel, one can test any explicit theory of network information processing by programming a computer to mimic a network.[10] These models produce output vectors when given input vectors, as described earlier.[11]

For example, consider a possible network computer model of free association processes in humans. The behavior to be modeled occurs when people are asked to name the first word that comes to mind when a given word is read to them. There are great consistencies for some pairs of words: given "knife," most people say "fork"; "bread" spurs "butter"; and so on. For other words, there is not much consistency. For example, when given "rug" some people say "floor," others say "feet," and still others say something else. The model is intended to explain the varying degrees of consistency in the associations.

This model is based on a theory that has two parts. One claim is that people associate objects that have similar distinctive properties. For example, "knife" and "fork" are both used for eating, "bread" and "butter" are often used together during a meal, and so on. The other claim is that objects differ in the "salience" of their features. And the more salient an object's features, the more likely everybody will notice the same ones.

Thus, a network could be designed that associates two named objects. The meaning of each word is specified as a set of features, and each feature corresponds to a single input unit. Each associated output object in turn corresponds to a single output unit, and the network is trained to produce the proper output when given an input. For some words (such as "knife" and "bread"), only one set of (salient) input features is presented and only one output unit can be activated, whereas for others (such as "rug") several different sets of (nonsalient, and hence variable) inputs are presented and several output units can be activated.

After the network is trained, it can be used to test the theory. The test depends critically on a characteristic of networks—and actual brains—known as *generalization.* The network is now given new words, which were not used during training. When given novel input (such as "cup" and "toast"), the network will generalize if it tends to produce the output associated with a familiar, similar input. So if the network had never been given "1101," but had been trained with "1100," it would generalize if it tended to produce the response associated with "1100" when given "1101."

The model, then, is intended to discover whether a particular set of input features will result in the right sort of generalization. Once the network has been trained, will new words tend to produce the appropriate responses? If the theory is correct, the network should mimic actual human behavior.

This simple example illustrates several important ideas. First, and probably most important, the network model tests only the theory that was used to specify it. From the start, someone must decide that a given task should be performed by a distinct subsystem; this is perhaps the most critical theoretical claim. A theory of a processing subsystem leads one to infer that a given input/output mapping is performed by one subsystem, which might correspond to one network. And then someone must decide how the input and output vectors will be set up and how the layers will be connected (there is no need for every unit to be connected to every other, as we shall see in the following chapter).

Second, although the theory must be specified in advance, what it implies in every possible situation is not. Networks often surprise their builders; humans cannot anticipate every possible situation or every possible interaction among factors in advance. Thus, we learn more about the implications of a theory by observing the way a model actually behaves.

Third, to the extent that the model can match the pattern of an organism's responses to novel stimuli, we have reason to take the theory seriously. For example, if the program produced the same free associations as people do when they are given a series of words, this is a form of evidence that the theory that underlies the model is correct.

Hence, we draw a distinction between a *computational analysis* and a *computer model*. A computational analysis is a logical exercise aimed at determining what processing subsystems are necessary to produce a specific behavior, given specific input. In contrast, a computer model is a program on a computer that mimics the operation of one or more subsystems. Ideally, the two go hand in hand: Computational analyses are used to motivate specific computer models, and computer models can be used to test the validity of computational analyses.

Peering into the black box. Another reason why it is worth programming computer models of neural networks is that one can analyze a network after it is trained and figure out how it performed the task. That is, the input/output associations arise because a particular pattern of weights develops on the connections. We sometimes can gain insight into how the task is performed by examining the patterns of weights in the network, noting which aspects of the input were used to establish the mapping to the output.

For example, Sidney Lehky and Terrence Sejnowski gave a network pictures of curved objects and trained it to classify them as concave or convex and to indicate the degree of curvature.[12] In this case, the input was a matrix with a number in each cell that indicated the intensity of light at that point, and the output was a classification and measure of curvature. After the network was trained, Lehky and Sejnowski gave it new pictures (which were not used in training). The network classified most of the new shapes correctly. They then observed what the hidden units were doing when simple line segments were presented. Some hidden units responded strongly when a line segment was presented with the end of the line in a particular position.

Lehky and Sejnowski's finding is interesting because similar results have been found for neurons in visual cortex; some (so-called *end-stopped*) cells respond very vigorously to the ends of lines. This property of neurons had been a puzzle for many years, given that the natural world in which we evolved does not have all that many terminating straight lines. Furthermore, although plenty of neurons respond to straight edges and are sensitive to the orientation of an edge, neurons that respond selectively to different degrees of curvature have not been discovered. But the world is full of curvy objects. Lehky and Sejnowski's model suggests a nonintuitive resolution to this conundrum: Curvature is extracted by sets of cells that are sensitive to the ends of lines. Once this relation is discovered, one can mathematically analyze why this would be true.

The network told us something about how the input/output mapping could be achieved; training led it to produce a good way of using the input to produce the output. By looking at patterns of weights between the input layer and the hidden layer, we could discover what information is being pulled out of the input in order to perform the task.[13]

Neural Plausibility

Although network computer models are "brain inspired," they do not capture the details of the actual neural networks in the brain in some important ways. First, real neural networks are much more complex than any model simulated to date. It is common for a neuron to have thousands (between 1,000 and 5,000) of synapses (connections);[14] few researchers have dared to build a network this complex on a computer. This may sound like a detail, but some input/output mappings that can be trained in small networks may not be able to be trained in larger ones (they do not "scale up"; the additional possible connections cause the network to get tangled up, as it were).

Second, real neurons do not have an arbitrary organization; many connections are prewired and do not change (except via death of neurons, which does happen at a high rate during childhood; this process is called *pruning*).[15]

Third, it is not clear whether a typical neuron can excite one neuron while inhibiting another.[16] A given neuron produces one neurotransmitter (which conveys a signal to another neuron across the physical gap between neurons), and in some parts of the brain some neurotransmitters can excite or inhibit, depending on other factors that affect the receiving cell. It is not known whether the same transmitter can serve either role within a single neural network. In most neural network models, the same unit can produce excitatory and inhibitory connections.

Fourth, it is unlikely that the "teacher" used in backward error propagation is a plausible model for learning.[17] Indeed, the deeper into the system processing occurs, the more layers of subsystems are interposed between perceptual stimulation and motor output—and hence the more difficult it would be to use the input and output of the overall system to adjust processing.

In this book we will treat the units of a network as corresponding to a group of neurons that have the same properties. Thus, we will not worry about the details of what an individual neuron does, but only consider the ways in which one set of neurons affects another set. In this context, the weights on connections may reflect the number of neurons in one set that influence the neurons in another. The present neural network models are only rough approximations to actual neural networks, but they nevertheless can tell us interesting things about network computation in the brain.

Five Principles

Neural network models are a valuable tool for understanding specific processes. But they are more than that. By studying the properties of these models we already, in the short time that cognitive neuroscience has existed as a discipline, have learned enough to formulate a handful of general principles about how the brain computes. These principles will have pervasive implications for our investigations.

Division of Labor

Different types of input/output mappings can be trained in a single network. However, because the same connections are used, very different kinds of mappings will interfere with one another and retard performance when they are established in the same network. In these situations, it is more efficient to have separate networks perform the different mappings.[18]

An extreme case of this situation occurs when the mappings are incompatible. For example, to encode information, one wants to remember the meaning of a word, independent of who said it or where it was written. On the other hand, to mimic an accent or calligraphy style, one needs to pay attention to the specific way the word was spoken or written. And in fact, as we shall see, separate networks apparently encode the two types of information.[19] Similarly, to recognize objects in different locations, one ignores where they are situated; on the other hand, to reach or navigate, one needs to know where they are located. Again, separate brain systems appear to have evolved that divide these functions to achieve visual perception.[20]

A complex Function can always be decomposed into sets of relatively simple functions. The brain appears to rely on this principle of division of labor, and our task is to understand the particular way in which it has broken processing down into relatively simple phases.

Weak Modularity

Individual neural networks are not independent, discrete "modules" within a larger system (in contrast to the types of components proposed by the philosopher Jerry Fodor).[21] The principle of weak modularity has two facets, which pertain to functional relations among processing subsystems and the localization of networks in the brain.

Functional relations among subsystems. We assume that a group of networks may work to compute complex input/output mappings, and so a processing subsystem may have an internal structure. In at least some cases, the same subnetwork may be a member of more than one processing subsystem. For example, neurons in visual area MT respond selectively to motion, and motion is used to distinguish shapes from background as well as to track objects.[22] Thus, it is plausible that neurons in area MT work with subsystems that distinguish shapes and with subsystems that track moving objects.[23] This observation suggests that some parts of the brain may be like letters in a crossword puzzle, serving as components of more than one word. Such an arrangement makes sense if brain structures that originally evolved for one purpose later may become recruited to subserve another, as has been claimed by some evolutionary biologists.[24]

This breakdown in modularity does not imply that a network computes more than one function. By definition, the set of input/output mappings performed by a network is the function it computes (and in fact one technical method for defining a function is simply to list all of the input/output pairs). Hence, we always can regard a network as computing a single function, although in some cases it will be difficult to characterize the function using common sense or ordinary language.

If we characterize a subsystem properly at a coarse level of analysis, we usually should be able to break it down into component subsystems. It is impossible to know in advance when the more specialized subsystems that comprise one larger subsystem will be shared with those that comprise another. Perhaps paradoxically, we can have the most confidence that subsystems are independent at the coarser levels of analysis, when we are characterizing what is accomplished by very large brain regions, because these subsystems differ qualitatively in the type of inputs received and outputs produced. When we consider subnetworks at a finer level of analysis, all of which may receive a given type of input (e.g., visual, auditory, etc.), we will find some that may work with several groups of other subsystems within the more general domain.

Localization in the brain. The reconciliation of the localizationist/globalist debate was that simple, mechanical operations—like those performed by neural network models—are localized to specific brain sites. It is important to realize that not all of the neurons that subserve a given computation need to be in the same place: In Chapter 1 we argued that functions are localized because the neurons that accomplish them use the same input, project the same output, and must interact quickly. However, not all of the units in a network are so described; indeed, using these criteria, one could argue that the only neurons that should be localized are those that fulfill the role of the hidden units or that project or receive recurrent connections. These neurons are loci where information comes together and then flows out to influence other parts of the network, and hence lie at the heart of the process that computes a given input/output mapping. This idea is similar in some respects to the idea of *convergence zones* proposed by the neurologist Antonio Damasio.[25]

Thus, when we later speak of subsystems as localized to a particular site, this will be shorthand for speaking of these critical members of the networks. We do not assume that all of a network needs to be localized to a given region of the brain. Furthermore, there is no reason why two or more subsystems (which operate on input in different ways) cannot be implemented in the same region. Indeed, neurons that participate in separate networks may be interdigitated in some regions of the brain.[26]

Finally, we must note that even though processing subsystems may not be entirely independent, in many cases their functions can be understood by treating them as if they were. By analogy, we can treat the rooms on the same floor of a house as largely independent when we heat them, even though there is considerable leakage through the walls. The influence of the leakage is much smaller than the influence of the radiator. Until we have understood the major factors that influence the heat in a room (the operation of the radiator), there is little point in considering the leakage.[27]

Constraint Satisfaction

Much of the brain's operation appears to be governed by constraint satisfaction. Consider the following metaphor. One of us likes to move into old houses and fix them up every few years. This hobby entails a lot of moving and figuring out how to arrange furniture in new rooms. Each piece of furniture has some weak constraints associated with it. For example, the bed must go against a wall because the headboard is rickety; two small tables go on either side of the bed; the couch is missing its back legs and so sits on books, which means it must go against a wall so that the back is not visible, and so on. The constraints associated with each piece of furniture are "weak" because each one can be satisfied in many ways; the bed, for example, can be put against any of several walls. However, once the bed is placed, the entire arrangement may be determined: There may be only one other wall large enough for the couch, the tables must go next to the bed, and so forth.

The brain often seems to use many different sorts of information at the same time, trying to satisfy all the constraints simultaneously. For example, many of the neurons in visual area V4 respond selectively to the orientation of stimuli, but also respond selectively to their color.[28] At first glance, this seems odd, given that we perceive color and orientation independently. However, we earlier noted that multiple cues taken together are a better indicator of edges than any single cue; this area may play a critical role in a process that depends on such multiple cues, each of which constrains where an edge could be located.

The requirement that all of the weak constraints must be satisfied at the same time is itself a very strong constraint, and often dictates what output will be produced from a set of inputs to a subsystem. Thus, it will not be a surprise to find that many subsystems accept a variety of inputs, using them to converge on the proper output.

Coarse coding. One reason why constraint satisfaction is important is that the input/output mappings computed by individual networks are not precise. This lack of precision underlies the fact that networks generalize; similar inputs can produce the same output. Neural computation appears to take advantage of what may appear to be sloppiness, not only by utilizing generalization effectively but also by utilizing *coarse coding.*[29]

Perhaps the best way to explain coarse coding is by example. The eye contains only three types of cells that register different colors, called *cones*.[30] One type responds maximally when the wavelength corresponds to red, another to green, and the third to blue. Although each type of cone responds maximally to a single wavelength, it responds less vigorously to a range of longer and shorter wavelengths. Indeed, the responses of the three kinds of cones overlap considerably. And it is this overlap that allows us to see so many colors: We see maroon, orange, magenta, and so forth as a result of the *mixture* of the outputs from the three types of cones. Given a particular mixture, a particular stimulus is implicated. Coarse coding is this method of using the degree of overlap in responses from units (or entire networks) that have different sensitivities to specify precise values.

Coarse coding is a way of exploiting the fundamental idea of constraint satisfaction; each input is only a weak constraint, and is effective only when multiple weak constraints must be satisfied at the same time. Coarse coding is a very efficient way of specifying information; for example, rather than needing a different type of cone for each color, we need only three kinds.[31]

Concurrent Processing

All networks are always operating; neurons are rarely "off," but rather typically have some resting level of activity all of the time.[32] This principle is realized in two ways, in subsystems that "race" each other in parallel and in subsystems that form a series of "cascades."

Parallel races. First, networks that comprise separate systems (lying along distinct neural pathways) operate simultaneously, at times being in "races" with each other. That is, there may be more than one way of producing a behavior, and the different "strategies" correspond to different combinations of subsystems. These combinations of subsystems function at the same time, and whichever combination produces the appropriate output behavior most quickly will "win." As we shall see when considering the effects of brain damage on behavior, the behavior may have different properties when different sets of subsystems win.

Serial cascades. Second, concurrent processing also occurs in networks that are organized sequentially, along a single "pathway." By analogy, one can chew food while the stomach is digesting, and the stomach can operate while the intestines are operating. This kind of processing is called "pipelining." Furthermore, a network is not quiescent until it receives an appropriate input. Rather, networks operate constantly; they do not "know" when an appropriate input is present. They merely map whatever input is present to the corresponding output. Thus, networks often operate on partial information, and produce partial outputs for the next subsystem in line—forming a series of "cascades."[33] The presence of so much degraded information is one reason why constraint satisfaction and recurrent feedback are important.

Opportunism

Finally, we perform a task using whatever information is available, even if that information typically is not used in that context. That is, the output of a given set of subsystems may be used to accomplish different ends, depending on the situation. For example, as will be discussed in the following chapter, the parietal lobes of the brain may be specialized for guiding action; nevertheless, in some contexts the information used to guide action may also be used to distinguish one object from another. Similarly, although the frontal lobes may have evolved to control fine motor movement, they can be pressed into performing arithmetic and other serial activities.

The Cognitive Neuroscience Triangle

We want to specify the components of information processing used to identify objects, form and use mental images, read, use language, remember, and so forth. The Wet Mind approach is schematized in Figure 2.7, a triangle with *Behavior* at the top, and *Computation* and *Brain* at the bottom. Behavior is at the top because our goal is to explain specific abilities, all of which ultimately are revealed by behavior. Research in cognitive psy-

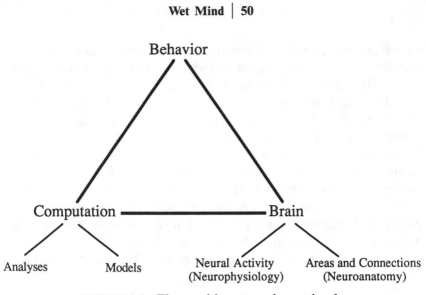

FIGURE 2.7   **The cognitive neuroscience triangle**

chology, linguistics, and similar fields plays an invaluable role in deepening our understanding of the phenomena to be explained. The kind of account we are seeking is symbolized by the vertices at the bottom. To reiterate, we want to understand the nature of the information processing that allows the brain to produce the observed behavior; therefore, we will consider how one could build a computational system that would behave like the brain. The goal of computational analyses and computer modeling is not merely to fathom *any* possible way in which the behavior could be produced; instead, we want to know how a device *with the structure and properties of the brain* could generate the behavior. Our analyses and modeling therefore must be performed in the context of facts about the brain itself. The two kinds of considerations will be used jointly in posing hypotheses about the underlying causes of our behavior.

Decades of work by Dry Mind researchers have shown that rigorous studies of behavior, computational analyses, and computer modeling can progress independently of any thought about the brain.[34] And decades of work in physiological psychology and psychobiology have shown that studies of brain/behavior relations can yield important findings independently of hypotheses about information processing.[35] Nevertheless, in this book we shall argue that maximum progress towards understanding mental abilities is made by considering all three sorts of factors together.[36]

We can use the language of computation, particularly as applied to neural networks, to specify the little-f functions carried out by particular parts of the brain. To do so, we analyze how the system is composed of interconnected processing subsystems. The computations performed by the individual processing subsystems must be capable of bridging the gap between the input to the brain (physical energy impinging on sensory receptors) and the output (behavior). Clearly, this bridge is not simple or direct. The same input can have many consequences, depending on the goals, context, and previous experience of the organism. Given the complexity of the tasks performed by the brain, it is not surprising that it has many distinct areas—each of which appears to carry out distinct functions.

We will draw inferences about processing subsystems by observing specific types of behaviors and then performing computational analyses of what is likely to be required to build a brain-like system to produce the observed behaviors. Once we have drawn inferences about the operation of the normal system, we will see how they illuminate the effects of brain damage on behavior.

Thus, in the remainder of the book we work through different types of abilities and make inferences about the underlying processing subsystems. The subsystems we infer for one ability will often be drawn upon by others, and hence the picture we paint will be cumulative. We will begin with visual perception, which will help us to lay the foundations for much of what is to come.

3

Visual Perception

Vision is not a single process. This is nowhere more apparent than in the variety and kinds of aberrations that can occur following brain damage. Oliver Sacks claimed that one man's vision was so disturbed that he mistook his wife for a hat![1] This was a rather extreme case of dysfunction, but many other examples of similarly bizarre behavior have been documented in the neurological literature. Such deficits can only be understood once we have a grasp of what the normal system does. Thus, our task in this chapter is to understand the fundamental structure of normal vision, and then to use this understanding to glean insights into the causes of different types of visual dysfunction that occur following brain damage.

We now have a great wealth of information about the neural bases of vision—in some ways, too great. Many researchers went into this field, drawn by the successes of previous researchers, and they have filled pages and pages with their discoveries. It is easy to become overwhelmed when opening one of the many journals and books in which research on the neural bases of vision is published. Fortunately, once one has a particular problem in hand, and is actively looking for relevant information, this literature falls into place.

Much of what we know about the neural systems underlying vision comes from work on monkeys. Because monkeys have visual abilities that are similar to ours, and the neuroanatomy and neurophysiology of their visual systems are similar to ours, it is relatively safe to extrapolate from them to humans.

We focus here on *high-level vision.* High-level visual processing involves the use of previously stored information. In contrast, *low-level* visual processing does not involve stored information; it is driven solely by the information striking the eyes, and is concerned with using such input to carry out the preliminaries, such as finding edges, delineating regions of homogeneous texture or color, establishing depth, and other tasks that will help one to discover which part of the input is likely to correspond to an object—not to figure out what that object actually is. High-level visual processes are the most "mental."

In this and all following chapters, we will take the approach schematized in the cognitive neuroscience triangle at the conclusion of the previous chapter. We will describe individual abilities of a system, and then will analyze how computations in the brain could produce the behavior.

Components of Vision: An Overview

When one has *identified* a stimulus, one knows more about it than is obvious from its visible properties per se. For example, as soon as one identifies an object as an apple, one knows that it has seeds inside—even though one cannot see the seeds. One knows its name, what it can be used for, where one typically finds it, and so on. The brain systems underlying object identification allow one to *know more about a stimulus than is apparent in the immediate input.* This is achieved by activating information previously stored in memory that applies to the object. In contrast, one has *recognized* a stimulus when it has been matched with a piece of information stored in memory, so one knows that it is familiar without knowing its identity or associations.

It has turned out to be extraordinarily difficult to build computer systems that can visually identify objects. People find vision so easy that researchers expected it to be easy to program a computer to see. (Indeed, in the early days of artificial intelligence research a student was supposedly asked to build a vision system as a summer project!) The reason vision is so easy for us is that we come equipped with an enormous amount of sophisticated machinery. These inborn abilities are ours for the using; we do not need to learn to see.

One of the main reasons it is so hard to understand vision is that we can identify objects in an astounding range of circumstances. The ability to identify objects in various situations appears to arise from the joint action of a number of subsystems working in concert.

Six Groups of Subsystems

It is useful to organize these subsystems into six groups, which are illustrated in Figure 3.1. Input from the eyes produces a pattern of activity in a set of visual areas (in the occipital lobe), which we call the *visual buffer*. These areas are spatially organ-

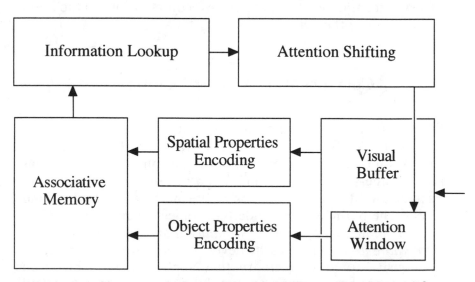

FIGURE 3.1 Six groups of subsystems used in high-level vision. *(Adapted from Kosslyn, Flynn, Amsterdam & Wang, 1990. Reprinted with permission.)*

ized, with the image from the eyes being physically laid out along the surface of the brain.[2] The *attention window* selects some region of the visual buffer for detailed processing.[3] The pattern in the attention window then is sent to two systems.

The *ventral system* is a set of brain areas that runs from the occipital lobe down to the inferior (i.e., lower) temporal lobe, and the *dorsal system* is a set of brain areas that runs from the occipital lobe up to the parietal lobes. These two pathways have different properties: The ventral system deals with *object properties,* such as shape and color; the dorsal system with *spatial properties,* such as location and size.[4] Leslie Ungerleider and Mortimer Mishkin call these the *what* and *where* systems, respectively.[5] The two pathways in the monkey brain are illustrated in Figure 3.2.

The distinction between the two pathways was discovered by examining monkeys who were trained to lift a lid covering one of two food containers placed in front of them.[6] Only one of the lids concealed food, and the monkey had to learn which one. In one version of the task, each lid had a different pattern. For example, one lid had a checked pattern, and the other had stripes. The food would always be under one of the lids, and

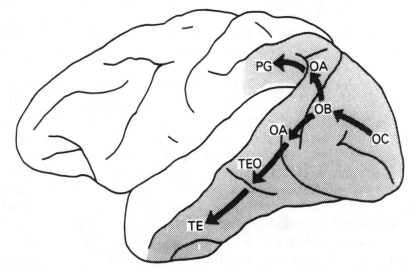

FIGURE 3.2 Two cortical visual systems. The letters refer to an older labeling scheme. *(From Mishkin, Ungerleider & Macko, 1983. Reprinted with permission.)*

they were switched from the right to the left side randomly from trial to trial. The monkey only got fed if it lifted the correct lid, which required learning to tell the patterns apart; the monkey had to learn to discriminate shape in order to find the reward.

In another version of the task, the monkey did not discriminate shape, but instead discriminated location: Now both lids were gray, and a small tower (a "landmark") was placed near the lids. The tower was closer to one lid than the other. The lid that was closer to the tower was the one that concealed the food, and the monkey's job now was to learn this spatial relation.

These tasks are interesting because different sorts of brain damage disrupt them. The shape task becomes exceedingly difficult for a monkey after its *temporal lobes* are removed. But if the parietal lobes are left intact, the monkey can still perform the location task. And exactly vice versa if the *parietal lobes* are removed (but the temporal lobes are left intact): The location task becomes very difficult, but the shape task is still manageable.[7]

Moreover, when researchers insert very small electrodes in brain cells in the two regions of the brain, they find that the cells fire to different sorts of stimuli. Cells in the inferior temporal lobes, in the ventral system, fire most vigorously when specific shapes are shown to the animal. Some of these cells even fire only when the animal sees a face or hand,[8] and some will only fire for a face when the eyes are pointed in a certain direction.[9]

On the other hand, cells in some parts of the parietal lobe, in the dorsal system, are sensitive to spatial properties. These cells fire when objects are in different locations, but are influenced not only by the location of the object but also by the position of the eyes.[10] We will consider such findings in more detail shortly.

The ventral (object-properties-encoding) system in the temporal lobes not only registers key properties of shapes, but also encodes color and texture; this information is matched to that of objects stored in visual memory.[11] This temporal-lobe memory stores information in a visual code, which cannot be accessed by input from other sensory modalities. The goal of this processing is to discover which stored object is most like the object being viewed. If a good match is obtained, the object is recognized; however, in some cases the input may not match any particular stored object very well.

The dorsal (spatial-properties-encoding) system in the parietal lobes appears to encode information that is used primarily to guide actions, such as moving one's eyes or reaching; indeed, virtually all of the neurons in the posterior parietal lobe either register the consequences of a movement, such as current eye position, or discharge immediately prior to a movement.[12] In addition, this system allows one to use spatial properties for other purposes, such as discriminating among spatial properties of objects.[13]

The outputs from the ventral (object properties) and dorsal (spatial properties) encoding systems come together at an *associative memory* (which relies on tissue in various places in the brain, as we shall discuss in Chapter 8), where they are matched to stored information. Information in associative memory can be matched by output from all sensory systems, and once the appropriate information is accessed, one knows the name of the object, categories to which it belongs, sounds it makes, and so forth. In many circumstances, the match in visual memory is good enough to select the appropriate representation in associative memory, especially in conjunction with information about the size, orientation and location of the object that is sent to associative memory by the dorsal system. However, in some circumstances the input does not match a visual memory very well; for example, if one sees a dog on its back with its legs splayed to the side, the overall shape may not match one stored in memory. Indeed, in such cases perhaps only one part could be matched to a stored shape. If so, then additional information must be collected.

We do not look around randomly when we seek additional information. Rather, stored information is used to make a guess about what we are seeing, and this guess then guides further encoding.[14] One actively seeks new information that will bear on the hypothesis. This use of stored information is called *top-down processing*. The first step in this process is to look up relevant information in associative memory. As will be discussed, there is ample evidence that the frontal lobe plays a critical role in this process.[15]

Finally, top-down processing must involve mechanisms that actually shift attention to a location where an informative part should be located, and the new part then is processed in turn. This part is matched to stored shapes in the ventral system, and its spatial properties are extracted in the dorsal system. The matching shape and spatial properties may in fact correspond to the hypothesized part. If so, enough information may have accumulated in associative memory to identify the object. If not, this cycle is repeated until enough information has been gathered to identify the object or to reject the first hypothesis, formulate a new one, and test it.

Visual Areas

Each of the visual pathways has many subareas.[16] The arrangement of these areas is clearly illustrated in Figure 3.3, which was constructed by taking advantage of some fundamental facts about the structure of the cortex. The cortex contains six major layers, with cells in different layers sending connections either downstream (deeper into the system, away from area V1—the first visual area, hence "V" and "1") or upstream (against the flow of information from V1). Specifically, cells in layers near the surface send connections downstream to cells in layer 4 (these are *afferent* connections); in contrast, cells in layers near the surface and cells in layers deep in cortex send connections upstream, typically to cells in layers 1 or 6—but almost never to layer 4 (these are *efferent* connections). Figure 3.3 was constructed by providing a computer program with information about the connections to and from each area, and having it place each area just above the farthest area downstream from which it receives input.[17]

The diagram illustrates the cortex as it was understood in 1983. A more recent version includes 32 areas, with over 300 connections;[18] this diagram is overwhelmingly complex. The areas and connections illustrated in Figure 3.3 are correct, and will serve us as a good foundation; we will consider additional information not in this diagram as it becomes relevant.

The areas along the left side of Figure 3.3 typically lie along the ventral pathway, whereas those along the right side typically lie along the dorsal pathway. There are three important features of the diagram that are worth noting now. First, it is orderly; everything is not connected to everything else. Second, there is a large amount of serial processing; in many cases, areas receive input from lower areas only via intermediate areas. Third, the lines connecting the areas do not have arrow heads. The reason for this is that virtually every area that sends information downstream to another area also receives information from that

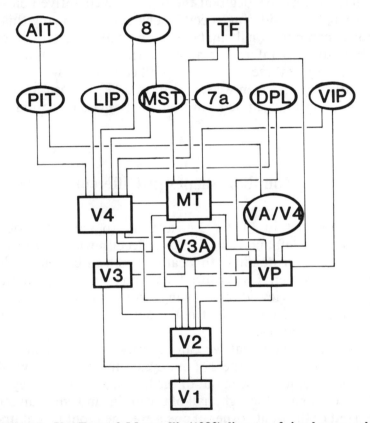

FIGURE 3.3 Van Essen & Maunsell's (1983) diagram of visual areas and their connections. See text for a discussion of how this diagram was constructed. Specific areas will be discussed as they become relevant. *(From A. Peters & E. Jones, eds.,* Cerebral Cortex, *vol. 3. Copyright © 1985 by Plenum Publishing Corporation. Reprinted with permission.)*

area. Indeed, the efferent connections are as large as the connections going downstream! A huge amount of information flows backwards in the visual system.[19]

It is clear that the visual system respects the principle of division of labor. We shall break the groups of subsystems illustrated in Figure 3.1 into more fine-grained subsystems as we consider what sorts of computations are needed to produce the observed visual abilities, keeping in mind key constraints from the neural substrate.

In the following three sections of this chapter we will draw inferences about what specific parts of the brain do when one identifies objects. We begin at the top of the cognitive neuroscience triangle, considering specific behaviors. Following this, we combine computational analyses with facts about the neural substrate to draw inferences about processing subsystems. Specifically, in these three sections we shall consider how we are able to identify objects when we see them in different locations, with parts missing or occluded, and when they assume unfamiliar shapes.

Identifying Familiar Shapes in Different Locations

Stare at the dot in Figure 3.4, and try to name the objects pictured at the left and right. Let us reflect on what you just did. You identified the dog in both locations with ease. You would be able to do this even if we ensured that you stared at the center of the page, and so viewed the drawings without moving your eyes. Furthermore, you could identify the objects if you viewed them at different distances.

The simple fact that we can identify objects when we see them out of different corners of our eyes is important; as we shall see, when an object is seen out of the left corner of one's eye, the input is sent first to the right half of the brain, and when an object is seen out of the right corner of one's eye, the input is sent first to the left half of the brain. Nevertheless, the image is treated as equivalent, even though the input is sent to different parts of the brain. The puzzle of how this ability arises is often called *the problem of stimulus equivalence across retinal translation.*[20] The

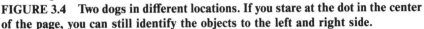

FIGURE 3.4 Two dogs in different locations. If you stare at the dot in the center of the page, you can still identify the objects to the left and right side.

retina is the light-sensitive layer of cells at the back of the eye; it is the first place where light causes neurons to respond. These cells convert the physical energy of the light into neural impulses, which then travel back into the brain. In this section we consider how the visual system recognizes familiar shapes when their images fall on different locations of the retina, which will lead us to infer an initial set of processing subsystems.

Charles Gross and Mortimer Mishkin offered one possible account for how the brain accomplishes this feat.[21] They noticed that neurons in the inferior temporal lobe (part of the ventral system that is involved in encoding object properties) have very large receptive fields. Recall that a cell's receptive field is the area of visual space in which a stimulus can trigger it. Cells in the inferior temporal lobe that are highly tuned for specific shapes respond to the right kind of object when it is in a wide range of positions in the field. This feature is convenient for identifying objects in different positions; these neurons fire when the object appears in numerous locations, and hence presumably play a role in recognizing it when it is seen in different positions. In a sense, they simply ignore spatial location (over a particular range).

This solution to the problem itself raises other problems. If the visual system ignores location so that it can recognize objects when they appear in different places, how can we reach for an object, walk around it, or throw something towards it? Hence a second system is needed to register location. And, as was mentioned earlier, separate systems are used for "what" and "where." Dividing the labor lets the system have its cake and eat it too.

Gross and Mishkin's idea is essentially a computational theory; they have a theory of how a system might be built to produce specific behaviors. Jay Rueckl, Kyle Cave, and Kosslyn tested this theory directly.[22] They thought about the problem in terms of input/output mappings. The question, as rephrased by them, was whether it is easier computationally to map a shape in a location (the input) to a name of the object and its location (the output) in a single system or in two separate systems (one that registers what the stimulus is, and the other that registers where it is).

To answer this question, Rueckl and his colleagues constructed a three-layer feedforward network computer model (structured rather like the octopus network discussed in the previous chapter). The input was a grid, in which nine simple figures were presented. Each figure appeared in nine different locations in the grid. The output was 18 units, nine of which were used to indicate shape (with one unit per object), and nine of which were used to indicate location (with one unit per location).

In one version of the network, each input unit was connected to each hidden unit, and each hidden unit was connected to each output unit. This was the single-system network. In another version of the network, half of the hidden units were connected to the shape output units and half were connected to the location output units. This was the two-system network. The architecture of this model is illustrated in Figure 3.5.

The question was: Which design would allow the proper input/output mapping to be specified more easily? A single system that registers "what" and "where" at the same time, or a division of labor approach, with separate systems for each classification? To answer this question, the back propagation learning procedure was used to establish the necessary input/output mappings. The goal here was not to understand learning, but rather to use the training procedure to measure the difficulty of the mapping: After 300 training trials, the networks were stopped and the amount of error in the output was measured. Recall that these networks start off producing random output, and are trained by comparing this output to the desired output. Each time the obtained and desired outputs are compared, a

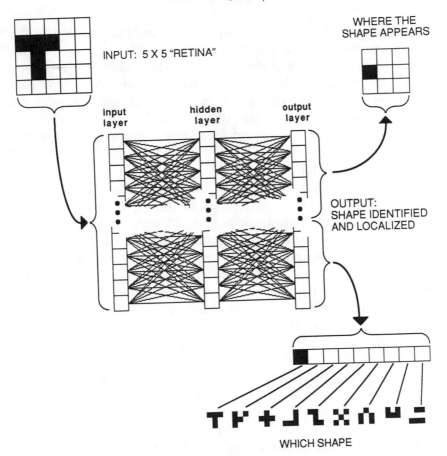

FIGURE 3.5 The organization of Rueckl et al.'s "what" versus "where" model. *(From Rueckl, Cave & Kosslyn, 1989. Reprinted with permission.)*

measure of error (based on the difference between the obtained and desired number at each output unit) is computed. The goal of training is to minimize the measure of error.

Experimentation revealed that if the net was split with the right proportions of connections going to the "what" and "where" output units, the two-system model was far superior to the single-system model. The shape mapping was more difficult, and so more of the hidden units had to be assigned to it (i.e., be connected to shape output units). This finding is consistent with the fact that many more neurons in the brain belong to the object-properties-encoding ("what") system than belong to the spatial-properties-encoding ("where") system.

The performance of the networks tells us about the structure of the mapping problem; identifying shape is a more complex problem than identifying location. If processing resources are properly allocated, then splitting "what" and "where" into separate subsystems is a good idea; when objects move around, this kind of split allows input/output mappings to be established more efficiently than can be done in a single system.

The connections from input units to the hidden units were analyzed in these networks. Units in the input array that have large weights on the connections to a hidden unit are in large part responsible for the behavior of that hidden unit. Hence, those input units are treated as the "receptive field" of the hidden unit. Rueckl and his colleagues found that, indeed, many hidden units that were used to encode shape developed large "receptive fields." These units were registering shape properties by monitoring large regions of the input array. Some of these hidden units responded to parallel vertical lines; others to parallel horizontal lines; and others to diagonal lines. These units responded to these patterns when they appeared in many locations in the array. In short, some of the hidden units in the "what" stream ignored location, so to speak, allowing the hidden units in the "where" stream to register location. This finding supported Gross and Mishkin's hypothesis, and suggested that the division of "what" and "where" is indeed a critical part of how the visual system is able to identify objects in different locations.

The network models studied by Rueckl et al. had it easy. They only had to deal with nine locations and nine patterns, and the input was always perfectly unambiguous. The networks in our heads are not so fortunate. Objects rarely appear in only a fixed number of locations, and there are a truly gargantuan number of objects that can be seen in each possible location. The mapping problem faced by our visual system is much more challenging than the one solved by the computer model.

The principle of division of labor leads us to expect numerous subsystems in the object-properties-encoding and spatial-properties-encoding systems, which confer much greater power than can be accomplished by a single input/output mapping. Let us now consider subsystems that are helpful for identifying objects when they are seen in different locations.

Stimulus-based Attention Shifting

First, we are led to infer a *stimulus-based attention shifting subsystem,* which draws one's eyes to a novel stimulus. This subsystem operates according to a simple principle: Whenever there is a relatively large change in one region of the visual field, it reflexively moves the eyes to that location. Clearly, when an object appears, the first thing one must do is to focus on it. Because images outside the high-resolution central region of the retina are difficult to see, we must be able to bring attention to objects not currently being attended (otherwise we would only see what we already have been seeing). In fact, infants under about two months old may exhibit an extreme form of stimulus-based attention control called "perceptual capture"; their eyes are drawn towards a moving object or flashing pattern, and then they are "stuck" there until some other stimulus draws their attention away.[23] It is of interest that this phenomenon disappears at about the time that the visual cortex becomes functional,[24] which suggests that visual capture may reflect the operation of subcortical structures which can be overridden (at least to some extent) by cortical ones later in development.

The process of being "grabbed" by a stimulus appears to depend in large part on a distinct visual pathway. Not illustrated in Figure 3.3, there are two major subcortical pathways from the eyes into the brain, the *geniculo-striate* and the *tecto-pulvinar.* The geniculo-striate pathway projects from the retina to the lateral geniculate nucleus (of the thalamus), which in turn projects to the occipital lobe (and leads into the areas illustrated in the figure). In contrast, the tecto-pulvinar pathway projects from the retina to the superior colliculus, from the superior colliculus to the pulvinar (which is another nucleus of the thalamus), and then to various parts of cortex (including the parietal lobe).

Insight into the functions of these two pathways was provided by research with golden hamsters, which could not identify patterns properly when the geniculo-striate pathway was disrupted, but had no trouble orienting towards a tickled whisker.[25] In contrast, the reverse pattern of deficits occurred when the tecto-pulvinar pathway was disrupted. These findings suggested that the geniculo-striate pathway plays a central role in object identification, whereas the tecto-pulvinar pathway plays a key role in orienting one towards a stimulus. This interpretation is consistent with a recent finding reported in studies of human patients who were blind in one half of the visual field.[26] This blindness was apparently caused by damage to area V1 and possibly other areas subserved by the geniculo-striate pathway. In these studies, a pattern was flashed into the blind field, which the patients did not see; nevertheless, this pattern apparently began to lure the eye towards it, which inhibited moving the eye subsequently to a visual target in the good field. The tecto-pulvinar pathway apparently was intact in these patients, and could direct eye movements to novel stimuli even when the geniculo-striate pathway or associated cortical structures were disrupted. Indeed, in his book *Blindsight,*[27] the neuropsychologist Lawrence Weiskrantz makes a compelling case that some otherwise blind patients can use this second pathway to "see" movement and some other kinds of spatial information.[28]

Such stimulus-based attention shifting often simplifies the problem of stimulus equivalence across retinal translation enormously: One simply moves one's eyes so that one is looking at the center of the stimulus object, and identifies it the same way no matter where the image initially fell on the retina. However, this is not the whole story: We can identify objects seen out of the corner of the eye even when they are flashed up so briefly that there is not enough time to move our eyes. To understand this seemingly simple ability, we must infer several additional subsystems.

A Visual Buffer

Input from the eyes (primarily via the geniculo-striate pathway) arrives at a structure we have called the visual buffer. This structure is spatially organized in much the same way that an array in a computer can be spatially organized. Indeed, in Rueckl et al.'s computer model, an array was used as a spatially organized input structure, which provided useful input to networks that classified shape and location; some of the "receptive fields" developed by the hidden units clearly took advantage of the spatial structure of the input array, monitoring parallel stripes at different orientations. The spatial organization of the array makes explicit such geometric properties.

The brain appears to have a structure that plays a role similar to the array in the model. In the brain, the visual buffer corresponds to areas that preserve the spatial structure of the images that strike the backs of our eyes. Roger Tootell, Martin Silverman, Eugene Switkes, and Russell De Valois provided dramatic evidence for the existence of such spatially organized areas.[29] They trained a monkey to stare at a pattern that looked something like a bulls eye with spokes coming out of the middle. There were little light bulbs spaced along the circles and spokes, which blinked on and off. The animal was then injected with 2-deoxyglucose, a radioactive kind of sugar. The more a given neuron worked as the animal viewed the pattern, the more of this sugar it used and the more radioactivity lodged in it. The animal was sacrificed and its brain, in essence, "developed" (much like one can develop certain kinds of photographs). The radioactive tracer allowed Tootell and his colleagues to observe which cells were most active when the animal was seeing the pattern. The pattern they saw on the brain is illustrated in Figure 3.6.

As expected, an image of the pattern was spread out over the back of the animal's brain, particularly in area V1; the pattern was magnified at its center, and slightly distorted, as is evident in Figure 3.6. This visual area, V1, is *retinotopically organized:* The pattern that falls on the retina is itself sent into the brain, and this pattern is physically laid out on the surface of area V1. This area is organized in the same way as the retina, and hence preserves

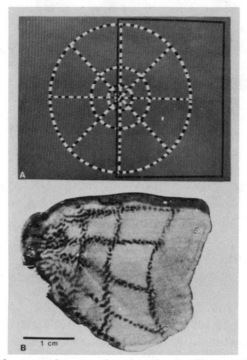

FIGURE 3.6   After a monkey stared at the stimulus illustrated at the top, it was injected with a radioactive metabolic tracer. This tracer revealed that neurons illustrated at the bottom (from one hemisphere) were active while the animal viewed the pattern. *(From Tootell, Silverman, Switkes & De Valois, 1982, copyright © 1982 by AAAS. Reprinted with permission.)*

the spatial properties of images that fall on the retina. If you had held up your hand during the experiment, and kept the animal focused on it throughout, presumably a "picture" of your hand would have appeared on its brain.[30]

However, although the pattern of activity of cells in these areas mirrors the pattern of activity on the retina, these patterns are not faithful copies; they usually have a disproportionately large number of cells devoted to the fovea (the central, high-resolution part of the retina), and often distort the input in other ways.[31] Further, most of these areas register only half (or less) of space.

Peter Fox and his colleagues at the Washington University School of Medicine used positron emission tomography (PET) scanning to show that V1 is retinotopically mapped in humans.[32] They asked people to view a checkerboard pattern on a small disk, which flashed regularly. These subjects had just been injected with water (H_2O) in which some of the oxygen was ^{15}O, a radioactive isotope. This form of water has a half-life of about 2 minutes (which means that the amount of radioactivity decreases by half every 2 minutes). The water gets mixed into the blood, and thereafter is transported to the brain. And the more that different parts of the brain need oxygen and nutrients, the more blood is shunted to them. Thus, by recording the amount of radioactivity in different parts of live, thinking human brains, one can discover which areas are most active during a given task. This technique is particularly exciting because it requires only about 40 seconds to get an image from a human brain, with a small amount of radioactive material.

Analogous to the findings with monkeys, viewing a small flashing disk causes the most activation in the part of V1 that receives input from the high-acuity, central (foveal) part of the retina. Fox and colleagues also asked people to view rings, which had flashing checkerboard patterns on them. The rings were larger than the disk; in fact, the small disk could fit in the hole in the smallest ring. Thus, it is of interest that the flashing rings did not activate the central parts of V1, but instead activated parts that receive input from the periphery. In fact, the larger the ring, the more the activation moved towards the peripheral part of V1. These findings, then, demonstrated that human V1 is spatially organized, with a systematic relation between the parts of the retina that are stimulated and the corresponding parts of cortex that are activated.

Although V1 is the largest retinotopically organized area, Tootell et al. reported that several other areas displayed the same type of pattern, and about 15 of the visual areas of the monkey are retinotopically organized.[33] As of this writing, 32 distinct areas concerned with processing visual information have been discovered in the cortex of monkeys;[34] these areas cover over half the surface of a macaque monkey's brain. The cortex is running out of room for much else! These animals have brains that are a little larger than two walnuts (our brains are about 15 times bigger). The human brain affords many, many additional opportunities for more areas.

The retinotopically organized areas that comprise the visual buffer store an image that indicates edges and regions of homogeneous color and texture. This representation also specifies the relative distance of each region from the viewer. It does not, however, identify objects or even necessarily pick out complete objects from the background.[35]

The spatial nature of the visual buffer allows us to restate the problem of how we recognize objects in different locations. We now can ask how we recognize the same pattern when it appears in different locations in the visual buffer. This is useful because we now are led to consider processes that can select a pattern in different locations in the buffer.

Attention Window

One reason it is useful to have the input to the visual identification system stored as a spatial pattern is that it is easy to allocate attention over such a pattern. Even if one cannot move one's eyes, to pay attention to a particular visible region of space one needs only to pick out a particular region of the visual buffer. The spatial structure of the buffer preserves the spatial relations among locations in space, with nearby locations in the buffer corresponding to small separations between objects (ignoring depth for now). Attention is the key to understanding how we identify objects when we see them out of different corners of our eye.

Consider the following experiment conducted by George Sperling, which shows that we can shift attention over an image without using eye movements.[36] Subjects were shown three rows of random letters, each of which contained three letters (e.g., the top row might be R, C, K, the middle, S, L, F, and the bottom A, M, H). This table was flashed up for less than one quarter of a second. Subjects were asked to name the letters, and they typically succeeded in naming only four or five. However, they claimed that they *saw* them all, but the letters faded too quickly to be reported. To demonstrate the validity of these reports, Sperling presented a high, medium, or low tone immediately *after* the display was turned off. He asked the subjects to report the top row if they heard the high tone, the middle row if they heard the medium tone, and the bottom row if they heard the low tone. People could do this perfectly, even though the display was turned off by the time they heard the tone. They apparently were able to shift attention to the required letters, even though the stimulus was no longer present.

This finding not only tells us that there is more information in the visual buffer than can be processed in detail, but also that the buffer can be scanned internally—even when eye movements are not possible. Only some of the information in the buffer can be sent downstream; the stimulus-based attention subsystem gives other input a cursory once-over to make sure it is not signaling a change of circumstances (if it is, then it may be important and so will be considered further).

Attention is the selective aspect of perception. We can think of visual spatial attention as a "window" moving in the visual buffer. Whatever is subsumed by the window is passed on to the dorsal and ventral systems. This arrangement is also useful because it sends information to the two visual pathways and yet keeps them coordinated. Because a single source of input feeds the two systems, processing in them is initiated at the same time—which need not happen if there were more than a single focus of attention.[37]

Jeffrey Moran and Robert Desimone described some properties of neurons in the inferior temporal lobe that support the idea that an attention window serves as a gateway to the object-properties-encoding system.[38] They recorded from individual neurons in different visual areas, and located neurons that responded to particular stimuli (e.g., a vertical green bar). They then mapped out the receptive fields of the neurons, and trained the animal to expect a reward only when it responded to the stimulus when it fell in a smaller region. They found that when the stimulus fell in that smaller portion of the receptive field, cells in area V4 responded as vigorously as before the training. But when the stimulus fell in a part of the receptive field that was outside the trained region, now the cells began to respond, but were quenched within about 60 milliseconds of when they began to fire.

These findings suggest that the "receptive field" of a cell is the range of locations in the visual buffer in which the attention window can provide input to the cell. At any one time the cell responds only to the current contents of the attention window, and training can restrict the regions that the window will occupy. The attention window can be shifted voluntarily, and information within this window receives additional processing downstream.[39]

The attention window helps us to understand how we can identify objects when they fall in different locations in the field; the attention window is shifted in the visual buffer, which picks out a region for additional processing. This shift can be initiated by the stimulus-based attention shifting subsystem, which can move the attention window in the absence of overt eye movements.[40] The pattern of activation in the attended region is then sent further into the system for identification. If the image of the object is in one location, we shift the attention window there; if it is in another, we shift it accordingly. Thus, regardless of where the image falls in the visual buffer, the attention window can send similar information further into the system.

Not only can the attention window shift its location in the visual buffer, but it also can expand or shrink its scope. For example, look at the room you are in. Can you "pay attention" to the entire room or to a detail? You should be able to adjust not only the location of your attention, but also the scope of your attention.[41] Because the scope of the attention window can be adjusted, one can pay attention to an object when it is at different distances—and so it projects different-sized images in the visual buffer. When the attention window encompasses a large area, it can subsume an image of an object seen close up; when it encompasses a small area, it can subsume an image of an object seen far away. Thus, this relatively simple mechanism helps us to understand how we can identify objects when we see them at different distances.

But these inferences are valid only if various distortions do not disrupt processing downstream. For example, if an object is outside the central regions of the visual buffer, its shape will be fuzzier because of decreased resolution; furthermore, images that fall in different positions in the buffer will be distorted in different ways. In addition, when an object is seen relatively far away, fine levels of detail will be blurred.

The ability to identify objects in different locations clearly reflects processing in the ventral system, and can only be understood by breaking that system into additional subsystems that perform particular functions. We begin with a subsystem that extracts key sorts of information from the image, and then consider a subsystem that uses this information to match input to stored patterns.

Preprocessing

Our approach leads us to consider how we could build a machine that behaves in certain ways. The distortions that occur when an object appears in different locations correspond to a set of novel inputs, assuming that one has not seen the object in all positions previously. If we observe equivalent output from a variety of novel inputs, the output could not have been directly associated with each input in the past. To understand how the system generalizes correctly, the first thing to do is to look for properties of the input that cut across the circumstances. In order to identify objects even when their images are distorted by falling in different locations in the visual field or at different distances, we must be picking up on something that is preserved in the different situations. Such considerations lead us to infer a subsystem that extracts types of properties that reliably signal the presence of specific objects in a wide range of conditions. We call this the *preprocessing subsystem.*

A specialist in computer vision named David Lowe noticed that certain aspects of an object's image remain relatively constant when the object is seen at different distances and from different points of view.[42] For example, hold up a pencil and twist it around in front of you. Imagine that you took photographs of it in each position. Now, imagine that you traced the edges of the pencil in the photos. In almost all of them, the parallel edges would produce roughly parallel lines in the photo—and would project roughly parallel lines onto the retina. Similarly, symmetrical shapes almost always project a roughly symmetrical image onto the retina. Hold up a coin or a playing card and shift it around. If you took photos of them in the different positions, the shapes would usually be roughly symmetrical. In addition, places where edges intersect will virtually always project intersecting lines in the image, places along a single edge will project line segments that line up, and so on. Lowe defined some half-dozen of these kinds of properties.

These features of the image are similar enough from case to case that they probably do not arise by chance. For example, although parallel edges do not project precisely parallel lines (because of perspective effects), in most cases the lines are roughly parallel. Lowe calls these features of the image its *nonaccidental properties*. He found that by using such properties he could program a computer to identify objects such as disposable razors even when they were jumbled up in a pail; these properties are relatively constant under a wide range of situations.

Irving Biederman and his colleagues have shown that nonaccidental properties are in fact useful for identifying objects.[43] Look at Figure 3.7. The intact drawings are on the left, and ones with missing properties are in the middle and on the right. The drawings in the middle and on the right have the same total length of missing contour, but the versions on the right are missing nonaccidental properties whereas the ones in the center include these properties. It should be clear immediately that the versions on the right are very difficult (sometimes impossible) to identify, whereas those in the center are not so bad.

The idea that there is a subsystem that marks nonaccidental properties helps us to understand the deficit exhibited by some patients with brain damage, who appear to represent only a few nonaccidental properties at one time. For example, one patient had particular trouble identifying overlapping figures, naming line drawings and objects, and determining whether a shape corresponded to an object.[44] If his problem was that he could not extract enough nonaccidental properties to make a match to stored information, then he should have had an easier time identifying simpler drawings. And in fact, he was able to decide

FIGURE 3.7 Biederman's (1987) illustration of the importance of nonaccidental properties. The objects on the right are missing nonaccidental properties, whereas those in the middle are missing the same amount of material from other regions of the figure. *(Reprinted with permission of Academic Press, Inc.)*

whether a silhouette shape corresponded to an object better than he was able to judge whether a line drawing corresponded to an object (which makes sense if the line drawings added additional nonaccidental properties, which further taxed the preprocessing subsystem). In addition, this patient was able to decide whether two drawings depicted the same object (even when seen from some different points of view), could draw reasonably well, and could identify many individual features of objects (such as an elephant's legs). His examiners noted that each of these tasks can be performed piecemeal, a part at a time. This strategy would allow him to extract the maximal number of nonaccidental properties over a smaller region, which would allow him to match a part better than the whole object.

Opportunistic encoding. Nonaccidental properties are based on configurations of edges. Unfortunately, many natural objects cannot be described easily using such properties. For example, a pine tree does not have sharply defined edges, nor does a shaggy dog, or a field of grass. These sorts of observations led the perceptual psychologist J. J. Gibson to emphasize the role of surfaces and textures in recognition.[45] Gibson noticed that certain objects have distinct textures, which provide a critical cue for recognizing them. For example, a brick wall, cobblestone street, and field of wheat all have distinctive textures that are not related to their shapes per se.

Our view is that the brain in general, and the visual system in particular, is opportunistic: Depending on what needs to be distinguished, different kinds of information are exploited. This observation leads us to infer that the preprocessing subsystem groups edges and regions using two kinds of principles. First, as was posited by Lowe and the Gestalt perceptual psychologists who preceded him, the preprocessing subsystem groups the input on the basis of nonaccidental properties and similar features. In addition to edges, we also infer that regions of common color and texture are grouped together.[46] For example, look at someone's shirt; it seems to be a single entity in large part because it (usually, at any rate) is a single color and texture.

Second, we assume that the preprocessing subsystem can be "tuned" to organize material in ways that have turned out to be useful for distinguishing among different objects. A particularly striking example of such tuning was described by Irving Biederman and Margaret Shiffrar.[47] It is very important to distinguish male and female baby chicks because the females lay eggs, and "chicken sexers" are very well paid to do this (indeed, this apparently was one of the professions that was not hurt too badly during the Great Depression). These experts have no conscious knowledge of how they discriminate between the sexes. Biederman and Shiffrar discovered that naive subjects could learn to categorize the sex of day-old chicks by attending to the shape (convex versus concave or flat) of a particular cloacal structure. By noticing these subtle changes, perceptual learning apparently altered the way the experts organized the perceptual input, allowing them to make the discrimination rapidly and easily.

In this case, the organization of the input may not be determined by the edges, color, or texture, but rather by one's previous experience of what is useful. As noted earlier, areas in the visual system receive feedback from higher areas; indeed, the feedback connections typically are of the same size as the connections sending information downstream. These feedback connections may have a role in "training" the preprocessing subsystem so that it can more easily encode visual characteristics that have proven useful in the past. These characteristics can be anything; they can be a peculiarly shaped blotch, a configuration of intensity of light, or a pattern of bumps on a surface. We may recognize our chair because it has a distinctive wrinkle on its cushion. In Chapters 8 and 9 we shall discuss ways in which such perceptual learning may take place.

The preprocessing subsystem merely sets the stage for recognizing a pattern. We must consider subsequent processes that use the information computed in the preprocessing subsystem to select the stored information that most closely corresponds to the input pattern. Because these matching operations are so different from those performed by the preprocessing subsystem, we posit a distinct subsystem that stores and matches visual patterns. Before turning to that subsystem, however, we must consider a completely different kind of input that helps us to recognize objects and events.

Motion Relations

We easily recognize moving objects. In fact, in many circumstances it is easier to recognize a moving object than a still one.

For example, if a caterpillar is still against a twig, it may be very difficult to notice. But if it is moving, we may identify it immediately. Computing motion relations appears to be qualitatively distinct from computing the organization of portions of static images, and distinct regions of the brain apparently encode motion (particularly areas MT and MST; see Figure 3.3). There appears to be a distinct *motion relations subsystem.* The motion relations subsystem extracts key aspects of motion fields, and operates concurrently with the preprocessing subsystem.

Motion serves two functions in recognition. First, it provides another way of organizing the input. Things that move in similar ways tend to be grouped perceptually into a single unit. We obtain *structure from motion.*[48] For example, if we see a flock of ducks flying by, we see the flock as a unit, not a collection of individual ducks. As is evident in Figure 3.3, MT and V4 are not connected in the usual ways; rather, they have rich interconnections between corresponding layers (which is why they are connected by a horizontal line in the diagram), and it seems likely that they often work together. As noted earlier, neurons in area V4 are known to be sensitive to color and orientation, which could be used effectively in conjunction with motion to compute perceptual units. For example, a bird's wings might be organized as a unit based on distinctive color, texture, and motion.

Second, different objects move in distinct ways, and this information itself can be used to identify objects. For example, the Swedish psychologist Gunnar Johansson attached lightbulbs to people's joints, and observed the patterns of moving lights in the dark.[49] He found that it is easy to recognize a human form solely on the basis of the patterns of movements of the joints. Similarly, people can recognize many individuals purely on the basis of movements.[50] Thus, the motion output from area MT (and other related areas, such as MST) may not only help to define perceptual units, but itself may be a cue used later downstream to identify objects.

Like the preprocessing subsystem, the motion relations subsystem organizes the input in two ways. First, properties of patterns of movement per se define how moving objects will be grouped. For example, things that move together will be grouped into a single unit; this is called the Gestalt Law of Common Fate. Second, patterns of motion that have previously proven useful for distinguishing objects will come to be grouped; this process relies on the kind of "feedback training" that allows one to become adept at classifying the sex of baby chicks. For example, if one has found that a particular wobble is useful for distinguishing one bird from another, this pattern of motion will come to be organized as a unit.

These inferences are consistent with properties of neurons in some of the higher visual areas of the macaque monkey brain. These neurons respond selectively to different patterns of motion. For example, some neurons in the inferior temporal lobe respond selectively to different patterns of gait.[51] Furthermore, areas MT and MST are clearly involved in encoding motion relations; neurons in these areas are sensitive to the direction and rate of motion,[52] and also to patterns of motion (such as expansion versus contraction of a field of dots).[53] These areas provide information not only to the ventral system, which presumably is used in the recognition of object properties, but also to the dorsal system, which presumably is used to update locations of objects. To complicate the picture further, it is likely that the motion relations subsystem also receives input from the preprocessing subsystem— which allows it to compute relations among organized units in the input, not simply relations among the edges and regions delineated in the visual buffer.

Pattern Activation

The fact that we can identify objects visually and can visualize objects in their absence implies that we store visual information. We assume that there is a special subsystem that stores only visual memories (this is a *unimodal* memory) for two reasons. First, recall that one of the important features of neural networks is that they generalize (i.e., they produce the same output from a range of similar inputs). For example, if trained to identify one set of dogs versus birds, a network can then identify other members of these categories. To generalize properly when recognizing shapes, "similarity" must be defined over properties of the visual input itself. Thus, there must be a memory that stores purely visual information, which can be matched to visual input. Second, the principle of division of labor suggests that it is easier to break down the problem of identifying an object into a number of stages. It would be very difficult to design a single memory that stores information in all sensory modalities and matches input from these modalities. Such a memory would need to overlay representations of visual input, auditory input, and so on. It is much more efficient if separate unimodal memories match the input, and provide a symbol that stands for the object as output; these symbols then can be matched easily to those stored in another, integrative memory.[54]

We call the unimodal visual memory the *pattern activation* subsystem because stored patterns can be activated by input. The patterns can correspond to entire objects or parts of objects, and these patterns can be activated in several ways; as will be discussed in the following chapter, mental images can be formed by activating these representations "top down." In addition, they are activated by the output from the preprocessing and motion relations subsystems; in this case, the output of the pattern activation subsystem indicates which stored visual memory best matches the input.[55]

The key idea is that we identify objects by matching both the input perceptual units and motion relations to those of stored objects. The match is made by a process of constraint satisfaction: If an object has two parallel lines a certain distance apart, and of such-and-such a length, and the lines come to a point at one end, there are only so many objects it can be. The challenge is a little like that of doing a crossword puzzle: Once enough letters are in place, there are only a few possible words that can be formed, even if a letter or two are missing. Lowe showed that this idea works well if the objects are familiar, and so relatively complete sets of nonaccidental properties (and their relative positions) previously have been stored.

The inferior temporal lobe not only is involved in encoding object properties, but also in storing visual memories. For example, in one experiment monkeys were trained to view one pattern, remember it for a brief period, and then decide whether a second pattern matched the first.[56] Some cells in the inferior temporal lobe responded selectively to different patterns when they were in view. Furthermore, some of these cells continued to respond during the interval that a monkey is holding a pattern in mind, after the initial stimulus was removed but before a to-be-matched stimulus was presented. These cells are presumably involved in maintaining the memory of the first pattern. This result is as expected, given the finding that visual memories are disrupted when the temporal lobes are removed.[57]

In addition, David Perrett and his colleagues describe cells in the superior temporal sulcus (STS, which defines the upper boundary of area IT in the temporal lobe) that respond selectively to static views of the head (area IT is subdivided into an anterior, AIT, and posterior, PIT, area in Figure 3.3).[58] Some of these neurons have remarkably specific taste in stimuli (so to speak), responding to the head in specific orientations or to the eyes in specific positions (different directions of gaze). Other cells in this area, in contrast, are tuned more broadly, responding to the head or eyes when they are in a number of different orientations or positions. Perrett and his colleagues report that some 69% of the cells that respond selectively to a face or head respond best when the object is seen from a particular vantage point.

The fact that some cells in STS are highly tuned for particular points of view is interesting in light of connections between portions of STS and parts of the parietal lobe. These cells may pass information to subsystems that are used to guide motor movements. As will be discussed shortly, one needs to know the precise position of parts of objects to be able to reach properly.

In short, perceptual units and motion relations are matched against stored memories in the pattern activation subsystem, and the representation that is most consistent with the input is activated. Because such networks generalize appropriately, even incomplete inputs can produce the proper output.

Recap: Identifying Familiar Shapes in Different Locations

When a shape is seen, a pattern of activity is evoked in the visual buffer. The stimulus-based attention shifting subsystem moves the attention window to the region of the visual buffer in which a new pattern of activity occurs, and the attention window selects that pattern. The information in the attention window then is sent to the ventral and dorsal systems. Because the visual buffer has different resolution and distortion in different locations, slightly different patterns of activation are evoked when an image appears in different locations or at different sizes. To recognize the object even when the image varies, the preprocessing subsystem marks nonaccidental properties, which do not vary when the shape is slightly distorted; it also marks perceptual units, which may signal a distinctive characteristic of an object. At the same time, the motion relations subsystem encodes patterns of movement, which also can be distinctive cues. The outputs from the preprocessing and motion relations subsystems are matched with information stored in the pattern activation subsystem. If the object is familiar, we assume that this or similar information was stored previously, and so it will match the input better than other stored patterns. If this match is good enough, the object is recognized.

Although this processing allows one to match the corresponding stored visual representation of a shape, it does not provide the name or any other information associated with the object. To activate this information, the visual identity output must be sent to an associative memory. For example, if the input matches best the stored features and motion relations of a cat, the "cat" output vector is produced by the pattern activation subsystem. This vector then enters associative memory, where it can activate the object's name. We can draw inferences about the properties of associative memory by considering another visual ability.

Identifying Partially Occluded Shapes

Another one of our visual abilities can now be easily understood: We can identify objects when they are partially occluded or are

FIGURE 3.8 A variety of objects that are missing parts or are partially occluded

missing parts. For example, you probably can identify all of the objects in Figure 3.8, even though parts are occluded or missing. In many situations, we identify objects when only a part is peeking out from under or from behind something else. This is a basic human ability; even young babies can identify their bottles when only a part can be seen from under a blanket.

The principle of constraint satisfaction is the key to understanding this ability. This principle is relevant at two levels of processing. First, there is redundancy in the information encoded in the ventral system. Not only are nonaccidental properties and distinctive perceptual units encoded by the preprocessing subsystem often redundant, but also these characteristics often are redundant with distinctive movements encoded by the motion relations subsystem. For example, even if the edges delineating an eraser are missing, those that define its parallel edges and its point may be enough to identify the pencil. Indeed, the output from the preprocessing subsystem typically is sufficient to recognize an object even if it is not moving, and distinctive motions alone sometimes are sufficient to recognize the object. Thus, recognition may still be possible if parts are occluded or missing, provided that the visible properties implicate only a single shape.

Second, the information from the ventral system is combined with information from the dorsal system. Recall that the dorsal system encodes spatial properties, including the location, size, and orientation of the stimulus. This information also provides clues as to the identity of an object. If the object were six feet long, we would not identify it as a typical pencil even if it had the right sort of parallel edges and point at the end.

We assume that if the input is too degraded, the match in the pattern activation subsystem will not be very good. In this case, the output from the subsystem will have a low "strength." Either it will be noisy, or it might shift between several possible objects. In this case, the output will not match a single representation in associative memory very well, and hence the spatial information encoded by the dorsal system will play an important role. To understand how this sort of spatial information is combined with the output of the ventral system, we must consider associative memory in more detail.

Associative Memory

The mere fact that we can recall where furniture is located in a given room of our house, or where objects are on our desk top, indicates that the relations between shape and location come together and are stored. Furthermore, we can identify a cat not only by seeing it, but also by hearing or feeling it rub against our shins. We clearly store more than unimodal visual memories, and we associate different sorts of memories together. Once we have identified the object, regardless of what input was used to make the identification, we have at our fingertips much of the information we know about cats—what to call it, what it eats, how to treat it, and so forth. We must posit a subsystem in which the outputs from the different perceptual processes come together and in which associations among different sorts of information are stored.

If the visual match in the pattern activation subsystem is very good, a particular pattern is identified and this pattern may in turn match only a single object in associative memory—allowing one to name it and recall the other information associated with it. If the match in the ventral system is very good, then the spatial properties of the object or part (its size, orientation, location) need not contribute to identification. However, if the match in the pattern activation subsystem is not very good because parts are occluded or missing, then integrating spatial properties with object properties in associative memory will help to identify the object.

Recall our furniture metaphor in Chapter 2: Each piece has weak constraints on where it can be located; the bed had to be against a wall, end tables had to be next to the bed, the sofa had to be against a wall, and so forth; nevertheless, there may be only one way to arrange the furniture so that each of these requirements is fulfilled at the same time. Each input to associative memory is a constraint, and the goal is to find the stored representation that is most consistent with all of the various inputs. Just as the bed could have been placed against several walls, the input from the pattern activation subsystem may match several objects in associative memory equally well. But not all of these objects may match the spatial properties as well. The more input properties there are that match those of a stored object, the more one can be confident that one is seeing that object.

These ideas illuminate an insight of the great Austrian philosopher Ludwig Wittgenstein.[59] Wittgenstein noticed that there rarely is a single defining attribute that allows us to pick out members of a category. Instead, most natural categories are like ropes: they have overlapping strands, not a single strand running the entire length. Wittgenstein noticed that members of families are similar in this way. There is no single nose, mouth, chin, eyes, or forehead feature that defines the Kennedy Look, but all Kennedys share many of these properties. To identify a Kennedy, one need only register a large number of these properties—but it does not matter whether every single one is present. The input features are like pieces of a picture puzzle, with very specific shapes; even given only 80% of the pieces of a puzzle, it often is possible to figure out the picture.[60]

We can draw two more inferences about the process of matching input to representations in associative memory. First, depending on the context, the *threshold* can be varied. The threshold determines how many consistent properties are required for an object to be identified. For example, if one is searching for one's cat and has looked everywhere but in the living room, the very tip of its tail sticking out from under the sofa may be enough to identify it. Context has adjusted the threshold in associative memory so that relatively few cat attributes must be encoded before identification occurs. In this case, "context" corresponds to additional input into a neural network (from other senses and from reasoning processes), which supplements the input from the ventral and dorsal systems; thus, context can affect how much perceptual input is required to identify the stimulus.

Second, the various properties of an object are not equally important. If one encodes three very important properties, that may be enough to identify the object, whereas one may need six relatively unimportant properties and one important property to identify it. For example, if a puzzle were a picture of an outdoor scene, pieces that illustrate sky would not contribute much to identifying the scene, whereas pieces that depict the foreground would.

Thus, it is not really 80% or some other fixed percentage of properties that must be encoded to identify an object, but rather the percent depends on the context and on the relative importance of the properties.

Recap: Identifying Partially Occluded Shapes

Objects that are partially occluded or are missing parts are identified by the same processes that allow us to identify familiar shapes in different locations. Now, however, the shape may be identified solely in the ventral system, or may also require integrating spatial information in associative memory. On the one hand, if the visible portions of the shape include distinctive nonaccidental properties, perceptual units, or patterns of motion, constraint satisfaction processes in the pattern activation subsystem may implicate a single representation. If so, then the output from the pattern activation subsystem will be sufficient to implicate a single representation in associative memory, and the object will be identified. For example, a fork can be identified as soon as its tines are seen. On the other hand, if the input does not provide such distinctive information, the output from the ventral system will have relatively low "strength," and so will not match any particular representation in associative memory very well. In this case, information about the location, size, and orientation encoded by the dorsal system will contribute to identification. If one representation is consistent with all of the properties of the object, and others are not very consistent, the object can be identified.

In many situations, however, even the sum total of the input may not be sufficient to implicate a single object; more than one representation in associative memory may be relatively consistent with the various input information. In these circumstances, one must take a "second look," encoding more information. The processes that are used to accomplish this lie at the heart of another of our abilities, discussed in the following section.

Identifying Unfamiliar Shapes

The existence of nonaccidental properties, perceptual units, and motion relations cannot account for all of our abilities to identify objects. For example, you probably had no trouble identifying the two cats in Figure 3.9, even though they have different shapes. In fact, their shapes probably did not exactly match the shapes of cats you have previously seen. We can identify a cat when it is running, curled up asleep, or sharpening its claws. In addition, think about a contorted person or bicycle on the ground, which can assume many different shapes—and these shapes disrupt some of the nonaccidental properties that are present in other situations. Flexible objects can appear in many novel configurations. If one simply takes in the entire object in a single attention fixation, the pattern may fail to match a stored pattern. This is one of the fundamental problems confronting researchers in computer vision.

FIGURE 3.9 **Two cats that have different shapes, but can be easily identified nevertheless**

Imagine overlaying the pictures of the cats presented in Figure 3.9 and seeing how much they overlap. Not much. In the early days of computer vision, researchers tried to store pictures in a computer and then simply match the input with each of the stored pictures. The stored picture that overlapped the most was assumed to correspond to the object. This idea died a quick death as soon as it was tested with actual computer programs: Those cats may not have very similar shapes to ones you've seen before, but you can identify them nonetheless. Thus, we do more than simply match overall shape to stored shapes when we identify objects.

Notice also what you do when you see chairs: You can identify them as chairs even though they have different arms and a differently shaped back and legs from other chairs you have seen. The parts themselves may vary. Furthermore, we can identify an object when it does or does not have optional parts, such as arms for a chair. All of these variations change the shape of the object, but we still can identify it even if we have never seen that particular shape before.

How might we build a system that copes with this problem? The approach is the same as before: We look for properties of the input that stay constant across the different variations. For example, consider what stays the same as a person crouches, stands on one foot, and curls into a fetal ball. The first thing to notice is that no parts are added, and most remain visible, as an object contorts. Thus, if we can identify the parts, we go a long way towards identifying the object.

And in fact there is good evidence that we perceptually organize objects into parts, which are stored in visual memory. For example, Stephen Reed and his colleagues showed subjects geometrical forms, such as a Star of David.[61] They later showed these people parts of figures, and asked them to indicate whether a particular part had been included in a previously viewed figure. People were very accurate at telling that a large triangle was part of a Star of David, but were not good at reporting that a parallelogram was part of it. When we see the star, we apparently organize the pattern as two overlapping triangles, which are then stored, not a hexagon with six small attached triangles or a parallelogram with four small triangles.[62] Consistent with these findings, Perrett et al. found cells in the inferior temporal lobe that respond best to eyes per se; these cells respond as well to eyes alone (seen through a slit) as to an entire face.[63] Biederman specifies a simple set of shapes called "geons" (for "geometrical ions") that might be used to organize objects into parts.[64]

Thus, we could begin to build a system that ignores irrelevant shape variations if we break objects down into their constituent parts, which are then processed separately in the ventral system. Each part would be identified by matching its nonaccidental properties, perceptual units, and motion relations, just as an entire object can be. The ventral system does not match objects per se; it just matches patterns. The pattern activation subsystem may store representations of a number of parts, especially if an object can have very differently shaped parts (consider the possible shapes of the backs of chairs).

But as soon as we start to attend to parts individually, we are faced with a problem: Their locations are registered by a separate system, and the arrangement of parts is a critical aspect of shape. For example, the letters b, d, p, and q can be drawn to differ only by the arrangements of their parts. In most cases, we probably simply match each letter as a single shape to a stored pattern. But we can look at each part separately, which forces us to register object properties and spatial properties in separate subsystems (the extreme example of this is when the parts are presented one at a time on a screen). Even so, we can identify the letter; we somehow put the parts together. Similarly, when we view objects close up, we may often see the parts individually and must somehow integrate them. This sort of processing forces us to consider in more detail subsystems of the spatial-properties-encoding dorsal system.

Spatiotopic Mapping

We can infer the existence of another subsystem by analyzing how to build a visual system that behaves like ours. We see objects as located relative to ourselves and other objects, but the visual buffer is composed of retinotopically organized areas; information in this structure is laid out as it is on the retina. The position on the retina is useless for reaching, navigation, or identification: Every time one's eyes shift, the location is different. Thus, there must be a transformation from a retinotopic to a spatiotopic (space-based) frame of reference.

And in fact neurons in area 7a of the parietal lobe respond selectively to the location of a stimulus in space, but these responses are modulated by the position of the eyes.[65] David Zipser and Richard Andersen built a neural network computer model that showed that this information is all that is needed to establish a spatiotopic frame of reference (location relative to the head, in their model).[66] They presented a network with a spot in a "retinal" array, and trained it to report the location of the spot in space. The network received not only the location of the spot on the "retina," but also a signal indicating where the eyes were pointed. After the network had been trained appropriately, they analyzed the weights on the connections from the input to the hidden units, mapping out the "receptive field" for each hidden unit (i.e., the input units that have large weights on the connections to the hidden unit). The most interesting result from Zipser and Andersen's network was that it developed "receptive fields" that were very similar to those found in area 7a of the parietal lobe; apparently, combining location on the retina with eye position is an effective way to compute location—which was also adopted by the brain.

However, if we infer that the spatiotopic mapping subsystem is embodied in the parietal lobe, we are faced with an apparent paradox: the receptive fields in this area are very large, and in fact are roughly the same size as the receptive fields of neurons in the inferior temporal lobe. And yet we infer that neurons in the parietal lobe register location, whereas those in the temporal lobe do not—thereby allowing one to identify objects when they appear in different parts of the visual field. Indeed, we inferred that this property is at the root of the division of labor between the ventral system and dorsal systems. Thus, we are faced with the question, how can large receptive fields in the ventral system allow the system to ignore location, but equally large receptive fields in the dorsal system allow it to encode location?

Our first response to the observation that the neurons have large receptive fields is to infer that coarse coding is used, as was discussed at the end of Chapter 2; in this case, the mix of outputs from neurons with overlapping receptive fields would signal a specific location. From this perspective, the question then becomes whether there are critical differences in the receptive field properties of the two types of neurons—those in the inferior temporal lobe and those in the parietal lobe—that would explain why only one sort can be used effectively in this type of coarse coding.

Randall O'Reilly, Kosslyn, Chad Marsolek, and Christopher Chabris combed the literature on the response properties of neurons in the two areas,[67] and found that the neurons respond in strikingly different ways to stimuli in different parts of their receptive fields. Neurons in the inferior temporal lobe virtually always respond most vigorously when a stimulus is placed so that its image falls on the fovea (the high-resolution, central part of the retina). In contrast, neurons in area 7a of the parietal lobe rarely respond most vigorously when the image strikes the fovea; in fact, about 40% of these neurons do not respond when the image falls on the fovea. Some neurons in this area are most sensitive to stimuli along one edge of the receptive field, others are most sensitive to stimuli in one quadrant, and so on.

O'Reilly et al. reasoned that coarse coding of location might be easier with receptive fields like those of neurons in area 7a than with receptive fields like those of neurons in the inferior temporal lobe. Their reasoning was based on the intuition that there is less variety in the outputs of the neurons if they all respond most vigorously to stimuli at the same location (i.e., the fovea). Coarse coding operates by using different mixtures of outputs to implicate a specific stimulus; if the mixtures do not differ very much, coarse coding will not be as effective.

To test this idea, O'Reilly et al. constructed a neural network model. This network received a point in an array as input, and specified the X and Y coordinates within the array as output. The network was constructed so that the receptive field properties of input units could be varied, with different regions of the input array sending stronger input into the system. O'Reilly et al. then observed the ease of mapping the input to the output when the network was constructed with a variety of different sorts of receptive fields.

And in fact, the network model showed that it is more difficult to map a dot in an array to explicit X and Y coordinates if the input receptive fields all produce the strongest output when the dot is in the center of the array. The greater the percentage of receptive fields that were most sensitive to inputs off the center, the more effectively the network recovered the location of the dot.

Thus, O'Reilly et al. received support for their hypothesis and eliminated the apparent paradox. Even though neurons in the parietal lobe and in the inferior temporal lobe have very large receptive fields, they differ critically in how the receptive fields are organized. If virtually all of the fields are most sensitive to stimuli at the center, as is true of neurons in the inferior temporal lobe, the overlap in their outputs cannot be used effectively to compute location. If, on the other hand, neurons that have large, overlapping receptive fields respond maximally when stimulated at various places outside the center of their receptive fields, they can use coarse coding effectively to compute location.

The O'Reilly et al. model was constructed with the assumption that the spatiotopic mapping subsystem receives information not only from the attention window, but also from unattended regions of the visual buffer. This assumption is warranted by a number of observations. Specifically, if it only received input from the attention window, we would be aware only of the locations of objects to which we were attending. Clearly, this is not the case. In fact, we voluntarily can shift our attention to look directly at an object seen out of the corner of our eye—and so must have information about where the object is located. Furthermore, because our eyes move, this location information cannot be retinotopic; it must be spatiotopic in order to allow a moving eye to settle on the correct position.

Information from the spatiotopic mapping subsystem not only feeds directly into the motor system, but also is sent indirectly into associative memory, where it is combined with information about shape and other object properties encoded by the ventral system. In order to understand how we can identify contorted shapes, we need to consider how spatial relations are encoded, and how this information is combined with information about the identity of an object's parts.

Categorical Spatial Relations Encoding

Let us continue our computational analysis of the Contorted Person Problem (i.e., how we identify objects when their parts are positioned in novel ways). We are trying to figure out what is preserved across the different postures. A contorted human shape certainly looks different from pose to pose but we identify it nonetheless. In considering what kinds of properties remain the same as we take photographs of a person kneeling, standing, walking, rolling over, and so on, we noticed that no parts are added or deleted (although some parts are occluded in some postures). In addition, notice that the spatial relations among the parts remain the same, *if we characterize the relations at a rather abstract level of analysis.* For example, the forearm remains "connected to" the upper arm, no matter how the person twists and turns, and the ears remain on the "sides of" the head, and so forth. Categories such as "connected to," "above," "inside," and so on are abstract because they group over a wide range of variation; they treat positions that share a single attribute of the spatial relation as equivalent.

Thus, one way to build a machine that exhibits our abilities might be to include a subsystem that computes *categorical spatial relations* among objects or parts of objects. These abstract spatial relations often remain constant when the positions of parts or objects vary, and hence capture what is stable across the various positions of flexible objects. Such categorical spatial relations differ qualitatively from one another; "above" is not a finer or different version of "left of."

Because the parietal system encodes location in a way that feeds directly into the processes that guide action, additional processing is necessary to encode spatial information into memory. This categorical spatial relations encoding subsystem presumably receives high-quality input only about material captured by the attention window. Indeed, Ullman suggests that some spatial relations can be computed only if one shifts attention systematically over the stimulus.[68,69]

Coordinate Spatial Relations Encoding

By considering what the visual system can do, we are led to infer that categorical spatial relations are not enough: What makes them well-suited for identifying flexible objects makes them ill-suited for other purposes. Specifically, to guide movements effectively, we need to represent not a category of relations, but the precise locations of objects. Indeed, consider which is easier, throwing something into a basket or estimating its distance from you in feet and inches (using numbers that specify categories); most people have much better metric information available for guiding movement than for estimating distance. Similarly, when viewing a familiar scene, we can direct our eyes to a given position rather precisely.[70]

Such representations of precise location can also be stored. For example, consider the ability to walk around in one's house in the dark, not bumping into furniture. If we only store categorical information, we would only remember qualitative spatial relations, such as "the chair is next to the couch"—which are not very useful for navigation or reaching.

In order to guide action, we need to specify information relative to our bodies. We do not, however, simply store movements per se. We can navigate around our house in the dark along any number of pathways, and can look to a familiar location from any number of vantage points. Rather, we store information about the coordinates of objects relative to the body, and can alter these coordinates so that this information remains current as we move about. We infer that a separate *coordinate spatial relations encoding* subsystem probably exists to encode such spatial relations into memory.

Evidence for the distinction. Two sorts of evidence exist for the distinction between categorical and spatial relations representations. One sort comes from computer models that examine the differences between the two kinds of mappings, and the other sort comes from studies of differences in how the cerebral hemispheres encode spatial relations. We will briefly consider each type of finding in turn.

Intuitively, the mapping from an input (two objects or parts) to a categorical spatial relation (e.g., "above") seems very different from the mapping of the same input to a coordinate spatial relation useful for guiding action. If we could determine that these mappings are in fact qualitatively distinct, this would be an argument that different subsystems compute them.

To examine this possibility, Kosslyn, Chabris, Marsolek, and Koenig trained network computer models to determine whether a dot was above or below a bar and whether a dot was within a criterion distance of a bar.[71] They used the same method used by Rueckl et al., examining both a single network that performed two tasks and a split network, with half of it doing one task and the other half doing the other task. The results were as expected: The split networks did much better than the networks that produced both judgments in a single system. This was true over a wide range of network sizes. This result is consistent with the idea that the two kinds of mappings are distinct.

Given only these results, it seemed possible that split networks generally may tend to do better than unsplit ones. To examine this possibility, Kosslyn et al. examined the ease of mapping two metric judgments in split and unsplit network models. These mappings should share patterns of input/output connections. In sharp contrast to the earlier results, splitting the network—so that each judgment was done by a separate group of hidden units—hurt performance dramatically. In this case, the single network was able to perform both input/output mappings more efficiently because they were qualitatively similar. When the mappings are qualitatively distinct, however, adjusting the weights on the connections to produce one mapping interferes with adjusting the weights to produce the other.

In addition, a number of researchers have collected neuro-psychological evidence that supports the distinction between the categorical and coordinate relations encoding subsystems.[72] These experiments rested in part on the idea that categorical information (e.g., as used in language) is generally processed better in the left cerebral hemisphere of right-handed people. Hence, it seemed possible that the categorical spatial relations encoding subsystem might be more effective in the left cerebral hemisphere.

On the other hand, the ability to navigate and reach properly relies on encoding precise metric information, and there is evidence that the right cerebral hemisphere plays a special role in this ability.[73] Indeed, the right hemisphere apparently can initiate reaching to a point more quickly than the left,[74] which is consistent with the idea that it can compute the precise location of the target more quickly. Hence, it seemed possible that coordinate relations encoding might be more effective in the right hemisphere.

A set of experiments has been conducted to test these hypotheses. In these experiments, people were asked to stare straight ahead while stimuli were flashed to the left or right side. A remarkable fact about the retina is that it is actually part of the brain that has been pushed forward during development. The left side of each retina is an extension of the left side of the brain, and sends fibers only to the left cerebral hemisphere, and vice versa for the right. It is not that the left eye sends information only to the left part of the brain and the right eye sends information only to the right part of the brain. Rather, each eye sends information to both halves of the brain, but the left half of each eye sends information only to the left cerebral hemisphere and the right half of each eye sends information only to the right cerebral hemisphere.

Thus, if we present something to the right of center to someone who is staring straight ahead, the visual image will fall onto the left half of each retina—which means that the left hemisphere initially will receive the visual input. In these kinds of experiments, the stimuli are presented for less time than is required to make an eye movement (which requires about a fifth of a second), and so only one hemisphere sees the stimulus initially. The hemispheres are connected by massive bundle of nerve fibers (called the *corpus callosum*), but time is required for information to cross between them.

If the left hemisphere is in fact better at computing categorical spatial relations, then a person ought to make such judgments faster when stimuli are presented to the right side than when they are presented to the left side. In contrast, if the right hemisphere is better at computing coordinate spatial relations, then one ought to make such judgments faster when stimuli are presented to the left side. This prediction has been confirmed in numerous experiments. For example, Joseph Hellige and Chikashi Michimata showed subjects a horizontal line and a dot, and asked them whether the dot was above or below the line (which requires computing a categorical relation) or whether the dot was within 3 millimeters of the line (which requires computing a coordinate relation).[75] Subjects were faster in the categorical task when the line and dot were presented to the right-visual-field/left-hemisphere, and were faster with the coordinate task when the stimuli were presented to the left-visual-field/right-hemisphere. Corresponding findings have been reported when people judge on/off and left/right (categorical judgments) and evaluate distances of 1 inch and 2 millimeters (coordinate judgments).[76,77]

The important finding here has nothing to do with the specializations of the cerebral hemispheres. Rather, we are interested in the evidence for the existence of distinct processing subsystems. If there were only a single subsystem that computes all spatial relations, either it would be better in one hemisphere or the other, or would be equally effective in both hemispheres. The findings show that there cannot be a single subsystem, given that one hemisphere was better for one type of relation and the other was better for the other type of relation. Thus, we have strong evidence for the existence of separate subsystems for computing categorical and coordinate spatial relations, which are relatively more effective in the left and right cerebral hemispheres, respectively.

The idea that the hemispheres compute spatial relations in different ways is supported by many other findings in the literature. For example, a number of researchers have reported that patients who suffered right-hemisphere damage have selective difficulty registering the locations of dots, compared to patients who suffered left-hemisphere damage.[78] Similarly, others have found that the ease of determining whether misoriented figures are the same or different depends on which hemisphere initially receives the input; the left hemisphere showed no effects, whereas the right did.[79] This result makes sense if the left hemisphere assigns categorical relations that are invariant over orientation (e.g., "connected to").[80] Furthermore, a well-known facet of "Gerstmann's syndrome" is inability to judge left/right, a categorical relation;[81] this syndrome usually arises following damage to the posterior left hemisphere.

In summary, we have good reason to infer that the dorsal system includes at least three distinct subsystems. One of these subsystems transforms retinotopic coordinates to spatiotopic coordinates; these representations are useful for guiding actions. In order to encode this kind of spatial information into memory, a coordinate spatial relations encoding subsystem registers the metric spatial relations between objects or parts within the attention window (which are the only material registered with high resolution); this subsystem encodes location in coordinates that are useful for guiding subsequent movements. In addition, a categorical spatial relations encoding subsystem categorizes the relation between parts or objects within the attention window, and passes this information downstream.

Convergence in Associative Memory

This computational analysis has led us to seek properties of contorting objects that are preserved when the shape changes. We noted that no parts are added or deleted, and that some categories of spatial relations between the parts remain the same. Thus, if the brain encodes an object's parts in the ventral system and their spatial relations in the dorsal system, the same input will converge on associative memory when the object is seen in different configurations—and the same stored representation in associative memory can be accessed when the object assumes many different shapes.

The process of constraint satisfaction operates best when

there is a steady stream of information flowing into associative memory (which occurs because the ventral and dorsal systems operate concurrently); as the object and spatial properties are matched, eventually a single object is implicated.[82] If one is encoding a sequence of information over time, the system is faced with a fundamental problem: it must decide where to move the eyes. To see why, hold out your thumb and look at it with one eye closed. Your thumb covers about the region of space that we can see with high acuity (approximately 2° of visual angle). We seem to see a much greater region clearly because we move our eyes around while we look at objects.

When thinking about how to build a system that mimics our visual systems, one is confronted with a decision: What principles should determine where one looks next at any given time? There are only three ways in which such shifts of attention can be guided: They can be random; they can be drawn to particular stimulus qualities (such as sharp changes in color or intensity) by the stimulus-based attention shifting subsystem; or they can be guided by knowledge, belief, or expectation. Even the most casual examination of patterns of eye fixations, such as those illustrated in Figure 3.10, shows that we often use knowledge to guide our eye movements. We humans do not just sit there and wait for information to come in; we actively seek information and actively test hypotheses. If one has an inkling of what one is seeing, one can seek out confirmatory evidence by looking for particular parts.

Top-down Hypothesis Testing

If a good match to an object is not made in the pattern activation subsystem, and the total constraints entering associative memory do not implicate one object, we will need to collect more information. If one representation in associative memory is relatively more consistent with the range of inputs than the others, it can serve as an hypothesis. That is, one can actively seek properties of the input that should be present if that object is in fact being viewed. For example, one of the authors is very myopic. As an experiment, he left various objects scattered around the house and several days later took off his glasses and

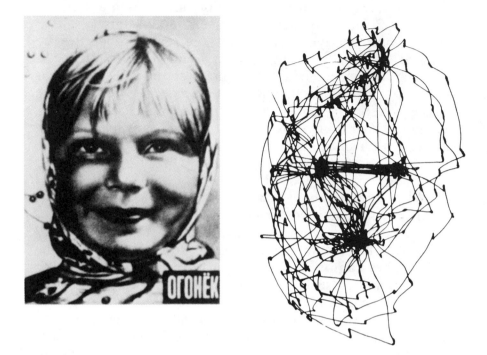

FIGURE 3.10 Patterns of eye movements observed when a person studied pictures (from Yarbus, 1967). *(From* Higher Cortical Functions in Man, *2nd edition, by A. R. Luria. Copyright © 1966, 1979 by A. R. Luria. Reprinted by permission of Basic Books, a division of HarperCollins Publishers Inc.)*

walked around, trying to identify objects. One of the objects, a shampoo tube, was not immediately identified. Rather, he only tentatively identified it, and then looked for a cap. Finding it, he decided that it probably was a shampoo tube. Such a process occurs normally, but so quickly that we are usually unaware of taking such second looks. Several areas in the frontal lobes are probably involved in directing attention to potentially informative sites.[83]

The first step in this process is to look up in associative memory the properties the suspected object should have. A subsystem with this function would be most efficient if it began by looking up particularly distinctive properties, such as unique parts, colored patches, or texture. For example, if you wanted to tell Spot from Fido, looking for four legs would not be useful. You would be better off looking for a particularly shaped head or a peculiar blotch on the dog's back.

Depending on the way spatial relations were stored, different processes would be required to use the stored information. In addition, it is clear that the processes that look up stored information are distinct from those that use that information to direct attention. We can infer that several subsystems likely exist to look up salient information in associative memory and to use this information to shift attention to a new location.

Coordinate property lookup.   We have argued that spatial information can be encoded into memory in two forms, using a coordinate representation that is suitable for guiding movements or a categorical representation. If an object's shape does not vary much from example to example, it is useful to look up a coordinate representation of the location of a distinctive characteristic and simply look in that location. This sort of metric code can easily be used to direct attention to a particular location. However, this method is not satisfactory in exactly those situations in which it is useful to encode categorical spatial relations.

Categorical property lookup.   If an object is contorted in an odd way, its shape will not match a single shape stored in the pattern activation subsystem, nor will its distinguishing characteristics be in their usual locations. For example, if a dog is curled up with a leg over its head, its face may be difficult to locate at first glance. In cases such as this, categorical spatial relations are useful. If one has stored information about what is connected to what, this information can guide attention to allow one to encode important characteristics.

Thus, we posit a *categorical property lookup subsystem,* which accesses qualitatively different representations from those accessed by a *coordinate property lookup subsystem.* Stored coordinates can be used immediately to guide attention, but stored categories must be converted to specific scanning strategies.[84] For example, if the categorical property lookup subsystem accesses the fact that "the head is at the front of the body," the body must be located before attention can be shifted to the appropriate relative location to focus on the head.

The computations required to look up categorical information are so different from those required to convert it to coordinates that we hypothesize a distinct *categorical-to-coordinates conversion subsystem*. This subsystem accepts categorical spatial relations (such as "at the front of") and coordinate information and produces a range of coordinates that indicates which location, in the present image, is specified by the representation. Coordinate information is necessary because a specific relation (such as "at the front of") implies different positions in space depending on the orientation, size, and distance of the object. Depending on how the dog is positioned, a different range of coordinates will be produced to specify the location of its face.

The property lookup and categorical-to-coordinate conversion subsystems are probably implemented in the frontal lobe. As we shall discuss in Chapter 9, the frontal lobe is known to be involved in setting up plans.[85] More important, the frontal lobe clearly has a role in formulating and testing hypotheses. A critical indicator of a frontal lobe disorder is the existence of *perseveration*. For example, as we shall discuss in more detail in Chapter 9, the Wisconsin Card Sorting Task is often used to diagnose frontal lobe disorders. In this task, the patient is asked to sort cards into piles. The cards have different shapes in different colors. The examiner might start off by having the patients sort the cards into red and green piles. The examiner provides the patients with feedback, telling them when they have made an error. The patients quickly learn to sort the cards correctly. But then the examiner switches criteria (e.g., to circular and angular shapes). The patients are not told that a switch has been made, but receive feedback that cues them that the rules of the game have been changed. Patients with frontal lobe damage require an abnormally long time to discover the new rule. They have difficulty abandoning their previous strategy and considering new alternatives, which is a critical component of hypothesis testing. These patients seem to suffer from a kind of psychological inertia. If they are doing nothing, they continue to do so; if they are doing a particular task, they continue to do so.[86]

In addition, the frontal lobe contains two neural structures that are critical in locating stored representations of distinctive properties and searching for them. Area 8 (see Figure 3.3) is called the *frontal eye fields*. This area is topographically mapped; if a region is electrically stimulated, the animal's eyes will shift to a corresponding position. Near this area is area 46, which has been shown to store locations of objects for a brief period of time;[87] this sort of information is clearly useful for planning eye movements. Perhaps not surprisingly, area 46 has rich and precise neuroanatomical connections to the parts of the parietal lobe that register location.[88] In short, there is good reason to believe that the frontal lobe is involved in looking up information to formulate hypotheses about what an object might be, and then using this information to shift eye positions to examine the object.[89]

Subsystems used to shift attention. Finally, our inferences so far imply that there must be mechanisms that actually shift attention, adjusting the location and size of the attention window as well as the positions of the eye, head, and body, as appropriate. Michael Posner and his colleagues have learned a great deal about these subsystems with a very simple task:[90] A subject is asked to stare at a point in the center of a screen. The subject then is cued to attend either to the left or right of that point by a box that lights up on one side. Shortly thereafter, an asterisk appears to the left or right, and the person simply presses a key—as quickly as possible—as soon as the asterisk appears. The trick is that the box leads the subject to attend to the same side as the asterisk most, but not all, of the time.

Normal people respond to the asterisk faster when it appears on the same side as the box; the box "primes" (biases) them to attend to that side—which is a good bet because the asterisk usually is on the same side as the box. People who have had brain damage sometimes do not respond normally in this task. Some patients have abnormal difficulty responding when the asterisk appears on the unexpected side. These patients typically have lesions in the parietal lobe on the opposite side to the asterisk, which suggested to Posner and his colleagues that they had suffered damage to a subsystem that *disengages* attention from a location. Other patients have abnormal difficulty *moving* attention to either side. These patients typically have lesions in a subcortical structure, the superior colliculus. The superior colliculus has long been known to have a role in shifting the eyes. And a third group of patients has trouble using the priming cue to help them detect the asterisk in the cued location, which suggests that they had suffered damage to a subsystem that *engages* attention. These patients typically have damage in another subcortical structure, the thalamus. The thalamus is a kind of switching station, connecting many parts of the cortex.[91]

Thus, there are at least three subsystems involved in allocating attention to a specific location and attention can be disrupted in different ways, depending on which of these subsystems is impaired. These subsystems are the final pieces that allow the entire system to identify objects even under poor conditions, as summarized below.

Recap: Identifying Unfamiliar Shapes

The subsystems we have inferred are schematized in Figure 3.11. When confronted with a shape such as that in Figure 3.12, the identification process is as follows. As usual, it begins when the image of the object causes a pattern of activation to be evoked in the visual buffer. This pattern is surrounded by the attention window, which allows these neurons to send output to the ventral and dorsal systems for further processing. The ventral system encodes object properties, such as shape, color, and texture. We have divided it up into three component subsystems: The preprocessing subsystem extracts nonaccidental properties (such as the symmetrical edges, parallel lines, and point at the front) and perceptual units (such as regions of the same color or blotches that have proven distinctive in the past), and marks them on the image. The motion relations subsystem extracts relative patterns of motion. The marked image and the motion information is then sent to the pattern activation subsystem, where the input is matched against information associated with stored patterns. In this example, the iron is seen from an unusual point of view so that not enough nonaccidental properties and perceptual units are seen to make a good match to stored patterns in the pattern

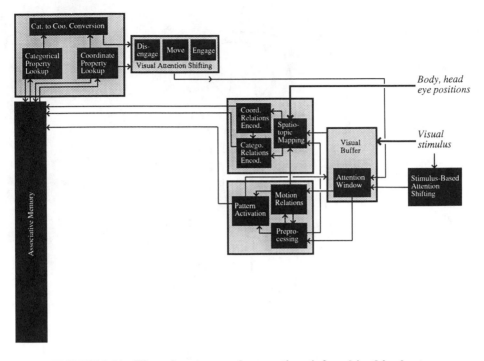

FIGURE 3.11 The subsystems and connections inferred in this chapter

activation subsystem. However, the best match is to an iron; enough of the nonaccidental properties are recovered to match this stored pattern better than any other one. This information is sent to associative memory.

At the same time that the ventral system is encoding object properties, the dorsal system encodes the location, size, and orientation of the stimulus. The spatiotopic mapping subsystem computes the location in space, actual size, and orientation of the object. The spatial properties of objects within the attention window are processed further; the spatial relations are categorized by the categorical spatial-relations-encoding subsystem (as "at center of field," "medium small," and "vertical"), and motor-based coordinates are encoded by the coordinate spatial relations encoding subsystem. These outputs are then sent to associative memory.

Because the match to a stored shape was not very good in the

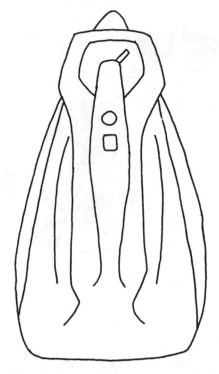

FIGURE 3.12   An iron seen from an unusual point of view

pattern activation subsystem, the output from the ventral system is not sufficient to implicate a single object in associative memory. But the match is consistent with the spatial properties, causing the iron representation in associative memory to be most active.

The property lookup subsystems now access associative memory in search of distinctive stored properties (parts and characteristics) of the candidate object and their locations. In this case, the place where water is poured into the iron is particularly distinctive, and it is stored using categorical spatial relations: "at the top front of the handle." The stored location of this property is converted to instructions to scan to the front end of the image, which are sent to the attention shifting subsystems. Once the attention window is repositioned, new object and spatial properties are encoded. In this case, the spout is identified in the pattern activation subsystem, and it has the proper spatial characteristics. Thus, the additional input to associative memory is sufficient to incriminate an iron; no other object has these hallmarks. If the part were not unique, another might need to be sought. The number of times this cycle must be repeated depends on how distinctive the object's properties are and on the context.

If the candidate object is incorrect, then the input will match some other representation in associative memory better. This will cause another object to become the new candidate, and this new hypothesis will then be tested. This hypothesis testing cycle is repeated until enough information has been encoded to implicate a particular object in associative memory.

We now have considered how we identify objects when they are seen in different locations, when parts are occluded or missing, and when they project unusual shapes. In so doing, we have inferred a set of processing subsystems that interact in specific ways. This system provides us with a powerful framework for understanding the effects of brain damage, as is illustrated in the following section.

Understanding the Effects of Brain Damage

Taking the Wet Mind approach, we make much of the fact that brain damage produces very specific deficits. However, the logic of inference from the brain-damaged mind to the intact one is not simple or straightforward. Any given ability is not usually disrupted all of a piece; rather, the deficits often are a matter of degree. Such graded deficits are consistent with damage within a neural network. Computer models of neural networks have shown that they degrade "gracefully" following damage; they limp along, making mistakes, instead of simply ceasing to function altogether (as a traditional computer would).

Think about the way the octopi interacted in the neural network model discussed in Chapter 2. If one octopus in the hidden unit layer died of food poisoning, the rest would still continue to function, but the system would not perform as well. If two died, the rest sometimes would not squeeze or tickle quite enough to cause the output octopi to respond appropriately. However, if the network were large enough, and only a small percentage of the octopi in the network succumbed to the bad food, the survivors could carry on acceptably. In the worst case, following an epidemic, they might have to compensate by changing how much they squeeze or tickle their compatriots. If major damage occurred, this would not always be sufficient to allow the network to function as well as it did when fully staffed, but moderate amounts of damage would not be completely devastating. So too with the brain.

Damage not only can disrupt processing subsystems, but also can impair the connections among them.[92] These connections rarely are completely severed; rather, damage often appears to degrade the information transmitted, not entirely terminating it.

Furthermore, damage can produce spurious inputs to subsystems that themselves are spared. Thus, the behavioral deficit can reflect damage to a processing subsystem that is not usually involved in a task, but this subsystem affects other subsystems that are used to carry out the task.

And this is not all we must consider when trying to understand the implications of a deficit. Consider an analogy. Say that a dog had a life-threatening tumor on its front left leg, and so the limb had to be surgically removed. The other three legs would not continue to operate just as they had before the operation. Rather, the gait would change, the musculature would develop to compensate for the imbalances, and so on. Similarly, the brain-damaged person is not a normal person who simply is missing an ability or two. Rather, initially untouched functions will "automatically" adjust their processing to operate in the new context. The "ecological balance" of the brain will be awry, and this can be reflected by widespread disturbance of function.

Consider another analogy: Say the three-legged dog encountered a log. Previously, it would have put its front legs up, and jumped over. But one front leg is insufficient, so it puts its head on the log and uses its chin to help lever itself over. The head and neck muscles are operating as before (they have not "automatically adjusted"), but they are operating in a new context. The brain too exhibits such opportunistic processing, using subsystems in new combinations to form new strategies.

Furthermore, the most common general consequence of damage is that the system slows down. It seems to have less activation. This *quantitative* change can lead to *qualitative* changes if particular functions require a lot of activation. For example, say that multiplication requires more effort than adding. If damage to some region not directly involved in multiplication disrupts the overall activation level of the system, this may result in a deficit in multiplication too. But because adding is easier than multiplication, the person may still be able to add. The selective deficit, then, would not necessarily indicate that the lesion hit a "multiplication center" in the brain.

Thus, we must consider four possible bases, operating alone and in combination, for the effects of brain damage: *impaired processing subsystems, impaired connections among subsystems, compensatory changes,* and *reduced activation.* The radio howls when the resistor is removed not because the resistor is used to suppress howls.[93] We are trying to understand a complex system, with many interacting components.[94]

It should be clear why a computer model is a helpful tool for understanding the effects of brain damage. It fills the same role as a notepad when one is doing complicated arithmetic; it saves one the effort of trying to keep track of everything operating at once. Kosslyn, Rex Flynn, Jonathan Amsterdam, and Gretchen Wang built a computer model of most of the processing subsystems and their interactions that are summarized in this chapter.[95] Each subsystem was built to mimic a neural network in the brain, operating on input to produce specific output.[96] The model identified a few simple pictures of objects, both at a class level (e.g., a pattern was identified as a face) and an exemplar level (a pattern was identified as Jack's face). In addition, the model identified these objects when they were partially occluded, twisted, or rotated. Examples of the stimuli given to the computer are provided in Figure 3.13. The model could identify more than one object in a scene, and also could determine whether two objects were the same.

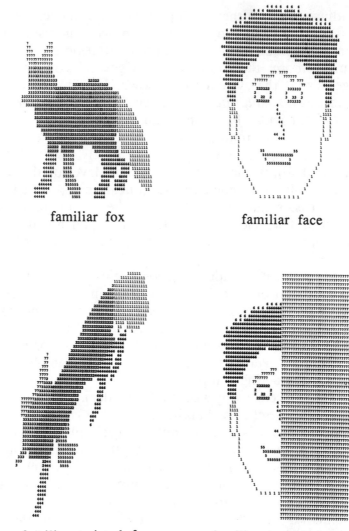

familiar fox   familiar face

unfamiliar twisted fox   familiar occluded face

FIGURE 3.13 Examples of stimuli given to the Kosslyn, Flynn, Amsterdam & Wang (1990) computer model. *(Reprinted with permission.)*

The computer model is interesting in part because each subsystem and connection could be damaged prior to running it. Subsystems could not only be entirely disrupted, but also could be partially damaged so that they functioned differently; for example, one type of partial damage to the categorical property lookup subsystem caused it to look up the same information repeatedly, so that the system kept looking for the same property. (As we shall see, human patients sometimes exhibit similar behavior.) By observing the tasks the model could and could not do after damage, insight was gained into possible underlying causes of visual deficits that are found after brain damage. Some of the results of running the computer model are discussed below.

The fact that brain damage can disrupt vision has been known for over a hundred years. However, the idea that brain damage can disrupt the mental aspects of vision has sometimes been at issue, and only relatively recently has it been fully documented. And in fact, a wide variety of different types of damage has now been described.[97]

Visual Object Agnosia

Visual object agnosia occurs when a brain-damaged patient has trouble identifying objects that is not due to blindness, difficulty in finding the name, problems in focusing attention, or to general mental deterioration. Rather, the patient has trouble interpreting the visual input.[98] Visual agnosia has also been called "mind blindness" or "psychic blindness," and was first demonstrated in a dog by Munk in 1881.[99] The term "agnosia" was originally coined by Sigmund Freud,[100] and is now the standard name for the syndrome. A person with visual agnosia usually is able to identify an object by touch or sound.

Consider a typical example of a patient who was diagnosed as having visual object agnosia:

> A sixty-year old man, almost blind in his right eye from an old injury, woke from a sleep unable to find his clothes, though they lay ready for him close by. As soon as his wife put the garments into his hands, he recognized them, dressed himself correctly and went out. In the streets he found he could not recognize people—not even his own daughter. He could see things, but not tell what they were.[101]

Visual object agnosia is often divided into two types.[102] Patients who are diagnosed as having *apperceptive* agnosia have difficulty putting together visual information to form an integrated perception of an object. Some such patients describe the world as fragmented or chaotic. These patients cannot determine whether two objects are the same or different, let alone identify an object they see. However, even these patients are not blind. Patients who are diagnosed as having *associative agnosia,* in contrast, have difficulty associating the perceptual input with previously stored information.[103] Patients who have "pure" associative agnosia can discriminate between and properly compare shapes, even though they cannot identify the shapes. The patient just described (and the one described at the beginning of Chapter 1) could tell whether objects were the same or different, but not what they were. In short, a problem appreciating the shape of an object is apperceptive; a problem identifying the object while being able to distinguish its shape is associative.

Given the inferences we have made about the functions of individual subsystems and their interconnections, we are led to conclude that a very large number of types of damage could produce apperceptive agnosia; indeed, all that is required is that the visual buffer be relatively intact, which would imply that the person is not blind, but the ventral system cannot function. Indeed, apperceptive agnosia can arise if the visual buffer itself is degraded overall, so that only low-quality information is passed into the system.[104] Martha Farah,[105] in summarizing this literature, notes that apperceptive agnosia often follows carbon monoxide poisoning, which tends to produce "many small disseminated" lesions in the occipital lobe. Thus, the visual buffer may be so degraded that nonaccidental properties subsequently cannot be extracted by the preprocessing subsystem. However, these patients often perceive the shapes of moving objects, which is consistent with Johansson's finding that motion relations can be computed on the basis of even very impoverished input.

Perhaps of more interest is associative agnosia. Patients who display such behavior often compare objects very slowly, painstakingly comparing one portion of the objects at a time.[106] This sort of behavior would arise if the preprocessing or pattern activation subsystem or their connections were damaged, so that relatively little information could be processed. Furthermore, damage to associative memory or connections to it would also disrupt identification. Moreover, if the shapes are unfamiliar, damage to subsystems or connections used in top-down processing would impair identification.

In addition, it is possible for any combination of subsystems or connections in the ventral system to be completely disrupted, so that the patient is opportunistically using spatial properties to compare the objects. In this case, the dorsal system would be used to encode location, size, and orientation; this information would be sent to associative memory, where it would be stored for each object to be subsequently compared (by other processes that access associative memory).

Such a compensation might occur if the activation level in the ventral system were reduced by damage. In this case, the ventral system itself may not be damaged, but may nevertheless not be able to function normally.

In short, we expect that "visual object associative agnosia" is not a single deficit; different patients who have been so diagnosed may in fact have very different underlying problems. In many cases, however, visual agnosia is associated with damage to the temporal lobes or damage to the occipital-temporal area; the locus of the damage parallels the locations of lesions that produce similar deficits in monkeys.[107] This fact suggests that the deficit is caused by disruption to the preprocessing or pattern activation subsystems or their connections.

Prosopagnosia

Prosopagnosia is a relatively rare variety of associative object agnosia, which impairs one's ability to identify faces (the term "prosopon" means face in Greek). Some of the descriptions of patients with prosopagnosia are startling. For example, one patient bumped into a mirror and apologized.[108] He apparently thought he had bumped into another person! Many of these patients can describe individual features of a face, but cannot put them together.

The idea that this deficit is limited to faces has had to be revised recently. More careful testing of many patients with prosopagnosia has often revealed that they also have difficulty identifying individual examples of other types of objects. For example, a farmer who had prosopagnosia could not identify his individual cows, and a bird watcher could no longer identify different types of birds.[109] However, other patients appear to have deficits that are in fact specific to faces.[110] Thus, there are probably at least two types of this disorder.

Prosopagnosia is particularly puzzling because at least some of these patients apparently recognize faces unconsciously, and never become aware that they have done so; patients with prosopagnosia showed changes in the electrical properties of their skin (i.e., increased electrodermal skin conductance responses) when they were viewing familiar faces, compared to unfamiliar ones, even when they claimed to have no idea whom they were looking at.[111] The stimulus must be matching a stored memory of a face in the pattern activation subsystem (at least to some degree), but processing stops early—and the person is never aware that a match was made.

Finally, it is worth noting that some patients can identify faces better than objects! At least in some cases, a patient with associative agnosia need not also display signs of prosopagnosia.[112] Thus, not all varieties of the disorder can simply reflect a problem in registering details clearly.

The computer model was also asked to identify specific faces. The model had selective trouble naming a face after 24 types of damage. Of these, 16 types of damage allowed it to name the face as a face, but not as a particular person. In every one of these cases, the pattern activation subsystem was still able to match the input to stored patterns. Following some types of damage, not enough information left the pattern activation subsystem. Other types of damage disrupted the matching process in some way, so that the match could not be good enough to identify the object. But even so, the fact that a match was made might be registered by the skin conductance response.

The computer model neatly accounted for the fact that some prosopagnosic patients have difficulty identifying a particular individual object (be it a dog, bird, or face). The model had this deficit when the preprocessing subsystem or its outputs were damaged, so that the input to the pattern activation subsystem was partially degraded. It also displayed this deficit when the pattern activation subsystem itself was partially damaged, so that the stored patterns were "blurred" (as would occur if connections in a neural network were randomly damaged). If the input to the pattern activation subsystem or representations within it are degraded enough, the input cannot be used to discriminate among similar stored patterns.

But what about the patients who have trouble only with faces? This deficit could reflect specific damage to the pattern activation subsystem. Perhaps the patterns representing faces simply get wiped out. Although this is logically possible, it seems rather implausible: The damage would have to disrupt just those connections in the network that mapped face stimuli to the appropriate recognition outputs. This kind of a "surgical strike" seems unlikely because having a stroke generally is more like being hit with a hammer than poked by a pin; a stroke typically affects literally millions of nerve cells. Alternatively, the preprocessing subsystem or its connections could be disrupted so that information that is specifically useful for faces is not registered. This sounds good, but it is vacuous unless we can specify the type of information in question.

Consider a different idea: One of us saw a prosopagnosic patient who could identify people immediately upon hearing their voices, which is typical for such patients. When asked what faces looked like to him, he was at a loss for words. "Like a pizza with the parts jumbled around, so you can see the pepperoni and the mushrooms one at a time but not all at once?" he was asked (this was obviously a leading question, but the interviewer was fishing for whatever he could get!). The patient's reply was vague, and then he said something very interesting: As soon as he heard a person's voice, his or her face "snapped into focus" all at once. And in fact, testing revealed that he had excellent visual mental imagery for faces: For example, when given two names (such as Jimmy Carter and Richard Nixon), he could easily decide which person had the rounder face, the longer nose, and similar properties by forming mental images of the faces.

This particular patient had a clear case of the more general (and apparently more common) type of prosopagnosia; he could not identify his own watch, his own car, and so on, in addition to individual faces. However, his remarks may provide an important hint into a detail of visual processing we have not yet considered: In the following chapter we will see that mental imagery sometimes is used as part of the visual matching process in the pattern activation subsystem, which makes sense because the nonaccidental properties are not sufficient to discriminate among very similar visual shapes. Faces are a good example of such shapes, and imagery may commonly be used when faces are recognized. If so, then patients who have "pure" prosopagnosia (i.e., limited only to faces), unlike the patient just described (who had a complex of other visual encoding problems), could have a deficit in forming images of faces: Faces are complex surfaces, and these patients may have damage that prevents them from forming such complex images to be used in object recognition.

Finally, following some types of damage the computer simulation model could identify faces better than some objects. Thus, it is comforting that such patients have been documented (indeed, at the time this prediction was made, the authors were unaware that relevant findings already had been reported).[113] In faces, the eyes stay the same distance apart and the same distance above the nose, no matter whether one is smiling or grimacing. Thus, coordinate spatial relations representations can usefully guide attention to specific features. As we discussed earlier, whenever an hypothesis must be tested, categorical or coordinate spatial relations representations must be looked up in associative memory and used to direct attention to a location of a distinctive part or property. Furthermore, categorical or coordinate spatial relations must be used to encode the location of a part or property. Recall that categorical spatial relations allow one to ignore variation among individual examples. Thus, if the categorical encoding process is disrupted, a person may have trouble identifying objects when they are viewed close up, so that parts are encoded over the course of several eye fixations. But if the coordinate encoding and lookup processes are spared by the damage, we expect the patient to be able to find parts of specific examples of objects, such as particular faces; coordinate spatial relations can be used to specify the locations of parts when the locations are always exactly the same.

Acquired Achromotopsia

Some people are color blind from birth, usually due to deficiencies in different kinds of retinal cells. Other people become color blind following brain damage, which is called *acquired achromotopsia*. One of the interesting features of this deficit is that it often accompanies prosopagnosia.[114] This correlation could occur because the cortical areas that process color happen to be near those that are critically involved in face perception (and thus are likely to be damaged together by the same lesion), or because face perception and color encoding share processing subsystems. Many researchers assume that the former alternative is correct, in part because it is not obvious what color vision and face perception share.

But consider the following fact: In area V1 of the visual system, a certain stain (cytochromoxydase) reveals "blob" patterns on the cortex. When tiny electrodes are placed in the cells in these blob regions, researchers have found that they respond selectively to different colors. However, it turns out that even some animals that do not have color vision have these blob structures; these cells appear to be involved in processing contrast and textural density, as well as color.[115]

Area V1 presumably is used in "low-level" visual processing (which is driven purely by what comes in from the eyes). We have been intentionally vague about the workings of low-level processes, only asserting that the raw material for high-level vision is present in the visual buffer (such as the locations of edges). It is well known that subtle variations in shading contribute to color perception; for example, the Land Effect is a demonstration that differences in color can be produced by variations in shading in special circumstances.[116] And variations in shading are important for reconstructing the third dimension from the two-dimensional images on the retina; this is called *shape from shading*.[117] Because shading may be detected by registering variations in contrast and textural density, it seems possible that at least one low-level visual subsystem may be critically involved in computing color and in computing subtle information about shape; if so, then damaging that mechanism may lead to acquired achromotopsia and the first (more general) type of prosopagnosia.

Color Agnosia

Acquired achromotopsia must be distinguished from a very different neurological deficit. *Color agnosia* is a problem in associating shapes and colors appropriately. For example, consider what happened to an artist following a stroke:

> He was not colour blind, however, for he could name most colours and pick out colours correctly to command. He could not associate colours with objects except by reference to rote memory.[118]

Patients like this one cannot recall which colors belong to objects unless the association has been memorized by rote. For example, if given a black-and-white drawing of a strawberry and asked to select the appropriate crayon to color it, patients with color agnosia will select the correct crayon only if they have a verbal association of the color of the object, remember it, and then laboriously name each color and see which one has the right name. They cannot color in most objects properly.

As we shall discuss in the following chapter, tasks like this one typically require mental imagery. And the simplest account of the deficit is that there is a deficit in the processes that activate stored visual information to generate visual mental images. We will defer discussing this process further until the following chapter, in which we will consider imagery in some detail.

Metamorphopsia

This is a very rare disorder that affects the experience of seeing. Patients who have this deficit may identify objects correctly, but they report that objects look odd. In one variant of this disorder, called *macropsia,* patients see objects as larger than they are, whereas in another variant, called *micropsia,* they see objects as smaller than they are. Furthermore, some of these patients have reported that objects appear fragmented, compressed, tilted, "turned around," and so on. One patient complained that faces looked like fish heads.[119] And the distortions are not necessarily static: One patient reported that people's eyes would swell and contract, going to "nothing at all" and then coming back "like a pimple."[120]

This deficit is intriguing because the patients typically can still recognize and identify objects even though they look distorted. This makes sense if the preprocessing and pattern activation subsystems are intact, but the spatiotopic mapping and/or motion relations subsystems are awry.

Simultanagnosia

Simultanagnosia, or *simultaneous agnosia* is an inability to see more than one shape at a time. For example, Moyra Williams describes the following patient:

> It was found that if two objects (e.g., pencils) were held in front of him at the same time, he could only see one of them, whether they were held side by side, one above the other, or one behind the other. Further testing showed that single stimuli representing objects or faces (including pictures) could be identified correctly and even recognized when shown again, whether simple or complex (newspaper photographs or simple sketches). If stimuli included more than one object, one only would be identified at a time, though the other would sometimes "come into focus" as the first one went out . . .
>
> If the patient was shown a page of drawings, the contents of which overlapped (i.e., objects drawn on top of one another), he tended to pick out a single object and deny that he could see any others. Moreover the figure selected at the first exposure of such stimuli was the only one seen on all subsequent presentations. If shown a drawing which might be seen in two different ways, and which to the normal person usually appears first in one configuration and then in the other (reversible figures), he would pick out one configuration only and was quite unable to reverse it.[121]

This deficit not only affects one's ability to see separate objects, but also sometimes one's ability to see the individual parts of a single object. For example, Tyler describes a patient who "could see only one object or part of one object at a time. . . . She reported seeing bits and fragments. For instance, when shown a picture of a U.S. flag, she said 'I see a lot of lines. Now I see some stars.' "[122] The patient described at the outset of Chapter 1 apparently had a similar deficit, combined with prosopagnosia—which probably reflected a degraded visual buffer, preprocessing, or pattern activation subsystem (he apparently could encode only low-resolution patterns, given the nature of his errors).

One clue regarding the nature of at least some forms of simultanagnosia was provided by Marcel Kinsbourne and Elizabeth Warrington.[123] They asked such patients to read a word, and then to read a second word that replaced it. Although these patients could identify the first word in a roughly normal amount of time, they had great difficulty with the second word. However, these patients were better with the second word when it was shown after a relatively long lag following the first word. These results may suggest that something in the visual system gets "locked onto" the first word, and takes time to disengage before being available for the second word. It is intriguing that Posner and his colleagues infer that the parietal lobes disengage visual attention, and many of these patients have damaged parietal lobes.

The idea that the parietal lobes are involved in simultanagnosia is consistent with the one condition in which the computer simulation model exhibited something like this deficit. The only time the computer model failed to name two objects that were presented at the same time was when the spatiotopic mapping subsystem was partially damaged, leading it to assign the same location to all stimuli—and so not to "look for" another object once the most salient one was encoded. Farah suggests that there are in fact two types of simultanagnosia,[124] one that reflects damage to attentional mechanisms (which feed information into the spatiotopic mapping and ventral subsystems, in our terms) and another that corresponds to difficulty in matching more than a single input at a time to stored visual memories. However, it seems clear that many types of disruptions could produce the deficit. For example, if the damage greatly slowed down the ventral system, associative memory might compensate by "refusing" to accept a second input until the first one was processed. In this case, the system might lock up, and not register more than one object unless they were presented sequentially after a delay.

Visuospatial Disorientation

Some patients are unable to locate objects in space by eye, even though they still can identify them. The difficulty in localizing stimuli is usually diagnosed by difficulty in visually guided reaching, which is called *optic ataxia.* Gordon Holmes may have provided the first detailed reports of such patients,[125] who not only were unable to use vision to guide reaching for objects, but also could not look at named objects, estimate distance correctly, or navigate correctly. Some of these patients would bump into objects, so poor was their ability to locate objects relative to their bodies.

Difficulty in localizing objects may arise following damage to the occipital-parietal area, typically in both hemispheres. This deficit could arise from disruptions of the spatiotopic mapping, spatial relations encoding, attention shifting, and the property lookup subsystems, or their connections. In the computer model, some of these deficits also disrupt processing when multiple parts must be found during object identification. And in fact, visuospatial disorientation sometimes is accompanied by simultanagnosia (indeed, the two are critical components of a single syndrome, "Balint's syndrome"). However, the combination of being able to identify objects while not being able to locate them properly occurred in the model only when objects could be identified purely on the basis of processing in the ventral system (without needing to encode individual parts and relations).

Disorders of Visual Search

Paralysis of gaze occurs when a patient is riveted to a stimulus, and has trouble moving his or her eyes voluntarily to another one. Such visual scanning disorders are also called *ocular apraxia*. Paralysis of gaze may reflect a problem in attention. As discussed earlier, Michael Posner and his colleagues identified three subsystems that are involved in attention, and this disorder could arise if these subsystems were disrupted. One kind of damage may impair the ability to disengage attention from the previous stimulus, which would produce this deficit. Another kind of damage may impair scanning ability per se, which would also produce the deficit. And yet another kind of damage may impair the ability to engage attention at a new location, which might produce something like this deficit.

This disorder also arises in the computer simulation model following a variety of types of damage. First, if the property lookup subsystems are damaged, so that they become "stuck" (i.e., they perseverate), the same information will be looked up over and over and no new instructions will be sent to the attention shifting subsystems. Second, if the spatiotopic mapping subsystem is damaged, so that it registers only a single location (directly in front, in the model), the system will not be "aware" that other objects are available to be seen. Third, if the ventral system is damaged so that object processing is slowed down, the dorsal system may compensate, slowing down so that its outputs are produced in tandem with those of the ventral system. In this case, the system would spend an abnormal amount of time focused on an object if the object must be identified before a new instruction can be sent to the attention shifting subsystems.

Unilateral Visual Neglect

Damage to one parietal lobe, typically on the right side, sometimes will lead a patient to ignore everything to one side of space (the left, following right-hemisphere damage).[126] When these patients are asked to copy a flower, they draw only the petals on the right side of the plant; when asked to copy a clock, they

Model   Patient's copy

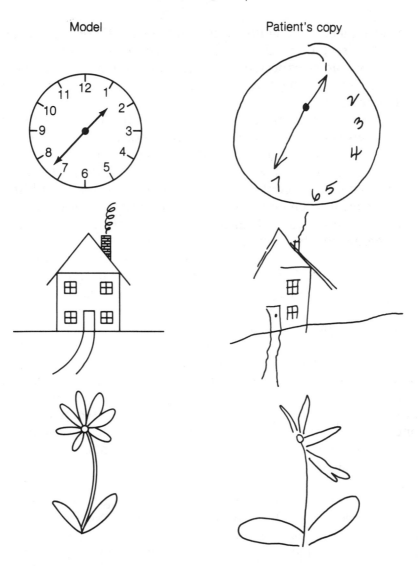

FIGURE 3.14 Drawings made by patients with unilateral visual neglect (reprinted from Kolb & Whishaw, 1990). *(From* Brain, Mind and Behavior, *2nd edition, by Floyd E. Bloom and Arlyne Lazerson. Copyright ©1985, 1988 by Educational Broadcasting Company. Reprinted by permission of W. H. Freeman and Company.)*

sometimes ignore the digits on the left side, and sometimes either cram all of the digits onto the right side or have them spilling off the clock face, running down the right side. If these patients are asked to bisect a line, they place the bisector too far towards the right, as would be expected if they are not aware of the left side of the line. Some of the drawings made by such patients are shown in Figure 3.14.

These patients must be distinguished from those with *homonymous hemianopia*. Patients with homonymous hemianopia are blind in one visual field. These patients typically learn to compensate, moving their heads around so that they see objects on the bad side. In contrast, patients with neglect are not blind; they sometimes can be led to pay attention to the neglected side, but only with great difficulty. These patients rarely learn to compensate for the deficit.

Unilateral visual neglect has a typical course of recovery. Dramatic ("florid") neglect is most common during the first six weeks or so following the injury. Following this, the neglect becomes less severe and is present only when there are two stimuli, one in each visual field. For example, if an examiner wiggles a finger to the patient's left or right side, the patient initially will not be able to see it on the neglected side. After a month or so, the patient will come to be able to see the wiggle on either side. However, if two fingers are wiggled at the same time, one in each field, the patient will revert back to seeing only the one on the good side. This phenomenon is called *extinction to double simultaneous stimulation*. Neglect patients, unlike those with simultanagnosia, have a deficit that is limited to one side of space.

One of the most intriguing aspects of the neglect syndrome is that it appears to affect consciousness itself. Neglect is often accompanied by *anosognosia;* these patients do not realize that they have a visual problem. Patients who have neglect with anosognosia do not try to compensate by moving their heads around or the like, and deny that they have a problem. Indeed, one of us heard an anecdote at a hospital that a neglect patient thought she might be going crazy because she "kept hearing voices"—namely those of people who were standing to her neglected side. She thought the voices were coming out of nowhere!

The computer simulation model suggests that damage to the

spatiotopic mapping subsystem could produce neglect. Such damage is consistent with the neurologist Robert Rafal's idea that simultanagnosia is a "double neglect," with both sides being ignored and only the central field being attended.

The idea that neglect has something to do with registering locations in space receives support from a curious aspect of the syndrome: These patients draw better if their eyes are closed! What is going on here? One answer is suggested by the fact that when asked to copy a flower with their eyes open, these patients virtually always draw the circle at the center correctly; they do not copy half a circle, whereas they do copy only half the petals. The circle is probably stored as a single representation, which is used to produce the pattern in one fell swoop—the patient does not visually monitor the drawing process, using feedback to guide the movement. By closing the eyes, the visual feedback is removed even when more complex patterns are drawn, and the attempt to use feedback may be the source of the problem: It is only when the patient tries to see where to put parts that he or she becomes confused; if he or she uses memory to guide drawing, the problem is circumvented.[127]

Finally, we must note that unilateral neglect can arise following damage to at least four different locations in the brain.[128] Hence, it seems likely that there will be more than one type of neglect, and we are just beginning to understand the ways in which it can vary.

The visual system is perhaps the best understood of all the "cognitive" systems. Not only can we characterize its behavioral abilities relatively easily, but also the study of animals that have similar visual systems has produced a rich body of knowledge about the neural substrate of vision. Furthermore, computer vision is an active area of research in artificial intelligence, and so we can take advantage of careful analyses of what is required to build a system that can see. Our approach is schematized by the cognitive neuroscience triangle. We characterized a specific visual ability, and then considered facts about the brain when analyzing how to build a system that could produce that ability.

In this chapter we saw the influence of each of the five principles noted in Chapter 2. The principle of division of labor lies at the heart of the segregation of the system into subsystems. Some of our inferences also suggest weak modularity, given that some of the subsystems must be used to carry out more than one type of task. For example, the motion relations subsystem presumably is used not only to recognize shapes in the ventral system, but also to track them—which requires processing in the dorsal system. Furthermore, it is likely the preprocessing subsystem sends output not only to the pattern activation subsystem for object recognition, but also to the dorsal system to help guide movements; we need to know where the handle is on a mug to reach properly, and hence shape information must be combined with spatial information to guide action. Indeed, Harries and Perrett have found connections between the posterior portions of the superior temporal sulcus (STS) and the inferior parietal lobe.[129] These connections appear to link the parietal lobe to regions of STS that have a high density of cells that respond to specific views of faces. We will consider the import of these connections in more detail in Chapter 7, where we consider movement control.

We also found that the principle of constraint satisfaction is critical in processing. Specifically, it helps to explain matching both in the pattern activation subsystem and in associative memory. We saw how coarse coding allows neurons in the parietal lobe to encode location, even though they have very large receptive fields. These neurons typically are most sensitive to stimuli that fall off the fovea, and computer models revealed that this property allows them to specify location effectively using coarse coding. Similarly, the principle of concurrent processing was necessary to understand how constraint satisfaction could operate effectively; multiple sources of information arrive at about the same time at the pattern activation subsystem and associative memory, which facilitates matching input to stored representations. Furthermore, some of our accounts of the effects of brain damage on behavior rest on the idea that subsystems are operating simultaneously. Finally, the various possible compensations following brain damage are examples of opportunistic processing; intact processes are drawn into the breach left by damaged subsystems, and contribute to performance in new contexts.

This chapter is a springboard for the following chapters. Vision is integral to many cognitive activities, and plays a critical role in visual cognition and reading. Once we have reviewed these topics, we will be in a good position to consider language, movement, and memory.

4

Visual Cognition

Many people report that they often think by visualizing objects and events. In this chapter we will explore the nature of visual cognition, which is the use of visual mental imagery in thinking. Visual mental imagery is accompanied by the experience of seeing, even though the object or event is not actually being viewed. To get an idea of what we mean by visual mental imagery, try to answer the following questions: What shape are a German Shepherd dog's ears? Which is darker green, a Christmas tree or a frozen pea? How many windows are there in your living room? If you are like most people, you visualized the objects and "looked" at the appropriate part or property. In all of these cases, an image did not arise until you tried to answer the question, and did not linger long after you used it. In addition, consider what seems to happen when you answer this question: If an uppercase version of the letter *n* were rotated 90° clockwise, would it be another letter? To answer, you probably mentally rotated the letter, and "looked" at the new pattern. We not only can examine objects in images, but we can transform them in various ways.[1]

These examples illustrate only a few of the characteristics of our imagery abilities, but are sufficient to allow us to distinguish imagery from perception. In perception, one sees objects that are physically present, whereas in imagery one "sees" objects that are not currently being viewed. Furthermore, we can change images at will, whereas the world is rarely so accommodating during perception.

The examples also allow us to distinguish visual imagery from visual memory proper. Visual images often are built on the basis of visual memories, like those involved in recalling what a German Shepherd's ears look like. Although the image itself was fleeting, the visual memory endures, and can be used later to form a new image. In addition, some visual images are not "replays" of material stored in visual memory. We can "mentally draw," making scribbles that we have never actually seen. Visual imagery is central to visual cognition in part because we use it creatively, forming novel patterns to be viewed before the "mind's eye."

Architects, engineers, gymnasts, and some mathematicians, among others, probably would be in dire straits if their imagery were completely disrupted. Indeed, imagery is often used by many people in the course of their everyday lives. To study the uses of imagery, researchers simply asked people to keep diaries, recording every use of imagery they experienced.[2] The reports from this study, as well as material in the previously published literature,[3] suggested that imagery can be used in four ways: to access information in memory, help one reason, learn new skills, and aid comprehension of verbal descriptions.

In this chapter we will consider how one could begin to build a system that would produce these abilities. We will argue that imagery shares mechanisms with visual perception, and will show how the subsystems inferred in the previous chapter can account for various facets of imagery. Because of the intimate relationship between imagery and perception, considerations about imagery will in turn lead us to augment further the inferences we drew about the subsystems used to identify objects in perception.[4]

Using Imagery to Access Stored Information

Imagery has long been known to be an aid to memory. For example, the ancient Greeks discovered that imaging objects in a sequence of familiar locations greatly enhances memory for the objects.[5] Once the objects have been visualized and the images stored, one later can remember the information by visualizing the locations and associated objects again. For example, if you want to remember a shopping list effectively, simply visualize walking through the market and "seeing" each item on the shelf, perhaps in a particularly large size. Later, when you are in the market, shut your eyes and imagine walking through it, "seeing" the objects that you previously had visualized. Allan Paivio summarizes much evidence that techniques such as this can greatly improve one's memory.[6]

People often use imagery to recall information even if they did not set out to store it as images,[7] and use imagery in recall when thinking about visual properties of objects that have been considered relatively infrequently and which cannot easily be inferred from verbal material. For example, people use imagery to determine whether the tip of a horse's tail is above or below its rear knees, but not whether it has two eyes. In both cases, the properties are visual and not very often considered, but it is easy to infer that a horse, like all mammals, has two eyes. In contrast, it is not easy to infer the relation between the tip of the tail and the rear legs, and so imagery is used; you may have had an image in both cases, but only really needed it when considering the tail and legs.[8]

Visual Imagery and Visual Perception

Part of the key to understanding how imagery allows us to recall information is inherent in the vocabulary we use to describe imagery. We speak of "seeing" objects in visual mental images because the experience of visual mental imagery is in many ways like that of visual perception. This observation suggests immediately that common mechanisms may be involved in imagery and perception. And in fact, there is now an enormous amount of evidence that visual mental imagery recruits some of the same processing subsystems used in visual perception.[9] The idea that imagery and perception rely on common mechanisms has been popular at various times at least since the writings of Aristotle, and was brought into scientific psychology at its inception.[10]

One fact about the neuroanatomy of the visual system proves to be very interesting in the context of visual mental imagery: Virtually every visual area that sends information to another area also receives fibers from that other area.[11] For example, there are anatomical connections that run from the higher visual areas in the temporal lobe to the retinotopically organized areas in the occipital lobe. Figure 3.3 does not have arrowheads for a reason; and the arrowheads in Figure 3.2 are misleading—information actually flows both ways. Indeed, the fibers running backwards are as large as those running downstream. This finding is fascinating because it implies that an enormous amount of information is flowing backwards in the system.

Brain scanning techniques have demonstrated that visual areas in the occipital, temporal, and parietal lobes are also activated during visual mental imagery. For example, in one study subjects were asked to imagine that they were walking along a path through their neighborhood, alternating between making right and left turns.[12] The subjects had inhaled ^{133}Xe, a radioactive gas that is transported to the brain; after the brain is saturated with this substance, the subject begins the task. The more active a particular brain area during the task, the more quickly fresh blood comes in and washes out the radioactive blood. This technique is usually called "Xenon-133 rCBF," or rCBF for short, which stands for regional cerebral blood flow.[13] Using this technique, the researchers could assess which parts of the cortex were differentially used in this task by observing the patterns of blood flow that occur while people perform the task, and comparing these patterns with blood flow in other, equally difficult, nonimagery tasks. Compared to a mental arithmetic task and to an auditory imagery/verbal task, they found that visual mental imagery resulted in large increases in blood flow in the occipital lobe, posterior superior parietal lobe, and posterior inferior temporal lobe—all of which are areas that are also used in high-level visual perception.[14]

Very similar results were reported by Georg Goldenberg and his colleagues in different kinds of tasks.[15] These researchers asked subjects to evaluate two kinds of questions. One kind typically evoked imagery (such as "Is the green of pine trees darker than the green of grass?"), whereas the other kind typically did not (e.g., "Is the categorical imperative an ancient grammatical form?"). Subjects were asked to evaluate the two kinds of questions, and the pattern of regional cerebral blood flow was recorded as they did so.[16] In the imagery condition there was increased blood flow in the occipital regions, relative to the low-imagery condition. These results show once again that brain areas concerned with vision are also used in visual imagery.[17]

In addition, different patterns of blood flow in the left and right hemispheres have been found during some imagery tasks (using the ^{133}Xe rCBF technique).[18] The most interesting results were obtained by monitoring blood flow while subjects imagined three-dimensional figures rotating: There was more flow in the right parietal lobe than the left, and more flow in the right frontal lobe than in the left. The parietal and frontal lobes are tightly interconnected,[19] and so it is not surprising that these asymmetries should go hand in hand. As was discussed in Chapter 3, Patricia Goldman-Rakic and her colleagues showed that the frontal lobes contain a spatial short-term memory; if area 46 in the frontal lobe of one hemisphere is damaged, the animal loses the ability to remember the locations of objects in the side of space processed in that hemisphere. Mental imagery obviously involves memory, and so it is of interest that the frontal lobe is active during this image transformation task.

In addition, numerous correlations between the location of brain damage and a behavioral deficit have provided hints regarding the neural substrate of visual imagery. For example, David Levine and his colleagues describe two brain-damaged patients who had complementary imagery disorders.[20] One patient could use images of shape but not spatial relations, whereas the other could use images of spatial relations but not shape. For example, one patient could decide whether George Washington had a beard (a shape imagery task), but not how to get from one location to another (a spatial relations imagery task), and vice versa for the other patient. Both patients had corresponding impairments in perception, which is consistent with the idea that the same subsystems are recruited in both kinds of processing. As expected from the findings discussed in Chapter 3, the patient who had trouble imaging shape had a lesion in the occipital-temporal region, whereas the patient who had trouble imaging location had a lesion in the occipital-parietal region.

Because visual imagery shares processing mechanisms with visual perception, we begin with a leg up when considering how it operates. At the outset, we gain insight into what an image representation is. The uses of imagery summarized earlier all depend on its spatial/visual properties. For example, to decide whether George Bush could see over the top of an elephant's head if he were sitting on its back, one needs to have Mr. Bush and the elephant in the same spatial frame of reference. Images must serve to make explicit the spatial structure of objects.

Thus, it is of interest that the visual buffer, as characterized in the previous chapter, is spatially organized. This structure is a set of topographically mapped areas in the occipital lobe. And the occipital lobe "lights up" when people perform visual imagery tasks, as noted earlier. Indeed, PET scanning has revealed that the primary visual cortex in humans is selectively activated during visual imagery,[21] and this area is known to be spatially organized in humans.[22] A spatial pattern in the visual buffer can be invoked from memory as well as from the eyes. By analogy, imagine that the visual buffer is a screen, which is connected to a camera and also to a videotape recorder. A picture on the screen can be displayed either from the camera (the eyes, during perception) or from the videotape recorder (previously seen information, during imagery). The buffer is not literally a screen, but the analogy is useful nevertheless.

Image Inspection

Part of what it means to "have an image" is to be able to interpret the imaged pattern. If one could not "inspect" patterns in images, for all intents and purposes they would not exist—and hence imagery would be useless for recalling information. For example, if asked whether there is an empty space in the uppercase version of the first letter of the alphabet, most people not only can answer properly but also can describe the shape of that empty space. They "inspect" the pattern in the image, and "see" the shape of the triangle.

Our accounts of how we interpret parts, properties, or spatial relations of objects in images hinge on the claim that images are patterns of activity in the visual buffer, mimicking those that are evoked during perception. As such, they can depict both object and spatial properties. If so, then image inspection can be accomplished in the same way as perceptual identification: Patterns in the visual buffer are encompassed by the attention window, and information is sent to the dorsal and ventral systems, just as was described in the previous chapter.

Zooming. This idea allows us to explain some of the more detailed observations about our ability to inspect objects in images. For example, consider the effects of imaging objects at different sizes. Another imagery exercise might prove illuminating: Try imaging a honeybee at a very small size, and then decide what color its head is. More time is required to do this than to make the same judgment when the honeybee first is imaged at a normal size.[23] When it is small, people report that they have to "zoom in" to "see" the head. In general, more time is required to inspect objects when they are imaged at tiny sizes than at larger sizes.[24]

The idea that one "zooms in" to "see" parts of an object imaged at a small size makes sense if images are patterns of activity in the visual buffer. Because the eye itself is limited in its resolution, the brain only needed to be able to encompass a specific level of resolution. And these resolution limits of the visual buffer will affect all patterns of activation within it, both when they arise from previously stored information (mental imagery) and from incoming information (perception).[25] All images will be subject to the "grain" of the buffer—whatever their origin. Hence, when an object is imaged too small (i.e., the corresponding pattern occupies too small a region of the visual buffer), zooming will be necessary. Such zooming requires that new information be added as the image is scaled up to cover a larger region of the visual buffer (we will consider the mechanisms underlying such processing shortly).

Image overflow. In addition, objects in images can only seem so large before they appear to "overflow" the image. For example, when people are asked to image walking towards a named object, they claim that it seems to loom larger as they get closer. There comes a point, however, where they cannot "see" the whole object at once—it seems to "overflow" the image. Try imaging a rabbit, seen from the side and off in the distance and imagine walking towards it; is there a point where the edges cannot all be "seen" at the same time? Now try it with an elephant. Which seemed closer at the point of overflow, the rabbit or the elephant? When this task is done carefully (showing subjects pictures, having them indicate distance using a tripod apparatus, and so on),[26] it has been found that the larger the object, the farther away it seems when it first overflows. Furthermore, very similar effects were found when the objects were actually physically present.

The inference that the visual buffer is used in imagery also explains why an object can extend only over a limited scope in an image before it seems to "overflow" the available "space." There is only a limited amount of "space" in the visual buffer in which a pattern can be formed. Indeed, this idea neatly explains why the "size" of the "mental screen" used in imagery and perception is about the same.[27]

Detecting parts. Some parts of imaged objects are easier to "see" than others in images. For example, say we showed you a Star of David, asked you to image it, and then to decide whether specific patterns were present. Just as is found in perception,[28] a triangle is easier to "see" as a subpattern of an imaged Star of David than is a parallelogram.[29]

This finding can be understood if, during both imagery and perception, the nonaccidental properties and perceptual units sent downstream as input to the pattern activation subsystem (as discussed in Chapter 3) will serve to define some parts of objects but not others. For example, if symmetry and points of intersection are used to identify shapes, parts such as a triangle of a Star of David will be particularly easy to spot. These parts are defined by sets of nonaccidental properties (the lines that form two large, overlapping triangles). On the other hand, in order to "see" a parallelogram embedded in the star, one must break up nonaccidental properties into smaller segments and reorganize them; one must see portions of the long lines that form the large triangles as the sides of the embedded figure, ignoring the extensions of the lines. The sides of the parallelogram will be particularly difficult to spot in imagery because the image is not like a picture; it is fading almost as soon as it is generated.[30]

Scanning. Image inspection often involves scanning an image, shifting attention while searching for a specific part or object in the image. For example, try imaging Snoopy the dog and "mentally staring" at his feet, and then judge the shape of his ears. If you start at the feet, you would require more time to respond than if you had started out staring at the center of his body. And this would have required more time than if you started off staring at his head.[31] Typically, the time to make a decision about a characteristic of an imaged object depends in part on how far one has to scan to "see" the characteristic. Indeed, the time to make a decision about a property at one location of an imaged object increases with each added increment in the distance scanned. This increase occurs when one scans images of pictures or of three-dimensional scenes; in the latter case, time typically increases with distance in three dimensions.[32]

Detailed observations of the behavior of image scanning mechanisms have led researchers to infer that two separate mechanisms are used. One simply involves shifting the attention window, so that different portions of an imaged object are selected for further processing.[33] This mechanism is good for "fine tuning," but has a fundamental limitation: this sort of scanning will "bump into the edge" of the visual buffer if shifted too far. However, in imagery one can scan around the walls of a room, never bumping into an edge. Indeed, subjects scan to "off screen" objects as quickly as they can scan to objects they can "see" initially.[34] For example, if you scan along the walls in an image of your bedroom, you scan across the first wall you "see" at the same rate as you scan over the other walls that become "visible" only later in the process.

The ability to scan to a location "off screen" suggests that a second scanning mechanism is also at work. In this case, scanning is accomplished by shifting the imaged object under a fixed attention window, filling in new portions along the leading edge. By analogy, it is like the shifting image on a TV screen as a camera sweeps along. When this mechanism is used, the image is transformed incrementally as it is slid across the buffer (reasons for an incremental shift will be developed when we consider image transformations below). The increase in time required to scan further distances over imaged objects follows from both scanning mechanisms.

Image Generation

The process of using imagery to recall information hinges not only on being able to inspect imaged objects, but also on the ability to form the image in the first place. For example, if one is asked about the shape of one's kitchen, one must form the image before one can scan it to determine its spatial properties. The process of forming images is called *image generation.*

Although it is not obvious, the time to form an image of something you've seen before increases for every additional part included in the image. For example, imaging the letter *L* is faster than imaging *F,* which is faster than imaging *E.* We build up visual mental images one part at a time; if you are like most people, when you image a letter *F,* for example, you in fact very quickly visualize the vertical segment on the left, then the horizontal segment at the top, and then the horizontal segment half-way down.

Consider, for example, the results of experiments reported by Kosslyn and his colleagues.[35] They first asked people to study block letters in grids,[36] such as those illustrated in Figure 4.1. Later, these people were shown grids that contained only two *X* marks, and asked whether a specific block letter would cover the *X* marks if it were present in the grid.[37] The block letters included from two (for the letter *L*) to five segments (for *G*). Half of the time the letter would have covered both *X* marks, and half of the time it would have covered only one.

The key to this experiment was that the two probe marks appeared in the grid only half a second after a lowercase letter appeared, which cued the subjects to image a particular block

Perception   Imagery

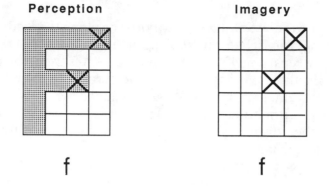

f   f

FIGURE 4.1 Stimuli used to study the process of forming images

letter. A half a second is not enough time to finish forming the image of the letter. Hence the time to respond should in part reflect the time to finish forming the image. The X marks "catch the image on the fly." And, as expected, response time increased with the visual complexity (number of segments) of the queried letter.

In addition to varying the complexity of the stimuli, Kosslyn et al. varied the positions of the X marks along the segments of the block letters.[38] If the image is being constructed a segment at a time, they reasoned, then a different number of segments will need to be imaged to evaluate X's in different locations—and hence X's on different segments should require different amounts of time to evaluate. And in fact, more time was required when an X fell on a segment that people typically draw later in the sequence of segments. For example, if an X was where the middle horizontal segment of an F should be, this took longer to affirm than if the X was on the top horizontal segment. Print an uppercase letter F; if you are like 94% of the population, the middle segment should be the last you print. This effect of probe position did not occur when the block letters were actually present or when people were allowed to form the image fully before the probe marks were presented. Similar results were found for novel two-dimensional patterns[39] and three-dimensional shapes.[40] In short, it appears that patterns in images are built up by activating parts individually, and that parts are imaged in roughly the order in which they are typically drawn.

Hence, the ability to generate images can be divided into two distinct abilities. First, and most basic, we must understand how one can activate stored visual information, reconstructing the spatial layout of objects and their parts. Second, we must account for how one not only can activate a single stored perceptual unit, but also can activate multiple units and compose them into a single image.[41]

We can go a long way towards understanding these abilities if the subsystems inferred in Chapter 3 can also operate in a slightly different way. In perception, the system as a whole is driven by external input. In contrast, in imagery, processes must be initiated by an internal command, which we assume arises from processing subsystems that employ imagery for the purposes discussed at the outset of this chapter. These subsystems set the state of the system (so that processes are initiated in the absence of the usually necessary external input) and provide the initial input, as is described below.[42] We shall briefly consider the operation of such processes in Chapter 9.

Activating images. In imagery, the situation is reversed from that of perception; the goal is to produce a spatial pattern of activation in the visual buffer when given a name, not the other way around. In order to function in perception, we inferred that the pattern activation subsystem must have a representation of an object's shape; in perception, this subsystem receives a set of cues as input and produces a single response for the object as output. It seems safe to assume that images of objects are based on previously encoded representations of shape, and we have inferred that such representations are stored in the pattern activation subsystem. Thus, we infer that images are formed by providing an input from memory to the pattern activation subsystem, which in turn "paints" the pattern onto the visual buffer.

Indeed, this very same imagery process may play a role in perception proper. David Lowe, the researcher who developed the theory of nonaccidental properties, also noted that nonaccidental properties alone are often not enough to make a good match to stored visual memories. For example, a pen and a mechanical pencil may share the same nonaccidental properties.

Lowe built a computer vision system that could identify objects in very noisy surroundings. For example, he would aim his TV camera at a bucket full of staplers, and ask the computer to identify what was in the bucket. In such situations, objects are partially hidden and are at odd angles. Lowe found that the nonaccidental properties sometimes were most useful as a first stage in a visual match process. Although they eliminated a large number of potential objects, they might match the nonaccidental properties of a few objects reasonably well. Thus, the input from the preprocessing subsystem may sometimes only serve to narrow down the number of alternatives. However, the goal of processing in the pattern activation subsystem is to select a single candidate object.

In such cases, Lowe's computer vision system used a second stage of processing: An image of the best-fitting pattern was projected backwards and matched against the input pattern itself. We briefly discussed this process in Chapter 3 when we suggested that a very specific deficit in recognizing faces may arise if a patient cannot form images to match against the input. The mental image makes explicit geometric patterns that are only implicit in the information stored in visual memory; for example, once one has imaged an uppercase letter *A,* it is obvious that it includes a particular enclosed shape. In Lowe's system, the image was a spatial pattern, formed by filling in cells of an array, as was the input pattern. The image could be rotated and expanded or shrunk until it overlapped an input pattern as well as possible. If the image overlapped the pattern well, the object or part was identified; if it did not, another image was formed and matched. The end result of this process was that a single pattern was matched—as well as possible—in visual memory. The kinds of images Lowe programmed are exactly what we are talking about here. And in fact, there is evidence that imagery is used when one is trying to identify an object that is partially covered, in just the way Lowe described.[43]

Lowe's ideas suggest that imagery is a consequence of opportunistic processing. Imagery may have developed for use in recognizing objects. And once this ability was available, it was recruited into other uppercase-*F* Functions. One now could use the process in the absence of immediate sensory input, and work with the image itself as if it were engendered by sensory input.

Thus, we can account for the basic fact of image generation very easily: Visual information stored in the temporal lobes is activated, which evokes a spatial pattern in the visual buffer. The higher visual areas in the temporal lobe are not spatially organized,[44] and hence this process reconstructs the implicit spatial knowledge stored in these higher structures. The situation is analogous to storing visual information as patterns of magnetic flux on videotape: the tapes must be played to reconstruct the spatial information implicit in the representation.

Arranging multiple parts. Computationally, it is easiest to generate multipart images if a low-resolution envelope of the entire object is imaged first.[45] This overall "skeletal image" indicates the "lay of the land," providing a frame of reference that allows one to establish the locations of key parts, such as the head, tail, and legs of an animal—which is essential if one is to know where to add additional parts when building up an image.

If a multipart image is needed to "see" the sought information (such as the relation between a horse's tail and knees), the system can generate one by operating as it does when it is testing an hypothesis during perception. In perception, the property lookup subsystems access a salient part in associative memory, which specifies where the part is located. That information is then sent to the attention shifting subsystems, which shift the attention window. In perception, a new part is then encoded and the hypothesis tested. In contrast, in image generation, once the attention window is properly positioned, a new part is generated at that location, using the pattern activation subsystem. For example, in perception one might see a cat out of the corner of one's eye, which leads to the hypothesis that a cat is present. The property lookup subsystems would access a description of a salient part of cats, perhaps the whiskers, and their location, at the front of the face. The location information is used to shift the attention window over the image of the object to a specific place, the front of the face. In image generation, the whiskers may not initially be present, and so now a new image is generated at the front of the face, adding the whiskers to the skeletal image.

Thus, the image can be built up a part at a time, using mechanisms that exist for other reasons; we need only assume that the property lookup subsystems can access a spatial relation and visual code for the part in associative memory, and send the relation to the attention shifting subsystems and the visual code for the part to the pattern activation subsystem.

Presumably, as in perception, the categorical property lookup subsystem and the coordinate property lookup subsystem operate at the same time, both seeking representations of parts in associative memory. Recall that in the previous chapter we inferred that not all parts are equally important for identifying an object, and so we assumed that more distinctive parts contribute more to reaching threshold during perception. Similarly, we assume that more salient parts are used to elaborate a skeletal image first (provided that the place where they belong is evident in the image). Thus, whichever lookup subsystem accesses the most salient part will "win," and will direct subsequent processing.

If the salient part is associated with a coordinate spatial representation, one may need to run a motor program to use it to position objects or parts in an image. For example, imagine what you would see when you first enter your living room. Most people make eye movements when imaging the furniture. This makes sense if the location information is stored in a motoric form, and the movement is performed as part of accessing the stored information. Each eye movement occurs when one "runs" a motor program, which serves to shift the attention window to the relevant location; following this, one forms an image of the object at that location.

Now try imaging your living room again. And then again. Do you move your eyes as much on the third time as you did on the first? By the third time, you should have recorded the location information into a categorical form. You may have coded the couch as something like "against the far wall in the center of the room," and the chair as "to the right when you first walk in"; these representations rely on categorical spatial relations (which are not necessarily verbal) and do not involve motor commands. Thus, one need not move one's eyes when retrieving this sort of information.

In short, we infer that there are two ways to construct multipart images: one in which parts are arranged in accordance with coordinate spatial relations representations and one in which they are arranged in accordance with categorical spatial relations representations. Depending on which kind of spatial representation is used, different sequences of processing will be necessary. If the location of the to-be-imaged part is specified in motor coordinates that are relative to one's body (e.g., directly in front, off in a specific direction up and to the right, and so on), it will be easy to find the correct location; one simply runs the program. But spatial relations need not be based on one's body. Indeed, recall our analysis that led us to infer the existence of categorical spatial relations representations; we suspected that they would be useful for organizing parts of flexible objects. In such cases, the spatial relations specify one part relative to another part or object. Categorical spatial relations often may also be useful for encoding the rough location of objects in scenes (e.g., the couch is "against the wall").

Finding the proper location of a to-be-imaged part is much more difficult if locations are specified relative to other parts. The system must look for a reference point in the image before the part can be placed correctly. For example, when asked to image a cat, and then asked whether a cat has curved claws, it is unlikely that you included the claws in the initial image. The claws must be added to the image when they become relevant. First, the system must look up where claws belong. The property lookup subsystem would access associative memory, and might find that claws are "at the front of the paws." Paws are the reference part, and now the problem becomes one of locating the paws. If the paws are specified relative to legs, then the problem is pushed back a step: Where are the legs? At some point, the sought part will be a portion of the skeletal image, and it will be relatively easy to compute its location and then work back to the appropriate reference part.

Once the location of the reference part, the paws, is computed, the attention window can be shifted to that location. The contents of the attention window will then go to the ventral and dorsal systems, and the reference part would be recognized and its location verified. Following this, the spatial relation ("front of") between the reference part and the to-be-imaged part must be converted to relative coordinates, and the part properly imaged. This part-integration process is repeated until the image is sufficiently detailed to perform the task at hand.

This line of reasoning allows us to understand the key characteristics of the processes that form images of objects and scenes. First, the reason more complex images require more time to generate is simple: Each part is imaged individually, and it takes time to look up the spatial relation, adjust the attention window to the appropriate location, and form an image of the part. The information stored in associative memory must include not only the names of parts, but also a symbol (i.e., corresponding to a vector of activation, as described in Chapter 2) that can prompt the pattern activation subsystem to form an image of the part, and a representation of the location of the part, which can be used to form the image in the proper position.

This idea also explains why parts are imaged one at a time. When stored categorical spatial relations representations are used to arrange parts, the stored representation is like a description of how parts are structured. For example, an uppercase letter *F* might be described as "a vertical segment on the left, with the left end of a horizontal segment connected to the top of the vertical segment, and the left end of another horizontal segment connected to the middle of the vertical segment." This sort of description can be accessed by the categorical property lookup subsystem, which prompts imaging of the proper segments in the proper locations. But only one location can be attended to at a time (the attention window cannot be divided), and so only one part is activated at a time. And if the same description is used to guide one while drawing a block letter and while imaging it, then it makes sense that the parts are imaged in the same order as they are drawn, as has been found.[46]

Recap: Accessing Stored Information Using Imagery

We use imagery to access stored information about an object by generating an image and then inspecting the imaged object for the sought information. This is accomplished by first looking up a description of the object in associative memory, and then using the code corresponding to the object to activate the appropriate visual memory of the object. This will produce a spatial pattern of activation in the visual buffer, which is the image proper. We need not infer any additional subsystems to understand this process; rather, we need only to augment our inferences about the property lookup subsystems, now allowing them not only to send location information to the attention shifting subsystems, but also to send a code to the pattern activation subsystem; this code activates stored patterns.

If the representation of the object includes more than one part, the property lookup subsystems access representations of spatial relations to arrange multiple images into a single composite form. The property lookup subsystem that accesses the most salient part directs subsequent processing, sending a spatial relation to the attention shifting subsystem and a code to the pattern activation subsystem. The attention window is moved to the location of the to-be-imaged part, and the image of that part is then activated.

Once the image has been generated, the pattern in the visual buffer is scanned by shifting the attention window, employing the subsystems used for that purpose during perception, and also by moving the imaged object itself, so that different portions are within the attention window. The contents of the attention window are sent to the subsystems in the ventral and dorsal systems, where they are processed just as is done during perception. Thus, one can identify parts, colors, and spatial characteristics of imaged objects by using recognition mechanisms to unpack the information implicit in the image.

Reasoning Using Imagery

Some of the most famous discoveries in science were made when someone visualized possible events and "observed" their outcomes.[47] For example, Albert Einstein claimed that he had his first insight into the theory of relativity when he considered what he "saw" when he imaged chasing after and matching the speed of a beam of light. He noticed that if light were a wave, he should see a particular pattern when he paralleled its flight—but such patterns were never seen, which planted a seed of doubt about the then-current way of viewing physics. Einstein used imagery as a way of reasoning, mentally setting up possible scenarios and "observing" what would happen if nature worked that way.

Consider a more mundane imagery reasoning task: If you were trying to decide how best to pack luggage into the trunk of an automobile, you might generate an image of each piece, and then mentally move the pieces around in the image, "looking at" how well they fit in different positions. All the while you would have to retain the images of the other suitcases and bags, so that you could "see" the available spaces. Many problems are sufficiently difficult that one must maintain an image over the course of many seconds.

Thus, using imagery to reason involves not only inspecting imaged objects and generating them, but also transforming objects in imagery and retaining images long enough to work with them. The imaged object is "inspected" using the same processes that are used to "inspect" an imaged object when recalling visual information; the imaged pattern is processed in the same way as patterns that arise during vision. In order to understand the use of imagery in reasoning, however, we must consider additional facets of our ability to generate images, and then must consider the mechanisms underlying image transformation and maintenance.

Creative Image Generation

When we use imagery to recall information, we generate images of previously seen patterns. This process hinges on activating stored memories, and sometimes also relies on using stored representations of spatial relations among parts of an object. However, one of the reasons imagery is so useful in thinking is that we can imagine things we have never seen; many images are *not* replays of previous perceptions, but are novel creations.

We can distinguish between two kinds of creative image generation. In one, the image is created by combining familiar elements in new ways. For example, one can image a friend shaking the front right hoof of a donkey; one has stored the appearance of the friend and a donkey in visual memory, and uses the description to combine them properly in an image. These sorts of images can be created by using novel spatial relations to arrange images of familiar objects. Thus, this sort of image generation is just like the multipart process described earlier, except that a new spatial relation representation is used to arrange the parts. Much of the creativity arises from which spatial relation is used, which is selected by other subsystems that presumably are in the frontal lobes (as will be discussed in Chapter 9).

A second kind of creative image generation is a greater departure from that discussed earlier. Most people can imagine a line being drawn, creating patterns they have never actually seen. This sort of imagery is not produced by arranging parts of previously seen objects in new ways. Rather, the elementary components of the image themselves are created from scratch. This sort of imagery relies on moving the attention window through the visual buffer, leaving a pattern of activation in its wake. The path presumably originates in the center of the attention window, which is spread wide enough to be able to "see" the emerging pattern.

Both methods of amalgamating parts in an image, using coordinate or categorical spatial relations representations, may also be used when one images drawing novel patterns. If coordinate representations are used, motor programs allow one to shift the attention window as if one were actually viewing the pattern, but now an imaged line is left along the path of the attention window. Like other sorts of imagery, an imaged line corresponds to a pattern of activation in the visual buffer. Similarly, if categorical representations are used, stored descriptions of spatial relations are used to shift the attention window in the proper direction, mentally drawing the segments as one goes.

In either case, instructions somehow must be provided to the attention shifting subsystems; if the image is truly novel, the instructions cannot be previously stored. Thus, it is of interest that there are rich connections from the frontal lobes (which presumably direct the process), not only to parts of the parietal lobes known to be involved in attention, but also to the subcortical structures involved in shifting attention.[48]

Image Transformation

Many of the uses of imagery in reasoning involve anticipating the consequences of an action or event, which rely on our ability to transform patterns in our images. These transformations often appear to mimic the time course of the corresponding transformations of the actual object. For example, if you rotated the lowercase letter *b* 180°, would it be another letter? What if you rotated a lowercase letter *n* 90°? The time to image an object rotating depends on the amount that the object must be rotated: the more rotation required, the more time is required to carry out the operation.[49]

Apostolos Georgopoulos and his colleagues studied the neural mechanisms underlying mental rotation in a monkey.[50] The animal first saw a light in the center of a display, and moved a handle towards the light. After a variable period, the center light went off and a second light went on; this light was dim or bright, and appeared at one of eight positions. When the second light was dim, the monkey was trained to move the handle in the direction of the light; when it was bright, the monkey moved the handle in a counterclockwise direction to a position that was perpendicular to the target light. With the dim lights, a simple movement was required, but mental extrapolation was necessary with the bright lights.

As the animal was performing the task, Georgopoulos et al. recorded the activity level of cells in the primary motor strip (area M1). They compared activity before the light changed with activity afterwards. Different cells increased their activity when the arm was in different positions. By observing the responses during the trials with a dim light, they were able to discover the preferred orientation of various cells. The researchers also recorded every 10 milliseconds after the first light went out and the second came on during the mental rotation trials. At first, the cells tuned for the current arm position fired the most, but then an interesting change occurred: The maximal activity actually shifted gradually across cells that had different position tunings, and ended with cells that preferred the target orientation. This shift across the different orientations took place within the first 225 milliseconds or so after the light changed; in contrast, the actual movement began about 260 milliseconds after the light changed. Thus, all of the changes in neural activity occurred *before* the animal actually started to move its arm! Indeed, the shift in orientation was in a counterclockwise direction, anticipating the actual motion.

In short, mental rotation in at least one task intimately involves changes in the motor cortex itself. This finding is consistent with the rCBF brain scanning results in humans, which documented both frontal and parietal activity in humans during mental rotation;[51] both of these areas have clear roles in programming and executing actions.

Shape shift subsystem. The advantages of being able to imagine the results of altering objects are legion, saving one much time and effort in planning movements or actual modifications of objects. We infer a *shape shift subsystem* that alters patterns of activation in the visual buffer. This process is particularly important because much of the power of image transformations in reasoning arises from their flexibility. For example, people can image a rolled-up carpet unfurling and "see" how long it might be, a hinge opening and "see" how far it would extend, a cat climbing a ladder and "see" whether it can reach the rungs, and so on.[52] One cannot anticipate in advance all of the different ways in which one might want to imagine an object or scene rearranged or changed. Thus, we want an image transformation system that is quite open-ended and flexible. Such reasoning leads us to infer this additional subsystem, which can be used to modify imaged patterns in the visual buffer itself.

Altering the representations of spatial properties, such as location and size, in the dorsal system cannot be all there is to image transformations. In many cases, these alterations are only useful for drawing new inferences from the image if the shapes are actually altered in the visual buffer. For example, unless you can "see" the relations among the shapes, you will not be able to shut your eyes and decide whether a particular jar would fit in the space on the top shelf of the refrigerator, and so forth. Thus, it makes sense that the image representation itself would be modified during image transformations.

The shape shift subsystem alters a part's shape, location, or orientation in the visual buffer during image transformation. The idea that the visual representation in the buffer is altered is consistent with the finding that the occipital lobe is active during mental rotation.[53] In addition, in order to alter the position, orientation, or size of an imaged object or its parts in an arbitrary way, one must alter the position representations of the parts in the dorsal system. For example, the property lookup subsystems must provide instructions about how to rotate a given object, unless the object is rotated randomly. Thus, it is interesting that the right frontal lobe is more active than the left during image rotation; we inferred that the right hemisphere has a special role in encoding precise metric information into memory—and just that sort of information is needed to transform the orientation of an object. Furthermore, we inferred that metric spatial properties are encoded in the right parietal lobe, and this structure is more active than the left parietal lobe during mental rotation.[54]

The shape shift subsystem we posit works closely in conjunction with the attention-shifting subsystems discussed in Chapter 3. As a simple example, image a table top with a single Coke can sitting on it. Say you want to image the can sliding along the table to the other side. The imaged can is attended to by positioning the attention window in the proper region of the visual buffer. The shape shift subsystem "fixes" the pattern of activation corresponding to the can in the attention window. And then the attention shifting subsystems actually move the window, which results in the pattern being dragged along with it; the pattern is "unfixed" when the window is properly repositioned. The shape shift subsystem alters the orientation of multipart objects, by wheeling the location of each part around a pivot. This process is exactly the same as that used to shift location, only now the locations are shifted along circular paths.[55] This subsystem and the others inferred earlier are illustrated in Figure 4.2.

We also can alter the imaged size of objects. If only a single object or part is imaged, then the spatiotopic mapping subsystem need only specify a different size. This operation is not an image transformation because the pattern of activation in the visual buffer is not affected; the actual size of an object is, as far as we now know, only represented in the dorsal system and is represented separately from object properties. However, this tech-

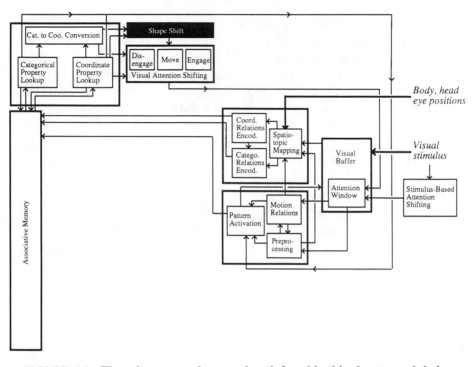

FIGURE 4.2   The subsystem and connections inferred in this chapter, and their relation to those inferred previously

nique will not work if the sizes of only some of the objects in an image are altered. One now wants to be able to answer questions such as, "If John were a foot higher, would he be able to see over the top of Sam's head?" (If so, then the milk crate over there can be impressed into use when the kids are watching the parade.) In such cases, the contents of the visual buffer must be altered. The subsystems we have already specified are sufficient to understand how this could be done. Specifically, the shape shift subsystem fixes a representation in the attention window, and then the window is shifted or its scope is adjusted. The representation is unfixed when the size is correctly adjusted, resulting in the pattern's subtending a larger angle in the visual buffer. This sort of transformation is necessary if occlusion is to occur naturally, so that a larger object covers more of the objects behind it, and if the relative sizes of parts of an object or scene are to be made explicit.[56]

Image transformations during perception. It is possible that mental image transformations are used not only in imagery, but also in perception as well. As noted earlier, Lowe showed that a computer vision system could profit from generating an image of a pattern and actively matching it to the input, rotating, shifting, and adjusting the size of the image to obtain the best match. And in fact, Pierre Jolicoeur and his colleagues have shown that people take progressively more time to name briefly presented objects when they are tilted farther from the upright.[57] This result only occurs the first time an object is seen, however, perhaps because more detailed visual information is stored after the object is seen that subsequently allows the input to be matched to a stored visual memory without generating an image. That is, presenting objects for a brief period presumably degrades the input, so that the nonaccidental properties and perceptual units are not sufficient to implicate a specific object. In this case, an image of the best-matching object might be projected back into the visual buffer, as suggested by Lowe.[58] If it did not match the pattern in the visual buffer very well, the image could be transformed until it matched it as well as possible.[59] If the initial input matches a stored pattern well, however, such imagery will not be necessary. This sort of intimate relation between imagery and perception makes sense, given the evidence that the same brain regions are used in both kinds of processing.

Image Retention

Retaining a mental image requires effort, and a limited amount of information can be held in an image for a limited amount of time. This is important because most imagery reasoning tasks cannot be carried out instantly; one needs time to complete them. Indeed, imagery is often used only when difficult problems arise.[60] For example, try to categorize each state along the Eastern seaboard of the United States as higher than it is wide or wider than it is high. This task requires many seconds; clearly, we can, with effort, maintain imaged patterns over some period of time.

By inferring that images occur in the same visual buffer that is used in perception, we expect that the properties of the buffer that affect perception also should affect imagery. If so, then the inability to maintain patterns in images for very long may be another consequence of this common mechanism. That is, in perception one does not want an image to linger; one wants to "clear the buffer" every time the eyes move. Indeed, if images did not fade rapidly, they would smear and become overlaid. Any animal that did this probably did not survive long enough to have many descendents! Thus, patterns in the visual buffer are transient in both perception and imagery.

Given these observations, it should not be surprising that mental imagery has only a limited capacity. This is true both in terms of the amount of material that can be held in an image and in terms of the amount of time one can hold an image. Indeed, images may be like objects seen in a brief flash, which then can be maintained only in a degraded form and only for a brief period of time.[61]

Image retention can be accomplished simply by reactivating representations in the pattern activation subsystem. If images are retained by repeatedly activating these representations, then the capacity limits make sense: Each part or object in the image is represented separately in the pattern activation subsystem, and hence would have to be activated and reactivated individually. The experiments on image generation have demonstrated that each such operation requires time. And as soon as a unit is activated in the visual buffer, it begins to fade. Thus, imagery may be like a juggling act: As each part is being refreshed, others are fading. The speed of the fading process, the speed of the refresh process, and the speed of shifting from one part to another defines the number of parts or objects one can maintain in an image.

Reasoning Symbolically with Imagery

One can use imagery to aid reasoning even when the task has nothing to do with visual or spatial information. For example, consider this problem: Susan is smarter than Sam, and Bill is dumber than Sam. Who is the smartest? If you imagine a line, and mentally place a dot for each person, the task is not hard.

All you need to do is order the dots from left to right in terms of relative intelligence, and then "see" which person's dot is at the far right after all of the statements are read.[62]

A symbolic use of imagery involves the same subsystems used in other kinds of imagery reasoning; one must generate the image and retain it long enough to operate on it and "see" the results. But there is one critical difference between this kind of symbolic imagery and the other sorts: One now must decide how to convert abstract material to particular patterns in the image. For example, one could visualize relative intelligence not only as dots on a line, but also as a set of circles, with larger ones standing for people with greater intelligence. We will consider reasoning processes in more detail in Chapter 9.

In general, the use of imagery in reasoning depends on high-level decision processes, presumably in the frontal lobes. Somewhere in the system decisions must be made about which object to image, how to transform it, and so on. The mechanisms discussed so far are like an engine, which pulls a car along in the directions dictated by how the front wheels are aligned; we have not yet considered what turns the steering wheel.

Recap: Using Imagery in Reasoning

In order to use imagery in reasoning one first must generate a pattern in the visual buffer. For some problems, one combines familiar objects or parts in new ways by employing novel spatial relations representations, using them just as one uses spatial relations accessed in associative memory when generating multipart images during recall. For other problems, one might "mentally draw" by shifting the attention window systematically and marking its path with a swath of activation in the visual buffer. Once the image is formed, the pattern is inspected exactly as is done when one is using imagery in recall.

In addition, if appropriate for solving a problem, one may alter the patterns in images by fixing them in the attention window and shifting it systematically. The dorsal and ventral subsystems "inspect" the object as the image is transformed, encoding properties that become evident.

Finally, many imagery problems require substantial

amounts of time to solve, and hence one often must retain the image by encoding the pattern and using the image activation process to refresh the visual buffer.

Using Imagery to Learn Skills

Imagery can also be used to help one to master new skills. For example, one can imagine shooting basketballs through a hoop—and will actually improve in doing so, as long as such imagined practice is intermixed with actual practice. However, such imagery practice is not as good as actual practice, in part because it does not provide one with feedback on the quality of the performance.[63]

One hint about how imagery can help one to learn new skills was suggested by the behavior of patient M.B., who was 82 years old when we tested her; she was suffering from an undiagnosed degenerative disease (perhaps early Alzheimer's disease), which resulted in some deficits in her visual abilities. We asked her to view pairs of objects on a computer screen, and to decide whether they could be made to match if one were rotated into the orientation of the other. She consistently held her hand to the screen, and twisted it as if she were actually able to rotate the object! For many years researchers who study mental rotation have noticed that subjects report feeling their hands twitch as they imagine rotating an object. In addition, Larry Parsons showed that people can imagine body parts moving in natural ways more easily than in unnatural ways.[64] For example, one can imagine rotating a hand more easily if it pivots around a wrist than if it pivots around its center.

These sorts of observations are consistent with the idea that the parietal lobe represents location primarily to guide action, and that metric information is stored in a form useful for this purpose (as was discussed in the previous chapter). If so, then when one needs to change the representation of metric location, one may need to perform an action; the action might be performed explicitly, such as by actually moving one's hands, or implicitly, such as by twitching the muscles to move one's hands but not actually doing so.

If so, then when one imagines moving in various ways, one

would actually affect the subsystems that are used to produce the actions. However, this idea in and of itself will not allow us to understand why imagining practicing can improve actual performance. To see why, consider how you would imagine yourself throwing a basketball through a hoop. Would you image seeing the ball in front of you as it would appear if you were about to throw it, holding it up, and then looking at the hoop and tossing it? Or would you imagine seeing yourself from the side, as if you were standing in front of the hoop and throwing the ball? In the first case, you would imagine what you would see, whereas in the second case you would imagine what someone else would see if you were performing the action. In a survey we discovered that most people report having images of the second kind; when they imagine practicing something, they see themselves from someone else's point of view.

This imagery ability would be easy to understand if we could explain how people imitate an action that they actually see. Whatever we do when we mimic someone we see, we can do the same when we imagine we see them (or ourselves) performing the action. Presumably, when we see someone else move in a particular way, we note how they moved and use that information to program our own muscles. As we shall discuss in Chapter 7, movement planning is based on computing the target coordinates of a movement; it is not concerned with the details of moving the individual muscles. The coordinate spatial relations encoding subsystem can encode the coordinates of the target of someone's movements (e.g., where the hands are supposed to end up to throw the ball properly), and these coordinates can be used in the future to help one move in the same way. We will consider this ability in more detail in Chapter 7.

Recap: Using Imagery to Learn Skills

In short, imagery helps one to learn a skill in much the same way that imitating a teacher helps one to learn a skill. The key idea is that the same representations in the parietal lobe are used to direct actual actions and imagined actions, and so refining these representations in imagery will transfer to actual movements.

Using Imagery to Comprehend Language

Imagery also can be used to help one to comprehend a verbal description, allowing one to extract new information from it and unpack its implications. For example, if one is hearing a description of a floor plan or the design of a complex machine, it will help to visualize the object. In this case, one uses an imaged scene as a kind of model to help one understand a statement.[65]

In order to understand this ability fully we must understand how individual words are comprehended, and how the meanings of individual words can be combined. We will defer these questions until Chapter 6, and for now will simply assume that the individual spoken or written words somehow activate the appropriate representations in associative memory. If so, then we do not need to posit any additional subsystems to understand our ability to use imagery to help us comprehend verbal statements. For example, when someone describes the shortest route to the train station, most people imagine the streets and landmarks and "inspect" the imaged map. In this case, the nouns name landmarks, which are imaged as described above; and the spatial relations name categorical spatial relations representations, which are used to arrange the imaged landmarks in the appropriate way. In some cases, one may also "mentally draw" lines, as described above, connecting landmarks when the description specifies a route between them.

In addition, because spatial relations are used to juxtapose objects or parts in an image, it is clear how we can generate images of novel verbally described scenes (e.g., your mother riding a surfboard down a giant wave). The nouns access stored visual memories of objects (via associative memory), and the verbs are converted to categorical spatial relations representations that are used to arrange the objects in the image. The resulting pattern can then be inspected, as described above, and new spatial relations discovered.

In many cases a description will lead one to construct a complex image, which is difficult to maintain. Imagery is particularly useful for comprehending complex statements if one can notice "perceptual units" which in turn can be encoded. For example, if one heard "go south for one block, turn right for one block, and then north for one block" and imaged the corresponding pathway, one should notice that the pattern was a U. This shape could then be stored as a single unit, instead of the more complex collection of three individual segments that were described. This is important because the limits on memory are defined by the number of units, not their individual structure.[66] Furthermore, when one constructs such an image one can notice that a shortcut might be better, and perhaps ask why one cannot simply go due west (and perhaps learn about one-way streets or the bad habits of the instructor).

Recap: Using Imagery to Comprehend Language

Imagery can be used to comprehend statements by generating an image of each named object, and using the described spatial relations to arrange the objects in a scene. Once the image is constructed, one "inspects" it using the subsystems used to inspect objects during perception. This process is particularly useful if one is interested in implicit spatial relations among the described objects.

Understanding the Effects of Brain Damage

If our analysis is on the right track, we should be able to use it to understand the ways in which brain damage affects imagery. In considering the various ways in which imagery is used, we found that four abilities were typically drawn upon, namely image inspection, generation, maintenance, and transformation; in this section, we will consider disruptions of the processing necessary to inspect, generate, and transform objects in images, but will not discuss clinical disruptions of image maintenance because there apparently has been no work specifically on this topic.

Image Inspection

As discussed in the previous chapter, patients (typically) with right parietal lobe damage sometimes show "unilateral visual neglect"; they ignore objects to their left sides. Edoardo Bisiach and his colleagues have found that some patients who neglect one side of objects in perception also do so in imagery—even when they image a scene that was very familiar prior to the injury. For example, in one study patients with right parietal lobe damage imagined that they were standing on one end of a plaza and were asked to describe what they could "see."[67] The patients described what would have been to their right had they actually viewed the plaza from that vantage point, but tended to ignore what was to their left. Following this, the patients were asked to imagine standing on the opposite side of the plaza, now facing where they first stood. The patients now described what they had just neglected, and neglected what they had just described!

One might try to argue that these patients simply were inhibited from talking about objects to their left, or perhaps they did not want to repeat themselves and so, when they shifted imaged vantage point, they named objects previously not mentioned. Such possible problems were neatly put to rest by the results of a clever experiment reported by Bisiach and his colleagues.[68] Bisiach et al. asked patients with damage to their parietal lobes (usually only on the right side) to perform a task that involves piecing together an image and inspecting it. The task requires subjects to look at a slit in a piece of cardboard, with the slit being placed directly in front of them. A form is then moved across the back of the cardboard, so that different parts of it are visible as it slides across the slit. Thus, in order to perceive the shape of the form, one has to build up an image of the whole, integrating together the various segments that are visible through the slit. (The actual stimuli were presented on film in a slightly different way, but this description conveys the general idea.) In their experiment, two blob-like forms were presented in succession, and the subjects were asked to decide whether the shapes were the same or different. If the forms were different, the difference could be on the left side or on the right side of the blobs. The neglect patients performed well when the difference was on the nonneglected side, but performed poorly when they had to "see" the difference on the neglected side of the image. Thus, even though the blobs were seen sliding across the central slit, when the critical difference was on the neglected side of the image, the patients failed to "see" it in their images.

The fact that patients who neglect one side of visible objects may also neglect one side of imaged objects is easily explained if the mechanisms responsible for attending to parts of real space are also involved in attending to parts of imaged space. The parallel disruption of visual imagery and perception makes perfect sense if the visual buffer contains patterns of activation used in both Functions. Indeed, all of the accounts we offered in Chapter 3 for unilateral neglect in perception are equally applicable for imagery. In both cases, if the attention window does not operate over half of the visual buffer (for whatever reason), one will not encode that material.

Image Generation

Introspectively, images seem to pop into mind all at once, but results of experiments suggest that this is not true. The discovery that images are built up a part at a time allows us to understand some selective disruptions of the process of image generation following brain damage.

Some disruptions of image generation can occur in the isolated cerebral hemispheres of "split-brain" patients. That is, the two hemispheres are connected primarily by a massive bundle of fibers (containing around 250–300 million individual fibers) called the corpus callosum (see Figure 1.1). For some types of epilepsy, cutting this structure helps to control the convulsions that plague the patient. When these operations were first performed, there was scant evidence that cutting the corpus callosum had any effects at all on behavior; more careful studies by Roger Sperry, Michael Gazzaniga, and their collaborators at Cal Tech revealed a host of deficits, however, and it has since been valuable to study such patients to discover what sorts of processing can be divided up, with some aspects carried out in different hemispheres.[69]

Try to answer the following questions: Is a St. Bernard dog larger than a goat (in cross section)? How about a fox? Do the fox's ears protrude above the top of its skull? What about the ears of an ape? Answers to questions such as these have provided insight into why the left hemisphere can sometimes generate images more effectively than the right. Kosslyn, Jeffrey

Holtzman, Martha Farah, and Michael Gazzaniga gave such questions to two split-brain patients,[70] and found that their right hemispheres had particular trouble generating images when multiple parts had to be arranged to answer a question. For example, only the left hemisphere could decide whether named animals have ears that protrude above the top of the head; this task requires positioning high-resolution details correctly. In contrast, both hemispheres were equally adept at forming images of an overall shape, such as is required to decide whether a named object is higher than it is wide (these objects had very similar heights and widths) or whether a goat is larger than a similar-sized other animal; these imagery tasks do not require "seeing" high-resolution details on the objects. These and similar results indicated that the right-hemisphere image generation deficit is selective; the right hemisphere has difficulty generating images when parts of an object must be properly arranged. The big-F Function of imagery per se is not better in one hemisphere or the other; rather, different small-f functions are more effective in one hemisphere or the other.

Particularly suggestive evidence for a selective deficit in arranging parts to form an image comes from a case study.[71] This patient reported impaired imagery following left-hemisphere damage, and claimed that, "When I try to imagine a plant, an animal, an object, I can recall but one part, my inner vision is fleeting, fragmented; if I'm asked to imagine the head of a cow, I know that it has ears and horns, but I can't revisualize their respective places. . . ."[72] These sorts of reports are exactly as expected if lesions can selectively disrupt processes that arrange parts in the proper locations when an image is formed.

Imagery that requires integrating parts together typically has been found to be better in the left hemisphere. This left-hemisphere superiority for the generation of multipart images makes sense if categorical spatial relations are not only encoded most effectively in the left hemisphere (as was discussed in the previous chapter), but also are stored and used most effectively there. Most objects vary from instance to instance, and hence categorical spatial relations will be most useful for representing the positions among their parts.

These ideas are consistent with the ways image generation can be disrupted following brain damage. Farah performed a sophisticated analysis of the relation between the location of brain damage and subsequent functional deficits in imagery.[73] She reviewed the literature reporting the deficits of individual cases of patients with brain damage, and inferred an imagery deficit when patients were described as having three major sorts of difficulty: First, most of these patients lost the ability to do the kinds of tasks that we can infer require imagery. For example, one patient was unable to describe a face when given the person's name, and another was unable to describe what you would see if you traveled along a familiar route. Second, some patients actually reported introspections about the loss of imagery. Third, imagery deficits were also inferred if patients had difficulty in drawing or making models of multipart, relatively unfamiliar objects. These objects were unlikely to have been described previously, and so one could not use a stored description to perform the task (unlike objects such as a stick figure of a human form, for which one probably can recall a description).

By looking at the patterns of tasks that a patient could and could not perform, Farah was able to draw inferences about the underlying deficit. She considered four kinds of tasks that often are used to test the patients: copying tasks, recognition tasks, perceptual tasks, and sensory tasks. Depending on which tasks the patient could or could not perform, Farah was able to zero in on the nature of the underlying deficit.

The most interesting result of Farah's analysis concerned the ability to generate images from memory; she inferred an image generation deficit if a patient could not answer questions that require imagery (e.g., did George Washington have a beard?), but could answer similar questions about visible stimuli and could identify objects. If a patient can answer questions about visible objects, the inspection mechanisms must be intact; and the ability to identify objects shows that representations of shape must be stored. Hence, a failure to generate images is probably at the root of the patient's inability to use imagery. Similarly, an image generation deficit was also inferred if a patient could not draw from memory, but could copy a visible object and could recognize objects. Thus, Farah garnered evidence that image generation is a distinct process, which could be damaged independently of other image processes.

The case studies revealed that imagery deficits could follow from damage to a host of different sites. At first glance, the localization data look like a complete mishmash. However, when only the patients who were inferred to have an image generation deficit were examined, a clear pattern emerged: these patients typically had damage to the left posterior part of the brain.[74]

These findings lead us to a puzzle: Why cannot left-hemisphere damaged patients image a particular example of an object, using motor-based, coordinate spatial relations to arrange the parts? For example, if asked whether George Washington has a beard, why don't these patients image a familiar painting of the first President seen from a familiar point of view? Farah found that brain damage that disrupts image generation usually leaves the frontal lobes intact.[75] Perhaps the frontal lobe-based categorical property lookup subsystem accesses categorical spatial relations representations, and tries to use them to form an image; but if the categorical spatial relations encoding subsystem is impaired, images cannot be formed: The system will not be able to position parts in the correct relative locations if it cannot compute categorical spatial relations. The trouble is that the frontal lobes may not "know" about the problem at the other end, and so don't try to switch strategies. It is as if a general does not know that the troops have been wiped out, and so keeps issuing orders and waiting for results.[76]

Thus, it is of interest that Kosslyn et al. eventually were able to train the right hemisphere of a split-brain patient to generate images of letters, after the hemisphere had failed to do so over the course of many testing sessions.[77] Once the man's right hemisphere got the idea of "drawing in his mind," it could generate not only images of a set of letters he practiced, but also new letters. In the isolated right hemisphere, the problem apparently was not with the troops, but with the general; the frontal system either was not used to thinking in terms of assembling images from parts or was persisting in trying an ineffective strategy, using categorical stored relations—which are not effectively processed in the right hemisphere.

The idea that both hemispheres can generate images was further supported by Michael Corballis and Justine Sergent.[78] They found that the right hemisphere of another split-brain patient could form images of letters in a similar task, which required him to decide whether lowercase letters are "short" or "tall." Although he was not perfect (he was correct on 83% of the trials), he performed better than one would expect if he were only guessing. Furthermore, in another study Sergent asked normal subjects to perform this task when the stimuli were presented initially to a single hemisphere, and found that they performed better when the stimuli were presented initially to the right cerebral hemisphere.[79] As Sergent noted, a variety of variables (such as the way stimuli are presented and the precise instructions) probably play a critical role in determining which hemisphere will be more proficient in forming images during a particular task.[80] In short, there is evidence that both hemispheres can generate images, although they apparently do so in different ways.[81]

Image Transformation

Our analysis of image transformations suggests that they are not carried out by a single process, which is located in a single brain locus. This inference allows us to understand what at first glance may appear to be contradictory effects of brain damage. On the one hand, there is evidence that the right cerebral hemisphere plays a critical role in mental rotation. For example, Graham Ratcliff found that damage to the right parietal lobe can selectively impair a patient's ability to decide whether a misoriented human figure is holding out the left or right arm,[82] which appears to require mental rotation. Similarly, such damage can selectively impair performance of a task that requires subjects to mentally fold a sheet into a cube,[83] and spatio-manipulation tasks were performed better by the isolated right hemisphere of a split-brain patient.[84] And, as already noted, there is greater blood flow in the right parietal area than in the left while subjects are mentally rotating patterns.[85]

On the other hand, there is evidence that the left hemisphere also plays a role in mental image transformations.[86] Indeed, in one study two aphasic patients rotated imaged patterns about ten times more slowly than did normal control subjects.[87]

These results are easily reconciled if we assume that image transformation, like image generation, is carried out by more than a single subsystem. If the shape shift subsystem is more effective in the right hemisphere, this would explain why damage to the right hemisphere disrupts mental rotation. Furthermore, to the extent that precise positions are necessary, coordinate representations may be used to direct the attention shifting subsystems—and the right hemisphere is generally better at coordinate processing. However, the categorical spatial relations encoding subsystem would be used to track the parts of objects as they rotate (and hence their positions no longer precisely match those of the coordinate representations stored in memory), and the categorical property lookup subsystem could be used to access a description of the local relations among parts. This sort of description may be needed to keep the basic shape intact as it is being shifted. And these categorical subsystems apparently operate more effectively in the left cerebral hemisphere.[88] Thus, damage to either cerebral hemisphere should impair image transformations, as has in fact been found.

In sum, our analysis of the processing subsystems used in imagery has given us insight into the possible bases of the behavioral dysfunctions that occur following brain damage. Although the fact that our inferences are consistent with these findings is not strong support for our reasoning, it may be stronger support than immediately meets the eye: The same set of inferences also allowed us to understand a wide range of deficits in visual perception proper. One sign that we are on the right track is that our ideas not only are internally consistent, but also help us to make sense of a wide range of phenomena that are very different from the ones that motivated our inferences in the first place.

By considering perceptual processing subsystems in a new light, we could understand many interesting characteristics of visual mental imagery. Using the inferences drawn in the previous chapter to understand mental imagery is not only consistent with the finding that many of the same parts of the brain are used in visual imagery and visual perception, but also with the computational analyses performed here and in the previous chapter. Indeed, when we drew additional inferences when reasoning about visual mental imagery, they sometimes reflected back and further informed our inferences about visual perception proper.

The notion that imagery grew out of more basic perceptual processes is an example of opportunistic processing at its best; once the brain could use stored visual information to form patterns in the visual buffer, other uses for this ability were discovered.

Like other sciences, cognitive neuroscience is cumulative: Once we have evidence for a specific set of subsystems, we can further our understanding by adding to the initial set. And this is exactly what we will continue to do in the following chapters.

5

Reading

One of the reasons why we know so much about how objects are visually identified is that monkeys identify them much as we do. Thus, when we learn about the neuroanatomy and neurophysiology of monkeys, we can extend our findings to humans. But monkeys do not use language, and it is unlikely that their brains can tell us much about many aspects of language.[1] Language has many facets, however, and we can begin to make headway if we approach language from the point of view of reading. Because reading is a visual activity, we can build on the inferences we drew in the previous chapters. An understanding of the visual processing used in reading will be a bridge to other language processes.

Nobody has yet constructed a machine that can read all handwritten addresses on envelopes. Given the amount of money to be made from such a machine, this failure is a good measure of how difficult it is to understand the mechanisms underlying reading. Nevertheless, the broad outlines of how we read are now becoming clear. Even if we do not know the details of how the individual networks operate, we do know something about the general structure of the system. Indeed, we know enough to gain insight into the reasons why brain damage impairs reading in many, remarkably distinct ways.

One key fact about reading is that we learn to speak before we learn to read. Thus, by the time we learn to read, the meanings of many words are already stored; and these familiar words are the ones we initially learn to read. Learning to read these words is learning to use an additional route into associative memory to access the information that is stored with words. The problem is that we initially learned to access the relevant memories on the basis of hearing sounds, hearing someone say the words. How are we able to use a pattern of lines to access these memories?

Another key fact about reading is that it is very unlikely that the species evolved to do it: Reading apparently is a relatively late cultural invention, which followed speaking and cave painting by many generations.[2] Thus, reading is an example of opportunistic processing at its best. Presumably, processing subsystems that were used to subserve other Functions—such as object identification—were then available for this role.

Reading involves a large number of distinct activities, ranging from combining individual letters into words, to combining words into sentences, to combining sentences into units of connected discourse. In this chapter we will focus on the fundamental reading skills used to interpret letters and organize them into words. We will consider the processes that underlie reading by taking our usual tack, considering key aspects of the ability one at a time and inferring a set of processing subsystems in the brain that could produce the behavior. We will be led to posit additional processes that operate in conjunction with associative memory; these processes are necessary to use written patterns to access stored information. Once armed with inferences about the mechanisms that underlie normal reading, we then will turn to the effects of brain damage on reading.

Reading at a Glance

Literate adults can read relatively short words with a single eye fixation; we do not need to examine each letter separately.[3] Like many visual abilities, this one seems deceptively simple. The fact that we take a little more time to read a word for each additional letter it contains, however, is one hint that the process is more complex than it might at first appear.[4]

The best clues about what different parts of the brain are doing during reading come from PET studies. These PET studies indicate that even reading single words is a complex activity, which involves several different parts of the brain. In particular, reading has a visual component and an associative memory component. The visual component clearly appears to involve the preprocessing and pattern activation subsystems, given the locus of the activation, and the associative memory component appears to involve the categorical property lookup subsystem.

In one such study, Steven Petersen, Peter Fox, Michael Posner, Mark Mintun, and Marcus Raichle examined the neural bases of reading single words.[5] Their subjects performed a number of tasks while their brain activity was being monitored by a PET scanner. As was discussed in Chapter 3, in this technique subjects are injected with water that contains a radioactive isotope of oxygen, ^{15}O, in some of the molecules. The water is carried with the blood into the brain, and more blood is used in parts of the brain that are working harder. Thus, by recording the radioactivity in different parts of the brain, one can observe how hard they are working when a person performs different tasks.

In these experiments, the subjects' brains were scanned for 40 seconds after they were injected. A new stimulus was presented to the subjects every second during this period. The key to the experiment is that the subjects were asked to do different things with the words, and the role of specific parts of the brain could be inferred by comparing the patterns of brain activation among these tasks. The specific tasks were as follows.

In one task, the subjects stared at a fixation point (a small +). This task should activate low-level visual processing, but the stimulus is so simple that very little effort should be required to process it.

In another task, the "passive" task, the subjects looked at individual words. Presumably, these instructions led the subjects to comprehend the meaning of the words, but not to use that meaning in any particular way.[6]

By subtracting the pattern of brain activation evoked by the fixation task from the pattern evoked by the passive reading task, Petersen et al. hoped to remove the contribution of visual encoding processes per se; what is left over should be due to reading the individual words. These results are illustrated by the triangle symbols in Figure 5.1. As is evident, the major activation was in the occipital-temporal junction area, particularly on the right side. This finding makes sense if only because the first task involved only a single symbol, whereas the second task involved words with multiple letters. Thus, we infer that the preprocessing subsystem must work harder to extract more nonaccidental

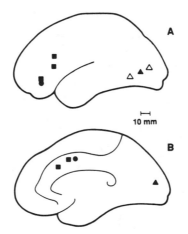

FIGURE 5.1 PET scanning results. Areas activated in visual word reading on the lateral aspect of the cortex (A) and on the medial aspect (B). Triangles refer to the passive task minus fixation (▲, left hemisphere; △, right hemisphere). Only occipital areas are active. Squares refer to generation minus repetition task. Circles refer to detection minus passive task. Solid circles and squares in (A) denote left hemisphere activation; however, in (B), on the midline it was not possible to determine whether activation is left or right. The lateral area is thought to involve a semantic network whereas the midline areas appear to involve attention. *(From Posner et al., 1988, reprinted by permission.)*

properties in the second task. And, as we shall argue later, the right hemisphere is better able to match precise patterns of lines to previously seen examples (see page 377).

The subjects also participated in three more tasks. In the "repetition" task, they saw a word and said it aloud. This task should involve not only the processes that are used when one reads a single word, but also those involved in programming and producing the speech output per se.

In another task, the subjects named a use for each of the objects. For example, when given the word "hammer," they may have said "pound." This "generation" task requires all of the processes used when one repeats a word, plus those that are involved in looking up the uses of objects in associative memory.

In the final, most complex task, they decided whether each word named a dangerous animal. They did not make these judgments aloud, and so the speech output mechanisms were not involved in the task. However, to ensure that the subjects actually performed this "detection" task, they were asked afterwards to estimate how often names of dangerous animals were presented. Detecting dangerous animals also requires accessing associative memory, but requires one to evaluate a specific piece of stored information, as opposed to retrieving it and generating a response (as was necessary to name a use for the object, in the generation task described above).

Thus, by subtracting the pattern of activation obtained in the word repetition task from that obtained in the generation task, these researchers could determine which parts of the brain are used when we access information in associative memory. These results are illustrated in Figure 5.1 by the square symbols. The left frontal lobe appears to play a role in accessing stored information associated with words; this is the locus we previously inferred for the categorical property lookup subsystem, and these results are consistent with this interpretation. In addition, however, the left cingulate gyrus, in the medial plane right above the corpus callosum, is selectively active (see Figure 1.1). Petersen et al. suggest that this area plays some role in preparing one for action, as will be discussed in Chapter 7.

Similarly, the pattern of activation evoked by the passive reading task was subtracted from that evoked by the dangerous animal detection task, which eliminated the contribution of processes used to encode and comprehend the individual words. What is left over should reflect processes that access specific information in associative memory. If the result of this subtraction is very similar to the previous one, then we can have confidence in the basic method. And indeed, as is illustrated in Figure 5.1, the results from the two subtractions are reasonably similar.[7]

More recently, Petersen and colleagues used PET scanning to provide additional hints about the roles of the different brain areas in reading.[8] They showed subjects four types of stimuli: (1) common nouns; (2) "pseudowords" (such as "floop" and "toglo," which were pronounceable and obeyed the spelling rules of English but were not actual words; (3) irregular sets of letters (e.g., "jvjfc") and; (4) strings of letter-like novel symbols, which they called "false fonts." In addition, the subjects viewed a set of cross hairs between sets of the other stimuli, which were used as a fixation point and provided a baseline condition for the subsequent subtraction analyses. The subjects simply passively viewed the stimuli, and the pattern of blood flow found during the baseline condition was subtracted from the patterns found during the other conditions. All of the stimuli activated the lateral occipital-temporal areas, which suggests that some process was operating on relatively complex visual stimuli. This process presumably is carried out by the preprocessing subsystem.

In addition, real words and pronounceable nonwords activated a region in the left, medial occipital-temporal area. We can interpret these data in two ways. On the one hand, this area may store feature extractors that develop with experience (like those used to determine the sex of baby chickens). If so, then the preprocessing stage itself can be further divided, with one smaller subsystem reflexively operating on all stimuli and another operating only on familiar stimuli (all stimuli would be entered into this second subsystem, since there is no way to "know" in advance which are familiar, but only the familiar ones would benefit from this processing). On the other hand, as Michael Posner and his colleagues seem to suggest, it is possible that the visual memories of words and combinations of letters are stored in this second area in humans.[9] It would be of interest if words are stored in posterior parts of the pattern activation neural network, given that the output from the preprocessing subsystem includes configurations of edges that are similar to what is actually stored for written words (for objects, there is much more information stored along with these properties, specifying texture, color, motion patterns, and so on). The lines and angles we use in writing neatly correspond to sets of nonaccidental properties.[10]

Moreover, when the activation caused by the false font, letter-like novel symbols was subtracted from that caused by the words, Petersen et al. found selective activation in the left frontal lobe—which suggested to them that the meanings of the words were extracted even during passive viewing. This interpretation is buttressed by the results of subtracting the activation induced by the letter-like novel symbols from that induced by the pronounceable nonwords: In this case, there was no selective activation of the frontal lobes. This makes sense because pronounceable nonwords are meaningless, and so there is nothing to be looked up in associative memory.[11]

Several inferences can be drawn from these studies. We inferred in the previous two chapters that visual memories are stored in the pattern activation subsystem. The visual encoding mechanisms are mechanical; they simply map input to output. They do not "know" whether they are seeing a drawing of a mountain range, a doodle, a word, or a pair of tangled shoelaces. Thus, we have every reason to expect the subsystems used in identifying objects visually also to be used in reading.

In this case, the nonaccidental properties of the entire word could be matched directly to stored patterns. If a familiar word appeared in a familiar font, it would be stored as a single pattern and could be recognized immediately. This kind of direct match would be equivalent to recognizing a familiar object when it assumes a typical shape (e.g., recognizing a front view of a face as a face). If so, then the increase in time to read words with more letters could occur because a greater proportion of a longer word falls towards the periphery, and so is not sharply delineated in the visual buffer. Alternatively, more time simply may be necessary to compare more complex input patterns to stored patterns.[12]

If the word is novel or not presented in a familiar font, it cannot be matched to a single stored pattern in the pattern activation subsystem. There is no choice but to match a smaller part of the pattern. On the one hand, the letters always can be matched individually—the simple fact that we can read individual letters indicates that their representations must be stored. On the other hand, we also can match intermediate representations, midway between individual letters and words. For example, people may match syllables, combinations of letters that form meaning units (called *morphemes,* such as "ing,"[13] frequently co-occurring letter pairs, or other combinations of letters.[14] Because combinations of letters are stored, if the entire word cannot be matched, these units can be. This procedure requires fewer matches to be made than when words are read a letter at a time, and hence is more efficient than reading each letter individually.[15]

As usual, the identity of each pattern that is matched in the pattern activation subsystem is passed to associative memory. At the same time, the categorical spatial relations encoding subsystem registers each pattern's relative position, and sends this information to associative memory. These inputs to associative memory in turn access the information stored with the word, allowing one to determine its meaning.

Recap: Reading at a Glance

We read at a glance by encoding a written word as a pattern of lines, which is processed in the same way as an object: The nonaccidental properties are marked, and then matched to those stored in the pattern activation subsystem. If a direct match cannot be made, then we identify the word by matching smaller portions of it to stored patterns and encoding their spatial relations. We cannot read at a glance when a word is so long that parts of it fall into low-resolution regions of the visual buffer.

Reading When Letters Are Obscured or Deformed

We decipher writing under a surprisingly large range of conditions. In particular, literate adults typically can read words even w | en letters are obscurxd or de*formed*. The first detailed theory of how we read words in such circumstances was formulated by James McClelland and David Rumelhart in 1981.[16] Their now-classic model of reading rested on a computational analysis. McClelland and Rumelhart noticed that regularities in words occur at three distinct levels of hierarchy, and posited that separate processing occurs at each level. At the first level, words are represented as collections of features, such as curved lines and straight lines at different orientations. At the second level, the features are organized into letters per se. At the third level, the letters are organized into words.

McClelland and Rumelhart's idea was that the neural network used to read words includes connections within and between these three levels, and activation is passed back and forth among the different types of information (using a variant of the recurrent network structure we discussed in Chapter 2). Thus, missing information at one level could be filled in by information at another, allowing one to read partially obscured or deformed words. To see how, let's consider a particularly puzzling discovery about reading, known as the *word superiority effect*. This intriguing laboratory phenomenon has turned out to place strong constraints on theories of reading.

Consider the following task: Subjects see a letter for a brief duration, and then it disappears. They then see that letter with another letter and indicate which of the two was just presented. For example, "A" might be shown for a tenth of a second, removed, and then "A/E" presented. The task, in this example, is to point to the "A." Do you think that this task would be more or less difficult than the following one? A four-letter word is flashed up (for the same amount of time that the single letter was presented in the first task), and then one of the four letters is presented along with another letter. The subject is told that one of those two letters was in the third position of the word (the position varies from trial to trial, sometimes being the first, second, third, or fourth), and is asked to indicate which one was in that position. For example, the word "PEAL" might be presented for a tenth of a second, and then three dashes and a pair of letters, such as "- - A/E -," are presented. In this example, the dashes indicate that the A or E appeared in the third position, and the subject is to point to the correct letter.

To most people's surprise, the letter flashed up by itself is seen *less* accurately than the letter seen in the context of a word. This is called the word superiority effect;[17] actually, it is only one example of several related phenomena that go by this name, but in this book we shall restrict the term to this one case.[18] Why should this effect occur? McClelland and Rumelhart analyzed the information available in the input and reasoned that it must have something to do with the redundancy present in words. If one is only seeing a few features at each position (because the word was only briefly shown), there may not be enough information encoded at any one position to recognize the letter unambiguously. But if one has sets of fragments at a number of positions, and knows that they must indicate a word, then there might be enough *mutual constraints* to implicate a single word.

For example, to distinguish REAR from READ one needs to notice some fragment of the lower region at the extreme right of the word. Just noticing this fragment in isolation usually will not be enough to distinguish among the various letters that have a line in that position. As an extreme example, say we presented the letter R in isolation for a very brief time, and all you saw was the "\" of the leg. The letters A, K, N, R, V, W, and X all have that part. You would be correct only one-seventh of the time by guessing among them. But if the same fragment were seen after the letters REA, only one of the possible letters, R, would complete a word. Knowing the context directs attention to the location of key information and also greatly constrains the alternative guesses one might make.

Such regularities also would help to explain why we can read words that are partially obscured. Take a look at the lower part of Figure 5.2. Those letters in isolation are all but impossible to identify. But as is evident at the top of Figure 5.2, a fragment embedded in a word may be enough to identify the word even when the fragment is not enough to identify the letter in isolation.

FIGURE 5.2 Top: words, which are difficult but possible to read. Bottom: isolated letters from those words, which are almost impossible to read.

In order to exploit this principle, McClelland and Rumelhart posited that each feature representation (which was an input unit in a network) is connected to the appropriate letter representations, which in turn are connected to the appropriate word representations. And these connections run both ways. Thus, the levels interact, with feedback from the word level affecting the letter level, and feedback from the letter level affecting the feature level. Not only do features send activation into the system, but as individual words are activated they send feedback to activate their constituent letters and features. For example, if "|\" "|_" "⊢" "| " were encoded at the feature level, the letters R, E, A, and R would be activated (along with many others). This would activate the word REAR, which would then further activate its letters and their features.

Furthermore, they assumed that the representations interact not only between levels, but also within each level. The representations of words tend to inhibit each other during reading, so that as one representation receives more appropriate input, it dampens the activation of the other representations. This kind of *winner take all* network results in only one representation's being fully activated after a short period of time, and hence causes the system to identify the input as corresponding to a single word.

McClelland and Rumelhart's account of the word superiority effect rests on the effects of feedback between the levels. Initially, different letters are activated to the degree that their constituent features are evident, which in turn activate words to the degree that their constituent letters are evident. We can illustrate this process with an analogy borrowed from an older model by Oliver Selfridge, which he called "Pandemonium:"[19] Imagine that each feature detector shouts its name whenever it sees its feature. Each letter detector listens for its features (e.g., "A" would listen for "diagonal line left"; "diagonal line right"; "horizontal line"). The more of its features it hears, the louder the letter detector shouts its name. The word detectors listen for their letters, and the more shouting each one hears from its letters, the more activated it becomes. And the more a word representation is activated, the more it encourages its letters and features by sending feedback to them via recurrent connections. This feedback "primes" the lower-level representations, sensitizing one to detect specific features of a letter that ought to be part of a word—which makes it easier to see the letter than when it is presented alone, without the benefit of such priming.

One problem with McClelland and Rumelhart's account, however, is that they posited separate, fixed regions in which each letter could appear. Four regions were defined, one for each position in a four-letter word. A separate set of representations of each feature and each letter was associated with each individual region, which permitted the reading of words that have the same letter in two positions, such as "REAR." This idea leads to immediate difficulties: What about five-letter words? Or 28-letter German nouns? And what about words in which the letters are spaced oddly? Or handwriting in which letters are not clearly separated?

In addition, McClelland and Rumelhart's model does not mesh well with the processes underlying visual perception in general. Specifically, the separation of object properties and spatial properties (discussed in Chapter 3) during encoding leaves McClelland and Rumelhart caught on the horns of a dilemma. On one horn, a person could attend to separate letters and encode them individually. But then (as was discussed in Chapter 3) the dorsal, spatial-properties-encoding system would keep track of the locations of the letters; one would not use duplicate features and letters for each position in space—as assumed by McClelland and Rumelhart. On the other horn, a person could attend to the entire word, encoding it as a single shape, in which case the letters and features have no special status, no distinct identity (they are simply parts of an overall pattern). Encoding the word as a whole does not fit with the hierarchical organization that lies at the heart of their account.[20]

Nevertheless, the computational analysis underlying McClelland and Rumelhart's theory has several things going for it. For one, the idea of different levels of representation accords well with our analyses of visual processing. Indeed, their feature level might correspond to processing in the preprocessing subsystem, their letter level to processing in the pattern activation subsystem (which could also match whole words), and their word level to processing in associative memory. In addition, the idea that the letters in words are mutually constraining is clearly correct, and this probably will be a critical component of any explanation of the word superiority effect. We can incorporate these insights into the picture developed previously to understand how partially obscured or deformed words are read.

Using Visual Mechanisms to Read

Consider how the subsystems we inferred in Chapter 3 may contribute to our ability to read. In many circumstances, objects we see do not match the appropriate stored visual pattern very well. If an object is partially hidden, or assumes an unusual shape, the input image may fail to match a single pattern well enough for the object to be recognized. In Chapter 3 we argued that when the input to the pattern activation subsystem does not match a stored visual pattern very well, the best match is sent to associative memory, where it is treated as an hypothesis to be tested. Alternatively, if no large shape matches the input very well, then smaller portions of the input are matched and used to form the hypothesis. In this situation, associative memory also receives representations of the spatial relations among the parts (via the dorsal system), and the representation that best matches the parts and their spatial relations serves as the hypothesis. The hypothesis is tested with a second encoding cycle, in which the system searches for information that would confirm or disconfirm the tentative identification. If the same mechanisms are used in reading, then we expect a deformed word also to be the basis of an hypothesis, leading to a second pass.

Additional information in associative memory. For objects, one seeks a distinctive part or characteristic (e.g., a spot on Fido's head) when testing an hypothesis. Each part and characteristic is stored with a spatial relation, which is used to guide the attention shifting mechanisms so that one can look for incriminating evidence. What kinds of information about words are stored in associative memory that can be used to guide attention during the second pass?

Consider the simple fact that we can read when shown a single letter at a time, as when individual letters slide across the movie screen when the title appears. For example, the letter "c" might move across a screen, followed by "a," and then "t." We have no trouble reading the word "cat." The individual letters presumably match individual representations in the pattern activation subsystem, but at some point they must be integrated with the spatial relations among them. Object properties and spatial properties are integrated only in associative memory (see Chapter 3). Hence, we infer that associative memory contains a representation of the letters of a word and their spatial relations.

This inference surely must be correct, if only because people can spell even irregular words, such as "aisle." Irregular words can only be spelled by looking up the letters and spatial relations in memory. Furthermore, we can verify whether somebody else spells words aloud correctly. These nonvisual representations in turn can be matched to visual ones, as when someone asks you to point to a specific word she names; this ability requires representation and integration across sensory modalities—which are hallmarks of representations in associative memory.

Using letters in hypothesis testing. As letters (encoded via the ventral system) and their spatial relations (encoded via the dorsal system) enter associative memory, the representation that best matches the input becomes most highly activated. The output of the associative memory network is information associated with the most activated word, including its letters and their locations. This processing is analogous to knowing the parts of an object once it is tentatively identified; for example, once the representation of an elephant is activated, one knows that it should have a tail, even if all that can be seen is its head. Similarly, once one identifies a word, one can access its constituent letters and their order—even if they all could not be seen clearly initially. Even fragmentary input may be enough to activate the proper representation, and information about the "parts" of the word is then available.

If the input to associative memory is treated as an hypothesis (because it does not clearly implicate a single word), the categorical property lookup subsystem can access the output from the associative memory network. The categorical property lookup subsystem would send information about which letters should be found in which positions to the subsystems that guide attention. Moreover, this subsystem would send input to the pattern activation subsystem to prime it to encode the expected letters (in any font).[21] This process is exactly the same as that used to form mental images, except that the representation is not fully activated. Instead, it is now only partially activated, biasing the subsystem to match the corresponding input pattern.

During reading, the hypothesis testing process would lead one to pay particular attention to the locations of distinguishing letters in words so that key fragments that might otherwise go unnoticed will be encoded. Such processing seems essential if one is to decode messy handwriting. In Chapter 3 we posited that properties of objects in associative memory have different "strengths," depending on how distinctive they are. In this case, a "distinctive" letter is one that discriminates between two similar words. For example, the final "r" of "rear" is important because it distinguishes "rear" from many other words. Thus, one would use top-down hypothesis testing to seek distinctive information that allows one to identify the word.

Before concluding, let us see how the inferences we have drawn so far, for different reasons, account for the word superiority effect. Visual information is encoded at each location on the retina at the same time, but when a stimulus is exposed for only a brief period, the encoding from any given location will be degraded. Thus, in a brief exposure the preprocessing subsystem may extract only, say, 75% of the nonaccidental properties at each location in the field (the exact number will depend on the lighting, precise exposure time, and so on). If only a single letter is present, 75% of its properties may be encoded. If four letters are encoded, on average 75% of each letter's properties may be encoded. For frequently seen words that are presented in familiar fonts, the available fragments may be sufficient in and of themselves to recognize the word in the pattern activation subsystem (in Chapter 8 we will review evidence that a modality-specific representation of words is in fact stored).[22] In most situations, however, one may not be able to recognize degraded words solely on the basis of constraint satisfaction processes in the pattern activation subsystem. Indeed, the word superiority effect occurs even when different fonts are used for different letters of a word, and so there is no stored visual pattern that corresponds to the entire word.[23] In such circumstances, tentative matches to individual letters or combinations of letters are made in the pattern activation subsystem, and their locations simultaneously are registered in the dorsal system. The two sorts of information are sent to associative memory and matched to stored representations of letters and positions there. In some situations, the input uniquely implicates a specific word, but in others more than one word is partially matched by the input. If the input does not implicate a single word, then the representation that most closely matches the set of inputs is used to direct a second encoding cycle to search for key letters. Finally, after one has identified the word, one simply spells the letters of the word and notes which is in the queried location.[24]

This account is appealing not only because it follows from inferences we drew earlier about object perception, but also because it leads us to expect parallels between reading and object identification. And in fact, researchers have found an *object superiority effect*.[25] In one experiment, subjects were shown a segment of a line drawing either in isolation or embedded in an object. Following this, they were shown two segments (both of which could have been in the object) and were asked to choose which they had seen before. Paralleling the word superiority effect, subjects detect parts of objects better when they are seen in context.[26]

The MORSEL model. Many ideas like the ones we have used to understand the word superiority effect were incorporated into a neural network model built by Michael Mozer.[27] This "Multiple Object Recognition and Attentional Selection" model (MOR-SEL) exploited specific types of interactions between an attentional mechanism and a semantic system (in an associative memory). Information in the semantic system was used to "pull out" specific patterns of activation from the input. This process allowed the model to use stored information about words to encode specific letters, which gave it an advantage when encoding a letter embedded in a word compared to when it was presented alone. This account of the word superiority effect was in many ways like that of McClelland and Rumelhart, but differed in an important way: The model did not merely send feedback to appropriate letters and features, but—like the process outlined above—it selectively attended to relevant regions and sought specific information. The model also had a visual short-term memory in which it built up an organized structure based on the location, the color, and the identity of a stimulus. In our terms, this short-term memory is part of associative memory, given that it integrates information about shape and location.

MORSEL read common words (i.e., those that had appeared more often during training, which used the back-propagation technique) better than rare words. It did so in part because familiar strings of letters were given more attention. In addition, it made specific types of errors that mirrored those made by humans. For example, letter transpositions occurred when position-specific information was lost; such transpositions occurred more often for random strings of letters than for words (because nonwords could not take advantage of stored information to organize the input or to pull out expected letters). The model could not account for errors based on visual similarity, however, because the encoding mechanisms were not well developed. In the present terms, such errors depend on which nonaccidental properties are not properly registered.

MORSEL is a good example of how a relatively simple model can help to reveal the power of some basic principles, such as using stored information to direct attention to the location of expected parts or properties of a stimulus. But it is too simple— we have inferred a much more complex system, which deals with a much wider range of phenomena.[28]

Recap: Reading When Letters Are Obscured or Deformed

We read partially obscured or deformed words in two ways. If the word is short, frequently encountered, and printed in a familiar font, we can match it to a whole-word pattern in the pattern activation subsystem. If so, then the redundancy in non-accidental properties may be enough to allow us to recognize an obscured word. Once the word is identified, one can access its letters and their positions in associative memory, and can deduce which letter belongs in each position.

Alternatively, if the word is relatively long, rarely encountered, or printed in an unfamiliar font, we match common combinations of letters in the pattern activation subsystem. This information is sent to associative memory, where it is integrated with spatial information encoded via the dorsal system. If the input to associative memory does not implicate a single representation, the best-matching representation in associative memory is used to guide top-down hypothesis testing to search for evidence of specific letters in specific positions. Thus, fragments that are not sufficient to identify letters on their own may be sufficient to implicate a word. In some situations, however, even after such processing two or more words might be consistent with the input. But if the word appears in a context, the context can now be used to select among the viable alternatives (we will have more to say about this in the next chapter).

Reading Words in Different Fonts

We can read words and letters that appear in multiple sizes and in different fonts. For example, **we can** read these WORDS even though *THEY each* **look** different. We can also read words in which the letters have different spacing, such as words like *t ree*. Notice, however, that we are slowed down when letters are staggered, or when the sizes and fonts are altered.[29] This too must be explained.

There are two ways in which these abilities can arise. On the one hand, if the deformations do not disrupt the nonaccidental properties (such as symmetries, points of intersection, and connected line segments) that characterize a "standard" set of letters, then the nonaccidental properties marked by the preprocessing subsystem will match the appropriate stored pattern. The nonaccidental properties are sufficiently stable that we expect many similar fonts to match a single stored pattern.

On the other hand, if the letters are written such that the nonaccidental properties of standard letters are disrupted (as in Gothic), then we must store a different representation of such letters in that particular font. Separate representations will be stored if a font is so distinct that the nonaccidental properties extracted from it do not match those of familiar letters.

Changing the size of the font slows one down if the scope of the attention window must be adjusted, which takes time.[30] In contrast, CHANGING THE font itself slows one down because new sets of nonaccidental properties must be extracted before the pattern can be identified. When the same sets are extracted over and over, the wheels are greased. For reasons that will be discussed in detail in Chapter 8, words bias (i.e., prime) the system so that it subsequently encodes words in the same font more easily than words in different fonts. Letters in the same font presumably are mapped to the proper outputs in the preprocessing and pattern activation subsystems by specific sets of connections. As will be discussed in Chapter 8, when the neurons that implement those connections are used repeatedly, *long-term potentiation* (LTP) causes them later to fire in response to less input.

In addition, in some situations the nonaccidental properties extracted from a new font do not access a multi-letter pattern in the pattern activation subsystem (a whole-word or letter-combination pattern). When this occurs, the input will match a relatively large number of letter patterns, thus requiring more time to pass to associative memory. Also, letters in some fonts may be relatively complex (such as Gothic) or may share many nonaccidental properties—and so are relatively similar to each other. In these cases, the input cannot be recognized until the preprocessing subsystem has processed it thoroughly, and hence it will take longer to read than when simpler or less similar letters are seen. Also, the more often one reads a particular font, the stronger will be the weights on the appropriate connections. Hence, the input/output mapping will be more reliable (i.e., able to be performed faster and with greater accuracy). *Thus, we are not surprised that people read some fonts more slowly than others.*

Finally, if unusual spacing between letters disrupts the overall pattern too much, the input may only match individual letters—and so we are slowed down. Moreover, spacing letters farther apart may cause some to fall outside the fovea, which slows down reading.[31] If the spacing perturbation is rather minor, the nonaccidental properties of the overall pattern may be preserved and the word read as usual.

Recap: Reading Words in Different Fonts

We read different fonts by matching nonaccidental properties to appropriate stored patterns. If the fonts are similar, the same set of nonaccidental properties will be extracted and matched to stored patterns; if they are very different, different sets of nonaccidental properties are extracted and subsequently matched to stored patterns in the pattern activation subsystem. If the font is relatively unfamiliar, whole-word patterns may not be stored, and so individual letters or combinations of letters are matched—which slows down processing. More frequently read fonts are also represented by patterns of stronger weights in the network than less frequently read fonts, and hence the input/output mapping is faster and more reliable. Finally, if the size changes, the scope of the attention window must be adjusted, which also slows processing.

The accounts of the three abilities we have just considered—reading at a glance, reading obscured or degraded words, and reading words in different fonts—are consistent with what is known about the neural substrate; they hinge on the role of the preprocessing and pattern activation subsystems, which are used to identify the visual patterns per se, and the categorical property lookup subsystem, which is used to test hypotheses as information enters associative memory and the system begins to converge on a possible identification. The PET scanning results had implicated these subsystems, and they turned out to play critical roles in our computational analysis.

Reading Unfamiliar Words

We can read aloud not only familiar words, but also unfamiliar words and even pronounceable nonwords (such as "glup" and "tuloperantic"). It is clear that we can pronounce written words even when we first see them, before we learn their meanings. "Hypha" is a word, for example, that refers to a type of filament in a fungus. You probably could read it aloud even before you learned its definition. In addition, a word like "fone" can be understood in context as soon as you pronounce it.

Indeed, when first learning to read, at least some children appear to pronounce a word and only then understand it (this is called "prelexical speech").[32] But it is an insult to say that an adult "moves his lips" while reading; fluent readers do not do this. It would seem that only with practice can a reader match the output from the pattern activation subsystem directly to stored representations in associative memory. Prior to that, and when we encounter unfamiliar words thereafter, we somehow say the word to ourselves and use the sound to understand it.

Logically, there seem to be only two ways in which patterns of lines could address information that was stored in associative memory when we learned to talk. First, as just discussed, the pattern could be processed in the same way as an object during object identification. The output from the pattern activation subsystem would then be sent to associative memory, where it could be stored and associated with other information. In this case, the child would learn the visual pattern that stands for a concept the same way he or she learned the sound, by rote memorization. Second, one might not identify the pattern of lines directly, but instead might first pronounce the word, and then use the sound to identify it—just as would be done if the word were heard spoken by someone else.[33] Young children find reading aloud easier than reading silently, which suggests that they often rely on this second method.[34]

Pronouncing Written Words

The mere fact that we can understand spoken words implies that there is a representation in associative memory that is accessed by auditory stimuli; even people who are illiterate can understand spoken speech. And so, if one can produce the sound corresponding to a word, the sound can then be used to identify it. We can infer two mechanisms that allow us to decode the pronunciation of written words. First, in some cases, the sound must be stored by rote as a property associated with a word.[35] The word "aisle," for example, cannot be sounded out using any general strategy. Second, the mere fact that we can pronounce novel words, or nonwords such as "flut," is evidence that there is a process that converts print to sound.[36]

In principle, there are several ways a *letter-to-sound conversion subsystem* could convert *graphemes* (printed symbols) to *phonemes* (language sounds).[37] On the one hand, it is possible that rules are stored and used to convert print to sounds.[38] For example, there is a rule that "s" produces a certain hissing sound, "t" a particular sound with the tongue behind the teeth, and so forth. This process will work well for languages such as Italian, where there are regular print-sound correspondences. English, however, suffers from many exceptions and irregularities, each of which would require a special-case rule. That is, in any given language, most words with a given sequence of letters are pronounced in a certain way. For example, in English "-ave" is usually pronounced as is in "wave," "save," "cave," and "gave"; these are called *regular* words. The exceptions to these rules, such as "have," are called *irregular* words.

On the other hand, it also is possible that sound conversion is done by analogy to memorized exemplars.[39] In this case, each example would have to have its pronunciation stored directly with it. For example, you might produce the sound of the pronounceable nonword "dard" by analogy to "bard," simply by substituting the initial sound "d" for "b" and then using the sound pattern stored with the visual form "bard."

A third possibility is that we use both techniques, reserving the rote memory case for exceptions to the usual pronunciation patterns (e.g., the word "yacht"); indeed, there does not seem any way around the idea that at least some pronunciations are stored by rote memory.[40] And given that they are stored by rote, they presumably can be used in various ways, including making analogies to new inputs.

A network model of print-to-sound conversion.   Recall from Chapter 2 that we can distinguish between "rule following" and "rule described" behavior (page 31). Although the motions of the planets can be described by rules, the planets themselves do not follow the rules. Similarly, although a computer program may actually follow rules, if the program is built into a chip, the rules may no longer be "mentioned" explicitly. In this case, the input/output mapping of the chip is determined purely by patterns of current flow and no rules can be pointed to in the system. Nevertheless, the behavior of the computer-with-a-program and the corresponding hard-wired chip both can be described using the same set of rules. Thus, the fact that a behavior can be described using rules does not imply that the underlying processing actually relies on those rules.

Mark Seidenberg and James McClelland make this point forcefully with a large network model that converts print to sound without using any stored rules at all.[41] Rather, print-sound correspondences were stored as patterns of weights in a network, which performed the requisite input/output mapping. The model could mimic aspects of normal reading as well as reading impairments in childhood and some types of deficits that occur following brain damage.[42] This model included three levels, one that represented the visual features (the orthographic level), a layer of hidden units, and the pronunciation output (the phonological level). The hidden units not only sent information up to the output units, but also sent feedback to the input units. The back-propagation learning procedure was used to train the network to make specific print-sound associations. The more frequently a word occurs in the language, the more frequently it was presented when training the model. After enough training, the model was able to pronounce correctly 97.3% of the words it was given. When it made an error, it did so in different ways. About 20% of the errors occurred when the model regularized words. That is, it gave a regular pronunciation to a word that has an irregular pronunciation (e.g., for "brooch," the model produced "broc," although it was trained to produce "bruc"). This type of error only occurred for words that appeared relatively infrequently during the training phase of the model. These regularization errors were produced on the basis of what the network had learned from exposure to other stimuli that had regular spelling-to-sound mappings (these types of words appeared often during training). Such regularization errors, the authors report, also occur when children learn to read,[43] and sometimes appear in cases of dyslexia following brain damage.[44] About 30% of the model's errors occurred when it produced incorrect vowels (e.g., "beau" was pronounced "bu"), and another 30% of the errors occurred when it produced incorrect consonants (e.g., hard G's instead of soft ones for words such as "gel," "gin," and "gist").

In addition, Seidenberg and McClelland investigated the performance of their network after specific types of damage had been inflicted on it. They trained the network on the same words with only half as many hidden units (100 instead of 200). The first result of interest was that decreasing the number of hidden units produced overall lower performance on all types of words (i.e., low-frequency irregular, low-frequency regular, high-frequency irregular, and high-frequency regular words). The second result of interest was that irregular words were read more poorly in the impoverished network, whatever their frequency during training, whereas only low-frequency irregular words were read relatively poorly in the 200-hidden-units network. This finding suggests that item-specific knowledge about pronunciation is less likely to be encoded when the number of hidden units decreases. These results, the authors suggest, simulate what occurs in children who have reading problems. A characteristic of dyslexic children is that they perform poorly even when they read higher-frequency irregular words.[45] In general, this model illustrated that properties of impaired reading, either during development or following brain damage, may simply occur because of limited computational resources.

This model did not store individual words per se; rather, it mapped spelling patterns onto pronunciation patterns. Thus, it was of interest to discover whether it could account for the simple fact that people can read words that appear frequently in the language faster than words that appear infrequently. In this model, word frequency was reflected by the weights of the connections: Words that were encountered frequently during training influenced the weights more than words encountered less often. And in fact, the model read common words correctly more often than relatively rare words. If we assume that the factors that make us more accurate also allow us to read more quickly (i.e., map input to output more easily), then the system would read common words more quickly than infrequent ones, as do people.

In addition, it has been found that people read regular words faster than irregular words, but only when both types of words occur relatively infrequently in the language.[46] Seidenberg and McClelland's model mimicked this result: When words were not presented often during training, special-purpose pathways were unlikely to be established for irregular words, and so the model read them more poorly. In contrast, when words were presented frequently during training, it set up weights to accomplish the mappings and read the words well—regardless of whether they were regular or irregular.

In short, we infer a letter-to-sound conversion subsystem, which maps a set of letters and their spatial relations onto phonemes. These phonemes in turn are input to another network that governs the subsystems that produce the sound (see Chapter 6). The relation between the letter-to-sound conversion subsystem and those we inferred earlier is illustrated in Figure 5.3.

Recap: Reading Unfamiliar Words

If a word is unfamiliar, it will not match a single stored pattern in the pattern activation subsystem. Thus, syllables, morphemes, or letters are matched, and this information is sent to associative memory. At the same time, the spatial relations among these units are encoded via the dorsal system. The letter-to-sound conversion subsystem converts this input to phonemes, which in

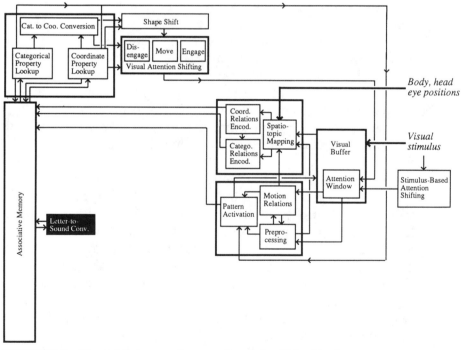

FIGURE 5.3 The subsystems and connections inferred in this chapter, and their relation to those inferred previously

turn are sent as input to other subsystems that pronounce words. This process need not involve use of rules per se. With repeated use, the entire pattern of lines becomes an entry in the pattern activation subsystem and the pattern recognized there is associated with the word in associative memory, which allows the word to be read in a single attentional fixation. Furthermore, with repeated use a set of phonemes can be directly associated with the word in associative memory. Hence, one can avoid having to compute the sound based on the visual input, but instead can simply look it up. In the brain, storage appears to be very cheap; indeed, we have yet to measure the capacity limits of long-term memory.[47] In contrast, computation requires effort. Thus, if it can, the brain appears to prefer to store information and simply look it up subsequently, instead of computing it anew each time it is needed.

Understanding the Effects of Brain Damage

Brain damage can impair a person's ability to read in various ways. This syndrome is called *alexia* in North America and *acquired dyslexia* or *word blindness* in Europe. The term acquired dyslexia is useful because it contrasts the syndrome that occurs in a previously literate adult with the inability to learn to read in the first place, *developmental dyslexia*. Acquired dyslexia may or may not be accompanied by an impaired ability to say the words aloud when reading.[48]

The ability to read is not usually completely disrupted; rather, it typically is impaired selectively. There are a surprising number of ways in which reading can be disrupted following brain damage, as we shall see. However, the various deficits are rarely all-or-none. Rather, the dissociations typically are a matter of degree. As was discussed in Chapter 3, such graded deficits are consistent with damage within a neural network. Computer models of neural networks have shown that they degrade "gracefully" following damage; they limp along, making mistakes, instead of simply ceasing to function altogether.[49]

Letters versus Words

In 1899, James Hinshelwood wrote a book entitled *Letter, Word-and-Mind-Blindness.*[50] In this book he described patients who had specific reading problems following brain damage. Some patients were "blind" when reading individual letters, but could read whole words. And other patients were "blind" when reading whole words, but could still read individual letters. These syndromes are now called *pure letter blindness* and *pure word blindness* or *literal alexia* and *verbal alexia,* respectively. (Recall from Chapter 3 that "mind blindness" was an early name for visual agnosia.) Although these syndromes are called "pure," they rarely—if ever—occur in complete isolation. Such reading deficits typically are relative; patients can have more difficulty in reading letters than words or vice versa.

"Pure letter blindness" could correspond to an inability to identify the letter (as revealed, for example, by a failure to match upper- and lowercase versions of the letter), or to an inability to say aloud the name of the letter. Both sorts of deficits have been reported to occur. We will focus here on the former sort of deficit, which does not reflect problems in accessing the name of the letter, pronunciation, or the like.

The most obvious way to account for these phenomena is as follows: Letter blindness might reflect a disruption of the representations of individual letters, whereas word blindness might reflect a disruption of the representations of words. Although possible, this notion is a little troublesome, for two reasons: First, it is dangerously close to being circular; the account is much like a description of the phenomenon itself. Second, it seems questionable whether the representations of individual letters and words would be stored far enough apart in the brain that damage could easily disrupt one while leaving the other intact.

Another account of letter blindness without word blindness is directly analogous to our account of the word superiority effect, only now the degradation is not produced because a word is flashed up quickly but rather because the brain has been damaged. As we saw earlier, because there are more possible constraints for words than letters, less information is necessary to match a word than to match an individual letter. If brain damage disrupts the preprocessing subsystem, the pattern activation subsystem, associative memory, or their connections, words might be matched but not individual letters—producing letter blindness but not word blindness.

Word blindness without letter blindness could result if damage reduces the *total* amount of information that can be encoded at one time. Even though a smaller *proportion* of the total number of nonaccidental properties is enough for word recognition, a larger absolute number must be encoded for words than for letters. One account for pure word blindness is that the preprocessing subsystem is able to process only a relatively few nonaccidental properties in a relatively small part of the field. Such a deficit would allow it to encode letters, but not words. Alternatively, damage might decrease the activation level of associative memory, preventing it from storing the incoming letters and spatial relations long enough to converge on a word—even though individual letters can be identified. Or, the constraint-satisfaction mechanism in the pattern activation subsystem or associative memory may be awry, so that input gets scrambled. In this case, the person may stumble on the compensatory strategy of narrowing the attention window to focus on individual letters—which may restrict the input so that the system can converge on the proper letter but will not allow it to encode words.

These accounts lead one to expect the damage that leads to alexia to have consequences in other domains. And indeed, alexia is often accompanied by prosopagnosia and/or visual object agnosia (which were discussed in Chapter 3).[51] In addition, brain damage generally slows people down, and affects general capacity as measured by a host of standard neuropsychological tests.

Visual Alexia

John Marshall and Frieda Newcombe described a kind of *visual paralexia* ("para" means "to the side of" and "lex" is a root for "word"), in which patients have difficulty decoding the visual form of a word.[52] These patients often read words as ones that look similar or that have some of the same letters as the correct word. Sometimes the patients can read the letters, but still not read the words (i.e., they are word-blind but not letter-blind). For example, one patient misread "lice" as "ice" or "like." She apparently realized that these responses were incorrect, but could not correct them.[53] Think about this for a moment: The patient had to have seen at least some of the correct features she was not using or she would not know that she was making an error, but she still could not read the word correctly!

Patients who have trouble decoding the visual form of a word may have disrupted preprocessing or pattern activation subsystems, disrupted spatiotopic or categorical spatial relations encoding subsystems (for registering positions of sets of letters), and/or disrupted information in associative memory. Disruptions of the associative memory network, so that it does not converge on the correct output mapping, could produce intrusion errors—which are often observed in these patients. An intrusion error occurs when another word preempts the correct one. Such a problem would account for how patients could realize that they were making errors, but not be able to correct them.

Some patients with visual alexia spontaneously adopt strategies to help them focus on the features of letters; they read by moving their fingers along the outline of a word. Other strategies are perhaps more interesting: Some patients move their fingers to depict the shape in the air.[54] The motor movements may allow additional spatial information to be encoded into associative memory. Indeed, it is possible that the representations of these movements themselves are compared to motor representations stored in memory that are used to print the shapes of the letters.[55] This would be a good example of opportunistic processing, if in fact it actually occurs.

The fact that some patients trace letters in the air is also of interest because it implies that information from the preprocessing subsystem (specifying the nonaccidental properties of the letters) is sent to the dorsal system, where it is used to guide action. Recall that we drew this inference in Chapter 3, based partly on the observation that one needs to know how parts of an object are oriented in order to reach properly. In addition, recall that there are connections between the posterior portion of the superior temporal sulcus and the inferior parietal lobes of monkeys, which may serve this role.[56] If so, then this is another example of weak modularity at work; the preprocessing subsystem may be able to play a role in both the ventral and dorsal systems during reading.

We suspect that the patients who benefit by moving their fingers along the outline of a word have difficulty in visually encoding the shapes per se, whereas those who motion in the air must be able to encode at least the individual visual features in the preprocessing subsystem.

Phonological Alexia

In addition to identifying written material directly, we can read by pronouncing a word and accessing memory via the sound pattern. This indirect route is used whenever we encounter a new word (such as "spectoculoid"), and the fact that some patients have difficulty reading unfamiliar or novel words *but not familiar* ones suggests that this route can be disrupted.[57] This deficit, *phonological alexia,* is particularly noticeable if patients are asked to read a pronounceable nonword, such as "tord." The patients typically misread the pronounceable nonword as a real word that looks similar, and sometimes will misread actual words as other ones that look similar.

Phonological alexia is often accompanied by visual paralexias, and sometimes makes itself apparent by these sorts of errors: If the patient can read only by matching visual patterns, errors often will reflect visual similarity. However, in these patients phonological alexia is seen only with relatively unfamiliar words or pronounceable nonwords; pure visual alexia results in such errors with all types of words. Patients with phonological alexia will often complain that they have trouble reading newspapers or books, but then seem reasonably unimpaired when asked to read common words in the clinic. If the words are unfamiliar, however, the deficit makes itself known.

These patients' deficits, then, could be caused by disruptions in the letter-to-sound conversion subsystem. Such deficits also could be caused by a disruption of the auditory information in associative memory. In addition, their errors reflect properties of the processes used in the other sort of reading, relying on direct visual matches. These processes are all they have to work with, and are what produces the behavior. The fact that such patients typically misread a pronounceable nonword as a real word that looks similar is easily explained: They simply respond on the basis of the representation that has the most constraints satisfied by the input, and because there is no correct match (the word is unfamiliar or novel), they make an error.

Neglect Dyslexia

This disruption is a consequence of unilateral visual neglect, which was described in Chapter 3. As we discussed, patients who display neglect are not blind, but rather ignore stimuli on the side opposite that of the damage. For purposes of discussion, we will consider patients with right parietal lesions who ignore the left half of space. Such patients show several interesting deficits when reading.

Words versus nonwords. These patients ignore the left side of nonwords, but can read relatively short words. For example, if asked to read "strowt" they might read "owt," but if asked to read "stroll" they do fine. They do not read entire nonwords even if they can easily be pronounced. It seems unlikely that the entire left part of the field is suddenly chopped off; if even a few fragments of input are available, then this finding can be explained exactly in the way we understood the word superiority effect. If these patients cannot see all of the first letters of a short word, they can use the other letters to constrain the possibilities —just as is done when a letter is missing in a word.

Short words versus long words. These patients tend to ignore the left side of words when the words are too long. Given a word such as "alphabetically," such patients typically will miss some of the first few letters. If the word is too long, too many letters often will be ignored to use the remainder to fill in the missing material.

Compound words. Words like "peanut" will be read better if there is no space between "pea" and "nut." Indeed, inserting a pound sign in the middle ("pea#nut") leads to better reading than inserting a space.[58] Inserting a space results in two separate perceptual groups, which may be encoded separately via the attention window. If the two groups are encoded separately, the one on the left will be ignored because its location will not be registered by the spatiotopic mapping subsystem. Hence, the constraint-satisfaction mechanisms in associative memory cannot be used to fill in the left portions of the word. Inserting a pound sign instead of a space leads the entire word to be encoded in a single attention fixation; it causes the letters to be seen as a single group, and hence constraint satisfaction mechanisms can be used to converge on the correct word at least some of the time.

Related words. But even when there is a space between words, both can be read some proportion of the time. The patients are more likely to read the left word when it could form a compound with the right word (such as "cow" and "boy") than when it could not (e.g., "sun" and "fly").[59] Again, this effect comes directly from the constraint-satisfaction mechanisms in associative memory.

Mirror-reversed words. Alfonso Caramazza and Argye Hillis described a patient with damage in the left hemisphere who neglected the last few letters of a word even when the word was mirror reversed (so that the first few letters were now on the patient's *left* side).[60] This patient also ignored the last few letters when the word was spelled vertically, and also tended to ignore the last few letters of the word when she was asked to spell the word backwards (which presumably involves imagery). But Marlene Behrmann and her colleagues showed precisely the opposite results with other patients! Their patients did not neglect when asked to read vertical words; rather, they neglected the letters to the patient's left side, regardless of whether the word was normal or mirror reversed, and they read words better when they were moved farther to the right of a fixation point (into the good field).

Behrmann et al.'s findings suggest that connections to or from the visual buffer had been disrupted; the visual buffer is retinotopic, and damage to these connections would disrupt processing to one side of the patient's body. Specifically, the damage could prevent the attention window from shifting to one side of the buffer, or could prevent information in one side of the attention window from being passed further into the system. In contrast, Caramazza and Hillis' result may suggest that the spatiotopic mapping subsystem or its output can be disrupted, which results in the attention window's not being positioned properly relative to an object. Damage to these structures might affect how the attention window is positioned on a word, so that one ignores part of it.

Alternatively, both types of dysfunctions might be caused by a damaged spatiotopic mapping subsystem, and the conflicting results may merely reflect subtle task differences that led the patients to define their frames of reference in different ways. The idea that frames of reference can be assigned by the spatiotopic mapping subsystem receives support from findings reported by other researchers, who asked patients with unilateral visual neglect to view displays while lying on their sides.[61] Thus the horizontal displays were vertical on the patients' retinas. These researchers found that neglect is partially based on the left side of the object, and partially based on the left side of the retina. This result makes sense if the spatiotopic mapping system can assign a frame of reference in different ways, and tends to vacillate when gravity and retinal position are in conflict. That is, normally the alignment of objects based on gravity is congruent with that based on the retina; up and down on the retina are up and down relative to gravity. However, when we are on our sides, the two frames of reference are in conflict, and the system may switch back and forth between them. Once a frame of reference is established, these patients would represent only a portion of space, and the attention shifting subsystems would never receive input to direct them to other regions. If the coordinate frame is based on the object, Caramazza and Hillis' results will be found; if it is based on the retina, Behrmann et al.'s results will be found.

Semantic Alexia

This problem is characterized by *semantic paralexias,* which are incorrect words whose meaning is somehow related to the proper word. The errors can be of a variety of types. These patients may read a synonym, antonym, subordinate, or an associated word.

For example, such a patient might misread "dog" as "cat" or "fox." Or, the patient might read a word that is a variant of the one actually shown. For example, a patient might say "twisted" when reading "twist," or "bought" when reading "buy." In addition, some patients have trouble reading function words, such as "of," "an," "not," and "and." If such a patient can read these words, it is only following a struggle, and these patients often substitute these function words for one another. Finally, although function words are most difficult, these patients also have more trouble reading verbs than adjectives, which are more difficult than nouns.

These disruptions would be caused if the normal process of constraint satisfaction in associative memory were awry. It is unclear exactly why these specific deficits occur, and we may not be able to say much more about them using commonsense concepts: A network model to be discussed shortly produces similar deficits when it is damaged, and the outputs arise because of the way weights are allocated on the connections in the network.[62] The precise allocation of weights depends on the process that establishes the input/output mapping in the first place—and our intuitions are not very good at fathoming the consequences of such computational processes.

Spelling Dyslexia

Some patients read words one letter at a time, even if they are short and familiar.[63] Sometimes the patients spell the words aloud when reading, but even when the patient does not say the name of each letter aloud, the time to read increases dramatically as the number of letters in a word increases: Normal people require about 30 milliseconds for each additional letter,[64] but these patients often require a second or more per additional letter.[65] These patients have the same problem with all types of words (nouns, verbs, adjectives, etc.), and sometimes have trouble identifying individual letters. This syndrome could reflect a strategy the patient uses to compensate for visual deficits; in some cases, it may be a consequence of simultanagnosia or a restricted attention window.[66] Recall that patients with simultanagnosia sometimes cannot register separate parts of a single visual form at the same time.

Daniel Bub and his colleagues found that one patient with spelling dyslexia did not need to register letters one at a time to encode a word, but was forced to do so when reading.[67] In their experiment, the subject saw either a short word, string of random letters, or pronounceable nonword for 650 milliseconds, and shortly thereafter saw the stimulus paired with a distractor that differed from it by a single letter. The patient was asked to select the original stimulus from the pair, and performed better for words and pronounceable nonwords than for random letter strings. Moreover, the patient was better when the random strings differed in the leftmost letter, and performed worse as the altered letter in the distractor was placed progressively to the right. This finding suggested that he scanned strings of random letters from left to right. In contrast, there was no such serial position effect for the words or pronounceable nonwords, which suggests that he did not scan these stimuli from left to right. Apparently he was able to take in groups of letters at once when viewing these stimuli, which suggests that the perceptual representations of the words were intact. Nevertheless, when reading aloud he required more time for each additional letter in a word.

These findings may suggest that the whole-word representations in the pattern activation subsystem were used to compare patterns but not to identify them. One possible explanation for this finding is that the output from the pattern activation subsystem is more complex when a word is recognized than when a letter is recognized, and damage impaired the ability to match complex patterns to representations in associative memory. If so, then the letter-by-letter reading might be a strategy that the patient developed to circumvent this problem.

Alexia Without Agraphia

Traditionally, clinicians have characterized reading difficulties in terms of clusters of related symptoms (and did not try to dissect these impairments into specific types of the sort we have been discussing thus far). Alexia without agraphia corresponds to problems in reading but not writing (*agraphia*). This syndrome is not caused by cortical damage alone, but—as we shall discuss shortly—involves subcortical damage. The so-called "pure" alexia (alexia without agraphia) has a number of associated symptoms, not all of which need be present.

Copying difficulties.   These patients often have trouble copying, both written material and drawings. This deficit may reflect problems in encoding subtle variations in visual shapes and/or spatial relations among them. That is, the deficit may result from disruption of the preprocessing, pattern activation, spatiotopic mapping, and/or spatial relations encoding subsystems or their interconnections.

Arithmetic.   These patients also have trouble doing written arithmetic. This problem may reflect visual encoding problems—especially if the patient has no trouble doing spoken arithmetic.

Color naming.   They often have trouble naming colors. This deficit suggests either a problem in perception, which can be ruled out by examining the ability to match two colors that are physically present, or a problem in accessing the proper name in associative memory. This problem would result if the input were degraded (due to a damaged preprocessing subsystem or connections from it), so that the recognition threshold could not be reached.

Spelling dyslexia.   Some patients will read each letter aloud as they are reading a word. Possible reasons for such a deficit were noted above.

No visual agnosia.   These patients rarely have visual agnosias.

Intact oral language.   However, in the face of these deficits, the patient's oral language is nearly normal, and his or her writing and oral spelling are virtually unimpaired. Thus, the deficit may reflect faulty encoding of visual forms and spatial relations and/or problems in using such information to converge on the correct representations in associative memory. The deficit probably does not involve associative memory per se, otherwise we would expect similar difficulties during oral spelling.

The apparent anatomical basis of pure alexia is thought to be damage to the left occipital lobe and a *disconnection* between the visual subsystems in the right occipital lobe and the left angular gyrus. *Right homonymous hemianopia* (blindness on the right side), which is usually present in cases of pure alexia, is one hallmark of left-hemisphere damage that has impinged on the visual mechanisms. Norman Geschwind claimed that this damage prevents input from the visual system from reaching associative memory on the left side, which is where word meanings are stored.[68] That is, the information that allows one to understand a word must be in associative memory, and possibly is stored only in the left hemisphere. (The left hemisphere is typically the site of the most language processing, and hence it would not be surprising if representations of word meaning were stored primarily in this hemisphere.) If so, then damaging the left visual cortex and disconnecting the right hemisphere visual cortex from the left hemisphere will prevent the person from reading. Note that visual input from both hemispheres must be blocked, often as a result of a lesion in the corpus callosum (the major pathway connecting the two hemispheres).[69] In our terms, the damage either disrupts the preprocessing or pattern activation subsystems on the left side, or their connections, and disconnects the right-hemisphere preprocessing subsystem from the left-hemisphere pattern activation subsystem, or the right-hemisphere pattern activation subsystem from the left-hemisphere associative memory. Hence, the input does not reach the left-hemisphere associative memory (which presumably implements the word shape/sound associations).

At first blush, however, the fact that these patients rarely have visual agnosia poses a serious challenge to the purported anatomical basis of the disruption. This disconnection seems to imply that object agnosia should go along with pure alexia, but it does not.[70] That is, if visual information is being choked off, why doesn't the patient have associative visual object agnosia (as described in Chapter 3)? Responding to this problem, Geschwind argued that objects have many more associations to a visual input than do words, and hence there are additional possible routes to language areas for object identification.[71] That is, the visual information makes contact with stored information in the right-hemisphere associative memory, and it is this information that crosses the callosum to language areas. Another possibility is that a lesion may be severe enough to disrupt word perception, but may still allow enough information to pass for objects to be identified.[72] Such a lesion would affect the preprocessing subsystems and/or their connections.

Alexia with Agraphia

These syndromes are sometimes called *parietal alexia* because they often arise following damage to this area (specifically, to the left angular gyrus, in right-handed people). Two of these syndromes are of particular interest.

Deep dyslexia. Researchers recently have characterized syndromes from a perspective different from the one just described. These syndromes are not anatomically based or inspired, but rather are defined functionally; they are characterized in terms of the component processes used in normal reading and ways in which they can go awry. So-called *deep dyslexia* is a syndrome that is always accompanied by agraphia, semantic alexia during oral reading, and phonological alexia (they cannot read aloud pronounceable nonwords).[73] Many have focused on the presence of visual and phonological alexias as key components of this syndrome.

Geoffrey Hinton and Timothy Shallice built a network model to mimic how we comprehend the meaning of written words without going through a sounding-out stage.[74] They assumed that the phonological alexia reflects damage to the grapheme-to-phoneme processes, and that the deficits in reading common words reflect partial disruption of the mapping from the visual form of words to sets of "semantic features" (between the pattern activation subsystem and associative memory, using the terminology we developed in earlier chapters). Hinton and Shallice investigated whether damaging their network would produce errors like those observed in these sorts of patients.

The input to the network was a set of three- and four-letter words composed of a restricted set of letters. The meaning of each word was represented by using a series of 68 semantic feature descriptions (such as "for breakfast," "does swim," "made of wood," "transparent," etc.), each of which corresponded to a single output unit. Forty words were used, which were members of five categories (indoor objects, animals, body parts, food, and outdoor objects). The network was trained so that when given a word, a high proportion of the correct semantic features were activated. As usual, there was a layer of hidden units between the input and the output layers, but in this network only 25% of the possible connections between contiguous layers were provided. Two other novel features of this network were a second layer of hidden units (a "clean-up group"), which received input from and provided feedback to the semantic feature units, and direct connections among the semantic feature units themselves. Thus, this network was a variant of the recurrent networks discussed in Chapter 2. Unlike standard feedforward networks, which simply map an input to an output, the activation in this recurrent network caused it to shift through a series of patterns of internal activity over time. The network would start off by producing a series of different, approximately correct outputs, but the patterns of feedback eventually caused it to have a stable pattern of activity that produced a single output. The weights on the connections among the units biased the system so that it eventually activated a particular combination of semantic features when given an input (in technical terms, they caused the network to develop "attractor basins").

After the network was trained to perform the correct input/output mapping reliably (using a variant of the back-propagation learning procedure), it was damaged. "Lesions" were made in a number of different ways: The weights on sets of connections were set to zero (which is equivalent to destroying them, since they no longer influence the units they are connected to), random values were added to some weights (introducing "noise" of the sort that could occur if neurons malfunctioned), or some units were removed from the hidden unit layers.

After suffering each of its "strokes," the network was retested with the words. Not surprisingly, it made more errors than it had while "healthy." Hinton and Shallice classified the errors as "visual," "semantic," "visual and semantic," or "other." One interesting consequence of doing violence to the network was that all types of errors occurred. Furthermore, the precise type of lesion was not critical; all ways of lesioning the network produced all types of errors. Nevertheless, the network was able to perform categorization tasks and discrimination tasks after damage to the semantic units. Thus, the network illustrated that the principle of constraint satisfaction in a damaged system can produce both the selective semantic alexia and visual paralexias that occur in deep dyslexia.

This model did not account for all features of the syndrome, however. The Australian neuropsychologist Max Coltheart suggested earlier that some of the other aspects of the disorder might occur because the patients have left-hemisphere damage, and hence the errors reveal how the right hemisphere may process language.[75] He hypothesized that only words that name visible objects or properties are stored in the right hemisphere, which would help to explain why these patients have particular trouble with abstract words (making derivational errors, such as reading "born" for "birth"). Coltheart argued that the different levels of difficulty of different types of words (function words being most difficult, followed by verbs, and then nouns) may reflect the elimination of the left hemisphere's specific contributions to language.[76]

Taking a different tack, David Plaut and Timothy Shallice showed that an extension of the Hinton and Shallice model may be able to account for the part-of-speech effect in deep dyslexia.[77] They trained the network to encode abstract words (such as "lack" and "past") as well as concrete words (such as "lock" and "post"), and built it so that abstract words had fewer associations to semantic features than concrete words. They found that all types of damage near the input layer resulted in more errors for abstract words than concrete ones, which would explain the finding with patients if different parts of speech have different numbers of associations to semantic features. (Although this seems reasonable, it is difficult to verify because we cannot precisely define or characterize "semantic features" in the brain.) They also found that severe damage near the output layer actually impaired concrete words slightly more than abstract ones—which corresponds to a rare disorder called "concrete word dyslexia."[78] Thus, actually building neural network models holds a clear promise of illuminating the complex interrelations among symptoms that occur following brain damage.

Surface dyslexia. Other patients make great use of a sound translation mechanism, which we have called the letter-to-sound conversion subsystem. They can read words and pronounceable nonwords well as long as the spelling leads to an unambiguous pronunciation. Irregular words typically are mispronounced. A fascinating aspect of this disorder is that the meaning of the word is tied to its pronunciation—if the word is mispronounced, it will be misunderstood. For example, "begin" might be mispronounced as "beggin" and understood as "collecting money."[79] These patients often will spell a word incorrectly, using the phonetic form; for example, "does" might be spelled as "duz."[80] These patients are all poor spellers, both in writing and in speech.

In addition to problems matching visual input to word-representations in associative memory, the poor spelling might suggest that the representations of letters in associative memory are disrupted, but the letter-to-sound conversion subsystem is still intact.

It should be clear that reading is an enormously complex process. It is no surprise that some people have trouble learning to read, and no surprise that many brain-damaged patients have trouble reading after the injury.

In summary, the general picture we have been painting has been elaborated in part by further articulating the nature of associative memory. We infer that associative memory includes representations of the meanings of words (we will discuss such information in the following chapter) and specifications of letters and the way they are ordered to spell the words, which can be matched by the output from the pattern activation and dorsal subsystems. Furthermore, associative memory must contain representations of the sounds of words, which are used by a letter-to-sound conversion subsystem.

In addition, when we considered the effects of brain damage, we emphasized the importance of degraded input and degraded representation. Such damage can result in selective deficits for representations that have few constraints (and hence little redundancy of input). This concept is consistent with properties of neural networks, as we discussed in Chapters 2 and 3. Moreover, we saw that the same network can produce different behaviors when damaged in different ways, which introduces a new level of complexity in interpreting the behavioral deficits. We also have pointed out the possible role of general declines in activation levels following brain damage, which can, for example, prevent sufficient amounts of information from accumulating in associative memory. The material reviewed in this chapter should leave no doubt about the critical role to be played by computer models in cognitive neuroscience; the patterns of deficits are simply too varied and complex to explain using common sense.

The five principles outlined at the conclusion of Chapter 2 were evident in our inferences and discussion. First, the principle of division of labor was apparent when we considered how one can read combinations of letters when they appear in different parts of the visual field; the ventral system registers letters and the dorsal system registers their locations. The locations of individual words also are critical when one is reading sentences; without knowing the relative locations of words, one cannot combine them properly. Second, weak modularity was revealed by the patients who make movements in the air while reading, which depend on information about shape. Presumably the preprocessing subsystem extracts the nonaccidental properties and sends this information to the dorsal system, which then uses this information to guide action. Third, constraint satisfaction is at the heart of the reading process, as revealed by the word superiority effect. Fourth, the very existence of reading is an example of opportunistic processing; reading is parasitic on aspects of the system that evolved for other purposes. In particular, we suspect that operation of the preprocessing subsystem has placed strong constraints on the development of writing, and the "phonological route" is a consequence of having auditory information available for spoken language, which is then recruited for reading. Finally, concurrent processing is necessary for combinations of letters and their positions to arrive at associative memory at the same time. Moreover, we expect much information to be flowing backwards in the visual system during reading, priming expected words and combinations of letters and completing partially encoded information.

We again consistently found that there is more than a single possible cause for each of the behavioral dysfunctions. This observation suggests that the dysfunctions may have been characterized too coarsely. If we know what to look for, we can probably distinguish one cause of a deficit from the alternatives by devising additional tests to administer to a patient. Such diagnoses are critical if we are ever to be able to treat these kinds of deficits.

The discussion so far has focused on perceptual processing. We have now dipped our toes into one of the major types of processes that stand between the input and the output: language. In the next chapter we will consider language more fully, and in the chapter following that we will consider writing and other forms of movement.

6

Language

A normal speaker produces about three words a second. These words are extracted from a stored mental dictionary (a *lexicon*) of somewhere between 20,000 and 50,000 words. On the average, only about one word per million is selected or pronounced incorrectly.[1] Our remarkable ability to produce words is equaled —or surpassed—by our ability to comprehend language; we can comprehend language at about the same rate, if not faster.

Such a performance is especially impressive because both language production and language comprehension require a wide variety of abilities. One must know facts about the grammatical structure of the language (its *syntax*), about the meanings of words and how meanings can be combined (its *semantics*), and about the sound structure of spoken words (its *phonology*). Furthermore, one must be able to integrate language into the nonlinguistic context, understanding the broader implications of what is being said.

Language is central to human life, and hence has rightfully been the focus of intense research interest. A massive literature describes the behavior of the systems that produce, comprehend, and use language. Indeed, there is an entire discipline, linguistics, that is concerned in large part with characterizing the intact, normal language system. In particular, Chomskian linguistics focuses on characterizing an "idealized speaker's" knowledge of a language (an idealized speaker has no memory limitations or the like), and tries to capture this knowledge in terms of a grammar.

In one chapter we cannot begin to describe in detail the known behavioral properties of our language system. However, as we have seen in previous chapters, the most basic behavioral properties are themselves powerful constraints on theorizing. Perhaps the most important property of language is that it is generative: We can produce and understand an infinite number of utterances. Thus, at the heart of language is the ability to combine a finite set of words in new ways. What is surprising is not that we sometimes make language errors, but rather that we make so few of them.

Following the format of previous chapters, we will take key aspects of these abilities one at a time and specify how a set of subsystems in the brain could produce the behavior. We will first consider abilities related to language comprehension, and then those related to language production. Then we will turn to the effects of brain damage on these abilities, using our inferences about the mechanisms that underlie the normal abilities to understand the deficits.

Language Comprehension

The British neurologist John Hughlings Jackson believed that more of the brain was involved in understanding a sentence than in understanding a word, and even more was involved in understanding connected discourse than in understanding a sentence. Jackson's idea was that as material becomes more complex, additional processes are recruited. This idea has withstood the test of time, and in this chapter we will explore how it is being fleshed out by cognitive neuroscientists.

As noted by Jackson, a host of relatively simple abilities are critical for comprehending language. In this section we will consider how one understands individual words spoken by different people, degraded words, combinations of words that form sentences, and the nonliteral implications of sentences, such as metaphors and jokes.

Understanding Words Spoken by Different People

Perhaps our most basic language ability, which appears very early in childhood, is understanding the meanings of individual words. Accounting for this ability is a challenge because the input is not constant; the actual acoustic stimulus that corresponds to a word varies considerably, depending on whether the speaker is a man or woman, adult or child, fast-talking New York salesman, or a relaxed Southerner. Nevertheless, the different physical stimuli striking our ears are all converted to a form that unlocks the same information stored in associative memory.

A spoken word corresponds to a wave in the air, analogous to a wave moving across water. In the simplest case, a sine wave, the amplitude rises and falls smoothly at a regular rate. For a sine wave, the frequency is determined by the distance between the peaks (the closer, the more frequent), which produces the pitch, and the amplitude is the height of the waves, which determines loudness. A sine wave is heard as a pure tone, which is not at all like language. Spoken words are complex waves composed of a mixture of different frequencies and amplitudes. To understand how one can identify a spoken word, we must explain how sets of physically different stimuli are mapped onto the same stored representation. In many ways this ability to map a wide variety of physical stimuli to the same output mirrors our ability to identify objects visually even when they project different shapes (see Chapter 3). Similar computational analyses can be performed for visual object identification and spoken word identification, which will lead us to infer analogous sets of processing subsystems.

As in vision, the brain appears to have relied on the principle of division of labor to solve this complex input/output mapping problem. Rather than attempting to map a wide range of wave-forms to the same word representation in associative memory in one fell swoop, the process is broken down into a set of relatively simple mappings. The same sort of reasoning used in Chapter 3 leads us to the following decomposition.

Auditory buffer. Sounds are represented initially in a cortical structure in the inner part of the superior (upper) temporal lobes. Heschl's gyrus, illustrated in Figures 6.1a and 6.1b (pp. 216–217), is the auditory analog to area V1; indeed, this structure is often called A1 (to indicate that it is the first cortical auditory area). As in vision, the raw auditory input is organized and represented in the auditory buffer prior to high-level processing. Ulrich Neisser posited that such a buffer serves as an "echoic memory"; this memory stores auditory input for very brief periods of time.[2] "Ringing in your ears" may reflect the way representations of loud noises linger in this buffer.

Area A1 has been shown to be *tonotopically* organized; it is spatially arranged so that higher frequency tones activate regions farther along the structure. In the visual buffer, variations in spatial position are used to represent variations in location, whereas in the auditory buffer they are used to represent variations in frequency. In vision, the first cortical areas preserve the organization of the retina; in audition, the first cortical area preserves the organization of the basilar membrane, the auditory analog (in the inner ear) of the retina.

The tonotopic representation of A1 was demonstrated as early as 1944 by Archie Tunturi in Oregon, working with dogs, and also in 1975, by Michael Merzenich and colleagues in San Francisco, working with cats.[3] This organization has also been demonstrated in other animals such as bats, in whom the cortical representation in A1 is extremely large for sounds of 61 kHz—which correspond to the bat's almost pure-tone echolocating sound frequency.[4]

The tonotopic organization of human A1 was revealed by using a type of brain scanning.[5] Researchers asked subjects to listen to a series of tone stimuli of different frequencies while a superconducting quantum interference device (SQUID) was placed on the side of the head. The SQUID detects tiny fluctuations in the magnetic field produced by the brain. When a group of neurons fires, it produces a faint magnetic flux, which is not distorted by passing through bone and does not spread out (unlike electric signals, which both are distorted and travel over the scalp and across the brain). Thus, one can discover which parts of the brain are active during a particular task by observing where magnetic fields arise.

The SQUID was placed in different locations on the head while subjects listened to the tones, and it was found that the locus of activity moved progressively farther along Heschl's gyrus with higher tones; researchers found a linear relationship between the cortical location and the logarithm of the frequency. Similar numbers of neurons apparently are used to process each octave of the acoustic spectrum.

The auditory buffer, as we conceive it, stores relatively unprocessed acoustic cues. These cues organize the amplitudes of different frequencies at different points in time, representing changes in loudness, pitch, pauses, patterns of rising and falling amplitude, and the like. As pointed out by Albert Bregman in his opus *Auditory Scene Analysis,* cues like these are the auditory analogs of edges and regions in early visual processing.[6]

Auditory attention window. More auditory information is represented in the auditory buffer than can be processed in detail. Furthermore, an individual word may be mixed with other words, such as occurs at a cocktail party.[7] Hence, the system needs a mechanism that can select some aspects of the representation in the auditory buffer and pass it on for additional processing. Paralleling the reasoning in Chapter 3, we posit an auditory attention window that selects some material in the auditory buffer. A pattern of activity within the window is sent to areas downstream for more detailed analysis.

Stimulus-based attention shift. We infer that a change in auditory input can draw attention to the stimulus, just as occurs in vision. For example, if the telephone rings while one is talking, one's attention is drawn to the sound. Recall that in vision there are two subcortical pathways from the eyes to the brain, the geniculo-striate and the tecto-pulvinar; the tecto-pulvinar pathway (eye,

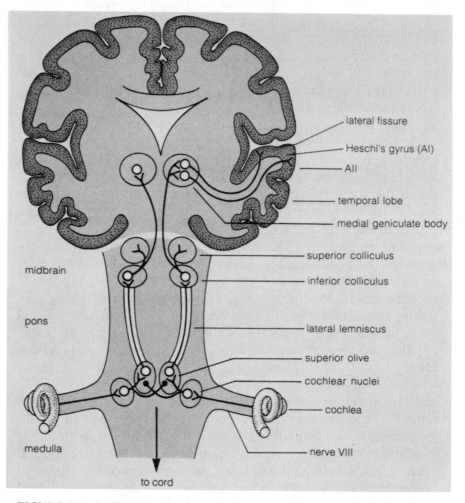

lateral fissure

Heschl's gyrus (AI)

AII

temporal lobe

medial geniculate body

superior colliculus

inferior colliculus

midbrain

pons

lateral lemniscus

superior olive

cochlear nuclei

cochlea

medulla

nerve VIII

to cord

FIGURE 6.1   Auditory areas and connections.   a. Front view. *(From* **Physiological Psychology** *by* **Robert Graham.** *Copyright © 1990 by Wadsworth, Inc. Reprinted by permission of the publisher.)*

superior colliculus, pulvinar, cortex) draws attention to potential regions of interest. The inferior colliculus and superior colliculus (see Figure 6.1a) play a similar role in audition.

The inferior colliculus projects to the deep layers of the superior colliculus, to cells that are aligned with motor output cells in another layer of the superior colliculus, which apparently allows the sensory input to produce a response to that location

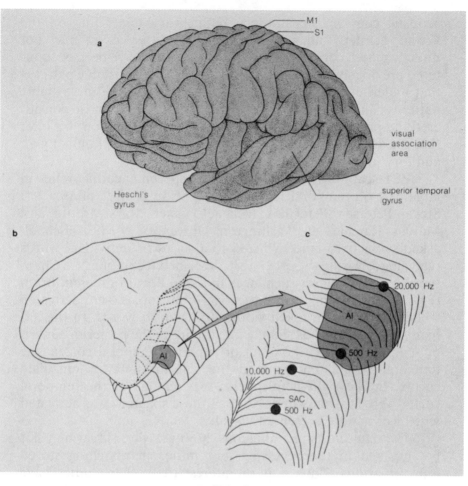

b. Side view

almost reflexively. In addition, the auditory receptive fields of neurons in the superior colliculus shift with changes in eye position, allowing the auditory and visual maps to remain aligned.[8] Hence, one typically pays attention to a single object, registering its appearance and sounds at the same time. It is relatively easy to conceive of a neural network that has this "reflex" property built into it.

Auditory preprocessing subsystem.   We are led to infer an auditory analog to the preprocessing subsystem, which computes auditory nonaccidental properties and distinctive groupings. Because the acoustic cues in the auditory buffer vary depending on the accent, gender, and age of the speaker, they often may not directly match corresponding sets of cues that have been encountered previously. It is much more useful to extract stable patterns that underlie combinations of such cues, and store these stable patterns. Thus, for the same reasons discussed when we considered the preprocessing subsystem in visual perception, we infer that the auditory cues are organized into perceptual units by an auditory preprocessing subsystem.

PET scanning results suggest that speech encoding relies in large part on temporal regions of the brain outside of area A1. Steven Petersen, Peter Fox, Michael Posner, Mark Mintun, and Marcus Raichle, at Washington University Medical School, asked subjects to read or listen to a series of individual words read aloud.[9] Using the previously described technique (see Chapters 3 and 5) to observe changes in blood flow in different brain regions, they found that six critical brain areas were activated when subjects were asked simply to listen to words. In the left hemisphere, there was significant activity in the posterior superior temporal cortex, the anterior superior temporal cortex, the temporal-parietal cortex, and the inferior anterior cingulate cortex. In the right hemisphere, two regions of the temporal cortex were also activated. None of these six areas was activated when words were presented visually.

These findings are ambiguous, however: these areas may not be involved in preprocessing, but rather in matching stored representations. Thus it is of interest that other studies have revealed that most of these areas are active when subjects hear speech and nonspeech auditory stimuli; only temporal-parietal and anterior superior temporal areas were activated by speech but not by nonspeech sounds.[10] The other regions of the temporal lobe appear to be used to encode both sorts of sounds. Indeed, patients with lesions in the temporal lobe often have difficulty encoding both speech and nonspeech sounds.[11]

The idea that speech sounds are registered by a more general preprocessing subsystem is supported by the results of an elegant experiment with monkeys.[12] Henry Heffner and Rickye Heffner first trained monkeys (Japanese macaques) to avoid drinking from a water spout when a certain type of monkey "coo" vocalization could be heard (otherwise a mild electrical shock was delivered through the water). When the monkeys were able to discriminate accurately between different examples of two types of vocalizations, an operation was performed to remove different parts of their brains.

The results showed that removing the left superior temporal gyrus impaired the monkeys' ability to discriminate the vocalizations. In contrast, when the corresponding area of the right hemisphere was removed, the monkeys did not have trouble discriminating among the vocalizations. However, after an average of ten additional training sessions, the monkeys with left-hemisphere lesions regained their ability to discriminate among the sounds. Presumably the memories of the sounds were stored elsewhere, and the lesions only impaired preprocessing temporarily.

This finding is fascinating in light of the results of further experimentation: When a second lesion was made in the intact right hemisphere, none of the monkeys now was able to discriminate among the vocalizations. Nor were they able to regain this ability with practice. A control operation showed that this result was not due to a general cortical trauma; rather, the superior temporal gyrus apparently is critical for the ability to discriminate between "coo" vocalizations. These findings suggest that the preprocessing subsystem is duplicated in each hemisphere, with the left being more efficient initially for mapping "coo" sounds; we will discuss the lateralization of function in Chapter 9.

These results indicate that an analog of the auditory preprocessing subsystem exists in monkeys, which is consistent with our inference that this subsystem is not devoted to language per se.

Tuning via experience. In Chapter 3, we argued that the visual preprocessing subsystem becomes "tuned" by experience to encode useful visual patterns—including the shapes of avian private parts, when determining the sex of day-old chicks. As was true in the visual system, the separate auditory areas are also connected with reciprocal connections: In general, an area that sends information to another also receives information from it.[13] Hence, the reasoning we used to infer that experience tunes the visual preprocessing subsystem also leads us to expect that stimulus properties that distinguish between words will be noted downstream, and feedback will reinforce the encoding of those properties in the auditory preprocessing subsystem. (We will consider a computational mechanism that uses such perceptual learning in Chapter 9.)

This idea allows us to understand why it is so much easier to distinguish the sounds speakers make when they are speaking in a familiar language. As an aside, an intuitive understanding of this effect may be the reason why people tend to talk loudly to someone who does not speak their language very well; the speaker knows that the person will have trouble encoding the sounds, and unconsciously tries to give him or her every opportunity to hear them.

The groundbreaking linguists Roman Jakobson and Morris Halle posited that we learn to encode the distinctions between relevant sounds in a language by organizing the speech stream into discrete *phonemes*.[14] A phoneme is an elementary unit of speech sound, somewhat like a letter in writing. A phoneme is a cue that is stable over the variations in how it is pronounced. For example, the sounds associated with "g" and "d" in the syllables "ga" and "da" are phonemes.

Alvin Liberman and his colleagues showed in the 1950s that humans hear speech sounds as discrete categories.[15] For example, people were asked to discriminate consonants such as "b" and "p" in the sounds "ba" and "pa." Linguists call "b" a *voiced consonant* because when one says "b," the vocal cords start vibrating at about the same time air is released. In contrast, "p" is called a *voiceless consonant* because the vocal cords start vibrating after the air has started being released. The delay before the vocal cords start vibrating is called *voice onset time* or VOT.

Liberman and his colleagues asked subjects to listen to a series of sounds, with a range of VOT values. Subjects were to indicate whether they heard "ba" or "pa." The subjects drew a sharp line, hearing "b" if the VOT was short (less than 25 milliseconds) and "p" when it was longer (greater than 25 milliseconds). This phenomenon is called *categorical perception,* and lies at the heart of what is accomplished by the auditory preprocessing subsystem. These categories are the equivalent of nonaccidental properties in vision; just as the same nonaccidental properties are encoded from many versions of an object, the same categories are extracted when a word is spoken by different people—and these categories help one to understand words spoken under different circumstances.

Peter Eimas and his colleagues have shown that even young infants display categorical perception for individual phonemes.[16] Thus, phonemes per se are not learned via experience. Rather, experience serves to organize these basic building blocks into more complex units, which correspond to the constituent sounds of a particular human language. Depending on which language an infant hears, some phonemes are used and others are not; unused phonemes later become difficult to distinguish.[17]

But why are phonemes themselves heard as categories? Insight into the structure of phonemes has come in part from studies of animals. For example, researchers studied how chinchillas discriminate the consonants "b" and "p" in the sounds "ba" and "pa."[18] A computer was programmed to produce a series of sounds, with VOT values ranging from 0 milliseconds ("ba") to 80 milliseconds ("pa") in 10 milliseconds steps. The experiment began by training the chinchillas to produce a different response for the 0 millisecond and the 80 millisecond VOT values. They were trained to go to one side of the cage after hearing "ba," and to remain drinking at a drinking tube when hearing "pa" (and vice versa for other animals). After this training, the chinchillas heard stimuli with the different VOTs.

This experiment produced two important results. First, the chinchillas—like humans—drew a sharp line, treating sounds on one side of the line as "ba" and on the other as "pa." Second, the boundary between the perception of "ba" and "pa" was virtually identical in chinchillas and in humans.

What do humans and chinchillas have in common that leads to such similar performance? One possible answer is that the phenomenon reflects basic properties of neural processing in the auditory system.[19] The auditory system may require more than 25 milliseconds or so to distinguish the arrival of some components of speech sounds. However, it is clear that we can distinguish clicks 3 milliseconds apart, as will be discussed shortly.

Furthermore, other animals—such as monkeys—have only weak categorical perception,[20] which is odd if this phenomenon reflects basic properties of neurons and the acoustic input per se.

Another possible answer rests on the observation that, for humans, categorical perception depends on specific relations in the input that define speech. Apparently our auditory systems develop certain *insensitivities* (which lead us not to make discriminations; i.e., to group within a category) because this is useful. Some acoustic aspects of speech sounds are not heard as members of categories when presented in isolation, but are perceived categorically when presented separately to the two ears in a way that allows one to "fuse" them into a single sound. The fact that chinchillas display categorical perception is important because it shows that categorical perception did not evolve solely in the service of language; rather, the way we encode acoustic information has apparently been shaped by the important perceptual discriminations we must make. Presumably, chinchillas engage in such processing because it helps them to recognize friend or foe, or otherwise discriminate important environmental sounds—and monkeys have only weak categorical perception because it would not help them to organize important stimuli in their environments. For this account to have force, however, we must discover exactly which relevant environmental stimuli lead to the evolution of categorical perception and which do not, but this research has yet to be reported.

We must say one final thing about the auditory preprocessing subsystem before continuing. In some circumstances the intonation pattern also carries meaningful information, even for single words. This information is carried in large part by changing pitch; for example, notice the difference in pitch when you say the word "rats?" with a rising note at the end of the word and "rats!" Indeed, the correct accentuation of certain syllables is sometimes critical to understand what is meant. Because it is the relative pitch that is important, the overall pitch of one's voice is not relevant to understanding the import of intonation. Thus, we can extract relatively invariant patterns of pitch even when speakers differ markedly in the pitch of their voices or their speech rate.

Although pitch is one of the acoustic cues in the auditory buffer, and is undoubtedly a cue used to interpret the meanings of words, it may be processed by separate mechanisms ("channels") in the auditory preprocessing subsystem, just as color is processed separately from shape in the visual preprocessing subsystem. Although one uses such stimulus properties in combination with other types of information when recognizing the stimulus, one can also attend to these dimensions individually.

Auditory pattern activation. Just as in vision, where there are stored representations of visual properties of objects, there also must be stored representations of speech sounds. Indeed, the mere fact that we can imagine songs (e.g., consider what seems to happen when you decide whether the first three notes of "Three blind mice" ascend or descend the scale), implies that auditory information per se must be stored.

In addition, there are good computational reasons why phonemes organized by the auditory preprocessing subsystem are matched to auditory representations of words, instead of being matched directly to information stored in a more general (not specific to any given sensory modality) associative memory. The reasoning that led us to posit an intermediate visual representation also applies here. Any given word can be spoken in a number of ways (e.g., with different accents), and so corresponds to a set of various combinations of phonemes. Because these sets of phonemes differ along perceptual dimensions, appropriate generalization requires that they be matched to a perceptual representation (recall the discussion on page 80 of Chapter 3). The representations in associative memory are not specific to any given sensory modality, and so there must be an auditory-specific memory. The representations in the auditory pattern activation subsystem serve to group sets of phonemes, which simplifies the later problem of matching the input to information in associative memory.

In the previous chapter we argued that letters and various combinations of letters must be represented in the visual pattern activation subsystem. Similar reasoning applies here. Because language is generative, unfamiliar words can always be produced, which will not correspond to a single stored representation in the auditory pattern activation subsystem. Thus, the input must be matched to smaller units, such as roots and common meaningful component sounds. For example, if one heard "fungible" for the first time, but had heard and stored "funge" and "able" previously, then only two matches would be needed; if one had not encoded "funge," but had encoded "fun" and the sound "guh," then three matches would be required. When hearing an unfamiliar word, usually one can encode two or three units, rather than the individual phonemes themselves.

Following our reasoning in Chapter 3, we conjecture that input is matched to the largest possible units, each of which accounts for "more variance" in the input (in addition, the larger the units that can be matched, the fewer individual matches need to be made). Hence, when one is confronted with a familiar word, it is matched to the corresponding auditory representation of a whole word, not its component sounds.[21]

Furthermore, if one is learning a new language, it may not be possible to match even these intermediate-level units. Indeed, one may not even be able to match to individual phonemes. For example, French includes a slightly different set of phonemes from English. In such cases, the preprocessing subsystem will need to encode new phonemes, using experience-based tuning like that which allows one to easily determine the sex of baby chicks (as was discussed in Chapter 3), which in turn will allow larger units to be organized and subsequently stored.

Such reasoning leads us to infer that the auditory pattern activation subsystem contains auditory representations of words and smaller units, which may correspond to roots, syllables, or even individual phonemes.

Posner, Petersen, Fox, and Raichle reported additional PET findings that suggest that temporal-parietal areas are involved in storing the auditory form of words.[22] In this study, the subjects were asked to judge whether two simultaneously presented written words rhymed. This task involves forming an auditory image of the sounds in sequence, and so we expect auditory memories to be activated. This task elicited activation in an area close to the supramarginal gyrus, which is distinct from but near the temporal areas that were activated when subjects were asked to listen to words and nonwords. Because the preprocessing subsystem (in the temporal areas) must pass information to the pattern activation subsystem, it makes sense that the two subsystems would be implemented in nearby tissue. Consistent with this inference, patients who have lesions in temporal-parietal areas (the angular gyrus and the supramarginal gyrus) often have difficulty recognizing speech sounds (i.e., they have phonological deficits),[23] as we would expect if this region is critically involved in matching input to stored auditory representations.

In short, we are led to infer that the representations of the sounds of individual words depend on temporal-parietal cortex. The various areas involved in encoding words are illustrated in Figure 6.2.

Because the temporal-parietal area is activated by the auditory representations of words, it may seem tempting to conclude that there is a separate auditory pattern activation subsystem for words. We have not done so, for two reasons. First, at the level of

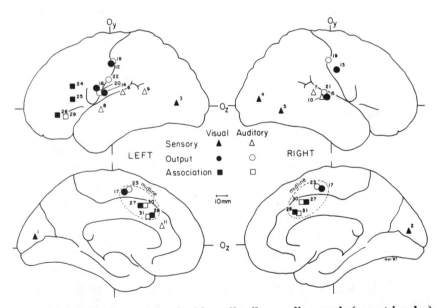

FIGURE 6.2 Brain areas involved in auditorily encoding words (open triangles) and pronouncing words (circles). The top figures are lateral views, and the bottom are medial views of the left and right hemispheres. For explanation of numbers, see Petersen et al., 1988. *(From Petersen et al., 1988. Reprinted by permission from Nature, 331: 585–589, copyright ©1988 Macmillan Magazines Ltd.)*

acoustic signals, the same sorts of input/output mappings seem to be required to recognize speech and other kinds of sounds (e.g., a bird call, a symphony, or a "dry" cough). In all cases, inputs must be matched to stored representations, and the identity of the best-matching representation (and, perhaps, a measure of how well it matches) in turn must be sent downstream. Second, words and nonwords differ in many ways, and it is not clear which factors are responsible for the results. For example, words have distinctive acoustic properties (such as a characteristic ratio of frequencies) and often simply are more familiar than nonspeech sounds. In Chapter 9 we will discuss a mechanism that explains how a network can become specialized for a particular type of material.

To summarize, we claim that the auditory preprocessing subsystem extracts specific cues to encode speech, and the auditory pattern activation subsystem contains representations of words and constituent parts of words. But we assume that there is sufficient continuity between speech and nonspeech sounds for the same subsystems to encode both.

Encoding meaning. Auditory encoding is the prelude to actual comprehension. A number of PET scanning results suggest that the perceptual encoding subsystems are localized differently from a second set of subsystems, which are used to access the meanings of words. For example, as was discussed in Chapter 5, Petersen et al. asked subjects to note—without saying anything —whether visually presented words named dangerous animals.[24] Subjects also passively viewed the word list; the pattern of activation in this baseline task was subtracted from that in the dangerous-animal detection task, which removed activation due to sensory processes. When this was done, Petersen et al. found that the dangerous-animal detection task selectively activated an area located in the left anterior frontal lobe, which suggests that the left frontal lobe plays a critical role in accessing semantic information.

Yet another task studied by the same group focused on semantic processes. Petersen et al. subtracted the activation engendered when subjects spoke words aloud from the activation engendered when they named a use for each object (for example, for "cake" they might have said "eat"). This technique allowed them to examine the brain areas involved in associating a verb to a noun, which is a type of semantic processing. When the words were presented auditorily or visually, the pattern of results led the authors to suggest that the left inferior frontal area is involved in processing semantic associations, whereas the anterior cingulate gyrus is involved in attending to different meanings of a word.

We now must consider how meaning is conferred, and how meaning can be used to help the auditory encoding process itself. Although recognition occurs when an appropriate representation is matched in the auditory pattern activation subsystem, the meaning of the sound is not accessed; the auditory pattern activation subsystem allows one only to recognize that a set of phonemes has been heard before. In Chapters 3, 4, and 5 we drew a set of inferences about the nature of an amodal associative memory structure, which is where the information corresponding to the meaning of a word is stored. We can elaborate on those inferences to understand how meaning is extracted from auditory input.

The process of understanding the meaning of a word begins with accessing the correct representation in associative memory when we hear the word. If the word is a key that unlocks the right stored memories, it is meaningful. If it is something like "peft," it is a key for a lock that does not exist, and it has no meaning.

In the previous chapter we were led to infer that an auditory representation of a word can be activated from memory, otherwise the "sounding-out" process could not take place. If we assume that unimodal memories are stored in the subsystem that encodes them,[25] then the sounding-out process must activate the appropriate representation in the auditory pattern activation subsystem, which in turn produces a representation that is sent to associative memory. This representation is compared to representations associated with words, which must be present in associative memory to match output from the auditory pattern activation subsystem during auditory perception.

In addition, we inferred that the individual letters that comprise a word must be stored with the word in associative memory. The mere fact that we can identify words when they are spelled aloud indicates that the individual letters must be represented in associative memory. The letters could be stored separately, and the sounds used to visualize the letters in sequence (as described in Chapter 4), or sets of sounds could be directly associated with individual letters in the auditory pattern activation subsystem, which in turn address letter representations in associative memory. In the first case, the word would be identified visually, by "seeing" the letters in the mental image; in the second, the sounds of each letter would directly access the word's representation. For example, when asked the meaning of the word "sluice" when touring a mill, it might be so hard to hear that you ask the questioner to spell the word. Upon hearing the letters, you might image them one at a time, and then "recognize" them and match them to the letters of the corresponding word.

Once a word's representation is accessed, it in turn activates a host of associated information. Some of this information corresponds to the meaning of the word. Philosophers distinguish between two aspects of meaning, "reference" and "sense." Reference concerns the connection between a representation and the actual object, property, or event. For example, the meaning of the word "snow" involves a cold white precipitate. Reference is a type of pointing; the word points to the object, property, or event. Sense, on the other hand, concerns the mutual implications of words. If someone understands the meaning of the word "danger," for example, they should act—and avoid acting—accordingly. As a first approximation, reference can be thought of as like the pictures in a dictionary, and sense as like the words in the definitions; the words set up a web of implications. The philosopher Gottlob Frege, who introduced this distinction, noted that the "morning star" and the "evening star" have the same reference—the planet Venus—but have different senses.[26]

For human beings to use both reference and sense, certain kinds of information must be stored in associative memory.[27] The representation of word reference consists of information that is used to identify the object, such as its distinguishing sounds, shape, color, texture, parts and the arrangement of parts. The representation of word sense consists of its abstract properties and the information that is implied by them.

For example, to understand the word "dog," one not only must recall specific information about that thing, such as what it looks like, but also whether the term is singular or plural, can be the subject of a sentence, and so on. Part of the representation of a word's sense must correspond to decomposed morphological forms. These forms allow us to combine roots (e.g., "walk") and suffixes (e.g., "ad") and affixes (e.g., "ed") in appropriate ways to construct inflections and derivations.

Semantic information is distinguished from *syntactic* information. Whereas semantic information specifies meaning, syntactic information specifies the type of the word, such as noun, verb, adjective, and so on; there are many words that belong to each of these syntactic categories. Each word is associated with a given *form class* (i.e., syntactic category), which places strong constraints on how the word can be combined with other words. Syntactic information must also be stored in associative memory. Each representation of a word specifies its form class; for example, "dog," "cat," and "pencil" are nouns, "eat," "run," and "write" are verbs, and so on.

Organization of associative memory. Semantic representations in associative memory are not randomly organized. Rather, it appears that words that share critical aspects of meaning are organized together. This inference helps us to understand why some patients who have had brain damage have trouble using only some types of words. For example, Elizabeth Warrington and Timothy Shallice described patient J.B.R., who was unable to name objects in some semantic categories.[28] In addition, he had the same pattern of deficits when he heard the names and was asked to provide a verbal definition. At first glance, it seemed that J.B.R. could understand words that referred to inanimate objects, but not animate ones. However, J.B.R. had trouble naming musical instruments (which are inanimate), but was relatively good at naming body parts (which are parts of living things). After carefully considering his specific pattern of deficits, Warrington and Shallice suggested that his deficit was in understanding words that name objects that are distinguished primarily by the way they look (e.g., plants, animals); in contrast, he was relatively good at understanding words that name objects that are distinguished primarily by the way we use them (e.g., tools, household objects).

Thus, it is possible that semantic information is organized along these lines, with appearance-based meanings segregated from use-based meanings. We find this idea attractive in part because different anatomical areas and connections may be more involved if stimuli typically evoke an action than if they typically simply activate information in associative memory. If so, then the representations of key aspects of objects may be different, depending on the typical consequences of activating the representation.

Another patient, V.E.R., at first glance seemed to have a similar type of deficit.[29] In this case, however, the deficit probably reflected impaired access mechanisms and not the semantic representations per se. V.E.R. had trouble comprehending the names of inanimate objects, but could comprehend the names of food, flowers, and animals relatively well (note that she presented the opposite pattern of deficits displayed by J.B.R.). But consider two additional observations about the patient's behavior. First, when words were read aloud and she was asked to select the corresponding pictures, V.E.R. improved when she was given more time between the trials. This suggests that the processes that access semantic information on the basis of auditory input may be degraded. Second, V.E.R.'s performance varied considerably from one day to another; words she failed to understand on one day were understood on another and vice versa. This finding also suggests that the patient had a problem in accessing (intact) semantic representations. If the representations were not intact, it is unclear how she could name objects she had previously failed to name. In the previous chapter we discussed possible problems in the constraint satisfaction process that underlies matching in associative memory, which may also account for this sort of deficit.

Left-hemisphere representation. Purely linguistic processing is performed primarily by the left cerebral hemisphere in right-handed people. Experiments with split-brain patients have been performed in which linguistic information is sent exclusively to one cerebral hemisphere. These experiments have demonstrated that the right hemisphere rarely can understand language, and almost never can produce it.[30] Similarly, when stimuli are presented initially to a single hemisphere in normal right-handed people, the right hemisphere has particular trouble using the rules of grammar to understand combinations of words and only the left hemisphere decomposes words into their simpler meaning constituents (e.g., "walking," which can be decomposed into "walk" and "ing").[31] Indeed, Koenig and his colleagues have shown that only the left hemisphere contains distinct representations of roots (e.g., the French stem "agit") and suffixes (e.g., the French suffix "at"). These findings are consistent with a wealth of material that reveals the special role of the left hemisphere (in right-handed people) in language.[32]

Moreover, in PET experiments cortex in the posterior medial left cerebral hemisphere was found to be activated by words and word-like letter strings, but not by strings of arbitrary symbols or strings of random letters.[33] The activated area is relatively close to a structure called the *planum temporale,* which is much larger in the left than in the right hemisphere.[34] These facts are intriguing because language comprehension deficits are traditionally associated with left posterior temporal lesions (in "Wernicke's area"). It is possible that this area is critically involved in storing word meaning per se, and the frontal lobe structures that are activated during semantic tasks implement property lookup subsystems, which direct search through stored information—as we have discussed in previous chapters. In fact, the *arcuate fasciculus* (a fasciculus is a bundle of direct connections) runs from the posterior temporal lobe to parts of the frontal lobe that may implement the property lookup subsystems,[35] which presumably would facilitate such processing.

Recap: Understanding Words Spoken by Different People

In order to understand words spoken by different speakers, acoustic information first is stored briefly in the auditory buffer. Some portion of this information is selected by the auditory attention window, and sent to the auditory preprocessing subsystem. This subsystem organizes the input into perceptual units that are relatively constant over variations in speech rate, gender, and accent. These units are called phonemes. These phonemes, plus information about changes in pitch and pauses, are then sent to the auditory pattern activation subsystem. If a familiar word is heard, the set of phonemes will match a whole word form. Once this perceptual match is made, a code for the word is sent to associative memory and the representation of the meaning of the word is activated. The meaning consists of information about reference and sense.

Understanding Degraded Words

We can understand words even when the speaker is holding a pencil in his or her mouth or background noise obliterates portions of the word. Just as in vision, one needs to comprehend words even when the input is degraded. Our account of this ability parallels our account of the corresponding visual ability. We again infer two mechanisms, both of which rely on constraint satisfaction.

Constraint satisfaction in the auditory pattern activation subsystem. The processing carried out by the auditory pattern activation subsystem also allows us to recognize words even when the input is degraded.[36] The principles that allow it to do so are like some of those that underlie the "word superiority effect" discussed in Chapter 5; the perception of some phonemes in a word helps one to perceive the other phonemes. Recall that if one sees a word with a missing letter, such as "ora-ge," the visible letters often allow one to read the word. In these cases, the visible letters in those positions place very strong constraints on what the word must be. Similarly, the perception of a given phoneme may make it more or less likely that certain other phonemes will immediately follow.

For example, when we hear the phonemes /a/, /k/, /t/, /o/, and /p/, the probability increases that the phoneme /s/ follows. In addition, the perception of initial speech sounds actually depends upon the sound that follows. Indeed, Francis Ganong used a computer to produce speech sounds that varied between "g" and "k."[37] He found that subjects perceived these sounds differently, depending on whether they were followed by "ift" (for "gift") or by "iss" (for *kiss*). Phonemes in particular orders are mutually constraining in the same way that letters are constraining during reading. If one encodes enough such information, even if it is relatively degraded, the pattern activation subsystem will be able to converge on the proper representation of the word.

Top-down processing. In some circumstances, such as talking near a waterfall or in a busy machine shop, the input is so degraded that it will not match a single representation in the auditory pattern activation subsystem, or matches several representations roughly as well, and so additional processing must take place. In these circumstances, one will take a "second hearing" of a word, just as one takes a second look at an object; this will be necessary, however, only if the input is badly degraded. In such cases, the pattern activation subsystem passes a representation of the best-matching word to associative memory, with the information that the match was poor. This word would then be treated as an hypothesis to be tested. The first step in testing the hypothesis is to access descriptions in associative memory of the perceptual properties of the best-matching word. As in vision, the property lookup subsystems access distinctive stored properties, and initiate the following two processes.

First, the categorical property lookup subsystem sends information to the pattern activation subsystem, which primes (i.e., biases) the pattern activation subsystem to encode the expected word. We expect such priming, if carried to an extreme, to produce auditory mental images, which operate analogously to their visual counterparts.

This sort of priming of the auditory pattern activation subsystem may underlie our ability to use context to fill in missing sounds. Indeed, Richard Warren showed that people "restore" missing phonemes if enough context is present. He snipped out part of words on magnetic tape, and replaced them with noise.[38] When people later heard them in the context of a sentence, they reported hearing the missing sound but also heard a "cough" at the same time. Presumably, feedback to the pattern activation subsystem allowed the representation of the sound of the word to be completed, which created this illusion.

Second, the property lookup subsystems direct attention to

search for an expected auditory property. We are led to infer top-down subsystems that adjust the attention window in the auditory buffer. The information received from the categorical property lookup subsystem is used to tune the attention window, seeking distinctive information in the auditory buffer. The auditory buffer stores the perceptual representation for enough time that one can tune the attention window, trying to encode a critical phoneme.[39]

This sort of selection is based on frequency, amplitude, and their time relations. Because this information is so different from the spatial characteristics of visual input, we need not assume that the three subsystems posited by Posner and his colleagues for visual attention (see Chapter 3) are also used here. Recall that Posner and his colleagues inferred subsystems that disengage attention, shift it, and engage it in a new location. These mechanisms (which were hypothesized to be carried out by the parietal lobes, superior colliculus, and thalamus, respectively), are closely tied to spatial properties of the visual buffer, and hence seem unlikely to be shared with audition. However, large portions of the parietal lobes contain cells that respond to visual and auditory input,[40] the superior colliculus contains cells that respond to auditory stimuli and cells that respond to visual stimuli (and, as noted earlier, their receptive fields are typically aligned), and the thalamus contains nuclei for each sensory modality.[41] Although distinct, visual and auditory attentional mechanisms appear to interact closely; indeed, the fact that the parietal lobe has many cells that respond to input in both modalities may suggest that the principle of weak modularity is evident once again.

Such top-down search in audition is apt to be relatively slow, which has at least two implications. First, it is more likely to be effective if the speaker slows down. Thus, it is no surprise that people generally seem to talk more slowly (if they want to be understood, that is!) when in noisy environs. Second, not all words will be encoded clearly, and so context will be especially important when one is trying to understand very degraded speech. In many cases, however, one will fail to encode the words.

If the "second hearing" does in fact encode the expected information, the word is recognized. We assume that information in the auditory pattern activation subsystem is accumulated over time. Unlike visual information, auditory input is defined temporally; it is a sequence of frequencies at different amplitudes that occur at different points in time. Thus, the auditory pattern activation subsystem always accumulates information over time, and the additional information encoded via the "second hearing" merely adds specific additional information to the pot. If the sought sound was in fact present in the auditory buffer, one additional encoding may be enough to implicate a single word representation in the pattern activation subsystem. If unexpected information is found, a different representation may be most activated in this network, which may result either in recognition or another hypothesis to be tested.

A Network Model

James McClelland and Jeffrey Elman built a network model of how individual words are encoded. Their TRACE model incorporated many of the features we have inferred.[42] The model was composed of three layers of units, which represented acoustic features, phonemes, and words; we identify these respective levels with the representations in the auditory buffer, preprocessing subsystem, and in the pattern activation subsystem/associative memory (they incorporated aspects of each representation in their word representations). The key to the model was that each level contained several copies of each detector; that is, there were several copies of each feature detector at the feature level, several copies of each phoneme detector at the phoneme level, and several copies of each word detector at the word level. Each copy was "centered" in a "time window" that was placed over a different time period.

This model was in many ways like McClelland and Rumelhart's model of reading, which was discussed in Chapter 5.[43] Recall that this model of reading duplicated each visual feature in each of four "windows," which focused on different letter positions; similarly, the TRACE model specifies a set of time windows, which are analogous to the spatial windows in the earlier model. In vision, we saw that neurons in the ventral system have large receptive fields, which is not consistent with the McClelland and Rumelhart model. We suspect that the

TRACE model will also fall prey to similar facts about audition, but—as was true in the earlier model—nevertheless embodied important computational principles.

This network model incorporated recurrent connections, as described in Chapter 2, which allowed "activation" to cycle through the network over time. An input into the system produced a pattern of activation over the entire network; this pattern was dynamic, with the processing elements at all levels continuing to interact as time went on. Thus, earlier segments of the input were still being processed while new segments entered the system. This characteristic of the model helped to simulate one important effect of context, namely, that what is entering the system at a given time influences both what was just perceived and what is about to be perceived.

The input into the system consisted of a series of acoustic features, which could activate more than a single phoneme at the second level. For example, a first feature might have activated both /b/ and /p/; a second, the phoneme corresponding to /l/; a third, /uh/; and a fourth, /g/. While the pattern of activation was developing over time, activation filtered up to the word level. In the present example, the word "plug" could be selected only after the /g/ had been activated. Before that, the candidates were "plug," "plus," "blush," and "blood." If "plug" won, activation was then fed back to the phoneme level, which caused /p/ to dominate /b/.[44]

McClelland and Elman showed that their model could account for many of the results of studies of human speech perception.[45] For example, both behavioral studies of humans[46] and experiments with the TRACE model show that embedding a phoneme in a word affects how it is perceived; furthermore, this effect is stronger if the phoneme appears towards the end of the word. This can be explained because when more previous input has been received, more top-down influences affect the encoding of subsequent inputs.

The same mechanism that explains phoneme identification also could explain word identification. At the phoneme level, each unit in a specific time slice shared excitatory connections with all the word units that contain that phoneme in that time slice. When activation flowed through the network, all the consistent word units started competing with each other. The word units that received input from the correct phonemes in the correct sequence were potential winners. But if no perfect match could be found—because of noise or underspecified phonemic units—the word that provided the best fit may have won. Hence, as in humans, the TRACE model had some ability to deal with degraded words.

In addition, the TRACE model could use information about the lexicon to determine where one word ended and another began, without needing direct cues about the boundaries between words. This is important because speech is virtually continuous; there are no consistent pauses between words. Thus, the acoustic stream does not always indicate directly where one word ends and another begins.[47]

In short, the TRACE model illustrated the power of some of the inferences we have drawn. Specifically, it shows how grouping acoustic features into phonemes allows a system to generalize properly, how mutual constraints between phonemes can implicate a specific word, and how top-down processing can enhance performance. It also illustrates the power of the principles of division of labor and constraint satisfaction, and exhibits weak modularity. However, this model is a minimal architecture of a system that can recognize spoken words. As noted above, when a word is understood, a variety of additional information is activated in associative memory. As we shall see in the following section, much of the information in associative memory is used when we comprehend sentences.

Recap: Understanding Degraded Words

Fragments of a word mutually restrict the possible matches to representations in the auditory pattern activation subsystem. If the proper phonemes are encoded, they may be consistent with only one word; the representation of this word is sent to associative memory and the representation of the meaning of the word is activated. We suspect that this sort of processing is adequate most of the time.

However, if the input is so degraded that there is no good match in the pattern activation subsystem, or there are several potential matches, the best-matching word will be sent to associative memory and treated as an hypothesis. The categorical property lookup subsystem then accesses a description of distinctive properties of the sound of the word, which is used to prime the auditory pattern activation subsystem and to guide the auditory attention window to select additional properties represented in the auditory buffer. These properties are then encoded into the preprocessing subsystem and then the pattern activation subsystem, where they are included in the match process; this information is integrated with that extracted from the whole word, and serves to implicate a specific representation. This top-down search process is repeated until a single representation is matched, just as in vision.

Understanding Sentences

The subsystems used to understand single words are also used to understand sentences, but this ability also requires the use of subsystems that compute relations among words. The relations among words are restricted in part by syntactic factors. That is, each word is assigned to a form class (such as noun, verb, adjective, adverb, and article), and the rules of grammar specify the ways in which form classes can be combined to produce sentences. Considering only these form classes, the rules of grammar specify that a sentence must have a noun phrase and a verb phrase, and that a noun phrase must include a noun and may include an adjective or article (but not an adverb); similarly, the verb phrase must include a verb and may contain an adverb. For example, in the sentence "The red car started quickly," the noun phrase is "The red car," which consists of an article, adjective, and noun; the verb phrase is "started quickly," a verb and adverb. One cannot say "The quickly car started red"; the rules of English grammar do not allow an adverb to modify a noun, or an adjective to modify a verb. (Note, however, that languages differ in the degree to which such rules constrain word order.)

We know an impressive number of words, and the rules of syntax help us to organize words in meaningful ways. Indeed, we can combine words into an infinite number of sentences; the rules regulate how members of form classes can be combined, and so they apply to an infinite number of sentences in which different words are plugged into "slots" defined by the form classes.

Sentence structure buffer. When we hear a sentence, we do not identify words individually, tucking away each one's meaning before turning to the next word in the sentence. Rather, we process several words concurrently, and use syntactic and semantic information to construct a structure of the entire sentence. We infer that the emerging syntactic and semantic structure of the sentence is stored temporarily in a *sentence structure buffer,* which is a special short-term memory store that retains information such as the presumed role of each word in the sentence (e.g., subject or object) and the meanings of combinations of words.[48] This inference is grounded on the following reasoning.

First, words are sometimes spoken in a noisy background, and hence we need to use top-down processing to encode them. As noted earlier, context affects our ability to identify words in such circumstances, and the context is determined in part by other words in a sentence. Studies of human speech recognition show that people use both previous *and* succeeding words to help them identify words in sentences. The auditory buffer stores information for only a very brief period; accordingly, some other memory structure is necessary.

McClelland and Elman's model illustrated one mechanism that might account for such prospective and retrospective influences of other words in a sentence. In this model, the dynamic pattern of activation throughout the network allowed succeeding and preceding stimuli to interact. However, such a mechanism cannot account for our ability to build up interpretations of sentences because the "whole is more than the sum of its parts." When one understands a sentence, one must compute a structure that organizes the words; the structure is apart from the words themselves.

This point was effectively argued by the linguist Noam Chomsky, who showed that direct associations between words would not allow one to understand their interrelations.[49] His elegant argument was stated mathematically, but the gist can be conveyed as follows. To understand a sentence such as "The dog that the cat scratched hated milk" one must keep track of the first part, "The dog," understand the embedded part, "the cat scratched," apply this part to the dog, and then apply "hated milk" to the dog. Chomsky proved that a separate syntactic structure is needed to organize such interrelations, where part of the sentence is interrupted by another part and must relate "over" the interruption.

In our terms, the interrelations would get tangled up in associative memory if each word merely were activated, even if there were an indication of its order in the sentence. The McClelland and Elman model works because the task they used is so simple and the network was set up only to perform that task.

In addition, a sentence structure buffer is necessary because some sentences fool us, requiring us to go back and reorganize what we heard before. For example, if someone read aloud the sentence "Through rapid righting with his right hand he was able to right the capsized canoe," you would probably think that the sentence was about "writing" until the very end.[50] If so, then when you heard the end of the sentence, the assumed structure would fall apart, and you would know that something was wrong with your interpretation. Similarly, if you heard "The horses raced past the barn fell," until the last word you would think that the horses were racing past the barn, not that they were being raced. This sort of *garden path* sentence requires one not only to go back and revise the interpretation of the individual words, but also to re-evaluate their syntactic classifications.[51]

This sort of revision-on-the-fly requires a special short-term sentence structure memory buffer, which stores previous words temporarily and allows succeeding words to influence their interpretation. This buffer differs from the auditory buffer in several ways. First, it must store information for many seconds, and hence is quite unlike the "fading echo" held transiently in the auditory buffer. Second, the sentence structure buffer must store not the sound per se, as is represented in the auditory buffer, but rather the syntactic and semantic information activated in associative memory by each word. If need be, associative memory can be entered again to find other words with the same sound (phonological specification), and a new organization evaluated. Third, the auditory buffer may have no fixed limit on the sheer amount of information it can store (albeit for a very brief period of time), whereas the sentence structure buffer appears to have a definite limit. That is, one briefly can hold a single beep or a complex sound produced by an orchestra in the auditory buffer, but if a sentence is too long or complex one cannot hold the underlying structure in the sentence structure buffer—and so it cannot be understood. As will be discussed later, this capacity may be affected by brain damage, which has dire consequences for one's ability to understand speech.

Sentence structure monitoring. The reasoning that led us to infer that the sentence structure is represented in a special buffer also implies that there must be processes that monitor the emerging structure of the sentence. If there is an internal inconsistency, these processes must seek other representations in associative memory that are consistent with the sounds of the words. These representations may correspond to alternative senses of a word (e.g., "book" can be a noun or a verb, meaning something one reads or something done in a police station), or to alternative words that sound alike (i.e., *homophones,* such as "write" and "right").

The sentence structure monitoring subsystem must check three kinds of information. First, it must monitor the *syntactic relations* among the words, checking that the emerging structure is grammatical. If it is not grammatical, representations of other words that sound the same will be activated in associative memory. Representations of these words then will be entered into the positions occupied by the previous interpretation of the sound (in the sentence structure buffer) until a grammatical string is formed.

Second, it must monitor the *semantic relations* among the words. A "colorless green idea" is unacceptable because the meanings of the words clash.[52] That is, even though the words are in the proper form classes to be combined, their meanings are contradictory; green cannot be colorless, and ideas do not literally have color. Note, however, that you may have tried to discover a metaphorical meaning for this phrase. As will be discussed shortly, if a literal meaning cannot be extracted, but the sentence is grammatically correct, then this subsystem will try to derive a metaphorical interpretation.

Third, the sentence structure monitoring subsystem must register the *prosody.* The prosody is the "melody" of the sentence, arising from variations in pitch, loudness, and phoneme duration (the word *prosody* is from the Greek for "song"). The prosody conveys a variety of types of information, including cues regarding the syntactic organization.[53] Moreover, the prosody can convey critical aspects of meaning. For example, depending on the pitch, the sentence "You are coming with us for lunch" may express a statement, a question, or an order—even though the literal meanings of the words and their relations are the same. The prosody also conveys information about the emotions of the speaker, which in turn provide hints as to possible nonliteral, metaphorical interpretations of a sentence.

All three kinds of information are used together to determine the meaning of the sentence. Indeed, errors in any one type of information can be overcome if the others are sufficiently distinctive; for example, we often understand ungrammatical statements. The sentence structure monitoring subsystem computes the meaning implied by these interlocking constraints and passes it to subsystems that use such information to make decisions about where to look, reach, or behave in some other way (as will be discussed in the following chapters).

The sentence structure monitoring subsystem clearly is not passive; as the structure emerges, it biases which words are likely to be activated next. This process is akin to the visual and auditory attention biasing we discussed earlier, but in this case it is word representations in associative memory that are primed by context.

Recap: Understanding Sentences

Understanding sentences begins with the processes used to understand individual words, as described in the first two sections of this chapter. The information in associative memory about the form class of each word, its meaning, and the interpretation of prosody place strong constraints on how words may be combined to form sentences. This information is stored temporarily in a sentence structure buffer, and is monitored by a subsystem that checks for internal consistency among the syntactic, semantic, and prosodic information. When an inconsistency is noted, this sentence structure monitoring subsystem must access associative memory to find an alternative representation that is consistent with the input from the auditory pattern activation subsystem. These processes continue until a structure is built up that is consistent with the various types of constraints. Furthermore, this subsystem notes the emerging structure of the sentence, and actively biases certain representations of words to be more likely to be activated. Because the entire emerging structure is represented, such biasing works in both directions: previous words bias succeeding ones, and vice versa. For example, "garden path" sentences fool the listener by leading to incorrect biases, which later must be overcome by reinterpreting the words in the buffer.

Beyond Literal Interpretation: Understanding Metaphor

Understanding language requires more than extracting the meanings of combinations of words. We also comprehend metaphors and "indirect speech acts." For example, if somebody asks, "Can you close the door?" you probably will not answer "Yes, I can," but instead will close the door. The literal interpretation of the sentence, using the syntactic relations and meanings of individual words, is as a question. But we understand it as a request.

The prosody, the melody of a sentence, often helps us to understand metaphor, humor, and irony. However, prosody is not a necessary or sufficient cue for such nonliteral interpretation. On the one hand, prosody changes when one is in different emotional states, which does not determine how a listener interprets whether one is speaking literally or metaphorically. On the other hand, one can understand written metaphors, humor, and irony—and prosody is not available at all. Furthermore, prosody cannot always provide cues to nonliteral interpretation even during speech. For example, consider the following two sentences: (a) "Don't cry during the night, Max!"; (b) "Don't cry over spilt milk, Max!" Although both spoken sentences may not differ in terms of prosody, it is clear that the first sentence will be taken literally, whereas the second sentence will not.

For many metaphors, the interpretation of the meaning of

the sentence is straightforward: There are a few dozen metaphorical sentences and phrases that have the status of fixed linguistic units. When such a sentence or phrase appears, the metaphorical meaning will be selected by default. Consider what happens when we change just one word in one of the previous sentences: "Don't cry over spilt coffee, Max!" It is less clear whether this sentence should be taken literally. With "milk," the sentence corresponds to a single entry in associative memory, and this entry is interpreted by activating the information associated with it.

We assume that the subsystem that monitors and processes the emerging sentence structure also compares the string to strings stored in associative memory. If a match is found between a sentence and such an entry in associative memory, the interpretation associated directly with the sentence in memory is applied to the input.

In principle, there is no reason why one would attempt to understand the literal meaning of a sentence before a metaphorical one; the monitoring subsystem could check for corresponding stored strings at the same time it is building up the structure of interrelated syntactic, semantic, and prosodic information. Indeed, there is evidence that if the sentence or phrase corresponding to an entire string is stored in associative memory, the metaphorical meaning is derived the same way as a literal one.[54]

Reasoning. In many cases, however, a metaphor, indirect request, or joke is novel (let us hope!); thus, there is no set string of words stored in associative memory. If the input cannot be construed as a set of words that have a coherent literal interpretation, one is forced to consider metaphorical or indirect interpretations.

Fortunately, prosodic or contextual cues often signal that the speaker is being "cute," making a joke or other indirect speech act. Indeed, cruel humor often omits such cues, and so the listener is not immediately aware that the utterance is a joke and considers seriously the meaning of the statement. (This allows the speaker to have it both ways: conveying a nasty message, but clothing it in humor.) When nonliteral meaning is employed and the phrase or sentence is novel, more general reasoning abilities must be brought into play, seeking a way to use some aspects of the meanings of the words to produce a coherent interpretation (we will discuss reasoning in Chapter 9). This is an example of the principle of weak modularity; these reasoning abilities are likely to be used in multiple contexts. Such computation is apt to be very complex, and we can only speculate tentatively about the specific subsystems and their interactions that subserve this ability. There are, however, a few seminal research findings that appear to provide important hints about what these subsystems do; these findings hinge on differences in how the cerebral hemispheres process language.

Although the left cerebral hemisphere is superior to the right in understanding literal meanings, there is good evidence that the right hemisphere has a special role in understanding metaphor, humor, and irony;[55] patients with damage to the right cerebral hemisphere may be insensitive to the metaphorical content of language. For example, when right-hemisphere patients were asked to select a picture that matched the metaphorical sentence "Sometimes you have to give someone a hand," they would choose the drawing of somebody offering someone a hand on a tray.[56] These patients seem to derive only the literal meaning of the sentence, and cannot derive its metaphorical aspect.

Similarly, right-hemisphere patients have particular trouble understanding humor. In one experiment, Hiram Brownell and his colleagues told these patients an incomplete joke and asked them to select the best punch line among a few alternatives.[57] Unlike left-hemisphere damaged patients, those with right-hemisphere damage often selected weird and bizarre endings, rather than humorous ones.[58]

These findings suggest that there are subsystems that abstract elements of the meanings of words and "generate a story" based on these elements. We can say little more than this about such subsystems, and will not attempt to elaborate them further. It seems likely, however, that such subsystems are distinct from those used in semantic and syntactic processing, given that these reasoning processes apparently are more effective in the right hemisphere than the left (for right-handed people), whereas the processes that compute the literal meanings of words and sentences are more effective in the left hemisphere. Such dissociations are one form of evidence for the existence of distinct subsystems.

Recap: Understanding Metaphor

Combinations of words can be understood literally or nonliterally. There are two ways in which nonliteral interpretations can be derived. First, if the sentence or phrase is a conventional expression, it is stored as a string in associative memory. In this case, the string can be identified as a single entry. We assume that the subsystems that monitor the emerging sentence structure also register such a match. Second, in some cases a string is not stored as a single entry in associative memory, but no literal interpretation of the sentence is possible, given the syntactic, semantic, and prosodic constraints within the sentence. In this circumstance, a metaphorical interpretation will be sought. Although a precise account for such processing is by no means clear, we can infer that reasoning is necessary to derive such an interpretation of a set of words. Such reasoning rests in part on prosody and contextual information, and apparently makes use of processes that are more efficient in the right cerebral hemisphere.

Language Production

We now turn to analogous abilities in language production. We begin by considering our ability to speak individual words, and then examine how we speak words in various ways, repeat them, say remembered sentences, and produce novel ones. By considering individual abilities in the context of facts about the brain, we again infer the existence of a set of distinct processing subsystems.

Speaking Individual Words

In this section we consider the most basic ability, simply saying a word. To build on previous chapters, we will assume that one has identified an object visually, and hence the representation of the object has been activated in associative memory. Because the task is to name the object, information associated with that object must be used to produce the appropriate sounds. For the most part, languages pair concepts and sounds arbitrarily; for example, the sound "cat" could have been used to refer to a part of a building, a food, or anything else. Thus, we must store the sound pattern of a word in memory.

Associative memory is implicated because this sound pattern must be paired with numerous other sorts of information; it can be activated by a written word, by a visual image, tactile stimulation, odor, or by input from another part of the brain (which may correspond to "having an idea"). In order to speak, speech output codes—the output equivalent of phonological representations—must be stored in associative memory.

Speech target sounds. Consider the task of building a machine that can pronounce words: The first issue we would need to decide is how to store the necessary information. Depending on how we store the information, different sorts of processing will be required. For example, if we store motion sequences with each word, which move the lips, tongue, and other components of the vocal apparatus, we simply look them up and activate them; alternatively, if we store more abstract specifications of the sounds, we will need to compute the actual movements. Clearly, only after we have some idea of how the information used to produce speech is stored will we be in a good position to infer the kinds of processes that produce the behavior.

Recall that phonemes are somewhat abstract; the same phoneme can be produced by many speakers in many circumstances. Hence, a phoneme cannot be identified with a particular set of frequencies at particular amplitudes. For the same reason, the stored information that allows one to produce phonemes cannot correspond to specific motor movements: One may want to sing a specific phoneme, produce it with one's mouth full, and so on. Furthermore, the precise movements that are needed to produce a sound depend on what sound one has just made; depending on where one's tongue is, how one's lips are held, and so on, one will need to make different motions to produce a subsequent sound.[59]

Hence, the instructions stored in associative memory define a target sound as a set of interlocking constraints of the form "the tongue is touching the teeth, the lips are pursed, the bottom teeth are separated from the top teeth," and so on; specific combinations of these constraints are needed to form the sound. These instructions define relative coordinates (positions) of components of the vocal apparatus, specifying how they are to be situated relative to one another to produce the sound. The coordinates are stored the same way that coordinate spatial relations are stored during visual perception, as was discussed in Chapter 3. In vision, the coordinates specify locations in space; in language, locations relative to other body parts. In both cases, however, the coordinates specify a target location; they do not specify particular motor movements.

There are many different ways in which the target sound can be produced, which are determined by the current position of the lips, tongue, and so forth. This is a classic example of a constraint satisfaction problem; once some movements have been specified, others are required. For example, try talking with your lips pursed, saying the words "My lips are pursed." Now trying talking normally. Did you notice what your tongue was doing in the two cases? To produce the (approximately) correct sound, the tongue had to compensate for the pursed lips.[60] This flexibility is critical because the mouth, tongue, and vocal apparatus will be in different positions depending on what word was just spoken previously.

Hence, we posit that speech sounds are represented in associative memory by a "packet" of separate combinations of coordinates. Each combination specifies a different way in which the vocal apparatus can produce the target sound.

Instructions generation subsystem. Figure 6.3 illustrates the subsystems inferred so far, plus the remaining ones inferred in this chapter. As is illustrated, if the speech output code stored in memory specifies the relative positions of the tongue, teeth, lips, and so forth to produce a target sound, then another subsystem is required to convert this information into specifications for how to move these components of the vocal apparatus. We infer a subsystem that receives speech output codes from the coordinate

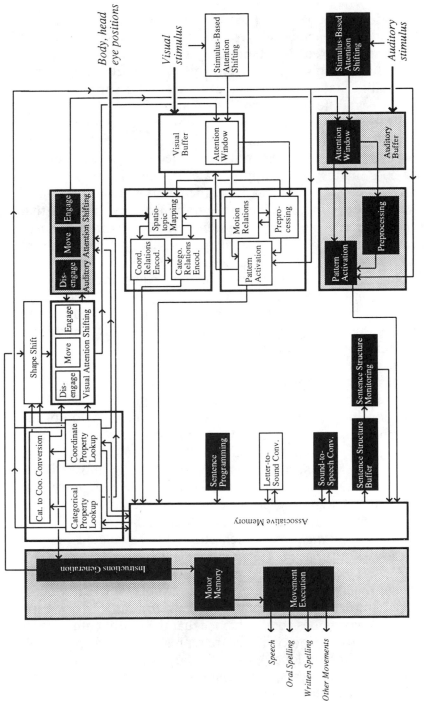

FIGURE 6.3 The subsystems and connections inferred in this chapter, and their relation to those inferred previously

property lookup subsystem (discussed in Chapter 3), and in turn orchestrates the various subsystems that control specific motor output systems. (Recall that the subsystems we infer here typically can be broken down into more finely characterized subsystems; it is possible that different frontal lobe lookup subsystems are used to access different sorts of information, but we have no firm grounds for drawing this inference at this point in time).

The instructions generation subsystem treats the speech output code as a set of constraints, and selects the combination of target coordinates that is appropriate for the current situation. Depending on what was just said, the components of the vocal apparatus will be in a specific configuration. We hypothesize that the instructions generation subsystem selects the combination of coordinates that requires the smallest modification of the present configuration to produce the sound (we will discuss in the following chapter how it receives feedback regarding the present configuration of the lips, tongue, jaw, and so on). Once these coordinates are selected, the instructions generation subsystem computes the proper trajectories for the tongue, jaw, and other components of the vocal apparatus.

The process of generating instructions to move the components of the vocal apparatus clearly involves memory. Indeed, when one learns how to make sounds, one not only learns the target coordinates but also how to shift the configuration of the vocal apparatus to reach those target coordinates. When one later wants to make the sound, this stored information is used to move the muscles. This sort of memory structure is more like a unimodal perceptual memory than like associative memory; it is specialized for a specific purpose and does not relate different sorts of information. Thus, we are led to hypothesize that there is a distinct *motor memory,* which stores pre-calculated instructions that will produce a specific movement when activated.

The left frontal lobe appears to have a special role in implementing the instructions generation subsystem. The neurological literature on the relation between frontal lobe function and language provides good evidence that the motor components of language production typically are represented in the posterior, inferior left frontal lobe.[61] Indeed, damage restricted to this region often produces speech disturbances such as dysarthria (trouble moving the mouth region) or dysprosody (disrupted melody). Doreen Kimura and Neil Watson reported a good example of the specific types of deficits that occur following damage to the left anterior part of the brain.[62] These authors found that such patients have difficulty rapidly repeating a syllable, such as "bababa. . . ." This task requires rapid, efficient articulation, which depends on the intact functioning of the instructions generation processes that "program" sequences of speech-like sounds.

Movement execution subsystem. The principle of division of labor leads us to expect more than a single subsystem to be at work in any complex task. We now infer a *movement execution subsystem* that coordinates the muscles that move the lips, tongue, jaw, and so on. As was true for comprehension, where the auditory buffer, attention window, and preprocessing subsystems operate for all types of sounds, at least some low-level motor subsystems are also used to make other sorts of noises; they are not specialized for language.

The inference that there are two subsystems used to produce speech is supported by results from PET and other brain scanning studies. For example, Petersen, Fox, Posner, Mintun, and Raichle reported PET results that isolated the brain areas used to produce speech.[63] They first observed which areas are activated when subjects received words but did not say them, and then examined which areas are activated when the subjects also pronounced the words. By subtracting the pattern of blood flow evoked when the words were presented but not pronounced from that evoked when they were also pronounced, what was left reflected the processes that underlie speaking the words per se.

The areas illustrated by circles in Figure 6.2 (page 225) were selectively activated by speaking the words. These areas included the mouth region of the primary motor area of the left hemisphere (area M1, which controls fine motor movements), the left buried sylvian cortex, the left premotor cortex (also called area 6), the right primary motor area, the right lateral sylvian cortex, and the supplementary motor area (SMA). When subjects were asked to move their mouths and tongues without speaking, the sylvian cortex was also activated in both hemispheres, which suggests that this area is not specialized for speech output, but rather for motor programming or monitoring of the mouth and tongue in general. It is not clear why the primary motor cortex was not activated by this task.

Petersen et al. also found that the same areas were activated when the words were presented visually or auditorily, which is consistent with the assumption that the subtractive method isolated the areas that contributed to speaking the word. By examining Figure 6.2, it is clear that some output areas activated in this experiment were different from those activated during language comprehension. The results are consistent with the idea that the generate instructions subsystem involves processes implemented in the supplementary motor area and premotor area.

The results from the PET studies imply that some brain areas are used to plan the output (and are active only when one is speaking) and some are used to produce the necessary movements.[64] Considerable details are now known about the neuroanatomical underpinnings of these subsystems.[65] Two distinct circuits, which are organized into loops, are involved in producing the movements critical for verbal output, the first of which actually controls the motor output. This loop includes cortical areas (such as M1 and Broca's area) involved in controlling the mouth, lips, tongue, jaw and vocal apparatus, and various subcortical structures, notably in the basal ganglia (the putamen and parts of the globus pallidus; plus the substantia nigra and the ventral lateral thalamic nucleus). And it appears to us that the second system is "wired" in a way that allows it to direct the movement execution subsystem so that the different organs work in concert to produce a specific sound. This loop runs from the supplementary motor area (SMA) to parts of the basal ganglia (the striatum and the globus pallidus, via the subcallosal fasciculus) and then back from the thalamus (ventrolateral nuclei) to the motor cortex. The organization of these two circuits into loops is critical because it offers tight feedback at all levels of motor control. We will say more about feedback and motor control in general in the following chapter.

Some motor aspects of language also have been studied in primates.[66] Paul MacLean and his collaborators have studied the cerebral structures that control the separation cry in the squirrel monkey. This is a very specific, easily differentiated cry that is produced when an animal is isolated (for even 15 minutes) in a sound-reducing chamber. These researchers tested the animal's ability to produce the separation cry after specific parts of their brains were removed. When the area corresponding to the human supplementary motor cortex was removed, the separation cry completely disappeared. However, nine weeks later, the animals had fully recovered this behavior.

This recovery of function is important in part because it points out possible differences between humans and nonhuman primates. Indeed, Terrence Deacon reviews the literature and concludes that monkey call production is probably controlled almost entirely by subcortical structures; it cannot be eliminated even when large lesions are placed in the motor cortical areas that control the mouth, tongue, and larynx.[67] Deacon suggests that human brain areas that correspond to the ones that produce calls in monkeys may be involved in laughter, shrieking, and other "innate" calls. The only cortical structures that appear to be involved in both primate calls and human speech are SMA and the cingulate gyrus. Lesions to these areas in humans result in hesitations, blockage of speech, or outright mutism—but not speech errors per se; these deficits are consistent with the idea that SMA in part implements the instructions generation subsystem, which produces the sound only when other processes provide it with the speech output codes for the necessary sounds.

Thus, we will not be able to learn very much about speech production by considering animal models. This is not to say, however, that all aspects of human language, with its capacity to combine words in new ways, are evolutionary discontinuities. Deacon, for example, makes a good case that human language recruited brain areas and circuits that were present in animals but being used for different purposes, such as regulating facial gestures, complex motions during eating, and learning sequential contingencies.[68]

Variability in cerebral localization.   Although there is good reason to believe that separate subsystems are used to control muscle movements and to orchestrate sets of muscles, the localization of these subsystems to specific regions of cortex is at issue. Some of the critical findings have been reported by the neurosurgeon George Ojemann and his collaborators.[69] Ojemann and his colleagues used a relatively unusual method to identify the cerebral areas used to produce words. These researchers delivered small electrical shocks to the cortex of patients who were about to have a brain operation. The patients were awake during this procedure, and the surgeons observed the effects of shocking different areas on the patients' ability to say words. Such shocks disrupt the normal functions of neurons, and so this technique can be used to discover which areas are critical for language; once the surgeon has identified the language areas, he or she tries to avoid cutting through them during the operation.

Ojemann, Ojemann, Lettich, and Berger report a study of 117 patients who were being operated on for the treatment of otherwise incurable epilepsy.[70] All of these patients apparently had damaged left hemispheres. They were selected on the basis of the Wada test, in which sodium amytal is injected into one carotid artery (a major vessel leading to one cerebral hemisphere), which momentarily "knocks out" that hemisphere. Thus, if the patient is talking at the time of the injection, language will cease if that hemisphere is critical for speech production.

If a to-be-operated-upon hemisphere was found to control speech production, then more careful testing was needed to discover whether a particular part of the hemisphere was involved in language.[71] Thus, these patients then were tested using the electrical stimulation procedure as they named objects. While a picture was presented, a specific cortical area was stimulated until the next picture appeared. Then, at least one picture was presented without stimulation, and then a new one was presented with stimulation, and so on. Two electrodes were used to provide the shock, which were 5 millimeters apart (allowing the surgeons to stimulate relatively small portions of cortex). Areas where a shock interfered with the naming task were inferred to be involved in language.

One of the most important results of this study was that the anatomical areas that apparently were involved in performing the task were highly localized in a given patient. Locations where a shock resulted in errors were separated by less than 1 centimeter in all directions from locations where shocks did not produce errors. Typically, several different sites produced errors when they were stimulated, and these sites were separated by noncritical regions—which resulted in "mosaics" of critical and noncritical sites.

A second important result was that different brain areas had to be shocked to disrupt naming in different patients. For example, delivering a shock to regions of the frontal lobes disrupted naming in one patient, but a shock to posterior regions did not; for another patient, the opposite pattern of results was found. For some patients, delivering shocks to areas that have long been thought to be critically involved in language production (e.g., Broca's area) did not disrupt naming. However, most of the patients were shown to have at least one critical region of the frontal lobe and one or more critical regions in the temporal-parietal area.

The finding of wide variability in localization of language functions must be taken with a grain of salt, for the following reasons. First, the subjects tested were not normal; they all had prior damage to the left hemisphere and had epilepsy. Thus, although they apparently did not have gross language problems prior to surgery, their brains may not have accomplished language normally.

Second, areas were stimulated near the region of diseased tissue (recall that the purpose was to discover whether the surgeons were about to cut into language areas). Thus, the areas stimulated were close to areas whose precise functions may have been modified or altered over the course of many years of seizures. Again, these patients may have developed a different functional organization from normal people because of their disease.

Third, the nature of the task and the method used do not isolate any specific cognitive operations, and so disruptions in naming could have occurred for different reasons in different patients. The task required visually encoding the picture and performing all of the processes described in Chapter 3, plus accessing the representation of the name and producing the word. Any one or combination of these processes could have been disrupted by the shock. The results show that naming is not possible when certain areas are shocked, but they do not indicate why.

Fourth, shocking a small area does not guarantee that only that area is affected. The affected tissue could transmit unusual signals to various remote areas, which causes them to function improperly. If so, then interpreting the results is not straightforward. Naming could be disrupted because the shock indirectly affects a remote area that is critical for any of the various types of processing that are necessary to perform the task.

Fifth, shocking an area may not only prevent that area from functioning normally, but also may release other areas from inhibition—which may allow the brain to perform a task in a novel way. For example, the left hemisphere may often inhibit corresponding motor control areas in the right hemisphere. Indeed, there are several descriptions of patients who stuttered, and who subsequently stopped stuttering after they had tumors removed from their right frontal lobes.[72] This result makes sense if prior to surgery both hemispheres tried to program speech, but fell out of synchronization, and the surgery disrupted the right hemisphere's ability to control speech. For normal people, cross-hemisphere inhibition may prevent such stuttering in the first place, but shocking the left hemisphere may eliminate such inhibition—allowing the right hemisphere to fill in. Thus, there is no simple relation between the normal function of a region and the effects of shocking it on one's behavior.

Even with all of these caveats, we cannot dismiss Ojemann and his colleagues' results out of hand. Indeed, the idea that language processes are not well localized is consistent with other findings. For example, the neurologist/linguist David Caplan reports that lesions in the same region are found in patients who have different behavioral deficits, and the same deficits can be present in patients who have lesions in different places.[73] However, others find that although a significant number of patients display such variability, the vast majority display production problems following frontal damage (in the vicinity of Broca's area) and comprehension damage following posterior damage (in the vicinity of Wernicke's area).[74]

The residual variability in lesion/deficit relations in language could reflect two kinds of factors. First, it is possible that the patients who do not fit the typical pattern have an undetected functional impairment in the appropriate area, which could be revealed by a PET scan. If a lesion cuts off input from a part of the brain, it may be dysfunctional even if the lesion does not directly affect it.[75]

Second, anatomical connections may place only weak constraints on the localization of many language processes. The connections from the sensory organs and to the muscles are highly localized, which places strong constraints on where in the brain perceptual and motor processes may occur. However, these anatomical connections place much weaker constraints on the localization of more "central" processes. Thus, a large region of tissue may be available to carry out language processes. But even if this is true, not any part of the brain can subserve language; the tissue still must receive the relevant input and be able to project output to the motor systems. And in fact, Caplan reports that lesions that disrupt language are always near the sylvian fissure, and these regions have the necessary connections. Unlike vision, language may not depend on specific structures that are pre-wired for just that purpose; rather, when people learn language, it is possible that there is considerable latitude regarding which brain areas are used.[76]

Recap: Speaking Individual Words

Producing a word begins with the activation of its representation in associative memory. The representation includes syntactic, semantic, prosodic, and phonemic information (in addition to a host of other sorts of information, including visual). The speech-output code is stored as a set of coordinates that specify how the various parts of the vocal apparatus should be positioned relative to each other to produce the appropriate sound. These coordinates are stored as a "packet," which indicates sets of alternative combinations of coordinates that can produce the sound—not the particular movements that need to be made in a given context to produce the sound. Depending on what word was just said, different movements will be used to say a subsequent word. The speech output code ("packet") associated with an activated word is sent to the instructions generation subsystem. This subsystem in turn selects the coordinates that will produce the sound with the smallest modification of the present vocal config-uration, and generates instructions for the movement execu-tion subsystem. This process involves accessing motor memory, where programs are stored for shifting combinations of mus-cles in specific ways. The movement execution subsystem uses these programs to control the individual muscles, causing the mouth, tongue, and vocal apparatus to work in concert to produce the appropriate sound.

Pronouncing Words in Different Ways

We can speak a word with a high voice or low one, and we can mimic accents or use clipped or drawled speech. We can (if need be) even talk with our mouth full of food. The subsystems we have inferred allow us to understand how one can pronounce words in different ways and in a wide variety of circumstances. These abilities arise for two reasons. First, speech output codes correspond to a packet of target coordinates. When a new accent is learned, new sets of target coordinates must be encoded; these specifications will produce different pitch contours and timing sequences to produce different accents. Second, the target coordinates define the relative positions of parts of the vocal apparatus, which can be reached in a number of different ways; if our mouths are full, we are forced to compensate by adjusting the tongue and vocal apparatus to produce the correct sound. We may speak in a novel way by imposing constraints on how movements of the vocal apparatus can be made (e.g., by pursing our lips); these constraints are analogous to having something in one's mouth, except that they are imposed from memory rather than by an object.[77]

Speaking with a pencil in our mouth or with pursed lips is different from the way we usually talk. We have spoken words so often that it is likely that the typical movement sequences are stored directly in motor memory. Usually, a "canned" motor program reconfigures an initial set of relative coordinates to a target set. However, if one is holding a pencil in one's mouth or the like, the "canned" motor programs may not be satisfactory, and the instructions generation subsystem must compute a novel set of movements to reach the target coordinates. As we will discuss in the next chapter, this computation also involves accessing stored information in motor memory, but this information specifies smaller segments of the trajectories that must be composed in new ways to fit the present circumstances.

Thus, the instructions generation subsystem often may produce instructions by selecting a combination of coordinates and then looking up stored commands that specify how to move the components of the vocal apparatus from their present positions to the target positions. In contrast, if we are talking around a pencil or the like, and we don't do this very often, it is unlikely that a canned program exists to produce the sound. In this case, a set of novel trajectories must be computed. In the following chapter we will consider in detail how such trajectories are generated.

Recap: Pronouncing Words in Different Ways

We account for the ability to produce words in different ways in exactly the same way we accounted for the ability to produce a word in a standard way. The stored target coordinates specify a sound, not particular movements. These coordinates are sent to the instructions generation subsystem, along with constraints based on the present position of the mouth, tongue, and so forth. Provided that one has the requisite information in associative memory (i.e., knows how to make the sound), these positions can be specified to produce different accents and so on. Furthermore, in the event that the vocal apparatus is in an unusual configuration, a novel set of trajectories can be computed to reach a target configuration.

Repeating Words

We also can repeat words we have just heard. At first glance, this ability may seem trivial. But consider the simple fact that one can repeat words in a familiar language much more easily than one can repeat words in an unfamiliar foreign tongue. Indeed, as noted earlier, it seems that one can distinguish familiar sounds more easily, which suggests that the auditory preprocessing subsystem becomes tuned with experience, allowing it to encode easily important distinctions in a language.

If familiar words are spoken, it is easy to explain how we can repeat them: A word is encoded, as discussed earlier, and the appropriate information is activated in associative memory. Once this set of information is activated, the associated speech output code is accessed and the word is produced just as discussed earlier.

In addition, we must note that Petersen et al. interpret their PET scanning results as suggesting that there is a direct route from phonological coding (in left temporal-parietal cortex) to articulatory coding (in the SMA, sylvian cortex, and the left premotor area).[78] If so, then one could repeat a word without having to go through associative memory. However, it is unclear computationally how a phonological representation could produce a movement without some intermediate translation to a motor code. In Chapter 8 we will discuss a direct stimulus-response connection process, which might be relevant here. But this process involves the basal ganglia—which apparently were not selectively activated in the PET studies. Thus, we will not consider such a direct route here.

But what about when unfamiliar words are heard and repeated? This is a much more difficult task, which increases in difficulty for increasingly unfamiliar words: Repeating "falciform" (which means curved) is much easier for a unilingual English speaker than repeating the unfamiliar French word, "effleurage." Part of an account for this observation was already discussed, when we considered the auditory preprocessing subsystem. As noted earlier, we learn to encode useful distinctions, and so can easily register the sounds of a familiar language. But this may not be the entire account. In addition, familiar words have representations in the pattern activation subsystem, and so can be encoded auditorily as a single unit; moreover, they also correspond to a single entry in associative memory, which is paired with a speech output code. In contrast, novel words do not correspond to a single auditory representation, and so must be encoded as two or more word-sounds; furthermore, when this information reaches associative memory, it does not evoke a single speech output code. Instead, for unfamiliar words this code must be computed for the encoded sound sequence.

Speech output code formulation.   Encoding the sounds of unfamiliar words is the first step towards repeating them; to understand how they are subsequently pronounced, we must draw further inferences. When discussing reading, we considered the ability to sound out unfamiliar words. We inferred that two possible mechanisms could be at work. One relies on a network that maps visual codes of letters to speech output codes; the other operates analogically, seeking similar words and modifying their output codes appropriately. Parallel alternatives are available for producing a speech output code when pronouncing a novel word. Because this computation (input/output mapping) is qualitatively distinct from those accomplished by the subsystems inferred so far, we hypothesize that another subsystem is used here. This *sound-to-speech conversion* subsystem could operate in two ways. On the one hand, it could include an associative network that accepts the specification of a sound (i.e., the output from the auditory pattern activation subsystem) as input, and produces speech output codes as output. For familiar words, this output would in turn be stored with the word in associative memory so that one could subsequently pronounce it by rote. Alternatively, the output codes associated with familiar words that sound like each of the encoded sounds could be accessed, and then modified appropriately to produce an appropriate code for the novel word.

It seems clear that we need something like the first sort of mechanism, if only because when we first learn to talk there are no previously encoded speech output codes to use as a basis for generalization. Rather, one hears a target sound, attempts to reproduce it, and then matches the sound produced to the target. If the pronounced sound did not match the target, the stored motor code is modified accordingly. In the following chapter we will discuss mechanisms that use feedback to correct movements. These observations do not rule out the second mechanism, however, and it is possible that both are at work.

Recap: Repeating Words

If words are familiar, they are encoded into associative memory in the same way that they are encoded during comprehension, and the stored speech output code is activated and used in the same way as in word production. If a word is not familiar, its sounds may be difficult to encode in the auditory preprocessing subsystem, and will not correspond to a single representation in the auditory pattern activation subsystem. Thus, several sound-units will be encoded into associative memory. A sound-to-speech conversion subsystem would then be required to generate a speech output code for the sounds, which in turn would be used to produce the word. This subsystem maps a sound to a speech output code, and is analogous to the letter-to-sound conversion subsystem discussed in Chapter 5.

Producing Remembered Sentences

We need to make a distinction between the processes that produce a sentence itself and those that "think up" a sentence. In this section, we consider the easier problem: How we speak a sentence after it has been conceived. The best example of such a sentence is one that was previously memorized. Hence, in this section we examine how one speaks the Pledge of Allegiance or similarly rote-memorized sentences.

No additional subsystems are needed to understand how we speak the words of a sentence. However, before we can begin to understand how such sounds are produced, we must consider a key fact about sentence production. The code used to speak much, if not most, of a sentence is "programmed" before we start to say it. This inference follows from the existence of common speech errors, such as *Spoonerisms*. William A. Spooner was an English clergyman and educator. Dr. Spooner was famous for making a particular kind of error, which today bears his name. A Spoonerism is a transposition of the initial sounds of two or more words (e.g., "tons of soil" for "sons of toil"). One of us once was asked whether his apartment was satisfactory, and answered "It seats my nudes" when intending to say "It suits my needs." The fact that "seats" picked up the sound intended for "needs" indicates that the later word was activated before that part of the sentence began to be produced.[79]

The inference that large sequences of sounds are "set up" before one begins to talk has received support of a very different kind. In these experiments, subjects are given a list of words and asked to repeat it as soon as they see a signal. The time between the presentation of the signal and the first response is measured, and it has been found that people require more time to begin talking if the list is longer. This finding is just as expected if the entire list is programmed before one actually begins to speak. Similarly, more time is required to begin saying longer sentences.[80] The fact that this result reflects a set-up stage, and not something having to do with talking per se, was demonstrated by showing the same effects in typing: More time is required to begin typing if a longer message must be typed.

Karl Lashley suggested one reason why large portions of a sentence may be programmed before one begins to speak.[81] If we waited to say each word before beginning to program the next, our output rate would be very much slower than what is possible if the sentence is programmed and then spoken without monitoring each word.

We earlier posited an instructions generation subsystem that converts speech output codes into a set of motor instructions. The subsystem that programs the speech output for a single word must have the capacity to program an entire sentence; indeed, some single words may be more complex (e.g., "antidisestablishmentarianism") than some sentences (e.g., "It is."). However, we must augment our inferences about the instructions generation subsystem in two ways. First, it must be capable of accepting an ordered set of speech codes, each corresponding to a different word. These codes must be stored in associative memory along with the words of the remembered sentence; the stored representation of the sentence must specify an ordered sequence of speech codes that is sent to the instructions generation subsystem. This process need not be perfect, and at least some speech errors may arise here. Second, it must generate instructions based on properties that span individual words. That is, when programming the movement execution subsystem, the instructions generation subsystem specifies the entire sequence of motor movements; it does not wait to say one word before the next is initiated. The constraint-satisfaction processes used here also could go awry, producing speech errors such as Spoonerisms.

A network model. Ways in which these two processes might produce speech errors are nicely illustrated by a model developed by Gary Dell.[82] This model of speech production accounts for several types of "slips of the tongue" speech errors. For example, the model can explain why people may say "I'll shut the darn bore" instead of "I'll shut the barn door." Such an error occurs because phonological units—here single phonemes—are exchanged.

Dell's model consisted of two networks; although Dell did not conceive of the networks in this way, they corresponded to different aspects of the associative memory we have inferred. The interesting properties of the model arose from how information in associative memory was activated and how patterns of activation interacted over the time course of producing a word. When a unit was activated, it excited or inhibited units to which it was connected, depending on the type of connection; the more the unit was activated, the more it influenced the other units. The *lexical network* contained only words and phonemes, and this network produced a phoneme string (which would be used to provide input to the instructions generation subsystem). Word units were linked to phoneme units by excitatory connections that ran both ways. The other, *word-shape network* specified *frames,* which are abstract definitions of a word that included the number of syllables, the internal structure (e.g., consonant-vowel; consonant-vowel-consonant), and a relatively abstract representation of the sound of the word; each word unit in the lexical network was connected to a frame in the word-shape network.

For example, consider how the model operated when it generated the expression "deal back."[83] Because the word "deal" was the first to be phonologically coded, a certain amount of activation was added to the corresponding word unit in the word-shape network. Because "back" was the second word, half of this amount was added to its word unit. Then, activation spread through the network, with units sending activation to every unit to which they were connected. This process caused the activated words (e.g., "deal" and "back") to activate the corresponding phonemes in the lexical network and thereby to be pronounced. Following this, a feedback mechanism turned off (i.e., set to zero) the activation at the phoneme level. This inhibition mechanism prevented the same phonemes from being selected again and again; in other words, it prevented the system from "stuttering."

The model's performance was improved by including sets of "built-in" features. For example, one feature increased the activation of all the words that were in the same phrase as a current word. This feature rested on the empirical finding that a current word is produced at the same time that the speaker is anticipating upcoming words. In addition, the model was sensitive to word frequency because another built-in feature produced higher resting activation levels for high-frequency words. Therefore, a phoneme from a high-frequency word was more likely to interfere with a phoneme from the current word than was a phoneme from a low-frequency word. The model also could vary the rate that activation decayed and the speech rate.

Phonological errors occurred when an incorrect phoneme unit was more strongly activated than the correct phoneme unit, which caused the wrong one to produce the output. In the model, as in humans, three types of errors occurred: anticipation, perseveration, and exchange. Anticipation errors occurred when upcoming phonemes were more activated than the appropriate ones at that point in time. For example, if /b/ was more activated than /d/ when "deal" was being pronounced, the model would produce the word "beal." In contrast, perseveration errors occurred if after producing "deal" the unit /d/ was more activated than /b/ when "back" was being produced, which caused the network to generate "dack." Finally, exchange errors were a combination of anticipation and perseveration errors. For example, an anticipation error could produce "beal back" instead of "deal back." When this occurred, the phoneme /b/ was immediately inhibited after it was activated in "beal." This could then cause the correct, but nonselected phoneme /d/ (for "deal") to be more activated than /b/, which has just been inhibited. Hence, /d/ then may have intruded when the second word was pronounced, and "dack" would be produced instead of "back." Hence, "beal dack" would be produced instead of "deal back."

In humans, these errors are more frequent with faster speech rates. The model behaved the same way when the number of time steps between syllables was set to mimic a high speech rate. This result occurred because, on the one hand, with less time between syllables there was more residual activation from previous phonemes, and, on the other hand, the effects of inhibition could persist longer. Consequently, errors were more likely to occur when many words were "said" very quickly.

Dell's model illustrated how previous and upcoming words and phonemes can produce interference with words as they are being pronounced, which may result in speech errors. However, there is no evidence that the neural networks in the brain actually accord with the model. It will be of interest to discover whether greater use of information about how the brain produces speech can further enhance such theorizing.

Cerebral localization. There is evidence that subsystems in the frontal lobe are involved in orchestrating the production of sentences. In one study, researchers measured regional cerebral blood flow while subjects performed a variety of tasks, some of which engaged the mechanisms underlying speech production.[84] Although the subjects were tested in six conditions, only two are relevant here. In one condition, the subjects produced random nonsense syllables; in another condition, they retold aloud magazine stories that they read 10 minutes before the test. The second condition is interesting because the subjects did not have to generate the sentences from scratch, but could rely in large part on information stored in associative memory. Thus, the results may reflect processes used to say sentences per se.

The pattern of blood flow evoked in the language condition was subtracted from that evoked in the syllable condition. Relative increases in blood flow were observed in the left frontal region (near Broca's area) and in the left anterior thalamic/pallidal region. In addition, a bilateral increase in blood flow was observed in the head of the caudate nucleus (of the basal ganglia) and in posterior ("retrorolandic") regions of the brain, both of which are known to be involved in motor control (see Chapter 7).

It is difficult to interpret these results for a number of reasons. For one, the subjects probably did not remember the actual words of the sentences in the language condition, but rather stored the "gist." The gist might be stored using representations that specify meanings of words, not the words themselves. This is called a *propositional representation.* These representations often are consistent with more than one set of words; for example, the same sentence said in English and French would express the same propositional content. Hence, when such representations are recalled and expressed, the subjects would paraphrase the original material. Thus, the results presumably also reflect the operation of the processes that select words to express the concepts (which are discussed in the following section). Furthermore, the syllable condition involved unspecified processes to generate meaningless syllables; subjects could have thought of words and edited them mentally (e.g., deleting or adding syllables), which would rely on a complex mix of processes. Presumably, however, low-level movement execution processes are shared in the two tasks, and so the difference in blood flow may reflect processing in associative memory and the generating instructions subsystem.

Hence it may be of interest that the frontal lobe and other areas known to be critical in orchestrating complex sequences of motor movements were selectively activated in the recall task.[85] There was no increase of activation in the left temporal area, however. Based on the locations of lesions that produce errors in language comprehension, Norman Geschwind and others inferred that the superior posterior temporal lobe is critical in storing word meanings.[86] This result may suggest either that recalling sentences from memory does not involve the type of semantic information processing used in comprehension, or that processes that access semantic information do not operate in the temporal lobe, but rather in the frontal lobes.[87]

Recap: Speaking Remembered Sentences

Sentences are produced by the same mechanisms used to produce single words. In both cases, the instructions generation subsystem programs a sequence of instructions, which then are executed by the movement execution subsystem. We need only to assume that the instructions generation subsystem can accept speech codes from a series of words and can set up motor instructions for the entire set. Speech errors may creep in either when the words are activated improperly in associative memory or when the output instructions are generated incorrectly— reflecting a failure of the constraint-satisfaction processes that produce the output.

Speaking Novel Sentences

As noted earlier, perhaps the most striking fact about language is that it is generative: We can produce an infinite number of different sentences by combining words in novel ways.[88] In order to produce a sentence, something must determine which words are to be activated in associative memory. If the sentence was previously memorized, the words and their order are stored in associative memory. But we rarely simply repeat verbatim what we have heard before.

Because sentences involve combinations of representations, two additional problems must be solved. First, some process must activate the appropriate representations in associative memory. Second, the speech codes associated with the words must be ordered appropriately.

Sentence programming subsystem. We assume that some undoubtedly very complex subsystem initiates saying a sentence. This *sentence programming subsystem* must activate the representations of words and their associated clusters of information ("concepts"). Furthermore, it must indicate the subject, verb, and object (if any) of the sentence, as well as the *topic* (old information to which it relates) and *focus* (new information introduced in the sentence) and other linguistic features. In short, this subsystem must specify what one is talking about.

It is not necessary, however, to assume that this subsystem also orders the speech codes and then passes the ordered set to the instructions generation subsystem. Rather, information associated with the representations in associative memory may almost force a specific order "automatically," using a process of constraint satisfaction. That is, once the appropriate information is activated in associative memory, words must be arranged in accordance with two types of rules. First, the meanings of words must be congruent. For example, we would not say "The apple took a bite out of Harry." Second, the words must be combined to respect the rules of grammar. We earlier noted that rules need not actually be stored explicitly, like recipes in a cookbook. Rather, individual words could have stored with them information that restricts the types of words with which they can be combined and how they can be used in a sentence.[89] For example, "cat" could have stored with it information like "animate, count noun (as opposed to mass noun), regular plural," and various restrictions (e.g., can be the subject of sentences with specific types of verbs, etc.) would in turn be represented with each of these delimiters elsewhere in associative memory (so they can be shared by many words). Information associated with verbs may provide particularly strong constraints on how words can be combined to form sentences.[90] In Chapter 9 we sketch out a way of representing "plans" that may allow such rules to be represented by combinations of networks that function in the way described in Chapter 2.

Both syntactic and semantic information force an ordering of words in sentences via a process of constraint satisfaction; each word specifies a set of constraints, and only certain combinations of words are therefore possible. Consider a metaphor of such constraint satisfaction that was developed by Jerome Feldman.[91] Feldman notes how the Necker cube in Figure 6.4 is seen either as facing up or as facing down at any particular point in time, but never as both. His explanation is that each

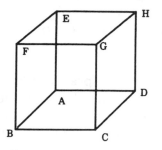

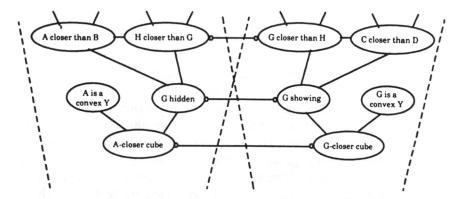

FIGURE 6.4 A Necker cube and Feldman's model of Necker cube reversal. *(From Feldman, 1985, by permission of the publisher.)*

interpretation is represented by a separate configuration of states, and these states are interrelated. Once one interprets the vertex labeled "A" as being part of the front face, the interpretation of every other vertex is determined if the various constraints are to be satisfied. For example, if "A" is part of the front face, then so must "D," and "B" cannot be part of the front face.

Similarly, as soon as linguistic characteristics such as the subject, verb, object, topic, and focus of a sentence are selected, only a few orderings of the speech codes may be possible given the various constraints associated with the concepts. But even so, more than one way of ordering the words usually is possible; for example, the sentence can incorporate active versus passive constructions. The precise order that emerges depends on the input provided by the sentence programming subsystem, which must also specify any specific properties of the sentence structure.

Finally, it is worth noting that the problem of selecting a set of words to express a thought is greatly exacerbated for some types of metaphor. If the metaphor is "pre-stored," speaking such a metaphor is exactly like speaking a memorized sentence, but much different processes must be used when one generates a novel metaphor to express an idea. This is likely to be a very complex activity, which may involve visualizing a scene and internally describing it in addition to selecting specific aspects of meaning to form sequences of words. We will not attempt to speculate about how such processes operate in concert.

Recap: Producing Novel Sentences

The sentence programming subsystem activates the representations of words in associative memory. It also specifies linguistic characteristics of the sentence, such as its subject, verb, object, topic, and focus. Given a set of inputs, the semantic and syntactic information associated with the representations of words in associative memory greatly constrain how the corresponding words can be ordered. Once the entire pattern of activation has been established, the speech output codes are passed as a unit to the instructions generation subsystem, which then sends input to the movement execution subsystem, which actually produces motor output.

Understanding the Effects of Brain Damage

Our inferences about comprehension and production suggest many possible reasons why patients with brain damage often have difficulty using language. An impairment or a loss of language abilities following brain damage is called *aphasia.*

Aphasia has been intensively studied over the past one hundred years, partly because language is widely appreciated as a uniquely human ability and partly because the deficits are dramatic and inescapable. These studies often have been extremely controversial, for a number reasons. First, researchers have tried to define taxonomies of language disorders, which have rested on coarse and broad descriptions. The problem is that until a phenomenon is relatively well understood, it is unclear what aspects of it should be used to define the categories. In the early stages of research in an area, taxonomies are likely to cut across distinctions that later theories deem important. Second, many conclusions about aphasia are based on results of group studies. The problem here is that each patient probably has a different lesion and different accompanying set of deficits. Averaging over these data may miss the mark altogether.[92] Third, the lesion sites rarely have been diagnosed precisely. In the early days, only X-rays were available, and then CT (also known as CAT—computerized axial tomography) scans produced X-ray images in three dimensions. These images were relative crude. Only recently has MRI (magnetic resonance imaging), which produces sharp images of damaged tissue, become widely available. But even MRI is not ideal: PET studies have revealed that lesions often cause disruption of function in tissue that appears structurally intact in an MRI scan. Many reports of lesion location may not be very useful for understanding language deficits. Fourth, it is not clear whether the various aphasic syndromes that have been described are any more than statistical clusterings of independent symptoms. That is, each syndrome is defined by the presence or absence of specific symptoms, each of which occur in various combinations.

Table 6.1 summarizes key symptoms of the major syndromes as traditionally characterized.[93] In most of these cases, there is now intense debate about whether these syndromes—as here characterized—even exist.[94] For example, patients who are

TABLE 6.1

Type	Behavior				
	Spont. speech	*Paraphasia*	*Comprehension*	*Repetition*	*Naming*
Broca's	nonfluent	uncommon	good	poor	poor
Wernicke's	fluent	common	poor	poor	poor
Conduction	fluent	common	good	poor	poor
Global	nonfluent	variable	poor	poor	poor
Mixed tr.	nonfluent	uncommon	poor	good	poor
Tr. motor	nonfluent	uncommon	good	good	poor
Tr. sensory	fluent	common	poor	good	poor
Amnestic	fluent	absent	good	good	poor
Subcortical	variable	common	variable	good	variable

Source: Adapted, by permission, from D. F. Benson in K. M. Heilman and E. Valenstein (Eds.), *Clinical Neuropsychology* (New York: Oxford University Press, 1985), p. 32. *Note:* "tr." indicates "transcortical."

classified as having Broca's aphasia have been shown to have comprehension difficulties,[95] in spite of the way they are traditionally characterized.

Thus, we will consider the individual symptoms of language disorders. For convenience, we will consider reasons why specific abilities could be obliterated, but the reader should keep in mind that we are dealing with a continuum: A patient's ability to understand or produce language is not often totally disrupted, nor is it often disrupted in isolation. Rather, language abilities rarely cease functioning altogether, and several abilities typically may be affected by a lesion.

The goal of the following discussion is to show that damaging the system could produce a given language deficit in multiple ways. If each symptom can arise in many ways, then a simple taxonomy is obviously inadequate for understanding how to treat a patient with the symptom. It is our hope that this exercise will lead to genuine understanding of the deficits in the future, when researchers explicitly investigate the kinds of alternative accounts we note.

Comprehension Deficits

In this section we consider symptoms that affect language comprehension. In the following section we consider deficits in language production instead of, or in addition to, deficits in comprehension.

Word deafness. Patients with this disorder can hear, but fail to register words or hear only fragments of words. They report that they can hear a sound, but cannot organize it into an interpretable word. However, they often seem to have good perception of nonverbal environmental sounds. In some cases, auditory comprehension is particularly impaired when words are presented in isolation, and is greatly improved when words are presented in the context of a sentence. This deficit can be observed in the absence of any problem in producing speech or reading.

Because speech production is usually spared, at least some of the representations in associative memory must be intact. However, it is possible that the representations of sound (corresponding to the output from the pattern activation subsystem) are damaged in associative memory. In addition, the deficit may arise from partial dysfunctions or disconnection at any stage of auditory encoding of speech sounds.

At first glance, the fact that nonspeech sounds are spared would seem to rule out a problem in the auditory preprocessing subsystem or the auditory pattern activation subsystem or their interconnections. However, it is possible that speech requires finer discriminations than nonspeech sounds, and the deficit in fact reflects a quantitative degradation of input at any stage; if nonspeech sounds do not require as high-quality information, a general degradation could produce a specific deficit in speech even when the input was good enough to encode nonspeech sounds.

And in fact, when careful laboratory analyses are performed, deficits can also be shown for less complex, nonverbal stimuli.

Indeed, the hypothesis of a disorder at the early level of auditory processing has been confirmed using nonspeech stimuli.[96] Normal subjects can perceive as distinct two clicks separated by a silence of 3 milliseconds, but patients with pure word deafness need an interval of silence ten times greater to distinguish the clicks. This result suggests that one source of the deficit is related to the ability to make fine temporal discriminations among acoustic signals. This explanation is consistent with the observation that these patients may sometimes comprehend a sentence if it is spoken very slowly and repeated many times.[97]

Recall that when the speech signal does not carry enough information, top-down search mechanisms are used, which first access associative memory for properties that would distinguish the best-matching stimulus from similar sounding words. However, in order for this mechanism to perform correctly, the analysis at the early stages of auditory processing must function properly; if a good hypothesis cannot be formed, the system will not be able to use the top-down mechanisms to identify the input.

In addition, some forms of word deafness may reflect problems in using context properly. As discussed earlier, context at the level of the word, the sentence, the text, and the situation (using visual and other nonlinguistic input) provides important constraints about what is being heard. If the top-down processes that use context to bias input are awry, the input may not be matched properly in associative memory.

Literal comprehension. Some patients (typically with right-hemisphere lesions) may be able to understand literal meanings, but fail to grasp metaphorical meanings or appreciate verbal humor. These patients may have otherwise normal language abilities.[98]

Such deficits may reflect a generally degraded amount of activation, making it difficult to perform complex processing. If these patients cannot understand common, cliché metaphors, they may be unable to access very long stored strings in associative memory; accessing such a complex representation—even if it can be accessed as a single entry—may require more activation than other, less complex representations. In addition, it is possible that the representations of some (or all) long strings in associative memory are damaged. Alternatively, if the patient can comprehend cliché metaphors but not novel ones, he or she may not be able to compute nonliteral interpretations that are consistent with the words. Such computation is very complex, involving many distinct subsystems; in essence, these subsystems attempt to generate a story that is consistent with some (not all) of the semantic and syntactic properties of the words. Even mild damage to any of the subsystems involved, or a decrease in overall activation levels, could hamstring this complex process. In addition, a deficit in decoding prosody could disrupt a person's ability to grasp metaphorical meaning or to appreciate verbal humor.

Prosody. As noted earlier, prosody is the melody of language, as defined by variations in pitch, loudness, and the relative durations of phonemes. Comprehension and production of prosody can be selectively impaired.[99] Impaired comprehension of prosody may arise for a number of reasons. First, the auditory preprocessing or pattern activation subsystems could be damaged so that they fail to encode pitch properly. Second, associative memory could fail to match incoming cues to the proper stored representations. Third, the sentence structure monitoring subsystem could fail to use prosodic cues properly.

Syntactic problems in comprehension. Some patients have trouble using grammatical information to comprehend sentences (which is sometimes called *agrammaticism*).[100] For example, these patients have difficulty comprehending sentences such as "The woman is being kissed by the man"; these sentences are called *reversible* because the subject and object are nouns that can fill either role, and hence the meaning of the words cannot help one to interpret the sentence. Instead, to realize who did what to whom, one must use the grammatical information inherent in the sentence itself. In contrast, in a sentence such as "Harry ate the apple," the meanings of the words themselves prevent one from thinking that the apple ate Harry. A selective failure to understand reversible sentences is one sign that grammatical information per se is not being properly processed. Many such types of comprehension deficits have been documented, with some patients having difficulty only for specific grammatical forms.[101] It is unclear whether comprehension deficits are always accompanied by corresponding production deficits. Although some patients have been described who cannot produce grammatical sentences but can use grammatical information to comprehend sentences,[102] it is not clear whether the opposite pattern of deficits can occur (although some Wernicke's aphasia patients have an asymmetry in their deficits in this direction).[103]

Some grammatical deficits in comprehension may result from damage to syntactic or semantic information in associative memory. If so, then such deficits should affect both comprehension and production because the same semantic and syntactic representations are used in both processes. Alternatively, grammatical deficits in comprehension could arise if the subsystem that monitors the emerging sentence structure is awry, or if the processes that activate syntactic or semantic information are disrupted. We shall consider such difficulties in more detail shortly.

Production Deficits

There are a relatively large number of ways in which speech production can be impaired following brain damage.

Articulation. Although some patients can produce noises, they cannot form them into words. Some can produce vowel sounds, but cannot combine them with consonants to produce syllables. We must distinguish between deficits in articulation and deficits in speech production that arise from dysfunction of the peripheral speech mechanisms of the throat and mouth; these latter disorders are not part of aphasia, but fall under the general rubric of *dysarthria*. In contrast, aphasic articulation problems reflect a deficit in generating the desired sound from memory. Patients with pure aphasic articulation problems can read and comprehend speech normally.

Aphasic articulation problems may arise if associative memory is damaged, so that the speech output codes are partially disrupted. Alternatively, damage to the instructions generation subsystem could make it difficult to translate speech output codes into the appropriate commands to move muscles. Again, the damage may be quantitative, and only appears to affect language production because saying words requires greater precision than making other sorts of noises. In addition, the connections between associative memory and the instructions generation subsystem and between the instructions generation subsystem and the movement execution subsystem could be partially disrupted. Finally, the movement execution subsystem also could be impaired, but not enough to affect producing simpler, nonlinguistic noises.

Anomia.   Virtually all aphasics have some difficulty in "finding" words, which is called *anomia* or *nominal aphasia.* There are early examples of this language impairment in the history of aphasiology.[104] For example, Napoleon's surgeon Baron Leary described the case of a soldier engaged in the Battle of Waterloo who received a "wound of the brain." The soldier subsequently returned to work as a drill sergeant, but he found himself unable to teach "naming of parts" without consulting the manual, nor could he call his men by name. The problem apparently was not in his visual system (he did not have agnosia or alexia); it was in digging out the proper words from memory. These patients often have particular trouble with words that are used relatively infrequently.

Consider the case of the patient E.S.T., who had great difficulty recalling names although he could define the meanings of words in detail.[105] E.S.T. had a clear idea of what he wanted to say, but could not use the appropriate words to communicate, especially if he was trying to talk about objects or actions. He replaced inaccessible words by similar, more common words or by phrases. Such *circumlocutions* are common in anomic patients. In addition, E.S.T. had trouble naming pictures, although he could describe perfectly the properties and functions of the pictured objects and he could accurately identify pictures he could not name. For example, when shown a picture of a snowman, he said: "It's cold, it's a man . . . cold . . . frozen." In addition, E.S.T. could sort pictures into semantic categories that could not be differentiated on the basis of visual cues. Moreover, when presented sets of four semantically related pictures and asked to select the picture corresponding to a word that was spoken aloud by the examiner, E.S.T. performed perfectly.

E.S.T. named pictures better when the experimenter gave him the initial phoneme of the name, which suggests that at least part of the output code was intact. Moreover, E.S.T. often produced phonological approximations to the real word (e.g., "sumberry" for "strawberry"). Finally, E.S.T.'s naming impairment was related to word frequency; he was more likely to name a word if he had seen or used it more often. These results suggest that the appropriate representation and associated semantic information were activated in associative memory, but the associated speech output code was damaged, could not be activated, or could not be used to generate output instructions.

There are several reasons why brain damage could make it difficult to activate the speech output codes associated with low-frequency words in associative memory. For example, damage could have affected some of the connections in a neural network in associative memory that stores the speech code. If so, then the effect of frequency can be explained if the more often one activates a representation, the stronger the weights on the relevant connections become; consequently, these entries are activated more effectively if the network is damaged. Similarly, the input to this part of associative memory could be degraded, which makes it more difficult to activate the stored information. In this case, the effects of word frequency can be explained if the more often a particular piece of information is used, the more redundancy is built into the network; if so, then less input will be needed subsequently for the network to produce the output.

In short, anomia could arise if there is loss of information associated with a word in associative memory or if the processes that activate words are awry. In addition, in many cases normal people may select appropriate words because so many constraints are entered into associative memory that only a single word can be activated. If there is a problem entering information into associative memory, this process will not operate properly, and the appropriate word sometimes may not be activated.

This deficit can occur without other aphasic symptoms. However, it often is found with a variety of other symptoms, as is evident in Table 6.1. In particular, it often is accompanied by *paraphasias,* which are described in the following section.

Paraphasia. A paraphasia occurs when one says an unintended syllable, word, or phrase. A paraphasia occurs when sounds are correctly articulated (and so it is not an articulatory problem), but the word is incorrect. It is common to distinguish between two types of paraphasias. A *literal* paraphasia occurs when the patient distorts the intended word (e.g., saying "pike" instead of "pipe"), and a *verbal* paraphasia occurs when the patient says an unintended word that may sound nothing like the intended word (e.g., "my mother" instead of "my wife"). These deficits are like the paralexias discussed in Chapter 5, but occur in free conversation rather than in reading.

Paraphasias may arise from milder versions of the same disruptions that produce anomias. In addition, literal paraphasias could arise following disruption of the instructions generation or movement execution subsystems. Furthermore, the sentence programming subsystem may be awry, causing inappropriate speech output codes to be activated and thereby producing a verbal paraphasia. It is of interest that many, if not most, verbal paraphasias are from the same semantic category as the intended words. This finding suggests that damage may have degraded the input of semantic constraints into associative memory or impaired the constraint-satisfaction process itself, which causes the wrong word representations to be activated in a given context.

Jargon. In some cases, patients produce a torrent of words, most of which are not useful for communication. Sigmund Freud in 1891 described this disorder as "impoverishment of words with abundance of speech impulse." These words are often loosely linked to ones that would have been appropriate. These patients tend to perseverate, "beating around the bush" and staying on a topic for an inappropriately long time, and often produce a stream of paraphasias. They also sometimes create new words, *neologisms,* that they treat just like actual words. A neologism is different from a literal paraphasia in that the patient does not treat it as an error, but instead as an actual word.

As pointed out in the literature,[106] the term "jargon aphasia" probably covers a variety of symptoms. Patients who produce neologisms and nonwords may have a different type of deficit from those who produce an incoherent message using real words. In the first case, which is referred to as *neologistic jargon aphasia,* patients not only produce many distorted words, but they also have trouble comprehending speech.[107] This deficit may arise from a disruption of the processes that activate word representations in associative memory. Unlike anomia, this deficit would not be selective to the speech output code, but rather would affect a variety of information associated with words. For example, if the associative memory network were damaged extensively, all sorts of inputs would have difficulty activating the proper representations. Hence, the patient would have trouble producing and comprehending a word because the appropriate representation would not be activated in either case. This interpretation is consistent with the finding that neologistic jargon aphasics produce high-frequency words better than low-frequency ones.[108] As before, we need only assume that there is the neural equivalent of stronger "weights" on the relevant connections of the network for more frequent words, and so they are more resistant to effects of damage.

The second sort of jargon aphasia is called *semantic jargon aphasia.* These patients seem unable to organize words into the proper sequence. This problem could reflect a dysfunction of the sentence programming subsystem and/or the constraint-satisfaction processes in associative memory that order words. Alternatively, damage may have eliminated, or eliminated access to, some of the semantic and syntactic information used to order words.

Some of these patients are perfectly able to decide whether a sentence spoken by somebody else is correct.[109] At least for these patients, the damage cannot have eliminated semantic or syntactic information. It is possible, however, that in these patients such information can only be accessed via the perceptual systems, and the relevant information cannot be activated by the sentence programming subsystem. If so, then they should be able to understand spoken speech but not activate the appropriate information to produce coherent speech themselves.

At least some of these patients are totally unaware of their speech defect, and deny it when explicitly asked about it. This kind of *anosognosia* (lack of awareness of a deficit; see Chapter 3) could result if no trace of the unused semantic and syntactic information can be accessed via the sentence programming or sentence structure monitoring subsystems. In this case, the complete absence of the information would provide no hints that something is amiss.

Syntactic difficulties. Some patients have difficulty using function words and (or) inflections correctly when speaking. These patients often have particular difficulty choosing the correct verb tense, and produce verbs using the stem (e.g., "walk" rather than "walks," or "walked"). In addition, they often speak almost "telegraphically," uttering phrases such as "He go." Such deficits would arise if the instructions generation subsystem were impaired, and so was not capable of producing long output sequences. Or, damage may have lowered the activation level of key parts of the brain, so that only a limited amount of information can be composed into a series of output codes. In either case, the sentence programming subsystem might compensate, providing input to associative memory so that only key words are activated and only the simplest forms of the words are used.

In addition, some patients cannot organize nouns and verbs correctly into a sentence. Such difficulties could arise because of degraded input to associative memory or disruption of the syntactic and semantic information associated with words in memory; these impairments would also produce a syntactic impairment in comprehension. Alternatively, the sentence programming subsystem may be damaged so that it fails to activate the proper syntactic information, which would result in a syntactic deficit in production but not in comprehension.

Repetition. Many aphasics have trouble repeating speech. Indeed, if they have severe trouble comprehending or producing language, it would be surprising if they did not also have trouble repeating it in at least some situations. However, some aphasics cannot repeat aurally presented material even though they can speak and understand relatively normally. Some of these patients have trouble repeating nonwords, but can repeat words almost normally.[110] In contrast, other patients have trouble repeating even familiar words.

According to our analyses, if the output from the auditory preprocessing subsystem is a set of phonemes that corresponds to a familiar word, one representation is activated in the pattern activation subsystem, which in turn activates a single entry in associative memory. If the set of phonemes does not correspond to a word, it will have to activate a set of syllables or similar relatively small sound sequences, which in turn will be used to generate speech output codes. Repeating words requires both encoding and production, which taxes the system. If the activation level is reduced enough, a partially damaged auditory pattern activation subsystem may not be able to make multiple matches and produce the appropriate set of outputs in this task. Similarly, damage to the connection between the pattern activation subsystem and associative memory can reduce how much information can be sent. Or damage to the processes used to generate novel speech output codes (as discussed earlier) could disrupt saying an unfamiliar word in this combined task. Any of these deficits would produce a selective problem in repeating unfamiliar words or nonwords if they are more difficult to encode or produce, as we have suggested earlier. Moreover, a reduced activation level could affect even the ability to repeat familiar words if the combined comprehension/production task taxes the system too much. In this case, speaking slowly and asking the patient to respond slowly might improve performance, as sometimes does in fact occur clinically.

Verbal fluency. Verbal fluency is the ability to speak smoothly, without long pauses between words. Patients who cannot speak fluently may or may not have difficulty finding words. It is clear that low verbal fluency could arise following mild damage to virtually any of the subsystems used to produce speech. If such damage is relatively mild, the system may slow down as a kind of compensation, allowing the proper output to be produced when each network either produces several outputs in succession and the subsequent one uses the pattern that occurred most frequently (which would correct for noisy outputs), or each network simply requires more time to perform its computation. Such a compensation would be learned, in the sense that higher-level "decision" processes (see Chapter 9) would discover that this strategy results in the proper output and so would set thresholds higher in associative memory; these decision processes would use feedback to "tune" the thresholds until processing becomes relatively accurate—slowing down speech output as a consequence.

Prosody. Production of prosody can be disrupted in three ways following brain damage:[111] (a) *hyperprosody,* which is rarely observed, is an exaggerated prosody; (b) *dysprosody* is a distorted prosody, which makes the patient sound as if he or she is speaking with a foreign accent; (c) *aprosody* is an attenuation or lack of normal prosody.

These disorders may arise if information about pitch is not used properly by the instructions generation subsystem, or if this information itself is disrupted. Similarly, it is possible that the movement execution subsystem is awry, so that it improperly modulates the output.

To our knowledge no network models have included a melodic contour to a sentence. It would be of interest to construct such models and then observe the kinds of errors they make when different amounts of the network are damaged. It is possible that the three varieties of problems in prosody reflect different amounts of damage to such a network.

We were able to apply much of the same reasoning to analyze visual perception and speech perception, and were able to infer that certain other functions must be performed in language processing. Specifically, we have inferred two sets of subsystems, which are used in comprehension and production.

For auditory speech comprehension, we inferred a total of eight subsystems. They were: the auditory stimulus-based attention shifting subsystem, which draws attention to a novel sound; the auditory buffer, which stores relatively "raw" acoustic input; an auditory attention window, which selects some representations in the buffer for further processing; an auditory preprocessing subsystem, which—among other things—organizes the input into phonemes; an auditory pattern activation subsystem, which matches sets of phonemes to stored representations of words or sound segments; and an auditory attention shifting subsystem (which itself could be decomposed into three subsystems), which shifts the auditory attention window to select specific sorts of information. We also were led to infer a sentence structure buffer, which holds semantic and syntactic information for a brief period of time, and a sentence structure monitoring subsystem, which checks the relations among the elements of the emerging sentence structure and re-enters associative memory if the structure is internally inconsistent. Comprehension occurs when the interlocking semantic and syntactic constraints produce an internally consistent structure in the sentence structure buffer, which in turn must feed into other subsystems that direct subsequent behavior. In addition, we were led to infer additional properties of associative memory and the coordinate property lookup subsystem.

For speech production, we inferred five subsystems. The movement execution subsystem actually moves the muscles, and the instructions generation subsystem receives output from the coordinate property lookup subsystem (which accesses associative memory) and produces an ordered string of commands. This subsystem relies in part on a motor memory. We also inferred a sound-to-speech conversion subsystem, which constructs speech output codes based on an auditory representation coming from the auditory pattern activation subsystem. And, finally, we inferred a sentence programming subsystem, which specifies key features of a sentence that in turn place constraints on how the words can be ordered.

Two general points have been made in this chapter. First, language is enormously complex. We have tried to be as conservative as possible in drawing inferences, and have avoided the kinds of details that typically force further differentiation. Nevertheless, we have inferred thirteen additional subsystems! Second, even with all of this we have just scratched the surface; we have not done justice to the rich descriptions of language that have been painstakingly assembled by linguists, nor have we dared to consider questions such as how language is learned, why all human languages have certain features in common, and so on.[112] We have largely avoided the technical issues that force one to specify details, such as the question of how the past tense is formed.[113] We simply do not know very much about how language is accomplished by the brain. Indeed, until very recently, when PET studies have become possible, we were severely limited in what we could learn about the neural bases of language.

We again see the five general principles of neural information processing at work: First, it is inconceivable that a system could comprehend and produce language without dividing up the labor. The component functions are too heterogeneous to be comfortably carried out by a single undifferentiated network. Second, having noted this, we must also note that some of these subsystems may be only weakly modular; the various processes may not be used solely in the service of specific linguistic abilities. For example, we noted that low-level speech encoding subsystems may also be used to code environmental sounds. Furthermore, it seems clear that associative memory cuts across a wide range of abilities, which leads us to expect parallel deficits in different domains when associative memory is damaged. And in fact, in the previous chapter we noted that some reading deficits are accompanied by deficits in comprehending spoken language. Third, the principle of constraint satisfaction is at the very heart of how individual words are identified and organized into sentences, and how individual words are ordered and pronounced as a string of sounds. Fourth, the principle of opportunism may lie at the root of our ability to use language. We assume that at least some of the peripheral aspects of language encoding and production were present for other purposes, and were adopted by language fairly late in the course of evolution. Indeed, even the basic structure of associative memory is mandated by other abilities. Thus, much of language itself may reflect opportunistic processing. Finally, it is clear that much of language relies on concurrent processing. For example, the sentence programming subsystem sets up a new sentence at the same time that the generate instructions subsystem computes instructions for the previous one, and the generate instructions subsystem operates at the same time that the movement execution subsystem is producing a yet earlier sentence.

We also have seen again the utility of our analyses for interpreting the effects of brain damage. Our inferences about normal processing led us to offer a host of possible interpretations of the effects of brain damage on language, which now can be investigated empirically. We suspect that different interpretations will be appropriate for different patients. This would be an important finding if for no other reason than it would suggest different courses of rehabilitation therapy, depending on the precise nature of the dysfunction.

7

Movement

We effortlessly reach to pick up a paperclip, lift a coffee cup to our lips, or walk to the refrigerator. These are in fact virtuoso performances, requiring the coordination of millions of muscle fibers. An enormous amount of computation is required to produce any given action, most of which is "automatic" and not under conscious control. This fact has become evident to researchers in robotics, who have discovered that it is very difficult to build robots that do even apparently simple, everyday things, such as buttoning a shirt.

In this chapter we consider first how the normal system performs actions in a variety of circumstances. As usual, our goal is to understand the componential structure of the processing system that gives rise to certain behaviors, not to understand the details of what occurs within each subsystem. In addition to considering action in general, we will consider the special case of writing. After we have discussed a variety of situations in which we can move and write appropriately, we will review and analyze the disorders of movement and writing.

Our abilities to produce actions in many ways mirror our perceptual abilities. In both cases, the underlying processing systems are remarkably flexible while at the same time being remarkably precise. We illustrate these properties by considering a few of the key abilities that allow us to make our way in the world. We begin by discussing how one can perform an individual simple action, and then move on to how one can compose simple actions in new ways, write, move "automatically," move encumbered limbs, move different limbs in the same way, and mimic others' actions.

Performing a Simple Action

Consider the apparently simple act of reaching to press a button to call an elevator. Depending on the particular elevator and one's distance from the wall, the target is in different locations relative to one's body. One visually encodes the coordinates of the button, and uses these coordinates to guide the reach. How are these spatial coordinates translated into specific movement instructions? In this section we consider how such seemingly simple actions are performed, and see that a considerable amount of processing must underlie them.

In the previous chapter we distinguished between two subsystems that are used to produce speech. Recall that the *instructions generation subsystem* computes the proper set of movements to satisfy constraints imposed by the target of a movement, the present position of the effector (jaw, tongue, lips, etc.), any impediments to movement, and the like, whereas the *movement execution subsystem* activates the muscles that produce those movements. The instructions generation subsystem computes a sequence of movements and functions in part as a buffer, storing a sequence of instructions for a brief period before, and while, they are executed; there is much evidence that such an output buffer exists.[1]

Further, we were led to infer that speech sounds are represented in associative memory as sets of combinations of "target coordinates"; these coordinates define the relative locations of different portions of the vocal apparatus at different points in time. Many combinations of coordinates can produce any given sound,[2] and the set of these combinations is represented in a single "packet." This packet is sent to the instructions generation subsystem, which takes into account the current coordinates of the lips, tongue, and so forth, in order to select a combination of target coordinates to produce a given sound in that context. The selected combination of coordinates specifies the locations of various components of the vocal tract that will produce the sound with minimal changes from the present configuration. These coordinates are then used to access a set of specific motor instructions, which then are sent to the movement execution subsystem.

In fluent speech, we assumed that the selected set of target coordinates usually corresponds directly to representations in motor memory; these motor representations specify which muscles to move to reach the target coordinates. Thus, the instructions generation subsystem is easily able to translate the selected set of target coordinates into specific instructions for the movement execution subsystem, which actually directs the muscles to move appropriately.

However, even for speech we saw that the instructions generation subsystem sometimes must compute a novel way to produce a target sound. If one talks with a pencil in one's mouth, it is unlikely (for most of us, anyway) that the necessary sets of coordinates or corresponding motor representations have been stored explicitly. Moreover, the language learner must have begun by computing how to produce each speech sound; he or she could not simply look up previously stored combinations of coordinates and motor representations.

Thus, we were led to infer that the instructions generation subsystem operates in two ways during speech production, one that hinges on looking up stored motor representations that allow the target to be reached by repeating a familiar action, and one that requires computing a novel combination of movements to produce a target sound.[3]

In the previous chapter we focused on fluent speech; we now turn to the processes that are responsible for generating novel actions. Many—if not most—actions are more like talking around a pencil than like fluent speech; we often must produce a new movement with the limbs, such as reaching in a slightly different way, and so cannot simply rely on previously stored information to meet the present task requirements. When we move in novel ways, we must compute a new trajectory.

Speech and Movement of the Limbs

We have been treating speech production as an example of movement production in general, which may not be entirely appropriate. In many ways, speech is special. For example, the goal is always to move the same body parts, which are highly specialized; each component of the vocal apparatus has a specific function, and they do not substitute for each other (except, perhaps, in very limited ways). One generates sound with the vocal cords, not by smacking the lips. In addition, the same basic sounds are used repeatedly, so that an adult usually can simply retrieve stored sets of coordinates and motor representations to produce the sounds. In contrast, we often can perform other sorts of actions—such as pressing a button—with a variety of limbs, and often cannot reach a goal using a previously stored trajectory.

On the other hand, although many aspects of speech are special, many other aspects are not. For example, novel sequences of actions can be composed, one can modulate the speed of output, more than a single muscle group must be coordinated, and so on. Furthermore, speech presumably evolved out of functions that controlled other sorts of motor output, and is unlikely to have shed all of the characteristics of those earlier types of processing.

Thus, the degree to which speech production shares subsystems with other types of motor control is an open question; it is likely that some, but not all, aspects of speech control characterize motor control in general. There is no guarantee that any specific aspects of the representation and control of speech are shared by other sorts of actions.

Hence it is of interest that, as is true for the representation of speech sounds, many sorts of movements are represented as sets of interlocking constraints. For example, researchers have studied how people grasp objects with two opposing fingers when one finger is displaced.[4] They found that people did not compensate by moving the finger that was directly affected, but by moving the other finger. It is clear that the grasping action was executed to satisfy multiple constraints at once, and as soon as one was changed, the overall configuration was altered. This is a good example of a constraint satisfaction problem; once some movements are perturbed, others are required.

Furthermore, the kinds of mistakes we make when ordering movements suggest that a sequence of instructions typically is computed before an action is initiated, just as occurs in speech. Indeed, many types of movement errors mirror speech errors; pre-entry (e.g., playing a note too soon on the piano), transposition, and the like occur in many types of actions.[5]

Thus, as a working assumption we will consider how the instructions generation and movement execution subsystems inferred in the previous chapter can produce movements more generally. The key problem we have not addressed is how the instructions generation subsystem actually computes a novel trajectory for moving a limb. This problem can be broken down into two aspects: the type of representation that is used to compute trajectories, and the computational process itself.

Representations Used to Compute Novel Trajectories

As noted when we discussed vision, different types of representations make different types of information explicit.[6] Depending on how the relative positions of body segments are represented, it will be more or less easy to compute a trajectory. Logically, the computation requires the spatial coordinates of the starting and target locations. The starting coordinates specify the initial location of the end of the body segment to be used for the task; for example, such coordinates might specify where the index finger of one's right hand is located prior to using it to press a button. The target coordinates specify the target location of the end of the body segment used for the task; for example, where a fingertip should be in order to call the elevator. What is at issue is how one gets from here to there.

Most contemporary theories of movement control posit that trajectories are specified as sets of *body segment coordinates,* as is true for speech. According to this view, a movement is represented in terms of coordinates that specify a sequence of locations of the end of a body segment (e.g., a fingertip). These coordinates not only indicate the location of the segment at the beginning and end of the trajectory, but also indicate intermediate positions along the trajectory itself. These intermediate locations are specified by *via point coordinates.*[7]

If movements are coded in terms of such coordinates, the instructions generation subsystem must perform an *inverse kinematics transformation. Direct kinematics* refers to the computations necessary to translate a specific set of joint angles (e.g., of the arm) into the corresponding position of a body part; *inverse kinematics* refers to the computations necessary to translate the position of a body part into the corresponding joint angles.

Successive solutions to the inverse kinematics problem specify a series of joint angles that will shift a body segment along a trajectory. But these computations do not indicate how those joint angles should in fact be produced. Actually moving limbs requires the system to cope with the effects of inertia, gravity, elasticity of muscles, and so forth. Each set of joint angles must be converted into a set of joint torques (forces), which activate the appropriate muscles to move the joints into particular positions; this is called the *inverse dynamics problem.* This is a difficult problem in part because the appropriate joint torque varies when the joints are in different positions and limbs are moving at different velocities and accelerations.[8]

The distinction between the inverse kinematics problem and the inverse dynamics problem can be illustrated as follows.[9] Consider how an artist would produce an animated cartoon of Mickey Mouse pounding a nail with a hammer. To make the cartoon, the artist prepares a succession of drawings, each of which differs by a small amount from the previous one; when the drawings are shown in rapid succession, it appears as though the arm and hammer are moving. In order to make Mickey Mouse's arm appear to move so that the hammer hits the nail, the artist essentially must solve the inverse kinematics problem repeatedly; he or she must figure out how to draw the angles at the shoulder, elbow, and wrist so that the hammer is swung along the series of positions. But not all solutions to these inverse kinematics problems would produce a realistic-looking cartoon. In some, Mickey would appear stiff and awkward, in others, he would seem to be moving under water, and so forth. To make Mickey's movement seem real, the artist would have to take into account how the succession of inverse dynamics problems would be solved. He or she would have to figure out exactly how factors such as the weight of the hammer, the effects of inertia, and the properties of muscles would influence the speed and position of the arm at each point along the trajectory.

As should now be apparent, a lot of computation is required to solve these two problems. This observation has led some researchers to suggest that movements are not represented in terms of body-segment coordinates, but rather are represented as joint angles. In this case, a trajectory is specified directly by a sequence of joint angles. The computational advantage of this representation is that the inverse kinematics transformation need not be performed at every step along the way; the inverse kinematics problem would need to be solved only to specify the joint angles at the start and finish of the movement.[10]

As attractive as this scheme might seem, it now appears that representations of joint angles are not used to compute novel trajectories. For example, when hand movements are observed carefully, it has been found that the hand moves smoothly towards a target, as would be expected if it traverses between sets of via point coordinates; in contrast, the joints move through complex angular changes.[11] The hand typically is moved through the shortest path in space, even if this does not correspond to the simplest sequence of possible joint angles. This would not be expected if the movement were being computed directly on the basis of sequences of joint angles. Furthermore, if joint angles were operated on directly we would expect even more variability in motion when barriers are placed between one's body and a goal, which requires complex changes in joint angles, but it appears that we can reach smoothly even here. These results make sense if barriers simply specify via points (i.e., locations that must be passed through), which in turn constrain the possible trajectories that can be computed by the instructions generation subsystem.

Indeed, the very fact that we can easily negotiate around barriers is difficult to reconcile with the idea that movements are represented directly as sequences of joint angles. The movement to the barrier, around it, and beyond it would have to be treated as three distinct events, each defined by distinct start and finish coordinates. If enough barriers are present, this sort of representation would become much like one that relies on spatial coordinates of the body segment. The major difference would be that separate events would need to be combined, as opposed to shifting between via points within a single movement. Presumably it is more complex computationally to compose separate events than to perform a single movement sequence.

As another possible alternative, one might argue that a trajectory could be computed on the basis of sets of *muscle coordinates*. This representation would specify sets of coordinated muscle movements that would move the limb to the correct relative location. Such a representation has the advantage of being easily converted to specific motor instructions, given that the representation directly specifies the appropriate pattern of muscle activation.

However, it seems very unlikely that actions are computed in terms of muscle coordinates; such representations are too restrictive. For example, we can easily change the size of an action, even one as overlearned as writing our signatures. When you sign your name very large on a chalkboard, it still looks about the same as when you sign a check. And yet very different muscle groups are used in the two cases.

Such observations allow us to argue that muscle coordinates are not used to compute trajectories by drawing a parallel to an argument we developed previously. In Chapter 3, we considered reasons why distinct unimodal memory representations may be used in perception (in the visual pattern activation subsystem). Recall that one wants to recognize stimuli that are similar to previously encountered stimuli; "similarity" in this case is defined in terms of physical properties of the stimulus (e.g., its shape). Networks are good at generalizing over variations in the input, but they generalize only over the dimensions that characterize the stored information. Thus, generalization based on physical properties is easy only if a representation preserves those properties, which suggests that unimodal representations exist.

Similarly, the fact that we can generalize easily over the size scale of an output suggests that the dimension of size characterizes the underlying representation. Size is not an aspect of specifications of muscle coordinates, but is inherent in specifications of via points. For example, if via points are used to compute trajectories, the distances between them can easily be multiplied to scale up the movement, or divided to scale it down.

In short, the problem of computing a novel trajectory can be recast as a problem of selecting via points and computing the trajectory through them. Although generating such spatial coordinates requires considerable computation, this scheme has many advantages; as we shall see, this representation allows one to use multiple limbs to achieve the same goal, to use visual feedback to correct movements, and promotes learning new movements by mimicking others. Presumably, barriers often impose the via points; alternatively, one could simply look at locations along a possible path, and encode these coordinates as via points, using the coordinate spatial relations encoding subsystem.[12]

Computing Trajectories: Network Models

We now turn to the most challenging part of the problem, how via points are used to compute novel trajectories. One of the reasons it is useful to build detailed models that compute trajectories is that the solution to this problem is not obvious. Computing trajectories is difficult because the input does not fully constrain the output. The problem is *ill-posed* (underspecified) in at least three respects.

First, in most cases the starting point, target location, and via points do not fully determine the trajectory. For example, consider the problem of determining a trajectory when only three points along it are specified: a starting point, target location, and one via point. An infinite number of trajectories can pass through these points; some would pass smoothly through all three, whereas others would zig and zag between them. How does the instructions generation subsystem determine which trajectory to use? Clearly, if additional constraints are added, such as requiring smooth trajectories, the number of possible alternatives is reduced dramatically.

Second, many combinations of joint angles can move a limb along a trajectory; that is, the series of inverse kinematics transformations is not fully determined by a trajectory. For example, to move a hand to a target, the coordinates of the hand at each point in time must be converted into a sequence of joint angles at the shoulder, elbow, and hand. Many combinations of joint angles can move the hand properly; the system must use only one.

Third, the same type of problem occurs again at the next level down, where joint angles are converted into specific patterns of muscle activation. Many combinations of muscles can produce any given set of joint angles; that is, the inverse dynamics transformation is not fully determined by a given set of joint angles.

On the face of things, neural networks might seem inherently ill-suited for controlling movements; these networks rely largely on parallel processing of multiple inputs, whereas movement control depends on serial ordering of individual events. However, key features of network models are consistent with properties of neural movement control.

For example, neural network models typically rely on "distributed representations," using patterns of activity in the network to represent information. Thus, it is of interest that there is evidence from single-cell recording studies that movements are represented by such distributed representations in area M1.[13] Although individual neurons fire at maximum frequency when a monkey moves its arm in a particular direction, these neurons tend to be broadly tuned, firing at some rate for a wide range of directions. Apostolos Georgopoulos and his colleagues suggest that the direction of reach is represented by a "population code"; it is the overlap of outputs from different neurons that codes a specific direction. This is, of course, none other than coarse coding, which is easily implemented in neural network models. Once again we see the principle of constraint satisfaction at work.

A good example of a neural network model of motor control was described by the Japanese computer scientist Mitsuo Kawato and his colleagues,[14] whose model was designed to simulate moving one's arm through a single plane. Their solution to the three ill-posed problems noted above hinges on a "smoothness performance index," which they used to produce the smoothest possible trajectories. This measure is based on minimizing changes in torque; Kawato and his colleagues used their smoothness index to determine the smoothest possible trajectory in terms of patterns of muscular activation. By minimizing torque, their model selects a single sequence of joint angles, thereby solving the inverse kinematics problem as well as the inverse dynamics problem.

Kawato and his colleagues incorporated this principle into a cascade neural network model (see Chapter 2), and observed whether such a model could mimic human performance. A cascade model, so named because it is like a series of waterfalls that tumble down a cliff, has multiple levels of processing and each level continuously sends input to the next; a level does not wait until it is finished before sending input to the next level. Their network was based on a multi-layer structure of the sort described in Chapter 2, and included four layers of units. Layer 1 represented successive torque values over time, whereas layer 3 represented the change in trajectory of the body part at each time unit. Layer 2 was designed to provide the necessary transformations between the representation of torque in layer 1 and the representation of the trajectory of a body part in layer 3. Finally, layer 4 represented the estimated time course of the trajectory of the limb itself. This four-layer structure was repeated many times, with each set defining the computation at a given unit of time. The cascade structure allowed the model to simulate processes that occur at different points in a sequence.

The network engaged in two distinct kinds of processing, learning and trajectory computation. In the learning phase, the network acquired an "internal model" of a body segment, in this case the arm.[15] This model corresponded to information in motor memory, and consisted of a complex function relating joint angles, their angular velocities, and the corresponding motor commands. The network was taught the internal model in the following way. A motor command was provided as input, and the corresponding trajectory taken by an actual arm was used as the teaching signal at layer 3; the standard back-propagation learning algorithm was used to train the network (see Chapter 2). Thus, the weights on the connections between layers 1 and 2 and layers 3 and 4 encoded the mapping from a set of motor commands to a movement of the arm (the hidden layer is needed because the mapping is very complex). Each level of the cascade was trained using the specific portion of the motor commands and trajectory that occurred at that interval of time.

After the network had been trained in this way, it was used to determine the trajectory that required the smallest changes in torque. A motor command was entered that corresponded to the one specifying the present position of the limb, and the estimated position of the hand (i.e., end of the arm segment) at layer 4 of the final set of units was compared to the desired target position. This target could be a via point or the end of the trajectory. The deviation between the estimated position and the target position was then used to send a correction signal backwards, through the different sets of network structures that form the cascade (using the back-propagation algorithm). This was a critical step in the simulation because it transformed errors in the position of the hand relative to the target at layer 4 into corrections of the motor commands themselves. The proper motor commands were thus discovered by the network in the course of computing the trajectory for the hand.

Thus, the error-correction feedback led the model to minimize the disparity between the present position of the hand and the desired target position successively over time, until the hand arrived at the target. A clever aspect of the model was that the smoothness performance index was used to constrain how weights between the first three layers could be adjusted when feedback was provided. Thus, the motor commands that subsequently were delivered to layer 3 were constrained by this index, forcing the network to produce a set of intermediate positions that required minimal changes in torque.

This model was used to simulate a two-link arm movement;[16] the first link corresponded to the upper arm and the second link to the forearm (and hence the corresponding joints were the shoulder and the elbow). After a training phase, the cascade model estimated the trajectory of the hand accurately, even for novel input.

This network model is interesting in part because it relied on processing in both directions, with information feeding forward and feeding backwards; the network exploited an interaction between the current state of the trajectory and information embedded in stored "models" of movements to control the next phase of the trajectory. This is useful because relatively few via points typically are imposed by barriers, and so the problem of specifying a trajectory is greatly underconstrained.

Consider another analogy to the visual system. When one sees a face, one does not recognize it as two eyes, a nose, a mouth, and so on; one recognizes a single object, namely a face. In Chapter 3 we assumed that the pattern activation subsystem accounts for as much of the input as possible with a single representation; thus representations of larger patterns inhibit representations of smaller ones. Similarly, when computing a trajectory, the instructions generation subsystem could attempt to access the motor representation that would encompass the largest possible segment of the trajectory. Kawato et al's network implicitly stores such information as part of the "model," which is used to establish the proper motor commands to produce a novel trajectory. This model does not store trajectories that are later produced, however. In contrast, Michael Jordan describes a model that is very similar to Kawato et al.'s, except that it also explicitly stores motor commands (after the model has been built in) so that they can be used to compute subsequent commands.[17] In the limit, a single motor representation would exist for familiar trajectories, such as those used to produce common speech sounds in normal circumstances. At the other extreme, only very small movement segments might be incorporated into complex novel trajectories, which would require multiple separate computations. Hence, a single process would generate instructions for novel and familiar trajectories.

There are several other impressive demonstrations that neural networks can compute trajectories effectively. For example, Jordan described a model that in many ways is similar to the one just described.[18] A major conceptual difference between

Jordan's model and the one devised by Kawato et al. centered on the smoothness performance index. Kawato et al. used changes in torque to compute smoothness, whereas Jordan used an index based on the minimum rate of change of acceleration (i.e., amount of jerk).

In addition, perhaps the earliest, and in some ways classic attempt to simulate arm movements in neural network models was reported by Daniel Bullock and Stephen Grossberg.[19] Their model was referred to as the "vector-integration-to-endpoint" (VITE) model. This model simulated both passive and active arm movements, but we will consider only how it computed trajectories during active arm movements. Two kinds of inputs were provided to compute a trajectory; one specified a target position, and the other specified the overall speed of the desired movement (the speed was specified by a "GO" signal, which also initiated the movement). The network computed the difference vector between the target location and the present position of the arm, and then altered the present position to reduce this disparity. The difference vector represented both the direction to move and the distance between the body segment and the target. The present position was continuously updated; the model integrated all the difference vectors over time, and hence the term "vector-integration-to-endpoint." As the present position was updated, the model generated a new movement command and activated specific muscle groups, thereby reducing the value of the difference vector. Opponent interactions occurred in the network that regulated the activation of antagonist muscular groups. The VITE model accounted for a surprisingly large range of phenomena.[20]

Bullock and Grossberg noted that some cells in the motor cortex have properties that mirror those of vector-computing nodes in their model. For example, the overlap in outputs from broadly tuned neurons in area M1 corresponds to their characterization of a vector.[21] As noted earlier, this overlap of outputs is the critical feature of coarse coding, which characterizes the operation of all of the network models.

In short, it is clear that neural network models can in fact simulate the process of generating instructions to control trajectories. At this early stage of research, it would be surprising if the details of any of the current models were correct. Perhaps most important is the simple demonstration that these sorts of networks can in fact control serial processing.

Recap: Performing a Simple Action

The target, starting point, and via point coordinates are used by the instructions generation subsystem to compute a trajectory. This computation relies in part on the representations in motor memory, and seeks to use the largest prestored trajectory segment that will allow a smooth transition between the three types of positions.

Combining Simple Movements in New Ways

Actions, like sentences in a language, are produced by a generative system. We can perform an infinite number of actions. Nevertheless, most actions are composed of sets of simple movements. This is particularly evident when one is learning a new sport, dance, martial art, or other skill. A good teacher will emphasize a "vocabulary" of simple movements and ways in which they are combined. When performing such sequences of movements, one must combine the "words" properly into motion "phrases," "sentences," and so forth.

This analogy to language suggests that our reasoning about speech production again might apply to action more generally. However, the process of combining actions cannot be accomplished by the subsystems inferred so far. We are led to infer a (no doubt very complex) *action programming subsystem* that provides an ordered set of subgoals to the instructions generation subsystem. Each subgoal is defined as a set of target coordinates and possibly one or more sets of via point coordinates. Given these two sorts of information, the individual components of the trajectory are then computed as described in the previous section.

We infer a separate subsystem from that used in speech because a different input/output mapping is required; this mapping differs in two important ways from that performed by the sentence programming subsystem. First, the action programming subsystem not only specifies the target for each movement, but also must specify which limbs should be moved and in what order. Recall that in language, the target sound greatly constrains which parts of the vocal apparatus will be used, and syntactic and semantic constraints in associative memory play a major role in ordering words; the corresponding mechanical constraints (due to the structure of the joints and the like) on the ordering of movements of the limbs are weaker, and hence often may not dictate a specific order of individual movements.[22]

Second, in speech, sounds are arbitrarily paired with individual concepts, and so associative memory must be accessed prior to generating the proper sounds. In contrast, when one combines simple nonlinguistic movements in a novel way, such stored associations are not used. Nevertheless, associative memory is accessed to use information from the perceptual systems and to use other sorts of stored information, as described in the following section.

Composing Complex Actions

There is good evidence that actions are composed hierarchically: An action is organized in terms of major segments, such as reaching, lifting, and drinking, and each segment in turn is organized in terms of simpler movements. For example, a movement to reach for a glass might consist of extending the arm, opening the hand, and grasping the glass tightly. However, the individual components of the action are not initiated sequentially, with each one waiting for the previous one to finish; rather, the instructions are generated in advance (as is true in language), and are executed during overlapping intervals of time. For example, when reaching for a glass we open our hand and begin to grasp well before it reaches the target. Indeed, the individual components of an action typically are coordinated so that it is performed quickly and smoothly.[23]

At first glance, the idea that motor representations are organized hierarchically seems inconsistent with the following simple finding: Expert typists, who can type around 90 words a minute, could stop typing almost instantly when given a signal; on average they typed only a single character after an auditory "stop" signal was presented.[24] If the representation were stored in terms of higher-level units, such as syllables or words, one might think that it should have been more difficult to stop. However, this result may reflect nothing more than the way that the movement execution subsystem controls the muscles. If it uses inhibition as well as excitation to coordinate muscles, then the result may not bear on the nature of the underlying representation. Instead, it merely indicates that humans can inhibit motor instructions relatively rapidly. In their attention experiment discussed in Chapter 3, Moran and Desimone found that it took a total of only about 90 milliseconds for attention to inhibit neural responses in a visual task (this process began 60 milliseconds from when the stimulus appeared, and required an additional 30 milliseconds to be completed),[25] and there is no reason such inhibitory processes could not also regulate motor output as effectively.

Presumably, when a new action is learned, hierarchical representations are stored.[26] These stored representations are analogous to the descriptions of shapes in associative memory that we discussed in Chapter 3; just as associative memory stores a description of an object in terms of the locations of its parts, it stores a description of an action in terms of individual movements and their order.

Neural Implementation

Researchers who study movement control often describe three levels of computation. At the coarsest level, a path must be planned, such as deciding whether to step over or around an obstacle. At the next level the inverse kinematics problem must be solved at each point along the path; one must compute the proper joint angles. And at the finest level, the inverse dynamics problem must be solved at each point; one must compute the muscle forces needed to move the joints into the proper positions. We assume that the action programming subsystem deals with planning at the coarsest level, the instructions generation subsystem solves the inverse kinematics problem and the inverse dynamics problem together, and the movement execution subsystem actually controls the muscles.

However, it is not obvious that we have divided processing into the biologically correct subsystems. Nor is it clear that the traditional way of dividing the problem is the best; as the neural network models have shown, these levels are not necessarily independent. Logically, a decision at any one of these three levels has direct implications for decisions at the others; for example,. one path would result in a more difficult inverse dynamics problem than another, given a present posture. Thus, it is important to discover whether the brain seems to respect our proposed division of processing.

At least one cortical area appears to be involved in carrying out the computations of the action programming subsystem,[27] namely the supplementary motor area (SMA). This area lies in the medial surface of the frontal lobes, as is illustrated in Figure 7.1. Damage to this area causes monkeys to have great difficulty producing complex sequences of finger movements and impairs their ability to coordinate their hands in even relatively simple tasks, such as using one hand to push a piece of food off a table into the other hand.[28] Perhaps the most compelling evidence that SMA is involved in high-level planning of movements comes from a PET scanning study.[29] Subjects were asked to move their fingers in a specific sequence, and both SMA and M1 were activated. In contrast, when the subjects simply *imagined* making a finger movement, only SMA was activated—not M1. The process of planning a movement, but not actually executing it, apparently takes place at least in part in SMA.

Additional evidence suggests that SMA plays a special role in programming actions that are not directed at an environmentally defined target. For example, monkeys with lesions to SMA have great difficulty learning a sequence of three movements that are not structured by environmental stimuli, but can easily learn to move a handle in response to a color cue.[30] In addition, researchers have found that patients with damage to SMA could not wave "bye bye," nor could they be taught to do so![31] In contrast, these patients could point to visible targets.

Another cortical area, the *premotor cortex (area 6),* appears to be involved in carrying out the computations of the instructions generation subsystem. Premotor cortex is located directly anterior to area M1 on the lateral surface, and does not extend quite as far forward as SMA. This area receives a large amount of input from the posterior parietal lobe, which we have inferred encodes spatial properties. This makes sense if the instructions

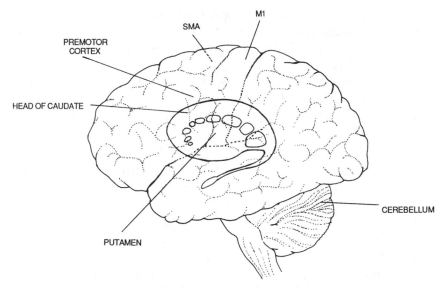

FIGURE 7.1 Key brain structures that produce movements

generation subsystem is embodied in the premotor cortex because it requires the coordinates not only of the target, but also of
any barriers or other environmentally imposed via points.

In addition, neurons in this area have been found that fire
after a monkey has been cued that it will have to reach in a given
way, but before a "go" signal is presented. This activity seems to
be involved in "setting" the animal so that it will respond
properly when the signal is presented.[32] Also, lesions of the
premotor cortex impair an animal's ability to reach around a
transparent barrier to grasp food.[33] This finding is remarkable
because the animal could see the goal, the barrier, and the effects
of the barrier on reaching. The finding makes sense if the lesion
disrupted the instructions generation subsystem, preventing it
from making use of environmentally imposed via points to
compute a trajectory.

Furthermore, other researchers have found increased blood
flow in the premotor area when human subjects were asked to
move their fingers in specific ways.[34] In contrast, the premotor
area did not become more active when subjects performed
previously memorized sequences of finger movements; this
makes sense if the instructions generation subsystem did not

need to compute a novel trajectory for memorized sequences and hence did not have to work very hard in this condition. However, increased blood flow occurred in SMA when subjects performed memorized actions, which suggests that the planning process was active even in this task; presumably, planning is required even if the trajectories of individual actions have been stored previously. (As we shall see shortly, however, we would not expect such activity if the sequence were highly overlearned, so that it could be performed "automatically.")

Results such as these indicate that the premotor area is not simply executing instructions formulated elsewhere in the system, but has some role in setting up the actual movement itself. The premotor system apparently plays a critical role in the process of computing a novel trajectory, when one cannot simply look up a stored motor memory to compute a trajectory. If so, then it makes sense that neurons in this area are involved in "setting" an animal to behave in a specific way, and that disruptions of this area are particularly severe when complex sequences of movements are necessary (such as those required to reach around a barrier).

It is also of interest that some neurons in the premotor area seem to control sets of large muscles, particularly those that move the trunk and arms. If movements are composed hierarchically, large movements usually would be initiated before finer ones; until the arm is in motion, there is no reason to begin opening the hand. Thus, once the movement instructions are generated, these initial movements can commence, but the movement execution subsystem is needed to compute the precise movements required later in the sequence. The fact that some neurons in this area appear to be involved in executing movements is another example of the principle of weak modularity.

Parts of the *basal ganglia* are also involved in planning actions and generating instructions. Indeed, our distinction between the two subsystems just considered and the movement execution subsystem is consistent with the idea that two distinct motor "loops" (i.e., circuits) pass through the basal ganglia.[35] The so-called "complex" loop is involved in planning and composing movements, and the "motor" loop is involved in executing them. The complex loop includes areas in the frontal lobe, which presumably are neural underpinnings of the action programming and instructions generation subsystems. These instructions are then sent to the caudate nucleus portion of the basal ganglia. We note further that the instructions could then be sent to a structure immediately adjacent to this nucleus; neurons in the globus pallidus portion of the basal ganglia fire immediately before a monkey makes a voluntary movement.[36] These areas in turn send information to the thalamus, which feeds information back up to the frontal lobe (in addition to other parts of cortex).

The role of the basal ganglia in planning movements is dramatically illustrated by the plight of patients with Parkinson's disease, which affects this structure. These patients shake, have trouble initiating movements, walk with a shuffle, and generally move very slowly. Their limbs often seem stiff; for example, if an examiner tries to bend the arm, the patient seems to be resisting. However, these symptoms can disappear if the patient does not try to plan movements in advance. For example, his or her gait improves dramatically if two-by-four pieces of wood are placed at regular intervals across a path, and the patient is asked not to step on them. This finding suggests that the patients can generate and execute movements properly, but have difficulty planning them. If the environment is structured so that relatively simple movements are elicited individually, without requiring advanced planning, the patients behave almost normally. Other diseases of the basal ganglia, such as Huntington's disease, also impair voluntary movement execution.

Finally, a number of other neural structures implement the movement execution subsystem. Area M1 (also called the precentral gyrus, motor strip, primary motor cortex, and area 4) is clearly involved in this process. Neurons in M1 control fine motor movements on the opposite side of the body. Recall from Chapter 1 that Fritsch and Hitzig applied small electrical shocks to parts of dogs' brains and found that different muscles moved when the shocks were delivered to different sites; we would expect this finding if they had stimulated M1. Indeed, as noted earlier, Wilder Penfield and his colleagues performed similar experiments on humans prior to brain surgery, and found that the body is spatially represented along this strip of cortex, with the hands, face, and vocal apparatus being controlled by relatively large regions.[37]

Many of the neurons in M1 have a direct connection to motor neurons in the spinal cord, which is consistent with the inference that M1 is involved in actually executing the movements rather than planning them. Indeed, some of these neurons synapse onto individual motor units, and may control individual muscles.[38]

Other areas are also involved in executing motor commands. For one, the "motor loop" apparently is initiated by the premotor area (area 6) and M1, and is mediated by another portion of the basal ganglia, the *putamen*. Thus, the basal ganglia are involved in carrying out the computations of both the movement execution and instructions generation subsystems. In addition, the *cerebellum* appears to play a critical role in movement execution, and might be a site of motor memories. The cerebellum contains over half of the neurons in the human brain, and probably has many functions.[39] Patients with damage to the cerebellum often exhibit flacid muscle tone, have trouble maintaining balance, and have problems in "coordination"; for example, they may overshoot when trying to reach towards a target and cannot perform motor tasks that involve interweaving several motions repetitively (e.g., walking heel-to-toe). It is as if the damaged cerebellum cannot easily "reset" to a response that was just inhibited. A good simulation of some of this behavior is exhibited by someone who has had too much to drink; alcohol appears to have specifically strong effects on the cerebellum.[40] Patients with cerebellar damage sometimes have been misdiagnosed as simply being drunk!

Furthermore, patients with damaged cerebella have trouble tapping at a constant rate,[41] but the deficit is different in patients who had damage to the lateral portions of the cerebellum compared to those who had damage to the medial portions. Patients with lateral damage had abnormal variability in timing the taps, but normal ability to execute the tapping movement itself; in contrast, those with medial damage had trouble executing the movements but could space them normally. These results have been taken to imply that timing is carried out by a separate process from execution per se.

We assume that the instructions generation subsystem controls timing, and that input from this subsystem to the cerebellum can be disrupted by lateral damage. However, we cannot rule out the possibility that portions of the instructions generation subsystem are actually embodied in the cerebellum; similarly, feedback from the cerebellum to motor cortex may play a critical role in the process of generating instructions. Indeed, if motor memories are accessed in the course of generating instructions for movements, as is suggested by the neural network models, then this might be a good example of the principle of weak modularity; motor memories may play an integral role in both generating instructions for movements and actually executing those movements.

In short, there is good neurophysiological evidence for our distinction between the action programming, instructions generation, and movement execution subsystems. Given the number of distinct areas that are involved, and the differences in their properties, we expect these three subsystems to be divided into more precisely specified subsystems (in the same way that the ventral and dorsal subsystems were decomposed in vision). However, we shall not attempt to push this analysis further here.

Movement Monitoring

Karl Lashley argued that we produce a spoken phrase without using feedback, in part because we would talk too slowly if we had to listen to each word before saying the next one.[42] It is in this context that two special aspects of speech are relevant: We speak relatively quickly, and there are strong constraints on the ways in which words can be combined (see Chapter 6). In contrast, when one combines portions of a new dance or the like, the action usually takes place over a much longer time scale than speaking a phrase or sentence. Furthermore, many movements can be composed in a large variety of ways. If one is composing movements in a new way over a long period of time, there may be "slippage at the junctures"—small errors in composing pairs of movements can compound, leading the action to miss the final target altogether.

Hence, we typically monitor each movement and use this feedback to correct slippage. Properties of this function lead us to posit a *movement monitoring subsystem,* which receives two kinds of input: feedback from perceptual systems about the position of a moving limb and output from the instructions generation subsystem about the expected trajectory. The movement monitoring subsystem compares the actual limb position to the expected position, and provides a "correction signal" to the instructions generation subsystem. This correction signal allows the instructions generation subsystem to adjust the trajectory appropriately. We hypothesize a distinct subsystem because this input/output mapping is qualitatively distinct from those considered so far, and hence would be computed more effectively by a distinct network (or networks).

The movement monitoring subsystem must be distinguished from other, "reflexive" ways in which feedback alters movement. Our muscles contain two kinds of fibers, *extrafusal* and *intrafusal*. Extrafusal fibers are large, and are used to move or to stabilize limbs, whereas intrafusal fibers are used to measure how much a muscle is extended. Intrafusal fibers have sensory endings that are sensitive to the length and the motion of muscles; this information, along with information from proprioceptors that indicates the mechanical state of a body part (such as information about joint angles), is sent to the spinal cord. Some of these outputs result in immediate effects at the level of the spinal cord, whereas others are sent to the cortex for more complex processing.

When a limb is suddenly perturbed in the middle of a movement, intrafusal fibers will be stretched abnormally—and thereupon will send a feedback signal to the spinal cord. This feedback produces input to the extrafusal and related fibers, which in turn control the perturbation. This mechanism is called the *stretch reflex*. This reflex has two response components; a fast component (of about 25 milliseconds) that does not involve cortical processes, and a slow component (of about 100 milliseconds) that probably involves cortical processing.[43] The slow component of the stretch reflex may arise when the movement monitoring subsystem sends a correction signal to the instructions generation subsystem, which produces compensatory movements. This idea is consistent with the high density of intrafusal fibers in muscles used to produce fine movements, such as those in the hand, neck, and extraocular muscles.[44, 45]

In addition to feedback from receptors in the muscles, it has been discovered that there are feedback messages within the nervous system itself.[46] This feedback consists of a copy of the command to the muscles, which apparently is sent back to the movement execution subsystem itself; indeed, neurons in the primary motor cortex (area M1) receive feedback from the muscle fibers they activate.[47] The movement execution subsystem apparently checks how faithfully its output was received by the muscles.

It is of interest that when typists make an error, they press the key with less force than when they type correctly;[48] this finding may suggest that the typist knows that an error was made before the key was actually pressed—which presumably occurs via this sort of feedback. (Alternatively, it may simply indicate that the muscle command was incorrect, which resulted both in a weak key press and in pressing the incorrect key.) The function of this feedback is reminiscent of a feature of many computer terminals that are connected to remote computers. These terminals use a communication system called "full duplex," where the symbols on the screen are not produced by pressing a key directly, but rather are echoed back from the computer—which allows the user to ensure that the proper symbol was received.

Furthermore, some neurons in the posterior parietal lobes appear to play a role in registering and using feedback. The parietal lobes contain neurons that receive input in multiple sensory modalities and that appear to code for spatial properties, including the positions of limbs or targets of limbs. In addition, some of these neurons fire immediately before an intentional movement, and do not fire if the limb is passively moved to a location,[49] whereas others fire during the interval a monkey has to remember where to look next.[50] Properties like these are necessary if neurons are to compare the expected consequences of an action to the actual consequences; a representation of the expected effect must be compared with feedback to generate the correction signal.[51]

In summary, we are led to distinguish three types of feedback. One sort of feedback involves very fast corrections at the level of the spinal cord; this feedback is reflexive, and does not inform the movement monitoring subsystem as we conceive of it here. A second sort of feedback apparently is processed via cortical subsystems. This type of feedback confirms that a motor command to the muscles was accurately received; this feedback appears to operate solely within the movement execution subsystem itself. A third type of feedback is also processed in the cortex, and provides information about the current position or trajectory of a limb. This type of feedback is relatively slow, and apparently is processed by the movement monitoring subsystem.

We infer that the movement monitoring subsystem exploits not only kinesthetic information but also visual information about the positions of the limbs. The fact that we use visual feedback to guide actions was demonstrated long ago by George Stratton, who for eight days wore a lens that turned the world upside down. At first, he reached incorrectly for objects and was disoriented. After a few days, however, he learned to compensate for the effects of the lens, and interacted normally with objects in the world. After the lens was removed, another (but shorter) period of adaptation was required until he returned to normal. Note that the initial problem, the eventual compensation, and the subsequent readjustment all depended on using visual feedback to guide actions.[52]

In short, when we produce actions by juxtaposing relatively simple movements in new ways, we monitor the transitions. Kinesthetic and visual feedback is provided by perceptual encoding subsystems, and the movement monitoring subsystem compares this feedback to the expected positions of the limbs. If the observed and expected positions are different, the movement monitoring subsystem sends the appropriate "correction signal" to the instructions generation subsystem. This signal forces the instructions generation subsystem to produce new instructions for the movement execution subsystem. This correction process may be similar to the "back propagation" error-correction technique used to train neural networks, as was discussed in Chapter 2. Indeed, the movement monitoring subsystem fills the role of the "teacher" in this process, computing the disparity between expected and observed outputs. This subsystem apparently is implemented in part by structures in the parietal lobes.[53]

Additional findings support the distinction between movements that are guided by feedback from the movement monitoring subsystem and those that are guided by instructions executed without feedback. In one study, brain-damaged patients were asked simply to reach for a point of light, and the time to initiate the reach, to accelerate, and to decelerate was recorded.[54] Patients with damage to the left hemisphere could initiate the reach properly, but took longer to decelerate. Presumably, feedback is used to guide the hand during the find phase of reaching—

and this process is disrupted in these patients. In contrast, patients with damage to the right hemisphere had the opposite problem: They had trouble initiating the reach, but once it was under way, they behaved normally. This finding suggests that they had trouble accessing the relevant information in associative memory (which is unlikely, given how simple the task was), generating instructions, or executing them. But once the movement was under way, the patients could generate fine-tuning instructions and execute them properly. Additional sources of support for the distinction between an initial ballistic (unmonitored) movement and subsequent monitored movements have been provided for many years.[55]

Recap: Combining Simple Movements in New Ways

To compose a multi-movement sequence, the action programming subsystem sends the target coordinates (and possibly via point coordinates) of each component movement in the proper order to the instructions generation subsystem (via associative memory, where information from the perceptual encoding subsystems is available and specifications of movement sequences may be present). Hierarchical representations are often used so that segments can be initiated at the proper times. These instructions are sent to the movement execution subsystem. Because individual movements are composed for the first time, the sequence is often inaccurate; thus, the action must be monitored and errors corrected. The movement monitoring subsystem compares kinesthetic and visual feedback to the expected consequences of making the movement, and sends a "correction signal" to the instructions generation subsystem. This signal tunes the instructions to the movement execution subsystem appropriately.

Producing Written Words

Writing is a good example of an action in which we combine familiar movements in new ways: We combine letters to form words, and words to form sentences. It is unlikely that a distinct system exists in the brain to control writing per se; writing is a relatively recent invention, and probably a consequence of other evolutionary developments, not an "adaptation" in its own right.[56] Indeed, the process of combining written words into sentences is almost exactly the same as the process of combining spoken words into sentences, and it is reasonable to expect many of the same subsystems to be used in both activities.

The major differences between speaking and writing involve the kind of motor movements made. In writing, the goal is to control the hand and arm properly. Like speech, movement representations must be stored in associative memory to guide writing; arbitrarily assigned patterns are used to represent each letter. Different representations must be stored for different fonts (block letters, lowercase letters, etc.). Analogously to speech production, if handwriting is being used, each letter presumably is represented by a "packet" of combinations of coordinates; this kind of representation would allow the letter to be produced differently depending on the previous letter and following letter. We assume that one can access a specification of the letters that comprise a word, and that each letter is associated with appropriate target and via point coordinates; hence, writing can be produced when these coordinates are sent to the instructions generation subsystem. We assume that the sentence programming subsystem specifies the words, and the action programming subsystem specifies that they should be written.

During writing, the movement monitoring subsystem not only must monitor the individual movements, but also must ensure that letters and words are properly spaced. To position letters and words properly, the movement monitoring subsystem presumably uses visual information provided by the spatiotopic mapping and coordinate spatial relations encoding subsystems. The instructions generation subsystem takes into account such information as well as the present position of the hands and arm (which depends in part on what letter was just written and in part on where one is writing on a page); this information, in combination with the target and via point coordinates, allows the instructions generation subsystem to produce appropriate commands for the movement execution subsystem.

We need not store a separate movement representation directly with each word, but we must store such representations with each letter: We can immediately write new words upon being given their spellings—and hence can write before we can store a movement representation directly with the word in associative memory. Furthermore, we can write in cursive, lowercase, or uppercase; indeed, when shown a new way to print (e.g., with thicker lines on the right and very thin letters), we can use that method to write all words. A movement representation that specifies a particular way of writing a word cannot be stored until the word has been written that way at least one time.

Letter-to-Writing Conversion

We inferred in Chapter 5 that, for literate adults, associative memory typically contains an association between each word and the ordered set of letters that spell it. When learning to write using a new style, one may store an association between each individual letter of the alphabet and its target and via point coordinates. A word's spelling can be looked up by the categorical property lookup subsystem, which would send this information to another subsystem that converts these representations to target specifications for each of its letters. Because this process is computationally distinct from those considered so far, we are led to infer a *letter-to-writing conversion subsystem*. This subsystem takes representations of letters as inputs, accesses the corresponding coordinate specifications in associative memory, and sends these coordinates to the instructions generation subsystem. Presumably, new fonts are learned when new target specifications are associated with the letters of the alphabet in associative memory.

The letter-to-writing conversion subsystem we infer has a role like that of the "allographic conversion mechanism" inferred by others.[57] The allographic conversion mechanism, which computes a specific letter shape representation (e.g., in a specific font) from an abstract letter representation, apparently can be disrupted selectively by brain damage.[58] Alfonso Caramazza and his colleagues also posit an additional subsystem, referred to as the "graphemic buffer." They assume that the conversion is performed one letter at a time, and hence the input to the allographic conversion mechanism must be retained briefly until all letters have been processed. We assume that the instructions generation subsystem operates on multiple representations at the same time, and so functions as this buffer.

Sound-to-Writing Conversion

In addition, paralleling our ability to read, adults often can use the sound of a word to guess at its spelling. Indeed, some of us forget the spelling of many words, and use such a guessing process regularly (and hence often misspell irregular words). A distinct *sound-to-writing conversion subsystem* presumably performs this conversion process, which must make use of information in associative memory that pairs representations of the output from the auditory pattern activation subsystem with typical spelling patterns.

Following our reasoning about reading, we can infer two methods by which the sound-to-writing conversion subsystem may operate: First, there could be an associative network that simply pairs representations of sounds and letter patterns; second, the subsystem could access other words that have a similar sound, and substitute the appropriate letter. For example, when computing how to spell "frunk" when it is heard for the first time, a conversion subsystem might access "trunk," which sounds similar, and then substitute an "f" for the initial "t." To our knowledge, there are no data that implicate either method in particular, and it is possible that both are used.

Many researchers have inferred that the brain incorporates a mechanism that converts the sound of a word into letter representations.[59] Indeed, brain-damaged patients have been reported who have selective problems in using the sound of novel words to guess their spelling, and so cannot write these words; in contrast, these same patients have no problem spelling or writing familiar words.[60]

The additional subsystems we have inferred are illustrated in the context of the previously inferred subsystems in Figure 7.2.

Recap: Producing Written Words

Writing is performed the same way as other sorts of combinations of familiar movements, except that the coordinate specifications of words are produced by a letter-to-writing conversion subsystem. This subsystem accesses stored associations (in associative memory) between representations of a word and its letters

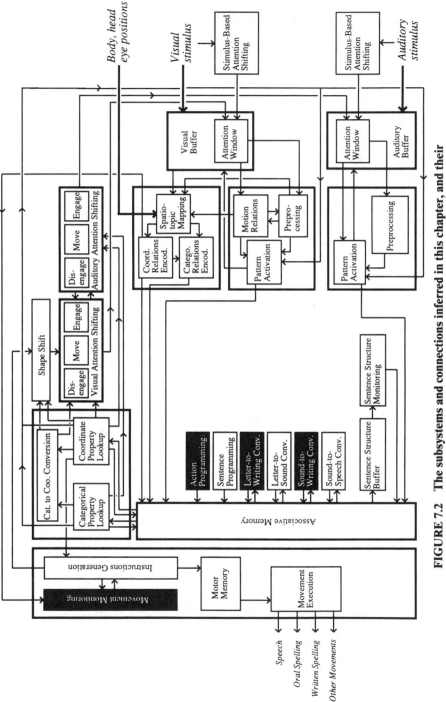

FIGURE 7.2 The subsystems and connections inferred in this chapter, and their relation to those inferred previously

316

and between the letters and specifications of their target and via point coordinates; the instructions generation subsystem uses these coordinate specifications in conjunction with information about the present position of the hand and arm to guide writing movements. A sound-to-writing conversion subsystem produces a set of letters for a word if they are not stored by rote.

Moving "Automatically"

When we are learning a new skill, we plan the sequence of individual movements and monitor them carefully as they are executed. But this can be exhausting! Fortunately, we soon are able to execute sequences of familiar movements "automatically," without having to think about each movement in turn. For example, when one is first learning to drive, one must think about each movement; coordinating the gas, clutch, and gear shift can be a major challenge. But after a few weeks, one can do all of this effortlessly. Similarly, children struggle to learn to write, whereas fluent adults write entire words automatically, without thinking about how to produce the individual letters. This shift is a consequence of several changes that occur when movements are generated repeatedly.

First, when movements are combined repeatedly, we store the sequence of coordinates as a single representation in associative memory. Second, when movements are combined repeatedly, we store a trajectory for the entire action in motor memory (we will discuss memory storage mechanisms in the following chapter). Thus, when the corresponding set of coordinates is present in the instructions generation subsystem, the appropriate trajectory can be computed by simply looking it up in memory. Third, if one has performed a movement enough times, the movement monitoring subsystem may have "tuned" the instructions to the point where additional monitoring is superfluous.

That is, we assume that once a trajectory has been modified by a correction signal, the new muscle commands can be stored in motor memory. With practice, the representations will become so good that the movement monitoring subsystem will not need to generate a correction signal, and much less processing will be required to perform the action.[61] The amount of practice that is necessary for an action to become automatic depends on the number of movements, the way they are arranged, and so forth.

Recap: Moving Automatically

"Automatic" actions occur when the coordinates of the target and via points for separate movements are stored in a single representation in associative memory, the corresponding motor representation is stored as a single unit in motor memory (as a "torque profile"), and these representations have been tuned by the movement monitoring subsystem so well that the action can be produced properly without using feedback.

Moving Encumbered Limbs

Just as we can speak with our mouths full, we can reach for a pencil even when wearing a ten-pound iron bracelet. We can move even when limbs are partially encumbered or restricted, compensating for current conditions. We must distinguish between three abilities that allow us to accomplish this feat.

First, if one is tugged off course, very low-level "homeostatic" mechanisms will try to correct the movement. These low-level mechanisms may be accomplished in part by the spinal cord, and involve no brain activity at all; as noted earlier, these processes occur relatively quickly. In addition, Andres Polit and Emillio Bizzi showed that once one begins to reach towards a target, the muscles act like springs that pull the limb back towards the target even when it is bumped far off course.[62]

Second, as one continues to reach, the movement monitoring subsystem sends information back to the instructions generation subsystem, which modifies the instructions sent to the movement execution subsystem. This cortical loop requires more time to act than the simpler spinal reflex.

Third, the movement instructions can be adjusted to anticipate certain conditions from the outset. For example, consider how you would reach if you were wearing the iron bracelet in the following situation: You were asked to reach under a large magnet, which exactly compensated for the extra weight of the bracelet. On some occasions the magnet was turned on, and on others it was off. If you were told in advance that the magnet was on, you would reach differently than if you were told that it was off. Indeed, if we fooled you, and told you that the magnet was off when it in fact was on, your wrist would probably fly up until the bracelet clanged against the magnet!

In this situation, you would compensate for an expected perturbation in advance of making the movement. When you initially hefted the bracelet (before reaching), information about its weight was encoded (via kinesthetic subsystems we have not discussed) and taken into account when the instructions generation subsystem produced new specifications. Thus, the initial reaching movement would be different depending on whether you thought that the magnet was on and whether you were wearing the bracelet.

The key to understanding our ability to compensate for encumbered limbs before beginning to move lies in the specifications sent to the instructions generation subsystem. We assume that when the weight was first lifted, the trajectory of the arm was perturbed and the movement monitoring subsystem provided the appropriate correction signal. The "tuned" movement representations were stored, and used for subsequent movements (as discussed above). This process will not be perfect, however, and thus the movement monitoring subsystem will be necessary in order to tune the instructions "on the fly."

Recap: Moving Encumbered Limbs

We move encumbered limbs using the same subsystems that we use to move unencumbered ones, and these subsystems operate in the same way in both cases. In particular, the movement monitoring subsystem uses feedback to compute correction signals, which allow the instructions generation subsystem to compensate for perturbations as they occur. In addition, the corrected movement representations that were required to compensate for prior perturbations are stored, and subsequently can be applied to a movement before it begins. This process makes it possible to anticipate the effects of a perturbation, and to compensate (at least in part) prior to performing an action.

Moving Different Limbs in the Same Way

In a pinch, most people can use a fork, open a door, or brush their teeth using their nondominant hand. Many of us can even write with a pencil when it is held in our mouths, albeit not very well. At first glance, one might be inclined to dismiss such transfer, focusing on how poorly we move in such situations. But one could argue that this is like a dog walking on its hind legs: What is remarkable is that it can do it at all, not that it does not walk as well as a human.

Thus, our ability to transfer actions to new limbs presents two puzzles: First, how can we transfer at all? If we learned to write, for example, with the right hand, how can we write with the left hand—or even with a mouth or a foot!—if we have to? And second, given that we can transfer actions to new limbs, why is such transfer not perfect?

Consider first why we can, at least in part, transfer familiar movements to new limbs. In associative memory, actions are stored as sets of target and via point coordinates, not instructions for specific movements. The instructions generation subsystem computes which movements are necessary to pass through the via points and reach the target coordinates within the constraints imposed by the current situation. If "decision subsystems" specify that a specific limb should be moved, this information can be sent to the instructions generation subsystem. Hence, the stored coordinates are used to generate commands for that limb.

But why, then, is it so hard to write with one's left hand? One answer is that if a movement is practiced, a particular representation will be stored in motor memory. But this representation specifies a particular sequence of muscle commands, which has been tailored by the movement monitoring subsystem to control a particular limb. Hence, the representation will not transfer well to another limb. For example, if one transfers hands, movement representations that are relative to the inner or outer side of the hand must be reversed. Thus, the instructions generation subsystem may be forced to compute a new trajectory, which may not be able to draw upon large motor sequences stored in motor memory.

Recap: Moving Different Limbs in the Same Way

Familiar movements are stored as sets of coordinates (target and via point) in associative memory, which do not specify individual motions; they also are stored as movement representations in motor memory, which are tailored for certain limbs. Although the target coordinates can easily be used to guide various limbs, the movement representations in motor memory cannot. Thus, familiar actions can be transferred, but only partially, to new limbs.

Mimicking Movements

We can mimic other people's movements. This ability can be broken into at least three abilities. We can observe and mimic a familiar movement; can observe and mimic a novel, relatively simple movement; and can observe and mimic someone who is combining movements in new ways. We will discuss each ability in turn.

First, consider how we can mimic someone when he or she performs a familiar movement. If the movement is familiar, we can identify it, and then can activate the corresponding representations as if we were performing it spontaneously. However, this is easier said than done. Consider the processing that may underlie this ability. In Chapter 4 we noted that mental imagery helps one to learn a skill; it does so, presumably, because it affords an opportunity to encode the coordinates of the end point and any via points of each movement, to generate the corresponding motor instructions (which are inhibited from being carried out), and to store these instructions in motor memory. These ideas are consistent with our inference that visual information can provide feedback to help guide one's own movements, which makes sense in part because coordinate spatial relations specify locations in a form that is useful for guiding movements (see Chapter 3).

Recall that the coordinate spatial relations encoding subsystem computes location relative to one's body or relative to objects in space; when reasoning about the spatiotopic mapping subsystem, we hypothesized that different objects can serve as the origin (anchor point) of the spatial representations. Thus, if one can encode the target and via point coordinates of another person's action relative to that person's body, these coordinates then can be compared (probably following much computation) to stored coordinates that are relative to one's own body. That is, once the other-body-centered coordinates are encoded, they can be compared to coordinates of actions stored in associative memory, which are relative to one's own body. If a stored representation is similar enough to the input, the action is identified (this is analogous to identifying an object visually, as discussed in Chapter 3), and it can be performed by sending the associated coordinates to the instructions generation subsystem. Indeed, the action can be performed well if the corresponding representation is also stored in motor memory.

Second, consider how we can mimic a new, relatively simple movement. In this case, the encoded coordinates do not match any that are associated with previously stored representations of movements. Thus, the encoded body-centered coordinates themselves will be sent to the instructions generation subsystem. This is not ideal, however, in part because the coordinates may not be encoded very precisely, and so the movement will be slightly awry. And perhaps more important, there is no corresponding motor representation that has been "tuned" to one's own musculature. The situation is in some ways analogous to writing with the nondominant hand, but now the coordinate specifications are derived from observation, not from associative memory. Thus, we should have more trouble mimicking a novel movement than mimicking a familiar one, which is clearly the case.

In addition, even if a novel movement is relatively simple, it may not be encoded as a single set of coordinates. One may encode the movement as relatively many small familiar movements that are arranged in a specific way. In a sense, no movement is completely novel; we are born with the ability to make a set of movements (some of which are only evident after considerable maturation), and can always discern familiar components of a movement. However, this sort of encoding strategy requires much more processing than does encoding familiar movements, where the units correspond to larger segments of the trajectory. This inference parallels the one we made in Chapter 5 when we discussed reading and hearing unfamiliar stimuli; when we do not have representations of relatively large segments, we must encode many smaller units—which requires more processing than is needed for familiar stimuli.

Third, consider how we mimic novel combinations of movements. For example, we might be shown how to play a new game, where one tosses balls in pockets in the side of a wall using a sideways throw. In this case, we encode coordinates that specify individual movements, as described above. In addition, the coordinate spatial relations encoding subsystem encodes into associative memory the coordinates of both the starting point and the target of each movement. The identity and order of the individual movements are stored in associative memory, which then can be used by the instructions generation subsystem to produce the movements in that order.

This process is very complex, and one may not encode all of the necessary coordinates to mimic an entire sequence. The pioneering Russian physiologist N. A. Bernstein suggested that when learning a new action one often encodes several subgoals that only approximate the action.[63] Hence, when one later produces the movement, one may lock joints together—which simplifies the problem of generating movement instructions on the basis of what has been encoded. There is evidence that this suggestion is correct.[64]

As more individual movements are composed into an action, the action will necessarily be increasingly imprecise; one has never combined the movements in this way before, and so the sequence has not been "tuned" for the properties of the limbs used to perform it. Thus, the movement monitoring subsystem will play a critical role in guiding mimicked actions.

Recap: Mimicking Movements

The target and via point coordinates of someone else's movements are encoded relative to his or her body by the coordinate spatial relations encoding subsystem, and then sent to associative memory. If these coordinates are similar to those associated with a movement stored in associative memory, this familiar movement is identified. The movement can then be performed in the same way it is performed spontaneously (as described earlier). However, if the encoded coordinates are not very similar to stored coordinates, then they must be stored and used to guide movement. In this case, the coordinates may not be very precise, and so the movement is not quite right; furthermore, the movement does not correspond to a motor representation of a large portion of the trajectory, and so requires more computation than is required for familiar movements. When a sequence of movements is imitated, the starting and target coordinates (plus via points) are encoded, and used to order the execution of specific movements. The movements and their ordering are "tuned" using the movement monitoring subsystem, and with practice become more precise.

Understanding the Effects of Brain Damage

In this section we consider breakdowns of motor control and writing that follow brain damage. There are a large number of putatively distinct types of these disorders, and they have been characterized in a wide variety of ways in the literature.[65] We have selected terminology that seems to illuminate the important distinctions among the varieties of disorders. We will consider first disorders of nonlinguistic movements, and then will turn to disorders of writing.

The Apraxias

The complexity of action is revealed by the patterns of breakdown following brain damage. These breakdowns in skill are collectively called the *apraxias* (derived from the Greek word *praxis,* meaning to do, action). The apraxias are due to mental problems, not problems in loss of muscular power (*paresis*) or problems in simple muscular control per se *(ataxia)*. However, the mental problems do not reflect a general intellectual deterioration, poor comprehension of the task, or poor cooperation with the examiner. In apraxia a person has reasonably full control of his or her muscles but is unable to carry out specific acts. That is, as was true in the agnosias, the apraxias are not due to deficits in more elementary processes, but reflect disruption of high-level processing. For example, Moyra Williams, in discussing an apraxic patient, notes that "when asked to touch his nose, he may touch the top of his head or his ears; when asked to comb his hair, he will turn the comb over and over in his hands two or three times or put it on the table; when asked to light a cigarette he will try to put the packet in his mouth and the cigarettes on the table."[66] There are several types of this disorder; as usual, we provide illustrative examples of the (many) ways these disorders can be explained.

Limb-kinetic apraxia. A person who has this disorder is unable to make precise movements with the limb on the side of the body opposite the lesion. For example, a patient with a left-hemisphere lesion will have trouble making precise movements with the right hand; such a patient has trouble following a request to pick up a dime from a table top because he or she cannot use the thumb and forefinger to pinch the dime, and often will brush it off the top of the table into his or her palm.[67] The problem is especially evident when the patient is trying to make fine finger movements, including simply tapping out a rhythm. The patient also has trouble imitating a series of movements.

This problem could reflect either difficulty in the action programming or instructions generation subsystems, components of which control only those limbs on the opposite side of the body. It is possible that either subsystem is degraded on one side, and hence has trouble precisely controlling movement. Alternatively, there may be a degraded connection from the instructions generation subsystem to one hemisphere's movement execution system. Care must be taken to distinguish this syndrome from ataxia, which is a general problem in making movements—not a problem in controlling the processes that "fine-tune" a gesture.

Ideomotor apraxia. This and all of the following apraxias are typically bilateral, affecting both sides of the body.[68] The patient with ideomotor apraxia is able to perform a sequence of movements, but has difficulty with the individual components. The required movement may be deleted, or "smeared" out, resulting in a kind of "motor slur." Sometimes two movements are conflated into a single gesture. For example, if asked to mime the action of using a match to light a candle, the patient might blur the movement of opening the match box with striking the match, and then move to holding the match to the top of the candle. In addition, patients with ideomotor apraxia improve little when they imitate a gesture or use actual objects as props.[69] This disorder typically occurs with lesions in the posterior left hemisphere.

Ideomotor apraxia could reflect problems in the action programming subsystem or its connection to associative memory; in this case, damage to the posterior left hemisphere could send spurious input to the frontal lobes (via several major fasciculi), and hence some individual target specifications will not be appropriately activated. In addition, the instructions generation subsystem could be disrupted, so that some steps are never generated. Furthermore, the disorder may in fact be a compensation for decreased activation, which precludes setting up complex sequences of movements; if so, then some movements will be deleted. This sort of account is parallel to a possible account for "telegraphic" speech output, which characterizes Broca's aphasia.

Ideational apraxia. The neurologist Hugo Liepmann first used this term to refer to a disconnection between the brain areas used to conceptualize a movement and the areas that allow one to make the movement.[70] The patient is often painfully aware of this disruption, which is increasingly evident for more complex and unfamiliar tasks. The main problem is in voluntarily performing a gesture that involves sequences of movements. For example, when explicitly asked to do so, a patient might be completely unable to carry out the steps required to light a candle (i.e., lift up the match book, open it, take out a match, light the match, put down the book, move the lit match to the candle, etc.). However, if the electricity went out, the patient would have no problem actually lighting a candle. Similarly, these patients might have no difficulty putting on their glasses when starting to read, but be completely unable to do so when the doctor specifically requests them to do so.

Harold Goodglass and Edith Kaplan noted that these patients often have disruptions in the ability to make gestures and to pantomime.[71] For example, when asked to demonstrate how one brushes one's teeth in the morning, these patients do not act as if they are holding a toothbrush and moving it back and forth; rather, they take the tip of a finger and rub it over their teeth. These patients are typically much better at imitating than at producing gestures.

This disorder could arise from a disconnection between the output of language comprehension processes and the action programming subsystem. The fact that the action can be carried out spontaneously indicates that the action programming subsystem must be able to activate the appropriate target specifications in associative memory, and that these targets can be used by the instructions generation subsystem to program the action. This disorder may also reflect disruptions of the movement monitoring subsystem, which may send spurious "correction signals" into the system. This makes sense given that the lesion is often in the parietal lobes, where we expect such processes to occur. Furthermore, the deficit is increasingly evident for more complex and unfamiliar tasks, which presumably rely more strongly on such monitoring. In addition, the patient can often perform an action "unconsciously" (e.g., light a candle). If the patient is not trying to guide an overlearned movement, he or she can do it; if the patient is trying to guide it, or has to—because the movement is novel—he or she is inept. Moreover, when one imitates a movement the external stimulus elicits the behavior, providing a guide for each individual motion. Thus, imitation requires less movement monitoring to sequence the motions than is required during spontaneous action. These notions are consistent with the fact that these patients will make errors by symbolic substitutions (e.g., brushing one's teeth with a finger) when asked to perform an action, which greatly simplify the necessary sequencing. This sort of substitution may reflect a compensatory strategy used if the movement monitoring subsystem is degraded.

Constructional apraxia. Constructional apraxia is evident when a patient is asked to copy a drawing, or to build a copy of a model. The patient is not only poor at copying novel stimuli, but is equally poor at copying stimuli that were highly familiar prior to the brain damage. There are now a number of standard tests for assessing constructional apraxia;[72] the responses to the different tests are not always correlated, suggesting that the disorder reflects impairment to a number of underlying components, which can be damaged independently.[73]

For example, patients who have constructional apraxia will not copy or draw accurately. They often will start the drawing too near an edge of the page, will draw it smaller or larger than the original, may duplicate lines or crowd them together, may rotate the figure, or may omit parts. These patients appear to have problems positioning parts correctly in a drawing, especially relative to a reference frame. In principle, this could reflect a deficit in the action programming, property lookup, and/or the coordinate spatial relations encoding subsystems. All of these subsystems are required to encode a shape and perform the necessary movements to draw it.

Similarly, these patients have trouble studying a design made of sticks of different lengths or a model made of blocks, and reproducing it with another set of sticks or blocks. These patients have trouble aligning sticks or blocks properly, so that they abut without overlapping. In addition, parts may be omitted or incorrectly arranged, and the patient sometimes will remove sticks or blocks from the original to use in making the copy.

In principle, these impairments could reflect at least three different kinds of disruptions: First, the action programming subsystem may be impaired, preventing it from specifying the proper sequence of movements. Second, the coordinate spatial relations encoding subsystem may be damaged, preventing one from knowing which stick or block is being copied. Third, the movement monitoring subsystem may be disrupted, preventing one from correctly adjusting the movements that position the sticks or blocks in the copy. In this task one cannot use shape variation to help arrange the parts (as can be done in drawing), and so the patients may become confused about "where they are" in the process; the strategy of removing a stick or block from the model would help to overcome this deficit, eliminating the chance of "re-copying" that part.

Studies of patients suffering from constructional apraxia have revealed that damage to either cerebral hemisphere can produce the disorder. It is sometimes stated that right-hemisphere damage results in a "piecemeal" approach to drawing and building a model,[74] where the individual parts are correctly placed but the overall design is awry. In contrast, left-hemisphere damage putatively results in a wholistic approach, in which the overall design is correct but details are deleted.[75] Patients with right-hemisphere damage often have particular difficulty copying complex or three-dimensional objects.

These clinical observations have proven difficult to document, however, and they often may have been based more on the way in which drawings are done—particularly the order in which segments are produced—than on the nature of the final product.[76] Sole use of categorical spatial relations (which could occur following damage to the right hemisphere) might result in a part-by-part chaining procedure and disruption of metric relations, and sole use of coordinate locations (which could occur following damage to the left hemisphere) might result in a haphazard absolute placement of parts, without the usual bias to include pairs of parts that are conjoined by categorical relations (being connected, adjacent, one within the other, and so on).

These ideas are consistent with the observation that these patients' lesions are usually in the posterior portions of the brain, and that damage to the frontal lobes (which are involved in action programming) does not produce these disturbances. However, if the frontal lobes receive spurious inputs as a consequence of this damage, then it is possible that an impaired action programming subsystem underlies this disorder.

Dressing apraxia. This disorder is immediately evident both in the clinic and at home: The patient has great difficulty in getting dressed. This difficulty is sometimes regarded as simply a special case of ideational apraxia, but it typically occurs even when the patient is moving spontaneously. The patient seems to have particular difficulties in sequencing separate actions (sometimes a jacket is put on before a shirt), including those required to put on even a single garment; for example, when trying to put on a jacket, the patient will get hung up trying to figure out where the arms go, and sometimes will end up with the jacket on backwards. Buttoning a garment is especially difficult.[77]

This disorder may also involve a component of unilateral neglect, making it difficult for the patient to attend to appropriate parts of the body. In keeping with this observation, this disorder is often a consequence of damage to the right posterior areas, particularly the temporal-parietal-occipital junction area. In addition to reflecting damage to the spatiotopic mapping subsystem (see Chapter 3), this deficit could also reflect disruption of the movement monitoring subsystem (possibly on only one side of the body) or disruption of the instructions generation subsystem.

Buccofacial (oral) apraxia. A patient who has this disorder has difficulty making skilled gestures using the facial muscles. For example, these people display some disruption of movements of the lips, tongue, and cheeks, as is evident in their inability to pretend to blow out a match, suck on a straw, or blow a kiss. These patients make several interesting types of errors,[78] such as substituting a verbal description for the action. For example, the patient might simply say the word "blow" when asked to pretend to blow out a match. In addition, these patients will sometimes substitute other movements for the one requested, or will perseverate, not stopping a given movement at the appropriate place.

Many of these patients become dramatically better at performing the action when given the object as a prop. So, for example, a patient unable to pretend to blow out a match will do just fine when given an actual lit match to blow out. At first glance, this disorder might sound similar to ideational apraxia, which might suggest that the movement monitoring subsystem is impaired. But this disorder typically follows damage to the frontal lobes, particularly the left frontal lobe—and the movement monitoring subsystem probably is implemented in the parietal lobes. It is possible that the frontal lobes send spurious input to the parietal lobes, and this input disrupts the movement monitoring subsystem. In addition, let us consider several other types of possible accounts.

This disorder may be related to a deficit we noted earlier, in which patients with damage to the supplementary motor cortex cannot wave "bye bye." We assumed that this area plays a special role in action programming. Facial muscles are controlled by different pathways from the rest of the body (i.e., directly from cranial nerves); these pathways may require different sorts of programming—which can be selectively disrupted. It would be worth knowing whether these patients always have problems producing other sorts of behaviors that are not tied to environmental cues. Alternatively, the lesion may damage tissue that is necessary for the coordinate property lookup subsystem to access information used to program facial movements. When the prop is encoded perceptually, this information may access the appropriate representations in associative memory, which in turn become activated. Furthermore, when asked to perform the action without the prop, many normal people report forming a visual image of the object, which is used to guide the action; this may be difficult for these patients because of damage to the property lookup subsystems (see Chapter 4) or decreased activation levels.

Disassociation apraxias. There are two types of disorders that seem to indicate a disconnection between input and output subsystems. In one, a patient will appear not to understand a verbal command to perform an action, but he or she can recognize the correct act when a doctor demonstrates it and can even imitate the action. Thus, these patients comprehend the act to which the request refers, but cannot carry it out. The final stages of the processes used to comprehend sentences apparently cannot provide input to the action programming subsystem, or the action programming subsystem cannot accept such input. These accounts are consistent with the finding that, in contrast to patients with ideomotor apraxia, these patients can imitate and use actual objects perfectly.[79] The deficit is a problem in getting from verbal input to action programming, not in understanding verbal input or programming actions per se.

The other disorder is similar, but is the obverse. That is, these patients cannot imitate a gesture, but can perform the act when given a verbal request. Apparently visual input cannot activate the appropriate target specifications in associative memory, or cannot provide feedback to the movement monitoring subsystem. Patients have also been described who did better with tactile stimuli than with verbal commands, and others did better with visual and verbal stimuli than tactile.[80] These findings suggest that tactile input also can fail to activate the appropriate target specifications in associative memory, or can fail to provide feedback to the movement monitoring subsystem.

The reader may have noticed at this point that more than one deficit may occur after one kind of damage. And in fact, many of these deficits can occur together in a single patient. However, one sometimes sees some forms of impairment without the others. Not only is damage often diffuse, but also we assume that different amounts of damage produce different degrees of decrement in overall activation levels. And because some behaviors require more complex computations than others, they may be affected by brain damage when other, less demanding, tasks are spared. Furthermore, the neural networks that carry out each type of computation presumably behave differently depending on the precise type of damage, as has been demonstrated with network models.[81] To understand the precise pattern of spared and impaired abilities in a single patient, one would need good network models of each subsystem and the connections among them, and would need to understand how the networks behave and interact with different degrees and types of damage.

The Agraphias

Agraphia is a disruption of the ability to write, which can occur in the presence or absence of the ability to read. When a similar ability is disrupted in both reading and writing, this is a strong hint that representations and processes in associative memory have been disrupted; when the two abilities are dissociated, this may be a hint that more peripheral subsystems have been impaired. The following disorders provide examples of both sorts of deficits. We begin with three types of disorders that seem to reflect more peripheral problems, and then turn to disorders that reflect language-related facets of the ability. These latter difficulties will help to tie material discussed in this chapter to material discussed in the previous one.[82]

Apraxic agraphia. Some patients have trouble performing learned movements, including holding a pen or pencil properly, which leads to illegible handwriting—both when they write spontaneously and to dictation. They can, however, spell aloud correctly; thus, the representations of words and their letters must be intact in associative memory. These patients usually write better when copying, and they often can learn to type or use anagram letters—which indicates that the problem is in performing writing movements per se. Lesions in the left parietal lobe are often associated with this problem (for right-handed people).

Because this deficit affects a variety of fine motor movements, it could reflect impaired function of the action programming, instructions generation, movement monitoring, or movement execution subsystems, or of the interconnections among these subsystems. The location of the lesion is perhaps most consistent with the idea that these patients have difficulty monitoring fine movements and correcting perturbations, but lesions may have remote effects—and so the other possible accounts cannot be rejected out of hand.

Apraxic agraphia without apraxia. Other patients also produce illegibly formed graphemes (i.e., letters and punctuation) in spontaneous writing and writing to dictation, but have preserved oral spelling. However, these patients can control movements normally, and can even properly imitate holding a pen or pencil.[83] Like the apraxic patients, they write better when copying. These patients also can read, and can pronounce a word upon hearing its spelling.

This deficit could reflect impaired function of the instructions generation subsystem, which may have difficulty coordinating very fine movements. In addition, the movement monitoring subsystem may play a critical role when one makes the sort of fine motor movements used in writing, and not when one makes common larger movements; if so, then if this subsystem is minimally disrupted, it may appear to produce a deficit in writing but not in other actions. Furthermore, this deficit may reflect a quantitative difference from the apraxic patients, rather than a qualitative change in the operation of the system; that is, holding a pen properly does not require such fine movement execution as actually writing.

Spatial agraphia. Patients with this disorder have difficulty putting lines in the correct places on a page. They (1) reiterate strokes, (2) cannot write in a straight line, and (3) insert inappropriate blank spaces. They have great difficulty copying, but can spell aloud and can pronounce a word upon hearing its spelling. This syndrome is frequently associated with unilateral visual neglect, and is often a consequence of nondominant hemisphere lesions (i.e., the right hemisphere in a left-hemisphere dominant person, which is the case for the majority of people).

The problem clearly is due to difficulty coordinating movement with lines on the page, which reflects difficulty in properly representing the location of the lines, the writing hand, or both. If the patient has unilateral visual neglect, the problem may be in attending to the proper places on the page or monitoring the results of prior portions of the action (i.e., seeing the previously written letters or words). This problem could also reflect damage to the spatiotopic mapping or coordinate spatial relations encoding subsystems, so that metric distance cannot be registered; these hypotheses are also consistent with the lesion location.

Unilateral (callosal) agraphia. Agraphia typically is evident when the patient tries to write with either hand. This form of agraphia affects only one hand, typically the left. If the corpus callosum is cut, the left hand of right-handed patients may be unable to write at all, whereas the right hand is intact. Although such patients may produce only an illegible scrawl with the left hand when writing, they may be able to type with this hand.[84] However, other patients can neither write nor type with the left hand following such a lesion.

This difficulty apparently reflects a selective disconnection of the right hemisphere from a lateralized language function on the left side. We can explain the results by positing that the left hemisphere has better representations of the coordinates of letters or the corresponding motor representations, and/or has more effective subsystems that access these stored representations and generate instructions for the movement execution subsystem.

Lexical agraphia. Most agraphias do not reflect problems in producing movements per se, but rather are caused by problems in language processing. By considering these disorders here, we see how the mechanisms underlying movement control are related to those discussed in the previous chapter. We noted earlier that adults apparently use two methods to spell words, one that involves accessing a stored representation of the word's spelling and one that involves accessing a stored representation of its sound. The first method requires looking up the representations of the letters and their ordering, which are associated with target specifications that in turn are used to generate the appropriate movement instructions. The ability to look up the spelling is necessary to spell irregular words (e.g., "island") and words that have homophones ("pear" vs. "pair"), which cannot be spelled correctly based only on the sound of the word. In contrast, the sound-based method uses representations of the sound of the word to infer the spelling. This process must make use of information in associative memory that assigns sounds to typical spelling patterns.

Dysfunction of the ability to use stored representations of spelling is called *lexical agraphia.* It has also been called *phonological spelling,* focusing on the operation of the intact ability. These patients cannot spell irregular and ambiguous words, but they are able to spell regular words and pronounceable nonwords. Errors are often nonwords that are phonologically correct, such as "gelosy" for "jealousy."[85] When researchers examined the overlap in CT scans from four patients suffering from lexical agraphia, they found damage to the left angular gyrus and the parieto-occipital gyrus in every case.[86]

The impairment could arise if damage decreased the activation level, and made accessing rote representations (of irregular words) more difficult than using the sounding out processes (which are based on highly practiced language processes). If so, then the damage would disrupt the more demanding processing while sparing the less demanding processing. Another possibility is that the sounding-out process is inhibiting the categorical property lookup subsystem from accessing the representation stored by rote or the letter-to-writing conversion subsystem from producing the target specifications. That is, when looking up an irregular word (which one does not know will be irregular in advance), the sounding out process must be inhibited (it will produce the wrong spelling). We assume that all processes typically are running at the same time (recall the principle of concurrent processing); the decision-making processes are good, but not good enough to sequence everything properly—in most cases parallel processes, such as those involved in constraint satisfaction, must be used. If so, then perhaps this deficit occurs because the sounding-out process improperly inhibits the rote lookup or letter-to-writing conversion process. Because the patient is relying on looking up the sound pattern associated with the word, and converting it to a set of letter instructions, the errors are often nonwords that are phonologically correct, such as "gelosy" for "jealousy."

In addition, this syndrome could arise if the individual letter representations in associative memory were disrupted and imagery was impaired; such disruptions would produce an impaired ability to spell irregular and ambiguous words in the face of an intact ability to spell regular words and nonwords. For irregular words one cannot rely on the sound of the word to produce the correct letters; one must access the stored letters themselves. This can be done in the normal system either by looking up the individual letters or by visualizing the entire word and "reading" the letters. As was discussed in Chapter 4, the imagery deficit could arise for numerous reasons; perhaps images of words cannot be formed, the individual letters cannot be recognized in the image, or images cannot be maintained long enough to be "read off"; if the patient can read, then we can infer that the visual interpretation processes are intact. It may be of interest that the common observed lesion site, the left angular gyrus and the parieto-occipital gyrus, may be associated with an image generation deficit.[87]

Phonological agraphia.   The sound-based method can be used to spell unfamiliar regular words and pronounceable nonwords (such as "glub" or "spab"). The fact that some patients cannot spell pronounceable nonwords but can spell both regular and irregular familiar words has been taken to indicate that the sounding-out process is awry. When the patient makes a mistake, the errors reflect the visual similarity of words, with errors resulting in a word that looks similar. Again examining overlap in CT scans from patients having this disorder, researchers found that the common site of lesion was in the supramarginal gyrus or the insula medial to it.[88]

In this disorder the sound-to-writing conversion subsystem or the route from it to the coordinate property lookup subsystem could be disrupted; hence, the patient cannot spell pronounceable nonwords but can spell familiar words, both regular and irregular. The sound input accesses a similar-sounding word (one that satisfies as many constraints posed by the input as possible), which is then spelled. Hence, erroneous words often will share many letters with the correct one. Alternatively, an analogy-based comparison process could be amiss, preventing novel words or pronounceable nonwords from matching the nearest word, and its spelling from being modified appropriately.

Deep agraphia. Recall that deep dyslexia is always accompanied by agraphia. The type of agraphia exhibited by these patients is called "deep agraphia." Patients suffering from deep agraphia have a syndrome that includes difficulty in spelling nonwords, conjunctions, prepositions, and adverbs. Moreover, they can spell nouns that name highly imageable objects better than those that label abstract concepts (e.g., "arm" versus "law"). These patients also make semantic paragraphias, which are spelling errors that result in real words that have a meaning related to the stimulus word—even though the words do not sound or look alike. For example, they might spell "flight" when asked to spell "propeller."[89]

According to our analyses, deep dyslexia reflects problems in associative memory (see pages 205–207). If so, then the same kinds of difficulties should be evident in reading and writing—in both deep dyslexia and deep agraphia. Many theories are possible to explain these disruptions, based on damage to representations and compensations that occur thereafter or disrupted inhibitory/excitory relations within associative memory (as was discussed in Chapter 5).

Patients with deep agraphia typically have lesions of the supramarginal gyrus or insula—and both areas are known to be involved in encoding auditory stimuli, and may be involved in storing semantic information associated with words. But their lesions typically are large, extending well beyond the area thought to be important for phonological agraphia per se. Having considered a few of these lesion localization findings, it is probably an appropriate time to remind the reader that although the area affected by a lesion certainly is not functioning as before, it is not the only area that functions abnormally; areas that receive input from the damaged area are also liable to be awry, and various compensations involving physiologically intact areas could also affect behavior. Thus, we must view these sorts of findings with caution.

Semantic agraphia. Patients with this deficit cannot write to express an idea; they write sentences that they do not understand, either when they read them or when someone else reads them aloud. Although these patients spell individual words correctly, they often supply incorrect words that sound the same as the correct ones (i.e., homophones). For example, when asked to spell "doe," a female deer, such patients may spell "dough." The lesions leading to this disorder are in similar locations to those affecting comprehension of spoken language.

This problem is at the level of comprehending words and their relations, not spelling or writing per se. The disorder may be the same as that underlying semantic problems in reading, but with a less severe disruption of the excitatory/inhibitory relations in associative memory (see Chapter 5).

We can understand many facets of how actions are controlled by adding only two subsystems, one that specifies the target and via point coordinates of a sequence of movements and one that monitors the consequences of moving in a specific way and sends a correction signal to the instructions generation subsystem to "fine-tune" the movement. We inferred two more subsystems to understand the particular case of writing, one that converts representations of letters to coordinate specifications and one that converts representations of sounds to sets of letters.

We again saw our five general principles at work. In particular, we saw the workings of the principle of weak modularity at every turn. We found that our inferences about the subsystems used in speech production helped us to understand movement more generally, and we inferred that the same subsystems are involved in writing and other sorts of movements. In addition, the mere existence of writing illustrates opportunistic processing at its best; virtually all of the necessary machinery was available for other purposes, and could be easily recruited in this new context. Furthermore, the principle of constraint satisfaction underlies the way actions are programmed and specific instructions are generated from target specifications, and lies at the heart of the use of "correction signals" sent by the movement monitoring subsystem. Indeed, even the movement execution subsystem appears to rely on constraint satisfaction; the neurons in area M1 are broadly tuned, and a specific direction of movement appears to be specified by the overlap in outputs of a population of neurons.

Moreover, the principle of division of labor again provides the foundation for the entire set of inferences we drew; we inferred new subsystems only when a necessary input/output mapping was very different from those performed by other subsystems, and hence was likely to be more effectively accomplished by a separate network. Finally, the idea of concurrent processing helped us to think about possible accounts for some sorts of agraphia; given that several processes are running at once, we were led to think about ways in which one could improperly inhibit the other.

In many cases, we noted that an apraxic disorder might reflect decreases in activation level; indeed, local pockets of "hypometabolism" can mimic the effects of a lesion in that area.[90] This possible basis of a disorder provides insight into a puzzle about apraxia. Specifically, although these patients usually are aware of their inability to perform the requested act, they cannot voluntarily correct their errors; in contrast, they often can perform the act if they are under emotional stress or if it is part of a well-learned sequence. For example, a person unable to dress may do just fine if awakened from sleep by someone screaming the word "fire" and the smell of smoke. John Hughlings Jackson noted such phenomena when he rejected strict localizationism, claiming that functions must be carried out by different systems that are evoked in different ways.

As we discussed earlier, one account of this phenomenon is that patients fail when they self-consciously monitor a movement, but can perform well if it is allowed to be executed "automatically." In addition, the present perspective leads us to suggest another account. In some cases, brain damage may reduce the activation level of specific neural loci, and stress may boost activation to a point where the computation can be performed. In many cases, both factors may be operating at once. This idea is consistent with the fact that such patients perform even worse than usual if they are urged to perform an action, which may reflect a deficit in the movement monitoring subsystem. But under extraordinary circumstances, the activation level may be raised to the point where even this damaged system may be able to perform normally.

8

Memory

Memory plays a critical role in many—if not all—aspects of cognition. Indeed, memory figured centrally in all of the abilities discussed in the previous chapters. It lies at the heart of our ability to understand written and spoken language because it enables us to identify words, to ascribe meaning to visual or auditory patterns, and to integrate the meanings of individual words into connected discourse. Similarly, it is critical in movement control and writing, in recognizing the face of a friend, in forming mental images, and so forth.

There is good reason to suspect that different sorts of memories underlie different abilities. Indeed, in previous chapters we inferred distinct unimodal visual and auditory memory structures, the visual and auditory pattern activation subsystems, respectively. We also discussed a special motor memory, which stores muscle commands to produce specific movements. Furthermore, in previous chapters we were led to infer that associations between "amodal" representations (which are not specific to any sensory modality) could be stored in yet another subsystem, which we called associative memory, and that associative memory contains a wide variety of different sorts of information —ranging from speech output codes to representations of visual output codes for specific shapes or letters of the alphabet.

In this chapter we will focus on the subsystems that allow us to enter various types of new information into memory. Even a moment's thought about memory encoding reveals that it has complex, even contradictory properties. In some circumstances, we cannot retain important facts for even very short periods of time; in others we can remember in great detail events of many years ago. We sometimes try hard to remember what we forgot, at other times we would prefer to forget what we do remember . . . These and other properties of our memories emerge from the joint action of several subsystems, which work together to store new information.

Components of Memory: An Overview

As is true in research on vision, detailed studies of nonhuman primates have revealed an enormous amount about the nature of the neural mechanisms underlying memory. These discoveries provide a firm foundation for inferences about the computations necessary to produce specific abilities. Before considering individual memory abilities in detail, it will behoove us to consider the general structure of the memory system. It is useful to organize the subsystems critical for memory into five groups, as illustrated in Figure 8.1.

Perceptual Encoding Subsystems

For convenience, we have summarized all of the perceptual subsystems inferred in previous chapters with a single box in Figure 8.1. Perceptual subsystems are critical for memory for at least three reasons. First, perception is often a prelude to

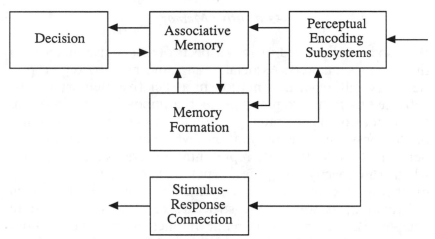

FIGURE 8.1 Overview of five groups of subsystems involved in encoding new memories

memory. Not only does perception provide much of the material one remembers, but it often defines the "context" that anchors memories to a particular time and place. Furthermore, we tend to remember important stimuli, and importance usually can be determined only after a stimulus is identified—which depends critically on perceptual subsystems.

Second, perceptual subsystems are relevant to memory because they are used to encode language. Verbal instructions not only define tasks in which memory is relevant, but also can direct one to remember something—which can lead to enhanced memory encoding. Similarly, language often defines a context, which in turn biases the perceptual systems so that we interpret —and later remember—stimuli in specific ways.

Third, perceptual encoding subsystems play a role in the storage of unimodal perceptual information. We inferred in Chapters 3 and 4 that unimodal visual information is probably stored in the inferior temporal lobe (in the object-properties-encoding subsystem), and we inferred in Chapter 6 that unimodal auditory information is probably stored in temporal-parietal cortex. We will build on these inferences in this chapter.

Associative Memory

We also have discussed various aspects of associative memory in the previous chapters. Associative memory has two key properties. First, although information in associative memory can be activated by input from any perceptual modality, this information is not stored perceptually. Rather, associative memory relies on "propositional" representations, which are not specific to any perceptual modality; these representations are like descriptions, which can specify categories, types of abstract relations (e.g., brother-of, member-of, and so on), and other nonperceptual information, as well as the structure of objects (as noted in Chapter 3).[1] Second, as its name implies, associative memory imposes an organization on stored information. Information in the unimodal subsystems is organized only in terms of simple part/whole relations, whereas associative memory is organized in complex ways that often rely on a variety of distinct types of associations (such as "is spelled as," "is a member of," "often is seen with," and so on).

Memory Formation Subsystems

The memory formation subsystems cause representations (of stimulus properties, spellings of words, and so on) and associations between representations to be stored.[2] Some representations of stimulus characteristics are stored in the perceptual subsystems, whereas others are stored in associative memory; similarly, associations can be established between representations in associative memory, or between these representations and representations in perceptual subsystems.

The memory formation subsystems rely on a set of anatomical structures located roughly in the middle of the brain, the principal members of this set being the *hippocampus* (and related cortex), the *limbic thalamus,* and the *basal forebrain.* Damage to any of these structures greatly impairs an animal's ability to store new information in memory.[3]

The hippocampus and related cortex. To be stored properly, incoming perceptual information must be processed by the hippocampus.[4] Before reaching the hippocampus, perceptual input converges on cortex under the front of the temporal lobe (i.e., the *parahippocampal gyrus* and the *perirhinal cortex*), which in turn projects to the *entorhinal cortex* and then to the hippocampus. The entorhinal cortex ultimately receives perceptual input in all modalities, and cells in the entorhinal cortex respond selectively to input in multiple perceptual modalities. A lesion in one or more of these structures typically results in memory deficits that are particularly evident when the subject tries to learn new material.[5]

In addition to receiving information from the entorhinal cortex, the hippocampus receives input from a number of other structures (the septum and the hypothalamus, via the fornix; the anterior thalamic nucleus and the subcallosal area, via the cingulum; and the amygdala). The hypothalamus is often grouped with the thalamus as constituting the *diencephalon*. The hypothalamus appears to be involved in motivation, and the amygdala appears to have a role in emotion;[6] clearly, both factors affect what we remember.

The hippocampus sends information to many parts of the brain: It sends output to the thalamus (anterior nucleus), the septum, the medial frontal cortex, and the mamillary bodies, via the fornix; it also sends output to the entorhinal cortex and then indirectly to the temporal cortex.[7] It is clear that the hippocampus not only receives information from perceptual subsystems, but it also sends information to those subsystems. The hippocampus plays a critical role in the storage of new perceptual representations.[8]

The hippocampus not only is involved in storing new representations of stimulus properties, but also plays a critical role in storing associations between representations.[9] These associations apparently depend in large part on the operation of specific neural microcircuits within the hippocampus.[10] The properties of some of these cells (e.g., dentate cells and pyramidal cells) change with use. As shall be discussed in detail shortly, this phenomenon is called *long-term potentiation*. Key anatomical areas involved in memory are illustrated in Figure 8.2.

Limbic thalamus. The limbic thalamus and related diencephalic structures shunt information from the hippocampus indirectly to

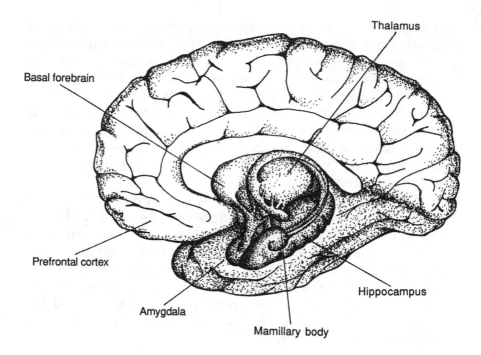

Thalamus

Basal forebrain

Prefrontal cortex

Amygdala

Mamillary body

Hippocampus

FIGURE 8.2 Many of the neural structures thought to be involved in encoding new memories

the basal forebrain (e.g., via the orbital frontal region). A lesion restricted to part of the limbic thalamus (e.g., the mediodorsal thalamic nucleus) causes a severe memory deficit in monkeys.[11] Although it is tempting to regard these structures simply as a relay, it is possible that they play a critical role in amplifying or augmenting the to-be-remembered information; many of the thalamic nuclei appear to be involved in attentional processes.[12]

Basal forebrain. The basal forebrain (which consists of the *nucleus basalis,* the *diagonal band of Broca,* and the *septal nuclei*) in turn issues a signal that new representations and/or associations should be stored.[13] This is a biochemical signal, consisting of the release of a neurotransmitter called *acetylcholine;* a neurotransmitter is a chemical messenger that carries signals across the synapses (connections) between neurons. A pathway of acetycholine-containing cells leads from the basal forebrain to various structures, including the cortical areas involved in perceptual encoding and the hippocampus. Presumably, this transmitter allows the "connection strengths" among neurons in a network to change, analogous to how information is encoded in computer simulation models of neural networks (as was discussed in Chapter 2).

Given that we define subsystems partly in terms of their inputs and outputs, it would be surprising if these varied anatomical areas embodied only a single subsystem. Rather, we shall decompose the memory formation subsystem into two more precisely characterized subsystems, just as we decomposed the ventral and dorsal systems in vision; these subsystems are involved in initiating the learning sequence, and in changing selected connection strengths in particular neural networks, respectively.

Stimulus-Response Connection Subsystem

Primates not only can store representations of facts, but also can store relatively direct connections between a representation of a stimulus and a representation that generates a response. Mishkin and his colleagues argue that the *striatum* plays a critical role in this sort of memory;[14] the striatum is part of the basal ganglia, which has five parts—only two of which, the *caudate nucleus* and the *putamen* (see Figure 7.1, page 304), comprise the striatum (these structures have the same cell types and are fused anteriorly, and appear to work closely with each other).[15] The striatum plays a critical role in skill acquisition, which makes sense in part because the striatum receives information from cortical perceptual areas and indirectly (in part via the thalamus) sends fibers to the premotor cortex and the supplementary motor cortex.

Decision Subsystem

The subsystems described so far are always operating. Thus, novel stimuli that are attended to and registered by perceptual subsystems are likely to be stored. Nevertheless, we sometimes want to raise the probability that specific, very important, information is stored. Hence, there must be a mechanism that receives input from associative memory (where "importance" is identified) and sends commands to the memory formation subsystems to store memories and associations between memories. This subsystem initiates and coordinates sets of individual processes, which constitute specific "strategies" that facilitate entering new information into memory. The decision subsystem may be localized in the dorsolateral frontal lobe, as will be discussed in the following chapter.

We now use this overview of the system to consider how different sorts of new information are entered into memory. We will discuss how new perceptual representations come to be stored, how such representations are associated with new contexts (such as occurs when one remembers which friends were at a party), how representations of object properties are associated in memory with representations of spatial properties, how representations of specific exemplars and prototypes are stored, how "intention" affects what information is stored, and how one stores "nonexplicit" knowledge. Finally, we will consider the effects of brain damage on such abilities, and use our inferences to generate possible accounts for these disorders.

Storing a New Stimulus

We can look at a novel object and later recognize it and visualize it; similarly, we can hear a novel sound and later recognize and image it. These observations indicate that we can store perceptual information in memory. To remember the perceptual qualities of a novel stimulus, a new representation must be formed in the appropriate pattern activation subsystem.

In a sense, the first step in storing new information is to determine that it is new. Recall from Chapters 2 and 3 that one of the properties of neural networks is that they generalize; a given output will be produced by a range of similar inputs. Even a novel object often will activate some of the stored representations to one degree or another. In many situations a stimulus can be matched closely to a previously stored representation, and hence a new representation of the stimulus is not stored.

However, if no single previously stored representation is activated over a threshold, this is a signal that the object is novel. It is important that the threshold be associated with a single representation because many novel objects may have individual parts that are similar to parts of familiar objects; thus, parts of novel objects may match parts of familiar objects, but no single stored representation corresponds to the entire input. When an input to a pattern activation subsystem does not match any single stored representation very well, a new representation may be stored. This process involves at least two distinct subsystems.

Print-Now Subsystem

As even our brief overview revealed, the memory formation subsystems clearly are very complex. However, just as we decomposed the ventral and dorsal systems in vision, we can begin to delineate sets of more specialized subsystems for entering new representations and associations into memory, each of which performs a more restricted type of input/output mapping.

One function of the memory formation subsystems is to trigger the "print now" process when new information is present, which is implemented at least in part in the basal forebrain. Because the input/output mapping is distinct from those of the subsystems we have inferred so far, and this mapping appears to depend on anatomical structures that have not been implicated in previous processing, we are led to posit a specialized *print-now subsystem* that performs this function. If novel stimuli are perceived, the input will not match a stored perceptual representation very well. When a match is not obtained, this information is sent to the frontal lobes and provides input to the print-now subsystem; recall that the perceptual encoding subsystems have anatomical projections into the frontal lobe.[16] Thus, the perceptual encoding subsystems send outputs to associative memory and to the print-now subsystem. It is common for a single neural structure to have projections to many other structures.[17]

The "print now" process is yoked to the patterns of activity that initiated the storage sequence; these patterns of activity are induced by the stimuli that are currently being attended (e.g., the image in the visual buffer that is surrounded by the attention window, the auditory representation that is selected in the auditory buffer, and so on), rather than any of the other myriad potential stimuli surrounding it. Structural changes are initiated that will allow the system later to reconstitute the pattern of activation evoked by the novel stimulus; these structural changes are analogous to changes of the weights on connections in a network model. Actually making these changes, however, depends on another subsystem.

Weight Adjustment Subsystem

The memory formation subsystems must also perform a very different kind of computation, which involves another set of anatomical structures. These considerations lead us to posit that a second subsystem is employed (recall our argument that very different sets of input/output mappings are probably accomplished by distinct subsystems; see Chapters 2 and 3). Once the "print-now" process is initiated, it must engage a mechanism that actually adjusts the strengths of the appropriate connections among neurons in the appropriate networks. We posit a *weight adjustment subsystem* that adjusts connections to conjoin the neurons that are activated together by a stimulus, thereby storing the properties of the stimulus.[18] This subsystem is critically dependent on processes that occur in the hippocampus and related cortex. When the hippocampus receives acetylcholine from the basal forebrain, it in turn provides input to the areas that embody the pattern activation subsystems and—presumably—associative memory; this input promotes changes in the strengths of the appropriate connections in order to store the configuration of activity evoked by the stimulus.

It seems unlikely that the hippocampus and related cortex "micromanage" the details of the changes in connection strengths. To micromanage the learning process, each connection to be changed would need to be monitored by neurons in the hippocampus. Given that a typical neuron has between 1,000 and 10,000 synapses (connections),[19] there would need to be many orders of magnitude more neurons in the hippocampus than in the areas in which the memories are actually stored. But the hippocampus is a relatively small structure. Thus, it is unlikely that the hippocampus monitors each and every changing connection, but it certainly defines contraints that lead to the appropriate changes; the hippocampus may serve to place a "catalyst" in a neural network, which leads it to change in a specific way.

The weight adjustment subsystem apparently requires a long time to finish adjusting the connection weights. If the hippocampus and related cortex are removed, a patient cannot remember any events within a year or two prior to the operation, although memories further removed in time are better preserved.[20] Indeed, memories from 10 to 20 years in the past are essentially normal. Consider an analogy: During the initial phases of memory encoding, it is as if one is preserving the shape of a letter by walking a particular route on a lawn. The pattern is dynamic, and is only evident in the way one moves. After a period of time, however, the grass will wear through, creating a dirt pathway. At that point, one can stop walking; the information is preserved structurally. The hippocampus and related cortex are involved in the walking process that eventually leads to the dirt path (i.e., changed connection strengths). Once this process is initiated, it "automatically" persists for some period of time; it is as if the spring in a mechanical man were "wound up," allowing it to march along for a period thereafter. As we shall discuss shortly, some events can "wind up" the spring more strongly than others, and the stronger the spring is wound, the more likely the man will walk long enough to wear a deep path through the grass. The additional subsystems are illustrated in the context of the system as a whole in Figure 8.3.

Synaptic Plasticity

The key to storing new information in memory is the ability to change the "strengths" of connections among neurons in just the right way. This is absolutely clear in computer simulation models of memory in neural networks (see Chapter 2), and has now been documented in actual neural networks.[21] The idea that changes in

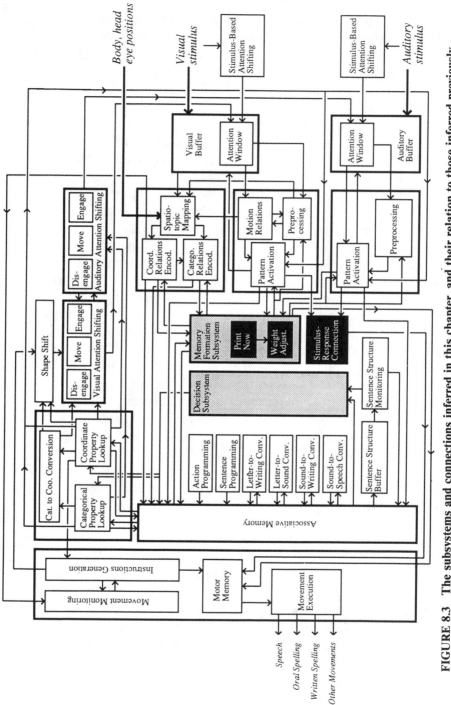

FIGURE 8.3 The subsystems and connections inferred in this chapter, and their relation to those inferred previously

synaptic connections are at the root of learning was popularized by the great Spanish histologist Ramon y Cajal at the turn of the century,[22] but such changes have only been documented relatively recently. These changes apparently begin in the hippocampus, and thus it is of interest that the functions of neural connections in the hippocampus change with use. Researchers first discovered these intriguing characteristics of hippocampal synapses in the rabbit.[23] After they provided intense electrical stimulation to areas that project to the hippocampus, they found that a single stimulation engendered a larger response than it had previously. As noted earlier, this phenomenon is called long-term potentiation, or LTP. Even more interesting is the duration of this effect; it can last hours, days, weeks, or even longer—depending on the age, health, and experience of the animal, as well as various properties of the stimulus.[24] This effect has been observed in different types of hippocampal neurons, such as granule cells and pyramidal cells.

Since these early discoveries, many experiments have been carried out to understand the biochemical events that underlie LTP and, more·precisely, to discover whether it depends on the sending neuron (i.e., has a *presynaptic* mechanism) or the receiving neuron (i.e., has a *postsynaptic* mechanism). Evidence has now accumulated for both pre- and postsynaptic contributions to LTP. Specifically, LTP relies on pairing the release of particular neurotransmitters (such as glutamate or aspartate) at the presynaptic neuron with the right level of voltage on the outer membrane of the postsynaptic neuron. That is, the transmitter must be present when the receiving neuron is ready. The neurotransmitter activates specific (glutaminergic) receptors on the receiving neuron called NMDA receptors (for N-methyl-D-aspartate); these receptors are referred to as NMDA receptors because NMDA selectively activates them—is their *agonist.*

These receptors give the synapses unusual properties. Like all neurons, the cell fires when ions rush into it from the surrounding fluid; the ions pass through small pores called *channels,* which are opened and closed under specific circumstances. The kind of ion channels associated with NMDA receptors are *voltage-gated.* That is, if the membrane of the receiving neuron has the proper voltage (i.e., is *depolarized* the right amount), a current flow of the sort necessary to induce the neuron to fire can occur;[25] if the membrane of the receiving neuron does *not* have the correct voltage, no transmission can occur (hence the term "gate").

But the most interesting feature of these neurons is that they have properties that change with use. Modifications within the cells occur after the sending neuron is stimulated with a high frequency while the receiving neuron has the proper voltage. After such modifications, only a small input will be necessary to activate the receiving neuron. The precise intracellular mechanisms responsible for these changes are still unknown.[26]

To summarize, NMDA receptors register the *conjunction* of the release of glutamate at the presynaptic level (by a sending neuron) and the depolarization at the postsynaptic level (by a receiving neuron). With use, less activity at the presynaptic level is required to trigger the receiving cell. The mechanism that underlies LTP is not limited to the hippocampus; it also is found in perceptual areas, such as area V1.[27] This makes sense if perceptual learning affects not only the networks that store new representations (the pattern activation subsystems), but also those involved in perceptual encoding. However, although we noted in Chapter 3 that the preprocessing subsystem could be tuned by experience, we did not infer that the visual buffer or low-level visual areas could be so tuned; we leave this possibility open until more direct evidence is available.

In 1949, Donald Hebb proposed that synaptic efficacy is changed when simultaneous activity occurs at the sending and receiving neurons.[28] Because Hebb proposed that synaptic changes may occur when such activity co-occurs, and because it has been demonstrated that NMDA receptors detect the conjunction of activity at the pre- and postsynaptic levels, synapses of the NMDA often are referred to as *Hebb synapses.*

Recap: Storing a New Stimulus

When a perceptual input does not match a single representation in the appropriate pattern activation subsystem very well, the pattern activation subsystem sends this information to the print-now subsystem (which is dependent on the basal forebrain). The print-now subsystem sends a signal to the weight adjustment subsystem (which is dependent on the hippocampus and related cortex). The weight adjustment subsystem then operates to change the connection strengths within the appropriate pattern activation subsystem(s), so that a representation of the stimulus will be stored. NMDA receptors may be critical in this process.

Associating Familiar Stimuli with New Contexts

In many cases, we do not store a new perceptual representation of an object, but rather store a new association between a familiar object and the context in which it occurs. For example, when you memorize a shopping list you do not form memories of new words; rather, you associate existing memory representations of the words with that particular list. Or, if you try to remember which friends were at a party, you are not memorizing the friends; you already know your friends. Rather, you are associating them with a particular context. The vast majority of laboratory research on memory in experimental psychology has this character. Subjects who are asked to memorize a list of words do not learn the words per se; they already know them before coming to the test, and instead learn to associate those particular words with the fact that they are on the list.

The problem, then, is to understand how associations between separately stored representations are established. The "context" can correspond to representations of other objects, and so one aspect of the problem is to determine how representations of stimuli are associated in memory. These representations could have been stored previously, or one or more of them could be stored on the spot, as described above.

Most of what we know about the neural bases of the association process has been inferred from studies of animals, particularly monkeys. Studies of animals make it possible to investigate precisely the role of specific brain structures in memory because specific structures can be removed; lesions of the human brain due to stroke and the like are usually less selective. Two research groups are particularly active in this domain, the group led by Mortimer Mishkin in Washington and the group led by Larry Squire in San Diego.

Memory processes in monkeys have been intensively studied

using the delayed nonmatching to sample task.[29] A monkey first is shown a sample object, it is removed, and then the monkey is shown two objects, one of which is identical to the sample. The monkey is required to select the new object (not the sample) in order to find a peanut that is placed under it. Different objects are presented on each trial. The key variable in this task is the amount of time that elapses before the two alternatives are presented, after the sample has been removed; the monkey must remember the sample during this interval.

If the stimuli are familiar, then a representation of the sample is associated with representations of contextual stimuli that are hallmarks of the task (e.g., the cage, the test table, and so on). When the monkey later must recognize the novel alternative, it looks at each of the test stimuli, which are encoded into the pattern activation subsystem and then into associative memory. We hypothesize that the decision subsystem monitors associative memory, noting when the appropriate context information is activated. When this information is activated, the decision subsystem initiates the process of picking up the other stimulus; the location (coordinates) of the novel stimulus has been encoded into associative memory (via the coordinate spatial relations encoding subsystem), and these coordinates are used to guide the movement, as was described in the previous chapter. If the stimuli are novel, then the system also must store a representation of the initial stimulus. This task, with familiar or novel stimuli, can be learned perfectly in a few days by a normal monkey.

Associative Memory as a Distinct Subsystem

One could challenge our assumption that associative memory is a separate structure. Why not simply establish direct connections between representations, without an additional memory store? One reason why this scheme will not work is that there are qualitatively different types of associations. Consider the difference between "is a" and "has a," as in "a lion is a zoo animal" and "a lion has a mane." It is not simply that "lion" is associated with "zoo animal" and with "mane"; different types of relations are part of the associations. Thus, a simple direct connection between different representations will not do the job; the nature of the types of associations themselves must be stored. This sort of information is not perceptual, and hence there must be a nonperceptual way of storing representations of associative relations.

One could still argue that direct connections are used, but posit that the type of associative relation (e.g., "is a," "has a") is specified by an intermediate representation. For example, the perceptual representation of lion might be associated with the representation "has the property," which in turn is associated with the representation of mane. Thus, the proper kind of relation is specified, but there is no separate associative memory store. This notion also has problems. Consider first the classic distinction between "types" and "tokens."[30] For example, there is only one actual painting of the Mona Lisa, which is the type, but there are many postcards of this painting, which are tokens. This distinction is useful for many reasons, but one stands out in this context. Without tokens, it is difficult to keep straight specific sets of associations. This is particularly clear for representations of associative relations.

For example, consider the possibility that there is only a single representation of the relation "has the property." Lion might be associated with "has the property," which in turn is associated with mane. Fine. But bird might be associated with "has the property," which in turn is associated with beak. So, two objects are associated with the representation "has the property," as are two properties. But there is no indication of which object is paired with which property. The object representations funnel into one side of the relation representation, and the property representations funnel into the other side; one cannot line up the connections going in with the proper connections going out.

This problem is solved if we have a separate token of the relation "has the property" and use it in each proposition. Thus, the representation of "has the property" that is used for lion is different from the representation of "has the property" that is used for bird. Similar problems arise in many domains if only a single representation of each object, property, or relation exists.[31] These tokens are not perceptual, and hence cannot be stored in the modality-specific perceptual memories. Therefore, we infer a distinct associative memory in which organized sets of tokens are stored.

This approach suggests that information in the perceptual memories (which function as types) is not actually copied into associative memory. And in fact, this seems highly unlikely, if only because associative memory would need to be larger than the sum of the perceptual memories, and no such structure has revealed itself neurologically. Rather, we need only assume that associations between perceptual representations are stored as relations between token symbols in associative memory, which serve as place holders. These symbols are arbitrarily assigned patterns of weights in a network, which in turn are associated with *pointers* back to the appropriate representations in perceptual encoding subsystems. A pointer is a representation that indexes ("points to") another representation. These pointers would allow the reference of the symbol to be "unpacked."

Hence, in some circumstances, the information in associative memory may be used only if it first engenders an appropriate perceptual representation. For example, if asked whether the word "tree" rhymes with "brie," the representations in associative memory are used to access representations in the auditory pattern activation subsystem, and auditory images are formed (by evoking the appropriate patterns of activation in the auditory buffer)—and the final phonemes are then attended to and compared.

The idea that associative memory hooks back into unimodal perceptual representations is consistent with a range of clinical findings. For example, patients with parietal lobe injuries sometimes have difficulty navigating not because they are disoriented in space, but rather because they cannot remember spatial information learned prior to the injury.[32] Consistent with our reasoning, after reviewing much of the clinical literature, Squire suggests that the perceptual systems that encode information may actually store much of it.[33]

Thus, associative memory serves in part as an organizational, cross-indexing system, not a repository of the primary representations themselves. The structures in associative memory organize place holders in various ways, specifying the arrangement of parts of an object, the letters of a word, membership in categories, the context in which a stimulus appeared, and so on.[34] This organizational system allows the memory formation subsystems to store complex relations among the individual pieces of information. We speculate that associative memory depends in part on the superior, posterior temporal lobe, if only because patients with lesions in this area often appear to have disrupted associations.

Deficits Following Lesions

Monkeys have a very difficult time performing the delayed nonmatching to sample task when the inferior temporal cortex is lesioned, for both short and long memory delays.[35] We expect this deficit because the process of entering a visual representation into memory begins with the perceptual subsystems, and the visual pattern activation subsystem apparently is implemented in the inferior temporal lobe (as we saw in Chapter 3).

Perhaps of greater interest here, animals perform normally on this task with short delays even after various neural structures underlying the memory formation subsystems are removed.[36] It is important to note that this task could be accomplished only if a very brief interval occurs between the standard and test stimuli. In this case, the animal could maintain a visual image of the standard and the weights on the connections of the network would not be adjusted; rather, the configuration of activity in the pattern activation subsystem induced by the stimulus would simply be retained. If so, then the decision subsystem can determine whether an object is new simply by noting whether the configuration of neural activity changes when attention is directed to the object. If it does change, the decision subsystem would in turn direct the coordinate property lookup subsystem to access the target coordinates of the object (encoded via the coordinate spatial relations encoding subsystem), and send them to the instructions generation subsystem, which causes the arm to select the stimulus being viewed. In contrast, if looking at an object does not change the configuration of activity very much, this information would lead the decision subsystem to initiate a reach for the other object. Such a process might be used, for example, if one were looking at hats in a store, turned away for a minute and heard someone put an additional hat on the shelf, and then turned back to the shelf. One could pick out the additional hat by looking at each one and determining whether it was familiar, as noted above.

If the delay is longer than a few seconds, an image of the

standard stimulus cannot be retained, and hence a new representation must be stored. The system cannot "know" in advance whether it needs to store new information or simply retain an image. Thus, the principle of concurrent processing suggests that both processes run at the same time; if the retention interval is too long to maintain the image, then the task can only be performed on the basis of the stored representations.

Thus, with a long delay (i.e., one or two minutes), we expect the animal to be severely impaired if the hippocampus and associated cortex or the diencephalon (i.e., the thalamus and mamillary body of the hypothalamus) are removed; lesioning the diencephalon disconnects the outputs from the hippocampus and related cortex from the rest of the system. Exactly this pattern of results has been found.[37]

In addition, Mishkin and his colleagues have reported that removing the amygdala also impairs memory encoding; indeed, they have suggested that this structure plays a critical role in memory, often being able to substitute for the hippocampus.[38] However, these experiments with monkeys failed to control for the fact that the overlying cortex was also being damaged when the amygdala was removed.[39] Indeed, the frontal half of the entorhinal cortex and the perirhinal cortex also were removed. To distinguish between the contribution of the amygdala per se and overlying cortex, Squire and his colleagues tested monkeys that had lesions in the hippocampus, entorhinal cortex, and perirhinal cortex; the amygdala was left intact in these animals.[40] These monkeys were impaired in a delayed nonmatching to sample task. In fact, these animals were impaired as severely as those with a lesion that included the amygdala. In addition, when a needle was used to deliver electric current that destroyed only the amygdala (all other structures were spared), the monkey did not have a memory deficit. These results strongly suggest that the cortex surrounding the amygdala and not the amygdala itself is critical in memory.[41]

Moreover, animals are impaired when the basal forebrain is lesioned.[42] This deficit occurs when there are long delays, which makes sense because the damaged basal forebrain does not release acetylcholine and hence the print-now command is impaired. However, only a relatively small deficit follows this lesion, which suggests either that other areas are also involved in releasing acetylcholine, and/or that other mechanisms are also involved in inducing the hippocampus and its surrounding cortex to induce the relevant synaptic changes.

Recap: Associating Familiar Stimuli with New Contexts

To remember a familiar stimulus, one typically does not store a new representation of the stimulus, but rather associates a previously stored representation with a specific context. When a familiar stimulus is perceived, the print-now and weight adjustment subsystems associate the perceptual representations of the stimulus with those of stimuli that are hallmarks of that context. The associations are stored using sets of "place holders" in associative memory. These place holders correspond to objects, properties, and relations; they are tokens that "point back" to representations of the corresponding types. The type-representations of perceptual characteristics of objects are stored in the perceptual encoding subsystems themselves.[43] When an object is later perceived and input enters associative memory, the relevant associations are activated. These associations identify the stimulus as having occurred in a specific context.

Forming Associations between Object Properties and Spatial Properties

We can easily remember where furniture is located in our living rooms. In Chapters 3 and 4, we considered alternative ways of storing spatial information, and also noted that the outputs from the ventral (object-properties) and dorsal (spatial-properties) systems must converge in an associative memory where the two sorts of information are conjoined.

Once again, much of what we know about the neural mechanisms underlying memory storage comes from studies of nonhuman primates. For example, monkeys have been tested in a shape-location association task in which they first are shown two objects, which then are removed.[44] After a brief delay, they are shown two copies of one of the objects, one of which is in the location previously occupied by that object. The monkeys must select the copy that is in the location occupied by that object when it was presented initially.

We can infer that the following computations are required in this task. First, the shapes and the locations of the initial objects must be encoded perceptually. Second, the representations of the shape and location of each object must be conjoined and stored in associative memory. Third, this information must be retained during the interval after the study stimuli are removed and before the test stimuli are presented. Fourth, the shape and locations of the test stimuli must be encoded perceptually and this information must be sent to associative memory. Fifth, the shape of the test stimuli must access the corresponding memory representation in associative memory, and the associated location information accessed. Finally, the stored representation of the location must be used to guide a reach to that copy of the object.

The shape of the object is entered into memory as described earlier: A new representation is stored in the pattern activation subsystem if the shape is novel, or a perceptual representation is simply activated if the shape is familiar. And the print-now and weight adjustment subsystems establish associations in associative memory between the perceptual representation of the object and those of contextual stimuli that are present at the same time. In addition, the locations of the objects are encoded via the categorical and coordinate spatial relations encoding subsystems, and this information is stored in associative memory. This information must be conjoined with the "place holders" that point to the relevant perceptual representations in the pattern activation subsystem.[45]

How are object properties and spatial properties correctly conjoined in associative memory? This is a special problem because the two kinds of information are encoded concurrently, by distinct subsystems. One way to pair the appropriate representations is by simple temporal contiguity: Both sorts of information reach the hippocampus at about the same time. This process will work well if only a single object is attended to at any one time, but what if two objects are seen at the same time? For example, one might see a large red ball and a small blue box, and must associate the sizes with the proper sets of object properties.

In this case, the problem is more complex; simple temporal contiguity cannot select and conjoin the appropriate members of different sets of object-properties and spatial-properties encodings that arrive at the hippocampus at about the same time. How is the representation of "large" assigned to the right object? One anatomical feature may hint at a solution to this problem, namely precise connections that run between the superior temporal sulcus and the inferior parietal lobe.[46] In the previous chapter we noted that such connections are useful if one is to reach appropriately to parts of objects (e.g., grasping the handle of a mug). In addition, however, these connections could serve to yoke specific object properties and spatial properties. Perhaps neuronal representations of connected regions are oscillating at the same rate,[47] which would allow the hippocampus to associate them properly.[48] Or some other distinctive "signature" could pair appropriate object properties and spatial properties representations during perceptual encoding. Logically, something like this seems to be required.

Thus, we are led to predict that this task should be impaired by lesions of: the inferior temporal cortex, which would disrupt perceptual encoding of shape; the hippocampus or related cortex, which are critical for encoding associations; the diencephalon, which serves as a routing (and possibly attentional) center for input from the hippocampus and related cortex; and the connection between medial temporal and diencephalic regions, which would also disconnect the inputs from the hippocampus and related cortex. All of these predictions have been borne out by the results of studies of monkeys with specific brain lesions.[49] We also expect deficits if the basal forebrain is damaged and if the dorsal system is damaged when subtle discriminations are required (and so parts and their locations must be stored), but the appropriate experiments have yet to be performed.

Neural Mechanisms

It has long been known that the hippocampus plays a critical role in spatial learning in rats,[50] monkeys,[51] and humans.[52] Indeed, in rats there are cells in the hippocampus that are tuned for particular spots in a maze or room; these so-called *place cells* appear to encode a special sort of contextual cue that is very relevant to rats (which are very spatial animals).[53] Richard Morris and his colleagues reasoned that given the large number of NMDA receptors within the hippocampus, they may play a critical role in the type of learning mediated by this structure.[54] These researchers tested the hypothesis that NMDA plays a critical role in spatial learning by injecting a specific NMDA *antagonist* (AP5; 2-amino-5-phosphonopentanoic acid) into the brains of rats, which interferes with normal processing at the NMDA receptors.[55] The rats were then given a spatial learning task or a visual discrimination learning task.

In their spatial learning task, rats were put into a pool of opaque water where a platform had been hidden under the surface. The animals tried to get out of the water, and hence sought the platform. When placed into the pool at different starting locations, the rats initially swam randomly until they found the hidden platform; but with increasing practice, normal rats required less and less time to locate the platform. Thus, the rats learned the location of the platform relative to the pool environment.

As would be expected if NMDA receptors play a role in spatial learning, rats could not learn this task very well when they were injected with the NMDA antagonist before being tested. Presumably, the antagonist interfered with learning processes in the hippocampus, so that the rats could not encode the location of the platform.

In another experiment reported by this group,[56] other rats were placed in the same pool, but now with two visually discriminable platforms that were placed two centimeters above the surface of the water. One was grey, and the other had black-and-white stripes. Only one of these platforms was rigid, and thus offered a respite from swimming; the other platform sank under the water every time a rat tried to clamber aboard. The locations of the two platforms were changed randomly from trial to trial, so that the rats could not learn to go to a specific location; rather, the animals had to learn to discriminate the patterns on the platforms.

In contrast to the results from the spatial task, injecting these rats with the NMDA antagonist did not affect learning; the treated rats learned the task as well as normal control rats. The fact that the drug impaired the spatial task, but not the pattern task, led Morris et al. to infer that the hippocampus plays a critical role in spatial learning but not in pattern discrimination.

However, this inference does not follow from their findings, for a number of reasons.[57] First, one problem is that only a single pair of patterns was used in the pattern discrimination task, and this sort of discrimination can be performed using the stimulus-response connection subsystem. In contrast, spatial learning apparently cannot be mediated by this system.[58] As will be discussed in more detail shortly, the stimulus-response connection subsystem appears to rely on different brain areas from the memory formation subsystem, and these brain areas may not be affected by drugs that interfere with NMDA receptors.

Second, lesions of the hippocampus and related cortex in monkeys greatly impair their learning visual discriminations among sets of stimuli, as noted earlier; such lesions in rats also impair their ability to learn associations between visually perceived stimuli.[59] Thus, there is strong evidence that the hippocampus is not restricted to encoding spatial information.

Third, Carolyn Cave and Squire showed that damage to the hippocampus in human patients does not impair spatial learning any more than it impairs learning properties of objects.[60] Cave and Squire also reviewed the relevant literature and showed that although the hippocampus clearly has a role in encoding spatial information into memory, it does not appear to have a special role in encoding this kind of information.[61]

Recap: Forming Associations between Object Properties and Spatial Properties

Shape is encoded by the ventral system, and location by the dorsal system. Thus, shape-location associations depend on information that is encoded concurrently, and the two sorts of information must be "bound" during encoding; the correct pointers must be established in associative memory. Anatomical connections between the ventral and dorsal systems serve to "tag" corresponding inputs in the two systems, setting up a "neural signature" that specifies how they are to be combined in associative memory. In all other respects, this sort of memory formation is the same as storing associations between pairs of objects, as described in the previous section.

Storing Exemplars and Prototypes

The abilities we have considered so far all involve remembering specific objects or locations. However, we not only remember individual objects, but we also "abstract out" properties of objects in a category and remember a *prototype*. For example, when asked to visualize a dog, most people report imaging an "average" dog, usually black, of medium size, with a medium tail, and so on. But some report that they never actually saw this particular dog; rather, it is a creation of their memory systems. Indeed, when we learn new words, we typically associate them not with individual objects, but with categories; proper names are the exception, not the rule. The way memory is organized appears to engender this abstraction process "automatically"; we do not need to ponder what multiple exemplars have in common in order to form a prototype.

To date, the neural mechanisms underlying memory for prototypes have not been studied in rats or monkeys. However, a confluence of behavioral data and computer simulation models offers insights into how the abstraction process may operate.

Perhaps the key behavioral finding is that categories are not represented in memory with sharp boundaries. Eleanor Rosch provided compelling evidence that categories have an internal structure, with some exemplars being "better" than others.[62] For example, people can more quickly affirm that a robin is a bird than that a penguin is a bird; the less typical the object is for the category, the more time people require to evaluate it—even though all of the exemplars are in fact members of the category. These and similar findings suggest that categories are not formed by a process that delineates sets of defining features and generates a list, which is then compared against the input. Rather, categories appear to have the properties of patterns of weights in neural networks, with some inputs generalizing better than others. Many variants of this idea have been developed,[63] but the following model illustrates key principles that characterize these models.

A Computer Model

McClelland and Rumelhart described a computer model that simulates how memory abstracts categories over the course of experience;[64] we interpret this model as reflecting processes in a pattern activation subsystem. Their model used a recurrent network design, as described in Chapter 2 and illustrated in Figure 8.4, with no intermediate level of hidden units. In this model, the units were organized into modules, each of which received input from and sent output to other modules. However, although any one module could be connected with many others, not all of them were connected.

In the model, a "mental state" corresponded to a pattern of activation over units in some of the modules; a particular pattern of activation in a given module could represent a specific aspect

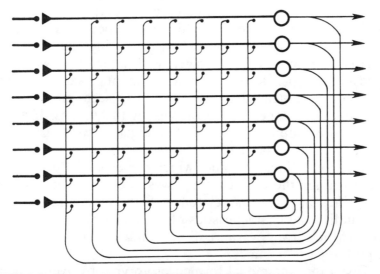

FIGURE 8.4 The structure of McClelland and Rumelhart's model of memory. *(From J. L. McCelland & D. E. Rumelhart [Eds.],* **Parallel distributed processing: Explorations in the microstructure of cognition.** *Copyright © 1986 by MIT Press. Reprinted by permission.)*

of the mental state. This pattern represented the synthesis of the patterns of activation in all the modules that sent information to this module.

Perceptual processes evoked a pattern of activation in each module, at which point the weights on the connections between the units might be modified. When the weights were modified, a new memory was encoded. However, once a pattern of activation was evoked, it began to decay; the pattern decayed quickly at first but the decay rate soon decreased and stabilized at a relatively slow rate (at a value above zero).

Information was retrieved when a fragment of the original mental state was presented, which reinstated the entire mental state; this is a kind of processing that such networks do well. Thus, recognition occurred when a similar form (or part) was encoded, as described in Chapter 3.

McClelland and Rumelhart illustrated how their model behaved in a series of simulated situations.[65] For example, they showed that the model was able to simulate what happens when someone sees many different dogs only once, with each having a different name. After a certain number of training trials, a set of weights developed that represented a prototypical dog that was never "shown" to the model. This process occurred "automatically" when the weights were changed during learning; earlier patterns of weights were averaged with later ones, which produced a prototype. However, this adjustment process was disproportionately influenced by the exemplar seen most recently, which does not appear to be the case with humans. If a larger number of examples were used in a larger network, this imbalance may not have occurred.

Because a different name (which corresponded to a pattern of activation in the "name units") was associated with each dog, no specific name was associated with the emerging prototype. Thus, individual characteristics of the exemplars, such as their names (which always varied), did not influence the formation of the prototype in memory.

Given that the model formed prototypes by averaging over the course of encountering individual exemplars, it was important to discover whether it sacrificed the ability to store individual exemplars in order to represent prototypes. We can, after all, remember a specific dog, not simply dogs in general. In another experiment, McClelland and Rumelhart simulated the following situation: A little boy sees two dogs very often; one next door, named Rover, and one at his grandmother's house, named Fido. The little boy also sees other dogs in the park from time to time, and his father always tells him that they are dogs. McClelland and Rumelhart simulated this situation using three name patterns, one for Rover, one for Fido, and one for dog. A different distorted version of the visual pattern for the prototypical dog was assigned to each exemplar (including the ones "in the park"). The model now only averaged over the various "in the park" exemplars, and preserved Rover and Fido as separate representations. After training, the model was given a name as input, and was able to produce the correct visual pattern for that exemplar. Similarly, it was able to retrieve the prototype visual pattern when the "dog" name pattern was provided. In addition, when given visual patterns as input, the network was able to produce the appropriate names of examples and the category. Therefore, the model had developed internal representations of both the prototype and the specific exemplars.

A critical feature of this model was its organization into modules, which were specialized for different purposes. This is another instance of the principle of the division of labor. In keeping with this principle, a perhaps simpler solution to the problem of forming prototypes while still retaining exemplars is simply to have two networks, one of which averages over inputs and one of which does not. If a large network had relatively sparse connections between input and output, it might not blur the representations as much and would store specific examples. In addition, there are different methods of adjusting the weights on the connections, some of which blur representations more than others;[66] it is possible that different methods are used in the two cerebral hemispheres. As we shall see in the following chapter, there is in fact some evidence that such specialization exists, with the network that stores prototypes being more effective in the left cerebral hemisphere and the network that stores exemplars being more effective in the right cerebral hemisphere.

Recap: Storing Exemplars and Prototypes

Prototypes are formed "automatically" when a set of stimuli is stored in a pattern activation network. Adjusting the weights on the connections to store each successive stimulus results in an averaging process, where the pattern of weights formed is a compromise between those formed for the individual stimuli. Specific examples are stored in a separate network, or module within a network, that does not average, either because it has a different pattern of connectivity or a different adjustment procedure is used.

Storing Information Intentionally

McClelland and Rumelhart's model depends on another interesting property of memory: We often store new information even if it has no obvious relevance to any goal or problem at hand. This is called *incidental* memory. It appears that the print-now and weight adjustment subsystems operate on input all the time; if one pays attention to a stimulus, it is likely to be stored "automatically," with no decision to do so.

On the other hand, one sometimes makes an effort to memorize something, and the effort pays off. For example, a student may need to remember specific shapes of cells for a biology exam, or one may need to remember how to get home from a friend's house. Hence, one tries to memorize the information, and is more likely to remember it than if the effort were not made. This sort of memory is called *intentional* memory.

We can infer at least five reasons why intentional memory is often better than incidental memory. First, if one is trying to memorize specific information, one will "pay attention" to it for a relatively long period of time. "Paying attention," in this sense, corresponds to two sorts of events: (1) the dynamic pattern of activation is retained in the pattern activation subsystems, which in turn provides a greater opportunity for the weight adjustment subsystem to operate effectively; and (2) the print-now subsystem sends a signal to the weight adjustment subsystem over a longer period of time. These events have the effect of "winding the mechanical man" more strongly, so that it "walks on the grass" more vigorously and for a longer period of time. Hence, the longer the information is attended to, the more likely it is that the memory formation subsystems eventually will store it in memory (i.e., form the "dirt path").[67]

Second, if the property lookup subsystems access more information about the to-be-remembered material, memory will be improved. There is a body of literature that indicates that the more information that is activated about a stimulus, the more likely one is to remember it—even if one has no intention of remembering it. This is usually called a *depth of processing* effect.[68] For example, if one thinks carefully about whether to purchase a piece of jewelry, considering which clothing it would complement, when it would be appropriate to wear, and so forth, it will be etched into memory for months (years?) to come; but if one simply makes up one's mind immediately, it would be easy to forget about it. In a typical laboratory experiment investigating this phenomenon, when subjects are asked to decide whether a word names a living object, one is more likely later to remember the word than if one is asked merely to decide whether the word rhymes with "tree." The semantic task requires one to activate representations of more properties of the object in associative memory than the acoustic task; the sound can be reconstructed by retrieving one piece of information, but it is unlikely that one stores the proposition "is living" with each living object, and hence one must infer this on the basis of other properties. Presumably, the more information about the object that is activated, the more opportunities there are for setting up new associations between to-be-remembered material and the context—which enhances memory.

Third, when one is trying to store information, the decision subsystem can be used to organize the information into fewer units (*chunks*),[69] and fewer units are easier to remember in part because the memory formation subsystems can spend proportionally more time on each one. For example, when viewing a new room for the first time, memory for the locations of furniture will be enhanced if one organizes the room into "seating groups," seeing configurations of furniture as units, rather than encoding each piece separately. Depending on how the attention window is set, material in different-sized regions of space will be encoded as a unit. In addition, one sometimes can organize a stimulus into parts that match previously stored representations. For example, if one is asked to remember the letters RCAIBMITTATT, one will do much better if one realizes that the letters correspond to the names of companies. This organization process could occur as follows: A set of letters, such as IBM, matches a stored pattern in the pattern activation subsystem, which sends input to associative memory. This pattern is associated with a company. The decision subsystem then directs the attention shifting subsystem to focus attention on groups of three and four contiguous letters, which may lead one to identify additional companies.[70]

Fourth, one can store information relatively effectively by inventing distinctive *retrieval cues*.[71] If the input A is paired with the output B in a neural network, and the input D with the output C, the outputs can be recovered more easily if A and D are distinct than if they are similar. For example, if you have to remember both your new license plate—provided it is a number—and your new personal ID code on a bank card, you will be better off if you associate the first number with a birthday you know well and the second number with a phone number you know well than if you associate both numbers with phone numbers. Indeed, in the latter case, you may have a hard time remembering which number was associated with which phone number. (Such strategies involve storing information in associative memory about a set of processing steps that specify what should be retrieved, and then what should be done with that information in turn.)

Fifth, one can try to visualize the material, as well as recall verbal descriptions. Upon hearing a word, for example, one can image the corresponding object and then associate that representation with a new context tag. Allan Paivio reviews a large amount of evidence that we remember information better when we use a "dual code" (visual and verbal) than when we store it in only a single way.[72] This makes sense because one later will have two shots at retrieving the information in associative memory, one via a visual association and one via a verbal association.

These various processes are often combined. For example, an effective way to remember information is to organize it hierarchically, in terms of categories and subcategories. One might remember a grocery list by organizing it into produce, paper products, canned goods, and so on; and then organize produce into fruits and vegetables; paper products into those for the kitchen and bathroom, etc. This process requires discovering a way to group the material into sets of categories (which may involve great "depth of processing"), organizing it into fewer units (at higher levels of hierarchy), and inventing distinctive retrieval cues (which may be facilitated by visualizing the objects); and while all of this is going on, one is paying attention to the to-be-stored material.[73]

Recap: Storing Information Intentionally

Intentional memory may be better than incidental memory for at least five reasons: (1) one pays attention to material longer, giving the memory formation subsystems more time to operate; (2) one activates more stored information that is associated with the to-be-remembered material, providing more opportunities for encoding associations to context; (3) the input can be organized into fewer units, and so more processing can be devoted to each; (4) distinctive retrieval cues can be employed; and (5) visual mental images can be formed and associated with context in addition to storing verbal material.

Storing Explicit Versus Implicit Memories

We have so far discussed memory representations that can be deliberately accessed and used for a variety of purposes. But this is not the only form in which memories are stored. Memories are the residue of experience. For example, recall that in Chapter 3 we discussed how the preprocessing subsystem can become tuned to allow one to make perceptual discriminations, such as those required to categorize the gender of baby chicks (by registering slight differences in the bumps at their bottoms). This is a form of memory, but one cannot recall—or use introspection to discover—how one categorizes the chicks. Indeed, when one becomes an expert in any domain, one often cannot report how one performs the task. Much, if not most, of the information in memory cannot be directly accessed and communicated.[74]

Thus, we can distinguish between *explicit* and *implicit* memory.[75] Although Peter Graf and Daniel Schacter probably characterized this distinction most clearly, it grew in part out of work with brain-damaged patients and in part from work in artificial intelligence,[76] and was applied to the brain largely to explain why patients who had amnesia still had some types of normal memory.[77] Explicit memories can be retrieved via internal processes, such as the property lookup subsystems discussed earlier in this book. Explicit memory representations of objects, sounds, and events, as well as the associations between them, can model the external world.[78]

Implicit memories, in contrast, cannot be looked up and used to produce novel actions or utterances, and cannot be used in reasoning; rather, implicit memories only make themselves known when they are activated in the course of processing a specific type of information or producing a specific type of response. It is worth considering in more detail the two types of implicit memory that have been studied intensively in recent years, *repetition priming* and *skill learning.*

Repetition Priming

Repetition priming is a kind of "greasing the wheels" that occurs when prior exposure to a stimulus facilitates later processing of that stimulus. Repetition priming ("priming," for short) has been extensively studied in carefully controlled experiments. Such experiments typically have two successive phases: an exposure phase and a test phase. In the exposure phase, the subject is shown a set of stimuli, such as words or pictures. The subject typically is asked to make a judgment about each stimulus during the exposure phase, such as whether it is pleasant or unpleasant, but never is asked to try to remember it; the judgment forces the subject to pay attention to each stimulus. In the test phase, the subject is usually given reduced perceptual information, such as words presented for just a few milliseconds, fragments of words, or the initial few letters of words. The subject is asked to identify the stimulus, complete the fragment, or say whether or not it is a word.

For example, consider the *stem completion* task. Subjects

are shown words during the exposure phase, such as "empty," "remember," and "subject," and are asked to report how much they like each word. During the test phase, only the first few letters of words are presented, such as "dro," "emp," and "sub"; each of these "stems" can be completed to form numerous different words. Some (usually half) of the stimuli in the test phase are letters from words that were presented during the exposure phase, and the remainder are novel. The subject is told to use these word stems to form the "first word that comes to mind." The subject is *not* told to try to recall the words in the exposure list; indeed, in these experiments, the test phase often is presented to the subject as a completely separate experiment. Different groups of subjects are tested, so that the stems that are novel for one group are taken from words in the exposure phase for the other group and vice versa. The result is straightforward: Subjects tend to complete stems to form words they saw in the exposure phase, although they often are not aware of having seen those words during the exposure phase. The representations of the words were *primed,* so that the stems alone were sufficient to activate them.

There is considerable evidence that priming tasks and explicit memory tasks rely on distinct processing subsystems. One finding that has been taken to support this claim is that certain drugs, such as scopolamine or even alcohol,[79] impair both recall and recognition in explicit memory tasks but do not affect the magnitude of priming.[80] Some researchers have assumed that if these two kinds of memory were mediated by the same brain system, a drug that affects one should also affect the other. However, one could argue that this result simply indicates that explicit memory requires more processing, and so is more susceptible to the effects of the drug. Thus, it is important that there is converging evidence from other sources that explicit memory and priming rely on distinct mechanisms. For example, subjects' performance on an explicit memory task is unrelated to their performance on a corresponding priming task.[81] Specifically, researchers have found that when subjects judge semantic properties of words during the exposure phase (e.g., judging whether it refers to an object or abstraction), their explicit memory for the words is better than it is when they judge superficial features of words (e.g., counting the number of "T junctions"—two intersecting lines—in the letters of words). This is the usual effect of engaging in greater "depth of processing," as noted above. In sharp contrast, the amount of priming during the test phase was not determined by the depth of processing during the exposure phase.

Other findings suggest that priming is mediated in large part by processes involved in perceptual encoding, prior to associative memory.[82] Perhaps the most compelling demonstration that priming can be induced by relatively low-level perceptual processing was reported by John Khilstrom and his colleagues.[83] They played a tape recording of pairs of words to subjects who were anesthetized during major surgery, and afterwards gave the subjects one word from each pair and asked them to "free associate" a second word. Although the patients had no explicit memory for the words on the tape, they did in fact show a priming effect by responding with the previously associated word more often than equally probable unpaired words. The words apparently were processed to some level within the system, even when the patient was fully unconscious.

The inference that priming arises in large part from the operation of perceptual encoding subsystems also receives support from the finding that maximal priming occurs only when the exposure stimuli and test stimuli have identical physical characteristics.[84] For example, much more priming occurs in the stem completion task when the exposure and test stimuli both are presented visually than when the exposure stimuli are presented auditorily and the test stimuli visually.[85] Similarly, more priming occurs when the same typographical font is used for the exposure and test stimuli than when different fonts are used. In both cases, however, some priming does occur when modality or font is changed—differences not found in explicit memory tasks.[86]

These findings clearly indicate that priming depends in part on modality-specific processes. In addition, Schacter and his colleagues examined implicit memory for novel three-dimensional objects, and found that implicit memory for objects depends on a modality-specific system that cannot operate on "impossible objects" (Escher-like drawings that do not depict physically possible objects).[87] These results are as expected if the preprocessing subsystem has been tuned to encode aspects of actual objects, and cannot encode drawings of physically impossible objects well enough for the pattern activation subsystem to store a good representation.

However, priming must involve more than partial activation of perceptual representations. For example, Chad Marsolek, Kosslyn, and Squire report a hemispheric dissociation between two components of priming.[88] They found that the advantage of having the exposure and test stimuli in the same sensory modality, or in the same typographical case, is specific to the right cerebral hemisphere. However, the left cerebral hemisphere shows the same amount of cross-modality or other-case priming as the right. Cross-modality priming cannot be based on perceptual representations, given that different representations are formed in different sensory modalities. This finding is consistent with the idea that the right hemisphere stores specific examples, whereas the left averages and stores prototypes. (We will have more to say about cerebral lateralization in the next chapter.) The important point for now is that priming has at least two components, only one of which is perceptual.

The inference that priming does not arise solely via perceptual processes is also supported by results of Graf and Schacter.[89] Graf and Schacter studied implicit memory for new associations between pairs of words. For example, subjects saw pairs such as "Ship-Castle" during the exposure phase, and stimuli such as "Ship-Cas—" during the test phase; during the test phase, the subjects were asked to complete the stem with the first word that came to mind. Graf and Schacter found that subjects showed greater priming when the stem was presented with the previously associated word, but *only* if the subjects had been asked to "elaborate" an association between the words during the exposure phase (e.g., by generating a sentence that linked the to-be-associated words). This finding is interesting in part because Graf and Schacter also showed that implicit memory for associations between words is modality-specific.[90] That is, the amount of priming from the previous exposure to a word-pair is reduced when the presentation modality is switched at the time of test (from auditory to visual).

Thus, Graf and Schacter's findings imply that priming occurs at two levels of processing. The existence of modality-specific priming indicates that some component of the implicit memory associations occurs during perceptual encoding of the words, and the fact that "semantic" elaboration is critical for instating these modality-specific implicit associations suggests that associative memory plays a key role in this effect.[91]

Mechanisms underlying priming. The perceptual and nonperceptual aspects of priming can be understood within the context of the inferences we have drawn so far. First, the modality- and form-specific aspect of priming is an expression of changes within the preprocessing and/or pattern activation subsystems. Priming occurs when prior exposure to a stimulus leaves a residual pattern of activity in these networks. This pattern of activity biases the subsystems to activate the representation of the prior stimulus when similar stimuli are presented subsequently.

Second, the aspect of priming that is not modality-specific arises from processes in associative memory. Again, prior exposure to a stimulus leaves a residual pattern of activity. Because the representations in associative memory are amodal, this sort of priming will occur even if the presentation modality or visual format of a stimulus is changed. This sort of priming apparently occurs in both cerebral hemispheres, although perceptual priming for specific forms relies on the right hemisphere.

In addition to affecting representations of stimuli themselves, priming can affect the representations of associations between stimuli. As discussed earlier, much learning consists of setting up associations between previously stored representations. We have distinguished between two types of associations, those between entries in associative memory and those between associative memory and the perceptual encoding subsystems (pointers).[92]

We now can return to Graf and Schacter's results, which indicated that modality-specific priming for novel associations occurs only when subjects are asked to elaborate an association between to-be-paired words. Our account hinges on the finding that subjects typically use visual mental imagery when asked to "elaborate an association" between two words.[93] Presumably, the pointers back to the perceptual representations are activated when images are formed. If so, then elaborative encoding of novel associations has two effects: First, it establishes the association between the to-be-remembered words, which is stored; thus, when one word is later presented it can activate the representation of the other. And second, it primes the associations (pointers) between the words and their corresponding perceptual representations, which in turn primes the perceptual representations themselves. For example, when presented with "Ship-Cas—," the first word activates all of the words with which it is associated, including "ocean," "sailor," and "castle." But "castle" is the only one that in turn has been primed to activate the corresponding representation in the visual pattern activation subsystem. Thus, when "cas" is encoded, it activates perceptual representations that include this pattern, which biases the subsystem to complete the stem as "castle."

In addition, it is conceivable that in some circumstances subjects could encode a pair of words as a single perceptual unit (in the pattern activation subsystem). In this case, the "association" would be implicit in the representation of the pair. This type of representation would produce priming of "new associations," but such priming should be modality-specific and form-specific. In principle, even amnesic subjects could show priming for new associations if this method were used. Presumably, the way the stimuli are encoded depends on the precise instructions given to the subjects and the precise nature of the stimuli, such as their size and separation on the page (smaller, closer words are more likely to be encoded as a single perceptual unit).

Finally, it is easy to understand the dissociation between priming and explicit memory. As noted above, explicit memory depends on associating the to-be-remembered information with the present context. This requires associating word-pairs (or whatever type of stimuli) with the fact that they are in the set used in the experiment. This sort of association plays no role in priming. Furthermore, all of the factors that enhance intentional memory affect explicit memory, but probably do not affect implicit memory. For example, explicit memory will be better if good retrieval cues are stored, but such cues are not used in accessing implicit memories. Hence, we do not expect to find that the level of performance when asked to recall the words explicitly (which relies on these additional sorts of associations and processes) will be related to the level of performance in priming tasks—as is in fact the case.

Skill Learning

The second type of implicit memory that has been studied in depth is skill learning. A (possibly) amusing characteristic of learning a new skill, such as learning to ice skate, is that we cannot anticipate the precise characteristics (amplitude, timing, muscular power, and so on) of our movements. Sometimes, it seems best not to think too much about what we are doing, because our deliberate attempts to move may actually impair performance. As discussed in the previous chapter, with practice feedback will no longer be necessary to guide a movement; the system will have tuned the stored motor representations to the point where a movement is performed "automatically." Such automatic movements are skills, and the underlying representations are good examples of implicit memories; one cannot access these representations in any way other than by executing them.

Mishkin and his colleagues suggest that a distinct neuroanatomical system may underlie some perceptual/motor aspects of skill.[94] Consider the following experiment with monkeys: The same pairs of objects are shown, once a day, with a reward always being placed under the same member of each pair. Eventually, the animal learns to select the object in each pair that is associated with a reward. After many trials, its reaching behavior becomes rapid and appears to be "automatic." If the hippocampus then is removed, the animal does *not* have a severe deficit in this task. The stimuli came to be associated "directly" with a particular response by the stimulus-response connection subsystem, which does not necessarily rely on the memory formation subsystems. As noted earlier in this chapter, in the discussion of Figure 8.2, the stimulus-response connection subsystem is implemented in the striatum, which serves to connect a perceptual input directly with a motor program in motor memory.[95] In this case, the action programming and instructions generation subsystems are bypassed; the input directly accesses a stored motor memory, which produces the response.

Mishkin suggests that a subcortical structure called the *substantia nigra* is critically involved in the "reinforcement" process that strengthens connections between perceptual states and responses.[96] The substantia nigra produces dopamine, another neurotransmitter, which plays a critical role in the function of the striatum.

In humans, many skills may be achieved using the stimulus-response connection subsystem. For example, when one first sees mirror-reversed print, it is difficult to read; but with practice, it becomes progressively easier to read such materials.[97] Such practice may occur because one learns to scan mirror-reversed words from right-to-left. In this task, the subjects generally are shown three or more words at a time, which require multiple fixations to encode properly. If the subjects initially scan the mirror-reversed words left-to-right, perceptual units (letters or groups of letters) will be encoded in the wrong order, and will not correspond to the order stored in associative memory. Hence, reading will be impaired. If the subjects learn to scan the words right-to-left, reading will be improved.

This modification of scanning could be easily learned using the stimulus-response connection subsystem; if the subject happens to scan right-to-left when presented with the words, the letter stream that is encoded would match representations in associative memory. This positive consequence would lead the stimulus-response subsystem to strengthen the connection between the stimulus (i.e., those reversed letters or groups of letters) and that response (scanning right-to-left). Thus, when that stimulus was encountered subsequently, one would adjust one's scanning pattern. This stimulus-response connection would be specific to particular words, but would generalize partially to novel mirror-reversed words.

Before continuing, it will behoove us to consider why a straightforward alternative account of the mirror-reading findings should be rejected. This account posits that mirror-reversed print is easier to read with practice because new representations of mirror-reversed letters, sequences of letters (e.g., "ion," "pre," etc.), and words are stored in visual memory.[98]

This alternative account can easily explain the key properties of the skill. For example, Neil Cohen and Squire found that normal subjects improved the most for the particular words they had seen during practice sessions, but the effects of practice partially generalized to new words.[99] According to this account, mirror-reversed words presented during the practice sessions were read better subsequently because they were likely to have been stored as a unit, and practice partially generalized to new words because some letters and common sequences of letters were also stored.

However, this account is troublesome, for empirical and theoretical reasons. First, the "new perceptual representations" account hinges on the operation of the memory formation subsystem. But even brain-damaged patients who cannot store new explicit information can learn to read mirror-reversed text.[100] Indeed, these patients develop the general skill at about the same rate as normal subjects—even though they do not remember having participated in the task before! These findings suggest that new explicit memories are not responsible for the general improvement. Second, the idea that representations of mirror-reversed text are encoded in the pattern activation subsystem conflicts with the finding that a *viewpoint consistency constraint* is exploited during object recognition. Apparently, the output from the preprocessing subsystem is matched to representations in the pattern activation subsystem regardless of left-right orientations. All that is important are the relative spatial relations among the nonaccidental properties, which must be consistent with seeing a stimulus from a single point of view—not their absolute locations. Not only does this process allow us to understand how we can read mirror-reversed print in the first place, before any practice, but it also is consistent with the fact that people have very poor memory for left-right orientation.[101] (Mirror-reversed words may be detected when the letters enter associative memory in the wrong order, or when spatial relations among letters or their component segments are encoded by the dorsal system and compared to representations in associative memory.)

Nevertheless, at least some of the improvement in normal subjects could reflect new explicit memory encodings. Specifically, normal subjects could associate new information with the stimulus words in associative memory, indicating that those words were mirror-reversed in the task. Subsequently, these representations could activate the corresponding perceptual representations via the appropriate pointers, which would prime those representations to encode the words more quickly. If so, then normal subjects would show greater improvement for repeated words than would subjects who could not encode new explicit memories. Cohen and Squire report this very finding;[102]

although the general skill develops at the same rate in patients who cannot encode explicit memories and normal control subjects, the normal control subjects learn to read specific repeated words more effectively than the patients.[103]

The sort of stimulus-driven "automatic" behavior that is mediated by the stimulus-response connection subsystem is qualitatively distinct from behavior that is deliberately initiated to achieve a goal (e.g., executing the specific movements to sew up a hole). Target and via point coordinates for performing specific movements that are stored in associative memory can be accessed in many different contexts, and combined in novel ways. Thus, the sort of "automatic" behavior discussed in Chapter 7 must be distinguished from that discussed here: one can decide to dance any time, and can drive one's car down any route—but a stimulus-response representation of a skill is restricted; the response can only be evoked by the appropriate stimulus. It appears that we can develop specific skills of this type without using the memory formation subsystems, which has two implications: Not only can new stimulus-response associations be established without using these subsystems, but also the processes that store new information in motor memory apparently do not depend on the memory formation subsystems.

Neural Mechanisms

Another type of synapse has been discovered that plays a critical role in establishing several forms of implicit memory. Because Eric Kandel has been at the center of this discovery, this type of synapse is sometimes called a *Kandel synapse*.[104] This synapse depends on changes in the availability of neurotransmitters in the presynaptic neuron, and does not depend on changes in the receiving neuron. Kandel and his colleagues have focused on understanding simple systems, primarily that of the Aplysia (a sea slug). Although this animal is very simple, it nevertheless engages in a surprisingly varied range of activities. Many of its neural circuits are being mapped out in great detail.[105]

The Aplysia is of interest in part because it can learn simple associations, and the neural changes that underlie such learning can be studied in detail. These associations are forms of implicit memory; they are evoked only in specific situations, and cannot be "looked up" or used in other ways. One kind of association underlies the phenomenon of *habituation*. Habituation is a very simple form of learning in which an organism progressively ignores a weak stimulus that is not noxious and not accompanied by a reward. If one stimulates an Aplysia's siphon, it initially withdraws both the siphon and its gill. However, with repeated stimulation, the response decreases. This habituation can last from minutes to weeks, depending on the number of times the animal is stimulated and the intensity of the stimulation.

The cellular mechanism responsible for habituation has been identified by Kandel and his colleagues. This mechanism hinges on the fact that more neurotransmitters are released at a terminal (the part of the synapse that releases neurotransmitters) after more calcium ions (Ca^{++}) flow into the terminal. Each time the cell fires, Ca^{++} normally flows into the neuron's terminals. Repeated stimulation of siphon sensory neurons inactivates Ca^{++} channels (small pores in the membrane those ions flow through) in the neuron; hence, less Ca^{++} flows into the terminal over the course of stimulation. Because the amount of transmitter that will be released depends on the influx of Ca^{++}, a decrease in the amount of Ca^{++} flowing in results in a decrease in the amount of transmitter that is released. This change occurs in the synapses between the sensory neurons that register stimulation of the siphon and the motor neurons that control the gill, and between the siphon motor neurons and interneurons (which do not receive direct input or control output, but rather modulate other neurons; these cells are roughly analogous to "hidden units" in neural network models, as discussed in Chapter 2).

Sensitization is another simple form of learning that results in implicit memory. Sensitization occurs when a prior stimulus leads an animal to respond more strongly to a subsequent stimulus. For example, if you suddenly heard a very loud noise, such as a nearby gun shot, you might react strongly. Then, if a few seconds (or minutes) later somebody slammed a door, you probably would react more strongly than you would have if the gun shot had not occurred. You had become sensitized to loud, sharp noises. In a sense, sensitization is a kind of priming, but it primes a response—not a perceptual encoding. Just as priming does not depend on specific associated knowledge about when and where the stimulus was perceived, sensitization does not depend on processes that access semantic or conceptual information in associative memory (as demonstrated by the mere fact that it occurs in Aplysia).

In their studies of Aplysia, Kandel and his collaborators observed that noxious stimulation of the tail enhances the normal withdrawal response of the gill and siphon to subsequent weak stimulation. Like habituation, sensitization can last from minutes to weeks, depending on the intensity and amount of stimulation. Similarly, the mechanism hinges on properties of synapses between the sensory neuron and its "central target cells." But in contrast to habituation, the learning process in sensitization involves an *increase* in the amount of transmitter released. A complex intracellular mechanism causes a greater amount of Ca^{++} to flow into the terminal, which causes more transmitter to be released.

Finally, classical conditioning is an even more complex form of learning that produces implicit memory. In classical conditioning, a neutral stimulus (the *conditioned stimulus,* or *CS*) is paired with a stimulus that induces a response (the *unconditioned stimulus,* or *US*). After a sufficient number of pairings, the CS will induce the response by itself. In Pavlov's classic experiments with dogs, the US was meat powder, which elicited the response of drooling. When a bell, the CS, was sounded prior to the US, it eventually came to elicit drooling by itself. For the Aplysia, a strong tactile stimulation of the tail is a US, which causes the gill and siphon to withdraw reflexively, and a mild tactile stimulation of the siphon is a CS. When this CS is paired with the US enough times, the CS alone comes to induce the withdrawal reflex. The association develops gradually over the course of many pairings of the CS and US, and once established, the conditioned response can persist for several days—and probably longer in some situations.[106]

Classical conditioning is also hypothesized to arise from an increase in the amount of Ca^{++} that flows into the terminals of the sensory neurons when the CS is present. In a sense, classical conditioning is a special form of sensitization; the animal becomes selectively sensitive to the CS. Thus, it makes sense that mechanisms involved in sensitization would also play a role in this sort of conditioning.[107] Kandel and his colleagues suggest that learning is subserved by a family of related processes; hence the same mechanisms used in simple forms of learning may also be used—along with other mechanisms—in more complex forms of learning. The mechanisms they suggest seem ideally suited for establishing new associations in the stimulus-response connection subsystem.

Thus, at least two neural mechanisms—Hebb synapses (as described earlier in this chapter) and Kandel synapses—are the basis of some forms of learning. These two types of neural mechanisms have been observed in a variety of organisms and in different parts of the nervous system.

Recap: Storing Implicit and Explicit Memories

Explicit memory corresponds to stored information that can be used in language, reasoning, and the production of novel behavior. In contrast, implicit memory reflects changes in representations that are only revealed when the representations are used in a specific kind of processing. Implicit memory is often revealed by repetition priming, where a previously perceived stimulus biases the system to encode a subsequent stimulus in the same way. Such priming occurs when a residual pattern of activation remains in a subsystem after a stimulus is perceived. Thus, priming in the preprocessing and pattern activation subsystems is modality-specific, whereas priming in associative memory is not. We also inferred that associations in associative memory, both among tokens and between tokens and modality-specific representations, can remain partially activated following use, which primes such associations. In addition, it is possible that under some circumstances pairs of stimuli can be perceptually grouped into a single unit in the pattern activation subsystem, and so if one stimulus activates the unit the other will be primed. Finally, we inferred that the stimulus-response connection subsystem may establish a relatively direct association between a perceptual state and a motor memory, which results in "automatic" performance that does not employ the action programming, instructions generation, or movement monitoring subsystems. Such behavior is inflexible, and only evoked by specific stimuli, in contrast to the "automatic" behavior considered in Chapter 7.

Using Short-term, Long-term, and Working Memories

It is now common to conceive of memory representations as being in one of three states.[108] First, material in *short-term memory* can be retained only for a very brief period of time, can specify a limited amount of information,[109] and we are aware of its contents. For example, one holds a telephone number in short-term memory by saying it over and over. The auditory buffer, the visual buffer, and corresponding structures in other modalities serve as short-term memory structures. In general, a short-term memory representation, on this view, is the same as a mental image; one retains perceptual information as was described in Chapter 4. The one exception to this generalization is the sentence structure buffer that we inferred in Chapter 6, which is a special-purpose short-term memory structure that stores syntactic and semantic information as the meaning of a sentence is built up over time.

Second, material in *long-term memory* is stored over a long duration, can specify very large amounts of information, and we are not aware of this information unless it has been activated and produced a representation in a short-term memory. We have inferred three types of long-term memories: Unimodal (modality-specific) representations are stored in the pattern activation subsystems, movement sequences are stored in motor memory, and amodal representations are stored in associative memory.

Finally, material in *working memory* is used to aid reasoning processes.[110] Reasoning processes only can operate on information in short-term memory, but relatively little information can be stored in short-term memory. Thus, decision processes in the frontal lobe selectively activate information in long-term memory and "swap" information in and out of short-term memory, as needed to perform a task. We interpret the short-term memory structures Patricia Goldman-Rakic reports in the frontal lobe[111] as extensions of the perceptual encoding subsystems, which serve to make perceptual information immediately available to the decision processes; according to this view, it is debatable whether one wants to conceive of the information as actually being stored—as opposed to monitored—in the frontal lobe.

Working memory, then, corresponds to the activated information in the long-term memories, the information in short-term memories, and the decision processes that manage which information is activated in the long-term memories and retained in the short-term memories.[112] The mere fact that priming occurs indicates that some information in long-term memory can be partially activated, even though it does not in turn engender a short-term memory representation. If we are not aware of it, the information is not in short-term memory; but the information may nevertheless still be partially activated, and capable of evoking a short-term memory representation quickly at some later time.

This kind of working memory system is necessary for a wide range of tasks, such as performing mental arithmetic, reading, problem solving and—as we shall see in the following chapter—reasoning in general. All of these tasks require not only some form of temporary storage, but also an interplay between information that is stored temporarily and a larger body of stored knowledge.

Thus, we do not need to posit any additional subsystems to conceive of the three states of memory representations. This conceptualization will prove useful when we consider accounts for various types of specific memory impairments following brain damage.

Understanding the Effects of Brain Damage

Amnesia is a neurological impairment of memory that is not caused by impaired perceptual, language, reasoning, attentional, motivational, or motor abilities. Amnesia can follow various injuries to the brain, including traumatic, surgical, chemical, viral, disease, or loss of blood (which reduces oxygen and nutrients), and can occur following electroconvulsive therapy.

Moreover, as our inferences about the mechanisms underlying memory storage lead us to expect, amnesia can result from lesions to different parts of the brain. Given the importance of the hippocampus in storing new memories, we expect a particularly dramatic form of amnesia following a lesion of the medial portions of the temporal lobe, including the hippocampus. This sort of amnesia does in fact occur, and is referred to as *medial temporal amnesia.* We will shortly present a detailed description of one such patient.

Another form of amnesia results from a lesion to the diencephalic structures, particularly the thalamus; this form is called *diencephalic amnesia.* For example, patient N.A. was 22 years old when he was accidently hurt with a small fencing foil. The foil went through his right nostril, up into his brain. He suffered multiple neurological deficits, all of which disappeared with time except for a severe and lasting memory impairment, particularly for verbal material.[113] A subsequent comprehensive magnetic resonance image (MRI) analysis revealed that N.A. had a large left diencephalic lesion.[114]

Perhaps the most frequent variety of amnesia accompanies *Korsakoff's syndrome,* which can be considered as a type of diencephalic amnesia. Korsakoff's syndrome may occur as an indirect result of alcohol abuse; drinking too much often results in eating too little, which results in a thiamine deficiency. This deficiency in turn can result in damage to different parts of the brain, in particular to two structures within the diencephaleon, the mamillary complex and the mediodorsal thalamic nucleus, which are involved in encoding new memories.[115]

Anterograde and retrograde amnesia. We have so far been discussing *anterograde amnesia,* which is the inability to form new memories. This sort of amnesia is to be contrasted with *retrograde amnesia,* in which patients forget events that occurred prior to an event that disrupted brain function. Destroying the hippocampus produces a retrograde amnesia for material learned a year or two before the event as well as a severe anterograde amnesia. The amnesia that follows damage to memory storage structures is *global;* it impairs learning in all perceptual modalities. Retrograde amnesia affects the recent past more than the remote past, and may extend from weeks to several years, depending on the severity of the anterograde amnesia and on the size and location of the lesion; in general, the more severe the anterograde amnesia, the more severe the retrograde amnesia.[116]

These observations make sense in the context of the inferences we have drawn. Recall that the weight adjustment subsystem depends on processes that occur in the hippocampus and related cortex. This subsystem creates the conditions under which the connection strengths change in a network to store new information. We inferred that this process requires a long time, like walking through the grass to create a dirt pathway; if the process stops "walking" too early (because of a lesion to the memory formation subsystem) the information will not be preserved structurally.

All forms of amnesia have two major characteristics.[117] First, the deficit is restricted to long-term memory; short-term memory and working memory are intact. Second, the deficit affects all explicit memories, but at least some forms of implicit memory are intact. We first will discuss these dissociations in more detail, and then will consider other sorts of memory disorders.

A Selective Long-term Memory Deficit

Even though their ability to store new information in long-term memory is severely impaired, amnesic patients typically have intact short-term and working memory; they can keep information in mind for a few minutes, provided that they attend to the material. This dissociation is dramatically illustrated by the amnesic patient H.M. In an effort to relieve his otherwise intractable epilepsy, H.M.'s medial temporal lobe (including the hippocampus) was removed when he was 27 years old.[118] Since the time of the operation, he has learned virtually no new facts (i.e., entered them into long-term memory), but he can store information temporarily in short-term and working memory.

For example, consider the following anecdote. Koenig and John Gabrieli tested H.M. seven days in a row, twice a day, for 30-minute sessions.[119] At the beginning and at the end of each session, they asked H.M. whether he knew where Koenig came from. Although they always told H.M. the correct answer after a while, he always said he did not know. Before they told H.M. the answer, he was always asked to guess. Probably because of Koenig's French accent, H.M. always suggested Canada, France, or New Orleans. Then, the researchers always told H.M. that he had made a good guess, but that the correct answer was Geneva, in Switzerland. H.M. always replied with surprise: "Oh,

Geneva, Switzerland!" The exact same discussion occurred at the beginning and end of each testing session.

On the last day of testing, H.M. was brought into another room immediately after the end of the testing session. About 10 minutes later, the researchers passed in front of the room where H.M. was sitting in a chair, waiting to be tested. A few seconds later, a research assistant ran to the researchers, and said, very excited, "When H.M. saw you walking in the hallway, he said: Have a good trip!" The assistant was very surprised and she asked him to repeat what he just said. H.M. replied that he had said "Have a good trip!" The assistant asked him to whom he said this. H.M. answered "I said this to the small one [Koenig] because he is going back to Geneva, Switzerland."

H.M. had gone into the waiting room immediately after he heard that Dr. Koenig was from Switzerland, and apparently no meaningful information had interfered with the working memory representation of the last thing he had been told. Therefore, this information remained available for about 10 minutes. It is unlikely that he rehearsed the information (i.e., repeatedly generated auditory images of the words) for the entire time, and so the information probably did not reside in short-term memory. But it is likely that the appropriate previously stored (before the operation) long-term memory representations remained activated for this interval.

Recall that when one understands a statement, the sentence comprehension process activates a specific a set of representations in associative memory (see Chapter 6). This constructive process creates a new pattern of activation for each statement, which is how H.M. can understand new concepts, such as the mere fact of Dr. Koenig's existence. This concept must have been built up on the basis of previously encoded information; furthermore, the sentence comprehension process must have built a temporary association between this representation and the fact that he was from Geneva. Similarly, H.M. can perform tasks over the course of many minutes because he is constantly involved in the task, and so the processes induced by the instructions remain activated. Unlike normal people, however, these patterns of activation could not be transformed into structural changes; the mechanical man could walk and form a pattern on the grass, but not wear through to the dirt.

Hence, if asked to remember a list of words, and then to recall as many as possible immediately after the last one is presented, amnesic subjects typically recall the last few items of the list, but do not recall items from the beginning of the list.[120] In contrast, normal subjects recall more words from the end and from the beginning of the list than from the middle. The tendency to recall relatively many words from the end of the list is called the *recency effect,* and is thought to occur because the last few words are still in short-term memory. The tendency to recall relatively many words from the beginning of the list is called the *primacy effect,* and is thought to occur because these were processed long enough that a representation was entered into long-term memory. However, this representation is dynamic; "the dirt path" may require years to be worn through permanently.[121]

This interpretation of the primacy and recency effects is consistent with the finding that amnesics show only a recency effect: Amnesics only have trouble when they must remember more information than they can hold in short-term memory; they simply do not enter new information into long-term memory.

If short-term memory for words and pictures relies on auditory and visual mental imagery, such as would occur when one "hears" words over and over while rehearsing them, then the limited capacity of short-term memory is easily interpreted: One can only retain a small amount of information in an image, and images decay quickly over time. Because the image generation process does not depend on altering strengths of connections, images of familiar material can be formed without using the memory formation subsystems; the appropriate representations in the pattern activation subsystem are activated by input from associative memory, and the decision subsystem causes them to remain active—causing a pattern of activity (an image) in the visual buffer (or auditory buffer, depending on the modality).

Alternatively, we can offer another account of the recency effect, which hinges on properties of working memory. In this case, recently encountered words would be available simply because their representations were still activated in long-term memory. This view is consistent with our anecdote about H.M. If so, then properties of short-term memory (and mental imagery) would have nothing to do with the spared memory for items near the end of a list.

In contrast, in order to store a long-term memory representation, the connections between the neurons must be altered via hippocampal function. Recall that the operation of the print-now subsystem relies in part on the basal forebrain's releasing acetylcholine; the acetylcholine is sent to the hippocampus and the appropriate perceptual areas. The hippocampus and related cortex play a critical role in the storage process, and diencephalic structures (i.e., the anterior nucleus of the thalamus and the mediodorsal thalamic nucleus) also play a critical role in the process because they serve as a routing (and perhaps attentional gating) center for output from the hippocampus and related cortex. Therefore, we are not surprised that damage to these structures typically engenders a long-term memory deficit.

The memory deficit following removal of the hippocampus and related structures does not arise because the representations stored in long-term memory are disrupted. These patients remember facts and events from well before the brain injury reasonably well. In addition, given that the patients can retrieve memories encoded before the onset of the amnesia, the medial temporal and diencephalic structures cannot play a critical role in looking up information in memory.

A Selective Explicit Memory Deficit

Studies with amnesic patients have revealed dissociations within long-term memory itself; some aspects of long-term memory can be spared while others are severely impaired. Specifically, amnesic patients typically perform well on a range of implicit memory tasks despite having very poor explicit memory. We have so far noted deficits in explicit memory; let us now consider evidence that implicit memory is relatively intact.

Priming. Amnesic patients often show priming in the face of otherwise devastating memory deficits. For example, researchers showed amnesic patients a series of fragmented drawings, each of which depicted a single object.[122] Several versions of each drawing were used, which included different amounts of the lines and regions that depicted the object. For each object, the patients first were shown a very fragmented version, and then a slightly less fragmented version, and so on, until they saw the complete object. At each stage, they were asked whether they could identify the object. The patients could identify the objects in a more fragmented form when they were shown the drawings in a second session than they could initially, even though they could not remember having previously participated in the study. Clearly, information about the drawings was encoded during the first session that primed performance during the second session. In addition, amnesic patients show priming in the stem completion task described earlier.[123]

Thus, priming occurs even following damage to the components of the weight adjustment subsystem that are located within the medial temporal areas and to their projections through the diencephalic areas. Presumably, this sort of priming arises because the preprocessing and pattern activation subsystems operate normally in these patients. Residual activation from the prior exposure could have biased the preprocessing subsystem to organize shapes in specific ways, and/or could have biased the pattern activation subsystem to match input to previously activated representations. As discussed earlier, we infer that the modality-specific component of priming arises because residual activation from previous processing persists, and hence influences subsequent encodings.

In addition, some cross-modality priming occurs even for amnesics, which is as expected because they have no problem comprehending language and performing other tasks that depend on activating associations in associative memory. Once these associations are activated, residual activation may linger to bias subsequent encodings. Peter Graf and his colleagues assessed priming in a word completion test in normal control subjects and amnesic patients.[124] Priming was observed in both groups, and the effect was larger within the same modality (i.e., visual exposure and visual test) than across modalities (i.e., auditory exposure and visual test) in both groups. These results are just as expected if priming corresponds to residual activation that occurs separately in the ventral system and associative memory.

Skill learning. Amnesic subjects also appear to learn skills virtually normally. For example, H.M. was taught to trace patterns while observing them in a mirror—which is a surprisingly difficult perceptual-motor skill. He was able to learn and retain this skill for several days, even though he was not aware of ever having performed the task.[125]

This sort of skill learning may depend on the stimulus-response connection subsystem. If so, then the result is easily interpreted: Mirror-writing develops by establishing new input/output mappings via the striatum, which allow one to move one's hand appropriately when viewing the stimulus. Such connections do not rely on storing new representations in perceptual subsystems or associative memory, and so this skill is not affected by damage to the memory formation subsystems. In addition, the stimulus itself may become easier to encode with practice if appropriate processes are primed in the preprocessing subsystem or perceptual representations become primed in the pattern activation subsystem.

However, this is not to say that explicit memory cannot contribute to the acquisition and use of skills. As noted earlier, Cohen and Squire found that although normal subjects and amnesic subjects were better able to read novel mirror-reversed words after practicing with other words, normal subjects improved with repeated words much more than did the amnesic patients.[126] This finding is consistent with our claim that this skill has two components, only one of which involves the stimulus-response connection subsystem (learning new patterns of eye movements); the other component involves using the memory formation subsystems to enter new information in associative memory, which subsequently primes perceptual representations. The normal subjects could engage in both sorts of learning, but the amnesics could only learn the striatum-mediated scanning. Thus, the normal subjects showed a larger improvement in this task with repeated words, where previously stored representations of those words primed performance, but both groups showed about the same level of improvement with novel words, where only the new scan path enhanced performance.

The Dementias

Recent studies of patients with Alzheimer's disease and Huntington's disease have revealed further dissociations within implicit memory. Alzheimer's disease patients have impaired priming, whereas Huntington's disease patients have relatively normal priming.[127] In contrast, Alzheimer's disease patients learn some skills normally (at least at relatively early stages of the disease), whereas Huntington's disease patients are impaired on tasks such as mirror reading.[128] The presence of this *double dissociation* between skill learning and priming is consistent with our inference that distinct neural mechanisms support skill learning and priming.

The fact that Huntington's disease patients have trouble learning skills may be a direct consequence of damage to part of the striatum (the caudate nucleus), which is not damaged in Alzheimer's disease patients. Indeed, some researchers have suggested that the striatum (specifically the caudate nucleus and the putamen) plays a critical role in learning to read mirror-reversed words.[129] This idea is consistent with the contention that the striatum implements the stimulus-response connection subsystem, which establishes relatively direct connections between a stimulus and a response. In contrast, Huntington's disease causes only minimal damage to parts of the brain involved in perceptual encoding, and hence our analysis leads us to expect Huntington's disease patients to have normal priming (if we assume that associative memory is also intact, which appears to be the case for the patients who were tested).

The fact that Alzheimer's disease patients have impaired priming may be a direct consequence of damage to cortical-cortical connections, including those in the temporal and parietal lobes. Indeed, Alzheimer's disease patients have been found to have neuronal loss in many cortical areas, in addition to pathology of the olfactory system, the enthorinal cortex, and the hippocampal formation.[130] On the other hand, their intact striata may allow them to learn skills normally (provided that all of the other necessary structures are intact, which appears to be the case, at least relatively early in the course of the disease).

A Selective Short-term Memory Deficit

In contrast to amnesic patients, other patients have been reported to have selective short-term memory deficits. For example, patient P.V. could not repeat sequences of digits, letters, or words longer than two or three items when they were presented auditorily.[131] In contrast, P.V. performed normally in at least some long-term memory tasks. For example, she was able to learn a list of ten words, and performed normally when asked to learn associations between pairs of words.[132]

The dissociation between the ability to hold information in short-term memory and to encode information into long-term memory, and vice versa, is consistent with our analyses. A deficit in short-term memory corresponds to a deficit within the perceptual areas (assuming that the deficit is not due to a lack of attention), which need not affect their functioning during perception proper. For example, information may decay faster from the auditory buffer, or the patient may not be able to generate or maintain auditory images, or the patient may not be able to organize information into relatively few "chunks," and so on. In contrast, the long-term memory deficits involve damage to any of the components of the memory formation subsystem, which are not used to retain information in short-term memory.

Source Amnesia

Some amnesic patients can learn new facts without remembering where and when these facts were learned. This dissociation is called *source amnesia*. Source amnesia appears to be unrelated to the severity of the memory deficit itself; some patients with source amnesia recall as many facts as patients without source amnesia.[133]

Source amnesia typically occurs following damage to the frontal lobes.[134] Thus, source amnesia may arise when the decision subsystem is damaged, which we hypothesize may be implemented in the dorsolateral frontal area. Perseveration is a common consequence of frontal lobe damage, which may account for the deficit if the decision subsystem repeatedly encodes one sort of information, not switching from the associations required to encode the fact itself to associations between the fact and contextual stimuli. This notion is consistent with the finding that these patients often recall the context itself, but not the association between the context and a fact.[135]

Alternatively, in some cases it seems possible that the damage affects the basal forebrain, so that memory encoding is not efficient. If so, then this deficit may reflect a compensation for sluggish processing. Logically, the associations that constitute a fact, such as between a property and an object, must be encoded before there is anything to associate with contextual stimuli. If the memory encoding process is slowed down, perhaps because of reduced amounts of acetylcholine, the decision subsystem may direct the memory formation subsystems to encode facts and context at the expense of setting up the association between the two; in many tasks, this strategy makes sense.

Moreover, there is evidence that the frontal lobe plays a critical role in accessing information,[136] as expected if the property lookup subsystems are implemented there. Perhaps the property lookup subsystems have been impaired, and so have difficulty accessing associations that are relatively weak, and most associations to context are weaker than the associations that compose a fact.

Furthermore, recall that Goldman-Rakic provides evidence that perceptual information ultimately projects to the frontal lobe;[137] if so, then perhaps damage to the frontal lobe degrades the perceptual information reaching the decision subsystem, so that it does not use this information effectively to set up "context" associations in associative memory.

It is clear that the inferences we drew when considering normal memory can help to illuminate possible problems in patients with brain damage. As usual, we found that alternative accounts often are possible, which may characterize different patients.

———

We have inferred three additional subsystems in this chapter. The "memory formation subsystems" were broken into two, more precisely characterized subsystems. The print-now subsystem initiates the process of encoding explicit memory representations; this subsystem is implemented in part in the basal forebrain, and its output initiates the process of modifying the strengths of connections in the appropriate networks (via the release of acetylcholine). The weight adjustment subsystem triggers processes that actually alter weights in networks to store representations of stimulus properties or associations between representations; this subsystem is implemented in part in the hippocampus and related cortex. And the stimulus-response connection subsystem encodes associations between perceptual representations and motor output programs that are not mediated by associative memory; this subsystem is implemented in part in the striatum.

We were able to account for a wide range of memory phenomena by considering properties of the perceptual encoding and motor output subsystems that we inferred (for other reasons) in previous chapters. For example, much of the work of memory is accomplished by machinery needed in perception and language, which again illustrates the principle of weak modularity at work. Indeed, the inferences we drew about memory interlocked so strongly with inferences drawn previously that it was often difficult for us to provide many alternative accounts for the effects of brain damage. We also saw evidence of the principle of division of labor; it would be very difficult to build a single network that accomplishes all of the functions of memory. For example, the computational requirements on a system that stores stimulus-response "reflexes" and on a system that stores explicit information for use in reasoning are contradictory—and hence it makes sense that distinct mechanisms exist for the different functions. And the principle of opportunism seems evident in the use of mental imagery as a form of short-term memory—which is interesting in part because imagery itself may have developed opportunistically out of perceptual processing (see Chapter 4).

Moreover, the principle of concurrent processing is evident in much of what we discussed: Information from the ventral and dorsal systems flows at the same time to associative memory, the print-now subsystem, and the weight adjustment subsystem. Furthermore, the print-now and weight adjustment subsystems, on the one hand, and the stimulus-response connection subsystem, on the other, must be operating at the same time; until efficient "direct" connections between a stimulus and a response are formed (if they can be at all), memory relies on the explicit representations stored by the memory formation subsystems.

Finally, the principle of constraint satisfaction is evident, this time at a more molecular level than we have considered previously. This principle underlies the operation of NMDA receptors; they only produce LTP if the proper conditions are satisfied at the same time. Similarly, the Kandel synapse operates according to the principle of constraint satisfaction. It is very exciting not only to see that similar principles may operate at different levels of analysis, but also simply to see that cognitive neuroscience is beginning to make contact with findings about the operation of ion channels and the like. This development holds the promise that the power of molecular biology and biophysics may soon be brought to bear on traditional questions about mental activity.

This chapter also illustrates the power of cognitive neuroscience to resolve old issues. At least since the time of the phrenologists, researchers have debated whether memory is distributed throughout the brain or localized to a specific area. The answer is both, at multiple levels of analysis. Clearly, many different structures are involved in memory; so in one sense memory is distributed. However, many of the structures may store distinct aspects of memory; so in another sense memory is localized. In yet another sense, memory is distributed throughout connections in individual neural networks, but even here aspects of it may be localized at specific synapses. Thus, the question that caused so much debate was couched in the wrong terms; rather than asking about "memory" as a single entity, it is better to focus on different aspects of memory and their inter-relations.

9

Gray Matters

This book is entitled *Wet Mind,* but one could argue that we have really only skirted the perimeters of what is commonly thought of as the "mind." Although we have discussed how human beings recognize and identify objects, use visual mental images, read, produce and comprehend language, move, and store new information in memory, we have been vague about the source of (free) "will," the ultimate source of decision making in the brain. What decides what to do next? We have inferred that there must be a "decision subsystem," but have not said much about it. We have eschewed talk of consciousness and emotion, and although we have frequently noted differences between the cerebral hemispheres, we have said nothing about how those differences arise. And we have not considered the practical side of research in cognitive neuroscience, such as its implications for rehabilitation.

The title of this chapter alerts the reader to its highly

401

speculative nature. We depart from our usual organizational scheme, and simply consider a set of relatively unrelated topics in the context of our previous inferences. Our discussion will not be as detailed as it was in previous chapters; not enough is known to warrant this treatment. Following this, we will draw some broad conclusions about how the brain produces the mind.

Reasoning

The first step in reasoning is to select a goal, and the second step is to devise a way to achieve it (which often involves deciding among possible alternative approaches). Such processes lie at the heart of many of our everyday activities. For example, they come into play when one cooks from a recipe and must have the appropriate ingredients ready at the right time, chooses the shortest route to carry out an errand, or curbs one's natural impulses and speaks tactfully to a rude colleague.

Reasoning is also required when one figures out how much to tip a waiter or considers exchange rates when deciding whether to make a purchase in a foreign country. Even the apparently simple operation of computing 15% of a total requires setting a goal and then devising a plan to achieve it—which involves the orchestration of many component processes (dividing, holding subproducts in memory, adding, and so forth).

Reasoning is perhaps the best example of a Function (as characterized in Chapter 1), so the principle of division of labor leads us to expect it to be accomplished by a host of processing subsystems working together. Indeed, we infer that most of the subsystems discussed earlier in this book play a role in reasoning, which also reflects the principles of weak modularity and opportunism at work. In particular, the perceptual encoding subsystems must play a critical role in reasoning because they determine how the stimulus situation is characterized; depending on how one "looks at" a situation, it will be responded to in different ways. The imagery processes may help one to construe a situation in different ways, as well as to anticipate the consequences of specific actions, as was discussed in Chapter 4. Moreover, the memory subsystems must play a critical role in reasoning, given that we often use plans that allowed us to cope with similar situations in the past. Perceptual input can access information in memory that pertains to similar previous circumstances, which can help one to decide how to behave in a current situation. Furthermore, the auditory subsystems are critical in part because they are used whenever one comprehends verbal instructions, which often define the problem. In addition, we earlier inferred that the decision subsystem initiates specific "strategies" to enhance memorization; for example, it governs how long one attends to a stimulus, which affects the probability that this material will be stored effectively. This subsystem could also be used more generally to initiate strategies. Finally, the action subsystems not only are necessary to produce the appropriate response, but also sometimes play a critical role in solving the problem. For example, one may write down intermediate steps when doing arithmetic and may draw a picture or build a model when designing a structure.

Nevertheless, the decision subsystem sits at the center of the reasoning process. This subsystem orchestrates the others so that a specific goal is achieved, and we must consider it in more detail.

Reasoning About Familiar Problems: An Overview

It is easiest to characterize the decision subsystem in more detail if we consider how it operates in the simplest types of reasoning, when one is familiar with the problem and already has an appropriate plan stored in memory to guide processing. Before considering specific examples of such reasoning, we will consider what they have in common. In these cases, the entire array of stimuli entering associative memory—including language and visual input—activates stored representations of plans. Analogous to the process of identifying objects (see Chapter 3), each plan is associated with a variety of conditions. To the extent that those conditions are satisfied by the input, the plan is activated. All else being equal, the most strongly activated plan will be used to guide processing.

We conceive of a stored plan in much the same way that we conceived of the representation of an action sequence in Chapter 7. Recall that an action sequence is stored as a set of movements, which are combined in a particular order when the action is produced. A stored plan is a representation in associative memory that specifies a sequence of operations, but these operations need not be overt movements. For example, one operation might be to form a visual mental image of an object (this operation, of course, decomposes into many distinct operations, as was discussed in Chapter 4), and another operation might be to "look" for a specific property in the imaged object or scene. Similarly, the arithmetic and logical operations all can be performed with no overt movements.

Each operation associated with a plan specifies an input for a specific subsystem. For example, a plan may specify that the categorical property lookup subsystem should look up the representation of a specific object in associative memory, then specify that certain associated representations should be sent to the subsystems that form an image of the object, and finally specify that a particular property should be sought on the imaged object. Depending on the problem, different objects would be imaged and different properties sought. Probably the vast majority of plans used in common, everyday reasoning are stored in a schematic form, and later fleshed out to apply to the objects and events in a particular situation.

In addition, each step may depend on the results of the previous step or steps. Indeed, plans may have a "branching" organization, allowing one to use several methods to reach a goal, depending on the requirements of the situation. The operations that define the branches (such as those that initiate mental imagery versus writing something down) are associated with a number of conditions (such as the number of digits that must be added). The stimuli that activated the plan, plus the results of performing previous operations, are fed into associative memory and are matched against the conditions associated with each branch. These inputs serve as constraints to activate the specific branch that most closely satisfies the conditions.

Two subsystems. We infer that the decision subsystem carries out at least two distinct functions in order to use representations of plans effectively, and this leads us to speculate that it can be subdivided into at least two subsystems.

First, as we have discussed in the previous chapters, the decision subsystems send instructions that activate individual operations. This is a different kind of input/output mapping from those accomplished by any of the other subsystems we have posited; in initiating an action, the most activated representation of a plan must be selected, and then the appropriate operations selected and carried out. Hence, we posit another subsystem, which we call the *run subsystem*.[1] The run subsystem selects the plan that is most activated, and then shunts the inputs associated with each step of the plan to the appropriate subsystems.[2] In some cases, the operation specifies an input to the action programming or sentence programming subsystems, which (in conjunction with the instructions generation and movement execution subsystems) produces a movement; in others, it specifies an input to other subsystems, which leads to a sequence of covert events. Based on PET results described in Chapters 5 and 6, we suspect that this subsystem is implemented primarily in the left dorsolateral frontal lobe.

Second, before being able to initiate a plan, one often must inhibit an ongoing plan. In this respect reasoning is similar to attention, which apparently involves a subsystem that disengages attention which is distinct from a subsystem that engages attention (see Chapter 3). The process of disengaging a plan is a qualitatively different function from those noted above, which leads us to hypothesize that there is an *interruption* subsystem that squelches a currently executing plan. The relation of these subsystems to those inferred in previous chapters is illustrated in Figure 9.1.

We will now consider how these subsystems confer four specific reasoning abilities. Following this, we will examine specific behaviors of the damaged system and offer accounts based on our inferences about the operation of the normal system.

Switching Behavior

Perhaps the most elementary form of reasoning involves using information from a previous situation to guide one to switch to a new behavior in a subsequent situation. The late Swiss developmental psychologist Jean Piaget developed the "A not B" task,[3] which has been used to study this ability in human infants and monkeys.[4] When the task is administered to infants, a toy is hidden in one of two identical bowls with lids while the

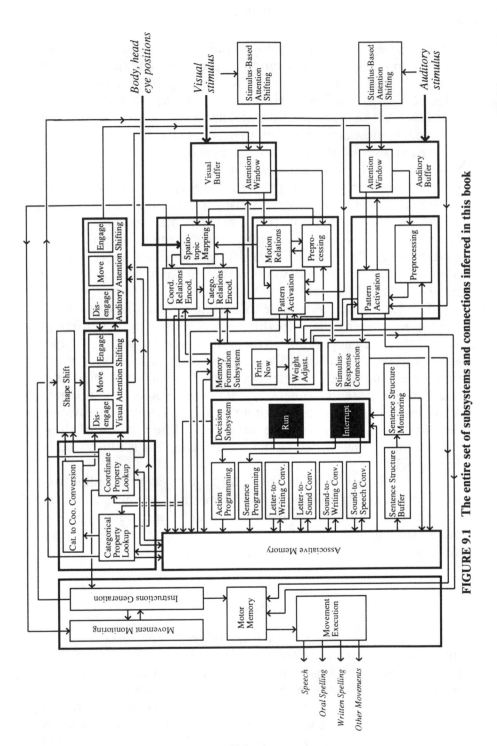

FIGURE 9.1 The entire set of subsystems and connections inferred in this book

406

infant is watching. The infant is briefly distracted so that he or she does not constantly stare at the location of the toy. After a delay (from 0 to 10 seconds), the infant is allowed to reach for the toy. Infants as young as 7½ months can be tested on this task, and even the youngest subjects can find the toy the first time the task is administered. However, when the toy is hidden at the other side on a subsequent test trial, these young infants persist in reaching back to the first location (hence the name "A not B"). A critical feature of this task is that the toy is hidden on the same side until it is found, and then it is hidden on the other side.

Researchers have also used a variant of this task, called the *delayed response task*. (This name is slightly misleading, given that the response also can be delayed in the A not B task.) This task is the same as the A not B task, except that the location of the toy is varied randomly from trial to trial. In addition, some researchers have used a variant called *the spatial reversal task,* which is similar to the A not B task (i.e., the hiding side is changed only after the object is found) except that the subjects cannot see where the object is hidden. Therefore, subjects must decide where the object is hidden solely on the basis of their memory of the previous trial. (When all three of these tasks are presented to monkeys, the toy is replaced by food.)

Human infants aged 7½ to 9 months perform the A not B task at the same level as infant monkeys aged 1½ to 4 months. In addition, adult monkeys with lesions in prefrontal cortex perform the delayed response task at a similar level. All three groups fail the task with a delay as brief as 1 to 2 seconds (i.e., they continue to make the initially successful response), although they can perform correctly when there is no delay.[5]

A not B errors appear to reflect the disruption of processes that rely on the frontal lobe; these errors do not arise following lesions to the parietal lobe or hippocampus.[6] Monkeys with lesions in the dorsolateral prefrontal cortex also are impaired in both the delayed response and the spatial reversal tasks. Adelle Diamond argues that processes in the frontal lobe play two critical roles in these tasks.[7] First, they play a key part in relating information over space and time. The tasks require the subject to watch where the object is hidden, to remember the location, and later to reach to the appropriate location. When memory is necessary, both the youngest human infants and monkeys with prefrontal lesions cannot perform the task; but when it is not, they can. Indeed, patients with frontal lobe damage often are reported to have difficulty keeping track of a temporal sequence or relating items in a sequence.[8] This idea dovetails nicely with one discussed in Chapter 3, that area 46—which plays a critical role in spatial short-term memory—might help processes that guide eye movements (which rely on the nearby area 8). However, it is not clear whether the frontal lobe actually stores information or merely has privileged access to information that is stored elsewhere.

Second, according to Diamond, processes in the frontal lobe inhibit action tendencies, which is consistent with our claim that an interruption subsystem is implemented in the frontal lobe. It seems clear that the tasks require the animal to inhibit dominant responses. For example, in the A not B task, the tendency to reach to the side where the reward has just been obtained must be inhibited. Some infants keep on reaching to the wrong side even though they were looking at the correct side—which we would expect if the frontal lobe were able to tap the correct memories, but the interruption subsystem were not yet fully functional.[9]

A neural network model. Stanislas Dehaene and Jean-Pierre Changeux designed a neural network model to simulate the performance of human infants and brain-damaged monkeys in the A not B task.[10] This network does not model a single cortical area, but rather mimics a very primitive organism composed of several subsystems that interact with the environment. In our terms, the network implements a system that can use very simple plans. The environment consists of objects that are represented in terms of features, such as location, shape, size, and color. Two objects can be presented as input on each trial. Reinforcement and punishment are provided to the "organism" while it is engaged in tasks with the following structure: (1) a single cue object is presented; (2) the object is removed, and a delay occurs; (3) two test objects are presented and a response is made; (4) depending on the response, reinforcement or punishment is provided; (5) an inter-trial interval occurs (and then a new cue object is presented). For the A not B task, the network was simply supposed to choose the location that was occupied by the cue object. The network was reinforced when it made a correct choice, and was punished when it made an incorrect choice.

As is illustrated in Figure 9.2, the network had two levels of organization. The first level consisted of the input and output layers, and the second level consisted of a memory layer and a rule-coding layer. In the input and output layers, each object dimension was coded by a specific cluster of units. In the output layer, the activity in a specific cluster (corresponding to a single value of a particular dimension, such as "red" for the color dimension) led the organism to choose one of the objects.

The memory layer consisted of units that were organized into clusters; the units within a cluster excited each other. In contrast, each cluster inhibited the other clusters. Finally, the rule-coding layer consisted of clusters of units that code for a

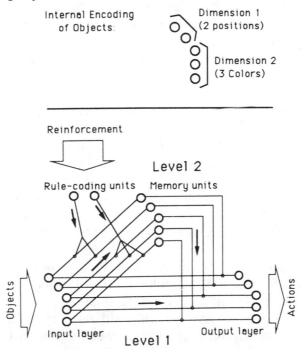

FIGURE 9.2 Architecture of the Dehaene and Changeux network. The top part (above the line) indicates the organization of the units at each level; in each set of five, the top two process position and the bottom three process color. *(Reprinted from* Journal of Cognitive Neuroscience *1:3, S. Dehaene and J.P. Changeux, A simple model of prefrontal cortex function: Delayed response tasks, by permission of The MIT Press, Cambridge, Massachusetts, and the authors. Copyright ©1989 by the Massachusetts Institute of Technology.)*

specific dimension of the input. The input layer was connected to the memory layer, and these connections were modulated by the activity of the rule-coding clusters. Moreover, the memory layer had connections that modulated the connections between the input and the output layers. In our terms, the rule-coding and memory layers embodied the run and interruption subsystems.

The organism had a general level of "satisfaction," which was altered whenever it was reinforced or punished. Depending on the level of satisfaction, different parts of the system were modified during learning. In particular, the strengths of connections in the rule-coding layer were changed when the satisfaction measure was highly negative. If this occurred, the activity of the rule-coding clusters was set to a random value.

Dehaene and Changeux first reported simulations performed with half of the model architecture, that is, with the input and output layers only. They found that their model produced the sort of A not B errors observed in human infants and frontally damaged adult monkeys. When the network was reinforced for choosing the object that appeared at the same location as the cue object, it eventually stopped behaving randomly and chose that object; the network could produce five successive correct responses in no more than eight trials. But when the cue was shifted to the other position, A not B errors appeared. That is, the model kept on selecting the object in the previous position. This fragment of the model appears to embody the stimulus-response connection subsystem discussed in Chapter 8; it has no decision-making subsystems, and so cannot regulate reflexive behavior.

When the memory layer and the rule-coding layer were included in addition to the input and the output layers, the model was able to perform the A not B task at least as well as 12-month-old infants and 4-month-old monkeys. The network was able to switch very quickly between tasks without going through a series of systematic A not B errors; hence, relearning was extremely fast. The added components allowed the model to interrupt its previous behavior and respond in a new way; this shift depended critically on the activity of the rule-coding layer.

Dehaene and Changeux also examined the effects of the delay between the cue and the opportunity to respond in the A not B task. They were able to simulate the improvement with age by altering the amount of "noise" within the clusters of memory units. It is possible that younger brains have more noise because the nerve fibers have not been fully myelinated (i.e., covered with a fatty sheath that serves as an insulator), which makes them more variable and less reliable.[11] When noise was added to the network, the performance depended on the delay between the cue and the response; when a large amount of noise was added, although the performance was nearly 100% correct with a short delay, it dropped to about 50% with a long delay.

Dehaene and Changeux suggest that there may be a direct relationship between the rule-coding units in their model and a similar set of neurons in the frontal lobe that code for hypotheses about the rules governing the stimuli. However, we wonder whether it is necessary that hypothesized rules be stored in the frontal lobes. A representation of such a rule has two components: a representation of an input/output regularity, and a representation of the conditions in which this regularity should apply. Let us consider each component separately.

First, it does not seem that the frontal lobe needs to be involved in storing input/output relations. Indeed, this seems to be just another instance of associative memory at work. For example, if one notices that cooking scrambled eggs at a low temperature results in creamier eggs, this reglarity can be stored using a "causes" association—which is stored like the "has" and "is a" relations discussed in Chapter 8. The motion relations subsystem registers changes over time, and might also be used to note temporal relations among inputs; alternatively, temporal relations might be registered by a separate subsystem, which in some ways would be analogous to the spatial relations encoding subsystems.[12]

Second, the rules of application also do not require representations in the frontal lobes. Again, associative memory can store the conditions in which specific input/output relations apply. This information in turn can be used by the run subsystem to initiate an appropriate action sequence. The fact that damage to the frontal lobe disrupts this task does not imply that the representations used are necessarily stored in the frontal lobe, only that one or more subsystems used to perform the task depend on this tissue's being intact. We conjecture that both the run and interruption subsystems rely on cortex in the frontal lobe.

Anticipating Sequences

The A not B task is a special case of a much more general situation, namely anticipating the appropriate next step in a sequence of steps. This task becomes much more challenging when one expects a particular sequence but the environment changes so that one's expectation is foiled.

The Wisconsin Card Sorting Task, briefly discussed in Chapter 3, appears to be a good measure of some types of processing carried out by the frontal lobe.[13] More specifically, it appears to be a good measure of the ability to form categories based on regularities in temporal sequences. The task employs a series of cards that can be sorted according to three dimensions: the number of elements on each card, their color, or their shape. The examiner selects one dimension and decides that one value of the dimension will go in one pile, and the other value will go in another pile, but the subject is not told which dimension has been selected. Rather, the examiner asks the subject to sort the cards, and tells him or her whether each choice is correct. For example, the examiner might decide that all red cards go in one pile and all green ones in another. The subject might initially sort based on how many symbols are on the card, but after hearing "no" each time a color is placed in the incorrect pile, should figure out the proper criterion for sorting.

After the subject learns to sort the cards correctly (and usually has sorted ten consecutive cards correctly), the examiner then surreptitiously changes the relevant dimension. After the switch, some subjects with frontal brain damage have tremendous difficulty shifting to the new dimension, even though the examiner repeatedly informs them that their sorting is incorrect. These patients tend to *perseverate* by persisting with the old dimension.[14]

In the Wisconsin Card Sorting Task, the initial input/output association is strengthened by reinforcement from the examiner. When the criterion is switched, the interruption subsystem must inhibit this response and allow a new association to be established. A mechanism that establishes associations seems to occur very early in phylogeny and ontogeny (that is, very early in both the evolution of the brain and the development of the individual organism);[15] indeed, we saw in Chapter 8 that such a mechanism exists at the level of the synapse itself. In contrast, the interruption mechanism may be a more recent development—both phylogenetically and ontogenetically. The frontal lobe clearly is a relatively recent evolutionary development,[16] and the interruption subsystem may not be possible without this cortex. The rule-coding layer in Dehaene and Changeux's model apparently plays a special role in this process. In fact, Dehaene and Changeux showed that another network model, similar to the one described above, can simulate subjects' performance in the Wisconsin Card Sorting Task.[17]

Selecting Among Competing Responses

In the laboratory, subjects are often shown a single stimulus at a time. But in the real world we typically are confronted by a rich array of stimuli, and different aspects of the input are likely to evoke different action sequences. In such situations, the system must select one response and inhibit the others. This process is central to performance of the famous Stroop Color Word Task.[18] This task requires one to name the color of the ink in which the name of a color is printed. In the interference condition, one color is used for the ink and another is named by the word (e.g., the word "blue" is printed in red and the task requires responding "red"). Subjects take more time and make more errors in this interference condition than they do when the word labels the color of the ink or when they name the color of the ink of colored blobs.

One account for this effect is that subjects read a word faster than they can name a color, and so the wrong response comes to mind first.[19] A control mechanism is therefore needed to avoid saying the color word. The role of the interruption subsystem is critical in this task, because an initial response must be inhibited. Patients with damaged frontal lobes have been found to be much slower, and make more errors, than normal control subjects on this task,[20] which again is consistent with the claim that the decision subsystems are implemented in the frontal cortex.

Koenig measured the time course of the color-word interference from 7-year-old children to adults.[21] He found that although the speed of reading increased more than the speed of naming colors from 7 to 10 years of age—which should result in greater interference—children actually exhibited less interference with age. Thus, some other process—such as the interruption subsystem—must have developed with age, and allowed older children to inhibit the incorrect response more effectively. This result is consistent with the finding that frontal lobes of school-aged children are not fully mature; neurons in the frontal lobes are among the last to be fully myelinated.[22] A network model of this task has been developed and is consistent with these ideas.[23]

Arithmetic

We have noted that not all reasoning culminates in overt behavior. In some cases, we activate a plan that leads us to perform not a series of overt movements, but rather a series of mental operations. A good example of such reasoning is arithmetic.

Even simple arithmetic requires a series of processing steps. For example, consider the processing that allows one to determine the sum of 22 + 23. First, the perceptual subsystems must encode the digits and operator. Second, the plan that corresponds to that arithmetic operation must be looked up. Third, the operations specified by the plan must be applied to those quantities. And fourth, the result must be produced.[24]

The third step can be complex, depending on the operation and the values of the digits. As noted earlier, a stored plan may specify subplans for specific parts of a process, and each subplan must be activated and used at the correct time. For example, to multiply 14 × 36, many people calculate 10 × 36, remember the result 360, then calculate 4 × 36, which itself is decomposed into (4 × 30) + (4 × 6), and then add this result (144) to 360 for a final result of 504. This process thus requires decomposing the whole operation into a set of more elementary operations, each of which then is performed by looking up a result stored in memory (i.e., in a multiplication table one memorized in elementary school) or using a simple "rule." Such rules could be implemented in an associative network or networks; for example, if a network received "10 × X" as input, it could simply append a zero to the second number in the output.

This procedure is performed in working memory (see Chapter 8). Recall that working memory corresponds to activated information in long-term memory, information in short-term memory, plus decision processes. The decision processes "swap" information from long-term memory in and out of short-term memory, including information about subproducts and the next step to perform in the plan.

The decision subsystems play a critical role in carrying out multistep computations. However, the results of simple and commonly performed complex calculations are stored in associative memory in a lookup table. Hence, these computations can be performed with only minimal involvement of the decision subsystems. Indeed, in most cases these subsystems serve merely to allow the stimuli to evoke the proper response.

Thus, it is not surprising that some adults with frontal lesions experience great difficulty solving a problem such as "if the price of 2 bowls is $30, how much do you have to pay for 5 bowls?" even though these patients have no difficulty solving problems such as "what is 30 divided by 2?" and "what is 15 times 5?"[25] The elementary computations can be performed, but the patient has trouble realizing which plan to activate or orchestrating the individual operations in sequence.

On the other hand, there are many ways to perform even very simple calculations, some of which will rely on the decision subsystems. Robert Siegler showed that at least four different strategies may be used by children 4 to 7 years old to solve simple addition problems, such as adding 5 + 3. Specifically, the child might respond based on (a) recalling the answer from memory; (b) guessing; (c) focusing on the maximum value of the pair (in this case 5) and counting up the number of the minimum value of the pair (3); and (d) beginning at zero, counting up to the number of one digit and continuing to count, adding an additional number until the sum is reached. The strategy may differ from individual to individual, and even from time to time for the same individual. Moreover, it has been shown that such strategies can be influenced by factors such as the notational system. For example, the quantity "three" can be represented in alphabetic (three), Arabic (3), Roman (III), and analogic (***) codes.[26]

The role of "mental models." We often may reason by constructing "mental models."[27] A mental model is a concrete example of a situation that is constructed in working memory. One mentally manipulates the model in some way, "observes" how it behaves, and then applies the results to the case at hand. As discussed in Chapter 4, visual imagery may be used to construct such mental models and to manipulate them in various ways. We saw in Chapter 4 that one also can use imagery to aid reasoning in tasks that apparently have nothing to do with visual or spatial information. In principle, a stored plan may specify sequences of various types of operations, and instructions to generate, manipulate, and inspect images are examples of sequences of such operations.

For example, visual imagery can be used in arithmetic in two ways. First, one may visualize quantities not by using digits, but by using a "model" that conveys the amounts. For instance, some people visualize digits as clusters of dots, and then simply count them up when adding.[28] Second, one may visualize digits as an aid to performing mental calculations. For instance, try to divide 3842 by 29. It is unlikely that you have the response previously stored in associative memory. If you visualize the operant and digits as they would appear if you used a scratch sheet, imagery may help you to retain the intermediate steps that are required to perform this calculation.

It seems likely that other sorts of mental models also can be used to perform arithmetic. For example, consider the case of patient N.A.U., who could judge approximate results even though he could not perform exact calculations.[29] For instance, N.A.U. judged $2 + 2 = 5$ as correct, but judged $2 + 2 = 9$ as incorrect. This observation led the investigators to suggest that arithmetic may be carried out using two distinct methods: one that uses exact number and calculation representations stored in memory, and another that uses a less precise but concrete model of quantities to perform approximate computations.

These findings may indicate that quantities can be represented by a mental scale (such as a number line), with greater distance along the scale indicating greater amount. This idea is consistent with the finding that normal subjects can determine that 99 is larger than 12 faster than that 15 is larger than 12.[30] In general, the larger the difference between the numbers, the faster the response times (up to a point; when the differences become sufficiently large, people evaluate the numbers very quickly and larger disparties do not decrease times appreciably). These results are very similar to what is found when line lengths or other perceptual qualities are judged, which suggests that increased quantities can be represented internally by an increased amount of activity in a network or a shift in the point of maximal activation within a network that is organized to represent a continuum.

This sort of scale-based representation lends itself to a process that obtains an approximate answer to a problem. In this case, one need only note differences in the amount of activity or position along the scale. For example, when we mentally divide 1534 by 118, we can determine that the result is a two-digit number between 10 and 20 without knowing the exact answer. It is possible that animals can use this system, which would be all that is necessary for their purposes, and that the methods used to obtain precise answers are by-products of the development of language.

Calculation deficits. Because calculation relies on cognitive operations that involve many subsystems, it is not surprising that lesions to several parts of the brain can result in calculation deficits.[31] Some researchers have found it useful to distinguish between three types of impairments in mental arithmetic following brain damage: (1) deficits in reading or writing numbers, which are referred to as *alexic* and *agraphic acalculia,* respectively; (2) a deficit in the spatial organization of the written numbers used in calculation, which is referred to as *spatial acalculia;* and, (3) a deficit in the process of calculation itself, which is referred to as *anarithmetria.*[32] The first two types of deficits can be explained by impairments in the visual system like those that produce alexia (see Chapter 5), or impairments in the output subsystems or associative memory, like those that produce agraphia (see Chapter 7). We have discussed such deficits in the earlier chapters, and will not review them again here. The abilities to encode and produce numbers clearly dissociate from the ability to perform calculations,[33] and so we shall focus on deficits that affect the calculation processes per se.

Group studies as well as single case studies typically report that deficits in calculation per se arise following damage to the posterior region of the left hemisphere.[34] There are many possible accounts for this finding. For example, the damage may disrupt part of associative memory that plays a special role in representing quantities. The damaged region is relatively near Wernicke's area, which may play a role as a repository of linguistically relevant information. Alternatively, the damage may send spurious input to the frontal lobes, thereby selectively disrupting one mode of operation of the action programming subsystem (which is recruited by a plan to process each number in sequence). Or, the damage may disrupt categorical spatial relations representations, which may often be used to specify the relative location of numbers along a spatial continuum (and possibly temporal relations, such as "before/after"). As usual, many accounts are possible.

In addition, our earlier discussion would suggest that patients with frontal lesions may also have calculation deficits. However, these deficits are only apparent when the task requires difficult, multicomponent calculations—presumably for the same reason that frontal patients are impaired in the A not B task, in the Wisconsin Card Sorting Task, and in the Stroop Color Word Task. All these tasks require the intact functioning of the decision subsystems.

In summary, much of our decision making may occur when stimuli activate a plan that is stored in associative memory. We assume that some stimuli and responses are more "salient" than others (in part because of associated emotions, as we will note below), and the salience of specific aspects of the stimuli and the response interacts with the degree to which a plan is activated by the input. The run subsystem presumably selects the plan that is evoked by the most salient aspects of the situation and that has the most salient response, and allows that plan to be executed. However, that plan will be acted upon immediately only if the present, ongoing plan is associated with less salient stimuli and responses; if so, then the interruption subsystem inhibits the ongoing plan.

Although this conception of reasoning may help to illuminate the process by which one figures out how to convert money to a foreign currency, fix a broken bicycle, or cook a meal, it seems woefully inadequate as an account of novel reasoning, such as that engaged in creative problem solving in uncharted waters. It also falls short as an account of long-range planning abilities. We will not dare to speculate about how one plans one's career, ponders whether to marry George rather than Sam, or makes other decisions that do not require responses relatively quickly. The pioneering split-brain researcher Michael Gazzaniga offers some intriguing ideas about an "interpreter" process in the left cerebral hemisphere that could be the key to this puzzle.[35] However, for now we will simply acknowledge that these are truly Gray Matters.

Cerebral Lateralization

In previous chapters we noted many examples of differences in the abilities of the cerebral hemispheres. For example, for right-handed people the left hemisphere typically is better than the right at encoding categorical spatial relations and written words; at forming visual mental images using categorical spatial relations to arrange parts; distinguishing phonemes; comprehending and producing most aspects of language; and sequencing a series of movements and fine-tuning a reaching movement. In contrast, the right hemisphere is better than the left at encoding coordinate spatial relations representations; forming visual mental images using coordinate spatial relations to arrange parts; storing form-specific representations of words; comprehending and producing metaphor; and initiating a reaching movement. The left hemisphere is often called the "dominant" hemisphere (for right-handed people) because it typically controls most aspects of language, controls the dominant (contralateral) hand, and contains more gray matter than the right hemisphere.[36]

Although research on the specialization of the cerebral hemispheres has progressed for over 100 years, the reasons why the cerebral hemispheres are specialized are still unclear.[37] At least part of the problem is that the differences between the hemispheres often are difficult to document with certainty; experiments sometimes do not even produce the same results when repeated.[38] Indeed, such variability is so pervasive that it seems unlikely that it merely reflects poor methodologies or sloppy experimentation;[39] at least some of the difficulty probably reflects individual differences among the subjects.[40] Such differences must be understood in their own right.

Another reason why progress has been slow in coming is that many researchers have thought in terms of simple dichotomies: The left hemisphere is "analytic," the right "synthetic"; the left "logical," the right "intuitive"; the left "serial," the right "parallel"; the left "linguistic," the right "perceptual," and so on.[41]

These terms are difficult to characterize clearly, and even more difficult to apply to specific research findings.[42] And, perhaps more important, it is unlikely that hemispheres differ at the level of Functions, given that Functions are not carried out by single processes. Even some aspects of language—which is probably the most strongly lateralized Function—are dealt with by the non-dominant hemisphere (see Chapter 6).

The approach we have taken in this book rejects sweeping generalizations about the functions of the cerebral hemispheres in favor of a more fine-grained approach; we focus on the relative efficacy of the various subsystems in the two hemispheres. We do not expect the two hemispheres to be specialized in absolute terms, but rather expect the differences to be ones of degree—not the presence or absence of particular subsystems. We assume that each subsystem is duplicated in the two hemispheres, but each version is not equally effective. If the relative efficacy of the individual subsystems in the hemispheres varies widely, then we expect wide variation in the characteristics of small samples of people.[43] And in fact, because most studies of cerebral lateralization involve relatively few subjects, the variability in the reported findings may not be surprising.

In this section we outline a theory of how cerebral lateralization arises, and this theory also accounts for individual differences in cerebral lateralization. To make the discussion more concrete, we explore such differences in the lateralization of visual processing. We take some relatively simple and uncontroversial ideas and show how they lead to a wide range of individual differences in lateralization. A computer simulation model was used to test some of these ideas, which we will briefly describe.[44]

The theory rests in part on the assumption that experience plays a role in how functions become lateralized in the brain. Perhaps the most striking support for this assumption is the plasticity evident following *hemidecortication* in infancy. Although the majority of subsystems that subserve language typically are more effective in the left hemisphere,[45] the right hemisphere can assume most of these functions if necessary. This point is dramatically illustrated when the cortex of the left hemisphere becomes so diseased during infancy that it must be removed, and yet these children learn to speak and comprehend almost normally. These right-hemisphere-based subsystems do not process language quite as well as would the coordinated subsystems of both hemispheres in a normal individual, but the resulting linguistic deficits are remarkably subtle and are readily apparent only during laboratory testing.[46] This phenomenon supports the assumption that there is considerable leeway in how functions become implemented in the cerebral hemispheres.

The theory is a theory of development, and is intended to describe events that take place approximately during the first two years of life (when the hemispheric bases of language functions are particularly malleable).[47] Some researchers have argued that lateralization is entirely innate and does not develop over time.[48] However, although it is absolutely clear that some aspects of laterality are innate (as will discussed shortly), there is no good evidence that *all* aspects of laterality are fully developed at birth; researchers who have assumed that laterality is fixed at birth typically have looked only at language, and then only at relatively coarse linguistic abilities—which may have led them astray.

Three Principles

The theory is a further refinement of one first proposed by Kosslyn in 1987.[49] It rests on three principles: adaptive subsystems, interhemispheric processing degradation, and "central" bilateral control.

Adaptive subsystems. Each subsystem "adapts" to perform frequently encountered tasks more effectively. This kind of adaptation underlies simple "practice effects"; with practice, subsystems more quickly and reliably produce information that is useful downstream in the flow of information processing. If each subsystem is implemented as a neural net (which must be true at some level of analysis), then practice works by adjusting the strengths of specific connections in the net (as discussed in Chapter 2). In the previous chapter, we argued that although the memory formation subsystems set the stage for learning, they do not "micromanage" the process of adjusting the weights in a network; we have not dealt with the problem of how the to-be-adjusted connections are selected so that the subsystem produces the output more effectively in the future.

One possible solution to this puzzle is suggested by the neuroanatomy of the visual system. As noted in Chapter 3, in the vast majority of cases examined so far, every visual area that sends information directly to another area also receives information directly from that area.[50] It is of particular interest that the two kinds of pathways typically are of comparable size, which implies a rich exchange of information in both directions. We discussed how the efferent (backwards running) pathways could provide "attentional" priming, which in the extreme produces visual mental images (see Chapter 4).

It is also possible that this feedback can be used to "train" the subsystem that produced useful output. That is, when a subsystem produces output that is useful for other subsystems downstream in the flow of information processing, those "receiving" subsystems provide feedback that allows the "sending" subsystem to learn to produce that output better in the future. Indeed, we inferred such a process when we considered how the preprocessing subsystem can become tuned to encode useful perceptual units, such as occurs when one becomes an expert at determining the sex of baby chicks.[51]

Interhemispheric processing degradation. The "training" feedback is more effective when it does not need to cross over to the other cerebral hemisphere. This inference is grounded in the fact that shape-sensitive cells in the inferior temporal lobe of one hemisphere of a monkey respond more vigorously when a stimulus is presented in the contralateral visual field (and so the input is sent directly to that hemisphere) than when it is presented in the ipsilateral field (and so information must cross over from the other side of the brain).[52] This asymmetry could reflect at least three factors. First, there are fewer projections to these cells across the commissures that connect the two hemispheres than there are within a hemisphere.[53] Moreover, this situation is exacerbated early in life. Indeed, the corpus callosum may not be fully mature until age 12 or so; at 6 years of age, only about two-thirds of the callosal fibers are myelinated.[54] Consistent with this observation, there is evidence that children improve with age in the ability to transfer information from one side of the body to the other.[55] All this fits well with the claim that feedback is less effective when it crosses to the other hemisphere.

Second, each hemisphere may inhibit high-level processing in the other hemisphere. Indeed, at higher levels of processing, attention seems to have its effects at least in part by inhibiting competing processing. For example, as discussed in Chapter 3, the responses of cells in areas V4 and IT in the monkey brain are inhibited when stimuli fall in parts of the cell's receptive field to which the animal's attention is not being directed.[56] Similarly, attention to a stimulus in one visual hemifield inhibits the ability to detect a stimulus in the other hemifield.[57] This mechanism makes sense from an information-processing point of view in that the two hemifields provide different inputs (typically the different halves of an object or scene), and competition between the hemispheres must be mediated somehow.

Third, there is evidence for a single "pool of capacity" that is drawn on by both hemispheres. If a stimulus first enters the other hemisphere, it may lead it to tie up capacity, leaving less available for the opposite hemisphere. This "capacity" may correspond to "activation" from deep brain structures, such as the reticular activating system. In this case, the more one hemisphere draws (e.g., by initially receiving a stimulus), the less capacity is available for processing in the other. For example, when more items had to be stored in short-term memory in one hemisphere of a split-brain patient, less could be stored in the other—even though there was no transfer of information between the two hemispheres.[58] (Recall that we discussed split-brain patients, who have had their hemispheres surgically disconnected for medical reasons, in Chapter 4.) This result makes sense if more "activation" is required to maintain more information, and once it is used in one hemisphere, less is available for the other.

For our purposes, the important idea is that when an output is produced by a subsystem in one hemisphere, the subsystems that receive that information are less effective in the other hemisphere. This effect should occur not only with input that is moving downstream, but also with information that provides feedback upstream. If so, then feedback will not be as effective when it crosses to the other hemisphere, and hence those subsystems will not be "trained" as effectively as are the corresponding ones on the same side as the subsystems providing feedback.

"Central" bilateral control.   So far we have discussed how subsystems come to produce specific outputs more effectively with practice, and why "training" feedback will be stronger to subsystems that are in the same hemisphere as the one providing the training. To draw inferences about how hemispheric specialization develops, we now must consider the circumstances in which feedback should originate on one side. Kosslyn originally argued that certain classes of activities are much more effective if directed from a single locus of control.[59] These activities involve coordinating rapid sequences of precise, ordered operations that extend over both halves of the body. One possible mechanism would simply duplicate the commands in each hemisphere, executing each copy simultaneously. However, it would be difficult to keep the corresponding subsystems coordinated across the two hemispheres. A more efficient mechanism would use a single subsystem in such circumstances, which would control the components of the movement execution subsystem that actually perform the movements on each side of the body. Kosslyn hypothesized that such "central" bilateral control subsystems are innately lateralized, which results in a single locus of control over both sides. These control subsystems are specialized components of the instructions generation subsystem.[60]

Kosslyn hypothesized that speech entails precise, ordered operations coordinated over both halves of the body, and hence it would be useful to have a unilateral speech output control process. In our terms, he assumed that the instructions generation subsystem in the left hemisphere would play a special role in producing speech. The claim that the left hemisphere plays such a role is supported by much evidence, both from studies of focal lesion patients and from studies of the suppression of activity during direct electrical stimulation of cortex. The results from these studies indicate that speech output is typically controlled by only one side of the brain.[61] Furthermore, there is evidence that such unilateral control is present very early in life.[62]

Similarly, Kosslyn assumed that one component of the right-hemisphere instructions generation subsystem plays a special role in directing the eyes to focus on different locations in space. In this case, one wants to examine new objects or regions before returning to previously considered ones, and such an exhaustive search strategy would be easier to perform if a single control process governed search over both halves of the field.[63]

The Snowball Effect

The ideas discussed above can account for the development of cerebral lateralization via a "snowball effect." Consider a simple example. Assume that a baby makes an utterance to express a thought (for example, she wants a rattle). Even a single-word voluntary utterance must be formed by sending instructions to the speech output control process. Such instructions must be paired with the relevant information (the "concept") in associative memory. If so, then the categorical property lookup subsystem would operate on both sides to access the appropriate representation, and would activate the target coordinates of the sound that is paired with this representation—and these coordinates would be passed to the instructions generation subsystem (we assume that people generally are of one mind in their to-be-expressed thoughts). If the component of the instructions generation subsystem used for language is innately lateralized to the left side, then the output from the categorical property lookup subsystem on the left side need not cross the corpus callosum. But more important, when the left-side instructions generation subsystem is used, it sends more effective feedback to the categorical property lookup subsystem on the left side (for any of the three reasons cited above). Hence, over the course of many such training occasions, the categorical property lookup subsystem on the left side will become more effective than the corresponding subsystem on the right side.

This asymmetry in training initiates a snowball effect: Once the left-side categorical property lookup subsystem becomes more effective than its right-side counterpart, it then will come to play the role played by the innately lateralized subsystem that got the ball rolling initially. The stronger subsystem will provide more effective feedback to subsystems in the left hemisphere that give it input. And then the effect will further compound, affecting subsystems that in turn feed these subsystems, and so on, percolating through the system.

In short, according to this theory, cerebral lateralization develops because: (a) "central" control processes are innately dominant in a single hemisphere; (b) feedback from the control subsystem is less effective in training the "sending" subsystem on the other side; and (c) the subsystems that thereby come to be stronger in one hemisphere then play the same role as the control subsystems, providing more effective feedback to subsystems on the same side that give them input. This effect is compounded, snowballing through the system.

A computer simulation model was implemented that became lateralized via the snowball effect, and it produced a wide range of patterns of lateralization, depending on a number of factors.[64] For example, lateralization varied depending on the strength of the innate lateralization of the speech output control portion of the instructions generation subsystem, the amount of cross-hemisphere inhibition, and the relative frequency of different types of tasks. This model was relatively complex, and each subsystem was not implemented as an actual network; rather, the behavior of networks was mimicked by "black boxes" that produced appropriate input/output behavior.

The simulation model performed two tasks, which recruited different combinations of the processing subsystems discussed earlier. The first task required the model to answer the question, "What is it?" The response was made via the speech-output control process. In the simulations, the input was a picture of a sparrow, and the output was, "It's a bird." Under the stimulus conditions Kosslyn and his colleagues simulated, they assumed that one high-resolution encoding of a part and its location is needed for confident recognition, in addition to the overall shape. Because animals are not rigid, encodings of categorical relations among the parts would be most useful (because they remain constant when the object moves; see Chapter 3).

The second task required examining faces at a very close distance, and not producing a verbal response; rather, it indicated whether it "knew" the individual whose face was presented by "pressing" a "yes" or "no" simulated button. Kosslyn and his colleagues assumed that the search control processes would be critical in this task, as would representations of coordinate spatial relations among the eyes, nose, and so on (which are specific for given faces).

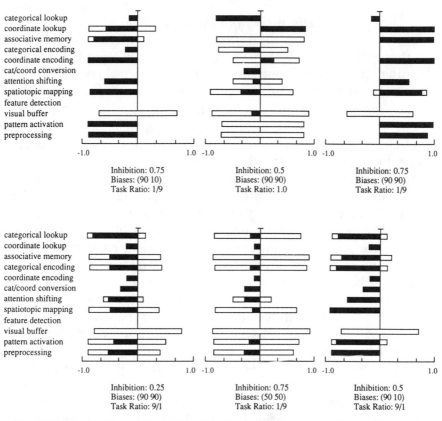

FIGURE 9.3 **Patterns of relative effectiveness in the cerebral hemispheres that developed in Kosslyn, Sokolov, and Chen's (1989) computer simulation. White bars to the left indicate strength in the left hemisphere, and white bars to the right indicate strength in the right hemisphere. The black bars indicate the difference in relative strength, which is a measure of the degree of hemispheric specializaton for the subsystem. (The "feature detection" subsystem was supplanted following more detailed analyses of the computations performed by the preprocessing subsystem.)** *(From Kosslyn, Sokolov & Chen, 1989, with permission.)*

Figure 9.3 illustrates some of the ways in which the different subsystems were affected by the various starting states of the model. The white bars indicate the strength of each subsystem on the left and right sides, respectively, and the black bars indicate the degree of asymmetry (lateralization) of these strengths. "Strength" indicates how quickly and accurately the subsystem could produce the appropriate output when given an input. The most obvious result illustrated in Figure 9.3 is that very different patterns of lateralization arise depending on the starting values.

Disproving the Initial Theory

A theory is good insofar as it makes strong predictions. A "strong" prediction is one that is difficult to wiggle out of. Thus, it is perhaps sad that this version of the theory was shot down rather quickly. J.W. is a split-brain patient who cannot read aloud words that are presented to his right hemisphere—even though he can point to named objects and produce other behaviors that show that his right hemisphere can comprehend words.[65] A clear prediction from the computer simulations of the snowball theory is that categorical spatial relations should be encoded more effectively in his left hemisphere. The left hemisphere clearly has a more effective "central" bilateral control process for speech output, and the categorical property lookup subsystem should be recruited to access instructions for this control subsystem, and hence should become more effective in the left hemisphere. And, as shown in the computer simulations, this subsystem ultimately should strengthen the categorical spatial relations encoding subsystem (which provides it with useful information).

This prediction has been disproved. In fact, J.W. can determine whether a dot is above or below a bar—a categorical spatial relation—more quickly and accurately in his right hemisphere (which cannot generate speech) than in his left. Furthermore, he can determine whether a dot is within 3 millimeters of a bar—a coordinate relation—more quickly and accurately in his left hemisphere than in his right hemisphere.[66]

Thus, the idea that a unilateral speech output control process drives left-hemisphere lateralization is probably incorrect. There is another way to conceive of the snowball process, however: Perhaps one or more of the perceptual encoding subsystems is innately lateralized. This idea makes sense because the cerebral hemispheres are somewhat lateralized even in animals that have no language abilities. As we discussed in Chapter 6, Heffner and Heffner showed that the left superior temporal lobe of Japanese macaques plays a special role in the perception of vocalizations.[67] A host of findings reveal other ways in which the cerebral hemispheres of monkeys are specialized. For example, the monkey left hemisphere is better able to discriminate which way a field of dots moves, the orientation of lines, and the location of a dot within a frame; on the other hand, the right hemisphere of monkeys appears to be better at discriminating facial expressions and determining identity.[68]

Considering findings such as these, Kosslyn, Chabris, Marsolek, and Koenig hypothesized a different process that would start the snowball rolling and would operate as effectively in animals as in humans.[69] Such a process follows from three observations. First, several researchers have proposed theories of lateralization that hinge on the fact that the right hemisphere is more mature at birth.[70] Second, infants rely primarily on stimulus properties to guide attention because they do not have information stored in memory to guide search. Typically, movement or a change seen "out of the corner of one's eye" draws attention. Acuity decreases towards the periphery in part because the cells that monitor these regions have large receptive fields. Hence, early in life the more mature right hemisphere processes information from large receptive fields to guide attention. Third, as the brain matures, other sorts of attention become possible; one becomes able to focus on a small area with high acuity. These processes require high-resolution input, which presumably arises from neurons with small receptive fields. The right hemisphere has already been configured to be used (i.e., "initialized") for bottom-up attentional processing, which relies on neurons with large receptive fields. Considerable neural reconfiguration would be required for it to perform this additional, competing function. And so, when the left hemisphere matures, it is a "clean slate" that is better able to carry out high-resolution, focal attention processing than the right hemisphere.[71] Thus, the right hemisphere develops with a bias to process input from neurons with relatively large receptive fields, whereas the left hemisphere develops with a bias to process input from neurons with relatively small receptive fields.

Kosslyn and his collaborators used network models to show that hemispheric specialization for categorical and coordinate spatial relations encoding can develop if the hemispheres monitor different-sized regions of space. One network encoded the distance of a dot from a bar, and performed better when its input was filtered through relatively large overlapping receptive fields than smaller, less overlapping, receptive fields. The large overlapping fields use "coarse coding" effectively to converge on the precise location of the dot (see Chapter 2). On the other hand, another network judged whether the dot was above or below the bar, and performed better when its input was filtered through smaller, less overlapping receptive fields. These fields were more effective for dividing space into discrete bins that correspond to spatial relations categories such as above/below or left/right.[72]

Once the categorical spatial-relations-encoding subsystem is stronger in the left hemisphere and the coordinate spatial-relations-encoding subsystem is stronger in the right, the snowball process can proceed as described above. Subsystems that send useful information to either will receive training feedback, which will be more effective if it does not have to cross to the other hemisphere.[73] The same kinds of variables that affected the computer simulation will also affect processing in this version of the model.

The claim that the left hemisphere typically monitors smaller local regions than the right hemisphere is consistent with a range of empirical findings. For example, patients with left-hemisphere lesions have trouble encoding parts of objects, whereas patients with right-hemisphere lesions have trouble encoding the global form of objects.[74] In addition, normal subjects categorize parts of objects faster when the objects are shown initially to the left hemisphere, whereas they categorize the overall shapes of objects faster when they are presented initially to the right hemisphere.[75]

The notion that the hemispheres differ in the sizes of the regions of space they monitor implies not only that they will be specialized differently for spatial relations encoding, but also that they may store different sorts of information about shape. Specifically, the left hemisphere may store smaller portions of shapes, but with higher resolution, than the right hemisphere. This idea is consistent with findings that were described in Chapter 7, namely that patients with left-hemisphere damage initiate a reaching movement normally, but have trouble controlling it (particularly in the deceleration phase); in contrast, patients with right-hemisphere damage have trouble initiating a reaching movement, but can control it normally.[76] As we discussed in Chapter 7, the first phase of reaching relies on computing and executing the initial trajectory, and does not rely on feedback, whereas the second relies on feedback to fine-tune the movement. The right hemisphere may be critical in the first phase because it processes the outputs from neurons with large receptive fields more effectively, which is useful for computing the location of the overall shape. In contrast, the left hemisphere may be critical in the second phase because it processes the outputs from neurons with small receptive fields more effectively, which is useful for encoding portions of objects; we typically reach for a portion of an object, such as the handle of a cup or the bottom segment of a pen.

Thus, the snowball theory is capable of explaining individual differences in lateralization, but the details of its operation will depend critically on what process or processes are innately lateralized. It remains to be seen, however, whether any version of this theory is on the right track.

Consciousness

As far as anyone knows, only brain activity is accompanied by states of consciousness. There has been much woolly speculation about consciousness over the years, and we have no desire to contribute to this morass. Rather, we want to establish criteria for an adequate theory of consciousness, and will sketch out a theory to illustrate some of the implications of the criteria.[77]

One reason why discussions of consciousness often degenerate is that theorists disagree about what is being discussed. It is impossible to fix the referent of the term—one cannot point to consciousness the way one can point to a book or even a brain, so there is no way to resolve disagreements. And in fact, many theories of consciousness simply try to explain it away.[78] However, people can be conscious of making a decision, being in love, seeing red, having a pain in the lower back, and so forth. And they clearly can distinguish being conscious of these events from not being conscious of them. The fact of consciousness should not be in doubt; there is something to be explained, not merely explained away. We will address here the everyday sense of the term; it refers to the phenomenology of experience, the feeling of red, and so forth.

Another reason why discussions about the nature of consciousness often bog down is that it is easy to conflate the information-processing or neural correlates of consciousness with the phenomenological texture of experience itself. We will focus on the nature of the private "feel" of experience, trying to show that its existence is not incompatible with the approach adopted earlier in this book.

Perhaps the most difficult problem in discussing consciousness is that we do not have a good vocabulary for theorizing about the phenomenon. As we have demonstrated in previous chapters, the vocabulary of computation has proven useful for understanding mental activity. But there is no corresponding vocabulary for understanding the texture of experience. Thus, we will not try to characterize the various facets of the phenomenon in detail, but rather will focus on how consciousness differs from brain states, how it arises, and how it functions in mental life.

Requirements for a Theory

Before beginning to consider what consciousness is, it will be useful to outline some key requirements for any adequate theory of consciousness.

Nonreducability. Consciousness is not the same thing as neural activity;[79] phenomenological experience cannot be described in terms of ion flows, synaptic connections, and so forth. Consciousness and brain events are members of different categories,[80] and one cannot be replaced by the other. Consciousness is like light that is produced by a hot filament in a vacuum: The physical events that produce the light cannot be equated with the light itself. Any theory of consciousness must describe a phenomenon that cannot be replaced by a description of brain events.

Unique role of consciousness. A theory can posit that consciousness is not functional, but rather is purely epiphenomenal—like the heat thrown off by a lightbulb while one reads, which plays no role in the reading process itself. Alternatively, a theory can posit that consciousness has a function. A theory based on the second supposition is a greater challenge to formulate, and we will assume it is our goal. If the theory posits that consciousness has a function, then it must posit a function that cannot be accomplished by brain events per se. For example, a theory should not posit that consciousness selects important information; one can imagine a computer model that has such a function, without relying on consciousness at all. There are at least two reasons for this requirement. First, if consciousness belongs in a different category from brain events, the two kinds of events should not be interchangeable—consciousness *is* a different kind of thing, and so presumably *does* a different kind of thing. Second, evolution does not favor the maintenance of "fifth wheels"—if a function can be carried out by brain events, it is unclear why consciousness would have developed and been maintained to carry out that function.

Selectivity. Only some mental activities are accompanied by conscious experience. For example, we are introspectively aware of "rotating" objects in visual mental images, but are not conscious of how we build up objects a part at a time when we form images. Similarly, we often have no conscious experience of how we reach a decision or how we identify an object. We typically are conscious of the result of a specific type of processing (e.g., the decision or the identity of an object), but are not aware of the full sequence of events that led to that outcome. A theory of consciousness must specify why some mental processes are accompanied by conscious experience whereas others are not.

Association with brain states. Consciousness arises from activity in the brain, and is not produced by another organ of the body. We can be certain of this because of the many findings of causal links between changes in brain states and consciousness; for example, consciousness is altered when one perceives different objects or takes drugs. Furthermore, electrical activity in the brain (as measured by "evoked potentials") occurs immediately before one is conscious of a stimulus.[81] Thus, even though a description of consciousness cannot be replaced by a description of brain activity, brain activity is a necessary prerequisite to consciousness. By analogy, changing the nature of the filament or the glass of the lightbulb will change the quality of the light.

Impact on brain states. If consciousness is not epiphenomenal, it plays a role in a causal sequence of events. Logically, it is possible that states of consciousness could merely affect other states of consciousness. But these experiences would just "be along for the ride"; they would not affect behavior, and from this perspective could be considered epiphenomenal. If consciousness affects the way one behaves, then it probably affects the brain rather than operating more directly on muscles. Thus, we assume that the relation between the brain and consciousness cuts both ways: Activity in the brain affects consciousness, and vice versa. This requirement is daunting. Indeed, at first glance it seems paradoxical: Something that is not a physical event not only must arise from a physical event, but also must be capable of feeding back and altering it.

Parity Theory

These requirements are so stringent that a viable theory of consciousness may seem impossible. Thus, it is useful to see at least one example of a theory that respects these constraints, even if that theory is entirely speculative. Kosslyn sketches out one direction of a viable theory.[82] At the heart of this theory is the idea that consciousness serves as a kind of "parity check." This idea is best understood in terms of a computer metaphor. Computers store information in terms of "bytes," which are sets of 8 "bits." A bit is the simplest possible code, which always specifies either 0 or 1. One of the bits in each byte is sometimes used as a "parity bit"; after a pattern of 0's and 1's in the first 7 bits is used to code a letter, digit, or some other symbol (just as an input vector specifies information in a neural network), the parity bit is set to 0 or 1 so that the sum of all 8 bits is always odd (or is always even, depending on the convention used in that machine). The computer later can discover whether stored information has been disrupted by checking whether the bits in each byte sum up properly; if they do not, a cosmic ray or the like has disrupted storage.

The key idea of Parity Theory is that consciousness is a parity check; if we have normal consciousness, this indicates that the system is functioning properly. According to this conception, consciousness is an interaction among physical energies produced by the brain, which provides a sign that neural activity in diverse locations is mutually consistent. Kosslyn develops two variants of Parity Theory;[83] we will briefly summarize only the so-called "weak" version here, and see how it satisfies the five requirements described above.

Nonreducability. Neural discharges in different brain areas that process the same stimulus apparently oscillate in phase together at around 40 Hz.[84] This finding has suggested to many that these oscillations serve to associate representations in different regions of the brain;[85] if the neural discharges that underlie the representations of "ball," "red," "large," and "moving to the right"— which occur in different brain regions—are all oscillating in the same way, this could indicate that the representations should be conjoined in associative memory. According to Parity Theory, consciousness has the same relation to these brain events as a chord does to individual notes that are played on a guitar. Consciousness arises from the interaction of the electromagnetic rhythms set up in individual brain loci, but cannot be reduced to the individual brain events any more than a chord can be reduced to individual notes.

Unique role of consciousness. Mental activity arises via the joint activity of billions of neurons, which change activity levels constantly. Even if it were possible to have a process that checked each neuron (to perform a parity check) and compared its state to that of every other neuron—and did this many times per second!—such a process would have a flaw: What would check to ensure that this process itself was operating correctly? If another process were required here, what additional process would be needed to check that process, and so on, in infinite regress? According to Parity Theory, consciousness is like a chord that is consonant or dissonant; if the neural states do not mesh properly, it is as if the instrument is out of tune. Thus, consciousness has a unique role; it performs a function that cannot be replaced by a brain process.

Selectivity. Benjamin Libet and his colleagues find that conscious experiences reliably lag behind the brain events that presumably evoke them.[86] This finding suggests that the "chord" takes time to establish, even after all "notes" are present. Thus, a delay period is necessary before each conscious experience. If so, then we should be conscious only of processes that are relatively slow. Subsystems that encode information perceptually, store it, and use it to generate movements generally operate very quickly, and so we are not conscious of their workings. These functions are essential to virtually all multicellular organisms, and they presumably have become efficient over the course of evolution. But once these processes have produced a result, the corresponding brain state may exist for enough time for us to become conscious of the result itself (for example, to see an object or feel an associated emotion). Similarly, we are not conscious of the very fast processes that compose parts into a visual mental image, but we are conscious of the relatively slow processes that rotate objects in images.

Recall that the principle of opportunism rests on the idea that neural structures that evolved for one purpose can be recruited to perform an entirely different Function; by analogy, although noses evolved to warm air and assist the sense of smell, once present they can be used to hold up glasses.[87] But when a function is used in a new context, it may operate relatively slowly; it did not evolve for this use, and so has not been selected to be relatively efficient in this way. Thus, we are conscious of the relatively slow processes that coordinate perceptual, memory, and motor events during reasoning, a relatively recent development on the evolutionary scale.[88]

Association with brain states. A chord cannot arise unless individual notes are played. Similarly, without the electromagnetic rhythms that are established in different parts of the brain, there can be no consciousness. The contents of consciousness (a percept, sensation, etc.) are determined by the kinds of processing described in previous chapters, which give rise to the individual "notes" that comprise the chord. If parity is preserved, one is aware only of the contents of consciousness (the object being viewed, the meaning of a phrase, etc.)—and one is not aware of consciousness itself. It is only when dissonance arises that one typically becomes aware of one's conscious state.

Impact on brain states. If a note is out of tune, a dissonant chord will be produced. According to Parity Theory, dissonance can arise if different portions of the brain are not oscillating compatibly. In a guitar, if a dissonant chord is played, one can feel it on the neck of the instrument; the dissonance feeds back and causes changes in the resonance of the instrument itself. When such dissonance arises in the brain, the brain areas that produce the electromagnetic rhythms are affected, and hence they do not process information normally. Thus, consciousness seems fragmented or weird. Drugs can have a similar effect by disrupting the rhythms directly, producing abnormal interactions.

According to this theory, the most common result of dissonant consciousness is the equivalent of pressing a "reset" button. When something is awry, the system starts over again. Indeed, neural network computer models sometimes "get stuck" and need to be reset in just this way. It is as if one closed one's eyes and tried to get from the top of a mountain to the bottom by feeling around the slope to the front and to both sides, and always stepped down the steepest slope. This method can get one stuck in a pit. When this happens, one could retrace one's steps back to the top, and start down a different trail altogether. Similarly, in networks the initial set of connection strengths sometimes can get the network stuck so that it cannot change the strengths properly to learn an input/output mapping (it is stuck in a *local minimum*); in these cases, it may be necessary to start over, with a different pattern of initial connection strengths.[89]

Kosslyn develops a number of predictions of Parity Theory,[90] but for present purposes we have said enough. It should be clear that the approach taken in this book is not antithetical to a theory of consciousness. If nothing else, our approach has led us to offer a set of requirements for an adequate theory of consciousness—which is a first step in developing insight into this most mysterious phenomenon.

Emotion

Without question, emotion plays a critical role in mental life. We must distinguish between two facets of emotion, the functional and the experiential. First, consider emotion as a type of information stored in memory. When we recall an event or scene, an emotional penumbra surrounds it; similarly, an emotional state sometimes brings to mind events or scenes previously colored by that emotion.

It is probably important that some of the same brain structures that store new memories also are involved in registering (and possibly storing) emotions. For example, consider the following experiment. Volunteer subjects who were being PET-scanned were told either that they would receive an electric shock at some point during the scanning session, or that no shock would be presented. In fact, no shock was ever presented, but during one session the subjects were anxiously anticipating the shock. This anxiety was related to unusually high activation of the amygdala.[91] This is of interest in part because the amygdala has strong connections to the hippocampus, and the hippocampus plays a critical role in memory (see Chapter 8).

The emotional associations with information in memory probably play a role in generating and "prioritizing" possible responses to a stimulus. That is, we noted earlier that in most circumstances more than one response to a stimulus is possible. All else being equal, the run subsystem would select the activated plan that has the strongest emotional salience. Moreover, if another goal is being pursued and a very salient plan is activated by the input, the ongoing plan will be interrupted and a new one initiated. For example, even if one is rushing to the store to buy some food before it closes, one will stop if one's child steps into the street and a car is coming. If additional plans are not as salient, the more salient are these plans, the more distracting the evoking stimuli will be.

Like other sorts of information, emotion is characterized not simply by a content (the type of emotion), but also by a strength. But the strength component plays a critical role in emotion; an emotion has different consequences, depending on its strength. For example, if one is slightly repelled by a stimulus (e.g., bird droppings), one may step over it, but if one is strongly repelled by a stimulus (e.g., an animal that has been run over by a car), one will have a very different reaction. For other kinds of information, the strength component simply affects how likely one is to be aware of the content; for emotion, the strength component also affects the way one responds to a stimulus in specific circumstances (i.e., which plan is used).

In addition, emotion is accompanied by an experience. The experience depends in part on the activation of specific information representations; it is well known that the same physiological state "feels" differently depending on how it is interpreted.[92] Depending on the strength of the emotion, consciousness is more or less dominated by the information that has been activated. In many cases, this information corresponds to associations to a stimulus. If highly emotional information is activated, it would induce strong "rhythms" in the brain, which are equivalent to a very loud note in a chord. The emotion not only colors the experience, but also may play a special role in how activity in brain areas is altered when dissonance occurs. By analogy, it may affect how much the neck of the guitar shakes when a dissonant chord is played. A dissonant "chord" that includes the rhythm of a strong emotion may act more quickly to reset the system than other sorts of dissonance, and may play a special role in activating the autonomic nervous system—readying one to fight or flee.

In short, it seems clear that the approach we have taken could lead towards detailed conceptions of the function of emotion and a way of thinking about some facets of the accompanying experiences.

Rehabilitation

In this book, we have outlined the architecture of Functions (with a capital F) such as reading, moving, and remembering. Our goal was to specify relatively simple subsystems that could operate together to produce complex behaviors. Such a conception of the normal system should play a critical role when a program of rehabilitation is designed for a brain-damaged patient. Ideally, the rehabilitation process should start by specifying what is impaired and what is intact in a given patient. In order to do so, one needs a theoretical framework that specifies the nature of the underlying component processes.

We are born with a finite number of neurons, and by adulthood no new neurons can be produced.[93] Thus, damaged neurons cannot be replaced by new, intact cells, nor is it likely that they can be repaired. However, we have argued throughout the book that the interactions among processing subsystems can be modified following a lesion to the brain, and such shifts give even the fully mature system considerable flexibility. Thus, a given Function may be performed in many ways, using processes that are implemented in different parts of the brain.

These considerations lead us to suggest that a good rehabilitation strategy would not consist of rote training in tasks that a brain-damaged patient cannot perform well. Rather, the best rehabilitation strategy would be to train a patient to perform such tasks using new methods that do not rely on the impaired subsystems: the rehabilitation program would take advantage of the principle of opportunism, teaching the patient a new way to perform such tasks. Unlike young children, mature adults cannot recruit new brain areas to perform damaged functions, so it is more effective to devise new ways of using preserved functions to accomplish tasks.

For example, one of us saw a patient with prosopagnosia. He was unable to recognize even the members of his own family. His lesions were in the occipital-temporal area and, as one would expect from the locus of his lesions (which spared the dorsal system; see Chapter 3), he had intact spatial abilities. Indeed, he could make very fine discriminations among height/width ratios. After determining this, he was asked to imagine a horizontal line connecting a person's eyes and then a vertical line connecting the center of the horizontal line to the bottom of the person's nose. He was asked to draw these "T" shapes for different people, and to note how the precise shape of this "T" varied from person to person. This patient seemed able to distinguish some people based on this spatial property. If he were in a restricted environment where he came into contact with a small number of other people, such as his place of work, this strategy might prove useful for distinguishing faces.

As another example, consider a patient with ideational apraxia, who has trouble performing actions in a sequence, such as those required to light a candle. Although we noted in Chapter 7 that such a behavior can result from the disruption of several different component processes, one type of possible disruption may affect the movement monitoring subsystem. If so, then the patient should improve if he or she were trained to perform this action "automatically." For instance, the patient may be better off performing the action with his or her eyes closed.

Having a theory to describe the subsystems that can be used to perform a task is indeed a critical step in the rehabilitation process. Designing or choosing the task(s) to diagnose which subsystems are impaired is also a critical step, as is designing new strategies that circumvent impaired subsystems. It is unlikely that a fixed set of training regimes can be created to cover all possible configurations of damage. Therefore, it seems likely that the clinician of tomorrow will be steeped not only in cognitive neuroscience, but also in research methods and task design.

Several themes have cut across the different topics we have discussed in this book. First of all, we repeatedly found evidence that the brain is organized according to the principle of division of labor. This led us to infer many distinct processing subsystems, which in turn provided not only the bases for diagnosing the effects of brain damage on behavior, but also the foundation of an approach to rehabilitation. But this principle is not hard-and-fast; the system is only weakly modular. Indeed, in this chapter we saw that the same mechanism that trains the preprocessing subsystem to encode useful patterns also may underlie the development of cerebral lateralization. But more than that, the tissue that implements the subsystems sometimes may be shared by more than one subsystem, as noted in Chapter 2. Indeed, recall Damasio's idea that what we call subsystems are merely loci of convergence of highly overlapping patterns of activity.[94]

Furthermore, time and time again we found evidence that constraint satisfaction was at work, taking advantage of the broad tunings of neurons rather than fighting this property. This sort of coding set the stage for our conception of consciousness, in that Parity Theory rests on the mutual consistency of the levels of activity of many individual neurons. In addition, we saw that the brain often is opportunistic, using structures that may have evolved in one context to carry out different sorts of tasks. This idea lies at the heart of our observations about the process of successful rehabilitation for mature people. Finally, concurrent processing is the rule. The idea that everything runs at once allows winner-take-all processes to govern some forms of decision making, which is far easier computationally than weighing each alternative individually, one at a time. In this chapter we saw how reasoning and decision making are not mysterious abilities, and can be conceptualized in the same way as the other Functions we discussed earlier in this book.

These principles have several corollaries, which are apparent throughout the book, although we did not develop them when we initially considered neural network computation. For one, areas that receive inputs from other areas typically send information back to those areas; the two areas are cooperating to perform a computation. Furthermore, the various subsystems operate in a cascade. Although we sometimes described the system as if it were an assembly line, marching forward in discrete time units, this clearly is an oversimplification. As was discussed in Chapter 2, not only is there a lot of information flowing backwards, but partial results are being sent forward constantly. Subsystems do not wait to finish before producing an output, but rather begin to produce an output stream as soon as they receive input.[95]

Another principle that appears to emerge from our investigations is that storage is used instead of computation, if at all possible.[96] Neural networks are very good at storing associations, but not very good at the kind of serial processing that underlies much of reasoning. In this sort of system, the results of previous decisions would be easy to store and to access later when appropriate. If so, then one reason why some older people may become wise is that they have stored the results of many previous decisions, and are able to generalize properly to similar cases when they arise subsequently.[97]

In addition, we have several times noticed that inhibition lies at the heart of control processes, as noted above when we discussed cerebral lateralization. This idea fits neatly with the principle of concurrent processing; the system runs constantly, and is managed by selectively turning off parts of it. This use of inhibition is a radically different perspective on how the flow of information processing is managed from that adopted in most specialists in artificial intelligence, and may be an example of where Wet Mind can contribute to this endeavor.

The study of Wet Mind is a very ambitious enterprise, and it would be easy to be discouraged. The conceptual issues are daunting, it is difficult to carry out such interdisciplinary work, and the methodologies are often too new to have been fully explored. Nevertheless, it is clear that researchers have begun to part the mists, and that a new field has coalesced. The previous pages illustrate that not only have a wide range of important discoveries been made, but an explanatory framework is emerging. Although our formulation of this framework probably will be modified by future research, it summarizes fundamental findings and ideas—and invites one to pose alternative possible accounts that can be discriminated among by further observations and rigorous experimentation. Our analyses and synthesis reveal that the field has in fact made remarkable progress in a very short time, and we hope we have conveyed to the reader why we believe that this is just a taste of what is to come.

Notes

1. WET MIND/DRY MIND

1. Benson & Greenberg, 1969.

2. For good examples of the Dry Mind approach, see Anderson, 1983; Kosslyn, 1980; Newell & Simon, 1972; and Fodor, 1968, who presents a good treatment of the philosophical foundations of this approach.

3. For brief reviews of the history of cerebral localization, see Churchland, 1986, and Walsh, 1987; Clarke & O'Malley, 1968, and Harrington, 1987, provide more comprehensive treatments.

4. See Gall, 1812 (excerpted and translated in Clarke & O'Malley, 1968).

5. Flourens, 1824 (translated in von Bonin, 1960).

6. Hitzig & Fritsch, 1870 (translated in von Bonin, 1960).

7. Munk, 1881.

8. See Harrington, 1987.

9. Dax, 1865 (translated in Diamond, 1974).

10. Broca, 1863.

11. Wernicke, 1874.

12. See Geschwind, 1966, pp. 4–5.

13. Jackson, 1864 (reprinted in Taylor, 1932); see also Jackson, 1874.

14. Gregory, 1961.

15. Ramon y Cajal, 1888 (excerpted and translated in Clarke & O'Malley, 1968).

16. Brodmann, 1909.

17. Lashley, 1929; see also Lashley & Clark, 1946.

18. See Milner, 1970, p. 109.

19. See Lashley, 1929, 1933, 1937.

20. E.g., Penfield & Perot, 1963; see also Penfield & Roberts, 1959.

21. Luria, 1973, 1980.

22. Cf. Geschwind, 1966.
23. E.g., see Mesulam, 1981; Squire, 1987.
24. Critchley, 1953.

2. COMPUTATION IN THE BRAIN

1. For further comparisons of brains and computers, see Kosslyn & Hatfield, 1984.

2. The output from a unit is not directly proportional to the simple sum of the inputs. Rather, networks typically use a nonlinear (sigmoidal) function, in which there is less effect of additional input when the sum is either very small or very large. The technical reasons for this feature are described by Rumelhart, Hinton & Williams, 1986a, 1986b.

3. Rumelhart, Hinton & Williams, 1986a, 1986b; see also Rumelhart & McClelland, 1986.

4. In actual computer models of neural networks, activation over a certain level at an output unit (e.g., .9) is treated as a "1" and activation under another level (e.g., .1) is treated as a "0" (which reduces the time to train the network).

5. E.g., see Grossberg, 1987, 1988.

6. For a simple presentation of how a computer works, see Kosslyn, 1983.

7. Recurrent networks exhibit these properties only if the pattern of feedback connections is appropriate for the particular set of input/output vectors associated by the network. Moreover, if the input vectors are too similar, the network will generalize (see page 40) and fail to complete the vector properly.

8. For an overview, see Marr, 1982.

9. Cf. Marr, 1982, p. 66.

10. McClelland & Rumelhart, 1988, have written versions of these types of models that one can experiment with on IBM-compatible or Macintosh personal computers.

11. Neural network computer models consist of a set of interlocking elements that function as if they were all operating at once ("in parallel"). Such a "parallel" neural network can be mimicked on a serial computer, even though the computer operates one step at a time. This is done by having the computer "pretend" that the input is being received all at once. Typically, processing is divided into very small "ticks" (time units). A little bit of each computation is done in each tick, and then with the next tick a little more is done. (This is like "time sharing" in a standard computer.) Thus, each part stays "neck and neck" with

the others. In general, as long as no processing is logically dependent on prior processing, it does not matter in what order (or over what period of real time) the processes are performed: the system can function as if the various processes were occurring at the same time.

For example, consider how one would program a computer to simulate a horse race. One would include a host of information about each horse and about the track. The program would then compute the location of each horse at 30 seconds after the start (say), at 1 minute after the start, at 1.5 minutes after the start, and so on, as the horses ran around the track. The program would use information about how well each horse runs on curved track, straight track, near other horses, and so on, to compute where it would be at each point in time. For each time slice, it would in fact compute what was going on at each location separately, updating both the information about the track and about the other horses (perhaps some horses are particularly competitive, and respond when others pull ahead). Even though the computer was working serially, it would mimic what would happen if the horses were running simultaneously. Depending on how frequently locations are updated during the race (i.e., the number and length of the time slices) and how one interprets the interval covered by each time slice, one can mimic true parallelism to any desired degree of accuracy. (People have actually written such programs and proceeded to lose money by betting on the horses that win in the simulation. Remember: A model is only as good as the theory that underlies it.)

12. Lehky & Sejnowski, 1988a, 1988b.

13. The networks we have discussed so far represent information by patterns of activity distributed over a set of units. There is no single place that corresponds to the representation of an association between two things or pieces of information. There are other types of networks that are not like this. Each unit in these networks stands for something, and the connections often have special meanings (such as "is a member of" when objects are organized into classes). For example, a unit might stand for a letter of the alphabet, or for a word. We will consider both types of networks later in the book. The evidence for such "local" representations in the brain is rather slim, but we suspect there must be at least some cases in which they are used (cf. Feldman, 1985).

14. Stevens, 1979, p. 15.

15. See Kandel & Schwartz, 1985; Shepherd, 1988.

16. Crick & Asanuma, 1986.

17. Cf. Grossberg, 1987, 1988.

18. E.g., see Kosslyn, Chabris, Marsolek & Koenig, in press;

Rueckl, Cave & Kosslyn, 1989.

19. Marsolek, Kosslyn & Squire, in press.
20. Ungerleider & Mishkin, 1982.
21. Fodor, 1983.
22. Allman, Miezin & McGuinness, 1985; Van Essen, 1987.
23. See Van Essen, 1985.
24. Gould & Lewontin, 1979.
25. Damasio, 1990a, 1990b.
26. E.g., see Livingstone & Hubel, 1987.
27. Cf. Simon, 1981.
28. Van Essen, 1985, 1987.
29. Hinton, McClelland & Rumelhart, 1986.
30. E.g., Kandel & Schwartz, 1985.
31. Another way of thinking about the breakdown of modularity at intermediate levels of analysis is that coarse coding may be used not only at the level of individual neurons, but also at the level of networks. In this case, outputs from multiple areas are combined to perform a computation.
32. Shepherd, 1988.
33. Cf. McClelland, 1979.
34. E.g., Anderson, 1983; Newell & Simon, 1972.
35. E.g., Kimble, 1988; Rosenzweig & Leiman, 1982.
36. It is worth emphasizing that by putting behavior at the top of the triangle we do not mean to imply that behavior always must be studied before turning to the brain or computational analyses. Progress can be made by starting from any vertex of the triangle and working outward, for example a new anatomical finding can lead to studies of behavior or computational analysis. No one type of consideration has priority; all are necessary to understand how the brain produces behavior. "Behavior" is at the top to remind us that our goal is to understand behavior, not to claim that studies of behavior per se are paramount.

3. VISUAL PERCEPTION

1. Sacks, 1985.
2. E.g., Daniel & Whitteridge, 1961; Tootell, Silverman, Switkes & De Valois, 1982.
3. For discussions of this aspect of attention, see Posner, 1988; Treisman & Gelade, 1980; Treisman & Gormican, 1988.
4. See Farah, 1990; Haxby et al., 1991; Maunsell & Newsome, 1987.
5. Ungerleider & Mishkin, 1982.
6. Pohl, 1973.

7. See also Ungerleider & Mishkin, 1982; Desimone & Ungerleider, 1989.

8. Desimone, Albright, Gross & Bruce, 1984; Gross et al., 1981; Gross, Desimone, Albright & Schwartz, 1984.

9. Perrett et al., 1985.

10. Andersen, Essick & Siegel, 1985.

11. See Desimone, Albright, Gross & Bruce, 1984; Desimone & Ungerleider, 1989; Miyashita & Chang, 1988.

12. Andersen, Essick & Siegel, 1985; Lynch, Mountcastle, Talbot & Yin, 1977; for a review, see Andersen, 1987.

13. Spatial properties apparently can be used to distinguish objects only under special circumstances, however, when the animal adopts a specific strategy. Monkeys apparently do not devise such strategies, although at least some human patients with brain damage apparently do (see Kosslyn, McPeek, Daly, Alpert & Caviness, submitted). We will have more to say about this shortly.

14. Gregory, 1966; Neisser, 1967, 1976.

15. E.g., Damasio, 1985a; Goldman-Rakic, 1987, 1988; Luria, 1980; Mesulam, 1981, 1990.

16. Van Essen & Maunsell, 1983; Van Essen, 1985; for slightly different versions of this analysis, see also Desimone & Ungerleider, 1989; Kaas, 1989.

17. See Cowey, 1981, and Kaas, 1989, for a number of accounts of why there are so many visual areas in the brain.

18. Felleman & Van Essen, 1991.

19. Van Essen, 1985.

20. E.g., Gross & Mishkin, 1977.

21. Gross & Mishkin, 1977.

22. Rueckl, Cave & Kosslyn, 1989.

23. E.g., see Bronson, 1974; see also Walsh & Hoyt, 1969.

24. Bronson, 1974.

25. Schneider, 1969.

26. Rafal et al., 1990.

27. Weiskrantz, 1986.

28. Information from the geniculo-striate pathway plays a key role not only in representing object properties, but also in representing spatial properties—including location. These spatial representations can be used to guide a wide variety of movements and can be stored for later use. In contrast, input from the tecto-pulvinar pathway apparently has a much more restricted function, being used primarily to draw the animal's attention to potentially important stimuli. This input does not produce general-purpose representations.

29. Tootell, Silverman, Switkes & De Valois, 1982.

30. See also Daniel & Whitteridge, 1961.

31. Van Essen, 1985.

32. Fox et al., 1986.

33. Felleman & Van Essen, 1991.

34. Felleman & Van Essen, 1991.

35. In some ways, the visual buffer is like a TV screen. Like a screen, the buffer is spatially organized, and the representations in it are produced by configurations of smaller regions. In other ways, however, the visual buffer is not at all like a TV screen. For one, it is not a display that something else uses to present information to a viewer; nothing "looks" at the screen. Rather, information in these areas is passed along for further operations by other visual areas. In addition, these brain areas do not serve merely as a display; rather, processes within the buffer actively work to define the edges and surfaces of objects.

36. Sperling, 1960.

37. The psychological reality of the attention window is further revealed in situations in which it is not used. For example, Anne Treisman and her colleagues have shown that people will sometimes experience "illusory conjunctions" when information is presented outside of attention. For instance, if shown a set of Z's and I's, people sometimes see a T; they mistakenly conjoin the vertical bar with a short horizontal bar at the top of the Z (see Treisman & Gelade, 1980; Treisman & Schmidt, 1982). If the attention window does not yoke the different sorts of information together, the separate processing streams can get out of synchronization.

38. Moran & Desimone, 1985.

39. Physiologically, the attention window may best be thought of as a set of switches, which regulate connections coming from the visual buffer, leaving on only a certain number at any one time. This mechanism appears to operate largely by inhibiting the unattended regions, and thus allowing only the attended regions to pass information further into the system.

40. Cf. Rafal et al., 1990.

41. Cave & Kosslyn, 1989; Larsen & Bundesen, 1978; Sekuler & Nash, 1972.

42. Lowe, 1985, 1987a, 1987b. This work is interesting in part because Lowe was inspired by the work of psychologists who study perception, such as J. J. Gibson, 1966—and hence, by relating his work to the brain, we illustrate the use of the cognitive neuroscience triangle.

43. For a review, see Biederman, 1987.

44. Riddoch & Humphreys, 1987; Humphreys & Riddoch, 1987a.

45. Gibson, 1950, 1966.
46. Cf. Chapter 12 of Kaufman, 1974; Neisser, 1967.
47. Biederman & Shiffrar, 1987.
48. Cf. Ullman, 1979.
49. Johansson, 1950, 1975.
50. Cutting & Kozlowski, 1977; see also Cutting & Proffitt, 1981.
51. E.g., see Gross, Desimone, Albright & Schwartz, 1984.
52. Allman, Miezin & McGuinness, 1985; Andersen, 1987.
53. Saito et al., 1986; see also Andersen, 1987; Maunsell & Newsome, 1987; Movshon, Adelson, Gizzi & Newsome, 1986.
54. Mumford (1991) suggests a way in which the thalamus may coordinate the results of a number of separate subsystems working in parallel.
55. One of our visual abilities is that we can ignore irrelevant variations in the shape of a single form (such as a cup). In order to do so, the pattern activation subsystem must be capable of producing one output from a range of similar inputs. However, such generalization must be held in check; we sometimes want to recognize a specific instance, and do not want to generalize. A relatively straightforward way to build a system with this property is to have the output from the pattern activation subsystem indicate not only the stored representation that best matches the input, but also how well it uniquely implicates that object or part. Hence, if a match is not very close, subsystems further downstream need not regard a particular instance as having been firmly recognized. The output from the pattern activation subsystem, then, might specify not only the pattern that matches the input best, but also how well it matches.
56. Miyashita & Chang, 1988.
57. E.g., Ungerleider & Mishkin, 1982.
58. Perrett et al., 1985.
59. Wittgenstein, 1953.
60. It is clear that context can also influence processing within associative memory. Depending on what one is trying to do, different sorts of stored information will be appropriate. For example, if one is asked to name the person and then shown a face, the response "face" must be suppressed. One wants to know who it is, not simply that the object is a face. Hence, associative memory must accept constraints that "set" it so that only representations with specific properties (such as a particular level of specificity) can be activated by the input. In later chapters we will discuss language comprehension and decision subsystems that presumably play a role in this process.
61. Reed, 1974; Reed & Johnsen, 1975.

62. Note that we do not always recognize objects by recognizing their parts; as discussed in previous sections, we also encode the overall pattern and recognize it directly if it matches a stored pattern. Kosslyn, 1991, suggests that the pattern activation subsystem tries to match the largest pattern possible, and suppresses patterns that correspond to smaller parts. This idea receives support from the behavior of a patient described by Luria, 1959, who could name the Star of David when all of the lines were a single color, but could not name it when one triangle was red and the other blue (this patient had *simultanagnosia,* a disorder that will be described shortly). Similarly, when this patient was shown a picture of a face, he could identify it as a face only when all parts were the same color; when parts were drawn in different colors, he named only the parts. Apparently, when the parts were the same color, they were grouped into a single overall configuration, which could be matched directly, but when parts were different colors, they were not grouped—and the patient was forced to match individual parts, which he could only consider in isolation.

63. Perrett et al., 1985.

64. Biederman, 1987.

65. Andersen, Essick & Siegel, 1985.

66. Zipser & Andersen, 1988.

67. O'Reilly, Kosslyn, Marsolek & Chabris, 1990.

68. Ullman, 1984.

69. To form new categorical spatial relations representations, we may need first to encode motor-based coordinate representations, and then perform an explicit or implicit movement to "unpack" this information. This idea may help us to resolve an apparent paradox. Consider again the results from the what/where experiments with monkeys; monkeys could not distinguish patterns such as stripes and checks after their temporal lobes were removed, but they could distinguish relative locations. Location, size, and orientation information are thought to be processed by the dorsal system, which is intact in these animals. If so, then they should be able to discriminate checkboard patterns from stripes using the dorsal system alone: the stripes occupy fewer locations than the checks, are larger, and have a different orientation. Thus, the dorsal system should be able to make the necessary discrimination. But monkeys without temporal lobes are greatly impaired when they must make this discrimination, even when the dorsal system is intact.

This result makes sense if we accept two assumptions. First, a spatial discrimination can be made only if categorical representations are encoded; coordinate representations are used to guide motor movements, not to make discriminations. Second, the dorsal system reflexively computes coordinate representations at the same time the ventral system is operating, and the motor codes must be actively unpacked to encode new spatial categories. Monkeys are not clever enough to realize this, and so do not shift their eyes or hands in a way that would allow them to encode the distinguishing spatial characteristics in a form that could be used to make the discrimination.

70. Cf. Loftus, 1983.

71. This task was based on one developed by Hellige & Michimata, 1989; see Kosslyn, Chabris, Marsolek & Koenig, in press.

72. E.g., Hellige & Michimata, 1989; Kosslyn, Koenig, Barrett, Cave, Tang & Gabrieli, 1989; see Kosslyn, Chabris, Marsolek & Koenig, in press, for a review.

73. See De Renzi, 1982.

74. Fisk & Goodale, 1988.

75. Hellige & Michimata, 1989.

76. See Kosslyn et al., 1989.

77. Sergent (in press) showed that the hemispheric specialization for the two types of spatial relations is only evident if the stimuli are rather dim; if they are presented with very high contrast, subjects are generally very fast and there is no hemispheric difference. Kosslyn et al. (in press) used neural network models to show that this result could occur even if separate subsystems compute the two types of relations, provided that high contrast causes more lower-level neurons to provide input to each network.

78. Taylor & Warrington, 1973; Warrington & Rabin, 1970; Hannay, Varney & Benton, 1976; but also see Ratcliff & Davies-Jones, 1972, for a failure to replicate using an easier task.

79. Hock, Kronseder & Sissons, 1981.

80. See also Mehta, Newcombe & Damasio, 1987; Olson & Bialystok, 1983.

81. E.g., Levine, Maini & Calvanio, 1988.

82. Cf. Damasio, 1989, 1990b; Kahneman, Treisman & Gibbs, in press.

83. See Damasio, 1985a; Goldman-Rakic, 1987; Luria, 1980; Mesulam, 1990.

84. Cf. Ullman, 1984.

85. E.g., see Damasio, 1985a; Goldman-Rakic, 1987; Luria, 1980.

86. See Milner, 1964.

87. Goldman-Rakic, 1987, 1988.

88. Goldman-Rakic, 1987, 1988.

89. See also Boch & Goldberg, 1989.

90. E.g., Posner, 1978/1986; Posner, Snyder & Davidson, 1980; Posner, Inhoff, Friedrich & Cohen, 1987.

91. For additional details, see Posner & Petersen, 1990.

92. Cf. Geschwind, 1965.

93. Gregory, 1961.

94. For further discussion of the difficulties of drawing inferences from behavioral deficits following brain damage, see Kosslyn & Van Kleeck, 1990; Kosslyn & Intriligator, in press.

95. Kosslyn, Flynn, Amsterdam & Wang, 1990.

96. Actual neural network models of each subsystem were not built, however, for technical reasons; namely, the computer would have required years to do anything interesting. Neural network models run on standard computers are very computation-intensive because the computer can only do one thing at a time, and each weight must be updated many times during the course of training. Instead, "black boxes" simulated neural networks with standard serial routines that operated on arrays and lists of facts.

97. Researchers in this area do not agree on the best way to classify the disruptions, and there is no widely accepted taxonomy of deficits. The taxonomy we use here is derived primarily from Damasio, 1985b; De Renzi, 1982; and Williams, 1970. Farah, 1990, offers a newer, perhaps more comprehensive, taxonomy which is motivated in part by discoveries and ideas that also motivated our analysis. We felt it would be more useful (and challenging) to address the traditional ways of characterizing the disorders, which do not incorporate these kinds of distinctions from the outset.

98. See Bauer & Rubens, 1985; Damasio, 1985b; Farah, 1990; Humphreys & Riddoch, 1987a, 1987b; Levine, 1982; Ratcliff, 1982; Riddoch & Humphreys, 1987.

99. Munk, 1881.

100. Freud, 1891.

101. Critchley, 1953, p. 289. This patient was first reported by Bay, 1952.

102. Lissauer, 1890.

103. E.g., De Renzi, 1982; Hecaen & Albert, 1978; Kolb & Whishaw, 1985.

104. Campion, 1987.

105. Farah, 1990.

106. De Renzi, 1982; Williams, 1970.

107. Levine, 1982.
108. Bauer & Rubens, 1985.
109. Damasio, 1985b.
110. See De Renzi, 1986, Case 4.
111. E.g., Tranel & Damasio, 1985.
112. E.g., see McCarthy & Warrington, 1986.
113. See Farah, 1990.
114. Damasio, 1985b.
115. See Allman & Zucker, 1991.
116. Land, 1972.
117. E.g., Lehky & Sejnowski, 1988a, 1988b; Marr, 1982.
118. Recounted in Critchley, 1953, p. 276.
119. See De Renzi, 1982.
120. Williams, 1970.
121. Williams, 1970, pp. 62–63.
122. Tyler, 1968.
123. Kinsbourne & Warrington, 1962, 1963.
124. Farah, 1990.
125. Holmes, 1919.
126. See De Renzi, 1982; Mesulam, 1981, 1985, 1990.
127. See Chapter 3 of Mesulam, 1985.
128. See Mesulam, 1981.
129. Harries & Perrett, 1991.

4. VISUAL COGNITION

1. When discussing imagery, we are not referring to the conscious experience of "seeing with the minds eye," "hearing with the mind's ear," or the like; the experience of "having a mental image" is a hallmark that the brain is processing information in a particular way, and it is these events that we want to understand. In the final chapter of this book we will briefly consider the relation between consciousness and brain function. For a more detailed discussion of much of the material in this chapter, see Kosslyn, 1983.

2. Kosslyn, Segar, Pani & Hillger, 1990.

3. E.g., see Shepard & Cooper, 1982.

4. One of the surprises of the study by Kosslyn, Segar, Pani & Hillger, 1990, was that most of the imagery that people reported did not seem to have any particular purpose; it simply arose as an association to other thoughts. Presumably, such imagery can remind one of things that might otherwise be overlooked. However, such "free association" imagery need not have any specific function. Evolutionarily, imagery could simply be a by-product of other processes, such as those used in

visual perception, and not all of the characteristics of imagery must be functional. In this chapter, we will consider how imagery can help one to perform a variety of tasks, but we do not assume that this is necessarily why imagery evolved; indeed, the visual subsystems may be like one's nose, which can be used to hold up glasses once one has it, even though it evolved for very different purposes (cf. Gould & Lewontin, 1979).

5. Yates, 1966.

6. Paivio, 1971.

7. Kosslyn & Jolicoeur, 1981.

8. For further discussion on the circumstances in which imagery is used, see Chapter 9 of Kosslyn, 1980.

9. E.g., see Farah, 1988; Finke & Shepard, 1986; Kosslyn, 1983; Shepard & Cooper, 1982.

10. See Park & Kosslyn, 1990.

11. Van Essen, 1985.

12. Roland & Friberg, 1985.

13. The rCBF technique is distinct from PET. For our purposes, perhaps the most important differences between the techniques are: (1) Unlike PET, rCBF produces images of activity only at the surface of the brain, and cannot localize activity in subcortical structures. (2) rCBF has much poorer resolution than PET, both spatially (in terms of the size of brain region it can resolve) and temporally (how long a brain area must be active to be detected). (3) rCBF is much less expensive than PET and—unlike PET—is commonly used as a clinical diagnostic tool, and so is available to greater numbers of researchers.

14. See Chapter 3.

15. Goldenberg, Podreka, Steiner, Willmes, Suess & Deecke, 1989.

16. Goldenberg, Podreka, Steiner, Willmes, Suess & Deecke, 1989, used yet another way of scanning the brain, called SPECT, for single photon emission computed tomography; this technique, a variant of PET, has poorer spatial and temporal resolution than PET but is less expensive to use.

17. See also Goldenberg, Podreka, Uhl, Steiner, Willmes & Deecke, 1989; Mazziotta, Phelps & Halgren, 1983; and Roland, 1982. See Farah, 1988, for a review of most of this literature.

18. Deutsch, Bourbon, Papanicolaou & Eisenberg, 1988.

19. Goldman-Rakic, 1987, 1988.

20. Levine, Warach & Farah, 1985.

21. Kosslyn, Alpert, Maljkovic, Weiss, Thompson, Hamilton, Chabris & Buonono, 1991.

22. Fox et al., 1986. See Chapter 3.
23. Kosslyn, 1980.
24. E.g., see Kosslyn, 1975, 1976.
25. Resolution limits in perception are caused in part by *spatial summation,* which is a neural averaging over adjacent regions of tissue; because the input is averaged over a region, variations in the light falling within that area are ignored. The same neural wiring may also constrain resolution in imagery.
26. See Kosslyn, 1980.
27. Kosslyn, 1978; Finke & Kosslyn, 1980
28. See page 89.
29. See Reed & Johnsen, 1975.
30. See also Finke, Pinker & Farah, 1989; Chambers & Reisberg, 1985.
31. See Finke & Pinker, 1982, 1983; Kosslyn, 1973, 1980; Kosslyn, Ball & Reiser, 1978; Pinker, Choate & Finke, 1984.
32. Pinker, 1980.
33. See Pinker, 1980.
34. Kosslyn, 1978. See also Chapter 3 of Kosslyn, 1980.
35. Kosslyn, Cave, Provost & Von Gierke, 1988; see also Roth & Kosslyn, 1988.
36. Kosslyn, Cave, Provost & Von Gierke, 1988.
37. This task was adapted from one developed by Podgorny & Shepard, 1978.
38. Kosslyn, Cave, Provost & Von Gierke, 1988.
39. Kosslyn, Cave, Provost & Von Gierke, 1988.
40. Roth & Kosslyn, 1988.
41. We assume that one must combine parts to form images when one has seen a series of parts of objects or scenes over time, as happens when parts of an object are encoded by different eye fixations, or when to-be-combined objects were initially viewed at different times. For example, if one uses imagery to decide whether the tip of a racehorse's tail is higher off the ground than its rear knees, one must compose an image in which the tail and knees are simultaneously "visible" at a high resolution; given the size of horses, and the resolution necessary to make the judgment, it is likely that the parts used to form the image were noted when one was relatively close to the horse, which would require making separate fixations. In this case, then, the requisite parts would be stored separately in memory, and generating the appropriate image would require mentally arranging the parts correctly. Kosslyn, Cave, Provost & Von Gierke (1988) showed that once an image is constructed, its parts are "visible" simultaneously; these

images were simple enough that all parts could be maintained at the same time.

42. Marvin Minsky, one of the fathers of artificial intelligence research, is reputed to have once said that whenever you are confronted with a complicated flow chart, look for the box labeled THINK. Thinking in the brain is not done in a single location or by a single subsystem. In Chapter 9 we will see that the frontal lobe clearly plays a critical role in initiating strategies, and a strategy is executed by a particular combination of subsystems. Because a subsystem is mechanical, producing the same response when given the same input, a complex chain of processing can be initiated by relatively simple inputs to specific subsystems.

43. Cave & Kosslyn, 1989.

44. E.g., see Gross, Desimone, Albright & Schwartz, 1984; Van Essen, 1985.

45. Kosslyn, 1980.

46. Kosslyn, Cave, Provost & Von Gierke, 1988.

47. For a good review, see Shepard & Cooper, 1982.

48. Goldman-Rakic, 1987, 1988; Posner & Petersen, 1990.

49. See Shepard & Cooper, 1982.

50. Georgopoulos et al., 1989.

51. Deutsch, Bourbon, Papanicolaou & Eisenberg, 1988.

52. Kosslyn, unpublished data.

53. Deutsch, Bourbon, Papanicolaou & Eisenberg, 1988.

54. Deutsch, Bourbon, Papanicolaou & Eisenberg, 1988.

55. This idea allows us to understand the most striking finding about image transformations: they usually are incremental (see Shepard and Cooper, 1982). That is, the time to rotate, enlarge, or otherwise alter an imaged object typically increases with increasingly greater transformations. This finding is puzzling because mental images are not real objects and hence are not constrained by the laws of physics to rotate along a trajectory. The laws of physics require that real objects move through a trajectory when rotated because instantaneous translation of position is impossible, but images are not real objects, and hence in principle need not necessarily be transformed through a trajectory.

Image transformations apparently are not carried out by a single processing subsystem, and subsystems in both cerebral hemispheres are involved. One reason the image is altered in small increments may hinge on the use of the spatial relations encoding subsystems (categorical and coordinate) to monitor the progress of the manipulation, which is important if one is to stop rotation or some other transformation at the correct time. Such a gradual transformation is in part necessary if the categorical spatial relations encoding subsystem is used to monitor image transformation, allowing one to stop when the shape is properly altered; it behooves one to rotate or otherwise alter the object in relatively small increments so that one does not overshoot the correct orientation.

However, this requirement cannot be the entire solution to the puzzle; it does not explain the apparently constant rate of rotation. If monitoring were the only factor, one should initially use large steps and slow down only when approaching the target orientation. The constant rate of rotation may reflect entirely different factors. Kosslyn (1987) argues that there is noise in the system, and hence the locations of individual parts are not altered by precisely the same amount, with the variance among their locations increasing with the step size of the individual shift operations. Hence, the image becomes scrambled in direct proportion to the size of the shifts, and smaller shifts are used to allow one to realign the image more easily. A series of such small shifts produces the typical linear increase in time to rotate increasing amounts (see Kosslyn, 1987, for further details).

56. Another way in which objects in images could be transformed corresponds to the "blink" transform described by Kosslyn (1980). In these cases, an image is allowed to fade, and an image of the object in another size, orientation, location, or configuration is generated. (The name reflects the discontinuous nature of the transformation; no intermediate positions are represented.) This method is not always very useful, however, because it cannot be utilized to alter the shapes of individual parts and it requires relatively difficult calculations to figure out where to peg each part. Thus, it is not surprising that the other, incremental method of image transformation is available.

57. For a review, see Jolicoeur, 1990.
58. Lowe, 1987a, 1987b.
59. See Ullman, 1989.
60. See Chapter 9 of Kosslyn, 1980.
61. See Kosslyn, 1983; Weber & Harnish, 1974.
62. Cf. Huttenlocher, 1968.
63. Cf. McBride & Rothstein, 1979; Richardson, 1967.
64. Parsons, 1987.
65. See Denis, 1982a, 1982b, 1988.
66. Ericsson, Chase & Faloon, 1980; Newell & Simon, 1972.
67. Bisiach & Luzzatti, 1978.
68. Bisiach, Luzzatti & Perani, 1979.

69. We must be cautious when drawing conclusions about left-brain and right-brain function in normal people from the results of studies of such patients: They did not have normal brains to begin with (they had severe epilepsy), and certainly do not have normal brains after the operation (they are split in half). However, it is valuable to study the dissociations that occur in such split brains; such results can provide insight into how a process may be carried out by distinct subsystems.

70. Kosslyn, Holtzman, Gazzaniga & Farah, 1985.

71. Deleval, De Mol & Noterman, 1983.

72. Translated by O. Koenig and by Farah, Levine & Calvanio, 1988, p. 71.

73. Farah, 1984.

74. Although Farah's characterization of the individual cases can be challenged (see Sergent, 1990), there is now enough convergent evidence from other sources to take seriously the idea that damage to the posterior left hemisphere disrupts visual mental imagery. For example, see Grossi, Orsini & Modafferi, 1986; Grossi, Modafferi, Pelosi & Trojano, 1989; Riddoch, 1990. Many researchers were surprised by the idea that mental imagery depends on processes carried out by the *left* cerebral hemisphere. The common wisdom had it that imagery is a right hemisphere activity, in contrast to language, which is primarily a left hemisphere activity (e.g., see Erlichman & Barrett, 1983; Ley & Bryden, 1983; Springer & Deutsch, 1981; Kosslyn, Holtzman, Gazzaniga & Farah, 1985). But when Erlichman & Barrett reviewed the neuropsychological literature on imagery, they discovered that imagery is not systematically associated with only right- or left-hemisphere processing. Imagery deficits arise following damage to a wide range of loci in the brain, which makes sense if imagery arises from the operation of many subsystems working in concert, with different subsystems residing in different parts of the brain.

75. Farah, 1984.

76. Alternatively, forming an image of a specific example may simply require too much effort for someone with brain damage, assuming that the damage lowers general activation levels.

77. Kosslyn, Holtzman, Gazzaniga & Farah, 1985.

78. Corballis & Sergent, 1988.

79. Sergent, 1989.

80. Sergent, 1989.

81. See also Corballis, 1991; Goldenberg, Podreka, Uhl, Steiner, Willmes & Deecke, 1989; Paivio, 1989.

82. Ratcliff, 1979.

83. Weisenberg & McBride, 1935.

84. Le Doux, Wilson & Gazzaniga, 1977.
85. Deutsch, Bourbon, Papanicolaou & Eisenberg, 1988.
86. E.g., see Butters, Barton, & Brody, 1970; De Renzi & Faglioni, 1967; see Chapter 6 of De Renzi, 1982, for a review.
87. Kosslyn, Berndt, and Doyle, 1985.
88. For additional details, see Kosslyn, 1987.

5. READING

1. In our opinion, if monkeys could read and otherwise use language properly, we could not ethically use them as laboratory animals. A major justification for experimenting on (or eating, or otherwise using) animals, as least as we see it, rests on a basic conception of ethics: Rights only exist because there are complementary duties (e.g., see Frankena, 1963). For example, if you have a right to live, the rest of us have a duty not to kill you. Thus, ethics is embedded in a community of responsible citizens who can perform the necessary duties that allow rights to be conferred. If a monkey, or anything else, could understand the necessary duties, it would become a member of the community to which the rights apply. However, monkeys cannot participate in such social contracts.

That said, we must acknowledge that in the best of all possible worlds we would not need to sacrifice living creatures to further our own ends. It is an unfortunate fact that although there are good substitutes for using animals for food, clothing, and so forth, there is no other way to learn about the detailed neurophysiology and neuroanatomy of the brain. The potential benefits from learning about the brain are immense, not only for treating people with brain disorders but also for building intelligent machines that could help the blind and infirm; these benefits must be weighed against the loss of animal life. At least for the near term, the benefits appear to outweigh the drawbacks. We will need to reassess this balance continually, however, as alternative methods for learning about the details of neurophysiology are developed.

2. Marshack, 1991.
3. Besner, Davelaar, Alcott & Parry, 1984.
4. See Just & Carpenter, 1980, 1987.
5. Petersen et al., 1988.
6. It is well known that certain aspects of reading words are "automatic," in the same way that seeing a color is automatic (Posner & Snyder, 1975; Shiffrin & Schneider, 1977). We have no choice but to perform such processing. For example, try not to read "stop" next time you see a stop sign. As will be discussed in Chapter 9, a famous demonstration of these automatic processes is called the Stroop Color

Word Task. In this test, one is asked to name the color of the ink used to print a word; the trick is that the word names either the same color or a different color. For example, the word "red" might be written in red ink or blue ink. It is much harder to name the color of the ink if that color is different from the color named by the word than if it is the same. One cannot help reading the word and perceiving the color, and if the word names another color there is interference. Thus, simply asking subjects to look at words will invoke basic processes that assign meaning.

7. As will be evident by the end of this chapter, many studies have reported different patterns of reading problems following brain damage. In many cases, however, patients have lesions in areas that are not activated during reading in the normal brain. At first blush, this seems peculiar; intuitively, it seems that damaging an area that is activated during reading should cause a reading deficit, and an area that causes a deficit when damaged should be activated during reading. The disparity between the two types of findings must be interpreted with caution, for several reasons. First, recall from Chapter 3 that a deficit in a given behavior following brain damage does not necessarily mean that the damaged area is responsible for producing this behavior. Brain damage can produce behavior deficits through a variety of indirect means. Second, for at least two reasons, it is difficult to interpret a *failure* to find activity with PET. On the one hand, PET images are usually obtained by subtracting patterns of blood flow in two conditions; if a process is "automatic," it may occur in both—and hence would not be evident after the subtraction. On the other hand, if the process is used very often, it may become highly practiced and efficient—and thus may not require additional oxygen or nutrients during the task. If so, then it may not be detected even if it is being used in a task. Caveats like this underscore the need for multiple different methods, all of which produce results that converge on the same conclusion. The inferences we draw here typically are based on some combination of computational analyses, behavioral findings with normal subjects, results from PET or other brain scanning studies, and effects of brain damage on behavior.

8. Petersen, Fox, Snyder & Raichle, 1990.

9. Posner, Petersen, Fox & Raichle, 1988.

10. The fact that words are defined by nonaccidental properties probably is not a coincidence; we write as we do because our visual systems are sensitive to certain types of patterns of lines. As writing developed, patterns of lines that were easily deciphered presumably were retained whereas patterns that were not easily deciphered were discarded. This is cultural evolution in action.

11. However, in previous experiments noted earlier, Petersen et al. did not find evidence that passive viewing of single words activated the

frontal lobe. When seeing the false fonts, the subjects in the present experiment may have set a high criterion in associative memory for identifying words; because the false-fonts were similar to real letters, they often would have partially matched representations in the pattern activation subsystem and hence might have been mistaken for words if the criterion were low. When the criterion is high, this leads to a top-down hypothesis testing cycle (as described in Chapter 3). When real words were presented, representations of words could be accessed in associative memory and this information could be used to direct attention; but this could not occur with novel symbols (because no corresponding representations were stored in associative memory). Thus, the hypothesis-testing process could operate fully only with real words. The hypothesis-testing process would rely on the categorical property lookup subsystem, and hence we would expect the left frontal lobe to be activated selectively when actual words were presented in this experiment.

12. This is a common assumption in cognitive psychology; for example, see Townsend, 1974; Luce, 1986.

13. See Caramazza, Laudanna & Romani, 1988.

14. Gibson & Levin, 1975; Mason, 1975.

15. As usual, we assume that any given input matches many representations in the pattern activation subsystem. These representations presumably have a mutually inhibitory relation, so that only a single pattern is matched at any given time (cf. Kahneman, Treisman & Gibbs, 1991). In this case, we need only assume that, all else being equal, larger patterns inhibit smaller ones. Thus, if a whole-word pattern is stored, it will "win" and suppress letter-combination and individual letter representations, which also will match the input.

16. McClelland & Rumelhart, 1981.

17. Reicher, 1969; Wheeler, 1970.

18. For reviews, see Henderson, 1982; McClelland & Rumelhart, 1981.

19. Selfridge, 1959.

20. McClelland and Rumelhart's model was the first of a long series of similar neural network models of reading. Some of these models were developed to account for both normal and pathological reading. In most of these models, word identification occurs only after letters have been identified. However, as will be discussed, brain damage can sometimes impair the ability to read letters but spare the ability to read words; this fact throws a shadow on these types of models. Nevertheless, each of them typically contains at least one nugget, one important insight, and it is always interesting to reflect on the computational analyses that motivated the models. In most cases,

however, there have been only minimal computational analyses; intuition and an exploratory urge have often been the primary source of motivation for these models.

McClelland (1986) was concerned about the limitations imposed by a set of fixed windows (those German nouns can really cause a problem to such a system!). Thus, he developed a model that contains a *Connection Information Distributor* (CID). The connections among units are not fixed, but are programmed from a central network where knowledge about processing is represented. He posited a set of "programmable modules," each of which included a set of programmable letter units; these units combine to produce a series of 32 programmable four-letter word units.

This particular model did not work very well when it processed only a single word. It is interesting to note, however, that it made human-like errors when given two separate words at the same time. In this situation, it would migrate and transpose letters. These errors arose because the programmable modules contained information about each other and there was interference between them; letters from one word were replaced by letters from the other word in a pair.

CID was followed by a more elaborate model, the "Programmable Blackboard model of reading" (PABLO; see McClelland, 1986). The goal of this model was to mimic the way humans integrate information over successive fixations while reading. One novel feature of this model was an attentional mechanism that sequentially selected material (up to 20 characters) along a row of text. This mechanism was very much like the attention window we inferred in Chapter 3, and was posited for many of the same reasons. On each fixation, the focus of attention was on two different regions, the "center"—which consisted of several letter positions around the fixation point—and the "penumbra"—which consisted of additional positions further to the right. Letters from both the center and the penumbra were projected to corresponding letter units in the network, but letters from the penumbra produced weaker activation than letters from the center.

The computer model was tested with words, random strings of letters, and "pseudowords" (pronounceable strings of letters that could be a word, but don't happen to be). Mimicking human performance, the model read pseudowords better than random strings, because pseudowords often are similar to words—and hence receive some feedback from word representations. However, the model produced one finding that is strikingly different from that found with humans: It read long words better than short ones, because short words receive less feedback than long words.

21. Cf. Adams, 1979.

22. See McClelland, 1976, and Schacter, et al., 1990, which

appear immune to the criticisms levied by Henderson (1982) of other studies that support this view.

23. Adams, 1979; McClelland, 1976.

24. Some earlier accounts of the word superiority effect rest on the idea that stored information changes perceptual encoding by using feedback. There is something odd about these accounts, however. How does the system "know" which kind of feedback to use? The correct word representation must provide feedback, if feedback is to help; and hence, the information necessary to produce the right kind of feedback must already implicate the sought word. If this information is already in memory, why bother with the perceptual tuning?

A slightly different account of the word superiority effect is as follows:

(a) Most fragments may fit several letters quite well, and only a few fragments serve to distinguish among them.

(b) The better the unique fit of the input to a stored pattern, the greater the "activation" of that memory representation (see text).

(c) Because only certain letters can occur in each position if a word is to be spelled (e.g., "bk" can never occur at the beginning or end of a word in English), there will be a smaller number of words that will "almost fit" the pattern as a whole than there will be letters that will "almost fit" at each position taken separately.

(d) Thus, the correct word will be activated more than will individual letters in isolation (because of less inhibition from other representations; see text).

(e) Finally, the level of activation of a representation will begin to decay, once the stimulus is removed. By the time the subject is asked to respond, the initially lower level of activation for an individual letter may have totally decayed, whereas the initially higher activation of the entire word may ensure that some activation persists. If the word representation is still active, then the subject can report which letter must have been in a specific position—producing the word superiority effect (cf. Johnston & McClelland, 1980).

Additional experimentation is necessary to distinguish between this account, which rests in part on the time for activation to decay, and the slightly simpler one described in the text. Of course, there is no need for only one account to be correct; the system may operate in both ways.

25. Weisstein & Harris, 1974.

26. See also Biederman, 1972.

27. Mozer, 1987, 1991; see also Mozer & Behrmann, 1990.

28. Other computational models of reading have been developed that do not involve neural networks. For example, Just & Carpenter (1987) developed a model of reading that was based on the patterns of eye fixations people make during normal reading. According to this model, a sequential letter-by-letter encoding process takes place before any semantic knowledge about the word is accessed. Each time a letter is analyzed in a given position, a series of possible words that fits the pattern is activated. And with each additional letter, additional constraints are added and the number of potential candidates becomes smaller. Such processing also relies on constraint-satisfaction processes, and it is unclear how it ultimately differs from the processing performed by neural network models.

29. E.g., see McClelland, 1976; Pollatsek et al., 1975; Taylor, Miller & Juola, 1977.

30. E.g., see Larsen & Bundesen, 1978.

31. For information about the relation between word length and reading time, see Just & Carpenter, 1987.

32. See Just & Carpenter, 1987.

33. See Patterson, Marshall & Coltheart, 1985.

34. Cf. Just & Carpenter, 1987, p. 96.

35. Cf. Coltheart, 1978.

36. Cf. Henderson, 1982, pp. 122–124.

37. Cf. Coltheart, 1978; Friedman & Albert, 1985; Patterson, 1982.

38. E.g., see Pinker & Prince, 1988.

39. Cf. Baker & Smith, 1976; Baron, 1977; Brooks, 1978.

40. Pinker, 1991, develops a similar idea. Note that both processes would operate at the same time, and if an irregular representation is found, the other process is inhibited; there is no way to "know" in advance whether a word has an irregular spelling.

41. Seidenberg & McClelland, 1989.

42. Patterson, Seidenberg & McClelland, 1989.

43. See Backman, Bruck, Hébert & Seidenberg, 1984.

44. See Patterson, Marshall & Coltheart, 1985.

45. Velluntino, 1979.

46. Taraban & McClelland, 1987.

47. See Shepard, 1967; Standing, 1973; Standing, Conezio & Haber, 1970.

48. E.g., see Coltheart, 1980; Friedman & Albert, 1985; Henderson, 1982; Patterson, Marshall & Coltheart, 1985.

49. Unless otherwise noted, the following material is based on

discussions in Coltheart, 1980; Friedman & Albert, 1985; and Patterson, Marshall & Coltheart, 1985.

50. Hinshelwood, 1899.
51. See also Farah, 1990.
52. Marshall & Newcombe, 1973.
53. Friedman & Albert, 1985, p. 63.
54. See Karanth, 1981; Luria, 1980.
55. Cf. Luria, 1980.
56. Harries & Perrett, 1991; see also Andersen, Asanuma, Essick & Siegel, in press.
57. Beauvois & Derouesne, 1979.
58. Behrmann, Moscovitch, Black & Mozer, 1990.
59. See Behrmann, Moscovitch, Black & Mozer, 1990.
60. Caramazza & Hillis, 1990.
61. Calvanio, Petrone & Levine, 1987; Gazzaniga & Ladavas, 1987.
62. Hinton & Shallice, 1991.
63. See Kinsbourne & Warrington, 1963.
64. Just & Carpenter, 1987.
65. Bub, Black & Howell, 1989.
66. See Chapter 3; see also Bub, Black & Howell, 1989; Farah, 1990.
67. Bub, Black & Howell, 1989.
68. Geschwind, 1965.
69. See Geschwind, 1965.
70. For additional problems, see Friedman & Albert, 1985; see also Hécaen & Kremin, 1977.
71. Geschwind, 1965.
72. See Oxbury, Oxbury & Humphrey, 1969.
73. See Coltheart, 1980.
74. Hinton & Shallice, 1991.
75. Coltheart, 1980.
76. Zaidel, 1976, 1990, reports that the right hemispheres of split-brain patients can in fact comprehend abstract words if they occur as frequently in the language as concrete words. However, one could argue that his stimulus presentation technique (presenting words to one ear while the other was preoccupied) could have allowed both hemispheres to receive the input, and his response (pointing) might be controlled by both hemispheres. With these caveats in mind, it is of interest that Zaidel still found that the right hemisphere has more difficulty with function words (e.g., "of," "and," "or") than concrete words.
77. Plaut & Shallice, 1991.

78. Warrington, 1981.
79. Marshall & Newcombe, 1973.
80. See Deloche & Seron, 1982; Marshall & Newcombe, 1973; Patterson, Marshall & Coltheart, 1985; Shallice & Warrington, 1980.

6. LANGUAGE

1. Levelt, 1989.
2. Neisser, 1967.
3. For a review, see Shepherd, 1988.
4. See Suga, 1978.
5. Romani, Williamson & Kaufman, 1982.
6. Bregman, 1990.
7. See Norman, 1970.
8. Jay & Sparks, 1984.
9. Petersen et al., 1988.
10. Compare the results for words reported by Petersen, Fox, Snyder & Raichle, 1990, with their findings for nonwords and the findings for nonspeech stimuli reported by Lauter, Herscovitch, Formby & Raichle, 1985, and Mazziotta, Phelps, Carson & Kuhl, 1982.
11. Ulrich, 1978.
12. Heffner & Heffner, 1984.
13. Felleman & Van Essen, 1991; Van Essen, 1985.
14. Jakobson & Halle, 1956.
15. See Liberman, Cooper, Shankweiler & Studdert-Kennedy, 1967.
16. E.g, Eimas, Sigueland, Jusczyk & Vigorito, 1971; Eimas, Miller & Jusczyk, 1987.
17. Strange & Jenkins, 1978.
18. Kuhl & Miller, 1978.
19. Cf. Pisoni, 1973.
20. Morse & Snowdon, 1975.
21. Foss & Swinney, 1973; Savin & Bever, 1970.
22. Posner, Petersen, Fox & Raichle, 1988.
23. E.g., Shallice, 1981.
24. Petersen et al., 1988.
25. As does Squire, 1987.
26. For further discussion on this topic, see Austin, 1962.
27. But information in memory is not all there is to meaning. For example, Putnam (1975) argued that part of the meaning of the word "water" is embedded in the nature of the substance itself. If natives of another planet used the word to refer to a substance with a different

chemical formula, the word would mean something different even if they had the same information in associative memory that we do. The present claim is not that meaning consists merely of information in memory, but rather that the psychological representation of meaning *depends* on it: No information in associative memory, no psychological representation of meaning.

28. Warrington & Shallice, 1984.

29. Warrington & McCarthy, 1983.

30. E.g., see Sidtis et al., 1981. Unless otherwise noted, all references to left and right hemispheres will apply to right-handed people.

31. E.g., see Code (1987) for evidence that the right hemisphere has difficulty using grammar, and Koenig, Wetzel & Caramazza (in press) for evidence that the right hemisphere does not decompose meaning into its simpler constituents.

32. E.g., Hecaen & Albert, 1978.

33. Petersen, Fox, Snyder & Raichle, 1990.

34. E.g., see Galaburda, 1984; Geschwind & Levitsky, 1968; Nieuwenhuys, Voogd & van Huijzen, 1988.

35. See Geschwind, 1972.

36. Warren, 1970.

37. Ganong, 1980.

38. Warren, 1970.

39. A critical distinction exists between the role of the category lookup subsystem in vision and audition. In vision, when more information is needed, the stimulus typically is still present, and one simply takes a second look. In contrast, in audition, the stimulus typically is present only fleetingly, and it lingers only briefly in the auditory buffer (except perhaps in music, when a note is sustained for a long time—but that does not bear on speech perception). Hence the top-down search process is more limited in audition than in vision.

40. Andersen, 1987; Hyvarinen, 1982.

41. Mumford, 1991; Kelly, 1985.

42. McClelland & Elman, 1986.

43. McClelland & Rumelhart, 1981.

44. Most of the principles that underlie the operation of this model can be traced to Miller & Isard, 1963.

45. McClelland & Elman, 1986.

46. Marslen-Wilson & Welch, 1978.

47. See Liberman, Cooper, Shankweiler & Studdert-Kennedy, 1967.

48. Cf. MacDonald, Carpenter & Just, in press.

49. Chomsky, 1957.

50. Lashley, 1951.

51. See Lashley, 1951.

52. Cf. Chomsky, 1957, 1965.

53. Selkirk, 1988.

54. Swinney & Cutler, 1979.

55. E.g., Brownell, Potter, Michelow & Gardner, 1984.

56. See Winner & Gardner, 1977.

57. Brownell, Michelow, Powelson, & Gardner, 1983.

58. Right-hemisphere damage also impairs the ability to identify a person by his or her voice and to interpret the emotional content of a speaker's voice (see Ellis & Young, 1988; Ross & Mesulam, 1979). Although this disruption in prosody may affect the ability to comprehend spoken metaphors or jokes, it probably is not a necessary part of the deficit: These patients also have trouble understanding written nonliteral language.

59. E.g., see Halle, 1990; Rosenbaum, 1991.

60. See MacNeilage, 1970.

61. Alexander, Benson & Stuss, 1989. See also Friston, Frith, Liddle & Frackowiak (1991) for a novel PET methodology that provided convergent evidence. These findings also showed that the left dorsolateral prefrontal cortex may regulate activity in the superior temporal lobes, which is consistent with the idea that top-down processing modulates processing in the auditory pattern activation subsystem.

62. Kimura & Watson, 1989.

63. Petersen et al., 1988.

64. In addition, several studies that have used the ^{133}Xe regional cerebral blood flow (rCBF) technique report results that may be relevant here. These results suggest that producing words leads to higher activity in the left cerebral hemisphere than in the right cerebral hemisphere. For example, Gur & Reivich, 1980, tested 36 right-handed men engaged in solving verbal analogies (from the Miller Analogies Test). The subjects spoke aloud while performing the task. Gur & Reivich compared the brain activity during the verbal task to the brain activity at rest (the subjects were relaxed with their eyes open). The researchers observed a larger increase in left-hemisphere activity than in right-hemisphere activity in 32 of the 36 subjects (see also Gur et al., 1988).

The problem with this and similar studies, however, is that the tasks are very complex, and it is not clear what aspect or aspects of processing underlie the results. The verbal analogies task required understanding the words, abstracting metaphorical interpretations, comparing different interpretations, and so forth, as well as speaking aloud. In addition, compared to PET techniques, these results do not provide good anatomical localization of activity. Reviews of these studies are provided by Ingvar, 1983, and Raichle, 1987.

65. Wise & Strick, 1984.

66. See MacLean, 1987.

67. Deacon, 1989.

68. Deacon, 1989; see also Galaburda, 1984.

69. Ojemann, 1983; Ojemann, Ojemann, Lettich & Berger, 1989.

70. Ojemann, Ojemann, Lettich & Berger, 1989.

71. The Wada test is dangerous and so is administered—with extreme caution—only when required for medical reasons; one major source of risk is that the injection can shake loose small pieces of plaque that adhere to the artery walls, which can be carried up into the brain and become lodged in the vessels, causing strokes.

72. Jones, 1966.

73. Caplan, in press.

74. For additional discussion, see Lecoeurs, Basso, Moraschini & Nespoulous, 1984.

75. E.g., see Kosslyn, McPeek, Daly, Alpert & Caviness, 1991. See also von Monakow, 1969.

76. Cf. Dennis & Whitaker, 1976; Ogden, 1988; but see also Curtiss, 1989. Also see Geschwind, 1965, for discussion of the importance of input/output connections.

77. See Rosenbaum, 1991.

78. Petersen et al., 1988.

79. For more about Dr. Spooner, see Potter, 1980.

80. Sternberg, Monsell, Knoll & Wright, 1978.

81. Lashley, 1951.

82. Dell, 1988; see also Dell, 1985, 1986.

83. Dell, 1988.

84. Wallesch, Henriksen, Kornhuber & Paulson, 1985.

85. Cf. Kimura, 1986.

86. Geschwind, 1972.

87. Many of the PET studies do not implicate the posterior temporal lobe when meaning presumably is extracted. As noted in note 7 of Chapter 5, we must be cautious about interpreting such negative findings.

88. Cf. Chomsky, 1957. This claim is not hyperbolic; the fact that adverbs can be repeated an infinite number of times, such as in "very, very, very happy," in and of itself guarantees that an infinite number of different sentences can be formed.

89. Cf. Bresnan, 1978; Fillmore, 1968.

90. Cf. Fillmore, 1968; Grimshaw, 1979. However, we must

acknowledge that some sort of representation of rules probably is also necessary to explain the generativity of language. Indeed, Bresnan, 1978, includes a representation of rules in addition to the information associated with individual words, and Pinker and Prince, 1988, make a good case that representations of rules are used in some types of language. In any event, because the brain physically is a network of neurons, at some level of analysis a network must be capable of carrying out all of our cognitive abilities. However, this observation does not imply that the best way to describe how the brain produces all kinds of behavior is necessarily in terms of network models of the sort we described in Chapter 2.

91. Feldman, 1985.

92. Cf. Caramazza, 1984.

93. Table 6.1 is intended merely as an overview of some key features of the syndromes; other behaviors have also been used to characterize each of them.

94. Caramazza, 1986; see also Zurif, Gardner & Brownell, 1989, for additional complexities.

95. Zurif & Caramazza, 1976.

96. Auerbach et al., 1982; see also Divenyi & Robinson, 1989.

97. See Ellis & Young, 1988.

98. Brownell et al., 1990; Brownell, Potter, Michelow & Gardner, 1984; for a review, see Caplan, in press.

99. See Danly & Shapiro, 1982; for a review, see Caplan, in press.

100. Goodglass & Berko, 1960; Zurif & Caramazza, 1976. See also Linebarger, Schwartz & Saffran, 1983, for a criticism of this characterization.

101. For a review, see Caplan & Hildebrandt, 1988.

102. E.g., Berndt, 1987.

103. See Ellis & Young, 1988.

104. E.g., see Clarke & O'Malley, 1968; Harrington, 1987.

105. Kay & Ellis, 1987.

106. E.g., by Butterworth, 1985, and Ellis & Young, 1988.

107. See Ellis & Young, 1988.

108. Ellis, Miller & Sin, 1983.

109. See Kinsbourne & Warrington, 1983.

110. McCarthy & Warrington, 1984; Beauvois, Dérousné & Bastard, 1980, cited in Ellis & Young, 1988.

111. E.g., Monrad-Krohn, 1947.

112. E.g., see Bickerton, 1990; Pinker, 1984.

113. Pinker, 1991, makes a good case that irregular (memorized) verbs are converted to the past tense by an input/output mapping of the sort performed by network models, and that regular verbs are converted using a set of rules. It remains to be seen, however, whether such

rules can be represented and processed by the types of network models discussed in Chapter 2.

7. MOVEMENT

1. Rosenbaum, 1991.
2. Cf. Abbs, 1986.
3. At first glance, one might argue that the distinction between two ways of generating instructions warrants the inference that two distinct subsystems are used. However, we only hypothesize distinct subsystems when the input/output functions are qualitatively distinct. In this case, we will argue that the same computation is used in both processes, as is discussed shortly.
4. Abbs & Gracco, 1983.
5. For reviews of these and other relevant findings, see Jeannerod, 1988; Rosenbaum, 1991; Rothwell, 1987.
6. Cf. Marr, 1982.
7. See Abend, Bizzi & Morasso, 1982; Hollerbach, 1990a; Hollerbach & Atkeson, 1987; Kaminski & Gentile, 1986; Rosenbaum, 1991; Viviani & Terzuolo, 1983.
8. See Hollerbach, 1990a.
9. This example was inspired by Michael Jordan.
10. See Soechting & Lacquaniti, 1983.
11. Morasso, 1981.
12. Although we believe that the evidence is strongly in favor of this conclusion, the reader should be warned that this view is not universally held (see Rosenbaum, 1991, for reviews). If one is willing to make various assumptions about the way sequences of joint angles are controlled, it is possible to show that a joint angle representation can mimic a coordinate representation. Using the principle of parsimony, we will adopt the simpler account for the phenomena and laboratory findings.
13. Georgopoulos, Kalaska, Caminiti & Massey, 1982; Georgopoulos, Schwartz & Kettner, 1986.
14. Kawato, Maeda, Uno & Suzuki, 1990; Kawato, 1991.
15. This idea appears to have originated with Jordan; see, for example, Jordan, 1990.
16. Kawato, Maeda, Uno & Suzuki, 1990.
17. Jordan, 1990.
18. Jordan, 1989, 1990.
19. Bullock & Grossberg, 1988.
20. See Rosenbaum, 1991, pp. 382–386, for a good summary.
21. See Georgopoulos, Kalaska, Caminiti & Massey, 1982.
22. We do not mean to denigrate the importance of biomechani-

cal aspects of motion in movement control. The effects of gravity, properties of pendulums, and the like clearly are exploited in motor programming. Indeed, by taking advantage of these characteristics the amount of computation necessary to produce a trajectory is dramatically reduced (e.g., see Saltzman & Kelso, 1987). We assume that these biomechanical properties are built into the network that corresponds to the instructions generation subsystem in the same way that a "smoothness performance index" or the like must be built in.

23. E.g., for reviews of relevant findings, see Rosenbaum, 1991.

24. Logan, 1982; see also Long, 1976; Rabbitt, 1978.

25. Moran & Desimone, 1985.

26. See Rosenbaum, 1991.

27. Cf. Wiesendanger, 1987.

28. For a review of these and related findings, see Rosenbaum, 1991.

29. Roland, Larsen, Lassen & Skinhoj, 1980.

30. See Passingham, 1986.

31. Watson, Fleet, Gonzalez-Rothi & Heilman, 1986.

32. Weinrich & Wise, 1982.

33. Wiesendanger, 1981.

34. Roland et al., 1982. For additional convergent evidence for the role of various cortical areas in motor control, using a novel and highly sophisticated way of analyzing patterns of electrical activity on the scalp, see Gevins et al., 1987.

35. DeLong et al., 1984; for a somewhat different treatment, see Kandel & Schwartz, 1985.

36. Iansek & Porter, 1980.

37. Penfield & Rasmussen, 1950.

38. Asanuma, 1981; Evarts, 1967.

39. See Ito, 1984; Llinas, 1981.

40. Cf. Marsden, Merton & Morton, 1977.

41. Ivry, Keele & Diener, 1988.

42. Lashley, 1951.

43. Cf. Hollerbach, 1990b.

44. See Shepherd, 1988.

45. It was originally proposed that the feedback mechanism operated as follows: A spindle (intrafusal fiber) is set to a reference value by a *gamma motor neuron;* the cell body of a gamma motor neuron is located in the spinal cord. A perturbation stimulates the spindle, which sends a signal to the spinal cord that is proportional to the amount it is perturbed. An *alpha motor neuron* (whose body is also located in the spinal cord) is then activated, which sends a command to the extrafusal fiber that compensates for the perturbation.

This mechanism leads us to predict that the gamma motor neuron should be activated before the alpha motor neuron. However, it is now known that both motor neurons fire at the same time (Vallbo, 1970; see also Hollerbach, 1990b, p. 177). Thus, it is unlikely that this mechanism is used even for very fast, reflexive corrections. The fact that the alpha motor neuron is activated as soon as a perturbation is detected is consistent with the notion that many of the control processes in the brain are carried out by inhibition; we assume that these brain control processes can reach down and also affect the alpha neurons in the spinal cord. That is, if all of the alpha motor neurons in affected areas are "turned on reflexively," they presumably will cancel each other out and the limb will not move; however, if some of them are then inhibited (via cortical processes) while others remain active, a compensatory movement will occur. We assume that the instructions generation subsystem computes the necessary inhibition, after receiving input about the perturbation from the movement monitoring subsystem.

Thus, it is worth noting that this feedback control mechanism is probably most useful when one is composing movements in a novel way, and hence is moving relatively slowly. One hundred milliseconds is probably too long for such feedback to help guide relatively fast movements; by the time the compensation was computed, the limb would be in a different position and the compensation would no longer be relevant. Therefore, we expect fast movements not to depend on feedback, as will be discussed shortly.

46. See Shepherd, 1988.

47. Asanuma, 1981.

48. Rabbitt, 1978.

49. E.g., see Mountcastle et al., 1975.

50. Gnadt & Andersen, 1988.

51. For a review of properties of such neurons, see Andersen, 1987.

52. See also Held, 1965.

53. Thus, movements are produced by a combination of *feedforward* and *feedback* control mechanisms (see Hollerbach, 1990a, 1990b). Feedforward control is provided by the instructions generation subsystem, which essentially "predicts" which movement instructions will move the muscles appropriately to reach the target position. To do so, the instructions generation subsystem takes into account information in motor memory when computing a trajectory. Feedback control is based on signals that register the errors between the actual and the intended position of a body segment during a movement. Comparing the state of the body segment with the intended state is especially critical when a perturbation occurs. In this case, feedforward

control alone would result in an inappropriate movement. Thus, the most powerful control mechanisms make use of both feedforward and feedback (c.f. An, Atkeson, & Hollerbach, 1988).

54. Fisk & Goodale, 1988.

55. E.g., see Woodworth, 1899; see Rosenbaum, 1991, pp. 205–223, for a review.

56. Cf. Gould & Lewontin, 1979.

57. E.g., Caramazza & Miceli, 1991.

58. See Goodman & Caramazza, 1986; Kinsbourne & Rosenfield, 1974.

59. Cf. Caramazza, Miceli, Villa & Romani, 1987; Ellis & Young, 1988; Shallice, 1988.

60. E.g., see Bub & Kertesz, 1982; Shallice, 1981.

61. The fact that a movement has become automatic does not imply that feedback cannot affect it—only that feedback is not necessary and typically is not used. For example, it is possible to delay one's speech electronically, so that it reaches one's ears a short time after it is spoken. This sort of feedback makes it almost impossible to speak clearly. In normal circumstances, there is no correction signal and the system operates automatically. But when a correction signal is introduced (e.g., by inserting a delay that mismatches the output instructions and feedback), the instructions generation subsystem tries to use it—and leads one to falter, if in fact it was fooled by the wonders of modern technology.

In addition, we must note that there is yet another sense in which movements can become automatic: Some stored representations are paired with instructions for the coordinate property lookup subsystems, so that the associated movement is carried out when the representation is activated. This sort of "bottom up" activation is automatic in the sense that the coordinate property lookup subsystem is not searching for such information initially, but rather responds reflexively to input from associative memory.

62. Polit & Bizzi, 1978; see also Bizzi & Mussa-Ivaldi, 1990.

63. Bernstein, 1967.

64. Arutyunyan, Gurfinkel & Mirskii, 1968.

65. E.g., compare Hecaen & Albert, 1978; Heilman & Rothi, 1985; Luria, 1980; Williams, 1970.

66. Williams, 1970, p. 93.

67. See Heilman & Rothi, 1985.

68. See Hecaen & Albert, 1978, pp. 97ff.

69. See Heilman, 1973.

70. Liepmann, 1905; see also Freeman, 1984; Rosenbaum, 1991.

71. Goodglass & Kaplan, 1963.

72. Critchley, 1953; Warrington, 1969.
73. Cf. Benton, 1962, 1969.
74. See Paterson & Zangwill, 1944.
75. Kirk & Kertesz, 1989.
76. Milberg, Hebben & Kaplan, 1986.
77. Williams, 1970.
78. Poeck & Kerschensteiner, 1975.
79. See Heilman, 1973.
80. De Renzi, Faglioni & Sorgato, 1982.
81. E.g., Wood, 1978.
82. Unless otherwise noted, the following material was drawn primarily from Marcie & Hecaen, 1979, and Roeltgen, 1985.
83. Roeltgen, 1985, p. 86.
84. Watson & Heilman, 1983.
85. See Roeltgen, 1985.
86. Roeltgen & Heilman, 1985.
87. See Farah, 1984.
88. Roeltgen & Heilman, 1986.
89. Bub & Kertesz, 1982.
90. E.g., Kosslyn, McPeek, Daly, Alpert, & Caviness, 1991.

8. MEMORY

1. The elements of propositional representations are not words per se; presumably, animals can employ propositional representations, and the same propositional representation may correspond to more than one word (synonyms; see page 266). Kosslyn, 1984, discusses the concept of propositional representation in more detail.
2. Cf. Squire, 1987.
3. Mishkin, 1978; Mishkin & Appenzeller, 1987.
4. Squire, in press.
5. Squire, in press.
6. Kandel & Schwartz, 1985; Reiman, Fusselman, Fox & Raichle, 1989; see also Raichle, 1990; Shepherd, 1988.
7. Amaral, 1987.
8. Squire, in press. As complicated as this sounds, there are even more connections to and from the hippocampus; further details on this and the other neuroanatomical facts reviewed in this chapter can be found in Amaral, 1987; Nieuwenhuys, Voogd & van Huijzen, 1988; see also Squire, in press.
9. Mishkin & Appenzeller, 1987; Squire, 1987, in press.
10. Fibers from the entorhinal cortex enter the hippocampus (*perforant fibers*) and terminate in an area called the *dentate fascia,* where they make connections with *dentate granule cells.* The dentate

granule cells project to *pyramidal cells* via short axons called the *mossy fibers*. These pyramidal cells send projections that ultimately exit the hippocampus.

The connections within the hippocampus form three distinct pathways, which constitute a circuit. All of these connections within the hippocampus, as well as the inputs to the hippocampus, are excitatory. In contrast, local interneurons (which are interposed between two or more other neurons) in the hippocampus have inhibitory connections. An interesting characteristic of the architecture of the hippocampus is that this circuit is repeated many times, forming a series of lamellae where similar neural processes can take place (for additional detail, see Amaral, 1987).

It is worth noting that Cotman and McGaugh, 1980, found that a lesion in the enthorinal cortex results in the destruction of perforant fibers in the same, ipsilateral side. Thus, synapses of perforant fibers on granule cells are lost. However, a few weeks later, new synapses appear on the dendrites of granule cells. These new synapses originate principally from the enthorinal cortex in the other cerebral hemisphere and the septal nucleus, and take over the now-vacated sites. These phenomena are referred to as "sprouting" and "migration," and may play a role in the memory formation process.

11. See Zola-Morgan & Squire, 1985a.

12. LaBerge & Buchsbaum 1990; Posner, 1988; Posner & Petersen, 1990; Rafal & Posner, 1987.

13. Mishkin & Appenzeller, 1987.

14. E.g., Mishkin & Appenzeller, 1987; Mishkin, Malamut & Bachevalier, 1984.

15. See Kandel & Schwartz, 1985, p. 524; for a slightly different treatment, see Nieuwenhuys, Voogd & van Huijzen, 1988.

16. E.g., Goldman-Rakic, 1987.

17. E.g., Felleman & Van Essen, 1991.

18. Cf. Hebb, 1949.

19. Stevens, 1979, p. 15.

20. See Squire, 1991.

21. For overviews, see Kandel & Schwartz, 1985; Shepherd, 1988.

22. Ramon y Cajal, 1888.

23. Bliss & Lømo, 1973.

24. See Tyler, Perkins & Harris, 1989.

25. See Mayer, Westbrook & Guthrie, 1984.

26. For additional details, see Bliss & Lynch, 1988; Lynch & Baudry, 1984; Malinow & Tsien, 1990; Shepherd, 1988; Stevens, 1989.

27. Tyler, Perkins & Harris, 1989.

28. Hebb, 1949.

29. See Mishkin & Appenzeller, 1987; Mishkin, Malamut & Bachevalier, 1984; Squire, in press.

30. E.g., see Sterelny, 1990.

31. See Valiant, 1988.

32. E.g., De Renzi, 1982; Squire, 1987.

33. Squire, 1987, in press.

34. Cf. Anderson & Bower, 1973; Damasio, 1990a, 1990b.

35. Mishkin & Appenzeller, 1987.

36. Mishkin & Appenzeller, 1987.

37. Mishkin & Appenzeller, 1987.

38. Mishkin, 1978; Mishkin & Appenzeller, 1987.

39. E.g., Mishkin, 1978; Zola-Morgan & Squire, 1985b.

40. Clower, Zola-Morgan & Squire, 1990.

41. For an excellent review of the issue and data, see Squire, in press.

42. Mishkin & Appenzeller, 1987; Mishkin, Malamut & Bachevalier, 1984.

43. Cf. Damasio, 1990a, 1990b; Squire, 1987. Note that if the to-be-distinguished objects can be easily discriminated from one another, then specific details will not need to be encoded into memory. In this case, information needs to be stored only in the ventral system and associative memory. However, if details must be encoded to distinguish the objects, then the dorsal system would be used to specify their spatial relations and the print-now and weight adjustment subsystems would conjoin these spatial representations with representations of the parts themselves.

44. Parkinson & Mishkin, 1982.

45. Again, the "place holders" may specify the structure of an object, including locations of its parts.

46. Harries & Perrett, 1991.

47. See Crick & Koch, 1990; Gray, Engel, König & Singer, 1990; Gray & Singer, 1989; Mumford, 1991; Von der Malsburgh & Schneider, 1986.

48. E.g., Hummel & Biederman, in press; this use of oscillation is said to solve the *binding problem:* the problem of how to coordinate separate representations that are computed by distinct processes in the system. See also Crick & Koch, 1990; Damasio, 1989; Von der Malsburgh & Schneider, 1986.

49. See Mishkin & Appenzeller, 1987; Squire, in press.

50. Morris, Hagan & Rawlins, 1986; Sutherland, Whishaw & Kolb, 1983.

51. Parkinson & Mishkin, 1982.

52. Smith & Milner, 1981.

53. Cf. O'Keefe & Nadel, 1978.

54. Morris, Anderson, Lynch & Baudry, 1986; Morris, Halliwell & Bowery, 1989.

55. Morris, Anderson, Lynch & Baudry, 1986.

56. Morris, Anderson, Lynch & Baudry, 1986.

57. See Squire & Cave, in press.

58. As implied by results reviewed in Mishkin & Appenzeller, 1987.

59. E.g., Sutherland, McDonald, Hill & Rudy, 1989.

60. Cave & Squire, 1991.

61. Cave & Squire, 1991.

62. Rosch, 1978; for reviews, see Cordier, 1980; Smith & Medin, 1981.

63. E.g., see Hinton & Anderson, 1981; Rumelhart & McClelland, 1986.

64. McClelland & Rumelhart, 1985, 1986.

65. McClelland & Rumelhart, 1986.

66. E.g., varying the "momentum" of the learning process or adding a separate set of "fast" weights; see Hinton & Plaut, 1986.

67. Cf. Atkinson & Shiffrin, 1968.

68. Cf. Craik & Lockhart, 1972.

69. See Miller, 1956.

70. See Bower, 1972; Paivio, 1971; Yates, 1966.

71. Cf. Tulving & Thompson, 1973.

72. Paivio, 1971.

73. For many related and similar observations, see Anderson & Bower, 1973; Baddeley, 1986.

74. This form of implicit memory, which we call *perceptual tuning*, should depend on the memory formation subsystems; thus, it should be distinguished from other forms of implicit memory that do not.

75. See Graf & Schacter, 1985.

76. E.g., see Milner, Corkin & Teuber, 1968; Warrington & Weiskrantz, 1968, for work with brain-damaged patients, and Winograd, 1975, for work in artificial intelligence.

77. See Squire, 1987.

78. Cf. Tulving & Schacter, 1990.

79. These drugs operate by blocking specific neurotransmitters. For example, there are two types of cholinergic synapses (i.e., nicotinic and muscarinic), which differ in the substance that blocks them (i.e., nicotine or muscarine, respectively). Nicotinic cholinergic synapses are typical at the neuromuscular junction, where synaptic action must be fast; in contrast, muscarinic cholinergic synapses, which are slower, can be found in various regions of the body (e.g., at the junction between motor nerves and glands, autonomic ganglia, smooth muscles, cardiac

muscles, and in various regions of the central nervous system). Other substances can also block the transmission of neurotransmitters (e.g., scopolamine at muscarinic cholinergic synapses).

80. Knopman & Nissen, 1987; Nissen, Knopman & Schacter, 1987. However, this finding must be distinguished from so-called *state dependent learning:* If one learns material in a specific state, one subsequently will recall it better in the same state—provided that the state itself does not impair memory. For example, if one was *slightly* inebriated or fatigued when one learned a new song, it will come back to one more easily when one later is in the same condition. This effect probably reflects the role of context in indexing memories; when the context is the same, there are more cues for retrieving the stored information, as was discussed earlier. For a discussion of state dependent learning, see Bower, 1983; Ellis & Ashbrook, 1989.

81. Graf & Mandler, 1984; Schacter & Graf, 1986.

82. See Tulving & Schacter, 1990.

83. Khilstrom et al., 1990.

84. Roediger & Blaxton, 1987.

85. See also Graf, Shimamura & Squire, 1985.

86. Tulving & Schacter, 1990.

87. Schacter, Cooper & Delaney, 1990.

88. Marsolek, Kosslyn & Squire, in press.

89. Graf & Schacter, 1985.

90. Graf & Schacter, 1985; see also Schacter & Graf, 1989.

91. Cf. Shimamura & Squire, 1989.

92. This distinction between associations among representations within associative memory and associations among representations in associative memory and those in perceptual subsystems dovetails with our earlier discussion of the representation of meaning. Recall that in Chapter 6 we distinguished between two aspects of the representation of meaning, sense and reference. Links between entries in associative memory are a critical part of the representation of sense, whereas pointers to representations in a pattern activation or spatial relations encoding subsystem are a critical part of some types of reference.

93. Cf. Bower, 1972; this observation has also been made by Kosslyn, but not published.

94. Mishkin & Appenzeller, 1987; Mishkin, Malamut & Bachevalier, 1984.

95. The radical behaviorists, who dominated much of experimental psychology during the first half of this century, eschewed all attempts to characterize internal processes. Their goal was to understand behavior by specifying stimulus-response associations (e.g., see Skinner, 1974; Watson, 1913). Thus, it is somewhat ironic that behav-

iorism not only provided many tools that have proven useful in cognitive neuroscience, particularly various ways of training animals, but also provided the conceptual basis for the "stimulus-response connection subsystem." The advent of neural network models, which are understood in terms of input/output mappings, paved the way for integrating key concepts in behaviorism with those developed in cognitive psychology, artificial intelligence, and neuroscience. This development was particularly smooth because some behaviorists (such as Herrnstein, 1977) were thinking about behavior in sophisticated ways that opened the way for theories of internal processing.

96. Mishkin & Appenzeller, 1987; Mishkin, Malamut & Bachevalier, 1984.

97. Cohen & Squire, 1980.

98. Cf. Kolers, 1983.

99. Cohen & Squire, 1980.

100. Cohen & Squire, 1980.

101. The idea of the viewpoint consistency contraint was introduced by Lowe, 1987b, and evidence for its psychological validity has recently been found by C. Cave and Kosslyn. For reviews of the literature on the perception and memory of left/right orientation, see Corballis & Beale, 1976, and Kosslyn, Dror, Park & Clegg, in preparation.

102. Cohen & Squire, 1980.

103. See also Musen, Shimamura & Squire, 1990.

104. Morris, Halliwell & Bowery, 1989.

105. E.g., see Hawkins & Kandel, 1984; Kandel, 1989.

106. Carew, Walters & Kandel, 1981.

107. See Hawkins & Kandel, 1984.

108. Cf. Baddeley, 1986.

109. See Miller, 1956.

110. Baddeley, 1986.

111. Goldman-Rakic, 1987, 1988.

112. See Kosslyn, 1991.

113. For an extensive description of the case, see Squire, 1987.

114. Squire et al., 1989.

115. For more information, see Squire, 1987.

116. For a review, see Squire, in press.

117. See Squire, 1987.

118. See Scoville & Milner, 1957.

119. Koenig & Gabrieli, submitted.

120. Baddeley & Warrington, 1970.

121. For additional discussion of such matters, see, for example, Norman, 1976.

122. Milner, Corkin & Teuber, 1968; Warrington & Weiskrantz, 1968.

123. See Graf, Shimamura & Squire, 1985; Graf, Squire & Mandler, 1984; Squire, Shimamura & Graf, 1987; Warrington & Weiskrantz, 1970.

124. Graf, Shimamura & Squire, 1985.

125. Milner, 1962.

126. Cohen & Squire, 1980.

127. Gabrieli, 1986; Heindel, Salmon, Shults, Walicke & Butters, 1989; Salmon, Shimamura, Butters & Smith, 1988; Shimamura, Salmon, Squire & Butters, 1987.

128. Gabrieli, 1986; Heindel, Butters & Salmon, 1988; Heindel, Salmon & Butters, 1991.

129. Martone et al., 1984.

130. For a review, see Moss & Albert, 1988.

131. See Baddeley, Papagno & Vallar, 1988.

132. Basso, Spinnler, Vallar & Zanobio, 1982. See also Baddeley & Wilson's, 1988, report of patient T.B.

133. Schacter, Harbluk & McLachlan, 1984; Shimamura & Squire, 1987.

134. See Janowsky, Shimamura, Kritchevsky & Squire, 1989; Schacter, Harbluk & McLachlan, 1984; Shimamura & Squire, 1987.

135. Shimamura & Squire, 1991.

136. E.g., Jetter, Poser, Freeman & Markowitsch, 1986.

137. Goldman-Rakic, 1987, 1988.

9. GRAY MATTERS

1. Many of these ideas about decision making were developed in discussions of the John D. and Catherine T. MacArthur Foundation Mind-Body Network, which includes J. Allan Hobson, Mardi Horowitz, Kenneth Hugdahl, Arthur Kleinman, Stephen Kosslyn, Robert Rose, and David Spiegel.

2. In a limited way the run subsystem acts like the central processing unit (CPU) of a computer. The CPU shunts information from memory to appropriate "registers" and special-purpose processors. This relation may not be coincidental. John von Neumann, 1958, the father of the modern computer, explicitly considered properties of the brain when designing the computer. As noted in Chapter 2, however, von Neumann did not incorporate many other features of the brain in his design.

3. Piaget, 1954.

4. See Diamond, 1988; Diamond & Doar, 1989; Diamond & Goldman-Rakic, 1989.

5. See Diamond, 1988, for a review of these findings.

6. See Diamond, Zola-Morgan & Squire, 1989.

7. Diamond, 1988.

8. E.g., Petrides & Milner, 1982; Shimamura, Janowsky & Squire, 1990.

9. Diamond, 1988.

10. Dehaene & Changeux, 1989.

11. Yakovlev & Lecours, 1967.

12. It is intriguing that time and space are often tied together in our language. When asked how far something is, the reply is often a measure of time (e.g., "20 minutes"); when asked how much time something required, the reply often notes its "length" (cf. Jackendoff & Landau, in press). It is possible that the spatial relations encoding subsystems themselves play some role in encoding temporal relations.

13. Berg, 1948.

14. E.g., see Milner, 1962; Janowsky, Shimamura, Kritchevsky & Squire, 1989.

15. The evolutionary argument can be made only indirectly, however, based on the prevalance of associative mechanisms in animals; e.g., see Schwartz, 1978.

16. See Kolb & Whishaw, 1990; Eccles, 1989.

17. Dehaene & Changeux, 1991.

18. Stroop, 1935.

19. Morton & Chambers, 1973.

20. Perret, 1974.

21. Koenig, 1989.

22. See O'Leary, 1990; Yakovlev & Lecours, 1967.

23. See Cohen, Dunbar & McClelland, 1990.

24. Calculation processes also often require shifting from one notational system to another. This ability, referred to as *transcoding,* is needed to transform "325" into "three hundred and twenty five" and vice versa. This ability rests on the ability to produce and comprehend Arabic and verbal numbers and to use related lexical and syntactic processes. Although these abilities have been intensively studied (e.g., Cohen & Dehaene, 1991; McCloskey & Caramazza, 1987; McCloskey, Sokol & Goodman, 1986; Deloche & Seron, 1982a, 1982b, 1987; Temple, 1989), we shall not consider them here; they are closely related to the processes we discussed in Chapters 5 and 6 that underlie reading and language.

25. See Barbizet, 1970.

26. See Siegler, 1987; for a discussion of the importance of

number format, see Cornet, Seron, Deloche & Lories, 1988; Gonzalez & Kolers, 1987.

27. See Johnson-Laird, 1983.

28. Hayes, 1973.

29. Dehaene & Cohen, 1991.

30. Moyer & Landauer, 1967, 1973; see also Moyer, 1973.

31. See Caramazza & McCloskey, 1987; Deloche & Seron, 1987; McCarthy & Warrington, 1990; McCloskey & Caramazza, 1987; Seron & Deloche, 1987; Warrington, 1982.

32. Hécaen, Angelergues & Houillier, 1961.

33. See McCloskey & Caramazza, 1987.

34. See Benton, 1987; Grafman, Passafiume, Faglioni & Boller, 1982; McCarthy & Warrington, 1990; Warrington, 1982; Warrington, James & Maciejewski, 1986.

35. Gazzaniga, 1985, 1989.

36. Gur et al., 1980.

37. E.g., see Bradshaw & Nettleton, 1983; Bryden, 1982; Kitterle, 1991; Springer & Deutsch, 1981.

38. E.g., for discussions of this problem, see De Renzi, 1982; De Renzi & Faglioni, 1967; Kosslyn, 1987; Springer & Deutsch, 1981; White, 1969.

39. Cf. Efron, 1991; Hardyck, 1983.

40. Cf. Kim & Levine, 1991.

41. E.g., see Bradshaw & Nettleton, 1983; Harrington, 1987; Springer & Deutsch, 1981.

42. E.g., see Marshall, 1981.

43. See Tversky & Kahneman, 1971, for a discussion of the "law of small numbers."

44. Kosslyn, Sokolov & Chen, 1989.

45. See Milner & Rasmussen, 1966; Rasmussen & Milner, 1977.

46. See Dennis & Kohn, 1975; Dennis & Whitaker, 1976; Ogden, 1988; but also see Curtiss, 1989.

47. Cf. Annett, 1985; Lenneberg, 1967.

48. Kinsbourne & Hiscock, 1983; see also Witelson, 1977.

49. Kosslyn, 1987.

50. Felleman & Van Essen, 1991; Van Essen, 1985; Van Essen & Maunsell, 1983.

51. Biederman & Shiffrar, 1987.

52. E.g., Gross, Rocha-Miranda & Bender, 1972; Schwartz, Desimone, Albright & Gross, 1984.

53. E.g., Desimone, Fleming & Gross, 1980.

54. Yakovlev & Lecours, 1967; Witelson & Kigar, 1988.

55. E.g., See O'Leary, 1980.

56. Moran & Desimone, 1985.

57. Hughes & Zimba, 1985, 1987.

58. Holtzman & Gazzaniga, 1982.

59. Kosslyn, 1987.

60. For related ideas, see Gazzaniga & LeDoux, 1978; Geschwind, 1976; Kimura, 1976, 1977; Levy, 1969; Mateer, 1978; Nottebohm, 1970, 1979; Summers & Sharp, 1979; Sussman & Westbury, 1978; Zangwill, 1976.

61. E.g., see Benson, 1967; Mazzocchi & Vignolo, 1979; Naeser, Hayward, Laughlin & Zatz, 1981.

62. For reviews, see Kinsbourne & Hiscock, 1983; Witelson, 1977.

63. For supporting evidence, see De Renzi, 1982; Efron, 1991.

64. Kosslyn, Sokolov & Chen, 1989.

65. E.g., see Sidtis, Volpe, Wilson, Rayport & Gazzaniga, 1981; Kosslyn, Holtzman, Gazzaniga & Farah, 1985.

66. Kosslyn, Koenig, Brown & Gazzaniga, in preparation.

67. For a review, see Hamilton & Vermeire, 1991.

68. Although the right-hemisphere specialization for face perception is like that found in humans, at first glance the left-hemisphere specialization for spatial tasks is not; as discussed in Chapter 3, in general humans perform metric spatial tasks better in the right hemisphere. However, it is possible that the monkey has more fine-grained spatial categories than those used by humans, which allows categorical spatial relations to be encoded in these tasks. If so, then the left-hemisphere specialization for spatial tasks in monkeys would not conflict with the pattern of human lateralization. In any case, the important point for now is that the cerebral hemispheres are lateralized in monkeys, even though they do not have language.

69. Kosslyn, Chabris, Marsolek & Koenig, in press.

70. Such theories have been developed by de Schonen & Mathivet, 1989, 1990; Hellige, 1989; and Sergent, 1988. For evidence that the right hemisphere is more mature at birth, see Geschwind & Galaburda, 1985; Geschwind & Behan, 1984; and Taylor, 1969.

71. See Kosslyn, Chabris, Marsolek & Koenig, in press.

72. This mechanism may not be sufficient to compute all categorical spatial relations. It is possible that relations such as "connected/ unconnected," "above/below," or "inside/outside" are computed in different ways, using different networks that together constitute the categorical spatial relations encoding subsystem. See Kosslyn, Chabris, Marsolek & Koenig, in press.

73. If coordinate relations are more useful in navigation, then so should be representations of specific shapes. For example, when navigating around a table, its shape is critical—a jutting corner is an obstacle in its own right. Hence, the snowball process would reinforce

these representations of specific examples in the right-hemisphere pattern activation subsystem. The lateralization processes not only can strengthen subsystems in general, but also can strengthen particular representations stored within them (see Kosslyn, 1987).

74. Delis, Robertson & Efron, 1986.

75. See Sergent, 1982; Van Kleeck, 1989, for a review.

76. Fisk & Goodale, 1988.

77. For more details, see Kosslyn, in press.

78. E.g., see Churchland, 1986; Dennett, 1991.

79. Many theorists, such as Crick & Koch, 1990, focus on the neural correlates or neural prerequisites for consciousness. Indeed, Crick & Koch develop ideas that are in some ways similar to those developed here. However, it is important to distinguish between such theories and theories of consciousness per se (as Crick & Koch did)—a theory of neural correlates or prerequisites is not a theory of the nature of consciousness itself.

80. Cf., Ryle, 1949.

81. Libet, 1987; Libet, Alberts, Wright & Feinstein, 1967.

82. Kosslyn, in press.

83. Kosslyn, in press.

84. Gray & Singer, 1989.

85. E.g., Crick & Koch, 1990; Mumford, 1991; see page 363.

86. E.g., see Libet, 1987; Libet, Alberts, Wright & Feinstein, 1967.

87. Cf. Gould & Lewontin, 1979.

88. For related ideas about the importance of the time scale, see Ericsson & Simon, 1980.

89. It is tempting to speculate further that laughter may sometimes accompany this process; when input "doesn't compute," laughter may disrupt further processing and lead the system to start over (for a similar idea, see Minsky, 1986).

90. Kosslyn, in press.

91. See Reiman, Fusselman, Fox & Raichle, 1989; see also Raichle, 1990.

92. E.g., for discussion of the relation between emotion and cognition, see Bower, 1983; Ortony, Clore & Collins, 1988; Schacter & Singer, 1962.

93. See Geschwind & Galaburda, 1987; O'Leary, 1990.

94. Damasio, 1990a, 1990b.

95. Cf. McClelland, 1979.

96. Cf. Newell, 1990, Chapter 2.

97. Note that a major part of this trick is to know how to characterize present and previous situations so that "similarity" is defined properly, which is not easy. See Goodman, 1973; Stanfill & Waltz, 1986.

Bibliography

Abbs, J. H. (1986). Invariance and variability in speech production: A distinction between linguistic intent and its neuromotor implementation. In J. S. Perkell, & D. H. Klatt (Eds.), *Invariance and variability in speech processes*. Hillsdale, NJ: Erlbaum.

Abbs, J. H., & Gracco, V. L. (1983). Sensorimotor actions in the control of multi-movement speech gesture. *Trends in Neuroscience, 6,* 391–395.

Abend, W., Bizzi, E., & Morasso, P. (1982). Human arm trajectory formation. *Brain, 105,* 331–348.

Adams, M. J. (1979). Models of word recognition. *Cognitive Psychology, 11,* 133–176.

Alexander, M. P., Benson, D. F., & Stuss, D. T. (1989). Frontal lobes and language. *Brain and Language, 37,* 656–691.

Allman, J., Miezin, F., & McGuinness, E. (1985). Direction- and velocity-specific responses from beyond the classical receptive fields in the middle temporal visual area (MT). *Perception, 14,* 105–126.

Allman, J., & Zucker, S. (1991). The relation between blobs and color vision. *The Brain: The Cold Spring Harbour conference seminar on quantitative biology.* Plainview, NY: Cold Spring Harbour Laboratory Press.

Amaral, D. G. (1987). Memory: Anatomical organization of candidate brain regions. In F. Plum (Vol. Ed.), & V. B. Mountcastle (Sec. Ed.), *Handbook of physiology, Section 1: The nervous system, Volume 5: Higher functions of the brain.* Bethesda, MD: American Physiological Society.

An, C. H., Atkeson, C. G., & Hollerbach, J. M. (1988). *Model-based control of a robot manipulator.* Cambridge, MA: MIT Press.

Andersen, R. A. (1987). Inferior parietal lobule function in spatial perception and visuomotor integration. In F. Plum (Vol. Ed.), & V. B. Mountcastle (Sec. Ed.), *Handbook of physiology, Section 1: The nervous system, Volume 5: Higher functions of the brain.* Bethesda, MD: American Physiological Society.

Andersen, R. A., Asanuma, C., Essick, G. K., & Siegel, R. M. (1990). Cortico-cortical connections of anatomically and physiologically defined subdivisions within the inferior parietal lobule. *Journal of Comparative Neurology, 296,* 65–113.

Andersen, R. A., Essick, G. K., & Siegel, R. M. (1985). Encoding of spatial location by posterior parietal neurons. *Science, 230,* 456–458.

Anderson, J. R. (1983). Spreading activation. In J. R. Anderson, & S. M. Kosslyn (Eds.), *Tutorials in learning and memory: Essays in honor of Gordon H. Bower.* San Francisco: W. H. Freeman.

Anderson, J. R., & Bower, G. H. (1973). *Human associative memory.* New York: V. H. Winston.

Annett, J. (1985). *Left, right, hand and brain: The right shift theory.* Hillsdale, NJ: Erlbaum.

Arutyunyan, G. H., Gurfinkel, V. S., & Mirskii, M. L. (1968). Investigation of aiming at a target. *Biophysics, 13,* 536–538.

Asanuma, H. (1981). The pyramidal tract. In V. B. Brooks (Vol. Ed.), J. M. Brookhart, & V. B. Mountcastle (Sec. Eds.), *Handbook of physiology, Section 1: The nervous system, Volume 2: Motor control.* Bethesda, MD: American Physiological Society.

Atkinson, R. C., & Shiffrin, R. M. (1968). Human memory: A proposed system and its control processes. In K. W. Spence, & J. T. Spence (Eds.), *The psychology of learning and motivation: Advances in research and theory, Vol. 2.* New York: Academic Press.

Auerbach, S. H., Allard, T., Naeser, M., Alexander, M. P., & Albert, M. L. (1982). Pure word deafness: An analysis of a case with bilateral lesions and a defect at the prephonemic level. *Brain, 105,* 271–300.

Austin, J. L. (1962). *How to do things with words.* Oxford: Clarendon Press.

Backman, J., Bruck, M., Hébert, M., & Seidenberg, M. S. (1984). Acquisition and use of spelling-sound correspondences in reading. *Journal of Experimental Child Psychology, 38,* 114–133.

Baddeley, A. D. (1986). *Working memory.* Oxford: Oxford University Press.

Baddeley, A. D., Papagno, C., & Vallar, G. (1988). When long-term learning depends on short-term storage. *Journal of Memory and Language, 27,* 586–595.

Baddeley, A. D., & Warrington, E. K. (1970). Amnesia and the distinction between long-term and short-term memory. *Journal of Verbal Learning and Verbal Behavior, 9,* 176–189.

Baddeley, A. D., & Wilson, B. (1988). Comprehension and working memory: A single case neuropsychological study. *Journal of Memory and Language, 27,* 479–498.

Baker, R. G., & Smith, P. T. (1976). A psycholinguistic study of English stress assignment rules. *Language and Speech, 19,* 9–27.

Barbizet, J. (1970). Prolonged organic amnesias. In J. Barbizet (Ed.), *Human memory and its pathology.* San Francisco: W. H. Freeman.

Baron, J. (1977). Mechanisms for pronouncing printed words: Use and acquisition. In D. La Berge, & S. Samuels (Eds.), *Basic processes in reading: Perception and comprehension.* Hillsdale, NJ: Erlbaum.

Basso, A., Spinnler, H., Vallar, G., & Zanobio, E. (1982). Left hemisphere damage and selective impairment of auditory verbal short-term memory: A case study. *Neuropsychologia, 20,* 263–274.

Bauer, R. M., & Rubens, A. B. (1985). Agnosia. In K. M. Heilman, & E. Valenstein (Eds.), *Clinical neuropsychology.* New York: Oxford University Press.

Bay, E. (1952). Der gegenwärtige Stand der Aphasie-Forschung. *Folia Phoniatrica, 4,* 9–30.

Beauvois, M. F., & Dérousné, J. (1979). Phonological alexia: Three dissociations. *Journal of Neurology, Neurosurgery, and Psychiatry, 42,* 1115–1124.

Beauvois, M. F., Dérousné, J., & Bastard, V. (1980). Auditory parallel to phonological alexia. *Proceedings of the Third European Conference of the International Neuropsychological Society.* Chianciano, Italy: International Neuropsychological Society.

Behrmann, M., Moscovitch, M., Black, S. E., & Mozer, M. C. (1990). Perceptual and conceptual mechanisms in neglect dyslexia: Two contrasting case studies. *Brain, 113,* 1163–1183.

Benson, D. F. (1967). Fluency in aphasia: Correlation with radioactive scan localization. *Cortex, 3,* 373–394.

———. (1985). Aphasia. In K. M. Heilman, & E. Valenstein (Eds.), *Clinical Neuropsychology* (2nd ed.). New York: Oxford University Press.

Benson, D. F., & Greenberg, J. P. (1969). Visual form agnosia: A specific deficit in visual recognition. *Archives of Neurology (Chicago), 20,* 82–89.

Benton, A. L. (1962). The visual retention set as a constructional praxis task. *Confinia Neurologica, 22,* 141–155.

———. (1969). Constructional apraxia: Some unanswered questions. In A. L. Benton (Ed.), *Contributions to clinical neuropsychology.* Chicago: Aldine.

———. (1987). Mathematical disability and the Gerstmann syndrome. In G. Deloche, & X. Seron (Eds.), *Mathematical disabilities.* Hillsdale, NJ: Erlbaum.

Berg, E. A. (1948). A simple objective technique for measuring flexibility in thinking. *Journal of General Psychology, 39,* 15–22.

Berndt, R. S. (1987). Symptom co-occurrence and dissociation in the interpretation of agrammatism. In M. Coltheart, G. Sartori & R. Job (Eds.), *The cognitive neuropsychology of language*. London: Erlbaum.

Bernstein, N. (1967). *The coordination and regulation of movements*. London: Pergamon.

Besner, D., Davelaar, E., Alcott, D., & Parry, P. (1984). Wholistic reading of alphabetic print: Evidence from the FDM and FBI. In L. Henderson (Ed.), *Orthographies and reading: Perspectives from cognitive psychology, neuropsychology, and linguistics*. Hillsdale, NJ: Erlbaum.

Bickerton, D. (1990). *Language and species*. Chicago: University of Chicago Press.

Biederman, I. (1972). Perceiving real-world scenes. *Science, 177,* 77–80.

———. (1987). Recognition-by-components: A theory of human image understanding. *Psychological Review, 94,* 115–147.

Biederman, I., & Shiffrar, M. M. (1987). Sexing day-old chicks: A case study and expert systems analysis of a difficult perceptual-learning task. *Journal of Experimental Psychology: Learning, Memory, and Cognition, 13,* 640–645.

Bihrle, A. M., Brownell, H. H., Powelson, J. A., & Gardner, H. (1986). Comprehension of humourous and non-humourous materials by left and right brain-damaged patients. *Brain and Cognition, 5,* 399–411.

Bisiach, E., & Luzzatti, C. (1978). Unilateral neglect of representational space. *Cortex, 14,* 129–133.

Bisiach, E., Luzzatti, C., & Perani, D. (1979). Unilateral neglect, representational schema, and consciousness. *Brain, 102,* 609–618.

Bizzi, E., & Mussa-Ivaldi, F. A. (1990). Geometrical and mechanical issues in movement planning and control. In M. I. Posner (Ed.), *Handbook of cognitive science*. Cambridge, MA: MIT Press.

Bliss, T. V. P., & Lømo, T. (1973). Long-lasting potentiation of synaptic transmission in the dentate area of the anaesthetized rabbit following stimulation of the perforant path. *Journal of Physiology, 232,* 331–356.

Bliss, T. V. P., & Lynch, M. A. (1988). Long-term potentiation of synaptic transmission in the hippocampus: Properties and mechanisms. In P. W. Landfield, & S. A. Deadwyler (Eds.), *Synaptic potentiation in the brain: A critical analysis*. New York: Alan Liss.

Boch, R. A., & Goldberg, M. E. (1989). Participation of prefrontal neurons in the preparation of visually guided eye movements in the rhesus monkey. *Journal of Neurophysiology, 61,* 1064–1084.

Bower, G. H. (1972). Mental imagery and associative learning. In L. Gregg (Ed.), *Cognition in learning and memory.* New York: John Wiley.

———. (1983). Affect and cognition. *Philosophical Transactions of the Royal Society of London, Series B, 302,* 387–402.

Bradshaw, J. L., & Nettleton, N. C. (1983). *Human cerebral asymmetry.* Englewood Cliffs, NJ: Prentice-Hall.

Bregman, A. S. (1990). *Auditory scene analysis: The perceptual organization of sound.* Cambridge, MA: MIT Press.

Bresnan, J. (1978). A realistic transformational grammar. In M. Halle, J. Bresnan, & G. A. Miller (Eds.), *Linguistic theory and psychological reality.* Cambridge, MA: MIT Press.

Broca, P. (1863). Localisation des fonctions cérébrales—Siège du langage articulé. *Bulletins de la Société d'Anthropologie, 4,* 200–204.

Brodmann, K. (1909). *Vergleichende Lokalisationslehre der Grosshirnrinde.* Leipzig: Barth.

Bronson, G. (1974). The postnatal growth of visual capacity. *Child Development, 45,* 873–890.

Brooks, L. (1978). Nonanalytic concept formation and memory for instances. In E. Rosch, & B. B. Lloyd (Eds.), *Cognition and categorization.* Hillsdale, NJ: Erlbaum.

Brownell, H. H., Michelow, D., Powelson, J., & Gardner, H. (1983). Surprise but not coherence: Sensitivity to verbal humor in right hemisphere patients. *Brain and Language, 18,* 20–27.

Brownell, H. H., Potter, H. H., Michelow, D., & Gardner, H. (1984). Sensitivity to lexical denotation and connotation in brain-damaged patients: A double dissociation. *Brain and Language, 22,* 253–265.

Brownell, H. H., Simpson, T. L., Bihrle, A. M., Potter, H. H., & Gardner, H. (1990). Appreciation of metaphoric alternative word meaning by left and right brain-damaged patients. *Neuropsychologia, 28,* 375–383.

Bryden, M. P. (1982). *Laterality: Functional asymmetry in the intact brain.* New York: Academic Press.

Bryden, M. P., & Ley, R. G. (1983). Right hemispheric involvement in imagery and affect. In E. Perecman (Ed.), *Cognitive processing in the right hemisphere.* New York: Academic Press.

Bub, D. N., Black, S., & Howell, J. (1989). Word recognition and orthographic context effects in a letter-by-letter reader. *Brain and Language, 36,* 357–376.

Bub, D. N., & Kertesz, A. (1982). Deep agraphia. *Brain and Language, 17,* 147–166.

Bullock, D., & Grossberg, S. (1988). Neural dynamics of planned arm movements: Emergent invariants and speed-accuracy properties during trajectory formation. *Psychological Bulletin, 95,* 49–90.

Butters, N., Barton, M., & Brody, B. A. (1970). Role of the right parietal lobe in the mediation of cross-modal associations and reversible operations in space. *Cortex, 6,* 174–190.

Butterworth, B. (1985). Jargon aphasia: Processes and strategies. In S. Newman, & R. Epstein (Eds.), *Current perspectives on dysphasia.* Edinburgh: Churchill-Livingstone.

Calvanio, R., Petrone, P., & Levine, D. N. (1987). Left visual spatial neglect is both environment-centered and body-centered. *Neurology, 37,* 1179–1183.

Campion, J. (1987). Apperceptive agnosia: The specification and description of constructs. In G. W. Humphreys, & M. J. Riddoch (Eds.), *Visual object processing: A cognitive neuropsychological approach.* Hillsdale, NJ: Erlbaum.

Caplan, D. (in press). *Language: Structure, processing, and disorders.* Cambridge, MA: MIT Press.

Caplan, D., & Hildebrandt, N. (1988). *Disorders of syntactic comprehension.* Cambridge, MA: MIT Press.

Caramazza, A. (1984). The logic of neuropsychological research and the problem of patient classification in aphasia. *Brain and Language, 21,* 9–20.

———. (1986). On drawing inferences about the structure of normal cognitive systems from the analysis of patterns of impaired performance: The case for single-patient studies. *Brain and Cognition, 5,* 41–66.

Caramazza, A., & Hillis, A. E. (1990). Spatial representation of words in the brain implied by the studies of a unilateral neglect patient. *Nature, 346,* 267–269.

Caramazza, A., Laudanna, A., & Romani, C. (1988). Lexical access and inflectional morphology. *Cognition, 28,* 297–332.

Caramazza, A., & McCloskey, M. (1987). Dissociations of calculation processes. In G. Deloche, & X. Seron (Eds.), *Mathematical disabilities.* Hillsdale, NJ: Erlbaum.

Caramazza, A., & Miceli, G. (1991). *The structure of orthographic representations in spelling.* Report of the cognitive neuropsychology laboratory, The Johns Hopkins University.

Caramazza, A., Miceli, G., Villa, G., & Romani, C. (1987). The role of the graphemic buffer in spelling: Evidence from a case of acquired dysgraphia. *Cognition, 26,* 59–85.

Carew, T. J., Walters, E. T., & Kandel, E. R. (1981). Classical conditioning in a simple withdrawal reflex in aplysia californica. *Journal of Neuroscience, 1,* 1426–1437.

Cave, C. B., & Squire, L. R. (1991). Equivalent impairment of spatial and nonspatial memory following damage to the human hippocampus. *Hippocampus, 1,* 329–340.

Cave, K. R., & Kosslyn, S. M. (1989). Varieties of size-specific visual selection. *Journal of Experimental Psychology: General, 118,* 148–164.

Chambers, D., & Reisberg, D. (1985). Can mental images be ambiguous? *Journal of Experimental Psychology: Human Perception and Performance, 11,* 317–328.

Chomsky, N. (1957). *Syntactic structures.* Mouton: The Hague.

———. (1965). *Aspects of a theory of syntax.* Cambridge, MA: MIT Press.

Churchland, P. S. (1986). *Neurophilosophy: Toward a unified science of the mind/brain.* Cambridge, MA: MIT Press.

Clarke, E., & O'Malley, C. D. (1968). *The human brain and spinal cord: A historical study illustrated by writings from antiquity to the twentieth century.* Berkeley: University of California Press.

Clower, R., Zola-Morgan, S., & Squire, L. R. (1990). Lesions of perirhinal cortex, but not lesions of the amygdala, exacerbate memory impairment in monkeys following lesions of the hippocampal formation. *Journal of Neuroscience Abstracts, 16,* 258.6.

Code, C. (1987). *Language, aphasia, and the right hemisphere.* Chichester: John Wiley.

Cohen, J. D., Dunbar, K., & McClelland, J. L. (1990). On the control of automatic processes: A parallel distributed processing model of the Stroop effect. *Psychological Review, 97,* 332–361.

Cohen, L., & Dehaene, S. (1991). Neglect dyslexia for numbers? A case report. *Cognitive Neuropsychology, 8,* 39–58.

Cohen, N. J., & Squire, L. R. (1980). Preserved learning and retention of pattern analyzing skill in amnesia: Dissociation of knowing how and knowing that. *Science, 210,* 207–209.

Coltheart, M. (1978). Lexical access in simple reading tasks. In G. Underwood (Ed.), *Strategies of information processing.* London: Academic Press.

———. (1980). Deep dyslexia: A right hemisphere hypothesis. In M. Coltheart, K. E. Patterson, & J. Marshall (Eds.), *Deep dyslexia.* London: Routledge.

Corballis, M. C. (1991). *The lopsided ape: Evolution of the generative mind.* New York: Oxford University Press.

Corballis, M. C., & Beale, I. L. (1976). *The psychology of left and right.* Hillsdale, NJ: Erlbaum.

Corballis, M. C., & Sergent, J. (1988). Imagery in a commissurotomized patient. *Neuropsychologia, 26,* 13–26.

Cordier, F. (1980). Gradients de prototypie pour cinq catégories sémantiques. *Psychologie Française, 25,* 211–219.

Cornet, J.-A., Seron, X., Deloche, G., & Lories, G. (1988). Cognitive models of simple mental arithmetic: A critical review. *European Bulletin of Cognitive Psychology, 8,* 551–571.

Cotman, C. W., & McGaugh, J. L. (1980). *Behavioral neuroscience.* New York: Academic Press.

Cowey, A. (1981). Why are there so many visual areas? In F. O. Schmitt, F. G. Warden, G. Adelman, & S. G. Dennis (Eds.), *The organization of the cerebral cortex.* Cambridge, MA: MIT Press.

Craik, F. I. M., & Lockhart, R. S. (1972). Levels of processing: A framework for memory research. *Journal of Verbal Learning and Verbal Behavior, 11,* 671–684.

Crick, F., & Asanuma, C. (1986). Certain aspects of the anatomy and physiology of the cerebral cortex. In J. L. McClelland, & D. E. Rumelhart (Eds.), *Parallel distributed processing: Explorations in the microstructure of cognition, Volume 2: Psychological and biological models.* Cambridge, MA: MIT Press.

Crick, F., & Koch, C. (1990). Towards a neurobiological theory of consciousness. *Seminars in the Neurosciences, 2,* 263–275.

Critchley, M. (1953). *The parietal lobes.* London: Edward Arnold.

Curtiss, S. (1989). The independence and task specificity of language. In A. Bornstein, & J. Bruner (Eds.), *Interaction in human development.* Hillsdale, NJ: Erlbaum.

Cutting, J. E., & Kozlowski, L. T. (1977). Recognizing friends by their walk: Gait perception without familiarity. *Bulletin of the Psychonomic Society, 9,* 353–356.

Cutting, J. E., & Proffitt, D. R. (1981). Gait perception as an example of how we may perceive events. In R. D. Walk, & H. L. Pick (Eds.), *Intersensory perception and sensory integration.* New York: Plenum Press.

Damasio, A. R. (1985a). The frontal lobes. In K. M. Heilman, & E. Valenstein (Eds.), *Clinical neuropsychology.* New York: Oxford University Press.

———. (1985b). Disorders of complex visual processing: Agnosias, achromatopsia, Balint's syndrome, and related difficulties of orientation and construction. In M.-M. Mesulam (Ed.), *Principles of behavioral neurology.* Philadelphia: F. A. Davis.

———. (1989). Time-locked multiregional retroactivation: A systems-level proposal for the neural substrates of recall and recognition. *Cognition, 33,* 25–62.

———. (1990a). Category-related recognition defects as a clue to the neural substrates of knowledge. *Trends in Neurosciences, 13,* 95–98.

———. (1990b). Synchronous activation in multiple cortical regions: A mechanism for recall. *Seminars in Neurosciences, 2,* 287–296.

Damasio, A. R., & Damasio, H. (1986). The anatomical substrate of prosopagnosia. In R. Bruyer (Ed.), *The neuropsychology of face perception and facial expression.* Hillsdale, NJ: Erlbaum.

Daniel, P. M., & Whitteridge, D. (1961). The representation of the visual field on the cerebral cortex in monkeys. *Journal of Physiology, 159,* 203–221.

Danly, M., & Shapiro, B. (1982). Speech prosody in Broca's aphasia. *Brain and Language, 16,* 171–190.

Dax, M. (1865). Lésions de la moitié gauche de l'encéphale coïncidant avec l'oubli des signes de la pensée. *Gazette Hebdomadaire de Médecine et de Chirurgie (Paris), 2,* 259–260.

De Renzi, E. (1982). *Disorders of space exploration and cognition.* New York: John Wiley.

———. (1986). Current issues in prosopagnosia. In H. D. Ellis, M. A. Jeeves, F. Newcombe, & A. Young (Eds.), *Aspects of face processing.* Dordrecht: Martinus Nijhoff.

De Renzi, E., & Faglioni, P. (1967). The relationship between visuo-spatial impairment and constructional apraxia. *Cortex, 3,* 327–342.

De Renzi, E., Faglioni, P., & Sorgato, P. (1982). Modality-specific and supramodal mechanisms of apraxia. *Brain, 105,* 301–312.

De Schonen, S., & Mathivet, E. (1989). First come, first served: A scenario about the development of hemispheric specialization in face recognition during infancy. *European Bulletin of Cognitive Psychology, 1,* 3–44.

———. (1990). Hemispheric asymmetry in a face discrimination task in infants. *Child Development, 61,* 1192–1205.

Deacon, T. W. (1989). The neural circuitry underlying primate calls and human language. *Human Evolution, 4,* 367–401.

Dehaene, S., & Changeux, J.-P. (1989). A simple model of prefrontal cortex function in delayed-response tasks. *Journal of Cognitive Neuroscience, 1,* 244–261.

———. (1991). The Wisconsin Card Sorting Test: Theoretical analysis and modeling in a neuronal network. *Cerebral Cortex, 1,* 62–79.

Dehaene, S. & Cohen, L. (1991). Two mental calculation systems: A case study of severe acalculia with preserved approximation. INSERM and CNRS, Laboratoire de Sciences Cognitives et Psycholinguistique, Paris, France, manuscript.

Deleval, J., De Mol, J., & Noterman, J. (1983). La perte des images souvenirs. *Acta Neurologica Belgica, 83,* 61–79.

Delis, D. C., Robertson, L. C., & Efron, R. (1986). Hemispheric specialization of memory for visual hierarchical stimuli. *Neuropsychologia, 24,* 205–214.

Dell, G. S. (1985). Positive feedback in hierarchical connectionist models: Applications to language production. *Cognitive Science, 9,* 3–23.

———. (1986). A spreading-activation theory of retrieval in sentence production. *Psychological Review, 93,* 283–321.

———. (1988). The retrieval of phonological forms in production: Tests of predictions from a connectionist model. *Journal of Memory and Language, 27,* 124–142.

Deloche, G., & Seron, X. (1982a). From three to 3: A differential analysis of skills in transcoding quantities between patients with Broca's and Wernicke's aphasia. *Brain, 105,* 719–733.

———. (1982b). From one to 1: An analysis of a transcoding process by means of neuropsychological data. *Cognition, 12,* 119–149.

———. (1987). Numerical transcoding: A general production model. In G. Deloche, & X. Seron (Eds.), *Mathematical disabilities.* Hillsdale, NJ: Erlbaum.

DeLong, M. R., Alexander, G. E., Georgopoulos, A. P., Crutcher, M. D., Mitchell, S. J., & Richardson, R. T. (1984). Role of basal ganglia in limb movements. *Human Neurobiology, 2,* 235–244.

Denis, M. (1982a). Imaging while reading text: A study of individual differences. *Memory and Cognition, 10,* 540–545.

———. (1982b). Images and semantic representations. In J. F. L. Ny, & W. Kintsch (Eds.), *Language and comprehension.* Amsterdam: North-Holland.

———. (1988). Imagery and prose processing. In M. Denis, J. Engelkamp, & J. T. E. Richardson (Eds.), *Cognitive and neuropsychological approaches to mental imagery.* Dordrecht: Martinus Nijhoff.

Dennett, D. (1991). *Consciousness explained.* Boston: Little, Brown.

Dennis, M., & Kohn, B. (1975). Comprehension of syntax in infantile hemiplegics after cerebral hemidecortication: Left-hemisphere superiority. *Brain and Language, 2,* 472–482.

Dennis, M., & Whitaker, H. A. (1976). Language acquisition following hemidecortication: Linguistic superiority of the left over the right hemisphere. *Brain and Language, 3,* 404–433.

Desimone, R., Albright, T. D., Gross, C. G., & Bruce, C. J. (1984). Stimulus selective properties of inferior temporal neurons in the macaque. *Journal of Neuroscience, 4,* 2051–2062.

Desimone, R., Fleming, J., & Gross, C. G. (1980). Prestriate afferents to inferior temporal cortex: An HRP study. *Brain Research, 184,* 41–55.

Desimone, R., & Ungerleider, L. G. (1989). Neural mechanisms of visual processing in monkeys. In H. Goodglass, & A. R. Damasio (Eds.), *Handbook of neuropsychology.* New York: Elsevier.

Deutsch, G., Bourbon, W. T., Papanicolaou, A. C., & Eisenberg, H. M. (1988). Visuospatial experiments compared via activation of regional cerebral blood flow. *Neuropsychologia, 26,* 445–452.

Diamond, A. (1988). Differences between adult and infant cognition: Is the crucial variable presence or absence of language? In L. Weiskrantz (Ed.), *Thought without language.* Oxford: Clarendon Press.

Diamond, A., & Doar, B. (1989). The performance of human infants on a measure of frontal cortex function, the delayed response task. *Developmental Psychobiology, 22,* 271–294.

Diamond, A., & Goldman-Rakic, P. S. (1989). Comparison of human infants and rhesus monkeys on Piaget's A not B task: Evidence for dependence on dorsolateral prefrontal cortex. *Experimental Brain Research, 74,* 24–40.

Diamond, A., Zola-Morgan, S., & Squire, L. R. (1989). Successful performance of monkeys with lesions of the hippocampal formation on A not B and object retrieval, two tasks that mark developmental changes in human infants. *Behavioral Neuroscience, 103,* 526–537.

Diamond, S. (1974). *The roots of psychology.* New York: Basic Books.

Divenyi, P. L., & Robinson, A. J. (1989). Nonlinguistic auditory capabilities in aphasia. *Brain and Language, 37,* 290–326.

Eccles, J. C. (1989). *Evolution of the brain: Creation of the self.* London: Routledge.

Efron, R. (1991). *The decline and fall of hemispheric specialization.* Hillsdale, NJ: Erlbaum.

Eimas, P. D., Miller, J. L., & Jusczyk, P. W. (1987). On infant speech perception and the acquisition of language. In S. Harnad (Ed.), *Categorical perception.* Cambridge: Cambridge University Press.

Eimas, P. D., Siqueland, E. R., Jusczyk, P. W., & Vigorito, J. (1971). Speech perception in infants. *Science, 171,* 303–306.

Ellis, A. W., Miller, D., & Sin, G. (1983). Wernicke's aphasia and normal language processing: A case study in cognitive neuropsychology. *Cognition, 15,* 111–144.

Ellis, A. W., & Young, A. W. (1988). *Human cognitive neuropsychology.* Hillsdale, NJ: Erlbaum.

Ellis, H. C., & Ashbrook, P. W. (1989). The "state" of mood and memory research: A selective review. *Journal of Social Behavior and Personality, 4,* 1–21.

Ericsson, K. A., Chase, W. G., & Faloon, S. (1980). Acquisition of a memory skill. *Science, 208,* 1181–1182.

Ericsson, K. A., & Simon, H. A. (1980). Verbal reports as data. *Psychological Review, 87,* 215–251.

Erlichman, H., & Barrett, J. (1983). Right hemispheric specialization for mental imagery: A review of evidence. *Brain and Cognition, 2,* 55–76.

Evarts, E. V. (1967). Representation of movement and muscles by pyramidal tract neurons of the precentral motor cortex. In M. D. Yahr, & D. P. Purpura (Eds.), *Neurophysiological basis of normal and abnormal motor activities.* New York: Raven Press.

Farah, M. J. (1984). The neurological basis of mental imagery: A componential analysis. *Cognition, 18,* 245–272.

———. (1988). Is visual imagery really visual? Overlooked evidence from neuropsychology. *Psychological Review, 95,* 307–317.

———. (1990). *Visual agnosia: Disorders of object recognition and what they tell us about normal vision.* Cambridge, MA: MIT Press.

Farah, M. J., Levine, D. N., & Calvanio, R. (1988). A case study of mental imagery deficit. *Brain and Cognition, 8,* 147–164.

Feldman, J. A. (1985). Four frames suffice: A provisional model of vision and space. *Behavioral and Brain Sciences, 8,* 265–289.

Felleman, D. J., & Van Essen, D. C. (1991). Distributed hierarchical processing in primate cerebral cortex. *Cerebral Cortex, 1,* 1–47.

Fillmore, C. (1968). The case for case. In E. Bach, & R. T. Harms (Eds.), *Universals in linguistic theory.* New York: Holt, Rinehart & Winston.

Finke, R. A., & Kosslyn, S. M. (1980). Mental imagery acuity in the peripheral visual field. *Journal of Experimental Psychology: Human Perception and Performance, 6,* 126–139.

Finke, R. A., & Pinker, S. (1982). Spontaneous mental image scanning in mental extrapolation. *Journal of Experimental Psychology: Learning, Memory, and Cognition, 8,* 142–147.

———. (1983). Directional scanning of remembered visual patterns. *Journal of Experimental Psychology: Learning, Memory, and Cognition, 9,* 398–410.

Finke, R. A., Pinker, S., & Farah, M. (1989). Reinterpreting visual patterns in mental imagery. *Cognitive Science, 13,* 51–78.

Finke, R. A., & Shepard, R. N. (1986). Visual functions of mental imagery. In K. R. Boff, L. Kaufman, & J. P. Thomas (Eds.), *Handbook of perception and human performance.* New York: Wiley-Interscience.

Fisk, J. D., & Goodale, M. A. (1988). The effects of unilateral brain damage on visually guided reaching: Hemispheric differences in the nature of the deficit. *Experimental Brain Research, 72,* 425–435.

Flourens, P. (1824). *Recherches expérimentales sur les propriétés et les fonctions du système nerveux dans les animaux vertébrés.* Paris: Crevot.

Fodor, J. A. (1968). *Psychological explanation: An introduction to the philosophy of psychology.* New York: Random House.

———. (1983). *The modularity of mind.* Cambridge, MA: MIT Press.

Foss, D. J., & Swinney, D. A. (1973). On the psychological reality of the phoneme: Perception, identification, and consciousness. *Journal of Verbal Learning and Verbal Behavior, 12,* 246–257.

Fox, P. T., Mintun, M. A., Raichle, M. E., Meizen, F. M., Allman, J. M., & Van Essen, D. C. (1986). Mapping human visual cortex with positron emission tomography. *Nature, 323,* 806–809.

Frankena, W. K. (1963). *Ethics.* Englewood Cliffs, NJ: Prentice-Hall.

Freeman, R. N. (1984). The apraxias, purposeful motor behavior and left-hemisphere function. In W. Prinz, & A. F. Sanders (Eds.), *Cognition and motor processes.* Berlin: Springer-Verlag.

Freud, S. (1891). *On aphasia* (translated by E. Stengel in 1953). New York: International Universities Press.

Friedman, R. B., & Albert, M. L. (1985). Alexia. In K. M. Heilman, & E. Valenstein (Eds.), *Clinical neuropsychology.* New York: Oxford University Press.

Friston, K. J., Frith, C. D., Liddle, P. F., & Frackowiak, R. S. J. (1991). Investigating a network model of word generation with positron emission tomography. *Proceedings of the Royal Society of London, Series B, 244,* 101–106.

Fritsch, G. T., & Hitzig, E. (1870). Über die elektrische Erregbarkeit des Grosshirns. *Archiv für Anatomie, Physiologie und wissenschaftliche Medizin, 37,* 300–332.

Gabrieli, J. D. E. (1986). *Memory systems of the human brain: Dissocations among learning capacities in amnesia.* Doctoral dissertation, Massachusetts Institute of Technology.

Galaburda, A. (1984). Anatomy of language: Lessons from comparative anatomy. In D. Caplan, A. R. Lecours, & A. Smith (Eds.), *Biological perspectives in language.* Cambridge, MA: MIT Press.

Gall, F. J. (1812). *Anatomie et physiologie du système nerveux en général, et du cerveau en particulier.* Paris: Schoell.

Ganong, W. F. (1980). Phonetic categorization in auditory word perception. *Journal of Experimental Psychology: Human Perception and Performance, 6,* 110–115.

Gazzaniga, M. S. (1985). *The social brain: Discovering the networks of the mind.* New York: Basic Books.

———. (1989). Organization of the human brain. *Science, 245,* 947–952.

Gazzaniga, M. S., & Ladavas, E. (1987). Disturbances in spatial attention following lesion or disconnection of the right parietal lobe. In M. Jeannerod (Ed.), *Neurophysiological and neuropsychological aspects of spatial neglect.* New York: Elsevier/North-Holland.

Gazzaniga, M. S., & LeDoux, J. E. (1978). *The integrated mind.* New York: Plenum Press.

Georgopoulos, A. P., Kalaska, J. F., Caminiti, R., & Massey, J. T. (1982). On the relations between the direction of two-dimensional arm movements and cell discharge in primate motor cortex. *Journal of Neuroscience, 2,* 1527–1537.

Georgopoulos, A. P., Lurito, J. T., Petrides, M., Schwartz, A. B., & Massey, J. T. (1989). Mental rotation of the neuronal population vector. *Science, 243,* 234–236.

Georgopoulos, A. P., Schwartz, A. B., & Kettner, R. E. (1986). Neural population coding of movement direction. *Science, 233,* 1416–1419.

Geschwind, N. (1965). Disconnexion syndromes in animals and man. *Brain, 88,* 237–294.

——. (1966). Carl Wernicke, the Breslau School and the history of aphasia. In E. C. Carterette (Ed.), *Language and communication.* Berkeley: University of California Press.

——. (1972). Language and the brain. *Scientific American, 226,* 76–83.

——. (1976). The apraxias: Neural mechanisms of disorders of learned movement. *American Scientist, 63,* 188–195.

Geschwind, N., & Behan, P. O. (1984). Laterality, hormones, and immunity. In N. Geschwind, & A. M. Galaburda (Eds.), *Cerebral dominance: The biological foundations.* Cambridge, MA: Harvard University Press.

Geschwind, N., & Galaburda, A. M. (1985). Cerebral lateralization. *Archives of Neurology, 42,* 428–459, 521–552, 634–654.

——. (1987). *Cerebral lateralization: Biological mechanisms, associations, and pathology.* Cambridge, MA: MIT Press.

Geschwind, N., & Levitsky, W. (1968). Human brain: Left-right asymmetries in temporal speech region. *Science, 161,* 186–187.

Gevins, A. S., Morgan, N. H., Bressler, S. L., Cutillo, B. A., White, R. M., Illes, J., Greer, D. S., Doyle, J. C., & Zeitlin, G. M. (1987). Human neuroelectric patterns predict performance accuracy. *Science, 235,* 580–584.

Gibson, E. J., & Levin, H. (1975). *The psychology of reading.* Cambridge, MA: MIT Press.

Gibson, J. J. (1950). *The perception of the visual world.* Boston: Houghton Mifflin.

——. (1966). *The senses considered as perceptual systems.* Boston: Houghton Mifflin.

Gnadt, J. W., & Andersen, R. A. (1988). Memory related motor planning activity in posterior parietal cortex of macaque. *Experimental Brain Research, 70,* 216–220.

Goldenberg, G., Podreka, I., Steiner, M., Willmes, K., Suess, E., & Deecke, L. (1989). Regional cerebral blood flow patterns in visual imagery. *Neuropsychologia, 27,* 641–664.

Goldenberg, G., Podreka, I., Uhl, F., Steiner, M., Willmes, K., & Deecke, L. (1989). Cerebral correlates of imaging colours, faces, and a map-I. SPECT of regional cerebral blood flow. *Neuropsychologia, 27,* 1315–1328.

Goldman-Rakic, P. S. (1987). Circuitry of primate prefrontal cortex and regulation of behavior by representational knowledge. In F. Plum (Vol. Ed.), & V. B. Mountcastle (Sec. Ed.), *Handbook of physiology, Section 1: The nervous system, Volume 5: Higher functions of the brain.* Bethesda, MD: American Physiological Society.

———. (1988). Topography of cognition: Parallel distributed networks in primate association cortex. *Annual Review of Neuroscience, 11,* 137–156.

Gonzalez, E. G., & Kolers, P. A. (1987). Notational constraints on mental operations. In G. Deloche, & X. Seron (Eds.), *Mathematical disabilities.* Hillsdale, NJ: Erlbaum.

Goodglass, H., & Berko, J. (1960). Agrammatism and inflectional morphology in English. *Journal of Speech and Hearing Research, 3,* 257–267.

Goodglass, H., & Kaplan, E. (1963). Disturbance of gesture and pantomime in aphasia. *Brain, 86,* 703–720.

Goodman, N. (1973). *Fact, fiction and forecast.* Indianapolis: Bobbs-Merrill.

Goodman, R. A., & Caramazza, A. (1986). Dissociation of spelling errors in written and oral spelling: The role of allographic conversion in writing. *Cognitive Neuropsychology, 3,* 179–206.

Gould, S. J., & Lewontin, R. C. (1979). The spandrels of San Marco and the Panglossian paradigm: A critique of the adaptationist programme. *Proceedings of the Royal Society of London, Series B, 205,* 581–598.

Graf, P., & Mandler, G. (1984). Activation makes words more accessible, but not necessarily more retrievable. *Journal of Verbal Learning and Verbal Behavior, 23,* 553–568.

Graf, P., & Schacter, D. L. (1985). Implicit and explicit memory for new associations in normal and amnesic subjects. *Journal of Experimental Psychology: Learning, Memory, and Cognition, 11,* 501–518.

Graf, P., Shimamura, A. P., & Squire, L. R. (1985). Priming across modalities and priming across category levels: Extending the domain of preserved function in amnesia. *Journal of Experimental Psychology: Learning, Memory, and Cognition, 11,* 385–395.

Graf, P., Squire, L. R., & Mandler, G. (1984). The information that amnesic patients do not forget. *Journal of Experimental Psychology: Learning, Memory, and Cognition, 10,* 164–178.

Grafman, J., Passafiume, D., Faglioni, P., & Boller, F. (1982). Calculation disturbances in adults with focal hemispheric damage. *Cortex, 18,* 37–50.

Gray, C. M., Engel, A. K., König, P., & Singer, W. (1990). Stimulus-dependent neuronal oscillations in cat visual cortex. Receptive field properties and feature dependence. *European Journal of Neuroscience, 2,* 607–619.

Gray, C. M., & Singer, W. (1989). Stimulus-specific neuronal oscillations in orientation columns of cat visual cortex. *Proceedings of the National Academy of Sciences of the United States of America, 86,* 1698–1702.

Gregory, R. L. (1961). The brain as an engineering problem. In W. H. Thorpe, & O. L. Zangwill (Eds.), *Current problems in animal behaviour.* Cambridge: Cambridge University Press.

———. (1966). *Eye and brain.* New York: McGraw-Hill.

Grimshaw, J. (1979). Complement selection and the lexicon. *Linguistic Inquiry, 10,* 279–326.

Gross, C. G., Bruce, C. J., Desimone, R., Fleming, J., & Gattass, R. (1981). Cortical visual areas of the temporal lobe. In C. N. Woolsey (Ed.), *Cortical sensory organization II: Multiple visual areas.* Clinton: Humana Press.

Gross, C. G., Desimone, R., Albright, T. D., & Schwartz, E. L. (1984). Inferior temporal cortex as a visual integration area. In F. Reinoso-Suarez, & C. Ajmone-Marsan (Eds.), *Cortical integration.* New York: Raven Press.

Gross, C. G., & Mishkin, M. (1977). The neural basis of stimulus equivalence across retinal translation. In S. Harnad, R. Doty, J. Jaynes, L. Goldstein, & G. Krauthamer (Eds.), *Lateralization in the nervous system.* New York: Academic Press.

Gross, C. G., Rocha-Miranda, C. E., & Bender, D. B. (1972). Visual properties of neurons in inferotemporal cortex of the macaque. *Journal of Neurophysiology, 35,* 96–111.

Grossberg, S. (1987). Competitive learning: From interactive activation to adaptive resonance. *Cognitive Science, 11,* 23–63.

———. (1988). *Neural networks and natural intelligence.* Cambridge, MA: MIT Press.

Grossi, D., Modafferi, A., Pelosi, L., & Trojano, L. (1989). On the different roles of the cerebral hemispheres in mental imagery: The "o'Clock Test" in two clinical cases. *Brain and Cognition, 10,* 18–27.

Grossi, D., Orsini, A., & Modafferi, A. (1986). Visuoimaginal constructional apraxia: On a case of selective deficit of imagery. *Brain and Cognition, 5,* 255–267.

Gur, R. C., Gur, R. E., Skolnick, B. E., Resnick, S. M., Silver, F. L., Chawluk, J., Muenz, L., Obrist, W. D., & Reivich, M. (1988). Effects of task difficulty on regional cerebral blood flow: Relationships with anxiety and performance. *Psychophysiology, 25,* 392–399.

Gur, R. C., Packer, I. K., Hungerbuhler, J. P., Reivich, M., Obrist, W. D., Amarnek, W. S., & Sackheim, H. (1980). Differences in distribution of gray and white matter in the human cerebral hemispheres. *Science, 207,* 1226–1228.

Gur, R. C., & Reivich, M. (1980). Cognitive task effects on hemispheric blood flow in humans: Evidence for individual differences in hemispheric activation. *Brain and Language, 9,* 78–92.

Halle, M. (1990). Phonology. In D. N. Osherson, & H. Lasnik (Eds.), *An invitation to cognitive science, Volume 1: Language.* Cambridge, MA: MIT Press.

Hamilton, C. R., & Vermeire, B. A. (1991). Functional lateralization in monkeys. In F. L. Kitterle (Ed.), *Cerebral laterality: Theory and research.* Hillsdale, NJ: Erlbaum.

Hannay, H. J., Varney, N. R., & Benton, A. L. (1976). Visual localization in patients with unilateral brain disease. *Journal of Neurology, Neurosurgery, and Psychiatry, 39,* 307–313.

Hardyck, C. (1983). Seeing each other's points of view: Visual perceptual lateralization. In J. B. Hellige (Ed.), *Cerebral hemispheric asymmetry: Method, theory, and application.* New York: Praeger.

Harries, M. H., & Perrett, D. I. (1991). Visual processing of faces in temporal cortex: Physiological evidence for a modular organization and possible anatomical correlates. *Journal of Cognitive Neuroscience, 3,* 9–24.

Harrington, A. (1987). *Medicine, mind, and the double brain.* Princeton, NJ: Princeton University Press.

Hawkins, R. D., & Kandel, E. R. (1984). Is there a cell-biological alphabet for simple forms of learning? *Psychological Review, 91,* 375–391.

Haxby, J. V., Grady, C. L., Horowitz, B., Ungerleider, L. G., Mishkin, M., Carson, R. E., Herscovitch, P., Schapiro, M. B., & Rapoport, S. I. (1991). Dissociation of object and spatial visual processing pathways in human extrastriate cortex. *Proceedings of the National Academy of Sciences of the United States of America, 88,* 1621–1625.

Hayes, J. R. (1973). On the function of visual imagery in elementary mathematics. In W. G. Chase (Ed.), *Visual information processing.* New York: Academic Press.

Hebb, D. O. (1949). *The organization of behavior.* New York: John Wiley.

Hécaen, H., & Albert, M. L. (1978). *Human neuropsychology.* New York: John Wiley.

Hécaen, H., Angelergues, R., & Houillier, S. (1961). Les variétés cliniques des acalculies au cours des lésions rétrorolandiques: Approche statistique du problème. *Revue Neurologique, 2,* 85–103.

Hécaen, H., & Kremin, H. (1977). Reading disorders resulting from left hemisphere lesions: Aphasic and "pure" alexias. In H. Whitaker, & H. A. Whitaker (Eds.), *Studies in neurolinguistics.* New York: Academic Press.

Heffner, H. E., & Heffner, R. S. (1984). Temporal lobe lesions and perception of species-specific vocalizations by macaques. *Science, 226,* 75–76.

Heilman, K. M. (1973). Ideational apraxia—a re-definition. *Brain, 96,* 861–864.

Heilman, K. M., & Rothi, L. J. (1985). Apraxia. In K. M. Heilman, & E. Valenstein (Eds.), *Clinical neuropsychology* (2nd ed.). New York: Oxford University Press.

Heindel, W. C., Butters, N., & Salmon, D. P. (1988). Impaired learning of a motor skill in patients with Huntington's disease. *Behavioral Neuroscience, 102,* 141–147.

Heindel, W. C., Salmon, D. P., & Butters, N. (1991). The biasing of weight judgements in Alzheimer's and Huntington's disease: A priming or programming phenomenon? *Journal of Clinical and Experimental Neuropsychology, 13,* 189–203.

Heindel, W. C., Salmon, D. P., Shults, C. W., Walicke, P. A., & Butters, N. (1989). Neuropsychological evidence for multiple implicit memory systems: A comparison of Alzheimer's, Huntington's, and Parkinson's disease patients. *Journal of Neuroscience, 9,* 582–587.

Held, R. (1965). Plasticity in sensory-motor systems. *Scientific American, 213,* 84–94.

Hellige, J. B. (1989). Endogenous and experimental determinants of cerebral laterality: What develops? *European Bulletin of Cognitive Psychology, 1,* 85–89.

Hellige, J. B., & Michimata, C. (1989). Categorization versus distance: Hemispheric differences for processing spatial information. *Memory and Cognition, 17,* 770–776.

Henderson, L. (1982). *Orthography and word recognition in reading.* New York: Academic Press.

Herrnstein, R. J. (1977). The evolution of behaviorism. *American Psychologist, 32,* 593–603.

Hinshelwood, J. (1899). *Letter-, word-, and mind-blindness.* London: Lewis.

Hinton, G. E., & Anderson, J. A. (1981). *Parallel models of associative memory.* Hillsdale, NJ: Erlbaum.

Hinton, G. E., McClelland, J. L., & Rumelhart, D. E. (1986). Distributed processing. In D. E. Rumelhart, & J. L. McClelland (Eds.), *Parallel distributed processing.* Cambridge, MA: MIT Press.

Hinton, G. E., & Plaut, D. C. (1986). Using fast weights to deblur old memories. In *Proceedings of the Cognitive Science Society.* Hillsdale, NJ: Erlbaum.

Hinton, G. E., & Shallice, T. (1991). Lesioning an attractor network: Investigations of acquired dyslexia. *Psychological Review, 98,* 74–95.

Hock, H., Kronseder, C., & Sissons, S. (1981). Hemispheric asymmetry: The effect of orientation on same-different comparison. *Neuropsychologia, 19,* 723–727.

Hollerbach, J. M. (1990a). Fundamentals of motor behavior. In D. N. Osherson, S. M. Kosslyn, & J. M. Hollerbach (Eds.), *Visual cognition and action: An invitation to cognitive science.* Cambridge, MA: MIT Press.

———. (1990b). Planning of arm movement. In D. N. Osherson, S. M. Kosslyn, & J. M. Hollerbach (Eds.), *Visual cognition and action: An invitation to cognitive science.* Cambridge, MA: MIT Press.

Hollerbach, J. M., & Atkeson, C. G. (1987). Deducing planning variables from experimental arm trajectories: Pitfalls and possibilities. *Biological Cybernetics, 56,* 279–292.

Holmes, G. (1919). Disturbances of visual space perception. *British Medical Journal, 2,* 230–233.

Holtzman, J. D., & Gazzaniga, M. S. (1982). Dual task interactions due exclusively to limits in processing resources. *Science, 218,* 1325–1327.

Hughes, H. C., & Zimba, L. D. (1985). Spatial maps of directed visual attention. *Journal of Experimental Psychology: Human Perception and Performance, 11,* 409–430.

———. (1987). Natural boundaries for the spatial spread of directed visual attention. *Neuropsychologia, 25,* 5–18.

Hummel, J. E., & Biederman, I. (in press). Dynamic binding in a neural network for shape recognition. *Psychological Review.*

Humphreys, G. W., & Riddoch, M. J. (1987a). *To see but not to see: A case study of visual agnosia.* Hillsdale, NJ: Erlbaum.

———. (1987b). *Visual object processing: A cognitive neuropsychological approach.* London: Erlbaum.

Huttenlocher, J. (1968). Constructing spatial images: A strategy in reasoning. *Psychological Review, 75,* 550–560.

Hyvarinen, J. (1982). Posterior parietal lobe of the primate brain. *Physiological Review, 62,* 1060–1129.

Iansek, R., & Porter, R. C. (1980). The monkey globus pallidus: Neuronal discharge properties in relation to movement. *Journal of Physiology, 301,* 439–455.

Ingvar, D. H. (1983). Serial aspects of language and speech related to prefrontal cortical activity. A selective review. *Human Neurobiology, 2,* 177–189.

Ito, M. (1984). *The cerebellum and neural control.* New York: Raven Press.

Ivry, R. I., Keele, S. W., & Diener, H. C. (1988). Dissociation of the lateral and medial cerebellum in movement timing and movement execution. *Experimental Brain Research, 73,* 167–180.

Jackendoff, R., & Landau, B. (in press). Spatial language and spatial cognition. In D. J. Napoli, & J. Kegl (Eds.), *Bridges between psychology and linguistics: A Swarthmore Festschrift for Lila Gleitman.* Hillsdale, NJ: Erlbaum.

Jackson, J. H. (1864). Clinical remarks on defects of expression (by words, writing, signs, etc.) in diseases of the nervous system. *Lancet, 1,* 604–605.

———. (1874). On the duality of the brain. In J. Taylor (Ed.), *Selected writings of John Hughlings Jackson.* London: Hodder and Stoughton.

Jakobson, R., & Halle, M. (1956). *Fundamentals of language.* The Hague: Mouton.

Janowsky, J. S., Shimamura, A. P., Kritchevsky, M., & Squire, L. R. (1989). Cognitive impairment following frontal lobe damage and its relevance to human amnesia. *Behavioral Neuroscience, 103,* 548–560.

Jay, M. F., & Sparks, D. L. (1984). Auditory receptive fields in primate superior colliculus shift with changes in eye position. *Nature, 309,* 345–347.

Jeannerod, M. (1988). *The neural and behavioral organization of goal-directed movements.* Oxford: Oxford University Press.

Jetter, W., Poser, U., Freeman, R. B., Jr., & Markowitsch, H. J. (1986). A verbal long term memory deficit in frontal lobe damaged patients. *Cortex, 22,* 229–242.

Johansson, G. (1950). *Configurations in event perception.* Uppsala, Sweden: Almqvist & Wiksell.

———. (1975). Visual motion perception. *Scientific American, 232,* 76–88.

Johnson-Laird, P. N. (1983). *Mental models.* Cambridge, MA: Harvard University Press.

Johnston, J. C., & McClelland, J. L. (1980). Experimental tests of a hierarchical model of word identification. *Journal of Verbal Learning and Verbal Behavior, 19,* 503–524.

Jolicoeur, P. (1990). Identification of disoriented objects: A dual-systems theory. *Mind and Language, 5,* 387–410.

Jones, R. K. (1966). Observations on stammering after localized cerebral injury. *Journal of Neurology, Neurosurgery, and Psychiatry, 29,* 192–195.

Jordan, M. I. (1989). Generic constraints on underspecified target trajectories. *Proceedings of the International Joint Conference on Neural Networks.* New York: IEEE Publishing Services.

———. (1990). Motor learning and the degrees of freedom problem. In M. Jeannerod (Ed.), *Attention and performance XIII.* Hillsdale, NJ: Erlbaum.

Just, M. A., & Carpenter, P. A. (1980). A theory of reading: From eye fixations to comprehension. *Psychological Review, 87,* 329–354.

———. (1987). *The psychology of reading and language comprehension.* Newton, MA: Allyn and Bacon.

Kaas, J. H. (1989). Why does the brain have so many visual areas? *Journal of Cognitive Neuroscience, 1,* 121–135.

Kahneman, D., Triesman, A., & Gibbs, B. J. (in press). The reviewing of object files: Object-specific integration of information. *Cognitive Psychology.*

Kaminski, T., & Gentile, A. M. (1986). Joint control strategies and hand trajectories in multijoint pointing movements. *Journal of Motor Behavior, 18,* 261–278.

Kandel, E. R. (1989). Genes, nerve cells, and the remembrance of things past. *Journal of Neuropsychiatry, 1,* 103–125.

Kandel, E. R., & Schwartz, J. H. (1985). *Principles of neural science* (2nd ed.). New York: Elsevier/North-Holland.

Karanth, P. (1981). Pure alexia in a Kannada-English bilingual. *Cortex 17,* 187–198.

Kaufman, L. (1974). *Sight and mind.* New York: Oxford University Press.

Kawato, M. (1991). Optimization and learning in neural networks for formation and control of coordinated movement. ATR Auditory and Visual Perception Research Laboratories, Kyoto, Japan, manuscript.

Kawato, M., Maeda, Y., Uno, Y., & Suzuki, R. (1990). Trajectory formation of arm movement by cascade neural network model based on minimum torque-change criterion. *Biological Cybernetics, 62,* 275–288.

Kay, J., & Ellis, A. W. (1987). A cognitive neuropsychological case study of anomia: Implications for psychological models of word retrieval. *Brain, 110,* 613–629.

Kelly, J. P. (1985). Anatomical basis of sensory perception and motor coordination. In E. R. Kandel & J. H. Schwartz (Eds.), *Principles of neural science* (2nd ed.). New York: Elsevier/North Holland.

Khilstrom, J. F., Schacter, D. L., Cork, R. C., Hurt, C. A., & Behr, S. E. (1990). Implicit and explicit memory following surgical anesthesia. *Psychological Science, 1,* 303–306.

Kim, H., & Levine, S. C. (1991). Inferring patterns of hemispheric specialization for individual subjects from laterality data: A two-task criterion. *Neuropsychologia, 29,* 93–105.

Kimble, D. P. (1988). *Biological psychology.* New York: Holt, Rinehart & Winston.

Kimura, D. (1976). The neural basis of language qua gesture. In H. Whitaker, & H. A. Whitaker (Eds.), *Studies in neurolinguistics.* New York: Academic Press.

———. (1977). Acquisition of a motor skill after left hemisphere damage. *Brain, 100,* 527–542.

Kimura, D., & Watson, N. V. (1989). The relation between oral movement control and speech. *Brain and Language, 37,* 565–590.

Kinsbourne, M., & Hiscock, M. (1983). The normal and deviant development of functional lateralization of the brain. In P. Mussen, M. Haith, & J. Campos (Eds.), *Handbook of child psychology.* New York: John Wiley.

Kinsbourne, M., & Rosenfield, D. B. (1974). Agraphia selective for written spelling: An experimental case study. *Brain and Language, 1,* 215–225.

Kinsbourne, M., & Warrington, E. K. (1962). A disorder of simultaneous form perception. *Brain, 85,* 461–486.

———. (1963). The localizing significance of limited simultaneous visual form perception. *Brain, 86,* 697–702.

———. (1983). Jargon aphasia. *Neuropsychologia, 21,* 27–37.

Kirk, A., & Kertesz, A. (1989). Hemispheric contributions to drawing. *Neuropsychologia, 27,* 881–886.

Kitterle, F. L. (1991). *Cerebral laterality: Theory and research.* Hillsdale, NJ: Erlbaum,

Knopman, D. S., & Nissen, M. J. (1987). Implicit learning in patients with probable Alzheimer's disease. *Neurology, 37,* 784–788.

Koenig, O. (1989). Hemispheric asymmetry in the analysis of Stroop stimuli: A developmental approach. *Developmental Neuropsychology, 5,* 245–260.

Koenig, O., & Gabrieli, J. D. E. (submitted). Computational constraints upon the acquisition of spatial knowledge in the cerebral hemispheres.

Koenig, O., Wetzel, C., & Caramazza, A. (in press). Evidence for different types of lexical representations in the cerebral hemispheres. *Cognitive Neuropsychology.*

Kolb, B., & Whishaw, I. Q. (1985). *Fundamentals of human neuropsychology* (2nd ed.). New York: W. H. Freeman.

———. (1990). *Fundamentals of human neuropsychology* (3rd ed.). New York: W. H. Freeman.

Kolers, P. A. (1983). Perception and representation. *Annual Review of Psychology, 34,* 129–166.

Kosslyn, S. M. (1973). Scanning visual images: Some structural implications. *Perception and Psychophysics, 14,* 90–94.

———. (1975). Information representation in visual images. *Cognitive Psychology, 7,* 341–370.

———. (1976). Can imagery be distinguished from other forms of internal representation? Evidence from studies of information retrieval time. *Memory and Cognition, 4,* 291–297.

———. (1978). Measuring the visual angle of the mind's eye. *Cognitive Psychology, 10,* 356–389.

———. (1980). *Image and mind.* Cambridge: Harvard University Press.

———. (1983). *Ghosts in the mind's machine.* New York: W. W. Norton.

———. (1984). Mental representations. In J. R. Anderson, & S. M. Kosslyn (Eds.), *Tutorials in learning and memory: Essays in honor of Gordon Bower.* New York: W. H. Freeman.

———. (1987). Seeing and imagining in the cerebral hemispheres: A computational approach. *Psychological Review, 94,* 148–175.

———. (1991). A cognitive neuroscience of visual mental imagery: Further developments. In R. Logie (Ed.), *Advances in mental imagery research.* Hillsdale, NJ: Erlbaum.

———. (in press). Cognitive neuroscience and the human self. In A. Harrington (Ed.), *So human a brain.* Boston: Birkhauser.

Kosslyn, S. M., Alpert, N., Maljkovic, V., Weise, S. B., Thompson, W. L., Hamilton, S. E., Chabris, C. F., & Buonanno, F. S. (1991). Visual mental imagery activates primary visual cortex. Harvard University manuscript.

Kosslyn, S. M., Ball, T. M., & Reiser, B. J. (1978). Visual images preserve metric spatial information: Evidence from studies of image scanning. *Journal of Experimental Psychology: Human Perception and Performance, 4,* 47–60.

Kosslyn, S. M., Berndt, R. S., & Doyle, T. J. (1985). Imagery and language: A preliminary neuropsychological investigation. In M. S. Posner, & O. S. Marin (Eds.), *Attention and Performance XI.* Hillsdale NJ: Erlbaum.

Kosslyn, S. M., Brunn, J. L., Cave, K. R., & Wallach, R. W. (1984).

Individual differences in mental imagery ability: A computational analysis. *Cognition, 18,* 195–243.

Kosslyn, S. M., Cave, C. B., Provost, D., & Von Gierke, S. (1988). Sequential processes in image generation. *Cognitive Psychology, 20,* 319–343.

Kosslyn, S. M., Chabris, C. F., Marsolek, C. J., & Koenig, O. (in press). Categorical versus coordinate spatial representations: Computational analyses and computer simulations. *Journal of Experimental Psychology: Human Perception and Performance.*

Kosslyn, S. M., Dror, I. E., Park, S. H., & Clegg, B. A. (in preparation). Memory for lateral orientation in the cerebral hemispheres.

Kosslyn, S. M., Flynn, R. A., Amsterdam, J. B., & Wang, G. (1990). Components of high-level vision: A cognitive neuroscience analysis and accounts of neurological syndromes. *Cognition, 34,* 203–277.

Kosslyn, S. M., & Hatfield, G. (1984). Representation without symbol systems. *Social Research, 51,* 111–133.

Kosslyn, S. M., Holtzman, P., Gazzaniga, M., & Farah, M. (1985). A computational analysis of mental image generation: Evidence from functional dissociations in split-brain patients. *Journal of Experimental Psychology: General, 114,* 311–341.

Kosslyn, S. M., & Intriligator, J. M. (in press). Is cognitive neuropsychology plausible? The perils of sitting on a one-legged stool. *Journal of Cognitive Neuroscience.*

Kosslyn, S. M., & Jolicoeur, P. (1981). A theory-based approach to the study of individual differences in mental imagery. In R. E. Snow, P. A. Federico, & W. E. Montague (Eds.), *Aptitude learning and instruction: Cognitive processes analysis of aptitude.* Hillsdale, NJ: Erlbaum.

Kosslyn, S. M., Koenig, O., Barrett, A., Cave, C. B., Tang, J., & Gabrieli, J. D. E. (1989). Evidence for two types of spatial representations: Hemispheric specialization for categorical and coordinate relations. *Journal of Experimental Psychology: Human Perception and Performance, 15,* 723–735.

Kosslyn, S. M., Koenig, O., Brown, H., & Gazzaniga, M. S. (in preparation). Relations of categorical and coordinate processing and visual sensitivities of the cerebral hemispheres: Studies with a split-brain patient.

Kosslyn, S. M., McPeek, R., Daly, P., Alpert, N. A., & Caviness, V. S. (1991). Using locations to encode shape: An indirect effect of a remote lesion. Harvard University manuscript.

Kosslyn, S. M., Segar, C., Pani, J., & Hillger, L. A. (1990). When is imagery used? A diary study. *Journal of Mental Imagery, 14,* 131–152.

Kosslyn, S. M., Sokolov, M. A., & Chen, J. C. (1989). The lateralization of BRIAN: A computational theory and model of visual hemispheric specialization. In D. Klahr, & K. Kotovsky (Eds.), *Complex information processing comes of age.* Hillsdale, NJ: Erlbaum.

Kosslyn, S. M., & Van Kleeck, M. H. (1990). Broken brains and normal minds: Why Humpty-Dumpty needs a skeleton. In E. L. Schwartz (Ed.), *Computational neuroscience.* Cambridge, MA: MIT Press.

Kuhl, P. K., & Miller, J. D. (1978). Speech perception by the chinchilla: Identification functions for synthetic VOT stimuli. *Journal of the Acoustical Society of America, 63,* 905–917.

LaBerge, D., & Buchsbaum, M. S. (1990). Positron emission tomography measurements of pulvinar activity during an attention task. *Journal of Neuroscience, 10,* 613–619.

Land, E. H. (1972). Experiments in color vision. In *Perception: Mechanisms and models. Readings from Scientific American.* San Francisco: W. H. Freeman.

Larsen, A., & Bundesen, C. (1978). Size scaling in visual pattern recognition. *Journal of Experimental Psychology: Human Perception and Performance, 4,* 1–20.

Lashley, K. S. (1929). *Brain mechanisms and intelligence.* Chicago: University of Chicago Press.

———. (1933). Integrative functions of the cerebral cortex. *Psychological Review, 13,* 1–42.

———. (1937). Functional determination of cerebral localization. *Archives of Neurology and Psychiatry, 38,* 371–387.

———. (1951). The problem of serial order in behavior. In L. A. Jeffress (Ed.), *Cerebral mechanisms in behavior.* New York: John Wiley.

Lashley, K. S., & Clark, G. (1946). The cytoarchitecture of the cerebral cortex of Ateles. *Journal of Comparative Neurology, 82,* 233–306.

Lauter, J. H., Herscovitch, P., Formby, C., & Raichle, M. E. (1985). Tonotopic organization in human auditory cortex revealed by positron emission tomography. *Hearing Research, 20,* 199–205.

Lauter, J. H., & Hirsh, I. J. (1985). Speech as a temporal pattern: A psychoacoustical profile. *Speech Communication, 4,* 41–54.

Lecoeurs, A. R., Basso, A., Moraschini, S., & Nespoulous, J. L. (1984). Where is the speech area, and who has seen it? In D. Caplan, A. R. Lecours, & A. Smith (Eds.), *Biological perspectives on language.* Cambridge, MA: MIT Press.

LeDoux, J. E., Wilson, D. H., & Gazzaniga, M. S. (1977). A divided mind: Observations on the conscious properties of the separated hemispheres. *Annals of Neurology, 2,* 417–421.

Lehky, S. R., & Sejnowski, T. J. (1988a). Network model of shape-from-shading: Neural function arises from both receptive and projective fields. *Nature, 333,* 452–454.

————. (1988b). Neural network model for the cortical representation of surface curvature from images of shaded surfaces. In J. S. Lund (Ed.), *Sensory processing in the mammalian brain.* Oxford: Oxford University Press.

Lenneberg, E. H. (1967). *Biological foundations of language.* New York: Wiley.

Levelt, W. (1989). *Speaking: From intention to articulation.* Cambridge, MA: MIT Press.

Levine, D. N. (1982). Visual agnosia in monkey and man. In D. J. Ingle, M. A. Goodale, & R. J. W. Mansfield (Eds.), *Analysis of visual behavior.* Cambridge, MA: MIT Press.

Levine, D. N., Maini, R. B., & Calvanio, R. (1988). Pure agraphia and Gerstmann's Syndrome as a visuospatial-language dissociation: An experimental case study. *Brain and Language, 35,* 172–196.

Levine, D. N., Warach, J., & Farah, M. J. (1985). Two visual systems in mental imagery: Dissociation of "what" and "where" in imagery disorders due to bilateral posterior cerebral lesions. *Neurology, 35,* 1010–1018.

Levy, J. (1969). Possible basis for the evolution of lateral specialization of the human brain. *Nature, 224,* 614–615.

Liberman, A. M., Cooper, F. S., Shankweiler, D., & Studdert-Kennedy, M. (1967). Perception of speech code. *Psychological Review, 74,* 431–461.

Libet, B. (1987). Consciousness: Conscious, subjective experience. In G. Adelman (Ed.), *Encyclopedia of neuroscience.* Boston: Birkhauser.

Libet, B., Alberts, W. W., Wright, E. W., & Feinstein, B. (1967). Response of human somatosensory cortex to stimuli below threshold for conscious sensation. *Science, 158,* 1597–1600.

Liepmann, H. (1905). Die linke Hemisphäre und das Handelin. *Münchener medizinische Wochenschrift, 49,* 2375–2378.

Linebarger, M., Schwartz, M., & Saffran, E. (1983). Sensitivity to grammatical structure in so-called agrammatic aphasics. *Cognition, 13,* 361–392.

Lissauer, H. (1890). Ein Fall von Seelenblindheit nebst einem Beitrage zur Theorie derselben. *Archiv für Psychiatrie und Nervenkrankheiten, 21,* 222–270.

Livingstone, M. S., & Hubel, D. H. (1987). Psychophysical evidence for separate channels for the perception of form, color, movement and depth. *Journal of Neuroscience, 7,* 3416–3468.

Llinas, R. (1981). Electrophysiology of cerebellar networks. In V. B. Brooks (Vol. Ed.), J. M. Brookhart & V. B. Mountcastle (Sec. Eds.), *Handbook of physiology. Section 1: The nervous system, Volume 2, Motor control.* Bethesda, MD: American Physiological Society.

Loftus, G. R. (1983). Eye fixations on text and scenes. In K. Rayner (Ed.), *Eye movements in reading.* New York: Academic Press.

Logan, G. D. (1982). On the ability to inhibit complex movements: A stop-signal study of typewriting. *Journal of Experimental Psychology: Human Perception and Performance, 8,* 778–792.

Long, J. (1976). Visual feedback and skilled keying: Differential effects of masking the printed copy and the keyboard. *Ergonomics, 19,* 19–110.

Lowe, D. G. (1985). *Perceptual organization and visual recognition.* Boston: Kluwer.

———. (1987a). Three-dimensional object recognition from single two-dimensional images. *Artificial Intelligence, 31,* 355–395.

———. (1987b). The viewpoint consistency constraint. *International Journal of Computer Vision, 1,* 57–72.

Luce, R. D. (1986). *Response times.* New York: Oxford University Press.

Luria, A. R. (1959). Disorders of "simultaneous perception" in a case of bilateral occipito-parietal brain injury. *Brain, 82,* 437–449.

———. (1973). *The working brain.* New York: Basic Books.

———. (1980). *Higher cortical functions in man.* New York: Basic Books.

Lynch, G., & Baudry, M. (1984). The biochemistry of memory: A new and specific hypothesis. *Science, 224,* 1057–1063.

Lynch, J. C., Mountcastle, V. B., Talbot, W. H., & Yin, T. C. T. (1977). Parietal lobe mechanisms for directed visual attention. *Journal of Neurophysiology, 40,* 362–389.

MacDonald, M. C., Carpenter, P. A., & Just, M. A. (in press). *Journal of Memory and Language.*

MacLean, P. D. (1987). The midline frontolimbic cortex and the evolution of crying and laughter. In E. Perecman (Ed.), *The frontal lobe revisited.* New York: The IRBN Press.

MacNeilage, P. F. (1970). Motor control and serial ordering of speech. *Psychological Review, 77,* 182–196.

Malinow, R., & Tsien, R. W. (1990). Presynaptic enhancement shown by whole-cell recordings of long-term potentiation in hippocampal slices. *Nature, 346,* 177–180.

Marcie, P., & Hécaen, H. (1979). Agraphia: Writing disorder associated with unilateral cortical lesions. In K. M. Heilman, & E. Valenstein (Eds.), *Clinical neuropsychology.* New York: Oxford University Press.

Marr, D. (1982). *Vision: A computational investigation into the human representation and processing of visual information.* New York: W. H. Freeman.

Marsden, C. D., Merton, P. A., & Morton, H. B. (1977). Disorders of movement in cerebellar disease in man. In F. C. Rose (Ed.), *Physiological aspects of clinical neurology.* Oxford: Blackwell.

Marshack, A. (1991). The Tai Plaque and calendrical notation in the Upper Paleolithic. *Cambridge Archaeological Journal, 1,* 25–61.

Marshall, J. C. (1981). Hemispheric specialization: What, how, and why. *Behavioral and Brain Sciences, 4,* 72–73.

Marshall, J. C., & Newcombe, F. (1973). Patterns of paralexia: A psycholinguistic approach. *Journal of Psycholinguistic Research, 2,* 175–199.

Marslen-Wilson, W., & Welch, A. (1978). Processing interactions and lexical access during word recognition in continuous speech. *Cognitive Psychology, 10,* 29–63.

Marsolek, C. J., Kosslyn, S. M., & Squire, L. R. (in press). Form-specific visual priming in the right cerebral hemisphere. *Journal of Experimental Psychology: Learning, Memory, and Cognition.*

Martone, M., Butters, N., Payne, M., Becker, J. T., & Sax, D. S. (1984). Dissociations between skill learning and verbal recognition in amnesia and dementia. *Archives of Neurology, 41,* 965–970.

Mason, M. (1975). Reading ability and letter search time: Effects of orthographic structure defined by single letter positional frequency. *Journal of Experimental Psychology: General, 104,* 146–166.

Mateer, C. (1978). Impairments of nonverbal oral movements after left hemisphere damage: A followup analysis of errors. *Brain and Language, 6,* 334–341.

Maunsell, J. H. R., & Newsome, W. T. (1987). Visual processing in monkey extrastriate cortex. *Annual Review of Neuroscience, 10,* 363–401.

Mayer, M. L., Westbrook, G. L., & Guthrie, P. B. (1984). Voltage dependent block by Mg2+ of NMDA response in spinal cord neurones. *Nature, 309,* 261–263.

Mazziotta, J. C., Phelps, M. E., Carson, R. E., & Kuhl, D. E. (1982). Tomographic mapping of human cerebral metabolism: Auditory stimulation. *Neurology, 32,* 921–937.

Mazziotta, J. C., Phelps, M. E., & Halgren, E. (1983). Local cerebral glucose metabolic response to audiovisual stimulation and deprivation: Studies in human subjects with positron CT. *Human Neurobiology, 2,* 11–23.

Mazzocchi, F., & Vignolo, L. A. (1979). Localisation of lesions in aphasia: Clinical-CT scan correlations in stroke patients. *Cortex, 15,* 627–654.

McBride, E., & Rothstein, A. (1979). Mental and physical practice and the learning and retention of open and closed skills. *Perceptual and Motor Skills, 49,* 359–365.

McCarthy, R. A., & Warrington, E. K. (1984). A two-route model of speech production. *Brain, 107,* 463–485.

———. (1986). Visual associative agnosia: A clinico-anatomical study of a single case. *Journal of Neurology, Neurosurgery, and Psychiatry, 49,* 1233–1240.

———. (1990). *Cognitive neuropsychology: A clinical introduction.* New York: Academic Press.

McClelland, J. L. (1976). Preliminary letter identification in the perception of words and nonwords. *Journal of Experimental Psychology: Human Perception and Performance, 2,* 80–91.

———. (1979). On the time-relations of mental processes: An examination of systems of processes in cascade. *Psychological Review, 86,* 287–330.

———. (1986). The programmable blackboard model of reading. In J. L. McClelland, & D. E. Rumelhart (Eds.), *Parallel distributed processing: Explorations in the microstructure of cognition, Volume 2: Psychological and biological models.* Cambridge, MA: MIT Press.

McClelland, J. L., & Elman, J. L. (1986). The TRACE model of speech perception. *Cognitive Psychology, 18,* 1–86.

McClelland, J. L., & Rumelhart, D. E. (1981). An interactive activation model of context effects in letter perception: Part 1. An account of basic findings. *Psychological Review, 88,* 375–407.

———. (1985). Distributed memory and the representation of general and specific information. *Journal of Experimental Psychology: General, 114,* 159–188.

———. (1986). A distributed model of human learning and memory. In J. L. McClelland, & D. E. Rumelhart (Eds.), *Parallel distributed processing: Explorations in the microstructure of cognition, Volume 2: Psychological and biological models.* Cambridge, MA: MIT Press.

———. (1988). *Explorations in parallel distributed processing: A handbook of models, programs, and exercises.* Cambridge, MA: MIT Press.

McCloskey, M., & Caramazza, A. (1987). Cognitive mechanisms in normal and impaired number processing. In G. Deloche, & X. Seron (Eds.), *Mathematical disabilities.* Hillsdale, NJ: Erlbaum.

McCloskey, M., Sokol, S. M., & Goodman, R. A. (1986). Cognitive processes in verbal-number production: Inferences from the performance of brain damaged subjects. *Journal of Experimental Psychology: General, 115,* 307–330.

Mehta, Z., Newcombe, F., & Damasio, H. (1987). A left hemisphere contribution to visuospatial processing. *Cortex, 23,* 447–461.

Mesulam, M.-M. (1981). A cortical network for directed attention and unilateral neglect. *Annals of Neurology, 10,* 309–325.

————. (1985). *Principles of behavioural neurology.* Philadelphia: F. A. Davis.

————. (1990). Large-scale neurocognitive networks and distributed processing for attention, language, and memory. *Annals of Neurology, 28,* 597–613.

Milberg, W., Hebben, N., & Kaplan, E. (1986). Boston process approach to neuropsychological assessment. In I. Grant, & K. M. Adams (Eds.), *Neuropsychological assessment of neuropsychiatric disorders.* New York: Oxford University Press.

Miller, G. A. (1956). The magical number seven, plus or minus two: Some limits on our capacity for processing information. *Psychological Review, 63,* 81–97.

Miller, G. A., & Isard, S. (1963). Some perceptual consequences of linguistic rules. *Journal of Verbal Learning and Verbal Behavior, 2,* 217–228.

Milner, B. (1962). Les troubles de la mémoire accompagnant des lésions hippocampiques bilatérales. *Physiologie de l'hippocampe.* Paris: Centre National de la Recherche Scientifique.

————. (1964). Some effects of frontal lobectomy in man. In J. M. Warren, & K. Akert (Eds.), *The frontal granular cortex and behavior.* New York: McGraw-Hill.

Milner, B., Corkin, S., & Teuber, H. L. (1968). Further analysis of the hippocampal amnesic syndrome: 14 year followup study of H. M. *Neuropsychologia, 6,* 215–234.

Milner, B., & Rasmussen, T. (1966). Evidence for bilateral speech representation in some non-right handers. *Transactions of the American Neurobiological Association, 91,* 306–308.

Milner, P. (1970). *Physiological psychology.* New York: Holt, Rinehart & Winston.

Minsky, M. (1986). *The society of mind.* New York: Simon & Schuster.

Mishkin, M. (1978). Memory in monkeys severely impaired by combined but not by separate removal of amygdala and hippocampus. *Nature, 273,* 297–298.

Mishkin, M., & Appenzeller, T. (1987). The anatomy of memory. *Scientific American, 256,* 80–89.

Mishkin, M., Malamut, B., & Bachevalier, J. (1984). Memories and habits: Two neural systems. In G. Lynch, J. L. McGaugh, & N. M. Weinberger (Eds.), *Neurobiology of learning and memory.* New York: Guilford Press.

Mishkin, M., Ungerleider, L. G., & Macko, K. A. (1983). Object vision and spatial vision: Two cortical pathways. *Trends in Neurosciences, 6,* 414–417.

Miyashita, Y., & Chang, H. S. (1988). Neuronal correlate of pictorial short-term memory in the primate temporal cortex. *Nature, 331,* 68–70.

Monrad-Krohn, G. H. (1947). Dysprosody or altered "melody of language." *Brain, 70,* 405–415.

Moran, J., & Desimone, R. (1985). Selective attention gates visual processing in the extrastriate cortex. *Science, 229,* 782–784.

Morasso, P. (1981). Spatial control of arm movements. *Experimental Brain Research, 42,* 223–227.

Morris, R. G. M., Anderson, E., Lynch, G. S., & Baudry, M. (1986). Selective impairment of learning and blockage of long-term potentiation by an N-methyl-D-aspartate receptor antagonist, AP5. *Nature, 319,* 774–776.

Morris, R. G. M., Hagan, J. J., & Rawlins, J. N. P. (1986). Allocentric spatial learning by hippocampectomised rats: A further test of the "spatial-mapping" and "working-memory" theories of hippocampal function. *Quarterly Journal of Experimental Psychology, 38B,* 365–395.

Morris, R. G. M., Halliwell, R. F., & Bowery, N. (1989). Synaptic plasticity and learning II: Do different kinds of plasticity underlie different kinds of learning? *Neuropsychologia, 27,* 41–59.

Morse, P. A., & Snowdon, C. T. (1975). An investigation of categorical speech discrimination by rhesus monkeys. *Perception and Psychophysics, 117,* 9–16.

Morton, J., & Chambers, S. M. (1973). Selective attention to words and colors. *Quarterly Journal of Experimental Psychology, 25,* 387–397.

Moss, M. B., & Albert, M. S. (1988). Alzheimer's disease and other dementing disorders. In M. S. Albert, & M. B. Moss (Eds.), *Geriatric neuropsychology.* New York: Guilford Press.

Mountcastle, V. B., Lynch, J. C., Georgopoulos, A., Sakata, H., & Acuna, C. (1975). Posterior parietal association cortex of the monkey: Command functions for operations within extrapersonal space. *Journal of Neurophysiology, 38,* 871–908.

Movshon, J. A., Adelson, E. H., Gizzi, M. S., & Newsome, W. T. (1986). The analysis of moving visual patterns. In C. Chagas, R. Gattass, & C. Gross (Eds.), *Pattern recognition mechanisms.* Vatican City: Pontifical Academy of Sciences.

Moyer, R. S. (1973). Comparing objects in memory: Evidence suggesting an internal psychophysics. *Perception and Psychophysics, 13,* 180–184.

Moyer, R. S., & Landauer, T. K. (1967). The time required for judgements of numerical inequality. *Nature, 215,* 1519–1520.

———. (1973). Determinants of reaction time for digit inequality judgements. *Bulletin of the Psychonomic Society, 1,* 167–168.

Mozer, M. C. (1987). Early parallel processing in reading: A connectionist approach. In M. Coltheart (Ed.), *Attention and performance XII: The psychology of reading.* Hillsdale, NJ: Erlbaum.

———. (1991). *The perception of multiple objects: A connectionist approach.* Cambridge, MA: MIT Press.

Mozer, M. C., & Behrmann, M. (1990). On the interaction of selective attention and lexical knowledge: A connectionist account of neglect dyslexia. *Journal of Cognitive Neuroscience, 2,* 96–123.

Mumford, D. (1991). On the computational architecture of the neocortex: I. The role of the thalmo-cortical loop. *Biological Cybernetics, 65,* 135–145.

Munk, H. (1881). *Über die Funktionen der Grosshirnrinde.* Berlin: Hirschwald.

Musen, G., Shimamura, A. P., & Squire, L. R. (1990). Intact text-specific reading skill in amnesia. *Journal of Experimental Psychology: Learning, Memory, and Cognition, 6,* 1068–1076.

Naeser, M. A., Hayward, R. W., Laughlin, S. A., & Zatz, L. M. (1981). Quantitative CT scan studies in aphasia, I: Infarct size and CT numbers. *Brain and Language, 12,* 140–164.

Neisser, U. (1967). *Cognitive psychology.* New York: Appleton-Century-Crofts.

———. (1976). *Cognition and reality.* San Francisco: W. H. Freeman.

Newell, A. (1990). *Unified theories of cognition.* Cambridge, MA: Harvard University Press.

Newell, A., & Simon, H. A. (1972). *Human problem solving.* Englewood Cliffs, NJ: Prentice-Hall.

Nieuwenhuys, R., Voogd, J., & van Huijzen, C. (1988). *The human central nervous system: A synopsis and atlas* (3rd ed.). Berlin: Springer-Verlag.

Nissen, M. J., Knopman, D. S., & Schacter, D. L. (1987). Neurochemical dissociation of memory systems. *Neurology, 37,* 784–788.

Norman, D. A. (1976). *Memory and attention: An introduction to human information processing.* New York: Wiley.

Nottebohm, F. (1970). Ontogeny of bird song. *Science, 167,* 950–956.

———. (1979). Origins and mechanisms in the development of cerebral dominance. In M. S. Gazzaniga (Ed.), *Handbook of behavioral neurobiology.* New York: Plenum.

O'Keefe, J., & Nadel, L. (1978). *The hippocampus as a cognitive map.* London: Oxford University Press.

O'Leary, D. S. (1980). A developmental study of interhemispheric transfer in children aged five to ten. *Child Development, 51,* 743–750.

———. (1990). Neuropsychological development in the child and the adolescent: Functional maturation of the central nervous system. In C.-A. Hauert (Ed.), *Developmental psychology: Cognitive, perceptual-motor and neuropsychological perspectives.* New York: Elsevier/ North-Holland.

O'Reilly, R. C., Kosslyn, S. M., Marsolek, C. J., & Chabris, C. F. (1990). Receptive field characteristics that allow parietal lobe neurons to encode spatial properties of visual input: A computational analysis. *Journal of Cognitive Neuroscience, 2,* 141–155.

Ogden, J. A. (1988). Language and memory functions after long recovery periods in left-hemispherectomized subjects. *Neuropsychologia, 26,* 645–659.

Ojemann, G. A. (1983). Brain organization for language from the perspective of electrical stimulation mapping. *Behavioral and Brain Sciences, 6,* 189–230.

Ojemann, G. A., Ojemann, J., Lettich, E., & Berger, M. (1989). Cortical language localization in left, dominant hemisphere. *Journal of Neurosurgery, 71,* 316–326.

Olson, D., & Bialystok, E. (1983). *Spatial cognition: The structure and development of mental representations of spatial relations.* Hillsdale, NJ: Erlbaum.

Ortony, A., Clore, G. L., & Collins, A. (1988). *The cognitive structure of emotions.* Cambridge: Cambridge University Press.

Oxbury, J. M., Oxbury, S. M., & Humphrey, N. K. (1969). Varieties of colour anomia. *Brain, 92,* 847–860.

Paivio, A. (1971). *Imagery and verbal processes.* New York: Holt, Rinehart & Winston.

———. (1989). A dual coding perspective on imagery and the brain. In J. W. Brown (Ed.), *Neuropsychology of visual perception.* Hillsdale, NJ: Erlbaum.

Park, S., & Kosslyn, S. M. (1990). Imagination. In M. G. Johnson, & T. B. Henley (Eds.), *Reflections on the principles of psychology: William James after a century.* Hillsdale, NJ: Erlbaum.

Parkinson, J. K., & Mishkin, M. (1982). A selective role for the hippocampus in monkeys: Memory for the location of objects. *Society for Neuroscience Abstracts, 8,* 23.

Parsons, L. M. (1987). Imagined spatial transformations of one's hands and feet. *Cognitive Psychology, 19,* 178–241.

Passingham, R. E. (1986). Cues for movement in monkeys (Macaca mulatta) with lesions in premotor cortex. *Behavioral Neuroscience, 100,* 695–703.

Paterson, A., & Zangwill, O. L. (1944). Disorders of visual space perception associated with lesions of the right cerebral hemisphere. *Brain, 68,* 331–358.

Patterson, K. E. (1982). The relation between reading and phonological coding: Further neuropsychological observations. In A. W. Ellis (Ed.), *Normality and pathology in cognitive functions.* London: Academic Press.

Patterson, K. E., Marshall, J. C., & Coltheart, M. (1985). *Surface dyslexia: Neuropsychological and cognitive studies of phonological reading.* Hillsdale, NJ: Erlbaum.

Patterson, K. E., Seidenberg, M. S., & McClelland, J. L. (1989). Connections and disconnections: Acquired dyslexia in a computational model of reading processes. In R. G. M. Morris (Ed.), *Parallel distributed processing: Implications for psychology and neurobiology.* New York: Oxford University Press.

Penfield, W., & Perot, P. (1963). The brain's record of auditory and visual experience. *Brain, 86,* 595–697.

Penfield, W., & Rasmussen, T. (1950). *The cerebral cortex of man: A clinical study of localization of function.* New York: Macmillan.

Penfield, W., & Roberts, L. (1959). *Speech and brain mechanisms.* Princeton, NJ: Princeton University Press.

Perret, E. (1974). The left frontal lobe of man and the suppression of habitual responses in verbal categorical behavior. *Neuropsychologia, 16,* 527–537.

Perrett, D. I., Smith, P. A. J., Potter, D. D., Mistlin, A. J., Head, A. S., Milner, A. D., & Jeeves, M. A. (1985). Visual cells in the temporal cortex sensitive to face view and gaze direction. *Proceedings of the Royal Society of London, Series B, 223,* 293–317.

Petersen, S. E., Fox, P. T., Posner, M. I., Mintun, M., & Raichle, M. E. (1988). Positron emission tomographic studies of the cortical anatomy of single-word processing. *Nature, 331,* 585–589.

Petersen, S. E., Fox, P. T., Snyder, A. Z., & Raichle, M. E. (1990). Activation of extrastriate and frontal cortical areas by visual words and word-like stimuli. *Science, 249,* 1041–1044.

Petrides, M., & Milner, B. (1982). Deficits on subject-ordered tasks after frontal- and temporal-lobe lesions in man. *Neuropsychologia, 20,* 249–262.

Piaget, J. (1954). *The construction of reality in the child.* New York: Basic Books.

Pinker, S. (1980). Mental imagery and the third dimension. *Journal of Experimental Psychology: General, 109,* 354–371.

———. (1984). *Language learnability and language development.* Cambridge, MA: Harvard University Press.

———. (1991). Rules of language. *Science, 253,* 530–535.

Pinker, S., Choate, P., & Finke, R. A. (1984). Mental extrapolation in patterns constructed from memory. *Memory and Cognition, 12,* 207–218.

Pinker, S., & Prince, A. (1988). On language and connectionism:

Analysis of a parallel distributed processing model of language acquisition. *Cognition, 28,* 73–193.

Pisoni, D. B. (1973). Auditory and phonetic codes in the discrimination of consonants and vowels. *Perception and Psychophysics, 13,* 253–260.

Plaut, D. C., & Shallice, T. (1991). Effects of word abstractness in a connectionist model of deep dyslexia. *Proceedings of the Thirteenth Annual Meeting of the Cognitive Science Society, Chicago, IL.* Hillsdale, NJ: Erlbaum.

Podgorny, P., & Shepard, R. N. (1978). Functional representations common to visual perception and imagination. *Journal of Experimental Psychology: Human Perception and Performance, 4,* 21–35.

Poeck, K., & Kerschensteiner, M. (1975). Analysis of the sequential motor events in oral apraxia. In K. Zulch, O. Kreutzfeld, & G. Galbraith (Eds.), *Otfried Foerster symposium.* Berlin: Springer-Verlag.

Pohl, W. (1973). Dissociation of spatial discrimination deficits following frontal and parietal lesions in monkeys. *Journal of Comparative and Physiological Psychology, 82,* 227–239.

Polit, A., & Bizzi, E. (1978). Processes controlling arm movements in monkeys. *Science, 201,* 1235–1237.

Pollatsek, A., Well, A. D., & Schindler, R. M. (1975). Familiarity affects visual processing of words. *Journal of Experimental Psychology: Human Perception and Performance, 1,* 328–338.

Posner, M. I. (1978/1986). *Chronometric explorations of mind.* New York: Oxford University Press.

———. (1988). Structures and functions of selective attention. In T. Boll, & B. K. Bryant (Eds.), *Clinical neuropsychology and brain function: Research, measurement, and practice.* Washington, DC: American Psychological Association.

Posner, M. I., Inhoff, A. W., Friedrich, F. J., & Cohen, A. (1987). Isolating attentional systems: A cognitive-anatomical analysis. *Psychobiology, 15,* 107–121.

Posner, M. I., & Petersen, S. E. (1990). The attention system of the human brain. *Annual Review of Neuroscience, 13,* 25–42.

Posner, M. I., Petersen, S. E., Fox, P. T., & Raichle, M. E. (1988). Localization of cognitive operations in the human brain. *Science, 240,* 1627–1631.

Posner, M. I., & Snyder, C. R. (1975). Attention and cognitive control. In R. L. Solso (Ed.), *Information processing and cognition: The Loyola symposium.* Hillsdale, NJ: Erlbaum.

Posner, M. I., Snyder, C. R., & Davidson, B. J. (1980). Attention and the detection of signals. *Journal of Experimental Psychology: General, 109,* 160–174.

Potter, J. M. (1980). What was the matter with Dr. Spooner. In V. A. Fromkin (Ed.), *Errors in linguistic performance: Slips of the tongue, ear, pen, and hand.* New York: Academic Press.

Putnam, H. (1975). The meaning of "meaning." In K. Gunderson (Ed.), *Language, mind, and knowledge: Minnesota studies in the philosophy of science.* Minneapolis, MN: University of Minnesota Press.

Rabbitt, P. M. A. (1978). Detection of errors by skilled typists. *Ergonomics, 21,* 945–958.

Rafal, R. D., & Posner, M. I. (1987). Deficits in human spatial attention following thalamic lesions. *Proceedings of the National Academy of Sciences of the United States of America, 84,* 7349–7353.

Rafal, R. D., Smith, J., Krantz, J., Cohen, A., & Brennan, C. (1990). Extrageniculate vision in hemianopic humans: Saccade inhibition by signals in the blind field. *Science, 250,* 118–121.

Raichle, M. E. (1987). Circulatory and metabolic correlates of brain function in normal humans. In F. Plum (Vol. Ed.), & V. B. Mountcastle (Sec. Ed.), *Handbook of physiology, Section 1: The nervous system, Volume 5: Higher functions of the brain.* Bethesda, MD: American Physiological Society.

———. (1990). Exploring the mind with dynamic imaging. *Seminars in the Neurosciences, 2,* 307–315.

Ramon y Cajal, S. (1888). Estructura del cerebelo. *Gaceta Medica Catalana, 11,* 449–457.

Rasmussen, T., & Milner, B. (1977). The role of early left-brain injury in determining lateralization of cerebral speech functions. In S. Dimond, & D. Blizzard (Eds.) *Evolution and lateralization of the brain.* New York: New York Academy of Sciences.

Ratcliff, G. (1979). Spatial thought, mental rotation and the right cerebral hemisphere. *Neuropsychologia, 17,* 49–54.

———. (1982). Disturbances of spatial orientation associated with cerebral lesions. In M. Potegal (Ed.), *Spatial abilities: Developmental and physiological foundations.* New York: Academic Press.

Ratcliff, G., & Davies-Jones, G. A. G. (1972). Defective visual localisation in focal brain wounds. *Brain, 95,* 49–60.

Reed, S. K. (1974). Structural descriptions and the limitations of visual images. *Memory and Cognition, 2,* 329–336.

Reed, S. K., & Johnsen, J. A. (1975). Detection of parts in patterns and images. *Memory and Cognition, 3,* 569–575.

Reicher, G. M. (1969). Perceptual recognition as a function of meaningfulness of stimulus material. *Journal of Experimental Psychology, 81,* 275–280.

Reiman, E. M., Fusselman, M. J., Fox, P. T., & Raichle, M. E. (1989).

Neuroanatomical correlates of anticipatory anxiety. *Science, 243,* 1071–1074.

Richardson, A. (1967). Mental practice: A review and discussion I & II. *Research Quarterly, 38,* 95–107, 262–273.

Riddoch, M. J. (1990). Loss of visual imagery: A generation deficit. *Cognitive Neuropsychology, 7,* 249–273.

Riddoch, M. J., & Humphreys, G. W. (1987). A case of integrative visual agnosia. *Brain, 110,* 1431–1462.

Roediger, H. L., & Blaxton, T. A. (1987). Effects of varying modality, surface features, and retention interval on priming in word-fragment completion. *Memory and Cognition, 15,* 379–388.

Roeltgen, D. P. (1985). Agraphia. In K. M. Heilman, & E. Valenstein (Eds.), *Clinical neuropsychology* (2nd ed.). New York: Oxford University Press.

Roeltgen, D. P., & Heilman, K. M. (1985). Review of agraphia and a proposal for an anatomically-based neuropsychological model of writing. *Applied Psycholinguistics, 6,* 205–230.

Roland, P. E. (1982). Cortical regulation of selective attention in man. *Journal of Neurophysiology, 53,* 1219–1243.

Roland, P. E., & Friberg, L. (1985). Localization of cortical areas activated by thinking. *Journal of Neurophysiology, 53,* 1219–1243.

Roland, P. E., Larsen, B., Lassen, N. A., & Skinhoj, E. (1980). Supplementary motor area and other areas in organization of voluntary movements in man. *Journal of Neurophysiology, 43,* 118–136.

Roland, P. E., Meyer, E., Shibasaki, T., Yamamoto, Y. L., & Thompson, C. J. (1982). Regional cerebral blood flow changes in cortex and basal ganglia during voluntary movements in normal human volunteers. *Journal of Neurophysiology, 48,* 467–480.

Romani, G. L., Williamson, S. J., & Kaufman, L. (1982). Tonotopic organization of the human auditory cortex. *Science, 216,* 1339–1340.

Rosch, E. (1978). Principles of categorization. In E. Rosch, & B. B. Lloyd (Eds.), *Cognition and categorization.* Hillsdale, NJ: Erlbaum.

Rosenbaum, D. A. (1991). *Human motor control.* San Diego, CA: Academic Press.

Rosenzweig, M. R., & Leiman, A. R. (1982). *Physiological psychology.* Lexington, MA: D. C. Heath.

Ross, E. D., & Mesulam, M. M. (1979). Dominant language functions of the right hemisphere? Prosody and emotional gesturing. *Archives of Neurology, 36,* 144–148.

Roth, J. R., & Kosslyn, S. M. (1988). Construction of the third dimension in mental imagery. *Cognitive Psychology, 20,* 344–361.

Rothwell, J. C. (1987). *Control of human voluntary movement.* London: Croom-Helm.

Rueckl, J. G., Cave, K. R., & Kosslyn, S. M. (1989). Why are "what" and "where" processed by separate cortical systems? A computational investigation. *Journal of Cognitive Neuroscience, 1,* 171–186.

Rumelhart, D. E., Hinton, G., & Williams, R. (1986a). Learning internal representations by error propagation. In D. E. Rumelhart, & J. L. McClelland (Eds.), *Parallel distributed processing: Explorations in the microstructure of cognition, Volume 1. Foundations.* Cambridge, MA: MIT Press.

———. (1986b). Learning representations by back-propagating errors. *Nature, 323,* 533–536.

Rumelhart, D. E., & McClelland, J. L. (1986). *Parallel distributed processing: Explorations in the microstructure of cognition, Volume 1. Foundations.* Cambridge, MA: MIT Press.

Ryle, G. (1949). *The concept of mind.* London: Hutchinson.

Sacks, O. (1985). *The man who mistook his wife for a hat and other clinical tales.* New York: Harper Perennial.

Saito, H., Yukie, M., Tanaka, K., Hikosaka, K., Fukada, Y., & Iwai, E. (1986). Integration of direction signals of image motion in the superior temporal sulcus of the macaque monkey. *Journal of Neuroscience, 6,* 145–157.

Salmon, D. P., Shimamura, A. P., Butters, N., & Smith, S. (1988). Lexical and semantic priming deficits in patients with Alzheimer's disease. *Journal of Clinical and Experimental Neuropsychology, 4,* 477–494.

Saltzman, E., & Kelso, J. A. S. (1987). Skilled actions: A task-dynamic approach. *Psychological Review, 94,* 84–106.

Savin, H. B., & Bever, T. G. (1970). The non-perceptual reality of the phoneme. *Journal of Verbal Learning and Verbal Behavior, 9,* 295–302.

Schacter, D. L., Cooper, L. A., & Delaney, S. M. (1990). Implicit memory for unfamiliar objects depends on access to structural descriptions. *Journal of Experimental Psychology: General, 119,* 5–24.

Schacter, D. L., & Graf, P. (1986). Effects of elaborative processing on implicit and explicit memory for new associations. *Journal of Experimental Psychology: Learning, Memory, and Cognition, 12,* 432–444.

———. (1989). Modality specificity of implicit memory for new associations. *Journal of Experimental Psychology: Learning, Memory, and Cognition, 15,* 3–21.

Schacter, D. L., Harbluk, J. L., & McLachlan, D. R. (1984). Retrieval without recollection: An experimental analysis of source amnesia.

Journal of Verbal Learning and Verbal Behavior, 23, 593–611.

Schacter, D. L., Rapcsak, S. Z., Rubens, A. B., Tharan, M., & Laguna, J. (1990). Priming effects in a letter-by-letter reader depends upon access to the word-form system. *Neuropsychologia, 28,* 1079–1094.

Schacter, S., & Singer, J. (1962). Cognitive, social and physiological determinants of emotional state. *Psychological Review, 69,* 379–399.

Schneider, G. E. (1969). Two visual systems. *Science, 163,* 895–902.

Schwartz, B. (1978). *Psychology of learning and behavior.* New York: Norton.

Schwartz, E. L., Desimone, R., Albright, T. D., & Gross, C. G. (1984). Shape recognition and inferior temporal neurons. *Proceedings of the National Academy of Sciences of the United States of America, 80,* 5776–5778.

Scoville, W. B., & Milner, B. (1957). Loss of recent memory after bilateral hippocampal lesions. *Journal of Neurology, Neurosurgery and Psychiatry, 20,* 11–21.

Seidenberg, M. S., & McClelland, J. L. (1989). A distributed, developmental model of word recognition and naming. *Psychological Review, 96,* 523–568.

Sekuler, R., & Nash, D. (1972). Speed of size scaling in human vision. *Psychonomic Science, 27,* 93–94.

Selfridge, O. G. (1959). Pandemonium: A paradigm for learning. In *The mechanization of thought processes: Proceedings of a symposium held at the National Physical Laboratory, November, 1958.* London: H. M. Stationery Office.

Selkirk, E. O. (1988). *Phonology and syntax: The relationship between sound and structure.* Cambridge, MA: MIT Press.

Sergent, J. (1982). The cerebral balance of power: Confrontation or cooperation? *Journal of Experimental Psychology: Human Perception and Performance, 8,* 253–272.

———. (1988). Face perception and the right hemisphere. In L. Weiskrantz (Ed.), *Thought without language.* Oxford: Oxford University Press.

———. (1989). Image generation and processing of generated images in the cerebral hemispheres. *Journal of Experimental Psychology: Human Perception and Performance, 15,* 170–178.

———. (1990). The neuropsychology of visual image generation: Data, method, and theory. *Brain and Cognition, 13,* 98–129.

———. (in press). Judgments of relative position and distance on representations of spatial relations. *Journal of Experimental Psychology: Human Perception and Performance.*

Seron, X., & Deloche, G. (1987). The production of counting sequences by aphasics and children: A matter of lexical processing? In G.

Deloche, & X. Seron (Eds.), *Mathematical disabilities*. Hillsdale, NJ: Erlbaum.

Shallice, T. (1981). Phonological agraphia and the lexical route in writing. *Brain, 104,* 413–429.

———. (1988). *From neuropsychology to mental structure*. Cambridge: Cambridge University Press.

Shallice, T., & Warrington, E. K. (1980). Single and multiple component central dyslexic syndromes. In M. Coltheart, K. E. Patterson, & J. C. Marshall (Eds.), *Deep dyslexia*. London: Routledge.

Shepard, R. N. (1967). Recognition memory for words, sentences, and pictures. *Journal of Verbal Learning and Verbal Behavior, 6,* 156–163.

Shepard, R. N., & Cooper, L. A. (1982). *Mental images and their transformations*. Cambridge, MA: MIT Press.

Shepherd, G. M. (1988). *Neurobiology*. Oxford: Oxford University Press.

Shiffrin, R. N., & Schneider, W. (1977). Controlled and automatic human information processing: II. Perceptual learning, automatic attending, and a general theory. *Psychological Review, 84,* 127–190.

Shimamura, A. P., Janowsky, J. S., & Squire, L. R. (1990). Memory for the temporal order of events in patients with frontal lobe lesions and amnesic patients. *Neuropsychologia, 28,* 803–813.

Shimamura, A. P., Salmon, D. P., Squire, L. R., & Butters, N. (1987). Memory dysfunction and word priming in dementia and amnesia. *Behavioral Neuroscience, 101,* 347–351.

Shimamura, A. P., & Squire, L. R. (1987). A neuropsychological study of fact memory and source amnesia. *Journal of Experimental Psychology: Learning, Memory, and Cognition, 13,* 464–473.

———. (1989). Impaired priming of new associations in amnesia. *Journal of Experimental Psychology: Learning, Memory, and Cognition, 15,* 721–728.

———. (1991). The relationship between fact and source memory: Findings from amnesic patients and normal subjects. *Psychobiology, 19,* 1–10.

Sidtis, J. J., Volpe, B. T., Wilson, D. H., Rayport, M., & Gazzaniga, M. S. (1981). Variability in right hemisphere language function after callosal section: Evidence for a continuum of generative capacity. *Journal of Neuroscience, 1,* 323–331.

Siegler, R. S. (1987). The peril of averaging data over strategies: An example from children's addition. *Journal of Experimental Psychology: General, 106,* 250–264.

Simon, H. A. (1981). *The sciences of the artificial*. Cambridge, MA: MIT Press.

Skinner, B. F. (1974). *About behaviorism*. New York: Random House.

Smith, E. E., & Medin, D. L. (1981). *Categories and concepts*. Cambridge, MA: Harvard University Press.

Smith, M. L., & Milner, B. (1981). The role of the right hippocampus in the recall of spatial location. *Neuropsychologia, 19,* 781–793.

Soechting, J. F., & Lacquaniti, F. (1983). Modification of trajectory of a pointing movement in response to a change in target location. *Journal of Neurophysiology, 49,* 548–564.

Sperling, G. (1960). The information available in brief visual presentations. *Psychological Monographs, 74,* (11, Whole no. 498).

Springer, S. P., & Deutsch, G. (1981). *Left brain, right brain* (rev. ed.). New York: W. H. Freeman.

Squire, L. R. (1987). *Memory and brain.* New York: Oxford University Press.

———. (in press). Memory and the hippocampus: A synthesis from findings with rats, monkeys and humans. *Psychological Review.*

Squire, L. R., Amaral, D. G., Zola-Morgan, S., Kritchevsky, M., & Press, M. (1989). Description of brain injury in the amnesic patient N.A. based on magnetic resonance imaging. *Experimental Neurology, 105,* 23–25.

Squire, L. R., Shimamura, A. P., & Graf, P. (1987). Strength and duration of priming effects in normal subjects and amnesic patients. *Neuropsychologia, 25,* 195–210.

Standing, L. (1973). Learning 10,000 pictures. *Quarterly Journal of Experimental Psychology, 25,* 207–222.

Standing, L., Conezio, J., & Haber, R. N. (1970). Perception and memory for pictures: Single-trial learning of 2560 visual stimuli. *Psychonomic Science, 19,* 73–74.

Stanfill, C., & Waltz, D. L. (1986). Toward memory-based reasoning. *Communications of the ACM, 29,* 1213–1228.

Sterelny, K. (1990). *The representational theory of mind: An introduction.* Oxford: Blackwell.

Sternberg, S., Monsell, S., Knoll, R. L., & Wright, C. E. (1978). The latency and duration of rapid movement sequences: Comparisons of speech and typewriting. In G. E. Stelmach (Ed.), *Information processing in motor control and learning.* New York: Academic Press.

Stevens, C. F. (1979). The neuron. In *The brain.* New York: W. H. Freeman.

———. (1989). Strengthening the synapses [news]. *Nature, 338,* 460–461.

Strange, W., & Jenkins, J. J. (1978). The role of linguistic experience in the perception of speech. In R. D. Walk, & H. L. Picks (Eds.), *Perception and experience.* New York: Plenum Press.

Stroop, J. (1935). Studies of interference in serial verbal reactions. *Journal of Experimental Psychology, 18,* 643–662.

Suga, N. (1978). Specialization of the auditory system for reception and processing of species-specific sounds. *Federal Proceedings, 37,* 2342–2354.

Summers, J., & Sharp, C. A. (1979). Bilateral effects of concurrent verbal and spatial rehearsal on complex motor sequencing. *Neuropsychologia, 17,* 331–343.

Sussman, H. M., & Westbury, J. R. (1978). A laterality effect in isometric and isotonic labial tracking. *Journal of Speech and Hearing Research, 21,* 563–579.

Sutherland, R. J., McDonald, R. J., Hill, C. R., & Rudy, J. W. (1989). Damage to the hippocampal formation in rats selectively impairs the ability to learn cue relationships. *Behavioral and Neural Biology, 52,* 331–356.

Sutherland, R. J., Whishaw, I. Q., & Kolb, B. E. (1983). A behavioural analysis of spatial localisation following electrolytic, kainate- or colchicine-induced damage to the hippocampal formation in the rat. *Behavioural Brain Research, 7,* 133–153.

Swinney, D. A., & Cutler, A. (1979). The access and processing of idiomatic expressions. *Journal of Verbal Learning and Verbal Behavior, 18,* 523–534.

Taraban, R., & McClelland, J. L. (1987). Conspiracy effects in word pronunciation. *Journal of Memory and Language, 26,* 608–631.

Taylor, A. M., & Warrington, E. K. (1973). Visual discrimination in patients with localized brain lesions. *Cortex, 9,* 82–93.

Taylor, D. C. (1969). Differential rates of cerebral maturation between sexes and between hemispheres. *Lancet, 2,* 140–148.

Taylor, G. A., Miller, T. J., & Juola, J. F. (1977). Isolating visual units in the perception of words and nonwords. *Perception and Psychophysics, 21,* 377–386.

Taylor, J. (1932). *Selected writings of John Hughlings Jackson.* London: Hodder and Stoughton.

Temple, C. M. (1989). Digit dyslexia: A category-specific disorder in developmental dyscalculia. *Cognitive Neuropsychology, 6,* 93–116.

Tootell, R. B. H., Silverman, M. S., Switkes, E., & De Valois, R. L. (1982). Deoxyglucose analysis of retinotopic organization in primate striate cortex. *Science, 218,* 902–904.

Townsend, J. T. (1974). Issues and models concerning the processing of a finite number of inputs. In B. H. Kantrowitz (Ed.), *Human information processing: Tutorials in performance and cognition.* New York: John Wiley.

Tranel, D., & Damasio, A. R. (1985). Knowledge without awareness: An autonomic index of facial recognition by prosopagnosics. *Science, 228,* 1453–1454.

Treisman, A. M., & Gelade, G. (1980). A feature integration theory of attention. *Cognitive Psychology, 12,* 97–136.

Treisman, A. M., & Gormican, S. (1988). Feature analysis in early vision: Evidence from search asymmetries. *Psychological Review, 95,* 15–48.

Treisman, A. M., & Schmidt, H. (1982). Illusory conjunctions in the perception of objects. *Cognitive Psychology, 14,* 107–141.

Tulving, E., & Schacter, D. L. (1990). Priming and human memory systems. *Science, 247,* 301–306.

Tulving, E., & Thompson, D. M. (1973). Encoding specificity and retrieval processes in episodic memory. *Psychological Review, 80,* 352–373.

Tversky, A., & Kahneman, D. (1971). Belief in the law of small numbers. *Psychological Bulletin, 76,* 105–110.

Tyler, H. R. (1968). Abnormalities of perception with defective eye movements (Balint's syndrome). *Cortex, 4,* 154–171.

Tyler, T. J., Perkins, A. T., & Harris, K. M. (1989). The development of long-term potentiation in hippocampus and neocortex. *Neuropsychologia, 27,* 31–39.

Ullman, S. (1979). *The interpretation of visual motion.* Cambridge, MA: MIT Press.

———. (1984). Visual routines. *Cognition, 18,* 97–159.

———. (1989). Aligning pictorial descriptions: An approach to object recognition. *Cognition, 32,* 193–254.

Ulrich, G. (1978). Interhemispheric functional relationships in auditory agnosia: An analysis of the preconditions and a conceptual model. *Brain and Language, 5,* 286–300.

Ungerleider, L. G., & Mishkin, M. (1982). Two cortical visual systems. In D. J. Ingle, M. A. Goodale, & R. J. W. Mansfield (Eds.), *Analysis of visual behavior.* Cambridge, MA: MIT Press.

Valiant, L. G. (1988). Functionality in neural nets. *Proceedings of the American Association for Artificial Intelligence.* Los Altos, CA: Morgan-Kaufmann.

Vallbo, A. B. (1970). Slowly adapting muscle receptors in man. *Acta Physiologica Scandinavica, 78,* 315–333.

Van Essen, D. C. (1985). Functional organization of primate visual cortex. In A. Peters, & E. G. Jones (Eds.), *Cerebral cortex.* New York: Plenum Press.

———. (1987). Visual cortex, extrastriate. In G. Adelman (Ed.), *Encyclopedia of neuroscience.* Boston: Birkhauser.

Van Essen, D. C., & Maunsell, J. H. (1983). Hierarchical organization and functional streams in the visual cortex. *Trends in Neurosciences, 6,* 370–375.

Van Kleeck, M. H. (1989). Hemispheric differences in global versus local processing of hierarchical visual stimuli by normal subjects: New data and a meta-analysis of previous studies. *Neuropsychologia, 27,* 1165–1178.

Velluntino, F. R. (1979). *Dyslexia: Theory and research.* Cambridge, MA: MIT Press.

Viviani, P., & Terzuolo, C. (1983). The organization of movement in handwriting and typing. In B. Butterworth (Ed.), *Language production.* London: Academic Press.

von Bonin, G. (1960). *Some papers on the cerebral cortex.* Springfield, IL: Charles C. Thomas.

von der Malsburg, C., & Schneider, W. (1986). A neural cocktail-party processor. *Biological Cybernetics, 54,* 29–40.

von Monakow, C. (1969). Diaschesis. (Excerpt from "Die Lokalisation im Grosshirn und der Abbau der Funktion durch kortikale Herde" by J. F. Bergmann, Wiesbaden, 1914. Translated by G. Harris). In K. H. Pribram (Ed.), *Brain and behavior: Volume 1. Mood, states, and mind.* Baltimore: Penguin Press.

von Neumann, J. (1958). *The computer and the brain.* New Haven, CT: Yale University Press.

Wallesch, C. W., Henriksen, L., Kornhuber, H. H., & Paulson, O. B. (1985). Observations on regional cerebral blood flow in cortical and subcortical structures during language production in normal man. *Brain and Language, 25,* 224–233.

Walsh, F. B., & Hoyt, W. F. (1969). *Clinical neuro-ophthalmology.* Baltimore: Williams and Wilkins.

Walsh, K. (1987). *Neuropsychology: A clinical approach* (2nd ed.). Edinburg: Churchill-Livingstone.

Warren, R. M. (1970). Perceptual restoration of missing speech sounds. *Science, 167,* 392–393.

Warrington, E. K. (1969). Constructional apraxia. In P. J. Vinken, & G. W. Bruyn (Eds.), *Handbook of clinical neurology.* New York: Elsevier/North-Holland.

———. (1981). Concrete word dyslexia. *British Journal of Psychology, 72,* 175–196.

———. (1982). The fractionation of arithmetic skills: A single case study. *Quarterly Journal of Experimental Psychology, 34A,* 31–51.

Warrington, E. K., James, M., & Maciejewski, C. (1986). The WAIS as a lateralising and localising diagnostic instrument: A study of 656 patients with unilateral cerebral lesions. *Neuropsychologia, 24,* 223–239.

Warrington, E. K., & McCarthy, R. A. (1983). Category-specific access dysphasia. *Brain, 106,* 859–878.

Warrington, E. K., & Rabin, P. (1970). Perceptual matching in patients with cerebral lesions. *Neuropsychologia, 8,* 475–487.

Warrington, E. K., & Shallice, T. (1984). Category specific semantic impairments. *Brain, 107,* 829–853.

Warrington, E. K., & Weiskrantz, L. (1968). A new method of testing long-term retention with special reference to amnesic patients. *Nature, 217,* 972–974.

———. (1970). The amnesic syndrome: Consolidation or retrieval? *Nature, 228,* 628–630.

Watson, J. B. (1913). Psychology as a behaviorist views it. *Psychological Review, 20,* 158–177.

Watson, R. T., Fleet, W. S., Gonzales-Rothi, L. J., & Heilman, K. M. (1986). Apraxia and the supplementary motor area. *Archives of Neurology, 43,* 787–792.

Watson, R. T., & Heilman, K. M. (1983). Callosal apraxia. *Brain, 106,* 391–403.

Weber, R. J., & Harnish, R. (1974). Visual imagery for words: The Hebb test. *Journal of Experimental Psychology, 102,* 409–414.

Weingartner, H. (1984). Psychobiological determinants of memory failures. In L. Squire, & N. Butters (Eds.), *Neuropsychology of memory.* New York: Guilford Press.

Weinrich, M., & Wise, S. (1982). Premotor cortex of the monkey. *Journal of Neuroscience, 2,* 1329–1345.

Weisenberg, T., & McBride, K. E. (1935). *Aphasia: A clinical and psychological study.* New York: Commonwealth Fund.

Weiskrantz, L. (1986). *Blindsight: A case study and its implications.* New York: Oxford University Press.

Weisstein, N., & Harris, C. S. (1974). Visual detection of line segments: An object superiority. *Science, 186,* 752–755.

Wernicke, C. (1874). *Der aphasische Symptomenkomplex.* Breslau: Cohn & Weigert.

Wheeler, D. D. (1970). Processes in word recognition. *Cognitive Psychology, 1,* 59–85.

White, M. J. (1969). Laterality differences in perception: A review. *Psychological Bulletin, 72,* 387–405.

Wiesendanger, M. (1981). Organization of secondary motor areas of cerebral cortex. In V. B. Brooks (Ed.), *Handbook of physiology.* Bethesda, MD: American Physiological Society.

————. (1987). Initiation of voluntary movements and the supplementary motor area. In H. Heuer, & C. Fromm (Eds.), *Generation and modulation of action patterns.* Berlin: Springer-Verlag.

Williams, M. (1970). *Brain damage and the mind.* Middlesex: Penguin Books.

Winner, E., & Gardner, H. (1977). The comprehension of metaphor in brain damaged patients. *Brain, 100,* 717–729.

Winograd, T. (1975). Frame representations and the declarative/procedural controversy. In D. Bobrow, & A. Collins (Eds.), *Representation and understanding: Studies in cognitive science.* New York: Academic Press.

Wise, S. P., & Strick, P. L. (1984). Anatomical and physiological organization of the non-primary motor cortex. *Trends in Neurosciences, 7,* 442–446.

Witelson, S. F. (1977). Early hemispheric specialization and interhemispheric plasticity: An empirical and theoretical review. In S. Segalowitz, & F. Gruber (Eds.), *Language development and neurological theory.* London: Academic Press.

Witelson, S. F., & Kigar, D. L. (1988). Anatomical development of the corpus callosum in humans: A review with reference to sex and cognition. In D. L. Molfese, & S. J. Segalowitz (Eds.), *Brain lateralization in children.* New York: Guilford Press.

Wittgenstein, L. (1953). *Philosophical investigations.* New York: Macmillan.

Wood, C. C. (1978). Variations on a theme by Lashley: Lesion experiments on the neural model of Anderson, Silverstein, Ritz, and Jones. *Psychological Review, 277,* 582–591.

Woodworth, R. S. (1899). The accuracy of voluntary movement. *Psychological Review Monograph Supplements, 3*(3).

Yakovlev, P. I., & Lecours, A. R. (1967). The myelogenetic cycles of regional maturation of the brain. In A. Minkowski (Ed.), *Regional development of the brain in early life.* Oxford: Blackwell.

Yarbus, A. L. (1967). *Eye movements and vision.* New York: Plenum Press.

Yates, F. A. (1966). *The art of memory.* Chicago: University of Chicago Press.

Zaidel, E. (1976). Auditory vocabulary of the right hemisphere following brain bisection or hemidecortication. *Cortex, 12,* 191–211.

————. (1990). The saga of right-hemisphere reading. In C. Trevarthen (Ed.), *Brain circuits and functions of the mind: Essays in honor of Roger W. Sperry.* Cambridge: Cambridge University Press.

Zangwill, O. (1976). Thought and the brain. *British Journal of Psychology, 67,* 301–314.

Zipser, D., & Andersen, R. A. (1988). A back-propagation programmed network that simulates response properties of a subset of posterior parietal neurons. *Nature, 331,* 679–684.

Zola-Morgan, S., & Squire, L. R. (1985a). Amnesia in monkeys following lesions of the mediodorsal nucleus of the thalamus. *Annals of Neurology, 17,* 558–564.

———. (1985b). Medial temporal lesions in monkeys impair memory on a variety of tasks sensitive to human amnesia. *Behavioral Neuroscience, 99,* 22–34.

Zurif, E. B., & Caramazza, A. (1976). Psycholinguistic structures in aphasia. In H. Whitaker, & H. A. Whitaker (Eds.), *Studies in neurolinguistics.* New York: Academic Press.

Zurif, E. B., Gardner, H., & Brownell, H. H. (1989). The case against the case against group studies. *Brain and Cognition, 10,* 237–255.

Index